P9-BIA-103

FIRST REPUBLIC BANK
It's a privilege to serve you®

Greetings,

San Francisco and the surrounding communities are home to many of our wonderful clients and friends. And they represent areas of new and continued growth for First Republic.

In appreciation of the range of amazing restaurants in the San Francisco area, we're delighted to present a special First Republic/Zagat Survey guide, featuring restaurants in and around San Francisco, including Silicon Valley and the Monterey Peninsula.

We'd like to invite you to visit any of our Preferred Banking Offices, where we offer the full range of private banking and wealth management services.

Our mission is simple: to provide extraordinary service the old-fashioned way — on a personalized basis — with decisions made quickly and solutions customized to meet individual needs.

It's a privilege to serve you.

James H. Herbert, II, Chairman and CEO

Katherine August-deWilde, President and COO

ZAGAT
2013

San Francisco Bay Area Restaurants

LOCAL EDITOR
Meesha Halm
STAFF EDITOR
Cynthia Kilian

Published and distributed by
Zagat Survey, LLC
76 Ninth Avenue
New York, NY 10011
T: 212.977.6000
E: sanfran@zagat.com
plus.google.com/local

ACKNOWLEDGMENTS

We're grateful to our local editor, Meesha Halm, who is a Bay Area restaurant critic, cookbook author and youth garden-to-table educator. We also sincerely thank the thousands of people who participated in this survey – this guide is really "theirs."

We also thank Crista Bourg, Kathryn Carroll, Tara Duggan, Jon Fox, Kara Freewind, Danielle Harris, Ashley Hayes, Katie Hottinger, Gayle Keck, Michele Laudig, Mike Lima, Virginia Miller, Craig Nelson, Jamie Selzer, Hilary Sims, Stefanie Tuder, Alice Urmey, Sharron Wood and Samantha Zalaznick as well as the following members of our staff: Aynsley Karps (editor), Brian Albert, Sean Beachell, Maryanne Bertollo, Danielle Borovoy, Reni Chin, Larry Cohn, Bill Corsello, John Deiner, Nicole Diaz, Kelly Dobkin, Jeff Freier, Alison Gainor, Matthew Hamm, Justin Hartung, Marc Henson, Ryutaro Ishikane, Natalie Lebert, Mike Liao, Vivian Ma, James Mulcahy, Polina Paley, Emil Ross, Emily Rothschild, Amanda Spurlock, Chris Walsh, Jacqueline Wasilczyk, Sharon Yates, Anna Zappia and Kyle Zolner.

ABOUT ZAGAT

In 1979, we asked friends to rate and review restaurants purely for fun. The term "user-generated content" had yet to be coined. That hobby grew into Zagat Survey; 33 years later, we have loyal surveyors around the globe and our content now includes nightlife, shopping, tourist attractions, golf and more. Along the way, we evolved from being a print publisher to a digital content provider. We also produce marketing tools for a wide range of corporate clients, and you can find us on Google+ and just about any other social media network.

Our reviews are based on public opinion surveys. The ratings reflect the average scores given by the survey participants who voted on each establishment. The text is based on quotes from, or paraphrasings of, the surveyors' comments. Phone numbers, addresses and other factual data were correct to the best of our knowledge when published in this guide.

JOIN IN: To improve our guides, we solicit your comments – positive or negative; it's vital that we hear your opinions. Just contact us at **nina-tim@zagat.com.** We also invite you to share your opinions at plus.google.com/local.

Our guides are printed using environmentally preferable inks containing 20%, by weight, renewable resources on papers sourced from well-managed forests. Deluxe editions are covered with Skivertex Recover® Double containing a minimum of 30% post-consumer waste fiber.

© 2012 Zagat Survey, LLC
ISBN-13: 978-1-60478-515-9
ISBN-10: 1-60478-515-2
Printed in the
United States of America

Contents

Ratings & Symbols

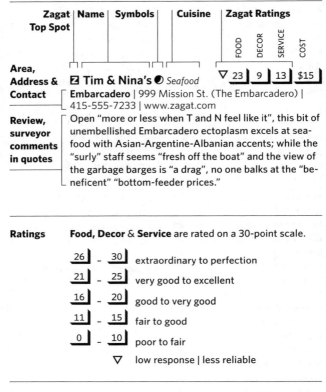

	Zagat Top Spot	Name	Symbols	Cuisine	Zagat Ratings			
					FOOD	DECOR	SERVICE	COST

Area, Address & Contact

▣ **Tim & Nina's** ◗ *Seafood*   ▽ 23 | 9 | 13 | $15

Embarcadero | 999 Mission St. (The Embarcadero) | 415-555-7233 | www.zagat.com

Review, surveyor comments in quotes

Open "more or less when T and N feel like it", this bit of unembellished Embarcadero ectoplasm excels at seafood with Asian-Argentine-Albanian accents; while the "surly" staff seems "fresh off the boat" and the view of the garbage barges is "a drag", no one balks at the "beneficent" "bottom-feeder prices."

Ratings   **Food, Decor** & **Service** are rated on a 30-point scale.

26	–	30	extraordinary to perfection
21	–	25	very good to excellent
16	–	20	good to very good
11	–	15	fair to good
0	–	10	poor to fair
	▽		low response	less reliable

Cost

The price of dinner with a drink and tip; lunch is usually 25% to 30% less. For unrated **newcomers,** the price range is as follows:

| I | $25 and below | E | $41 to $65 |
| M | $26 to $40 | VE | $66 or above |

Symbols

▣   highest ratings, popularity and importance
◗   serves after 11 PM
▣ Ⓜ   closed on Sunday or Monday
⌿   no credit cards accepted

Maps

Index maps show restaurants with the highest Food ratings in those areas.

About This Survey

- 1,636 restaurants covered
- 15,502 surveyors
- 84 notable openings
- Top Rated: **Gary Danko** (Food, Service, Most Popular), **Sierra Mar** (Decor), **Bi-Rite** (Bang for the Buck), **Cheesecake Factory** (Most Popular Chain)
- No. 1 Newcomer: **State Bird Provisions**

SURVEY STATS: Bay Area surveyors report eating out an average of 2.9 meals per week, vs. 3.1 nationally . . . The reported average tip is 18.6%, tied with Seattle for the lowest among major U.S. markets (the national average is 19.3%) . . . Service remains the top complaint (cited by 56%), followed by noise (22%) . . . 58% say they're eating out as often as a year ago, 23% say more, 19% less . . . 56% report spending the same amount per meal vs. last year, while 34% say more, 10% less . . . On a 30-point scale, the Bay Area rates 27 for culinary diversity, 26 for creativity, 19 for hospitality and 15 for table availability . . . Favorite cuisines: Italian (24%) followed by French (15%) . . . 36% occasionally engage in group dining discounts, 5% participate regularly . . . A whopping 79% of surveyors agree that restaurants should be required to post a health-inspection letter grade in the window.

GETTING TECHNICAL: 67% reserve via Internet or e-mail, 25% call . . . 46% have downloaded restaurant-related smartphone apps . . . 20% follow restaurants and food trucks via social media . . . 14% post on social media when they arrive . . . 58% feel it's rude and inappropriate to text, e-mail, tweet or talk on the phone while dining out, 38% say it's acceptable in moderation and 2% deem it perfectly acceptable . . . Taking photos of food or companions is considered acceptable in moderation by 67%, perfectly acceptable by 20% and rude and inappropriate by 11%.

NEW FROM NOTABLE CHEFS: AQ (Mark Liberman), **Brassica** (Cindy Pawlcyn), **Burritt Tavern** (Charlie Palmer), **Central Kitchen, Salumeria** (Thomas McNaughton), **Copita** (Joanne Weir), **Dixie** (Joseph Humphrey), **Haven** (Daniel Patterson), **Hawk's Tavern** (Tyler Florence), **Keiko à Nob Hill** (Keiko Takahashi), **La Condesa** (Rene Ortiz), **Namu Gaji** (Dennis Lee), **Redd Wood** (Richard Reddington), State Bird Provisions (Stuart Brioza & Nicole Krasinski), **The Thomas & Fagiani's Bar** (Brad Farmerie).

HOT NABE: Surveyors think the Mission (Namu Gaji, **Wise Sons**) is the neighborhood with the best restaurants. Particularly hot of late is Valencia Street (**Abbot's Cellar, Amber Dhara, Farina Pizza, St. Vincent Tavern & Wine Merchant, Tacolicious, West of Pecos, Wo Hing General Store**).

HOT TREND: Mexican tequilerias multiplied (**Comal,** Copita, La Condesa, **Mateo's Cucina Latina, Nopalito, Mosto** at Tacolicious, **Rumbo Al Sur**).

San Francisco, CA   Meesha Halm
October 10, 2012

KEY NEWCOMERS

maps.google.com

Fisherman's Wharf
San Francisco Bay

Gioia Pizzeria
Park Tavern
Dixie
North Beach
Umami Burger
Marina
Russian Hill
Parallel 37
Brasserie S&P
Keiko à Nob Hill
Presidio
Sweet Woodruff
Burritt Tavern
Presidio Heights
Bouche
Trace
State Bird
Downtown
South Beach
Two Sisters
Pläj
AQ Restaurant
Civic Center
SoMa
Maven
Lower Haight
Haight-Ashbury
Mozzeria
West of Pecos
Wo Hing
Farina Pizza
Izakaya Yuzuki
Castro
Southern Pacific Brewery
Central Kitchen/Salumeria
Craftsman & Wolves
St. Vincent Tavern
Ken Ken Ramen
Abbot's Cellar
Lolinda
Noe Valley
Mission
Portola Dr

903
Bernal Heights

Mateo's Cocina Latina
French Blue
La Condesa
Goose & Gander
Brassica
Healdsburg
St Helena
Davis
Santa Rosa
Redd Wood
Glen Ellen Star
Napa
Vacaville

Point Reyes National Seashore
San Rafael
Vallejo
Hawk's Tavern
Comal
Corners Tavern
Mill Valley
Copita
FuseBox
Walnut Creek
Sausalito
Haven
Rumbo Al Sur
San Francisco
Oakland
Hopscotch
Pacific Ocean
Livermore
Hayward
Pacifica

Rangoon Ruby
Asian Box
Fremont
Palo Alto

Google

6   Latest openings, menus, photos and more on plus.google.com/local

Key Newcomers

Our editors' picks among this year's arrivals. See full list at p. 37.

HOT CHEFS AND OPENINGS

AQ
Burritt Tavern
Central Kitchen/Salumeria
Comal/E
Copita/N
Dixie
Haven/E
Keiko à Nob Hill
La Condesa
Lolinda
Mateo's Cocina Latina/N
Park Tavern
State Bird Provisions
Wo Hing General Store

PIZZA

Farina Pizza
Gioia Pizzeria
Mozzeria
Redd Wood/N

QUICK SERVICE/CASUAL

Asian Box/S
Craftsman & Wolves
903
Sweet Woodruff
Umami Burger

LOCAL JOINTS

Bouche
Corners Tavern/E
French Blue/N
FuseBox/E
Glen Ellen Star/N
Goose & Gander/N
Hopscotch/E
Izakaya Yuzuki
Ken Ken Ramen
Pläj
Rangoon Ruby/S
Rumbo Al Sur/E
West of Pecos

REDO'S

Brasserie S&P
Brassica/N
Parallel 37
Trace

WINE/BEER/SPIRITS

Abbot's Cellar
Hawk's Tavern/N
Maven
Southern Pacific Brewery
St. Vincent Tavern
Two Sisters Bar & Books

NEXT UP: Much-anticipated openings expected near the legendary Fillmore theater include **Hapa,** the first brick-and-mortar noodle house from the popular food stall **Hapa Ramen; Brenda's Original Po' Boys** from **Brenda's French Soul Food**; and a second venture from the owners of the Bay Area's top newcomer, **State Bird Provisions.** At press time, la dolce vita is sweeping into town with the arrival of Yigit Pura's **Tout Sweet Patisserie** in Union Square; Michael Recchiuti's **Chocolate Lab Cafe** in Dogpatch; and Belinda Leong's **b. patisserie** in Pacific Heights.

Additionally, **Boulettes Larder** in the Ferry Building is expanding next door with **Bouli Bar,** and a link in the London-based **Hakkasan** Chinese chain is slated for Downtown. Finally, despite being one of the area's top restaurants, Douglas Keane's **Cyrus** in Healdsburg will close at the end of October.

Most Popular

This list is plotted on the map at the back of this book. Places outside of San Francisco are marked as: E=East of SF; N=North; and S=South. When a restaurant has locations both inside and out of the city limits, we include the notation SF as well.

1. Gary Danko | *American*
2. Boulevard | *American*
3. Slanted Door | *Vietnamese*
4. Kokkari Estiatorio | *Greek*
5. French Laundry/N | *Amer./Fr.*
6. Chez Panisse/E | *Cal./Med.*
7. House of Prime Rib | *Amer.*
8. Absinthe | *French/Med.*
9. Zuni Café | *Mediterranean*
10. A16 | *Italian*
11. Chez Panisse Café/E | *Cal./Med.*
12. Acquerello | *Italian*
13. Burma Superstar/E/SF | *Burmese*
14. Amber India/S/SF | *Indian*
15. Zachary's/E | *Pizza*
16. Yank Sing | *Chinese*
17. Alexander's/S/SF | *Japanese/Steak*
18. Tadich Grill | *Seafood*
19. Bouchon/N | *French*
20. Fleur de Lys | *Californian/French*
21. Arizmendi/E/N/SF | *Bakery/Pizza*
22. Delfina* | *Italian*
23. Scoma's/N/SF | *Seafood*
24. Buckeye/N | *Amer./BBQ*
25. Perbacco | *Italian*
26. Ad Hoc/N | *American*
27. Chow/E/SF | *American*
28. Nopa | *Californian*
29. Flour + Water | *Italian*
30. Chapeau! | *French*
31. Cotogna* | *Italian*
32. Evvia/S | *Greek*
33. Aziza | *Moroccan*
34. Quince | *Italian*
35. Jardinière | *Californian/French*
36. Bottega/N | *Italian*
37. Frances | *Californian*
38. Scott's Seafood/E/S | *Seafood*
39. À Côté/E | *Fr./Med.*
40. Bistro Jeanty/N | *French*

MOST POPULAR CHAINS

1. Cheesecake/E/N/S/SF | *Amer.*
2. In-N-Out/E/N/S/SF | *Burgers*
3. Amici's/E/N/S/SF | *Pizza*
4. Il Fornaio/E/N/S/SF | *Italian*
5. Boudin | *Amer./Sandwiches*
6. Buca di Beppo/S/SF | *Italian*
7. Ruth's Chris/E/SF | *Steak*
8. Cheese Steak/E/N/S/SF | *Cheesesteaks*
9. Benihana/S/SF | *Japanese*
10. Morton's/S/SF | *Steak*

Many of the above restaurants are among the San Francisco area's most expensive, but if popularity were calibrated to price, a number of other restaurants would surely join their ranks. To illustrate this, we have added lists of Best Buys on pages 14 and 15.

* Indicates a tie with restaurant above

Top Food

BY CUISINE

Excludes places with low votes, unless otherwise indicated; Top Food
excludes dessert-only spots

CHINESE

27 Mingalaba/S
26 Yank Sing
25 Ton Kiang
   R&G Lounge
   Tommy Toy's

CONTINENTAL

27 La Forêt/S
25 Ecco/S
   Bella Vista/S
24 Anton & Michel/S

DIM SUM

26 Yank Sing
25 Ton Kiang
24 Oriental Pearl
23 Hong Kong Lounge
   Koi Palace/E/S

ECLECTIC

27 Della Fattoria/N
25 Graffiti/N
   Firefly
   Willi's Wine Bar/N
   Va de Vi/E

FRENCH

28 Marinus/S
27 Masa's
   La Folie
   Madrona Manor/N
   La Forêt/S

FRENCH (BISTRO)

27 Bistro des Copaines/N
   Bistro Jeanty/N
   Chapeau!
26 Bouchon/N
25 Artisan Bistro/E
   Chez Spencer

INDIAN

27 Ajanta/E
26 Chutney
25 All Spice/S
   Vik's Chaat Corner/E
   Lotus of India/N

ITALIAN

28 Seven Hills
   Acquerello
27 Cucina Paradiso/N
   La Ciccia
   Delfina

JAPANESE

28 Kiss Seafood
27 Sushi Zone
   Ichi Sushi
   Zushi Puzzle
   Sushi Ran/N

MED./GREEK

28 Kokkari Estiatorio
   Evvia
   Chez Panisse Café/E
   Rivoli/E
   Chez Panisse/E

MEXICAN

25 La Victoria Taqueria/S
   El Castillito
   La Taqueria
   Loló
   C Casa/N

MIDDLE EASTERN

26 Saha
25 Dishdash/S
24 Helmand Palace
23 Kabul/S
   A La Turca

PERUVIAN

25 Pasión
   La Costanera/S
24 Piqueo's
   La Mar Cebicheria
   Mochica

PIZZA

27 Cheese Board Pizzeria/E
26 Diavola/N
   Tony's Pizza
   Pizzaiolo/E
   Gioia Pizzeria/E/SF

SANDWICHES

27 Fatted Calf/N/SF
   Lucca Deli
26 Downtown Bakery/N
   Saigon Sandwiches
   4505 Meats

SEAFOOD

27 Passionfish/S
26 Swan Oyster Depot
   Marica/E
   Sotto Mare
   Hog Island Oyster Co./N/SF

SPANISH/BASQUE

27| Piperade
25| Contigo
Fringale
24| Zarzuela
Gitane

STEAK

27| Cole's Chop House/N
Seasons
Ruth's Chris/E/SF
Harris'
26| Press/N

THAI

27| Sea Thai Bistro/N
Royal Thai/N

25| Marnee Thai
Basil
Lers Ros Thai

VEGETARIAN

27| Millennium
25| Greens
24| Gracias Madre
23| Udupi Palace/E/SF
Cha-Ya Vegetarian/E/SF

VIETNAMESE

26| Slanted Door
Thanh Long
Saigon Sandwiches
Tamarine/S
25| Vung Tau/S

BY SPECIAL FEATURE

BREAKFAST

27| Tartine Bakery
26| Downtown Bakery/N
Campton Pl.
24| Mama's on Washington
Zazie

BRUNCH

28| Erna's Elderberry/E
Redd/N
27| La Forêt/S
Nopa
26| Boulettes Larder

CHILD-FRIENDLY

26| Tony's Pizza
Cook St. Helena/N
Yank Sing
Rosso Pizzeria/N
22| Gott's Roadside/N/SF

HOTEL DINING

28| Erna's/E (Château du Sureau)
Marinus/S (Bernardus Lodge)
Sierra Mar/S (Post Ranch Inn)
27| Masa's (Hotel Vintage Ct.)
Farmhouse Inn/N

NEWCOMERS (RATED)

27| State Bird Provisions
25| AQ
Alex Rest./N
Redd Wood/N
Park Tav.

OPEN LATE

27| Nopa
26| Chutney
25| La Victoria/S
Ryoko's
Locanda

TRENDY

27| Delfina
Jardinière
Nopa
25| AQ
Locanda

WINE BARS

27| Sushi Ran/N
Étoile/N
25| A16
24| Barbacco
23| RN74

WINNING WINE LISTS

29| Gary Danko
French Laundry
28| Acquerello
Marinus/S
27| Boulevard

WORTH A TRIP

29| French Laundry/N (Yountville)
28| Erna's Elderberry/E (Oakhurst)
Marinus/S (Carmel Valley)
Sierra Mar/S (Big Sur)
Chez Panisse/E (Berkeley)

Top Decor Overall

29] Sierra Mar/S	Waterbar
28] Auberge du Soleil/N	26] Farm/N
Marinus/S	Seasons
Erna's Elderberry/E	Quince
Ahwahnee Dining/E	Meadowood Rest./N
Garden Court	Sutro's at the Cliff House
Pacific's Edge/S	La Forêt/S
27] Gary Danko	Bix
Farallon	Boulevard
Caprice/N	Madrona Manor/N
French Laundry/N	AQ
Big 4	Murray Circle/N
Kokkari Estiatorio	Grand Cafe
Jardinière	Plumed Horse/S
Twenty Five Lusk	El Paseo/N
Roy's at Pebble Beach/S	Restaurant at Ventana*/S
Étoile/N	Madera/S
Spruce	Coi
Fleur de Lys	Meritage at The Claremont/E
Wente Vineyards/E	Napa Valley Wine/N

OUTDOORS

Angèle/N	La Mar Cebicheria
Auberge du Soleil/N	Murray Circle/N
Bistro Don Giovanni/N	Nepenthe/S
Epic Roasthouse	Sociale
Étoile/N	Tra Vigne/N
Foreign Cinema	Waterbar

ROMANCE

Aziza	Garden Court
Bix	Gitane
Cafe Jacqueline	Jardinière
Casanova/S	La Forêt/S
Chez Spencer	Madrona Manor/N
Fleur de Lys	Shadowbrook/S

ROOMS

Ahwahnee Dining/E	Jardinière
AQ	Kokkari Estiatorio
Boulevard	Plumed Horse/S
Farallon	Redd/N
Garden Court	Twenty Five Lusk
Gitane	Waterbar

VIEWS

Beach Chalet	Pacific's Edge/S
Bella Vista/S	Sam's Chowder/S
Greens	Sierra Mar/S
Guaymas/N	Slanted Door
La Costanera/S	Sutro's
Navio/S	Wolfdale's/E

Top Service Overall

29 | Gary Danko

28 | French Laundry/N
Erna's Elderberry/E
Acquerello
Benu
Seasons

27 | Marinus/S
Coi
Sierra Mar/S
Madrona Manor/N
Meadowood Rest./N
Terra/N
La Folie
Chez Panisse/E
Baumé/S
Manresa/S
Fleur de Lys
Masa's
Étoile/N
Farmhouse Inn*/N

Auberge du Soleil/N
Kokkari Estiatorio
La Forêt/S
Boulevard
Michael Mina

26 | Saison
Allegro Romano
Atelier Crenn
Bistro des Copains/N
Cafe Gibraltar/S
Wolfdale's*/E
Cucina Paradiso/N
Chantilly/S
Commis/E
Chez Panisse Café/E
Marché aux Fleurs/N
Quince
Harris'
Big 4
Bistro Moulin

Best Buys Overall

BAKERIES

28 Bi-Rite
27 Tartine Bakery
Della Fattoria/N
26 Downtown Bakery/N
Bakesale Betty/E

DELI

27 Lucca Deli
26 4505 Meats
25 Boccalone Salumeria
Deli Board
23 Wise Sons Deli

DESSERT

28 Bi-Rite
27 Bar Tartine
Cafe Jacqueline
26 Downtown Bakery/N
25 Sandbox

DINERS

25 Bette's Oceanview/E
HRD Coffee Shop
24 Fremont Diner/N
22 Joe's Cable Car
Alexis Baking Co./N

FOOD TRUCKS

25 3-Sum
Cupkates
24 RoliRoti
Chairman Truck
23 Curry Up Now

HOLE-IN-THE-WALL

26 Saigon Sandwiches
24 Shalimar/E/S/SF
23 A La Turca
House of Nanking
Yamo

HOT DOGS

26 4505 Meats
25 Underdog
23 Top Dog/E
Caspers Hot Dogs/E
21 Showdogs

NOODLE SHOPS

25 O Chamé/E
24 San Tung
22 Katana-Ya
King of Thai/E/SF
Osha Thai

PUB FOOD

23 Biergarten
22 4th St. Bar & Grill
20 Wurst/N
19 Dear Mom
18 Gordon Biersch/S

SLEEPERS

28 Terrapin Creek/N
Kappou Gomi
27 To Hyang
Sazon Peruvian/N
25 Mr. Pollo

TAQUERIAS

25 La Taqueria
23 Taqueria Can Cun
Tacubaya/E
22 Picante Cocina/E
20 Mijita

TOP CHEF BARGAINS

28 Chez Panisse Café/E
26 Pizzeria Delfina
23 Hawker Fare/E
Out the Door
20 Burger Bar

BEST BUYS: BANG FOR THE BUCK

In order of rating.

1. Bi-Rite
2. Dynamo Donut
3. Blue Bottle/E/SF
4. Top Dog/E
5. Caspers Hot Dogs/E
6. In-N-Out/E/N/S/SF
7. Saigon Sandwiches
8. Let's Be Frank
9. Arinell Pizza/E/SF
10. Golden Boy/S/SF
11. La Victoria Taqueria/S
12. El Castillito
13. Ayola
14. Arizmendi/E/N/SF
15. Yellow Submarine
16. Taqueria La Bamba/S
17. AK Subs
18. HRD Coffee Shop
19. Java Beach Cafe
20. Buster's Cheesesteak
21. Taqueria Can Cun
22. Nation's Giant Hamburgers/S
23. Jim's Country/E
24. Cheese Steak Shop/E/N/S/SF
25. Marcello's Pizza
26. Taqueria San Jose/S/SF
27. El Farolito/E/N/S/SF
28. Cheese Board Pizzeria/E
29. Bakesale Betty/E
30. Curry Up Now/S/SF
31. El Metate
32. Cancun/E
33. Boccalone Salumeria
34. Ike's Place/S/SF
35. La Corneta/S/SF
36. Pearl's Deluxe Burgers/E/N/SF
37. Pancho Villa Taqueria/S/SF
38. Super Duper
39. La Taqueria
40. La Cumbre Taqueria/S/SF
41. Carmel Bakery/S
42. Kitchenette SF
43. American Grilled Cheese
44. Auntie April's
45. Actual Cafe/E
46. Taqueria 3 Amigos/S
47. One Hawaiian BBQ
48. Blue Barn Gourmet
49. Lucca Deli
50. Yamo

BEST BUYS: OTHER GOOD VALUES

Applewood Pizza/N
Asian Box/S
Bacon Bacon
Bo's BBQ/E
Brown Sugar Kitchen/E
Cafe Citti/N
Chairman Truck
Cool Café/S
Counter Palo Alto/S
Cupkates
Dasaprakash/S
Diavola/N
El Tonayense
Fremont Diner/N
Gayle's Bakery/S
Gioia Pizzeria/E
Gott's Roadside/N/SF
Graffiti/N
Grégoire/E
Hawker Fare/E
Homeroom/E
Kasa Indian
Le Cheval/E
Little Chihuahua
Mingalaba/S
Naked Lunch
903
Orenchi Ramen/S
Pizza Antica/E/N/S
Pizzeria Picco/N
Pizzeria Tra Vigne/N
RoliRoti
Sazon Peruvian/N
Tacubaya/E
Umami Burger
Vik's Chaat/E
Willow Wood/N
Wise Sons Deli
Xolo Taqueria/E
Zachary's/E

Latest openings, menus, photos and more on plus.google.com/local

OTHER USEFUL LISTS*

LOCATION MAPS

---

* All places are in San Francisco unless otherwise noted (East of San Francisco=E; North of San Francisco=N; South of San Francisco=S). These lists include low vote places that do not qualify for top lists.

Special Features

Listings cover the best in each category and include names, locations and Food ratings. Multi-location restaurants' features may vary by branch.

BREAKFAST

(See also Hotel Dining)

Tartine	**Mission**	27
Downtown Bakery	**Healdsburg/N**	26
Boulettes Larder	**Embarcadero**	26
Bette's Oceanview	**Berkeley/E**	25
Gayle's Bakery	**Capitola/S**	24
Mama's on Wash.	**N Beach**	24
Zazie	**Cole Valley**	24
Venus	**Berkeley/E**	24
Big Sur	**Big Sur/S**	24
Fremont Diner	**Sonoma/N**	24
Willow Wood	**Graton/N**	24
Mama's Royal	**Oakland/E**	24
Koi	**Daly City/S**	24
La Note	**Berkeley/E**	23
Oliveto Cafe	**Oakland/E**	23
Rick & Ann	**Berkeley/E**	23
Water St. Bistro	**Petaluma/N**	23
🆕 903	**Bernal Hts**	23
Chloe's Cafe	**Noe Valley**	23
Mo's	**N Beach**	23
Emporio Rulli	**Downtown**	22
Butler/Chef	**SoMa**	22
Model Bakery	**St. Helena/N**	22
Rose's Cafe	**Cow Hollow**	22
Kate's Kit.	**Lower Haight**	22
Alexis Baking	**Napa/N**	22
Il Fornaio	**multi.**	22
Town's End	**Embarcadero**	22
La Boulange	**multi.**	22
Farm:Table	**Civic Ctr**	21
Blackberry Bistro	**Oakland/E**	21
Sears	**Downtown**	21
Ella's	**Presidio Hts**	21
FatApple's	**multi.**	20
Jimmy Beans	**Berkeley/E**	20
Jimtown Store	**Healdsburg/N**	20
Pork Store	**multi.**	19
Dipsea Cafe	**Mill Valley/N**	19
Rigolo	**Presidio Hts**	18
Toast (SF)	**Noe Valley**	17
Mel's Drive-In	**multi.**	17

BRUNCH

Erna's	**Oakhurst/E**	28
Redd	**Yountville/N**	28
La Forêt	**San Jose/S**	27
Seasons	**Downtown**	27
Nopa	**W Addition**	27
Wente Vineyards	**Livermore/E**	26
Yank Sing	**SoMa**	26
Campton Pl.	**Downtown**	26
Zuni Café	**Hayes Valley**	26
Boulettes Larder	**Embarcadero**	26
Baker/Banker	**Upper Fillmore**	26
Brenda's	**Civic Ctr**	25
Universal Cafe	**Mission**	25
Greens	**Marina**	25
Bar Jules	**Hayes Valley**	25
Insalata's	**San Anselmo/N**	25
Navio	**Half Moon Bay/S**	25
Buckeye	**Mill Valley/N**	25
SPQR	**Pacific Hts**	25
Outerlands	**Outer Sunset**	25
Camino	**Oakland/E**	25
Foreign Cinema	**Mission**	25
Tra Vigne	**St. Helena/N**	24
Madera	**Menlo Pk/S**	24
Gayle's Bakery	**Capitola/S**	24
Girl/Fig	**Sonoma/N**	24
Zazie	**Cole Valley**	24
Venus	**Berkeley/E**	24
Fremont Diner	**Sonoma/N**	24
Tarpy's	**Monterey/S**	24
Willow Wood	**Graton/N**	24
Absinthe	**Hayes Valley**	24
Lark Creek	**Walnut Creek/E**	24
La Note	**Berkeley/E**	23
Rio Grill	**Carmel/S**	23
Rick & Ann	**Berkeley/E**	23
Anzu	**Downtown**	23
Slow Club	**Mission**	23
Waterbar	**Embarcadero**	23
Scott's Seafood	**multi.**	23
Mission Bch. Café	**Mission**	23
Chloe's Cafe	**Noe Valley**	23
Gabriella Café	**Santa Cruz/S**	23

Bar Agricole | **SoMa**	23
1300/Fillmore | **W Addition**	23
Bistro Liaison | **Berkeley/E**	23
Epic Roasthse. | **Embarcadero**	23
15 Romolo | **N Beach**	22
Picante Cocina | **Berkeley/E**	22
Rose's Cafe | **Cow Hollow**	22
Duck Club | **Lafayette/E**	22
Nob Hill Café | **Nob Hill**	22
Liberty Cafe | **Bernal Hts**	22
Kate's Kit. | **Lower Haight**	22
Baker St. Bistro | **Marina**	22
Catch | **Castro**	22
Alexis Baking | **Napa/N**	22
Tav./Lark Creek | **Larkspur/N**	22
Town's End | **Embarcadero**	22
Garden Ct. | **Downtown**	22
Ahwahnee | **Yosemite/E**	22
Marinitas | **San Anselmo/N**	22
Five | **Berkeley/E**	21
Mayfield | **Palo Alto/S**	21
Fandango | **Pacific Grove/S**	21
Chow/Park Chow | **multi.**	21
Elite Cafe | **Pacific Hts**	21
Ella's | **Presidio Hts**	21
Grand Cafe | **Downtown**	21
Q Rest. | **Inner Rich**	20
MoMo's | **S Beach**	20
Balboa Cafe | **Cow Hollow**	20
Piazza D'Angelo | **Mill Valley/N**	20
Luna Park | **Mission**	20
Le Zinc | **Noe Valley**	20
Trader Vic's | **Emeryville/E**	19
Park Chalet | **Outer Sunset**	17
Beach Chalet | **Outer Sunset**	17

BUSINESS DINING

Marinus | **Carmel Valley/S**	28
Kokkari | **Downtown**	28
Evvia | **Palo Alto/S**	28
Boulevard | **Embarcadero**	27
Masa's | **Downtown**	27
Cole's Chop | **Napa/N**	27
La Forêt | **San Jose/S**	27
Fleur de Lys | **Downtown**	27
Michael Mina | **Downtown**	27
Le Papillon | **San Jose/S**	27
Seasons | **Downtown**	27
Sent Sovi | **Saratoga/S**	27

Piperade | **Downtown**	27
Ruth's Chris | **Polk Gulch**	27
Harris' | **Polk Gulch**	27
Press | **St. Helena/N**	26
House/Prime | **Polk Gulch**	26
Picco | **Larkspur/N**	26
Alexander's Steak | **multi.**	26
Quince | **Downtown**	26
Flea St. Café | **Menlo Pk/S**	26
Chiaroscuro | **Downtown**	26
Yank Sing | **SoMa**	26
Cotogna | **Downtown**	26
Ame | **SoMa**	26
Campton Pl. | **Downtown**	26
Zuni Café | **Hayes Valley**	26
Perbacco | **Downtown**	26
Jin Sho | **Palo Alto/S**	26
Solbar | **Calistoga/N**	26
Dio Deka | **Los Gatos/S**	25
Morton's | **multi.**	25
Chantilly | **Redwood City/S**	25
All Spice | **San Mateo/S**	25
Bottega | **Yountville/N**	25
Plumed Horse | **Saratoga/S**	25
Fifth Floor | **SoMa**	25
Murray Circle | **Sausalito/N**	25
Boca | **Novato/N**	25
Farallon | **Downtown**	25
Ozumo | **multi.**	25
Viognier | **San Mateo/S**	25
Lark Creek Steak | **Downtown**	25
Tommy Toy | **Downtown**	25
Poggio | **Sausalito/N**	24
Madera | **Menlo Pk/S**	24
Prospect | **SoMa**	24
Barbacco | **Downtown**	24
Wexler's | **Downtown**	24
One Market | **Embarcadero**	24
Kanpai | **Palo Alto/S**	24
Pazzia | **SoMa**	24
Big 4 | **Nob Hill**	24
Amber India | **multi.**	24
Gitane | **Downtown**	24
Tadich Grill | **Downtown**	24
Roy's | **SoMa**	24
Bourbon | **Downtown**	24
Osteria | **Palo Alto/S**	24
Peasant/Pear | **Danville/E**	24
Alfred's Steak | **Downtown**	23

SPECIAL FEATURES

CELEBRITY CHEFS

Jesse Cool
  Flea St. Café | **Menlo Pk/S**   26
  Cool Café | **multi.**   21
Chris Cosentino
  Boccalone | **Embarcadero**   25
  Incanto | **Noe Valley**   25
Dominique Crenn
  Atelier Crenn | **Marina**   27
Gary Danko
  Gary Danko | **Fish. Wharf**   29
Traci Des Jardins
  Jardinière | **Civic Ctr**   27
  Manzanita | **Truckee/E**   23
  Mijita | **multi.**   20
  Public Hse. | **S Beach**   17
Brad Farmerie
  NEW Thomas/Fagiani's | -
  Napa/N
Ryan Farr
  4505 Meats | **Embarcadero**   26
Tyler Florence
  Wayfare Tav. | **Downtown**   24
  El Paseo | **Mill Valley/N**   23
  NEW Hawk's Tav. | 21
  Mill Valley/N
Ken Frank
  La Toque | **Napa/N**   27
  Bank Café | **Napa/N**   24
Mark Franz
  Farallon | **Downtown**   25
  Waterbar | **Embarcadero**   23
Ruggero Gadaldi
  Pesce | **Russian Hill**   25
  Beretta | **Mission**   24
  Delarosa | **Marina**   22
Tony Gemignani
  Tony's Pizza | **N Beach**   26
  Tony's Coal-Fired | **N Beach**   24
Charlie Hallowell
  Pizzaiolo | **Oakland/E**   26
  Boot/Shoe | **Oakland/E**   24
Bruce Hill
  Picco | **Larkspur/N**   26
  Pizzeria Picco | **Larkspur/N**   26
  Zero Zero | **SoMa**   24
  Bix | **Downtown**   24
Gerald Hirigoyen
  Piperade | **Downtown**   27
  Bocadillos | **N Beach**   23

Scott Howard
  Brick/Bottle | 19
  Corte Madera/N
Joseph Humphrey
  NEW Dixie | **Presidio**   -
Todd Humphries
  Kitchen Door | **Napa/N**   22
Philippe Jeanty
  Bistro Jeanty | **Yountville/N**   27
Laurence Jossel
  Nopa | **W Addition**   27
  Nopalito | **multi.**   24
Shotaro "Sho" Kamio
  Yoshi's | **Oakland/E**   23
  Yoshi's | **W Addition**   23
Laurent Katgely
  Chez Spencer | **Mission**   25
Douglas Keane
  Healdsburg B&G | 20
  Healdsburg/N
Hubert Keller
  Fleur de Lys | **Downtown**   27
  Burger Bar | **Downtown**   20
Loretta Keller
  Coco500 | **SoMa**   23
Thomas Keller
  French Laundry | 29
  Yountville/N
  Ad Hoc | **Yountville/N**   27
  Bouchon | **Yountville/N**   26
David Kinch
  Manresa | **Los Gatos/S**   27
Christopher Kostow
  Meadowood Rest. | 27
  St. Helena/N
Christopher Kump
  Fort Bragg | **Ft Bragg/N**   23
Mourad Lahlou
  Aziza | **Outer Rich**   26
Dennis Leary
  Canteen | **Tenderloin**   27
  Sentinel | **SoMa**   24
  Golden West | **Downtown**   21
Corey Lee
  Benu | **SoMa**   27
Dennis Lee
  Namu | **Mission**   -
Anthony Mangieri
  Una Pizza | **SoMa**   26

Joseph Manzare
Zuppa | **SoMa** — 19
Globe | **Downtown** — 18
Hecho | **Downtown** — 18

Thomas McNaughton
Flour + Water | **Mission** — 26
NEW Central Kitchen | **Mission** — -
NEW Salumeria | **Mission** — -

Michael Mina
Michael Mina | **Downtown** — 27
Arcadia | **San Jose/S** — 24
Bourbon | **Downtown** — 24
RN74 | **SoMa** — 23

Russell Moore
Camino | **Oakland/E** — 25

Masaharu Morimoto
Morimoto | **Napa/N** — 25

Nancy Oakes
Boulevard | **Embarcadero** — 27
Prospect | **SoMa** — 24

Daniel Olivella
Barlata | **Oakland/E** — 22
B44 | **Downtown** — 22

Rene Ortiz
NEW La Condesa | **St. Helena/N** — 24

Charlie Palmer
Dry Creek | **Healdsburg/N** — 24
NEW Burritt Tavern | **Downtown** — -

Roland Passot
La Folie | **Russian Hill** — 27
LB Steak | **San Jose/S** — 22

Daniel Patterson
Coi | **N Beach** — 27
NEW Haven | **Oakland/E** — 25
Plum | **Oakland/E** — 23

Cindy Pawlcyn
Mustards | **Yountville/N** — 25
Cindy's | **St. Helena/N** — 24
NEW Brassica | **St. Helena/N** — 22

Melissa Perello
Frances | **Castro** — 27

Charles Phan
Slanted Door | **Embarcadero** — 26
Out the Door | **multi.** — 23
NEW Wo Hing | **Mission** — 22
Academy Cafe | **Inner Rich** — 21

Heaven's Dog | **SoMa** — 20
NEW Moss Room | **Outer Rich** — -

Richard Reddington
Redd | **Yountville/N** — 28
NEW Redd Wood | **Yountville/N** — 25

Judy Rodgers
Zuni Café | **Hayes Valley** — 26

Mitchell and Steven Rosenthal
Town Hall | **SoMa** — 23
Salt Hse. | **SoMa** — 22
Anchor & Hope | **SoMa** — 22

Ryan Scott
3-Sum | **Loc varies** — 25
NEW Market & Rye | **multi.** — -

Gregory Short
Masa's | **Downtown** — 27

Joshua Skenes
Saison | **Mission** — 27

Hiro Sone
Terra | **St. Helena/N** — 27
Ame | **SoMa** — 26
Bar Terra | **St. Helena/N** — 25

Cal Stamenov
Marinus | **Carmel Valley/S** — 28

Craig Stoll
Delfina | **Mission** — 27
Pizzeria Delfina | **multi.** — 26
Locanda | **Mission** — 25

James Syhabout
Commis | **Oakland/E** — 28
Hawker Fare | **Oakland/E** — 23

Michael Tusk
Quince | **Downtown** — 26
Cotogna | **Downtown** — 26

Alice Waters
Chez Panisse Café | **Berkeley/E** — 28
Chez Panisse | **Berkeley/E** — 28

Joanne Weir
NEW Copita | **Sausalito/N** — -

Roy Yamaguchi
Roy's | **Pebble Bch/S** — 26
Roy's | **SoMa** — 24

Chris Yeo
Straits | **multi.** — 21
Sino | **San Jose/S** — 20

CHILD-FRIENDLY

(Alternatives to the usual fast-food places; * children's menu available)

Tony's Pizza* | **N Beach**	26
Cook St. Helena | **St. Helena/N**	26
Yank Sing | **SoMa**	26
Roy's* | **Pebble Bch/S**	26
Rosso Pizzeria* | **Santa Rosa/N**	26
Pizzeria Delfina | **multi.**	26
Zachary's Pizza | **Oakland/E**	26
Burma Superstar | **Inner Rich**	25
La Taqueria | **Mission**	25
Mustards | **Yountville/N**	25
Ton Kiang | **Outer Rich**	25
Insalata's* | **San Anselmo/N**	25
R & G Lounge | **Chinatown**	25
Buckeye* | **Mill Valley/N**	25
NEW Redd Wood | **Yountville/N**	25
Bette's Oceanview | **Berkeley/E**	25
Lark Creek Steak* | **Downtown**	25
O'mei | **Santa Cruz/S**	25
Vik's Chaat* | **Berkeley/E**	25
Lers Ros Thai | **multi.**	25
Fish* | **Sausalito/N**	25
Foreign Cinema* | **Mission**	25
Scoma's* | **multi.**	25
Zero Zero | **SoMa**	24
Mama's on Wash. | **N Beach**	24
Cindy's* | **St. Helena/N**	24
Tommaso's | **N Beach**	24
Arcadia* | **San Jose/S**	24
Lo Coco's | **multi.**	24
Luella* | **Russian Hill**	24
Tarpy's* | **Monterey/S**	24
Willow Wood | **Graton/N**	24
Bellanico | **Oakland/E**	24
Cetrella* | **Half Moon Bay/S**	24
Tony's Coal-Fired | **N Beach**	24
Koi | **Daly City/S**	24
Lark Creek* | **Walnut Creek/E**	24
Taqueria Can Cun | **multi.**	23
Original Joe's* | **San Jose/S**	23
Kuleto's | **Downtown**	23
Super Duper | **multi.**	23
Chenery Park | **Glen Pk**	23
Rick & Ann* | **Berkeley/E**	23
Shen Hua | **Berkeley/E**	23
Azzurro | **Napa/N**	23
Pancho Villa | **multi.**	23

Hurley's | **Yountville/N**	23
NEW 903 | **Bernal Hts**	23
Osteria Coppa* | **San Mateo/S**	23
Pauline's | **Mission**	23
Parcel 104* | **Santa Clara/S**	23
Great Eastern | **Chinatown**	23
Flavor* | **Santa Rosa/N**	23
Forbes Mill* | **Danville/E**	23
Eliza's | **Pacific Hts**	23
La Méditerranée* | **multi.**	23
Xolo Taqueria | **Oakland/E**	23
Caspers Hot Dogs | **multi.**	23
Parada 22 | **Haight-Ashbury**	23
Pizzeria Tra Vigne* | **St. Helena/N**	23
Mo's | **N Beach**	23
Duarte's* | **Pescadero/S**	23
Quattro* | **E Palo Alto/S**	22
Sam's Chowder* | **Half Moon Bay/S**	22
Picante Cocina* | **Berkeley/E**	22
Model Bakery | **multi.**	22
La Ginestra | **Mill Valley/N**	22
Bungalow 44* | **Mill Valley/N**	22
Joe's Cable Car | **Excelsior**	22
Bo's BBQ | **Lafayette/E**	22
Pizza Antica* | **multi.**	22
Aperto* | **Potrero Hill**	22
Pacific Catch* | **multi.**	22
Henry's Hunan | **multi.**	22
Kitchen Door* | **Napa/N**	22
Eric's | **Noe Valley**	22
Homeroom* | **Oakland/E**	22
Market | **St. Helena/N**	22
Tacko | **Cow Hollow**	22
Front Porch* | **Bernal Hts**	22
Fentons* | **Oakland/E**	22
Giorgio's | **Inner Rich**	22
Giordano | **N Beach**	22
Alexis Baking | **Napa/N**	22
La Cumbre | **Mission**	22
Gott's Roadside* | **multi.**	22
Goat Hill | **Potrero Hill**	22
Il Fornaio* | **multi.**	22
Cactus Taqueria* | **multi.**	22
Barney's* | **multi.**	22
Ahwahnee* | **Yosemite/E**	22
La Boulange | **multi.**	22
Barbara's* | **Princeton Sea/S**	22
Boudin* | **Fish. Wharf**	22

Basque Cultural* | **S San Francisco/S**	21
Alioto's* | **Fish. Wharf**	21
Lovejoy's Tea* | **Noe Valley**	21
Venezia* | **Berkeley/E**	21
Rustic* | **Geyserville/N**	21
Cool Café | **Stanford/S**	21
Caffè Macaroni* | **N Beach**	21
North Bch. Pizza | **multi.**	21
Amici's* | **multi.**	21
Cheesecake Fac.* | **multi.**	21
Sears | **Downtown**	21
Chow/Park Chow* | **multi.**	21
Juan's | **Berkeley/E**	21
Piatti* | **multi.**	21
Joe's Taco* | **Mill Valley/N**	21
NEW Hawk's Tav.* | **Mill Valley/N**	21
Brandy Ho's | **multi.**	21
Ella's | **Presidio Hts**	21
Showdogs | **Downtown**	21
FatApple's* | **multi.**	20
Norman Rose | **Napa/N**	20
Left Bank* | **multi.**	20
Jimmy Beans* | **Berkeley/E**	20
Q Rest. | **Inner Rich**	20
Citrus Club | **Haight-Ashbury**	20
Emmy's Spaghetti* | **Bernal Hts**	20
Jimtown Store | **Healdsburg/N**	20
Mijita* | **multi.**	20
Healdsburg B&G* | **Healdsburg/N**	20
Saul's Rest./Deli* | **Berkeley/E**	20
Brannan's Grill | **Calistoga/N**	20
Gar Woods* | **Carnelian Bay/E**	20
Rest. Peony | **Oakland/E**	20
Taqueria 3 Amigos* | **multi.**	20
Max's* | **multi.**	20
Alice's | **Noe Valley**	20
Fog City Diner* | **Embarcadero**	20
Juban | **multi.**	20
Wurst Rest. | **Healdsburg/N**	20
Yankee Pier* | **multi.**	19
Burger Joint | **Mission**	19
Rudy's Can't Fail* | **multi.**	19
NEW Roosertail | **Upper Fillmore**	19
Pasta Pomodoro* | **multi.**	19
Let's Be Frank | **multi.**	19
Dipsea Cafe* | **Mill Valley/N**	19
Mifune | **Japantown**	19
Jay's* | **multi.**	19

Rigolo* | **Presidio Hts**	18
Buca di Beppo* | **multi.**	18
Nepenthe* | **Big Sur/S**	18
Guaymas* | **Tiburon/N**	17
Toast (SF)* | **Noe Valley**	17
Park Chalet* | **Outer Sunset**	17
Mel's Drive-In* | **multi.**	17
Beach Chalet* | **Outer Sunset**	17
NEW 400 Degrees* | **Carmel/S**	–
NEW Gioia Pizzeria | **Russian Hill**	–

COCKTAIL SPECIALISTS

Redd | **Yountville/N**	28
Michael Mina | **Downtown**	27
Range | **Mission**	27
Jardinière | **Civic Ctr**	27
Nopa | **W Addition**	27
Aziza | **Outer Rich**	26
Slanted Door | **Embarcadero**	26
Wood Tav. | **Oakland/E**	26
AQ | **SoMa**	25
Bar Terra | **St. Helena/N**	25
Oswald | **Santa Cruz/S**	25
À Côté | **Oakland/E**	25
Locanda | **Mission**	25
Park Tav. | **N Beach**	25
Haven | **Oakland/E**	25
Foreign Cinema | **Mission**	25
Beretta | **Mission**	24
Prospect | **SoMa**	24
Boot/Shoe | **Oakland/E**	24
Zero Zero | **SoMa**	24
Girl/Fig | **Sonoma/N**	24
Parallel 37 | **Nob Hill**	24
Bix | **Downtown**	24
Betelnut Pejiu | **Cow Hollow**	24
Wayfare Tav. | **Downtown**	24
La Condesa | **St. Helena/N**	24
Absinthe | **Hayes Valley**	24
Plum | **Oakland/E**	23
Dosa | **multi.**	23
Flora | **Oakland/E**	23
Coco500 | **SoMa**	23
Alembic | **Haight-Ashbury**	23
Adesso | **Oakland/E**	23
Bar Agricole | **SoMa**	23
Le Colonial | **Downtown**	23
15 Romolo | **N Beach**	22

Salt Hse. | **SoMa**	22
Hog & Rocks | **Mission**	22
Starbelly | **Castro**	22
Revival Bar | **Berkeley/E**	22
Per Diem | **Downtown**	22
Sidebar | **Oakland/E**	22
Underwood Bar | **Graton/N**	22
Wo Hing | **Mission**	22
Plate Shop | **Sausalito/N**	22
Nombe | **Mission**	22
Delarosa | **Marina**	22
Rumbo | **Oakland/E**	21
Nihon | **Mission**	21
Heaven's Dog | **SoMa**	20
Spoonbar | **Healdsburg/N**	20
Café des Amis | **Cow Hollow**	19
Dear Mom | **Mission**	19
Brick/Bottle | **Corte Madera/N**	19
Tres | **S Beach**	18
NEW Brasserie S&P | **Downtown**	-
NEW Copita | **Sausalito/N**	-
NEW Dixie | **Presidio**	-

DANCING

Le Colonial | **Downtown**	23
Luka's Taproom | **Oakland/E**	20
Hopmonk Tav. | **multi.**	20
Uva Trattoria | **Napa/N**	19

ENTERTAINMENT

(Call for days and times of performances)

Marinus | piano | **Carmel Valley/S**	28
Ledford Hse. | jazz | **Albion/N**	27
Harris' | live music | **Polk Gulch**	27
Zuni Café | piano | **Hayes Valley**	26
Foreign Cinema | films | **Mission**	25
Albion River Inn | piano | **Albion/N**	25
Big 4 | piano | **Nob Hill**	24
Bix | jazz | **Downtown**	24
Sardine Factory | piano | **Monterey/S**	24
Cetrella | live music | **Half Moon Bay/S**	24
La Note | accordion | **Berkeley/E**	23
Ana Mandara | jazz | **Fish. Wharf**	23
Scott's Seafood | jazz/piano | **multi.**	23
Yoshi's | live jazz | **Oakland/E**	23
Blowfish Sushi | DJ | **San Jose/S**	23
Cascal | Latin music | **Mtn View/S**	23
Yoshi's | live jazz | **W Addition**	23
Giordano | live music | **N Beach**	22
Garden Ct. | live music | **Downtown**	22
Ahwahnee | piano | **Yosemite/E**	22
Rose Pistola | jazz | **N Beach**	21
Everett/Jones BBQ | jazz | **Oakland/E**	21
Max's | varies | **multi.**	20
Uva Trattoria | varies | **Napa/N**	19
Beach Chalet | live music | **Outer Sunset**	17

FIREPLACES

French Laundry | **Yountville/N**	29
Erna's | **Oakhurst/E**	28
Marinus | **Carmel Valley/S**	28
Kokkari | **Downtown**	28
Sierra Mar | **Big Sur/S**	28
Evvia | **Palo Alto/S**	28
Farmhse. Inn | **Forestville/N**	27
Madrona Manor | **Healdsburg/N**	27
Auberge du Soleil | **Rutherford/N**	27
Fleur de Lys | **Downtown**	27
Manresa | **Los Gatos/S**	27
Étoile | **Yountville/N**	27
Meadowood Rest. | **St. Helena/N**	27
Bistro Jeanty | **Yountville/N**	27
La Toque | **Napa/N**	27
Ledford Hse. | **Albion/N**	27
Harris' | **Polk Gulch**	27
Press | **St. Helena/N**	26
House/Prime | **Polk Gulch**	26
Alexander's Steak | **Cupertino/S**	26
Prima | **Walnut Creek/E**	26
Spruce | **Presidio Hts**	26
Ame | **SoMa**	26
Stark's | **Santa Rosa/N**	26
Dio Deka | **Los Gatos/S**	25
Village Pub | **Woodside/S**	25
Rest./Stevenswood | **Little River/N**	25
Chantilly | **Redwood City/S**	25
Chez Spencer | **Mission**	25
Sundance Steak | **Palo Alto/S**	25
John Ash | **Santa Rosa/N**	25
All Spice | **San Mateo/S**	25
Farm | **Napa/N**	25
Alex Rest. | **Rutherford/N**	25

Kenwood	**Kenwood/N**	25	PlumpJack	**Olympic Valley/E**	23
Terzo	**Cow Hollow**	25	St. Orres	**Gualala/N**	23
Plumed Horse	**Saratoga/S**	25	El Dorado	**Sonoma/N**	23
Haps Original	**Pleasanton/E**	25	Caprice	**Tiburon/N**	23
Murray Circle	**Sausalito/N**	25	Izzy's Steak	**Marina**	23
Ravens'	**Mendocino/N**	25	Epic Roasthse.	**Embarcadero**	23
Santé	**Sonoma/N**	25	Ma Maison	**Aptos/S**	23
Boca	**Novato/N**	25	Ravenous	**Healdsburg/N**	22
Navio	**Half Moon Bay/S**	25	Farmstead	**St. Helena/N**	22
Bistro Don Giovanni	**Napa/N**	25	Quattro	**E Palo Alto/S**	22
Viognier	**San Mateo/S**	25	Sam's Chowder		22
Buckeye	**Mill Valley/N**	25	**Half Moon Bay/S**	
Camino	**Oakland/E**	25	LB Steak	**San Jose/S**	22
Foreign Cinema	**Mission**	25	Duck Club	**Bodega Bay/N**	22
Albion River Inn	**Albion/N**	25	Moosse Café	**Mendocino/N**	22
Bella Vista	**Woodside/S**	25	Plouf	**Downtown**	22
Madera	**Menlo Pk/S**	24	Monti's	**Santa Rosa/N**	22
Casanova	**Carmel/S**	24	Cattlemens	**multi.**	22
Vic Stewart	**Walnut Creek/E**	24	Iberia	**Menlo Pk/S**	22
Gayle's Bakery	**Capitola/S**	24	Shadowbrook	**Capitola/S**	22
Applewood Rest.	**Guerneville/N**	24	Tav./Lark Creek	**Larkspur/N**	22
Lupa Trattoria	**Noe Valley**	24	Il Fornaio	**multi.**	22
Big 4	**Nob Hill**	24	Rest. LuLu	**SoMa**	22
Deetjen's Big Sur	**Big Sur/S**	24	Osha Thai	**Embarcadero**	22
Betelnut Pejiu	**Cow Hollow**	24	Speisekammer	**Alameda/E**	22
Postino	**Lafayette/E**	24	Barney's	**Berkeley/E**	22
Anton/Michel	**Carmel/S**	24	Guamenkitzel	**Berkeley/E**	22
Chez TJ	**Mtn View/S**	24	C Rest.	**Monterey/S**	22
Sardine Factory	**Monterey/S**	24	Davenport	**Davenport/S**	22
Wayfare Tav.	**Downtown**	24	Ahwahnee	**Yosemite/E**	22
MacCallum	**Mendocino/N**	24	Troya	**Inner Rich**	22
Soule Domain	**Kings Bch/E**	24	Another Monkey/Koh	**Mission**	21
Pacific's Edge	**Carmel/S**	24	Townhouse B&G	**Emeryville/E**	21
Flying Fish (Carmel)	**Carmel/S**	24	Nick's Cove	**Marshall/N**	21
Della Santina	**Sonoma/N**	24	Caffè Macaroni	**N Beach**	21
Tarpy's	**Monterey/S**	24	Fandango	**Pacific Grove/S**	21
Cafe Citti	**Kenwood/N**	24	Casa Orinda	**Orinda/E**	21
Cetrella	**Half Moon Bay/S**	24	Hilltop 1892	**Novato/N**	21
Mezza Luna	**Princeton Sea/S**	24	Chow/Park Chow	**multi.**	21
Rio Grill	**Carmel/S**	23	Metro	**Lafayette/E**	21
Kuleto's	**Downtown**	23	Piatti	**multi.**	21
5A5 Steak	**Downtown**	23	Toast	**Novato/N**	21
El Paseo	**Mill Valley/N**	23	Hawk's Tav.	**Mill Valley/N**	21
Wine Spectator	**St. Helena/N**	23	Mendocino Hotel	**Mendocino/N**	21
Scott's Seafood	**Palo Alto/S**	23	Samovar Tea	**Hayes Valley**	21
Brix	**Napa/N**	23	Left Bank	**Larkspur/N**	20
Parcel 104	**Santa Clara/S**	23	Skates on Bay	**Berkeley/E**	20
Flavor	**Santa Rosa/N**	23	Zibibbo	**Palo Alto/S**	20
Forbes Mill	**Los Gatos/S**	23	Brannan's Grill	**Calistoga/N**	20

Cottonwood | **Truckee/E** 20
Gar Woods | **Carnelian Bay/E** 20
Piazza D'Angelo | **Mill Valley/N** 20
Jake's/Lake | **Tahoe City/E** 20
Sunnyside Lodge | **Tahoe City/E** 20
Café des Amis | **Cow Hollow** 19
Café Gratitude | **Berkeley/E** 19
Dipsea Cafe | **Mill Valley/N** 19
Nepenthe | **Big Sur/S** 18
Half Moon Brew | 18
   Half Moon Bay/S
Guaymas | **Tiburon/N** 17
Lake Chalet | **Oakland/E** 17
🆕 Corners Tav. | –
   Walnut Creek/E

FOOD STANDS/ TRUCKS

3-Sum | **Loc varies** 25
Cupkates | **Loc varies** 25
RoliRoti | **Embarcadero** 24
Chairman | **Loc varies** 24
Curry Up Now | **Loc varies** 23
Bacon Bacon | **Loc varies** 23
El Tonayense | **Loc varies** 23
Sam's Chowder | **Loc varies** 22
Hapa Ramen | **Loc varies** 21
🆕 Del Popolo | **Downtown** –

GREEN/LOCAL/ ORGANIC

(Specializing in organic, local ingredients)

Gary Danko | **Fish. Wharf** 29
French Laundry | **Yountville/N** 29
Terrapin Creek | **Bodega Bay/N** 28
Erna's | **Oakhurst/E** 28
Marinus | **Carmel Valley/S** 28
Sierra Mar | **Big Sur/S** 28
Commis | **Oakland/E** 28
Chez Panisse Café | **Berkeley/E** 28
Rivoli | **Berkeley/E** 28
Chez Panisse | **Berkeley/E** 28
Cafe Gibraltar | **El Granada/S** 28
Boulevard | **Embarcadero** 27
Masa's | **Downtown** 27
Passionfish | **Pacific Grove/S** 27
Farmhse. Inn | **Forestville/N** 27
La Folie | **Russian Hill** 27
La Ciccia | **Noe Valley** 27
La Taquiza | **Napa/N** 27

Madrona Manor | **Healdsburg/N** 27
Tartine | **Mission** 27
Saison | **Mission** 27
Local Mission | **Mission** 27
Fleur de Lys | **Downtown** 27
Manresa | **Los Gatos/S** 27
Étoile | **Yountville/N** 27
Atelier Crenn | **Marina** 27
Wolfdale's | **Tahoe City/E** 27
Coi | **N Beach** 27
Ajanta | **Berkeley/E** 27
Millennium | **Downtown** 27
Della Fattoria | **Petaluma/N** 27
Range | **Mission** 27
Meadowood Rest. | **St. Helena/N** 27
La Toque | **Napa/N** 27
Canteen | **Tenderloin** 27
Frances | **Castro** 27
Ledford Hse. | **Albion/N** 27
Marché/Fleurs | **Ross/N** 27
Delfina | **Mission** 27
Jardinière | **Civic Ctr** 27
Nopa | **W Addition** 27
Cafe La Haye | **Sonoma/N** 27
Ad Hoc | **Yountville/N** 27
Press | **St. Helena/N** 26
Picco | **Larkspur/N** 26
Wente Vineyards | 26
   Livermore/E
La Posta | **Santa Cruz/S** 26
Quince | **Downtown** 26
Sebo | **Hayes Valley** 26
Aubergine | **Carmel/S** 26
Richmond | **Inner Rich** 26
Pizzaiolo | **Oakland/E** 26
Gioia Pizzeria | **Berkeley/E** 26
Slanted Door | **Embarcadero** 26
Table Café | **Larkspur/N** 26
Cafe Beaujolais | 26
   Mendocino/N
Lalime's | **Berkeley/E** 26
Spruce | **Presidio Hts** 26
Pizzetta 211 | **Outer Rich** 26
Flea St. Café | **Menlo Pk/S** 26
Cotogna | **Downtown** 26
4505 Meats | **Embarcadero** 26
Dopo | **Oakland/E** 26
Oliveto Rest. | **Oakland/E** 26
Zuni Café | **Hayes Valley** 26

Tamarine | **Palo Alto/S**	26		Fish | **Sausalito/N**	25
Commonwealth | **Mission**	26		Foreign Cinema | **Mission**	25
Flour + Water | **Mission**	26		North Bch. Rest. | **N Beach**	25
Mendo Bistro | **Ft Bragg/N**	26		Zatar | **Berkeley/E**	25
Boulettes Larder | **Embarcadero**	26		Anokha/Lotus | **San Rafael/N**	25
Pizzeria Picco | **Larkspur/N**	26		Poggio | **Sausalito/N**	24
Encuentro | **Oakland/E**	26		Tra Vigne | **St. Helena/N**	24
Solbar | **Calistoga/N**	26		Dry Creek | **Healdsburg/N**	24
Zazu | **Santa Rosa/N**	25		Maverick | **Mission**	24
Village Pub | **Woodside/S**	25		Gather | **Berkeley/E**	24
Harvest Moon | **Sonoma/N**	25		Madera | **Menlo Pk/S**	24
Artisan Bistro | **Lafayette/E**	25		Prospect | **SoMa**	24
Rest./Stevenswood | **Little River/N**	25		One Market | **Embarcadero**	24
			Garibaldis | **Presidio Hts**	24
Gialina | **Glen Pk**	25		Parallel 37 | **Nob Hill**	24
John Ash | **Santa Rosa/N**	25		Deetjen's Big Sur | **Big Sur/S**	24
John Bentley | **Redwood City/S**	25		Nopalito | **W Addition**	24
Pearl | **Napa/N**	25		Osteria Stellina | **Pt Reyes/N**	24
Contigo | **Noe Valley**	25		Marzano | **Oakland/E**	24
Firefly | **Noe Valley**	25		MacCallum | **Mendocino/N**	24
Farm | **Napa/N**	25		Txoko | **N Beach**	24
Kiji Sushi Bar | **Mission**	25		Pacific's Edge | **Carmel/S**	24
Bottega | **Yountville/N**	25		Hayes St. Grill | **Hayes Valley**	24
Willi's Wine | **Santa Rosa/N**	25		Della Santina | **Sonoma/N**	24
Terzo | **Cow Hollow**	25		Luella | **Russian Hill**	24
Greens | **Marina**	25		Fremont Diner | **Sonoma/N**	24
Bar Jules | **Hayes Valley**	25		Zin | **Healdsburg/N**	24
Mustards | **Yountville/N**	25		Piccino | **Dogpatch**	24
K&L Bistro | **Sebastopol/N**	25		Blue Plate | **Mission**	24
Grégoire | **Berkeley/E**	25		Bellanico | **Oakland/E**	24
Fifth Floor | **SoMa**	25		Montrio Bistro | **Monterey/S**	24
Insalata's | **San Anselmo/N**	25		Aquarius | **Santa Cruz/S**	24
Ravens' | **Mendocino/N**	25		Rocker Oysterfellers | **Valley Ford/N**	24
Woodward's Gdn. | **Mission**	25		Lark Creek | **Walnut Creek/E**	24
Barndiva | **Healdsburg/N**	25		Dragonfly | **Truckee/E**	24
Underdog | **Inner Sunset**	25		Plum | **Oakland/E**	23
Farallon | **Downtown**	25		Regalito Rosticeria | **Mission**	23
Blue Barn | **Marina**	25		Dosa | **multi.**	23
Incanto | **Noe Valley**	25		Serpentine | **Dogpatch**	23
Navio | **Half Moon Bay/S**	25		Super Duper | **multi.**	23
Bistro Don Giovanni | **Napa/N**	25		Oliveto Cafe | **Oakland/E**	23
Dynamo Donut | **Mission**	25		Water St. Bistro | **Petaluma/N**	23
Viognier | **San Mateo/S**	25		Slow Club | **Mission**	23
Station 1 | **Woodside/S**	25		Harmony | **Mill Valley/N**	23
SPQR | **Pacific Hts**	25		Wise Sons | **Mission**	23
O Chamé | **Berkeley/E**	25		Hawker Fare | **Oakland/E**	23
Outerlands | **Outer Sunset**	25		Pauline's | **Mission**	23
Camino | **Oakland/E**	25		Brix | **Napa/N**	23
Sol Food | **San Rafael/N**	25			

Parcel 104	**Santa Clara/S**	23
Il Cane Rosso	**Embarcadero**	23
Donato	**Redwood City/S**	23
Mixt Greens	**Downtown**	23
Green Chile	**W Addition**	23
Xolo Taqueria	**Oakland/E**	23
Pizzeria Tra Vigne	**St. Helena/N**	23
Gabriella Café	**Santa Cruz/S**	23
Bar Agricole	**SoMa**	23
Tacubaya	**Berkeley/E**	23
St. Orres	**Gualala/N**	23
Sutro's	**Outer Rich**	23
Epic Roasthse.	**Embarcadero**	23
Butler/Chef	**SoMa**	22
Ravenous	**Healdsburg/N**	22
Farmstead	**St. Helena/N**	22
Doña Tomás	**Oakland/E**	22
Magnolia	**Haight-Ashbury**	22
Oola	**SoMa**	22
Pizza Antica	**Lafayette/E**	22
Dante's Weird Fish	**Mission**	22
Pacific Catch	**Marina**	22
Grasing's Coastal	**Carmel/S**	22
Eureka	**Castro**	22
Revival Bar	**Berkeley/E**	22
Zaré/Fly Trap	**SoMa**	22
Tav./Lark Creek	**Larkspur/N**	22
Plant Cafe	**multi.**	22
Radius	**SoMa**	22
Locavore	**Bernal Hts**	22
Underwood Bar	**Graton/N**	22
Farmerbrown	**multi.**	22
Plate Shop	**Sausalito/N**	22
Marinitas	**San Anselmo/N**	22
Nick's Crispy	**Russian Hill**	22
Nick's Cove	**Marshall/N**	21
Cool Café	**multi.**	21
Meadowood Grill	**St. Helena/N**	21
Breads/India	**multi.**	21
Peter Lowell	**Sebastopol/N**	21
Chow/Park Chow	**Inner Sunset**	21
Golden West	**Downtown**	21
Academy Cafe	**Inner Rich**	21
Fish & Farm	**Downtown**	20
Jimtown Store	**Healdsburg/N**	20
Mijita	**multi.**	20
Heaven's Dog	**SoMa**	20
Spoonbar	**Healdsburg/N**	20
Yankee Pier	**San Jose/S**	19

Chez Shea	**Half Moon Bay/S**	19
Café Gratitude	**multi.**	19
Imperial Tea	**Embarcadero**	19
T Rex BBQ	**Berkeley/E**	18
Globe	**Downtown**	18
MarketBar	**Embarcadero**	18

HISTORIC PLACES

(Year opened; * building)

1800	Central Mkt.*	**Petaluma/N**	26
1800	Market*	**St. Helena/N**	22
1800	Boxing Rm.*	**Hayes Valley**	21
1848	La Forêt*	**San Jose/S**	27
1848	Cindy's*	**St. Helena/N**	24
1856	Garden Ct.*	**Downtown**	22
1857	Little River Inn*	**Little River/N**	22
1860	Della Fattoria*	**Petaluma/N**	27
1860	Pizza Antica*	**Lafayette/E**	22
1863	Sutro's*	**Outer Rich**	23
1863	Cliff Hse.	**Outer Rich**	21
1864	Rocker Oysterfellers*	**Valley Ford/N**	24
1867	Sam's Grill	**Downtown**	22
1870	Bottega*	**Yountville/N**	25
1870	Murray Circle*	**Sausalito/N**	25
1873	Farmhse. Inn*	**Forestville/N**	27
1875	La Note*	**Berkeley/E**	23
1878	Mendocino Hotel*	**Mendocino/N**	21
1880	Pianeta*	**Truckee/E**	21
1881	Madrona Manor*	**Healdsburg/N**	27
1881	Il Fornaio*	**Carmel/S**	22
1882	MacCallum*	**Mendocino/N**	24
1883	Celadon*	**Napa/N**	25
1884	Terra*	**St. Helena/N**	27
1886	Cole's Chop*	**Napa/N**	27
1886	Mendo Bistro*	**Ft Bragg/N**	26
1886	Willi's Wine*	**Santa Rosa/N**	25
1888	Tav./Lark Creek*	**Larkspur/N**	22
1889	Boulevard*	**Embarcadero**	27
1889	Pacific Café*	**Outer Rich**	24
1889	Wine Spectator*	**St. Helena/N**	23

1890	Scoma's*	**Sausalito/N**	25
1890	Chez TJ*	**Mtn View/S**	24
1890	Eureka*	**Castro**	22
1890	Yankee Pier*	**Larkspur/N**	19
1893	Cafe Beaujolais*	**Mendocino/N**	26
1893	Jimtown Store*	**Healdsburg/N**	20
1894	Duarte's*	**Pescadero/S**	23
1894	Fentons	**Oakland/E**	22
1895	La Posta*	**Santa Cruz/S**	26
1895	Restaurant*	**Ft Bragg/N**	22
1898	Slanted Door*	**Embarcadero**	26
1900	French Laundry*	**Yountville/N**	29
1900	Frances*	**Castro**	27
1900	Diavola*	**Geyserville/N**	26
1900	Bar Tartine*	**Mission**	25
1900	Girl/Fig*	**Sonoma/N**	24
1900	Pauline's*	**Mission**	23
1900	Bar Agricole*	**SoMa**	23
1900	Emporio Rulli*	**Downtown**	22
1900	La Ginestra*	**Mill Valley/N**	22
1900	Cha Cha Cha*	**Mission**	22
1900	Axum Cafe*	**Lower Haight**	21
1904	Bourbon*	**Downtown**	24
1904	Moosse Café*	**Mendocino/N**	22
1905	Hopmonk Tav.*	**Sebastopol/N**	20
1906	AQ*	**SoMa**	25
1906	Wayfare Tav.*	**Downtown**	24
1906	Coco500*	**SoMa**	23
1906	Davenport*	**Davenport/S**	22
1906	Pork Store*	**Haight-Ashbury**	19
1906	Chez Shea*	**Half Moon Bay/S**	19
1906	Imperial Tea*	**Embarcadero**	19
1907	Tony's Pizza*	**N Beach**	26
1907	Tony's Coal-Fired*	**N Beach**	24
1907	Town Hall*	**SoMa**	23
1908	Mezza Luna*	**Princeton Sea/S**	24
1908	Zaré/Fly Trap*	**SoMa**	22
1908	Bottle Cap*	**N Beach**	18
1909	Campton Pl.*	**Downtown**	26

1909	Fort Bragg*	**Ft Bragg/N**	23
1910	Harris'*	**Polk Gulch**	27
1910	Sasa*	**Walnut Creek/E**	26
1910	Catch*	**Castro**	22
1910	Rest. LuLu*	**SoMa**	22
1911	Hotel Mac Rest.*	**Richmond/E**	21
1912	Swan Oyster	**Polk Gulch**	26
1913	Zuni Café*	**Hayes Valley**	26
1913	Balboa Cafe	**Cow Hollow**	20
1914	Wexler's*	**Downtown**	24
1914	Healdsburg B&G*	**Healdsburg/N**	20
1915	Napa Wine Train*	**Napa/N**	22
1915	Café des Amis*	**Cow Hollow**	19
1916	Amer. Grilled*	**SoMa**	23
1916	Cafe Divine*	**N Beach**	21
1917	Pacific's Edge*	**Carmel/S**	24
1917	Tarpy's*	**Monterey/S**	24
1918	St. Francis	**Mission**	18
1919	Albion River Inn*	**Albion/N**	25
1919	Ana Mandara*	**Fish. Wharf**	23
1919	Sauce*	**Hayes Valley**	22
1920	Acquerello*	**Polk Gulch**	28
1920	Commonwealth*	**Mission**	26
1920	Albona Rist.*	**N Beach**	25
1920	Florio*	**Pacific Hts**	22
1920	Boogaloos*	**Mission**	20
1922	Benu*	**SoMa**	27
1924	Big 4*	**Nob Hill**	24
1925	John Bentley*	**Redwood City/S**	25
1925	Farallon*	**Downtown**	25
1925	Rist. Capellini*	**San Mateo/S**	22
1925	Alioto's	**Fish. Wharf**	21
1927	Bella Vista*	**Woodside/S**	25
1927	Chop Bar*	**Oakland/E**	24
1927	Ahwahnee*	**Yosemite/E**	22
1927	Townhouse B&G*	**Emeryville/E**	21
1928	Ma Maison*	**Aptos/S**	23
1928	Elite Cafe*	**Pacific Hts**	21
1928	Cottonwood*	**Truckee/E**	20
1929	Aubergine*	**Carmel/S**	26
1930	Lalime's*	**Berkeley/E**	26
1930	Foreign Cinema*	**Mission**	25

1930 | Soule Domain* | Kings Bch/E — 24

1930 | Lo Coco's* | **Oakland/E** — 24

1930 | Willow Wood* | Graton/N — 24

1930 | Caprice* | **Tiburon/N** — 23

1930 | Ravenous* | **Healdsburg/N** — 22

1930 | Guamenkitzel* | Berkeley/E — 22

1932 | Camino* | **Oakland/E** — 25

1932 | Casa Orinda* | **Orinda/E** — 21

1933 | Luka's Taproom* | Oakland/E — 20

1934 | Stark's* | **Santa Rosa/N** — 26

1934 | Caspers Hot Dogs | Oakland/E — 23

1935 | Tommaso's | **N Beach** — 24

1936 | Cafe La Haye* | Sonoma/N — 27

1936 | Gabriella Café* | Santa Cruz/S — 23

1937 | Buckeye* | **Mill Valley/N** — 25

1937 | Deetjen's Big Sur* | Big Sur/S — 24

1937 | Postino* | **Lafayette/E** — 24

1937 | 231 Ellsworth* | San Mateo/S — 23

1938 | Sears | **Downtown** — 21

1940 | Glen Ellen Inn* | Glen Ellen/N — 24

1941 | Brown Sugar* | Oakland/E — 26

1947 | Shadowbrook | **Capitola/S** — 22

1948 | Evan's* | **S Lake Tahoe/E** — 27

1949 | House/Prime | **Polk Gulch** — 26

1949 | Gott's Roadside | St. Helena/N — 22

1949 | Nepenthe | **Big Sur/S** — 18

1950 | Sea Thai/Modern* | Santa Rosa/N — 27

1950 | Sundance Steak* | Palo Alto/S — 25

1950 | Alexis Baking* | **Napa/N** — 22

1952 | Rivoli* | **Berkeley/E** — 28

1952 | Plumed Horse | **Saratoga/S** — 25

1953 | Mel's Drive-In* | **Inner Rich** — 17

1955 | Breads/India* | **Berkeley/E** — 21

1956 | Original Joe's | **San Jose/S** — 23

1957 | Mama's on Wash. | N Beach — 24

1959 | Red Hut | S Lake Tahoe/E — 23

HOTEL DINING

Ahwahnee Hotel
  Ahwahnee | **Yosemite/E** — 22

Albion River Inn
  Albion River Inn | **Albion/N** — 25

Applewood Inn
  Applewood Rest. | **Guerneville/N** — 24

Auberge du Soleil
  Auberge du Soleil | **Rutherford/N** — 27

Bardessono Hotel & Spa
  NEW Lucy | **Yountville/N** — -

Basque Hotel
  15 Romolo | **N Beach** — 22

Bernardus Lodge
  Marinus | **Carmel Valley/S** — 28

Best Western Plus Lighthse.
  NEW Moonraker | **Pacifica/S** — 26

Blue Heron Inn
  Moosse Café | **Mendocino/N** — 22

Blue Rock Inn
  Left Bank | **Larkspur/N** — 20

California, Hotel
  Millennium | **Downtown** — 27

Carlton Hotel
  Saha | **Nob Hill** — 26

Carneros Inn
  Farm | **Napa/N** — 25
  Boon Fly | **Napa/N** — 23

Casa Madrona
  Poggio | **Sausalito/N** — 24

Cavallo Pt. Resort (Fort Baker)
  Murray Circle | **Sausalito/N** — 25

Château du Sureau
  Erna's | **Oakhurst/E** — 28

Claremont Hotel
  Meritage/Claremont | Berkeley/E — 22

El Dorado Hotel
  El Dorado | **Sonoma/N** — 23

Fairmont San Jose
  Grill/Alley | **San Jose/S** — 24
  McCormick/Schmick | San Jose/S — 23

Fairmont Sonoma
  Santé | **Sonoma/N** — 25

Farmhouse Inn
  Farmhse. Inn | **Forestville/N** — 27

Sir Francis Drake Hotel
  Scala's Bistro | **Downtown** — 23

Solage Resort
  Solbar | **Calistoga/N** — 26

Sonoma Hotel
  Girl/Fig | **Sonoma/N** — 24

Stanford Inn & Spa
  Ravens' | **Mendocino/N** — 25

Stevenswood Lodge
  Rest./Stevenswood | **Little River/N** — 25

St. Orres Hotel
  St. Orres | **Gualala/N** — 23

St. Regis
  Ame | **SoMa** — 26

Taj Campton Pl. Hotel
  Campton Pl. | **Downtown** — 26

Clement Monterey
  C Rest. | **Monterey/S** — 22

Truckee Hotel
  Moody's Bistro | **Truckee/E** — 23

Valley Ford Hotel
  Rocker Oysterfellers | **Valley Ford/N** — 24

Ventana Inn & Spa
  Rest./Ventana | **Big Sur/S** — 23

Villa Florence Hotel
  Kuleto's | **Downtown** — 23

Vintage Ct., Hotel
  Masa's | **Downtown** — 27

Vitale, Hotel
  Americano | **Embarcadero** — 21

Waterfront Plaza Hotel
  Miss Pearl's | **Oakland/E** — 22

Westin St. Francis
  Bourbon | **Downtown** — 24

Westin Verasa Napa
  La Toque | **Napa/N** — 27
  Bank Café | **Napa/N** — 24

W San Francisco
  NEW Trace | **SoMa** — 21

LATE DINING

(Weekday closing hour)

Nopa | 1 AM | **W Addition** — 27
Korean Vill. BBQ | 2 AM | **Inner Rich** — 26
La Victoria | 3 AM | **San Jose/S** — 25
El Castillito | varies | **Mission** — 25
Marcello's Pizza | 1 AM | **Castro** — 25

Ryoko's | 2 AM | **Downtown** — 25
Don Pisto's | 12:30 AM | **N Beach** — 25
Taco Shop | 12 AM | **Outer Sunset** — 25
Sol Food | 12 AM | **San Rafael/N** — 25
Locanda | 12 AM | **Mission** — 25
Lers Ros Thai | 12 AM | **Tenderloin** — 25
North Bch. Rest. | varies | **N Beach** — 25
Beretta | 12 AM | **Mission** — 24
NEW Bouche | 1 AM | **Nob Hill** — 24
Big 4 | 12 AM | **Nob Hill** — 24
Brother's Korean | varies | **Inner Rich** — 24
Broken Record | 12 AM | **Excelsior** — 24
Kitchen | 1 AM | **Millbrae/S** — 24
Shalimar | 11:30 PM | **Tenderloin** — 24
Absinthe | 12 AM | **Hayes Valley** — 24
Tsunami Sush/Sake | 12 AM | **multi.** — 24
El Zocalo | 3:45 AM | **Bernal Hts** — 23
Taqueria Can Cun | varies | **Mission** — 23
Original Joe's | varies | **San Jose/S** — 23
Top Dog | 2 AM | **Berkeley/E** — 23
In-N-Out | varies | **multi.** — 23
Pancho Villa | varies | **Mission** — 23
El Farolito | varies | **Mission** — 23
Great Eastern | 12 AM | **Chinatown** — 23
Alembic | 12 AM | **Haight-Ashbury** — 23
Caspers Hot Dogs | 11:30 PM | **multi.** — 23
Spices | 12 AM | **Inner Rich** — 23
Mua Lounge | 12 AM | **Oakland/E** — 23
Adesso | varies | **Oakland/E** — 23
Emporio Rulli | 12 AM | **S San Francisco/S** — 22
15 Romolo | 1:30 AM | **N Beach** — 22
Katana-Ya | 11:30 PM | **Downtown** — 22
Sauce | 2 AM | **multi.** — 22
Magnolia | 12 AM | **Haight-Ashbury** — 22
Acme Burger | varies | **W Addition** — 22
Oola | 1 AM | **SoMa** — 22
Asian Pearl | 1 AM | **Millbrae/S** — 22
Rosamunde | 12 AM | **Mission** — 22

Hog & Rocks | 12 AM | **Mission** 22

Nation's Giant | 24 hrs. | 22
   Daly City/S

King of Thai | varies | **multi.** 22

Buster's Cheesesteak | 22
   2:30 AM | **N Beach**

Revival Bar | 12 AM | **Berkeley/E** 22

Giordano | 12 AM | **Mission** 22

Osha Thai | varies | **multi.** 22

Thai Hse. | varies | **Tenderloin** 22

Delarosa | 1 AM | **Marina** 22

Swiss Hotel | 1 AM | **Sonoma/N** 21

Waterfront | 12 AM | 21
   Embarcadero

Fonda Solana | 12:30 AM | 21
   Albany/E

North Bch. Pizza | 12 AM | **multi.** 21

Pi Bar | 12 AM | **Mission** 21

Metro | 12 AM | **Lafayette/E** 21

Brazen Head | 1 AM | **Cow Hollow** 21

Home of Chicken | varies | **multi.** 20

César | 11:30 PM | **Berkeley/E** 20

Luka's Taproom | varies | 20
   Oakland/E

Heaven's Dog | 1 AM | **SoMa** 20

NEW Maven | 12 AM | 20
   Lower Haight

Taqueria 3 Amigos | 12 AM | 20
   San Mateo/S

Cannery/Brew | 12 AM | 19
   Monterey/S

Rudy's Can't Fail | 1 AM | **multi.** 19

NEW Dear Mom | varies | 19
   Mission

Globe | 1 AM | **Downtown** 18

Naan/Curry | varies | **multi.** 18

NEW Southern Pacific | varies | 18
   Mission

Mel's Drive-In | varies | **multi.** 17

Dobb's Ferry | 1:30 AM | 16
   Hayes Valley

NEW Goose/Gander | 12 AM | —
   St. Helena/N

NEW Lolinda | 1 AM | **Mission** —

NEW Thomas/Fagiani's | —
   12 AM | **Napa/N**

MEET FOR A DRINK

Keiko | **Nob Hill** 29

Kokkari | **Downtown** 28

Redd | **Yountville/N** 28

Boulevard | **Embarcadero** 27

Bistro/Copains | **Occidental/N** 27

Auberge du Soleil | **Rutherford/N** 27

Michael Mina | **Downtown** 27

Range | **Mission** 27

Jardinière | **Civic Ctr** 27

Nopa | **W Addition** 27

Press | **St. Helena/N** 26

Bouchon | **Yountville/N** 26

Picco | **Larkspur/N** 26

Alexander's Steak | **SoMa** 26

La Posta | **Santa Cruz/S** 26

Marica | **Oakland/E** 26

Prima | **Walnut Creek/E** 26

Fig Cafe/Wine | **Glen Ellen/N** 26

Locanda Positano | **San Carlos/S** 26

Umami | **Cow Hollow** 26

Zuni Café | **Hayes Valley** 26

Tamarine | **Palo Alto/S** 26

Wood Tav. | **Oakland/E** 26

Rosso Pizzeria | **Santa Rosa/N** 26

Perbacco | **Downtown** 26

Encuentro | **Oakland/E** 26

Solbar | **Calistoga/N** 26

Dio Deka | **Los Gatos/S** 25

Morimoto | **Napa/N** 25

Chotto | **Marina** 25

AQ | **SoMa** 25

John Ash | **Santa Rosa/N** 25

John Bentley | **Redwood City/S** 25

Bar Terra | **St. Helena/N** 25

Soif Wine Bar | **Santa Cruz/S** 25

Farm | **Napa/N** 25

La Costanera | **Montara/S** 25

Bottega | **Yountville/N** 25

Arizmendi | **Mission** 25

Willi's Wine | **Santa Rosa/N** 25

Va de Vi | **Walnut Creek/E** 25

Kenwood | **Kenwood/N** 25

Terzo | **Cow Hollow** 25

Plumed Horse | **Saratoga/S** 25

Mustards | **Yountville/N** 25

Murray Circle | **Sausalito/N** 25

Oswald | **Santa Cruz/S** 25

Willi's Seafood | **Healdsburg/N** 25

Barndiva | **Healdsburg/N** 25

Farallon | **Downtown** 25

Ozumo | **multi.** 25

Bistro Don Giovanni | **Napa/N** 25

Buckeye	**Mill Valley/N**	25
Redd Wood	**Yountville/N**	25
Lark Creek Steak	**Downtown**	25
Park Tav.	**N Beach**	25
Haven	**Oakland/E**	25
HRD Coffee	**SoMa**	25
Foreign Cinema	**Mission**	25
Poggio	**Sausalito/N**	24
Tra Vigne	**St. Helena/N**	24
Beretta	**Mission**	24
Prospect	**SoMa**	24
Enoteca Molinari	**Oakland/E**	24
Oenotri	**Napa/N**	24
Barbacco	**Downtown**	24
Wexler's	**Downtown**	24
Tacolicious	**multi.**	24
Zero Zero	**SoMa**	24
One Market	**Embarcadero**	24
Mamacita	**Marina**	24
Cindy's	**St. Helena/N**	24
O3 Bistro	**Civic Ctr**	24
Girl/Fig	**Sonoma/N**	24
Garibaldis	**Presidio Hts**	24
Parallel 37	**Nob Hill**	24
La Mar	**Embarcadero**	24
Big 4	**Nob Hill**	24
Bix	**Downtown**	24
Betelnut Pejiu	**Cow Hollow**	24
Barolo	**Calistoga/N**	24
Amber India	**multi.**	24
Gitane	**Downtown**	24
Sardine Factory	**Monterey/S**	24
Wayfare Tav.	**Downtown**	24
Bank Café	**Napa/N**	24
Broken Record	**Excelsior**	24
La Condesa	**St. Helena/N**	24
Picán	**Oakland/E**	24
Txoko	**N Beach**	24
ZuZu	**Napa/N**	24
Chop Bar	**Oakland/E**	24
Della Santina	**Sonoma/N**	24
Oyaji	**Outer Rich**	24
Zin	**Healdsburg/N**	24
Bellanico	**Oakland/E**	24
Absinthe	**Hayes Valley**	24
Bar Bambino	**Mission**	24
Rocker Oystersfellers	**Valley Ford/N**	24
Bocadillos	**N Beach**	23
Cin-Cin Wine	**Los Gatos/S**	23
Leopold's	**Russian Hill**	23
Serpentine	**Dogpatch**	23
5A5 Steak	**Downtown**	23
Oliveto Cafe	**Oakland/E**	23
Flora	**Oakland/E**	23
Wine Spectator	**St. Helena/N**	23
Ana Mandara	**Fish. Wharf**	23
Slow Club	**Mission**	23
Moody's Bistro	**Truckee/E**	23
Waterbar	**Embarcadero**	23
Rest./Ventana	**Big Sur/S**	23
Amber Bistro	**Danville/E**	23
Osteria Coppa	**San Mateo/S**	23
Pauline's	**Mission**	23
Town Hall	**SoMa**	23
Colibrí	**Downtown**	23
Cascal	**Mtn View/S**	23
Donato	**Redwood City/S**	23
Flavor	**Santa Rosa/N**	23
Skool	**Potrero Hill**	23
Alembic	**Haight-Ashbury**	23
Yoshi's	**W Addition**	23
Jake's Steaks	**Marina**	23
Manzanita	**Truckee/E**	23
PlumpJack	**Olympic Valley/E**	23
Butterfly	**Embarcadero**	23
Mundaka	**Carmel/S**	23
RN74	**SoMa**	23
Adesso	**Oakland/E**	23
Uva Enoteca	**Lower Haight**	23
Bar Agricole	**SoMa**	23
Forchetta/Bastoni	**Sebastopol/N**	23
Biergarten	**Hayes Valley**	23
1300/Fillmore	**W Addition**	23
Joya	**Palo Alto/S**	23
Epic Roasthse.	**Embarcadero**	23
Le Colonial	**Downtown**	23
Emporio Rulli	**Larkspur/N**	22
15 Romolo	**N Beach**	22
Rose's Cafe	**Cow Hollow**	22
Little River Inn	**Little River/N**	22
Doña Tomás	**Oakland/E**	22
Cantinetta Luca	**Carmel/S**	22
Bungalow 44	**Mill Valley/N**	22
54 Mint	**SoMa**	22
Magnolia	**Haight-Ashbury**	22
Bo's BBQ	**Lafayette/E**	22

Salt Hse. | **SoMa**	22	Pi Bar | **Mission**	21
Xanh | **Mtn View/S**	22	Oxbow Wine | **Napa/N**	21
Barlata | **Oakland/E**	22	Pacific Crest | **Truckee/E**	21
Meritage/Claremont | **Berkeley/E**	22	Trace | **SoMa**	21
Grasing's Coastal | **Carmel/S**	22	Rose Pistola | **N Beach**	21
Café Rouge | **Berkeley/E**	22	Lavanda | **Palo Alto/S**	21
Hog & Rocks | **Mission**	22	Ristobar | **Marina**	21
Original Joe's (SF) | **N Beach**	22	Rumbo | **Oakland/E**	21
Eureka | **Castro**	22	25 Lusk | **SoMa**	21
Andalu | **Mission**	22	Elite Cafe | **Pacific Hts**	21
Starbelly | **Castro**	22	Hawk's Tav. | **Mill Valley/N**	21
Revival Bar | **Berkeley/E**	22	Mendocino Hotel | **Mendocino/N**	21
Zaré/Fly Trap | **SoMa**	22	Nihon | **Mission**	21
Giordano | **Mission**	22	Hapa Ramen | **Loc varies**	21
Palio d'Asti | **Downtown**	22	Brazen Head | **Cow Hollow**	21
Iberia | **Menlo Pk/S**	22	Norman Rose | **Napa/N**	20
Per Diem | **Downtown**	22	Left Bank | **multi.**	20
Tav./Lark Creek | **Larkspur/N**	22	Tropisueño | **SoMa**	20
Florio | **Pacific Hts**	22	César | **Berkeley/E**	20
Sidebar | **Oakland/E**	22	Skates on Bay | **Berkeley/E**	20
Rest. LuLu | **SoMa**	22	Zibibbo | **Palo Alto/S**	20
Jasper's Corner | **Downtown**	22	Luka's Taproom | **Oakland/E**	20
Radius | **SoMa**	22	Mijita | **S Beach**	20
Underwood Bar | **Graton/N**	22	Heaven's Dog | **SoMa**	20
Wo Hing | **Mission**	22	MoMo's | **S Beach**	20
Anchor & Hope | **SoMa**	22	Balboa Cafe | **Cow Hollow**	20
Sens | **Embarcadero**	22	Gar Woods | **Carnelian Bay/E**	20
Davenport | **Davenport/S**	22	Maven | **Lower Haight**	20
Marinitas | **San Anselmo/N**	22	Ottimista | **Cow Hollow**	20
Troya | **Inner Rich**	22	Spoonbar | **Healdsburg/N**	20
Miss Pearl's | **Oakland/E**	22	Tommy's Mex. | **Outer Rich**	20
Nombe | **Mission**	22	Luna Park | **Mission**	20
Vin Antico | **San Rafael/N**	22	Le Zinc | **Noe Valley**	20
Delarosa | **Marina**	22	Sino | **San Jose/S**	20
Another Monkey/Koh | **Mission**	21	Hopmonk Tav. | **Sebastopol/N**	20
Lion/Compass | **Sunnyvale/S**	21	Jake's/Lake | **Tahoe City/E**	20
Mateo's Cocina | **Healdsburg/N**	21	Sunnyside Lodge | **Tahoe City/E**	20
Townhouse B&G | **Emeryville/E**	21	La Trappe | **N Beach**	20
Five | **Berkeley/E**	21	Wurst Rest. | **Healdsburg/N**	20
E&O Asian Kit. | **Downtown**	21	Meritage Martini | **Sonoma/N**	20
Fonda Solana | **Albany/E**	21	Presidio Social | **Presidio**	19
Luce | **SoMa**	21	Bluestem Brass. | **SoMa**	19
Sea Salt | **Berkeley/E**	21	Trader Vic's | **Emeryville/E**	19
Rustic | **Geyserville/N**	21	Tokyo Go Go | **Mission**	19
Americano | **Embarcadero**	21	Cannery/Brew | **Monterey/S**	19
Meadowood Grill | **St. Helena/N**	21	Café des Amis | **Cow Hollow**	19
		Dear Mom | **Mission**	19
Boxing Rm. | **Hayes Valley**	21	Brick/Bottle | **Corte Madera/N**	19
Nettie's Crab | **Cow Hollow**	21	North Coast Brew | **Ft Bragg/N**	19

Gordon Biersch | **multi.** 18

Tres | **S Beach** 18

Bridgetender | **Tahoe City/E** 18

Southern Pacific | **Mission** 18

MarketBar | **Embarcadero** 18

Hecho | **Downtown** 18

Half Moon Brew | 18
   Half Moon Bay/S

Guaymas | **Tiburon/N** 17

Park Chalet | **Outer Sunset** 17

Public Hse. | **S Beach** 17

Beach Chalet | **Outer Sunset** 17

NEW Abbot's Cellar | **Mission** –

NEW Brasserie S&P | **Downtown** –

NEW Burritt Tavern | **Downtown** –

NEW Campo Fina | –
   Healdsburg/N

NEW Comal | **Berkeley/E** –

NEW Copita | **Sausalito/N** –

NEW Corners Tav. | –
   Walnut Creek/E

NEW Dixie | **Presidio** –

NEW French Blue | **St. Helena/N** –

NEW Goose/Gander | –
   St. Helena/N

NEW Lolinda | **Mission** –

NEW Lucy | **Yountville/N** –

NEW Mission Rock | **Dogpatch** –

NEW Rangoon Ruby | –
   Palo Alto/S

NEW Rich Table | **Hayes Valley** –

NEW St. Vincent Tav. | **Mission** –

NEW Surf Spot | **Pacifica/S** –

NEW Thomas/Fagiani's | –
   Napa/N

NEW West/Pecos | **Mission** –

NEWCOMERS

Keiko | **Nob Hill** 29

State Bird | **W Addition** 27

B-Side BBQ | **Oakland/E** 26

Moonraker | **Pacifica/S** 26

Castagna | **Marina** 26

AQ | **SoMa** 25

Alex Rest. | **Rutherford/N** 25

Redd Wood | **Yountville/N** 25

Deli Board | **SoMa** 25

Park Tav. | **N Beach** 25

Haven | **Oakland/E** 25

O3 Bistro | **Civic Ctr** 24

Parallel 37 | **Nob Hill** 24

Bouche | **Nob Hill** 24

La Condesa | **St. Helena/N** 24

Canela | **Castro** 24

Dragon Rouge | **Alameda/E** 24

903 | **Bernal Hts** 23

Izakaya Yuzuki | **Mission** 23

Forchetta/Bastoni | 23
   Sebastopol/N

Umami Burger | **Cow Hollow** 23

Brassica | **St. Helena/N** 22

Per Diem | **Downtown** 22

Wo Hing | **Mission** 22

Mateo's Cocina | **Healdsburg/N** 21

Ken Ken | **Mission** 21

Trace | **SoMa** 21

Rumbo | **Oakland/E** 21

Hawk's Tav. | **Mill Valley/N** 21

Joshu-ya Brass. | **Berkeley/E** 21

Maven | **Lower Haight** 20

Two Sisters | **Hayes Valley** 19

Roostertail | **Upper Fillmore** 19

Dear Mom | **Mission** 19

Southern Pacific | **Mission** 18

Asian Box | **Palo Alto/S** 17

Melt | **multi.** 17

Cedar Hill | **Marina** 17

Abbot's Cellar | **Mission** –

Brasserie S&P | **Downtown** –

Burritt Tavern | **Downtown** –

Campo Fina | **Healdsburg/N** –

Catheads BBQ | **SoMa** –

Central Kitchen | **Mission** –

Comal | **Berkeley/E** –

Copita | **Sausalito/N** –

Corners Tav. | **Walnut Creek/E** –

Craftsman/Wolves | **Mission** –

Del Popolo | **Downtown** –

Dixie | **Presidio** –

Farina Pizza | **Mission** –

400 Degrees | **Carmel/S** –

French Blue | **St. Helena/N** –

FuseBox | **Oakland/E** –

Gioia Pizzeria | **Russian Hill** –

Glen Ellen Star | **Glen Ellen/N** –

Goose/Gander | **St. Helena/N** –

Hayes Valley Bakeworks | –
   Hayes Valley

Hopscotch | **Oakland/E** –

Local's Corner | **Mission**	¬
Lolinda | **Mission**	¬
Lot 7 | **Mission**	¬
Lucy | **Yountville/N**	¬
Machine Coffee | **Downtown**	¬
Market & Rye | **multi.**	¬
Mission Rock | **Dogpatch**	¬
Moss Room | **Outer Rich**	¬
Mozzeria | **Mission**	¬
Pläj | **Hayes Valley**	¬
Rangoon Ruby | **Palo Alto/S**	¬
Rest. Mitsunobu | **Menlo Pk/S**	¬
Rich Table | **Hayes Valley**	¬
Salumeria | **Mission**	¬
Saru Sushi | **Noe Valley**	¬
SoMa StrEAT | **SoMa**	¬
Split Bread | **SoMa**	¬
St. Vincent Tav. | **Mission**	¬
Surf Spot | **Pacifica/S**	¬
Sweet Woodruff | **Nob Hill**	¬
Thomas/Fagiani's | **Napa/N**	¬
U-Sushi | **Downtown**	¬
West/Pecos | **Mission**	¬

OUTDOOR DINING

Sierra Mar | **Big Sur/S**	28
Redd | **Yountville/N**	28
Cole's Chop | **Napa/N**	27
Madrona Manor | **Healdsburg/N**	27
Tartine | **Mission**	27
Auberge du Soleil | **Rutherford/N**	27
Sushi Ran | **Sausalito/N**	27
Étoile | **Yountville/N**	27
Meadowood Rest. | **St. Helena/N**	27
Bistro Jeanty | **Yountville/N**	27
Piperade | **Downtown**	27
Marché/Fleurs | **Ross/N**	27
Press | **St. Helena/N**	26
Bouchon | **Yountville/N**	26
Wente Vineyards | **Livermore/E**	26
Prima | **Walnut Creek/E**	26
Slanted Door | **Embarcadero**	26
Cafe Beaujolais | **Mendocino/N**	26
Pizzetta 211 | **Outer Rich**	26
Hog Island Oyster | **Embarcadero**	26
Roy's | **Pebble Bch/S**	26
Dopo | **Oakland/E**	26
Zuni Café | **Hayes Valley**	26
Chez Spencer | **Mission**	25

Pasta Moon | **Half Moon Bay/S**	25
John Ash | **Santa Rosa/N**	25
Bottega | **Yountville/N**	25
Universal Cafe | **Mission**	25
Willi's Wine | **Santa Rosa/N**	25
Va de Vi | **Walnut Creek/E**	25
Kenwood | **Kenwood/N**	25
Grégoire | **Berkeley/E**	25
Murray Circle | **Sausalito/N**	25
Willi's Seafood | **Healdsburg/N**	25
Barndiva | **Healdsburg/N**	25
Boca | **Novato/N**	25
Celadon | **Napa/N**	25
Chez Papa Bistrot | **Potrero Hill**	25
Bistro Don Giovanni | **Napa/N**	25
Buckeye | **Mill Valley/N**	25
Redd Wood | **Yountville/N**	25
O Chamé | **Berkeley/E**	25
À Côté | **Oakland/E**	25
Fish | **Sausalito/N**	25
Foreign Cinema | **Mission**	25
Scoma's | **Sausalito/N**	25
Poggio | **Sausalito/N**	24
Tra Vigne | **St. Helena/N**	24
Dry Creek | **Healdsburg/N**	24
Angèle | **Napa/N**	24
Gather | **Berkeley/E**	24
Madera | **Menlo Pk/S**	24
Casanova | **Carmel/S**	24
LaSalette | **Sonoma/N**	24
Cindy's | **St. Helena/N**	24
Rutherford Grill | **Rutherford/N**	24
Girl/Fig | **Sonoma/N**	24
Pazzia | **SoMa**	24
Zazie | **Cole Valley**	24
Applewood Rest. | **Guerneville/N**	24
La Mar | **Embarcadero**	24
Blue Bottle | **SoMa**	24
Betelnut Pejiu | **Cow Hollow**	24
Bistro Aix | **Marina**	24
Postino | **Lafayette/E**	24
Sociale | **Presidio Hts**	24
Anton/Michel | **Carmel/S**	24
Chez TJ | **Mtn View/S**	24
MacCallum | **Mendocino/N**	24
Txoko | **N Beach**	24
Il Davide | **San Rafael/N**	24
Della Santina | **Sonoma/N**	24

Isa | **Marina**	24
Fremont Diner | **Sonoma/N**	24
Tarpy's | **Monterey/S**	24
Blue Plate | **Mission**	24
Cafe Citti | **Kenwood/N**	24
Absinthe | **Hayes Valley**	24
Lark Creek | **Walnut Creek/E**	24
Dragonfly | **Truckee/E**	24
La Note | **Berkeley/E**	23
Oliveto Cafe | **Oakland/E**	23
Rick & Ann | **Berkeley/E**	23
Chaya | **Embarcadero**	23
Wine Spectator | **St. Helena/N**	23
Water St. Bistro | **Petaluma/N**	23
Slow Club | **Mission**	23
Hurley's | **Yountville/N**	23
Waterbar | **Embarcadero**	23
Bridges | **Danville/E**	23
Amber Bistro | **Danville/E**	23
Parcel 104 | **Santa Clara/S**	23
Cascal | **Mtn View/S**	23
Flavor | **Santa Rosa/N**	23
Skool | **Potrero Hill**	23
Le Charm Bistro | **SoMa**	23
Manzanita | **Truckee/E**	23
PlumpJack | **Olympic Valley/E**	23
Mistral | **Redwood Shores/S**	23
Pizzeria Tra Vigne | **St. Helena/N**	23
Basin | **Saratoga/S**	23
Chloe's Cafe | **Noe Valley**	23
Gabriella Café | **Santa Cruz/S**	23
Mo's | **SoMa**	23
Bar Agricole | **SoMa**	23
El Dorado | **Sonoma/N**	23
Biergarten | **Hayes Valley**	23
Bistro Liaison | **Berkeley/E**	23
Epic Roasthse. | **Embarcadero**	23
Le Colonial | **Downtown**	23
Emporio Rulli | **multi.**	22
Ravenous | **Healdsburg/N**	22
Farmstead | **St. Helena/N**	22
Fumé Bistro | **Napa/N**	22
Sam's Chowder | **Half Moon Bay/S**	22
Picante Cocina | **Berkeley/E**	22
Rose's Cafe | **Cow Hollow**	22
71 St. Peter | **San Jose/S**	22
Doña Tomás | **Oakland/E**	22
Bungalow 44 | **Mill Valley/N**	22
Moosse Café | **Mendocino/N**	22
Bo's BBQ | **Lafayette/E**	22
South Park | **SoMa**	22
Plouf | **Downtown**	22
Pizza Antica | **multi.**	22
Aperto | **Potrero Hill**	22
Monti's | **Santa Rosa/N**	22
Baker St. Bistro | **Marina**	22
Grasing's Coastal | **Carmel/S**	22
Café Rouge | **Berkeley/E**	22
Café Tiramisu | **Downtown**	22
Brassica | **St. Helena/N**	22
Café Claude | **Downtown**	22
Front Porch | **Bernal Hts**	22
Fentons | **Oakland/E**	22
Catch | **Castro**	22
Iberia | **Menlo Pk/S**	22
Alexis Baking | **Napa/N**	22
Tav./Lark Creek | **Larkspur/N**	22
Underwood Bar | **Graton/N**	22
Barney's | **multi.**	22
Frantoio | **Mill Valley/N**	22
Bucci's | **Emeryville/E**	22
Town's End | **Embarcadero**	22
B44 | **Downtown**	22
La Boulange | **multi.**	22
Barbara's | **Princeton Sea/S**	22
Boudin | **Fish. Wharf**	22
Lion/Compass | **Sunnyvale/S**	21
Mateo's Cocina | **Healdsburg/N**	21
Townhouse B&G | **Emeryville/E**	21
Waterfront | **Embarcadero**	21
Fonda Solana | **Albany/E**	21
Sea Salt | **Berkeley/E**	21
Rustic | **Geyserville/N**	21
Cool Café | **Stanford/S**	21
Meadowood Grill | **St. Helena/N**	21
Cheesecake Fac. | **Downtown**	21
Nettie's Crab | **Cow Hollow**	21
Straits | **multi.**	21
Chow/Park Chow | **multi.**	21
Piatti | **multi.**	21
Rose Pistola | **N Beach**	21
Everett/Jones BBQ | **multi.**	21
Left Bank | **multi.**	20
Jimmy Beans | **Berkeley/E**	20
Zibibbo | **Palo Alto/S**	20
Jimtown Store | **Healdsburg/N**	20
Mijita | **multi.**	20
Healdsburg B&G | **Healdsburg/N**	20

SPECIAL FEATURES

MoMo's | **S Beach** — 20
Cafe Bastille | **Downtown** — 20
Piazza D'Angelo | **Mill Valley/N** — 20
Le Zinc | **Noe Valley** — 20
Jake's/Lake | **Tahoe City/E** — 20
Fog City Diner | **Embarcadero** — 20
Sunnyside Lodge | **Tahoe City/E** — 20
Meritage Martini | **Sonoma/N** — 20
Yankee Pier | **multi.** — 19
Bridgetender | **Tahoe City/E** — 18
Southern Pacific | **Mission** — 18
Nepenthe | **Big Sur/S** — 18
MarketBar | **Embarcadero** — 18
Half Moon Brew | — 18
  Half Moon Bay/S
Guaymas | **Tiburon/N** — 17
Park Chalet | **Outer Sunset** — 17
Lake Chalet | **Oakland/E** — 17
Beach Chalet | **Outer Sunset** — 17

PEOPLE-WATCHING

Evvia | **Palo Alto/S** — 28
Redd | **Yountville/N** — 28
Chez Panisse Café | **Berkeley/E** — 28
Boulevard | **Embarcadero** — 27
Tartine | **Mission** — 27
Michael Mina | **Downtown** — 27
Bistro Jeanty | **Yountville/N** — 27
Jardinière | **Civic Ctr** — 27
Nopa | **W Addition** — 27
Bouchon | **Yountville/N** — 26
Picco | **Larkspur/N** — 26
Umami | **Cow Hollow** — 26
Downtown Bakery | — 26
  Healdsburg/N
Flea St. Café | **Menlo Pk/S** — 26
Hog Island Oyster | **Napa/N** — 26
Zuni Café | **Hayes Valley** — 26
Tamarine | **Palo Alto/S** — 26
Central Mkt. | **Petaluma/N** — 26
Wood Tav. | **Oakland/E** — 26
Flour + Water | **Mission** — 26
Solbar | **Calistoga/N** — 26
Dio Deka | **Los Gatos/S** — 25
Village Pub | **Woodside/S** — 25
Morimoto | **Napa/N** — 25
Bottega | **Yountville/N** — 25
Va de Vi | **Walnut Creek/E** — 25
Plumed Horse | **Saratoga/S** — 25
Mustards | **Yountville/N** — 25

Insalata's | **San Anselmo/N** — 25
Oswald | **Santa Cruz/S** — 25
Barndiva | **Healdsburg/N** — 25
Ozumo | **Oakland/E** — 25
Bistro Don Giovanni | **Napa/N** — 25
Viognier | **San Mateo/S** — 25
À Côté | **Oakland/E** — 25
Locanda | **Mission** — 25
Park Tav. | **N Beach** — 25
Foreign Cinema | **Mission** — 25
Poggio | **Sausalito/N** — 24
Tra Vigne | **St. Helena/N** — 24
Beretta | **Mission** — 24
Gather | **Berkeley/E** — 24
Madera | **Menlo Pk/S** — 24
Prospect | **SoMa** — 24
Oenotri | **Napa/N** — 24
Barbacco | **Downtown** — 24
Mamacita | **Marina** — 24
La Mar | **Embarcadero** — 24
Bix | **Downtown** — 24
Betelnut Pejiu | **Cow Hollow** — 24
Postino | **Lafayette/E** — 24
Amber India | **Mission** — 24
Gitane | **Downtown** — 24
Wayfare Tav. | **Downtown** — 24
Picán | **Oakland/E** — 24
Txoko | **N Beach** — 24
Absinthe | **Hayes Valley** — 24
Poesia | **Castro** — 24
Tsunami Sush/Sake | — 24
  W Addition
Scala's Bistro | **Downtown** — 23
Dosa | **multi.** — 23
Cin-Cin Wine | **Los Gatos/S** — 23
Serpentine | **Dogpatch** — 23
Chez Papa Resto | **SoMa** — 23
5A5 Steak | **Downtown** — 23
Oliveto Cafe | **Oakland/E** — 23
Flora | **Oakland/E** — 23
Postrio | **Downtown** — 23
El Paseo | **Mill Valley/N** — 23
Ana Mandara | **Fish. Wharf** — 23
Moody's Bistro | **Truckee/E** — 23
Waterbar | **Embarcadero** — 23
Brix | **Napa/N** — 23
Town Hall | **SoMa** — 23
Blowfish Sushi | **Mission** — 23
Cascal | **Mtn View/S** — 23

Bocanova	**Oakland/E**	23
Donato	**Redwood City/S**	23
Yoshi's	**W Addition**	23
Manzanita	**Truckee/E**	23
Mundaka	**Carmel/S**	23
Farina	**Mission**	23
RN74	**SoMa**	23
Bar Agricole	**SoMa**	23
Pampas	**Palo Alto/S**	23
Joya	**Palo Alto/S**	23
Epic Roasthse.	**Embarcadero**	23
Emporio Rulli	**multi.**	22
Farmstead	**St. Helena/N**	22
15 Romolo	**N Beach**	22
Quattro	**E Palo Alto/S**	22
Rose's Cafe	**Cow Hollow**	22
Bungalow 44	**Mill Valley/N**	22
LB Steak	**San Jose/S**	22
54 Mint	**SoMa**	22
Magnolia	**Haight-Ashbury**	22
Xanh	**Mtn View/S**	22
Barlata	**Oakland/E**	22
Café Claude	**Downtown**	22
Andalu	**Mission**	22
Front Porch	**Bernal Hts**	22
Starbelly	**Castro**	22
Gott's Roadside	**Napa/N**	22
Sidebar	**Oakland/E**	22
Rest. LuLu	**SoMa**	22
Underwood Bar	**Graton/N**	22
Wo Hing	**Mission**	22
Anchor & Hope	**SoMa**	22
Cha Cha Cha	**multi.**	22
Marinitas	**San Anselmo/N**	22
Miss Pearl's	**Oakland/E**	22
Delarosa	**Marina**	22
Lion/Compass	**Sunnyvale/S**	21
Mateo's Cocina	**Healdsburg/N**	21
Five	**Berkeley/E**	21
Le Central	**Downtown**	21
Boxing Rm.	**Hayes Valley**	21
Nettie's Crab	**Cow Hollow**	21
Rose Pistola	**N Beach**	21
25 Lusk	**SoMa**	21
Nihon	**Mission**	21
Mario's Bohemian	**N Beach**	21
Left Bank	**Larkspur/N**	20
Fish & Farm	**Downtown**	20
César	**Berkeley/E**	20

Ace Wasabi's	**Marina**	20
Zibibbo	**Palo Alto/S**	20
Heaven's Dog	**SoMa**	20
Balboa Cafe	**multi.**	20
Boogaloos	**Mission**	20
Brannan's Grill	**Calistoga/N**	20
Cafe Bastille	**Downtown**	20
Cottonwood	**Truckee/E**	20
Gar Woods	**Carnelian Bay/E**	20
Ottimista	**Cow Hollow**	20
Spoonbar	**Healdsburg/N**	20
Sino	**San Jose/S**	20
Hopmonk Tav.	**Sebastopol/N**	20
Jake's/Lake	**Tahoe City/E**	20
Café/Presse	**Downtown**	20
Tokyo Go Go	**Mission**	19
Cannery/Brew	**Monterey/S**	19
Buck's	**Woodside/S**	19
Let's Be Frank	**Presidio**	19
Tres	**S Beach**	18
Bridgetender	**Tahoe City/E**	18
Frjtz Fries	**Mission**	18
MarketBar	**Embarcadero**	18
Guaymas	**Tiburon/N**	17
Public Hse.	**S Beach**	17
NEW Comal	**Berkeley/E**	–
NEW Copita	**Sausalito/N**	–
NEW Corners Tav.	**Walnut Creek/E**	–
NEW French Blue	**St. Helena/N**	–
NEW Goose/Gander	**St. Helena/N**	–
NEW Lolinda	**Mission**	–
NEW Mission Rock	**Dogpatch**	–
NEW SoMa StrEAT	**SoMa**	–
NEW Surf Spot	**Pacifica/S**	–
NEW Thomas/Fagiani's	**Napa/N**	–

POWER SCENES

Gary Danko	**Fish. Wharf**	29
Kokkari	**Downtown**	28
Evvia	**Palo Alto/S**	28
Redd	**Yountville/N**	28
Boulevard	**Embarcadero**	27
Masa's	**Downtown**	27
Auberge du Soleil	**Rutherford/N**	27
Michael Mina	**Downtown**	27
Seasons	**Downtown**	27
Jardinière	**Civic Ctr**	27

Press | **St. Helena/N**	26
Bouchon | **Yountville/N**	26
Alexander's Steak | **multi.**	26
Tony's Pizza | **N Beach**	26
Spruce | **Presidio Hts**	26
Zuni Café | **Hayes Valley**	26
Perbacco | **Downtown**	26
Dio Deka | **Los Gatos/S**	25
Village Pub | **Woodside/S**	25
Morton's | **multi.**	25
Plumed Horse | **Saratoga/S**	25
Fifth Floor | **SoMa**	25
Ozumo | **Embarcadero**	25
Viognier | **San Mateo/S**	25
Tommy Toy | **Downtown**	25
Park Tav. | **N Beach**	25
Prospect | **SoMa**	24
Barbacco | **Downtown**	24
One Market | **Embarcadero**	24
Parallel 37 | **Nob Hill**	24
Big 4 | **Nob Hill**	24
Arcadia | **San Jose/S**	24
Tadich Grill | **Downtown**	24
Wayfare Tav. | **Downtown**	24
Allegro Romano | **Russian Hill**	23
Postrio | **Downtown**	23
Ana Mandara | **Fish. Wharf**	23
Parcel 104 | **Santa Clara/S**	23
Town Hall | **SoMa**	23
Forbes Mill | **multi.**	23
Chef Chu's | **Los Altos/S**	23
Manzanita | **Truckee/E**	23
Mistral | **Redwood Shores/S**	23
RN74 | **SoMa**	23
Epic Roasthse. | **Embarcadero**	23
Le Colonial | **Downtown**	23
Quattro | **E Palo Alto/S**	22
Sam's Grill | **Downtown**	22
Original Joe's (SF) | **N Beach**	22
Il Fornaio | **Palo Alto/S**	22
Sens | **Embarcadero**	22
Lion/Compass | **Sunnyvale/S**	21
Le Central | **Downtown**	21
Balboa Cafe | **Mill Valley/N**	20
Ottimista | **Cow Hollow**	20
Buck's | **Woodside/S**	19
NEW Burritt Tavern | **Downtown**	-

PRIVATE ROOMS

(Restaurants charge less at off times; call for capacity)

Gary Danko | **Fish. Wharf**	29
Acquerello | **Polk Gulch**	28
Erna's | **Oakhurst/E**	28
Marinus | **Carmel Valley/S**	28
Kokkari | **Downtown**	28
Boulevard | **Embarcadero**	27
Masa's | **Downtown**	27
Passionfish | **Pacific Grove/S**	27
La Folie | **Russian Hill**	27
Madrona Manor | **Healdsburg/N**	27
La Forêt | **San Jose/S**	27
Auberge du Soleil | **Rutherford/N**	27
Fleur de Lys | **Downtown**	27
Manresa | **Los Gatos/S**	27
Le Papillon | **San Jose/S**	27
Seasons | **Downtown**	27
Millennium | **Downtown**	27
Ruth's Chris | **Polk Gulch**	27
Jardinière | **Civic Ctr**	27
Harris' | **Polk Gulch**	27
Press | **St. Helena/N**	26
Wente Vineyards | **Livermore/E**	26
Alexander's Steak | **Cupertino/S**	26
Aubergine | **Carmel/S**	26
Prima | **Walnut Creek/E**	26
Aziza | **Outer Rich**	26
Slanted Door | **Embarcadero**	26
Spruce | **Presidio Hts**	26
Flea St. Café | **Menlo Pk/S**	26
Yank Sing | **SoMa**	26
Sons/Daughters | **Nob Hill**	26
Tamarine | **Palo Alto/S**	26
BayWolf | **Oakland/E**	26
Boulettes Larder | **Embarcadero**	26
Perbacco | **Downtown**	26
Village Pub | **Woodside/S**	25
Morton's | **Downtown**	25
Chantilly | **Redwood City/S**	25
John Bentley | **Redwood City/S**	25
Kenwood | **Kenwood/N**	25
Plumed Horse | **Saratoga/S**	25
Pesce | **Russian Hill**	25
Fifth Floor | **SoMa**	25
Insalata's | **San Anselmo/N**	25
Barndiva | **Healdsburg/N**	25
Boca | **Novato/N**	25

Farallon | **Downtown** 25
Incanto | **Noe Valley** 25
Ozumo | **Embarcadero** 25
Navio | **Half Moon Bay/S** 25
R & G Lounge | **Chinatown** 25
Viognier | **San Mateo/S** 25
Buckeye | **Mill Valley/N** 25
À Côté | **Oakland/E** 25
Tommy Toy | **Downtown** 25
Foreign Cinema | **Mission** 25
North Bch. Rest. | **N Beach** 25
Bella Vista | **Woodside/S** 25
Poggio | **Sausalito/N** 24
Tra Vigne | **St. Helena/N** 24
Dry Creek | **Healdsburg/N** 24
Angèle | **Napa/N** 24
Prospect | **SoMa** 24
Zarzuela | **Russian Hill** 24
Casanova | **Carmel/S** 24
Carneros Bistro | **Sonoma/N** 24
Vic Stewart | **Walnut Creek/E** 24
One Market | **Embarcadero** 24
Cindy's | **St. Helena/N** 24
Big 4 | **Nob Hill** 24
Betelnut Pejiu | **Cow Hollow** 24
Gary Chu's | **Santa Rosa/N** 24
Postino | **Lafayette/E** 24
Anton/Michel | **Carmel/S** 24
Chez TJ | **Mtn View/S** 24
Sardine Factory | **Monterey/S** 24
Arcadia | **San Jose/S** 24
MacCallum | **Mendocino/N** 24
Pacific's Edge | **Carmel/S** 24
Roy's | **SoMa** 24
Tarpy's | **Monterey/S** 24
Blue Plate | **Mission** 24
Cetrella | **Half Moon Bay/S** 24
Absinthe | **Hayes Valley** 24
Montrio Bistro | **Monterey/S** 24
Scala's Bistro | **Downtown** 23
Alfred's Steak | **Downtown** 23
Rio Grill | **Carmel/S** 23
Soi4 | **Oakland/E** 23
Postrio | **Downtown** 23
Ana Mandara | **Fish. Wharf** 23
Hurley's | **Yountville/N** 23
Waterbar | **Embarcadero** 23
Scott's Seafood | **multi.** 23
Pauline's | **Mission** 23

Parcel 104 | **Santa Clara/S** 23
231 Ellsworth | **San Mateo/S** 23
Town Hall | **SoMa** 23
PlumpJack | **Olympic Valley/E** 23
Alegrias | **Marina** 23
Basin | **Saratoga/S** 23
St. Orres | **Gualala/N** 23
Caprice | **Tiburon/N** 23
Bistro Liaison | **Berkeley/E** 23
Le Colonial | **Downtown** 23
Little River Inn | **Little River/N** 23
Sauce | **Hayes Valley** 22
71 St. Peter | **San Jose/S** 22
Grasing's Coastal | **Carmel/S** 22
Café Rouge | **Berkeley/E** 22
Khan Toke | **Outer Rich** 22
Andalu | **Mission** 22
Palio d'Asti | **Downtown** 22
Iberia | **Menlo Pk/S** 22
Shadowbrook | **Capitola/S** 22
Florio | **Pacific Hts** 22
Il Fornaio | **multi.** 22
Rest. LuLu | **SoMa** 22
Indigo | **Civic Ctr** 22
Frantoio | **Mill Valley/N** 22
Cha Cha Cha | **Mission** 22
Lion/Compass | **Sunnyvale/S** 21
Fandango | **Pacific Grove/S** 21
Eulipia | **San Jose/S** 21
Straits | **San Jose/S** 21
Piatti | **Mill Valley/N** 21
Rose Pistola | **N Beach** 21
Lavanda | **Palo Alto/S** 21
Grand Cafe | **Downtown** 21
Left Bank | **multi.** 20
Zibibbo | **Palo Alto/S** 20
Piazza D'Angelo | **Mill Valley/N** 20
Trader Vic's | **Emeryville/E** 19
Zuppa | **SoMa** 19
Buca di Beppo | **multi.** 18

PRIX FIXE MENUS

(Call for prices and times)
Gary Danko | **Fish. Wharf** 29
French Laundry | **Yountville/N** 29
Kiss Seafood | **Japantown** 28
Acquerello | **Polk Gulch** 28
Erna's | **Oakhurst/E** 28
Sierra Mar | **Big Sur/S** 28

Wakuriya | **San Mateo/S**	28	Incanto | **Noe Valley**	25
Commis | **Oakland/E**	28	Chez Papa Bistrot | **Potrero Hill**	25
Chez Panisse Café | **Berkeley/E**	28	Navio | **Half Moon Bay/S**	25
Chez Panisse | **Berkeley/E**	28	Mr. Pollo | **Mission**	25
Cafe Gibraltar | **El Granada/S**	28	Lark Creek Steak | **Downtown**	25
Masa's | **Downtown**	27	Tommy Toy | **Downtown**	25
La Folie | **Russian Hill**	27	Vik's Chaat | **Berkeley/E**	25
Madrona Manor | **Healdsburg/N**	27	Ecco | **Burlingame/S**	25
La Forêt | **San Jose/S**	27	Scoma's | **Fish. Wharf**	25
Saison | **Mission**	27	Dry Creek | **Healdsburg/N**	24
Auberge du Soleil | **Rutherford/N**	27	Le P'tit Laurent | **Glen Pk**	24
Fleur de Lys | **Downtown**	27	One Market | **Embarcadero**	24
Michael Mina | **Downtown**	27	Girl/Fig | **Sonoma/N**	24
Manresa | **Los Gatos/S**	27	Garibaldis | **Presidio Hts**	24
Le Papillon | **San Jose/S**	27	Zazie | **Cole Valley**	24
Étoile | **Yountville/N**	27	Chez TJ | **Mtn View/S**	24
Seasons | **Downtown**	27	MacCallum | **Mendocino/N**	24
Sent Sovi | **Saratoga/S**	27	Pacific's Edge | **Carmel/S**	24
Coi | **N Beach**	27	Roy's | **SoMa**	24
Ajanta | **Berkeley/E**	27	Isa | **Marina**	24
Millennium | **Downtown**	27	Tarpy's | **Monterey/S**	24
Meadowood Rest. | **St. Helena/N**	27	Scala's Bistro | **Downtown**	23
		Espetus | **Hayes Valley**	23
La Toque | **Napa/N**	27	Mezze | **Oakland/E**	23
Canteen | **Tenderloin**	27	Chez Papa Resto | **SoMa**	23
Piperade | **Downtown**	27	Rick & Ann | **Berkeley/E**	23
Ledford Hse. | **Albion/N**	27	Postrio | **Downtown**	23
Jardinière | **Civic Ctr**	27	Hurley's | **Yountville/N**	23
Chapeau! | **Inner Rich**	27	Waterbar | **Embarcadero**	23
Ad Hoc | **Yountville/N**	27	Amber Bistro | **Danville/E**	23
Quince | **Downtown**	26	Unicorn | **Downtown**	23
Esin | **Danville/E**	26	Parcel 104 | **Santa Clara/S**	23
Aubergine | **Carmel/S**	26	231 Ellsworth | **San Mateo/S**	23
Marica | **Oakland/E**	26	Le Charm Bistro | **SoMa**	23
Aziza | **Outer Rich**	26	Alamo Sq. | **W Addition**	23
Slanted Door | **Embarcadero**	26	St. Orres | **Gualala/N**	23
Baumé | **Palo Alto/S**	26	Caprice | **Tiburon/N**	23
Lalime's | **Berkeley/E**	26	Bistro Liaison | **Berkeley/E**	23
Sons/Daughters | **Nob Hill**	26	Duck Club | **Lafayette/E**	22
Jin Sho | **Palo Alto/S**	26	South Park | **SoMa**	22
Capannina | **Cow Hollow**	26	Plouf | **Downtown**	22
Chantilly | **Redwood City/S**	25	Hyde St. Bistro | **Russian Hill**	22
Chez Spencer | **Mission**	25	Baker St. Bistro | **Marina**	22
Firefly | **Noe Valley**	25	Palio d'Asti | **Downtown**	22
Plumed Horse | **Saratoga/S**	25	Indigo | **Civic Ctr**	22
Greens | **Marina**	25	Sens | **Embarcadero**	22
Ton Kiang | **Outer Rich**	25	Town's End | **Embarcadero**	22
Santé | **Sonoma/N**	25	Basque Cultural | **S San Francisco/S**	21
Farallon | **Downtown**	25		

Waterfront | **Embarcadero**	21
Axum Cafe | **Lower Haight**	21
Metro | **Lafayette/E**	21
Lavanda | **Palo Alto/S**	21
Cliff Hse. | **Outer Rich**	21
Jimmy Beans | **Berkeley/E**	20
Zibibbo | **Palo Alto/S**	20
Charcuterie | **Healdsburg/N**	20
MoMo's | **S Beach**	20
Cafe Bastille | **Downtown**	20
Le Zinc | **Noe Valley**	20
MarketBar | **Embarcadero**	18

QUIET CONVERSATION

Gary Danko | **Fish. Wharf**	29
Keiko | **Nob Hill**	29
Acquerello | **Polk Gulch**	28
Chez Panisse | **Berkeley/E**	28
Masa's | **Downtown**	27
Farmhse. Inn | **Forestville/N**	27
Madrona Manor | **Healdsburg/N**	27
Terra | **St. Helena/N**	27
Auberge du Soleil | **Rutherford/N**	27
Fleur de Lys | **Downtown**	27
Manresa | **Los Gatos/S**	27
Le Papillon | **San Jose/S**	27
Benu | **SoMa**	27
Atelier Crenn | **Marina**	27
Seasons | **Downtown**	27
Sent Sovi | **Saratoga/S**	27
Meadowood Rest. | **St. Helena/N**	27
La Toque | **Napa/N**	27
Marché/Fleurs | **Ross/N**	27
Cafe Jacqueline | **N Beach**	27
Alexander's Steak | **multi.**	26
Quince | **Downtown**	26
Aubergine | **Carmel/S**	26
Richmond | **Inner Rich**	26
Baumé | **Palo Alto/S**	26
Lalime's | **Berkeley/E**	26
Flea St. Café | **Menlo Pk/S**	26
Campton Pl. | **Downtown**	26
BayWolf | **Oakland/E**	26
Solbar | **Calistoga/N**	26
Morton's | **San Jose/S**	25
Chantilly | **Redwood City/S**	25
All Spice | **San Mateo/S**	25
Alex Rest. | **Rutherford/N**	25
Plumed Horse | **Saratoga/S**	25

Fifth Floor | **SoMa**	25
Murray Circle | **Sausalito/N**	25
O Chamé | **Berkeley/E**	25
Ecco | **Burlingame/S**	25
Mescolanza | **Outer Rich**	25
Bella Vista | **Woodside/S**	25
Casanova | **Carmel/S**	24
Applewood Rest. | **Guerneville/N**	24
Postino | **Lafayette/E**	24
Chez TJ | **Mtn View/S**	24
Arcadia | **San Jose/S**	24
Soule Domain | **Kings Bch/E**	24
Pacific's Edge | **Carmel/S**	24
L'Ardoise | **Castro**	24
Luella | **Russian Hill**	24
Rest./Ventana | **Big Sur/S**	23
Scott's Seafood | **Palo Alto/S**	23
231 Ellsworth | **San Mateo/S**	23
Forbes Mill | **multi.**	23
St. Orres | **Gualala/N**	23
Quattro | **E Palo Alto/S**	22
Duck Club | **multi.**	22
Khan Toke | **Outer Rich**	22
Nordstrom Cafe | **Downtown**	22
Lovejoy's Tea | **Noe Valley**	21
Five | **Berkeley/E**	21
Luce | **SoMa**	21
Pianeta | **Truckee/E**	21
Two Sisters | **Hayes Valley**	19
NEW Brasserie S&P | **Downtown**	–
NEW Burritt Tavern | **Downtown**	–

RAW BARS

Ichi Sushi | **Bernal Hts**	27
Sushi Ran | **Sausalito/N**	27
Bouchon | **Yountville/N**	26
Swan Oyster | **Polk Gulch**	26
Slanted Door | **Embarcadero**	26
Hog Island Oyster | **multi.**	26
Ame | **SoMa**	26
Zuni Café | **Hayes Valley**	26
Central Mkt. | **Petaluma/N**	26
Chotto | **Marina**	25
Bar Crudo | **W Addition**	25
Anchor Oyster | **Castro**	25
Willi's Seafood | **Healdsburg/N**	25
Farallon | **Downtown**	25
Tataki | **Noe Valley**	25

Foreign Cinema | **Mission** _25_
Wayfare Tav. | **Downtown** _24_
Walnut Creek Yacht | **Walnut Creek/E** _24_
Absinthe | **Hayes Valley** _24_
Glen Ellen Inn | **Glen Ellen/N** _24_
Rocker Oysterfellers | **Valley Ford/N** _24_
Dragonfly | **Truckee/E** _24_
Wine Spectator | **St. Helena/N** _23_
Waterbar | **Embarcadero** _23_
Ferry Plaza Seafoods | **Embarcadero** _23_
El Dorado | **Sonoma/N** _23_
Woodhouse Fish | **Castro** _22_
Sam's Chowder | **Half Moon Bay/S** _22_
Fresca | **Noe Valley** _22_
Fish Market | **multi.** _22_
Monti's | **Santa Rosa/N** _22_
Café Rouge | **Berkeley/E** _22_
Hog & Rocks | **Mission** _22_
Nick's Cove | **Marshall/N** _21_
Credo | **Downtown** _21_
Boxing Rm. | **Hayes Valley** _21_
Metro | **Lafayette/E** _21_
Cliff Hse. | **Outer Rich** _21_
Grand Cafe | **Downtown** _21_
Zibibbo | **Palo Alto/S** _20_
Luka's Taproom | **Oakland/E** _20_
Fish Story | **Napa/N** _20_
Fog City Diner | **Embarcadero** _20_
Meritage Martini | **Sonoma/N** _20_
Yankee Pier | **multi.** _19_
Lake Chalet | **Oakland/E** _17_
NEW Local's Corner | **Mission** _–_
NEW Mission Rock | **Dogpatch** _–_
NEW Thomas/Fagiani's | **Napa/N** _–_

ROMANTIC PLACES

Gary Danko | **Fish. Wharf** _29_
Keiko | **Nob Hill** _29_
French Laundry | **Yountville/N** _29_
Acquerello | **Polk Gulch** _28_
Erna's | **Oakhurst/E** _28_
Marinus | **Carmel Valley/S** _28_
Sierra Mar | **Big Sur/S** _28_
Chez Panisse | **Berkeley/E** _28_
Boulevard | **Embarcadero** _27_
Masa's | **Downtown** _27_
Bistro/Copains | **Occidental/N** _27_

Farmhse. Inn | **Forestville/N** _27_
La Folie | **Russian Hill** _27_
Madrona Manor | **Healdsburg/N** _27_
La Forêt | **San Jose/S** _27_
Terra | **St. Helena/N** _27_
Auberge du Soleil | **Rutherford/N** _27_
Fleur de Lys | **Downtown** _27_
Le Papillon | **San Jose/S** _27_
Étoile | **Yountville/N** _27_
Sent Sovi | **Saratoga/S** _27_
Wolfdale's | **Tahoe City/E** _27_
Coi | **N Beach** _27_
Meadowood Rest. | **St. Helena/N** _27_
La Toque | **Napa/N** _27_
Ledford Hse. | **Albion/N** _27_
Marché/Fleurs | **Ross/N** _27_
Jardinière | **Civic Ctr** _27_
Cafe Jacqueline | **N Beach** _27_
Chapeau! | **Inner Rich** _27_
Wente Vineyards | **Livermore/E** _26_
Alexander's Steak | **Cupertino/S** _26_
Quince | **Downtown** _26_
Aubergine | **Carmel/S** _26_
Aziza | **Outer Rich** _26_
Baumé | **Palo Alto/S** _26_
Cafe Beaujolais | **Mendocino/N** _26_
Lalime's | **Berkeley/E** _26_
Flea St. Café | **Menlo Pk/S** _26_
Roy's | **Pebble Bch/S** _26_
Solbar | **Calistoga/N** _26_
Village Pub | **Woodside/S** _25_
Harvest Moon | **Sonoma/N** _25_
Rest./Stevenswood | **Little River/N** _25_
Chantilly | **Redwood City/S** _25_
Chez Spencer | **Mission** _25_
John Ash | **Santa Rosa/N** _25_
John Bentley | **Redwood City/S** _25_
All Spice | **San Mateo/S** _25_
La Costanera | **Montara/S** _25_
Bottega | **Yountville/N** _25_
Terzo | **Cow Hollow** _25_
Bistro Central | **W Addition** _25_
Fifth Floor | **SoMa** _25_
Heirloom | **Mission** _25_
Murray Circle | **Sausalito/N** _25_
Woodward's Gdn. | **Mission** _25_
Barndiva | **Healdsburg/N** _25_

Incanto	**Noe Valley**	25
Risibisi	**Petaluma/N**	25
Ozumo	**Oakland/E**	25
Navio	**Half Moon Bay/S**	25
955 Rest.	**Mendocino/N**	25
Viognier	**San Mateo/S**	25
Ecco	**Burlingame/S**	25
Mescolanza	**Outer Rich**	25
Albion River Inn	**Albion/N**	25
Bella Vista	**Woodside/S**	25
Madera	**Menlo Pk/S**	24
Zarzuela	**Russian Hill**	24
Casanova	**Carmel/S**	24
Applewood Rest.	**Guerneville/N**	24
La Mar	**Embarcadero**	24
Big 4	**Nob Hill**	24
Bix	**Downtown**	24
Deetjen's Big Sur	**Big Sur/S**	24
Amber India	**SoMa**	24
Gitane	**Downtown**	24
Anton/Michel	**Carmel/S**	24
Chez TJ	**Mtn View/S**	24
MacCallum	**Mendocino/N**	24
Soule Domain	**Kings Bch/E**	24
Txoko	**N Beach**	24
Pacific's Edge	**Carmel/S**	24
Venticello	**Nob Hill**	24
L'Ardoise	**Castro**	24
Luella	**Russian Hill**	24
Glen Ellen Inn	**Glen Ellen/N**	24
Peasant/Pear	**Danville/E**	24
La Note	**Berkeley/E**	23
Chez Papa Resto	**SoMa**	23
Ana Mandara	**Fish. Wharf**	23
Slow Club	**Mission**	23
Rest./Ventana	**Big Sur/S**	23
Brix	**Napa/N**	23
Donato	**Redwood City/S**	23
Le Charm Bistro	**SoMa**	23
Manzanita	**Truckee/E**	23
Gabriella Café	**Santa Cruz/S**	23
St. Orres	**Gualala/N**	23
Caprice	**Tiburon/N**	23
1300/Fillmore	**W Addition**	23
Pampas	**Palo Alto/S**	23
Epic Roasthse.	**Embarcadero**	23
Le Colonial	**Downtown**	23
Ma Maison	**Aptos/S**	23
Little River Inn	**Little River/N**	22

71 St. Peter	**San Jose/S**	22
Duck Club	**multi.**	22
Moosse Café	**Mendocino/N**	22
St. Michael's	**Palo Alto/S**	22
Khan Toke	**Outer Rich**	22
Zaré/Fly Trap	**SoMa**	22
Shadowbrook	**Capitola/S**	22
La Corneta	**Burlingame/S**	22
Tav./Lark Creek	**Larkspur/N**	22
Indigo	**Civic Ctr**	22
Napa Wine Train	**Napa/N**	22
Garden Ct.	**Downtown**	22
Ahwahnee	**Yosemite/E**	22
Matterhorn Swiss	**Russian Hill**	21
Nick's Cove	**Marshall/N**	21
Luce	**SoMa**	21
Sea Salt	**Berkeley/E**	21
Christy Hill	**Tahoe City/E**	21
Pianeta	**Truckee/E**	21
25 Lusk	**SoMa**	21
Sunnyside Lodge	**Tahoe City/E**	20
Katia's Tea	**Inner Rich**	20
NEW Thomas/Fagiani's	**Napa/N**	–

SINGLES SCENES

La Posta	**Santa Cruz/S**	26
Umami	**Cow Hollow**	26
Zuni Café	**Hayes Valley**	26
Universal Cafe	**Mission**	25
Barndiva	**Healdsburg/N**	25
Ozumo	**multi.**	25
Foreign Cinema	**Mission**	25
Beretta	**Mission**	24
Marlowe	**SoMa**	24
Barbacco	**Downtown**	24
Bix	**Downtown**	24
Betelnut Pejiu	**Cow Hollow**	24
Gitane	**Downtown**	24
Broken Record	**Excelsior**	24
La Condesa	**St. Helena/N**	24
Blue Plate	**Mission**	24
Poesia	**Castro**	24
Dragonfly	**Truckee/E**	24
Tsunami Sush/Sake	**W Addition**	24
Dosa	**Upper Fillmore**	23
Cin-Cin Wine	**Los Gatos/S**	23
Serpentine	**Dogpatch**	23
5A5 Steak	**Downtown**	23
Flora	**Oakland/E**	23

Slow Club | **Mission**	23
Moody's Bistro | **Truckee/E**	23
Blowfish Sushi | **Mission**	23
Cascal | **Mtn View/S**	23
Jake's Steaks | **Marina**	23
Butterfly | **Embarcadero**	23
Mundaka | **Carmel/S**	23
Bar Agricole | **SoMa**	23
Joya | **Palo Alto/S**	23
15 Romolo | **N Beach**	22
Quattro | **E Palo Alto/S**	22
Magnolia | **Haight-Ashbury**	22
Xanh | **Mtn View/S**	22
Barlata | **Oakland/E**	22
Hog & Rocks | **Mission**	22
Café Claude | **Downtown**	22
Andalu | **Mission**	22
Starbelly | **Castro**	22
Per Diem | **Downtown**	22
Anchor & Hope | **SoMa**	22
Davenport | **Davenport/S**	22
Cha Cha Cha | **multi.**	22
Miss Pearl's | **Oakland/E**	22
Nick's Crispy | **Russian Hill**	22
E&O Asian Kit. | **Downtown**	21
Luce | **SoMa**	21
Nettie's Crab | **Cow Hollow**	21
Rose Pistola | **N Beach**	21
Rumbo | **Oakland/E**	21
25 Lusk | **SoMa**	21
Elite Cafe | **Pacific Hts**	21
Nihon | **Mission**	21
Ace Wasabi's | **Marina**	20
Zibibbo | **Palo Alto/S**	20
Emmy's Spaghetti | **Bernal Hts**	20
Heaven's Dog | **SoMa**	20
MoMo's | **S Beach**	20
Balboa Cafe | **multi.**	20
Cafe Bastille | **Downtown**	20
Cottonwood | **Truckee/E**	20
Gar Woods | **Carnelian Bay/E**	20
Ottimista | **Cow Hollow**	20
Tommy's Mex. | **Outer Rich**	20
Luna Park | **Mission**	20
Sino | **San Jose/S**	20
Hopmonk Tav. | **Sebastopol/N**	20
Jake's/Lake | **Tahoe City/E**	20
La Trappe | **N Beach**	20
Tokyo Go Go | **Mission**	19

Cannery/Brew | **Monterey/S**	19
Gordon Biersch | **multi.**	18
Tres | **S Beach**	18
Frjtz Fries | **Mission**	18
Half Moon Brew | **Half Moon Bay/S**	18
Guaymas | **Tiburon/N**	17
Beach Chalet | **Outer Sunset**	17
NEW Lolinda | **Mission**	-
NEW Mission Rock | **Dogpatch**	-

SLEEPERS

(Good food, but little known)

Terrapin Creek | **Bodega Bay/N**	28
Kappou Gomi | **Outer Rich**	28
Wakuriya | **San Mateo/S**	28
Evan's | **S Lake Tahoe/E**	27
La Taquiza | **Napa/N**	27
Jole | **Calistoga/N**	27
Hachi Ju Hachi | **Saratoga/S**	27
To Hyang | **Inner Rich**	27
Zeni | **San Jose/S**	27
Café Fiore | **S Lake Tahoe/E**	27
Nama Sushi | **Walnut Creek/E**	27
Sazon Peruvian | **Santa Rosa/N**	27
Ledford Hse. | **Albion/N**	27
Naked Lunch | **N Beach**	26
La Posta | **Santa Cruz/S**	26
Locanda Positano | **San Carlos/S**	26
Papito | **Potrero Hill**	26
Table Café | **Larkspur/N**	26
Saravana Bhavan | **Sunnyvale/S**	26
Korean Vill. BBQ | **Inner Rich**	26
Sakae Sushi | **Burlingame/S**	26
Thai Buddhist | **Berkeley/E**	26
Emilia's | **Berkeley/E**	26
Encuentro | **Oakland/E**	26
Amasia Hide's | **Castro**	25
Chinois | **Windsor/N**	25
Rest./Stevenswood | **Little River/N**	25
Sai Jai Thai | **Tenderloin**	25
Pearl | **Napa/N**	25
Bar Terra | **St. Helena/N**	25
Soif Wine Bar | **Santa Cruz/S**	25
Kiji Sushi Bar | **Mission**	25
Rest. James | **Los Gatos/S**	25
Liou's Hse. | **Milpitas/S**	25
Moki's Sushi | **Bernal Hts**	25
Oswald | **Santa Cruz/S**	25

Ravens' | **Mendocino/N**	25
Sandbox | **Bernal Hts**	25
Santé | **Sonoma/N**	25
Sugo | **Petaluma/N**	25
Sumika | **Los Altos/S**	25
Battambang | **Oakland/E**	25
Navio | **Half Moon Bay/S**	25
Arun | **Novato/N**	25
Mr. Pollo | **Mission**	25
Naomi Sushi | **Menlo Pk/S**	25
Taco Shop | **Outer Sunset**	25
Truly Med. | **Mission**	25
Cajun Pacific | **Outer Sunset**	25
O'mei | **Santa Cruz/S**	25
Salang Pass | **Fremont/E**	25

THEME RESTAURANTS

Napa Wine Train | **Napa/N**	22
Miss Pearl's | **Oakland/E**	22
Stinking Rose | **N Beach**	21
Benihana | **multi.**	21
Max's | **multi.**	20
Buca di Beppo | **multi.**	18

TRENDY

Commis | **Oakland/E**	28
Range | **Mission**	27
Delfina | **Mission**	27
Jardinière | **Civic Ctr**	27
Nopa | **W Addition**	27
Bouchon | **Yountville/N**	26
Picco | **Larkspur/N**	26
Sebo | **Hayes Valley**	26
Slanted Door | **Embarcadero**	26
Umami | **Cow Hollow**	26
Spruce | **Presidio Hts**	26
Zuni Café | **Hayes Valley**	26
Tamarine | **Palo Alto/S**	26
Wood Tav. | **Oakland/E**	26
Commonwealth | **Mission**	26
Flour + Water | **Mission**	26
Pizzeria Picco | **Larkspur/N**	26
Pizzeria Delfina | **Mission**	26
Solbar | **Calistoga/N**	25
Morimoto | **Napa/N**	25
AQ | **SoMa**	25
Rest. James | **Los Gatos/S**	25
Bottega | **Yountville/N**	25
Terzo | **Cow Hollow**	25

Trattoria Corso | **Berkeley/E**	25
Mustards | **Yountville/N**	25
Oswald | **Santa Cruz/S**	25
Barndiva | **Healdsburg/N**	25
Ozumo | **multi.**	25
Bistro Don Giovanni | **Napa/N**	25
Bar Tartine | **Mission**	25
A16 | **Marina**	25
SPQR | **Pacific Hts**	25
À Côté | **Oakland/E**	25
Locanda | **Mission**	25
Park Tav. | **N Beach**	25
Lers Ros Thai | **multi.**	25
Foreign Cinema | **Mission**	25
Maverick | **Mission**	24
Beretta | **Mission**	24
Gather | **Berkeley/E**	24
Marlowe | **SoMa**	24
Boot/Shoe | **Oakland/E**	24
Zero Zero | **SoMa**	24
Mamacita | **Marina**	24
Bix | **Downtown**	24
Betelnut Pejiu | **Cow Hollow**	24
Amber India | **Mission**	24
Gitane | **Downtown**	24
Picán | **Oakland/E**	24
ZuZu | **Napa/N**	24
Limón | **Mission**	24
Tsunami Sush/Sake | **W Addition**	24
Plum | **Oakland/E**	23
Dosa | **multi.**	23
Bocadillos | **N Beach**	23
Serpentine | **Dogpatch**	23
5A5 Steak | **Downtown**	23
Flora | **Oakland/E**	23
Postrio | **Downtown**	23
Slow Club | **Mission**	23
Coco500 | **SoMa**	23
Waterbar | **Embarcadero**	23
Hawker Fare | **Oakland/E**	23
Town Hall | **SoMa**	23
Blowfish Sushi | **Mission**	23
Cascal | **Mtn View/S**	23
Yoshi's | **W Addition**	23
Farina | **Mission**	23
RN74 | **SoMa**	23
Adesso | **Oakland/E**	23
Bar Agricole | **SoMa**	23
Biergarten | **Hayes Valley**	23

1300/Fillmore | **W Addition** 23
Joya | **Palo Alto/S** 23
15 Romolo | **N Beach** 22
Doña Tomás | **Oakland/E** 22
Bungalow 44 | **Mill Valley/N** 22
Mission Chinese | **Mission** 22
Salt Hse. | **SoMa** 22
Xanh | **Mtn View/S** 22
Café Rouge | **Berkeley/E** 22
Hog & Rocks | **Mission** 22
Front Porch | **Bernal Hts** 22
Starbelly | **Castro** 22
Revival Bar | **Berkeley/E** 22
Sidebar | **Oakland/E** 22
Osha Thai | **multi.** 22
Underwood Bar | **Graton/N** 22
Anchor & Hope | **SoMa** 22
Cha Cha Cha | **multi.** 22
Miss Pearl's | **Oakland/E** 22
Delarosa | **Marina** 22
Fonda Solana | **Albany/E** 21
Boxing Rm. | **Hayes Valley** 21
Rumbo | **Oakland/E** 21
25 Lusk | **SoMa** 21
Hawk's Tav. | **Mill Valley/N** 21
Nihon | **Mission** 21
César | **Berkeley/E** 20
Ace Wasabi's | **Marina** 20
Zibibbo | **Palo Alto/S** 20
Emmy's Spaghetti | **Bernal Hts** 20
Heaven's Dog | **SoMa** 20
Balboa Cafe | **Cow Hollow** 20
Boogaloos | **Mission** 20
Maven | **Lower Haight** 20
Naked Fish | **S Lake Tahoe/E** 20
Ottimista | **Cow Hollow** 20
Piazza D'Angelo | **Mill Valley/N** 20
Spoonbar | **Healdsburg/N** 20
Sino | **San Jose/S** 20
Hopmonk Tav. | **Sebastopol/N** 20
Café des Amis | **Cow Hollow** 19
Dear Mom | **Mission** 19
Tres | **S Beach** 18
Southern Pacific | **Mission** 18
NEW Abbot's Cellar | **Mission** –
NEW Central Kitchen | **Mission** –
NEW Comal | **Berkeley/E** –
NEW Lolinda | **Mission** –
NEW Mission Rock | **Dogpatch** –

Namu | **Mission** –
NEW Thomas/Fagiani's | **Napa/N** –
NEW West/Pecos | **Mission** –

VALET PARKING

Gary Danko | **Fish. Wharf** 29
Marinus | **Carmel Valley/S** 28
Kokkari | **Downtown** 28
Sierra Mar | **Big Sur/S** 28
Evvia | **Palo Alto/S** 28
Boulevard | **Embarcadero** 27
Masa's | **Downtown** 27
La Folie | **Russian Hill** 27
Cole's Chop | **Napa/N** 27
Auberge du Soleil | **Rutherford/N** 27
Fleur de Lys | **Downtown** 27
Michael Mina | **Downtown** 27
Benu | **SoMa** 27
Seasons | **Downtown** 27
Coi | **N Beach** 27
Millennium | **Downtown** 27
La Toque | **Napa/N** 27
Ruth's Chris | **multi.** 27
Jardinière | **Civic Ctr** 27
Harris' | **Polk Gulch** 27
House/Prime | **Polk Gulch** 26
Picco | **Larkspur/N** 26
Wente Vineyards | **Livermore/E** 26
Alexander's Steak | **multi.** 26
Quince | **Downtown** 26
Aubergine | **Carmel/S** 26
Prima | **Walnut Creek/E** 26
Aziza | **Outer Rich** 26
Slanted Door | **Embarcadero** 26
Thanh Long | **Outer Sunset** 26
Spruce | **Presidio Hts** 26
Cotogna | **Downtown** 26
Ame | **SoMa** 26
Campton Pl. | **Downtown** 26
Zuni Café | **Hayes Valley** 26
Pizzeria Picco | **Larkspur/N** 26
Perbacco | **Downtown** 26
Baker/Banker | **Upper Fillmore** 26
Solbar | **Calistoga/N** 26
Dio Deka | **Los Gatos/S** 25
Morton's | **multi.** 25
Chantilly | **Redwood City/S** 25
Terzo | **Cow Hollow** 25
Plumed Horse | **Saratoga/S** 25

Fifth Floor | **SoMa**	25
Insalata's | **San Anselmo/N**	25
Santé | **Sonoma/N**	25
Boccalone | **Embarcadero**	25
Farallon | **Downtown**	25
Ozumo | **multi.**	25
Navio | **Half Moon Bay/S**	25
Buckeye | **Mill Valley/N**	25
Crustacean | **Polk Gulch**	25
Tommy Toy | **Downtown**	25
Park Tav. | **N Beach**	25
Foreign Cinema | **Mission**	25
Scoma's | **Fish. Wharf**	25
North Bch. Rest. | **N Beach**	25
Poggio | **Sausalito/N**	24
Prospect | **SoMa**	24
Barbacco | **Downtown**	24
Delica | **Embarcadero**	24
One Market | **Embarcadero**	24
Garibaldis | **Presidio Hts**	24
Parallel 37 | **Nob Hill**	24
Applewood Rest. | **Guerneville/N**	24
Big 4 | **Nob Hill**	24
Bix | **Downtown**	24
Postino | **Lafayette/E**	24
Arcadia | **San Jose/S**	24
Wayfare Tav. | **Downtown**	24
Pacific's Edge | **Carmel/S**	24
Venticello | **Nob Hill**	24
Hayes St. Grill | **Hayes Valley**	24
Bellanico | **Oakland/E**	24
Absinthe | **Hayes Valley**	24
Aquarius | **Santa Cruz/S**	24
Kuleto's | **Downtown**	23
5A5 Steak | **Downtown**	23
Postrio | **Downtown**	23
Chaya | **Embarcadero**	23
Anzu | **Downtown**	23
Wine Spectator | **St. Helena/N**	23
Waterbar | **Embarcadero**	23
Amber Bistro | **Danville/E**	23
Osteria Coppa | **San Mateo/S**	23
Scott's Seafood | **Walnut Creek/E**	23
Parcel 104 | **Santa Clara/S**	23
231 Ellsworth | **San Mateo/S**	23
Blowfish Sushi | **San Jose/S**	23
Bocanova | **Oakland/E**	23
Donato | **Redwood City/S**	23
Maykadeh | **N Beach**	23
Manzanita | **Truckee/E**	23
Farina | **Mission**	23
Sutro's | **Outer Rich**	23
Epic Roasthse. | **Embarcadero**	23
Hunan Home's/Gdn. | **Chinatown**	23
Quattro | **E Palo Alto/S**	22
LB Steak | **San Jose/S**	22
Duck Club | **Lafayette/E**	22
Rist. Capellini | **San Mateo/S**	22
Hudson | **Oakland/E**	22
Meritage/Claremont | **Berkeley/E**	22
Andalu | **Mission**	22
Tav./Lark Creek | **Larkspur/N**	22
Florio | **Pacific Hts**	22
Il Fornaio | **multi.**	22
Rest. LuLu | **SoMa**	22
Le Cheval | **Oakland/E**	22
Ahwahnee | **Yosemite/E**	22
Miss Pearl's | **Oakland/E**	22
Lion/Compass | **Sunnyvale/S**	21
Matterhorn Swiss | **Russian Hill**	21
Townhouse B&G | **Emeryville/E**	21
Cha Am Thai | **SoMa**	21
Five | **Berkeley/E**	21
Waterfront | **Embarcadero**	21
Luce | **SoMa**	21
Cupola Pizzeria | **Downtown**	21
Americano | **Embarcadero**	21
Casa Orinda | **Orinda/E**	21
Cheesecake Fac. | **Santa Clara/S**	21
Benihana | **Burlingame/S**	21
Straits | **Downtown**	21
Trace | **SoMa**	21
Rose Pistola | **N Beach**	21
25 Lusk | **SoMa**	21
Elite Cafe | **Pacific Hts**	21
Cliff Hse. | **Outer Rich**	21
Grand Cafe | **Downtown**	21
Fish & Farm | **Downtown**	20
MoMo's | **S Beach**	20
Balboa Cafe | **Cow Hollow**	20
Luna Park | **Mission**	20
Sunnyside Lodge | **Tahoe City/E**	20
Yankee Pier | **multi.**	19
Trader Vic's | **Emeryville/E**	19
Café des Amis | **Cow Hollow**	19
NEW Brasserie S&P | **Downtown**	-
NEW Pläj | **Hayes Valley**	-

VIEWS

Erna's | **Oakhurst/E**	28
Marinus | **Carmel Valley/S**	28
Sierra Mar | **Big Sur/S**	28
Rivoli | **Berkeley/E**	28
Cafe Gibraltar | **El Granada/S**	28
Cucina Paradiso | **Petaluma/N**	27
Boulevard | **Embarcadero**	27
Farmhse. Inn | **Forestville/N**	27
La Forêt | **San Jose/S**	27
Auberge du Soleil | **Rutherford/N**	27
Étoile | **Yountville/N**	27
Wolfdale's | **Tahoe City/E**	27
Meadowood Rest. | **St. Helena/N**	27
Ledford Hse. | **Albion/N**	27
Cafe La Haye | **Sonoma/N**	27
Press | **St. Helena/N**	26
Picco | **Larkspur/N**	26
Wente Vineyards | **Livermore/E**	26
Tony's Pizza | **N Beach**	26
Slanted Door | **Embarcadero**	26
Cafe Beaujolais | **Mendocino/N**	26
Downtown Bakery | **Healdsburg/N**	26
Hog Island Oyster | **Embarcadero**	26
Roy's | **Pebble Bch/S**	26
Frascati | **Russian Hill**	26
Chevalier | **Lafayette/E**	26
Boulettes Larder | **Embarcadero**	26
Zazu | **Santa Rosa/N**	25
Rest./Stevenswood | **Little River/N**	25
John Ash | **Santa Rosa/N**	25
Farm | **Napa/N**	25
La Costanera | **Montara/S**	25
Kenwood | **Kenwood/N**	25
Greens | **Marina**	25
Ike's Pl./Lair | **Stanford/S**	25
Murray Circle | **Sausalito/N**	25
Ravens' | **Mendocino/N**	25
Barndiva | **Healdsburg/N**	25
C Casa | **Napa/N**	25
Ozumo | **Embarcadero**	25
Navio | **Half Moon Bay/S**	25
Bistro Don Giovanni | **Napa/N**	25
HRD Coffee | **SoMa**	25
Fish | **Sausalito/N**	25
Scoma's | **multi.**	25
Albion River Inn | **Albion/N**	25

Bella Vista | **Woodside/S**	25
Dry Creek | **Healdsburg/N**	24
Angèle | **Napa/N**	24
Madera | **Menlo Pk/S**	24
Delica | **Embarcadero**	24
One Market | **Embarcadero**	24
Mama's on Wash. | **N Beach**	24
Rutherford Grill | **Rutherford/N**	24
Applewood Rest. | **Guerneville/N**	24
La Mar | **Embarcadero**	24
Big Sur | **Big Sur/S**	24
Chez TJ | **Mtn View/S**	24
Café Rustica | **Carmel Valley/S**	24
Pacific's Edge | **Carmel/S**	24
Venticello | **Nob Hill**	24
Le Garage | **Sausalito/N**	24
Cafe Citti | **Kenwood/N**	24
Chapter & Moon | **Ft Bragg/N**	24
Glen Ellen Inn | **Glen Ellen/N**	24
Aquarius | **Santa Cruz/S**	24
Dragonfly | **Truckee/E**	24
Mezza Luna | **Princeton Sea/S**	24
Chaya | **Embarcadero**	23
Wine Spectator | **St. Helena/N**	23
Red Hut | **S Lake Tahoe/E**	23
Water St. Bistro | **Petaluma/N**	23
Waterbar | **Embarcadero**	23
Rest./Ventana | **Big Sur/S**	23
Scott's Seafood | **multi.**	23
Brix | **Napa/N**	23
Il Cane Rosso | **Embarcadero**	23
Bocanova | **Oakland/E**	23
Flavor | **Santa Rosa/N**	23
Manzanita | **Truckee/E**	23
Mistral | **Redwood Shores/S**	23
Butterfly | **Embarcadero**	23
Ferry Plaza Seafoods | **Embarcadero**	23
Kincaid's | **Burlingame/S**	23
St. Orres | **Gualala/N**	23
Sutro's | **Outer Rich**	23
Caprice | **Tiburon/N**	23
Epic Roasthse. | **Embarcadero**	23
Sam's Chowder | **Half Moon Bay/S**	22
Little River Inn | **Little River/N**	22
Duck Club | **Bodega Bay/N**	22
Moosse Café | **Mendocino/N**	22
Meritage/Claremont | **Berkeley/E**	22

Hong Kong East | **Emeryville/E**	22
Catch | **Castro**	22
Shadowbrook | **Capitola/S**	22
McCormick/Kuleto | **Fish. Wharf**	22
Il Fornaio | **Carmel/S**	22
Fishwife | **Pacific Grove/S**	22
Napa Wine Train | **Napa/N**	22
Davenport | **Davenport/S**	22
Ahwahnee | **Yosemite/E**	22
Barbara's | **Princeton Sea/S**	22
Bar Bocce | **Sausalito/N**	22
Boudin | **Fish. Wharf**	22
Lion/Compass | **Sunnyvale/S**	21
Alioto's | **Fish. Wharf**	21
Nick's Cove | **Marshall/N**	21
Waterfront | **Embarcadero**	21
Rustic | **Geyserville/N**	21
Cool Café | **Stanford/S**	21
Americano | **Embarcadero**	21
Meadowood Grill | **St. Helena/N**	21
Hilltop 1892 | **Novato/N**	21
Cheesecake Fac. | **Downtown**	21
Rotunda | **Downtown**	21
Christy Hill | **Tahoe City/E**	21
Piatti | **Mill Valley/N**	21
Mendo Café | **Mendocino/N**	21
Cliff Hse. | **Outer Rich**	21
Mendocino Hotel | **Mendocino/N**	21
Cafe Divine | **N Beach**	21
Skates on Bay | **Berkeley/E**	20
Mijita | **Embarcadero**	20
MoMo's | **S Beach**	20
Cottonwood | **Truckee/E**	20
Gar Woods | **Carnelian Bay/E**	20
Jake's/Lake | **Tahoe City/E**	20
Café/Presse | **Downtown**	20
Sunnyside Lodge | **Tahoe City/E**	20
Trader Vic's | **Emeryville/E**	19
Café des Amis | **Cow Hollow**	19
Rudy's Can't Fail | **Oakland/E**	19
Brick/Bottle | **Corte Madera/N**	19
Imperial Tea | **Berkeley/E**	19
Bridgetender | **Tahoe City/E**	18
Nepenthe | **Big Sur/S**	18
Half Moon Brew | **Half Moon Bay/S**	18
Guaymas | **Tiburon/N**	17
Park Chalet | **Outer Sunset**	17

Beach Chalet | **Outer Sunset**	17
NEW Lolinda | **Mission**	-
NEW Mission Rock | **Dogpatch**	-

VISITORS ON EXPENSE ACCOUNT

Gary Danko | **Fish. Wharf**	29
Keiko | **Nob Hill**	29
French Laundry | **Yountville/N**	29
Acquerello | **Polk Gulch**	28
Erna's | **Oakhurst/E**	28
Marinus | **Carmel Valley/S**	28
Kokkari | **Downtown**	28
Sierra Mar | **Big Sur/S**	28
Wakuriya | **San Mateo/S**	28
Evvia | **Palo Alto/S**	28
Redd | **Yountville/N**	28
Commis | **Oakland/E**	28
Chez Panisse | **Berkeley/E**	28
Boulevard | **Embarcadero**	27
Masa's | **Downtown**	27
La Folie | **Russian Hill**	27
Cole's Chop | **Napa/N**	27
Madrona Manor | **Healdsburg/N**	27
La Forêt | **San Jose/S**	27
Terra | **St. Helena/N**	27
Auberge du Soleil | **Rutherford/N**	27
Fleur de Lys | **Downtown**	27
Michael Mina | **Downtown**	27
Manresa | **Los Gatos/S**	27
Benu | **SoMa**	27
Étoile | **Yountville/N**	27
Atelier Crenn | **Marina**	27
Seasons | **Downtown**	27
Sent Sovi | **Saratoga/S**	27
Coi | **N Beach**	27
Meadowood Rest. | **St. Helena/N**	27
La Toque | **Napa/N**	27
Ruth's Chris | **Polk Gulch**	27
Jardinière | **Civic Ctr**	27
Harris' | **Polk Gulch**	27
Hana | **Rohnert Pk/N**	26
Press | **St. Helena/N**	26
Alexander's Steak | **multi.**	26
Quince | **Downtown**	26
Aubergine | **Carmel/S**	26
Slanted Door | **Embarcadero**	26
Baumé | **Palo Alto/S**	26
Spruce | **Presidio Hts**	26

Flea St. Café	**Menlo Pk/S**	26
Roy's	**Pebble Bch/S**	26
Sons/Daughters	**Nob Hill**	26
Ame	**SoMa**	26
Campton Pl.	**Downtown**	26
Oliveto Rest.	**Oakland/E**	26
Village Pub	**Woodside/S**	25
Morton's	**Downtown**	25
Morimoto	**Napa/N**	25
John Ash	**Santa Rosa/N**	25
John Bentley	**Redwood City/S**	25
Bottega	**Yountville/N**	25
Plumed Horse	**Saratoga/S**	25
Greens	**Marina**	25
Fifth Floor	**SoMa**	25
Santé	**Sonoma/N**	25
Ozumo	**Embarcadero**	25
Navio	**Half Moon Bay/S**	25
Tommy Toy	**Downtown**	25
Dry Creek	**Healdsburg/N**	24
Prospect	**SoMa**	24
Barbacco	**Downtown**	24
Parallel 37	**Nob Hill**	24
Deetjen's Big Sur	**Big Sur/S**	24
Chez TJ	**Mtn View/S**	24
Wayfare Tav.	**Downtown**	24
Pacific's Edge	**Carmel/S**	24
Roy's	**SoMa**	24
Jai Yun	**Chinatown**	24
Bourbon	**Downtown**	24
5A5 Steak	**Downtown**	23
El Paseo	**Mill Valley/N**	23
Waterbar	**Embarcadero**	23
Rest./Ventana	**Big Sur/S**	23
Town Hall	**SoMa**	23
Forbes Mill	**Los Gatos/S**	23
Manzanita	**Truckee/E**	23
RN74	**SoMa**	23
Epic Roasthse.	**Embarcadero**	23
Sawa Sushi	**Sunnyvale/S**	23
McCormick/Kuleto	**Fish. Wharf**	22
Napa Wine Train	**Napa/N**	22
Garden Ct.	**Downtown**	22
Eulipia	**San Jose/S**	21
Sino	**San Jose/S**	20
NEW Brasserie S&P	**Downtown**	-
NEW Burritt Tavern	**Downtown**	-
NEW Rest. Mitsunobu	**Menlo Pk/S**	-

WINE BARS

Sushi Ran	**Sausalito/N**	27
Étoile	**Yountville/N**	27
La Toque	**Napa/N**	27
Picco	**Larkspur/N**	26
Wente Vineyards	**Livermore/E**	26
Prima	**Walnut Creek/E**	26
Fig Cafe/Wine	**Glen Ellen/N**	26
Frascati	**Russian Hill**	26
Rosso Pizzeria	**Santa Rosa/N**	26
Encuentro	**Oakland/E**	26
Soif Wine Bar	**Santa Cruz/S**	25
Willi's Wine	**Santa Rosa/N**	25
Va de Vi	**Walnut Creek/E**	25
Incanto	**Noe Valley**	25
Bar Tartine	**Mission**	25
A16	**Marina**	25
Viognier	**San Mateo/S**	25
Maverick	**Mission**	24
Enoteca Molinari	**Oakland/E**	24
Barbacco	**Downtown**	24
Carneros Bistro	**Sonoma/N**	24
ZuZu	**Napa/N**	24
Della Santina	**Sonoma/N**	24
Zin	**Healdsburg/N**	24
Bellanico	**Oakland/E**	24
Bar Bambino	**Mission**	24
All Seasons	**Calistoga/N**	24
Kuleto's	**Downtown**	23
Bocadillos	**N Beach**	23
Cin-Cin Wine	**Los Gatos/S**	23
Azzurro	**Napa/N**	23
Pauline's	**Mission**	23
RN74	**SoMa**	23
Uva Enoteca	**Lower Haight**	23
Emporio Rulli	**Larkspur/N**	22
Andre's Bouchée	**Carmel/S**	22
Cantinetta Luca	**Carmel/S**	22
Liberty Cafe	**Bernal Hts**	22
Brassica	**St. Helena/N**	22
Rest. LuLu	**SoMa**	22
Jackson Fillmore/Cucina	**San Anselmo/N**	22
Napa Wine Train	**Napa/N**	22
Vin Antico	**San Rafael/N**	22
Rustic	**Geyserville/N**	21
Oxbow Wine	**Napa/N**	21
Cafe Zoetrope	**N Beach**	20
Q Rest.	**Inner Rich**	20

Zibibbo	**Palo Alto/S**	20	Sent Sovi	**Saratoga/S**	27
Ottimista	**Cow Hollow**	20	Coi	**N Beach**	27
Le Zinc	**Noe Valley**	20	Millennium	**Downtown**	27
Two Sisters	**Hayes Valley**	19	Range	**Mission**	27
NEW Burritt Tavern	**Downtown**	–	Meadowood Rest.	**St. Helena/N**	27
NEW Copita	**Sausalito/N**	–	La Toque	**Napa/N**	27
NEW French Blue	**St. Helena/N**	–	Piperade	**Downtown**	27
NEW FuseBox	**Oakland/E**	–	Frances	**Castro**	27
NEW Glen Ellen Star	**Glen Ellen/N**	–	Ledford Hse.	**Albion/N**	27
NEW Lucy	**Yountville/N**	–	Jardinière	**Civic Ctr**	27
NEW St. Vincent Tav.	**Mission**	–	Nopa	**W Addition**	27

WINNING WINE LISTS

			Chapeau!	**Inner Rich**	27
Gary Danko	**Fish. Wharf**	29	Cafe La Haye	**Sonoma/N**	27
Keiko	**Nob Hill**	29	Press	**St. Helena/N**	26
French Laundry	**Yountville/N**	29	Bouchon	**Yountville/N**	26
Acquerello	**Polk Gulch**	28	Picco	**Larkspur/N**	26
Erna's	**Oakhurst/E**	28	Wente Vineyards	**Livermore/E**	26
Marinus	**Carmel Valley/S**	28	Alexander's Steak	**Cupertino/S**	26
Kokkari	**Downtown**	28	Quince	**Downtown**	26
Sierra Mar	**Big Sur/S**	28	Aubergine	**Carmel/S**	26
Redd	**Yountville/N**	28	Prima	**Walnut Creek/E**	26
Commis	**Oakland/E**	28	Fig Cafe/Wine	**Glen Ellen/N**	26
Chez Panisse Café	**Berkeley/E**	28	Slanted Door	**Embarcadero**	26
Rivoli	**Berkeley/E**	28	Lalime's	**Berkeley/E**	26
Chez Panisse	**Berkeley/E**	28	Spruce	**Presidio Hts**	26
Boulevard	**Embarcadero**	27	Flea St. Café	**Menlo Pk/S**	26
Masa's	**Downtown**	27	Cotogna	**Downtown**	26
Passionfish	**Pacific Grove/S**	27	Sons/Daughters	**Nob Hill**	26
Bistro/Copains	**Occidental/N**	27	Ame	**SoMa**	26
Evan's	**S Lake Tahoe/E**	27	Campton Pl.	**Downtown**	26
Farmhse. Inn	**Forestville/N**	27	Oliveto Rest.	**Oakland/E**	26
La Folie	**Russian Hill**	27	Zuni Café	**Hayes Valley**	26
Cole's Chop	**Napa/N**	27	Central Mkt.	**Petaluma/N**	26
Madrona Manor	**Healdsburg/N**	27	Flour + Water	**Mission**	26
La Forêt	**San Jose/S**	27	Mendo Bistro	**Ft Bragg/N**	26
Saison	**Mission**	27	BayWolf	**Oakland/E**	26
Jole	**Calistoga/N**	27	Pizzeria Picco	**Larkspur/N**	26
Terra	**St. Helena/N**	27	Baker/Banker	**Upper Fillmore**	26
Auberge du Soleil	**Rutherford/N**	27	Solbar	**Calistoga/N**	26
Fleur de Lys	**Downtown**	27	Dio Deka	**Los Gatos/S**	25
Michael Mina	**Downtown**	27	Zazu	**Santa Rosa/N**	25
Manresa	**Los Gatos/S**	27	Village Pub	**Woodside/S**	25
Sushi Ran	**Sausalito/N**	27	Morimoto	**Napa/N**	25
Le Papillon	**San Jose/S**	27	John Ash	**Santa Rosa/N**	25
Benu	**SoMa**	27	John Bentley	**Redwood City/S**	25
Étoile	**Yountville/N**	27	Bar Terra	**St. Helena/N**	25
Seasons	**Downtown**	27	Soif Wine Bar	**Santa Cruz/S**	25
			Contigo	**Noe Valley**	25
			Farm	**Napa/N**	25

SPECIAL FEATURES

Bottega | **Yountville/N**	25	Bistro Ralph | **Healdsburg/N**	24
Willi's Wine | **Santa Rosa/N**	25	Parallel 37 | **Nob Hill**	24
Va de Vi | **Walnut Creek/E**	25	La Mar | **Embarcadero**	24
Alex Rest. | **Rutherford/N**	25	Bistro Aix | **Marina**	24
Kenwood | **Kenwood/N**	25	Anton/Michel | **Carmel/S**	24
Terzo | **Cow Hollow**	25	Chez TJ | **Mtn View/S**	24
Plumed Horse | **Saratoga/S**	25	Sardine Factory | **Monterey/S**	24
Greens | **Marina**	25	La Condesa | **St. Helena/N**	24
Trattoria Corso | **Berkeley/E**	25	Picán | **Oakland/E**	24
Mustards | **Yountville/N**	25	Pacific's Edge | **Carmel/S**	24
Fifth Floor | **SoMa**	25	ZuZu | **Napa/N**	24
Heirloom | **Mission**	25	Della Santina | **Sonoma/N**	24
Santé | **Sonoma/N**	25	Roy's | **SoMa**	24
Woodward's Gdn. | **Mission**	25	Luella | **Russian Hill**	24
Willi's Seafood | **Healdsburg/N**	25	Zin | **Healdsburg/N**	24
Farallon | **Downtown**	25	Piccino | **Dogpatch**	24
Celadon | **Napa/N**	25	Bourbon | **Downtown**	24
Incanto | **Noe Valley**	25	Cetrella | **Half Moon Bay/S**	24
Navio | **Half Moon Bay/S**	25	Absinthe | **Hayes Valley**	24
Bistro Don Giovanni | **Napa/N**	25	Montrio Bistro | **Monterey/S**	24
955 Rest. | **Mendocino/N**	25	Bar Bambino | **Mission**	24
Bar Tartine | **Mission**	25	Glen Ellen Inn | **Glen Ellen/N**	24
A16 | **Marina**	25	All Seasons | **Calistoga/N**	24
Viognier | **San Mateo/S**	25	Scala's Bistro | **Downtown**	23
Redd Wood | **Yountville/N**	25	Rio Grill | **Carmel/S**	23
Naomi Sushi | **Menlo Pk/S**	25	Kuleto's | **Downtown**	23
SPQR | **Pacific Hts**	25	Bocadillos | **N Beach**	23
Lark Creek Steak | **Downtown**	25	Chez Papa Resto | **SoMa**	23
À Côté | **Oakland/E**	25	Oliveto Cafe | **Oakland/E**	23
Camino | **Oakland/E**	25	Postrio | **Downtown**	23
Locanda | **Mission**	25	El Paseo | **Mill Valley/N**	23
North Bch. Rest. | **N Beach**	25	Wine Spectator | **St. Helena/N**	23
Albion River Inn | **Albion/N**	25	Waterbar | **Embarcadero**	23
Bella Vista | **Woodside/S**	25	Rest./Ventana | **Big Sur/S**	23
Poggio | **Sausalito/N**	24	Bridges | **Danville/E**	23
Tra Vigne | **St. Helena/N**	24	Brix | **Napa/N**	23
Dry Creek | **Healdsburg/N**	24	231 Ellsworth | **San Mateo/S**	23
Beretta | **Mission**	24	Town Hall | **SoMa**	23
Angèle | **Napa/N**	24	Donato | **Redwood City/S**	23
Prospect | **SoMa**	24	Alembic | **Haight-Ashbury**	23
Oenotri | **Napa/N**	24	Forbes Mill | **multi.**	23
Barbacco | **Downtown**	24	Manzanita | **Truckee/E**	23
Casanova | **Carmel/S**	24	PlumpJack | **Olympic Valley/E**	23
LaSalette | **Sonoma/N**	24	Butterfly | **Embarcadero**	23
Carneros Bistro | **Sonoma/N**	24	Gabriella Café | **Santa Cruz/S**	23
Vic Stewart | **Walnut Creek/E**	24	RN74 | **SoMa**	23
One Market | **Embarcadero**	24	Adesso | **Oakland/E**	23
Cindy's | **St. Helena/N**	24	Uva Enoteca | **Lower Haight**	23
Girl/Fig | **Sonoma/N**	24	St. Orres | **Gualala/N**	23

Pampas | **Palo Alto/S** 23
Epic Roasthse. | **Embarcadero** 23
Farmstead | **St. Helena/N** 22
Andre's Bouchée | **Carmel/S** 22
Cantinetta Luca | **Carmel/S** 22
LB Steak | **San Jose/S** 22
54 Mint | **SoMa** 22
Liberty Cafe | **Bernal Hts** 22
Monti's | **Santa Rosa/N** 22
Barlata | **Oakland/E** 22
St. Michael's | **Palo Alto/S** 22
Grasing's Coastal | **Carmel/S** 22
Brassica | **St. Helena/N** 22
Zaré/Fly Trap | **SoMa** 22
Gott's Roadside | **Napa/N** 22
Tav./Lark Creek | **Larkspur/N** 22
Rest. LuLu | **SoMa** 22
Indigo | **Civic Ctr** 22
Underwood Bar | **Graton/N** 22
Wo Hing | **Mission** 22
Napa Wine Train | **Napa/N** 22
Plate Shop | **Sausalito/N** 22
Marinitas | **San Anselmo/N** 22
Vin Antico | **San Rafael/N** 22
Alioto's | **Fish. Wharf** 21
Mateo's Cocina | **Healdsburg/N** 21
Five | **Berkeley/E** 21
Nick's Cove | **Marshall/N** 21
Luce | **SoMa** 21
Rustic | **Geyserville/N** 21
Meadowood Grill | **St. Helena/N** 21
Fandango | **Pacific Grove/S** 21
Oxbow Wine | **Napa/N** 21
Rose Pistola | **N Beach** 21
Lavanda | **Palo Alto/S** 21
Pianeta | **Truckee/E** 21
Ristobar | **Marina** 21
Rumbo | **Oakland/E** 21
César | **Berkeley/E** 20
Zibibbo | **Palo Alto/S** 20
Heaven's Dog | **SoMa** 20
Balboa Cafe | **Mill Valley/N** 20
Ottimista | **Cow Hollow** 20
NEW Brasserie S&P | **Downtown** –
NEW Burritt Tavern | **Downtown** –
NEW Corners Tav. |
  Walnut Creek/E –
NEW Dixie | **Presidio** –

NEW French Blue | **St. Helena/N** –
NEW Glen Ellen Star |
  Glen Ellen/N –
NEW Goose/Gander |
  St. Helena/N –
NEW Moss Room | **Outer Rich** –
NEW Rich Table |
  Hayes Valley –
NEW St. Vincent Tav. | **Mission** –
NEW Thomas/Fagiani's |
  Napa/N –

WORTH A TRIP

Albion
  Ledford Hse. 27
  Albion River Inn 25
Berkeley
  Chez Panisse Café 28
  Rivoli 28
  Chez Panisse 28
  Lalime's 26
  Zachary's Pizza 26
Big Sur
  Sierra Mar 28
  Deetjen's Big Sur 24
  Rest./Ventana 23
Carmel
  Aubergine 26
  Pacific's Edge 24
  Cantinetta Luca 22
Carmel Valley
  Marinus 28
El Granada
  Cafe Gibraltar 28
Forestville
  Farmhse. Inn 27
Gualala
  St. Orres 23
Half Moon Bay
  Navio 25
Healdsburg
  Madrona Manor 27
  Dry Creek 24
Larkspur
  Emporio Rulli 22
Little River
  Little River Inn 22
Livermore
  Wente Vineyards 26

Cuisines

Includes names, locations and Food ratings.

AFGHAN

Salang Pass	**Fremont/E**	25
Helmand Palace	**Russian Hill**	24
Kabul Afghan	**multi.**	23

AMERICAN

Gary Danko	**Fish. Wharf**	29
French Laundry	**Yountville/N**	29
Commis	**Oakland/E**	28
Boulevard	**Embarcadero**	27
Evan's	**S Lake Tahoe/E**	27
State Bird	**W Addition**	27
Madrona Manor	**Healdsburg/N**	27
Saison	**Mission**	27
Jole	**Calistoga/N**	27
Terra	**St. Helena/N**	27
Michael Mina	**Downtown**	27
Manresa	**Los Gatos/S**	27
Benu	**SoMa**	27
Range	**Mission**	27
Lucca Deli	**Marina**	27
Cafe La Haye	**Sonoma/N**	27
Ad Hoc	**Yountville/N**	27
Press	**St. Helena/N**	26
House/Prime	**Polk Gulch**	26
Esin	**Danville/E**	26
Spruce	**Presidio Hts**	26
Flea St. Café	**Menlo Pk/S**	26
Nick's on Main	**Los Gatos/S**	26
Sons/Daughters	**Nob Hill**	26
Ame	**SoMa**	26
Commonwealth	**Mission**	26
Mendo Bistro	**Ft Bragg/N**	26
Boulettes Larder	**Embarcadero**	26
Baker/Banker	**Upper Fillmore**	26
Stark's	**Santa Rosa/N**	26
Zazu	**Santa Rosa/N**	25
Village Pub	**Woodside/S**	25
Rest./Stevenswood	**Little River/N**	25
Bar Terra	**St. Helena/N**	25
Farm	**Napa/N**	25
Universal Cafe	**Mission**	25
Nojo	**Hayes Valley**	25
Bar Jules	**Hayes Valley**	25
Mustards	**Yountville/N**	25

Fifth Floor	**SoMa**	25
Oswald	**Santa Cruz/S**	25
Woodward's Gdn.	**Mission**	25
3-Sum	**Loc varies**	25
Barndiva	**Healdsburg/N**	25
Celadon	**Napa/N**	25
Navio	**Half Moon Bay/S**	25
955 Rest.	**Mendocino/N**	25
Buckeye	**Mill Valley/N**	25
Outerlands	**Outer Sunset**	25
NEW Park Tav.	**N Beach**	25
Maverick	**Mission**	24
RoliRoti	**Embarcadero**	24
Madera	**Menlo Pk/S**	24
Prospect	**SoMa**	24
One Market	**Embarcadero**	24
Mama's on Wash.	**N Beach**	24
Rutherford Grill	**Rutherford/N**	24
NEW Parallel 37	**Nob Hill**	24
Big 4	**Nob Hill**	24
Bix	**Downtown**	24
Big Sur	**Big Sur/S**	24
Los Altos Grill	**Los Altos/S**	24
Kitchenette SF	**Dogpatch**	24
Sardine Factory	**Monterey/S**	24
Arcadia	**San Jose/S**	24
Wayfare Tav.	**Downtown**	24
Hillstone	**Embarcadero**	24
Soule Domain	**Kings Bch/E**	24
Pacific's Edge	**Carmel/S**	24
Tarpy's	**Monterey/S**	24
Zin	**Healdsburg/N**	24
Blue Plate	**Mission**	24
Bourbon	**Downtown**	24
Chapter & Moon	**Ft Bragg/N**	24
Mama's Royal	**Oakland/E**	24
Red Grape	**Sonoma/N**	24
Aquarius	**Santa Cruz/S**	24
Rocker Oysterfellers	**Valley Ford/N**	24
Lark Creek	**Walnut Creek/E**	24
Southie	**Oakland/E**	24
Il Postale	**Sunnyvale/S**	23
Original Joe's	**San Jose/S**	23
Serpentine	**Dogpatch**	23
Chenery Park	**Glen Pk**	23

CUISINES

Flora	**Oakland/E**	23
Rick & Ann	**Berkeley/E**	23
Postrio	**Downtown**	23
In-N-Out	**multi.**	23
Bacon Bacon	**multi.**	23
Red Hut	**S Lake Tahoe/E**	23
Slow Club	**Mission**	23
Moody's Bistro	**Truckee/E**	23
3rd St. Grill	**SoMa**	23
Scott's Seafood	**multi.**	23
231 Ellsworth	**San Mateo/S**	23
Town Hall	**SoMa**	23
Mission Cheese	**Mission**	23
Mixt Greens	**Downtown**	23
Amer. Grilled	**SoMa**	23
Basin	**Saratoga/S**	23
Mua Lounge	**Oakland/E**	23
Chloe's Cafe	**Noe Valley**	23
Kincaid's	**multi.**	23
Mo's	**multi.**	23
Duarte's	**Pescadero/S**	23
Mombo's Pizza	**multi.**	23
Caprice	**Tiburon/N**	23
1300/Fillmore	**W Addition**	23
Farmstead	**St. Helena/N**	22
15 Romolo	**N Beach**	22
Fumé Bistro	**Napa/N**	22
Sauce	**multi.**	22
Bungalow 44	**Mill Valley/N**	22
Duck Club	**multi.**	22
Magnolia	**Haight-Ashbury**	22
Liberty Cafe	**Bernal Hts**	22
Monti's	**Santa Rosa/N**	22
Restaurant	**Ft Bragg/N**	22
Salt Hse.	**SoMa**	22
Hudson	**Oakland/E**	22
Sycamore	**Mission**	22
Homeroom	**Oakland/E**	22
Hog & Rocks	**Mission**	22
Nation's Giant	**Daly City/S**	22
Original Joe's (SF)	**N Beach**	22
Market	**St. Helena/N**	22
Eureka	**Castro**	22
Boudin	**multi.**	22
NEW Per Diem	**Downtown**	22
Shadowbrook	**Capitola/S**	22
Gott's Roadside	**multi.**	22
Tav./Lark Creek	**Larkspur/N**	22
Citizen's Band	**SoMa**	22

Jasper's Corner	**Downtown**	22
Indigo	**Civic Ctr**	22
Buckhorn Grill	**multi.**	22
Town's End	**Embarcadero**	22
Ahwahnee	**Yosemite/E**	22
Lion/Compass	**Sunnyvale/S**	21
Hotel Mac Rest.	**Richmond/E**	21
Five	**Berkeley/E**	21
Farm:Table	**Civic Ctr**	21
Swiss Hotel	**Sonoma/N**	21
Hilltop 1892	**Novato/N**	21
Cheesecake Fac.	**multi.**	21
Eulipia	**San Jose/S**	21
Rotunda	**Downtown**	21
Sears	**Downtown**	21
Chow/Park Chow	**multi.**	21
NEW Trace	**SoMa**	21
Toast	**multi.**	21
Stacks	**multi.**	21
25 Lusk	**SoMa**	21
Elite Cafe	**Pacific Hts**	21
NEW Hawk's Tav.	**Mill Valley/N**	21
Cafe Divine	**N Beach**	21
Pine Cone Diner	**Pt Reyes/N**	21
Ella's	**Presidio Hts**	21
Brazen Head	**Cow Hollow**	21
Crepevine	**multi.**	21
Norman Rose	**Napa/N**	20
Fish & Farm	**Downtown**	20
Q Rest.	**Inner Rich**	20
Montclair Egg	**Oakland/E**	20
Skates on Bay	**Berkeley/E**	20
Healdsburg B&G	**Healdsburg/N**	20
MoMo's	**S Beach**	20
Balboa Cafe	**multi.**	20
Brannan's Grill	**Calistoga/N**	20
NEW Maven	**Lower Haight**	20
Mission Ranch	**Carmel/S**	20
Luna Park	**Mission**	20
Hopmonk Tav.	**multi.**	20
Java Beach	**Outer Sunset**	20
Fog City Diner	**Embarcadero**	20
Radish	**Mission**	20
Wurst Rest.	**Healdsburg/N**	20
Presidio Social	**Presidio**	19
Bluestem Brass.	**SoMa**	19
Pork Store	**multi.**	19
NEW Two Sisters	**Hayes Valley**	19
Cannery/Brew	**Monterey/S**	19

Buck's | **Woodside/S** 19
Rudy's Can't Fail | **multi.** 19
NEW Roostertail | **Upper Fillmore** 19
Campanula | **N Beach** 19
North Coast Brew | **Ft Bragg/N** 19
Gordon Biersch | **multi.** 18
Nepenthe | **Big Sur/S** 18
Bottle Cap | **N Beach** 18
Station Hse. | **Pt Reyes/N** 17
Toast (SF) | **Noe Valley** 17
Park Chalet | **Outer Sunset** 17
Beach Chalet | **Outer Sunset** 17
Dobb's Ferry | **Hayes Valley** 16
NEW Abbot's Cellar | **Mission** -
NEW Burritt Tavern | **Downtown** -
NEW Corners Tav. | -
Walnut Creek/E
NEW French Blue | **St. Helena/N** -
NEW Glen Ellen Star | -
Glen Ellen/N
NEW Goose/Gander | -
St. Helena/N
NEW Hayes Valley Bakeworks | -
Hayes Valley
NEW Hopscotch | **Oakland/E** -
NEW Thomas/Fagiani's | **Napa/N** -

ARGENTINEAN

Boca | **Novato/N** 25
NEW Lolinda | **Mission** -

ASIAN

House | **N Beach** 27
Chinois | **Windsor/N** 25
B Star | **Inner Rich** 25
NEW O3 Bistro | **Civic Ctr** 24
Betelnut Pejiu | **Cow Hollow** 24
Flying Fish (Carmel) | **Carmel/S** 24
Chubby Noodle | **N Beach** 24
Dragonfly | **Truckee/E** 24
Champa Gdn. | **Oakland/E** 23
Bridges | **Danville/E** 23
Unicorn | **Downtown** 23
Hawker Fare | **Oakland/E** 23
Butterfly | **Embarcadero** 23
NEW Forchetta/Bastoni | 23
Sebastopol/N
E&O Asian Kit. | **Downtown** 21
Spice Kit | **multi.** 18
NEW Asian Box | **Palo Alto/S** 17

AUSTRIAN

Leopold's | **Russian Hill** 23

BAKERIES

Bi-Rite Creamery | **Mission** 28
Tartine | **Mission** 27
Della Fattoria | **Petaluma/N** 27
Downtown Bakery | 26
Healdsburg/N
Bakesale Betty | **Oakland/E** 26
Arizmendi | **multi.** 25
Sandbox | **Bernal Hts** 25
Dynamo Donut | **Mission** 25
Gayle's Bakery | **Capitola/S** 24
Mama's on Wash. | **N Beach** 24
Big Sur | **Big Sur/S** 24
Fort Bragg | **Ft Bragg/N** 23
Emporio Rulli | **multi.** 22
Model Bakery | **multi.** 22
Liberty Cafe | **Bernal Hts** 22
Copenhagen Bakery | 22
Burlingame/S
Alexis Baking | **Napa/N** 22
Carmel Bakery | **Carmel/S** 22
Town's End | **Embarcadero** 22
La Boulange | **multi.** 22
Mayfield | **Palo Alto/S** 21
Golden West | **Downtown** 21
DeLessio Mkt. | **multi.** 21
NEW Craftsman/Wolves | -
Mission
NEW Hayes Valley Bakeworks | -
Hayes Valley

BARBECUE

NEW B-Side BBQ | **Oakland/E**
Buckeye | **Mill Valley/N**
Wexler's | **Downtown**
Addendum | **Yountville/N**
Bo's BBQ | **Lafayette/E**
BarBersQ | **Napa/N**
Baby Blues BBQ | **Missio**
Everett/Jones BBQ | **mu**
Q Rest. | **Inner Rich**
Memphis Minnie | **Low**
Southpaw BBQ | **Mis**
Ono Hawaiian | **Lak**
T Rex BBQ | **Berke**
NEW Catheads B

CUISINES

BELGIAN

Refuge	**San Carlos/S**	25
La Trappe	**N Beach**	20
Frjtz Fries	**Mission**	18

BRAZILIAN

Mozzarella/Bufala	**W Portal**	23
Espetus	**multi.**	23
Pampas	**Palo Alto/S**	23

BRITISH

Betty's Fish	**Santa Rosa/N**	24
Lovejoy's Tea	**Noe Valley**	21

BURGERS

900 Grayson	**Berkeley/E**	25
Pearl's Deluxe/Phat	**multi.**	24
Super Duper	**multi.**	23
Roam	**Cow Hollow**	23
In-N-Out	**multi.**	23
Mo's	**multi.**	23
NEW Umami Burger	**Cow Hollow**	23
Joe's Cable Car	**Excelsior**	22
Acme Burger	**W Addition**	22
Counter Palo Alto	**Palo Alto/S**	22
Nation's Giant	**Daly City/S**	22
Buster's Cheesesteak	**N Beach**	22
Barney's	**multi.**	22
ueburger	**Oakland/E**	21
ople's	**multi.**	20
Bar	**Downtown**	20
ister	**multi.**	20
B&G	**Healdsburg/N**	20
multi.	20
lti.	19
nterey/S	19
	17
26
25
24	rmel/S	—
24
22
22
21
21
20	lti.
r Haight	20
ion	19
eshore	19
ey/E	18
BQ	**SoMa**	—

CALIFORNIAN

Craw Station	**Inner Sunset**	2
Boxing Rm.	**Hayes Valley**	21
Elite Cafe	**Pacific Hts**	21
Terrapin Creek	**Bodega Bay/N**	28
Erna's	**Oakhurst/E**	28
Marinus	**Carmel Valley/S**	28
Sierra Mar	**Big Sur/S**	28
Redd	**Yountville/N**	28
Chez Panisse Café	**Berkeley/E**	28
Rivoli	**Berkeley/E**	28
Chez Panisse	**Berkeley/E**	28
Passionfish	**Pacific Grove/S**	27
Farmhse. Inn	**Forestville/N**	27
Local Mission	**Mission**	27
Auberge du Soleil	**Rutherford/N**	27
Fleur de Lys	**Downtown**	27
Étoile	**Yountville/N**	27
Sent Sovi	**Saratoga/S**	27
Wolfdale's	**Tahoe City/E**	27
Coi	**N Beach**	27
Meadowood Rest.	**St. Helena/N**	27
Canteen	**Tenderloin**	27
Frances	**Castro**	27
Ledford Hse.	**Albion/N**	27
Jardinière	**Civic Ctr**	27
Nopa	**W Addition**	27
Osake	**Santa Rosa/N**	27
Cafe La Haye	**Sonoma/N**	27
Picco	**Larkspur/N**	26
Wente Vineyards	**Livermore/E**	26
Asena	**Alameda/E**	26
Quince	**Downtown**	26
Aubergine	**Carmel/S**	26
Plow	**Potrero Hill**	26
Richmond	**Inner Rich**	26
Table Café	**Larkspur/N**	26
Cafe Beaujolais	**Mendocino/N**	26
Lalime's	**Berkeley/E**	26
Flea St. Café	**Menlo Pk/S**	26
Frascati	**Russian Hill**	26
Campton Pl.	**Downtown**	26
entral Mkt.	**Petaluma/N**	26
nd Tav.	**Oakland/E**	26
lf	**Oakland/E**	26
Calistoga/N	26
on	**Sonoma/N**	25
istro	**Lafayette/E**	25

61

🆕 AQ | **SoMa**	25
John Ash | **Santa Rosa/N**	25
John Bentley | **Redwood City/S**	25
Pearl | **Napa/N**	25
All Spice | **San Mateo/S**	25
Soif Wine Bar | **Santa Cruz/S**	25
Rest. James | **Los Gatos/S**	25
Hot Box Grill | **Sonoma/N**	25
Kenwood | **Kenwood/N**	25
Plumed Horse | **Saratoga/S**	25
Mustards | **Yountville/N**	25
Heirloom | **Mission**	25
Murray Circle | **Sausalito/N**	25
Santé | **Sonoma/N**	25
Woodward's Gdn. | **Mission**	25
900 Grayson | **Berkeley/E**	25
Blue Barn | **Marina**	25
Viognier | **San Mateo/S**	25
Station 1 | **Woodside/S**	25
Pappo | **Alameda/E**	25
Camino | **Oakland/E**	25
Ecco | **Burlingame/S**	25
🆕 Haven | **Oakland/E**	25
Foreign Cinema | **Mission**	25
Albion River Inn | **Albion/N**	25
Dry Creek | **Healdsburg/N**	24
Gather | **Berkeley/E**	24
Boon Eat/Drink | **Guerneville/N**	24
Marlowe | **SoMa**	24
Carneros Bistro | **Sonoma/N**	24
Cindy's | **St. Helena/N**	24
Bistro Ralph | **Healdsburg/N**	24
Garibaldis | **Presidio Hts**	24
Applewood Rest. | **Guerneville/N**	24
🆕 Bouche | **Nob Hill**	24
Blue Bottle | **multi.**	24
Deetjen's Big Sur | **Big Sur/S**	24
Venus | **Berkeley/E**	24
Bistro Aix | **Marina**	24
MacCallum | **Mendocino/N**	24
Café Rustica | **Carmel Valley/S**	24
Chop Bar | **Oakland/E**	24
Flying Fish (Carmel) | **Carmel/S**	24
Luella | **Russian Hill**	24
Beast/Hare | **Mission**	24
Piccino | **Dogpatch**	24
Montrio Bistro | **Monterey/S**	24
Glen Ellen Inn | **Glen Ellen/N**	24
Peasant/Pear | **Danville/E**	24

All Seasons | **Calistoga/N**	24
Dragonfly | **Truckee/E**	24
Rio Grill | **Carmel/S**	23
Actual Cafe | **Oakland/E**	23
Plum | **Oakland/E**	23
Mezze | **Oakland/E**	23
Anzu | **Downtown**	23
Wine Spectator | **St. Helena/N**	23
Boon Fly | **Napa/N**	23
Hurley's | **Yountville/N**	23
Coco500 | **SoMa**	23
Rest./Ventana | **Big Sur/S**	23
Bridges | **Danville/E**	23
Amber Bistro | **Danville/E**	23
La Rose Bistro | **Berkeley/E**	23
Brix | **Napa/N**	23
Parcel 104 | **Santa Clara/S**	23
Flavor | **Santa Rosa/N**	23
Manzanita | **Truckee/E**	23
PlumpJack | **Olympic Valley/E**	23
Butterfly | **Embarcadero**	23
Mission Bch. Café | **Mission**	23
Gabriella Café | **Santa Cruz/S**	23
Bar Agricole | **SoMa**	23
St. Orres | **Gualala/N**	23
El Dorado | **Sonoma/N**	23
Sutro's | **Outer Rich**	23
Aqui Cal-Mex | **multi.**	23
Ravenous | **Healdsburg/N**	22
Farmstead | **St. Helena/N**	22
Little River Inn | **Little River/N**	22
71 St. Peter | **San Jose/S**	22
Moosse Café | **Mendocino/N**	22
Oola | **SoMa**	22
St. Michael's | **Palo Alto/S**	22
Meritage/Claremont | **Berkeley/E**	22
Grasing's Coastal | **Carmel/S**	22
Café Rouge | **Berkeley/E**	22
Starbelly | **Castro**	22
Fresh/Lisa | **Santa Rosa/N**	22
Revival Bar | **Berkeley/E**	22
Zaré/Fly Trap | **SoMa**	22
Shadowbrook | **Capitola/S**	22
Sidebar | **Oakland/E**	22
Radius | **SoMa**	22
Locavore | **Bernal Hts**	22
Fishwife | **Pacific Grove/S**	22
Café Brioche | **Palo Alto/S**	22

CUISINES

Claudine | **Downtown**	22
Bucci's | **Emeryville/E**	22
Napa Wine Train | **Napa/N**	22
Garden Ct. | **Downtown**	22
Davenport | **Davenport/S**	22
Plate Shop | **Sausalito/N**	22
Ahwahnee | **Yosemite/E**	22
Vin Antico | **San Rafael/N**	22
Boudin | **Fish. Wharf**	22
Jackson's | **Santa Rosa/N**	21
Townhouse B&G | **Emeryville/E**	21
Five | **Berkeley/E**	21
Nick's Cove | **Marshall/N**	21
Flying Fish (HMB) | **Half Moon Bay/S**	21
Waterfront | **Embarcadero**	21
Luce | **SoMa**	21
Cool Café | **multi.**	21
Mayfield | **Palo Alto/S**	21
Meadowood Grill | **St. Helena/N**	21
Stinking Rose | **N Beach**	21
Hilltop 1892 | **Novato/N**	21
Christy Hill | **Tahoe City/E**	21
Oxbow Wine | **Napa/N**	21
Pacific Crest | **Truckee/E**	21
Metro | **multi.**	21
Cliff Hse. | **Outer Rich**	21
Mendocino Hotel | **Mendocino/N**	21
Calafia | **Palo Alto/S**	20
Spinnaker | **Sausalito/N**	20
Luka's Taproom | **Oakland/E**	20
Gar Woods | **Carnelian Bay/E**	20
Spoonbar | **Healdsburg/N**	20
Straw | **Hayes Valley**	20
Johnny Garlic's | **multi.**	20
Jake's/Lake | **Tahoe City/E**	20
Brick/Bottle | **Corte Madera/N**	19
Globe | **Downtown**	18
Half Moon Brew | **Half Moon Bay/S**	18
Park Chalet | **Outer Sunset**	17
Lake Chalet | **Oakland/E**	17
NEW Brasserie S&P | **Downtown**	–
NEW Central Kitchen | **Mission**	–
NEW Gioia Pizzeria | **Russian Hill**	–
NEW Lucy | **Yountville/N**	–
NEW Moss Room | **Outer Rich**	–
Namu | **multi.**	–
NEW Pläj | **Hayes Valley**	–
NEW Rich Table | **Hayes Valley**	–
NEW St. Vincent Tav. | **Mission**	–

CAMBODIAN

Battambang | **Oakland/E**	25
Angkor Borei | **Bernal Hts**	23

CARIBBEAN

Front Porch | **Bernal Hts**	22
Fishwife | **Pacific Grove/S**	22
Cha Cha Cha | **multi.**	22

CHEESE SPECIALISTS

Cheese Board | **Berkeley/E**	27
Mission Cheese | **Mission**	23
Amer. Grilled | **SoMa**	23

CHEESESTEAKS

Cheese Steak | **multi.**	23
Jake's Steaks | **Marina**	23
Phat Philly | **Mission**	22
Buster's Cheesesteak | **N Beach**	22
Jay's | **multi.**	19

CHICKEN

RoliRoti | **Embarcadero**	24
Il Cane Rosso | **Embarcadero**	23
Green Chile | **W Addition**	23
Home of Chicken | **multi.**	20
Goood Frikin' | **Mission**	20

CHINESE

(* dim sum specialist)

Mingalaba | **Burlingame/S**	27
Yank Sing* | **SoMa**	26
Ton Kiang* | **Outer Rich**	25
Liou's Hse. | **Milpitas/S**	25
R & G Lounge | **Chinatown**	25
O'mei | **Santa Cruz/S**	25
Tommy Toy | **Downtown**	25
San Tung | **Inner Sunset**	24
Chu | **Oakland/E**	24
Chairman* | **Loc varies**	24
Gary Chu's | **Santa Rosa/N**	24
Shanghai Hse. | **Outer Rich**	24
Z & Y | **Chinatown**	24
Bund Shanghai | **Chinatown**	24
Kitchen* | **Millbrae/S**	24
Oriental Pearl* | **Chinatown**	24
Hong Kong Lounge* | **multi.**	24
Jai Yun | **Chinatown**	24
Shanghai Dumpling | **Outer Rich**	24

East Ocean	**Alameda/E**	24
Koi*	**multi.**	24
Tai Pan*	**Palo Alto/S**	24
Shen Hua	**Berkeley/E**	23
Harmony*	**Mill Valley/N**	23
Great Eastern*	**Chinatown**	23
Hakka Rest.	**Outer Rich**	23
Eliza's	**Pacific Hts**	23
Chef Chu's	**Los Altos/S**	23
Spices	**multi.**	23
House/Nanking	**Chinatown**	23
Hunan Home's/Gdn.	**multi.**	22
Legendary Palace*	**Oakland/E**	22
Fang	**SoMa**	22
Happy Cafe*	**San Mateo/S**	22
Mission Chinese	**Mission**	22
Asian Pearl	**Millbrae/S**	22
Kingdom/Dumpling	**Parkside**	22
Henry's Hunan	**multi.**	22
Crouching Tiger	**Redwood City/S**	22
Eric's	**Noe Valley**	22
Hong Kong East*	**Emeryville/E**	22
Joy Luck Palace	**Cupertino/S**	22
NEW Wo Hing	**Mission**	22
Mayflower*	**multi.**	22
Good Luck*	**Inner Rich**	22
Jennie Low's	**Petaluma/N**	21
Shanghai Dumpling	**Millbrae/S**	21
ABC Cafe	**Chinatown**	21
Brandy Ho's	**multi.**	21
Just Wonton	**Outer Sunset**	20
Yuet Lee	**Chinatown**	20
Heaven's Dog*	**SoMa**	20
Rest. Peony*	**Oakland/E**	20
Sino*	**San Jose/S**	20
Alice's	**Noe Valley**	20
Imperial Tea*	**Embarcadero**	19

COFFEEHOUSES

Dynamo Donut	**Mission**	25
Blue Bottle	**multi.**	24
Bacon Bacon	**multi.**	23
Emporio Rulli	**multi.**	22
Java Beach	**Outer Sunset**	20
NEW Machine Coffee	**Downtown**	-

COLOMBIAN

Mr. Pollo	**Mission**	25

CONTINENTAL

La Forêt	**San Jose/S**	27
Ecco	**Burlingame/S**	25
Bella Vista	**Woodside/S**	25
Anton/Michel	**Carmel/S**	24

CREOLE

Brenda's	**Civic Ctr**	25
Angeline's LA Kit.	**Berkeley/E**	24
Craw Station	**Inner Sunset**	24
Boxing Rm.	**Hayes Valley**	21

CRÊPES

Crepevine	**multi.**	21

CUBAN

La Bodeguita/Medio	**Palo Alto/S**	23
Cha Cha Cha	**San Mateo/S**	22

DELIS

Lucca Deli	**Marina**	27
4505 Meats	**Embarcadero**	26
Boccalone	**Embarcadero**	25
NEW Deli Board	**SoMa**	25
Wise Sons	**multi.**	23
Il Cane Rosso	**Embarcadero**	23
AK Subs	**SoMa**	22
Miller's East	**multi.**	21
Jimtown Store	**Healdsburg/N**	20
Saul's Rest./Deli	**Berkeley/E**	20
Max's	**multi.**	20
Moishe's Pippic	**Hayes Valley**	18
NEW Machine Coffee	**Downtown**	-
NEW Market & Rye	**multi.**	-
NEW Salumeria	**Mission**	-
NEW Split Bread	**SoMa**	-

DESSERT

Bi-Rite Creamery	**Mission**	28
Tartine	**Mission**	27
Cafe Jacqueline	**N Beach**	27
Downtown Bakery	**Healdsburg/N**	26
Sandbox	**Bernal Hts**	25
Cupkates	**Loc varies**	25
Gayle's Bakery	**Capitola/S**	24
Emporio Rulli	**multi.**	22
Model Bakery	**multi.**	22
Chile Pies	**multi.**	22

Fentons	**Oakland/E**	22
La Boulange	**multi.**	22
Mayfield	**Palo Alto/S**	21
Cheesecake Fac.	**multi.**	21
DeLessio Mkt.	**multi.**	21
NEW Craftsman/Wolves	**Mission**	-
NEW Glen Ellen Star	**Glen Ellen/N**	-

DINER

Bette's Oceanview	**Berkeley/E**	25
HRD Coffee	**SoMa**	25
Fremont Diner	**Sonoma/N**	24
Red Hut	**S Lake Tahoe/E**	23
Joe's Cable Car	**Excelsior**	22
Alexis Baking	**Napa/N**	22
Gott's Roadside	**multi.**	22
Sears	**Downtown**	21
Pine Cone Diner	**Pt Reyes/N**	21
FatApple's	**multi.**	20
Jimmy Beans	**Berkeley/E**	20
Montclair Egg	**Oakland/E**	20
Fog City Diner	**Embarcadero**	20
Rudy's Can't Fail	**multi.**	19
Dipsea Cafe	**Mill Valley/N**	19
St. Francis	**Mission**	18
Mel's Drive-In	**multi.**	17

ECLECTIC

Sierra Mar	**Big Sur/S**	28
Della Fattoria	**Petaluma/N**	27
Graffiti	**Petaluma/N**	25
Firefly	**Noe Valley**	25
Willi's Wine	**Santa Rosa/N**	25
Va de Vi	**Walnut Creek/E**	25
Celadon	**Napa/N**	25
Willow Wood	**Graton/N**	24
Pomelo	**multi.**	24
Cin-Cin Wine	**Los Gatos/S**	23
Fort Bragg	**Ft Bragg/N**	23
Flavor	**Santa Rosa/N**	23
Alembic	**Haight-Ashbury**	23
Ravenous	**Healdsburg/N**	22
Restaurant	**Ft Bragg/N**	22
Kitchen Door	**Napa/N**	22
Andalu	**Mission**	22
Dead Fish	**Crockett/E**	22
360° Gourmet	**multi.**	22
Mendo Café	**Mendocino/N**	21
Academy Cafe	**Inner Rich**	21

Cottonwood	**Truckee/E**	20
Hopmonk Tav.	**multi.**	20
NEW Dear Mom	**Mission**	19
Chez Shea	**Half Moon Bay/S**	19
NEW SoMa StrEAT	**SoMa**	-
NEW Surf Spot	**Pacifica/S**	-

ETHIOPIAN

Zeni	**San Jose/S**	27
Asmara	**Oakland/E**	26
Café Colucci	**Oakland/E**	26
Addis Ethiopian	**Oakland/E**	25
Axum Cafe	**Lower Haight**	21

EUROPEAN

Bar Tartine	**Mission**	25
RoliRoti	**Embarcadero**	24

FILIPINO

Attic	**San Mateo/S**	20

FONDUE

La Fondue	**Saratoga/S**	23
Fondue Cowboy	**SoMa**	22
Matterhorn Swiss	**Russian Hill**	21

FRENCH

NEW Keiko	**Nob Hill**	29
French Laundry	**Yountville/N**	29
Erna's	**Oakhurst/E**	28
Marinus	**Carmel Valley/S**	28
Masa's	**Downtown**	27
La Folie	**Russian Hill**	27
Madrona Manor	**Healdsburg/N**	27
La Forêt	**San Jose/S**	27
Auberge du Soleil	**Rutherford/N**	27
Fleur de Lys	**Downtown**	27
Le Papillon	**San Jose/S**	27
Atelier Crenn	**Marina**	27
Coi	**N Beach**	27
Bistro Moulin	**Monterey/S**	27
La Toque	**Napa/N**	27
Marché/Fleurs	**Ross/N**	27
Jardinière	**Civic Ctr**	27
Cafe Jacqueline	**N Beach**	27
La Gare	**Santa Rosa/N**	27
Fig Cafe/Wine	**Glen Ellen/N**	26
Baumé	**Palo Alto/S**	26
Cafe Beaujolais	**Mendocino/N**	26

NEW Castagna | **Marina**	26
Chevalier | **Lafayette/E**	26
Chantilly | **Redwood City/S**	25
Kenwood | **Kenwood/N**	25
Bistro 29 | **Santa Rosa/N**	25
Grégoire | **multi.**	25
Fifth Floor | **SoMa**	25
Santé | **Sonoma/N**	25
Chez Maman | **Civic Ctr**	25
955 Rest. | **Mendocino/N**	25
Viognier | **San Mateo/S**	25
À Côté | **Oakland/E**	25
Angèle | **Napa/N**	24
Casanova | **Carmel/S**	24
NEW Bouche | **Nob Hill**	24
Bix | **Downtown**	24
Bistro Aix | **Marina**	24
Gitane | **Downtown**	24
Chez TJ | **Mtn View/S**	24
Bank Café | **Napa/N**	24
Pacific's Edge | **Carmel/S**	24
Isa | **Marina**	24
Chaya | **Embarcadero**	23
La Bicyclette | **Carmel/S**	23
La Rose Bistro | **Berkeley/E**	23
Brix | **Napa/N**	23
Manzanita | **Truckee/E**	23
Mistral | **Redwood Shores/S**	23
La Fondue | **Saratoga/S**	23
RN74 | **SoMa**	23
Vanessa's Bistro | **multi.**	23
Le Colonial | **Downtown**	23
Ma Maison | **Aptos/S**	23
Fresh/Lisa | **Santa Rosa/N**	22
Rest. LuLu | **SoMa**	22
Garçon | **Mission**	22
La Boulange | **multi.**	22
Basque Cultural | **S San Francisco/S**	21
Metro | **multi.**	21
Crepevine | **multi.**	21
Luna Park | **Mission**	20
Rigolo | **Presidio Hts**	18

FRENCH (BISTRO)

Bistro/Copains | **Occidental/N**	27
Bistro Jeanty | **Yountville/N**	27
Chapeau! | **Inner Rich**	27
Bouchon | **Yountville/N**	26

Artisan Bistro | **Lafayette/E**	25
Chez Spencer | **Mission**	25
Fringale | **SoMa**	25
Bistro Central | **W Addition**	25
K&L Bistro | **Sebastopol/N**	25
Chez Papa Bistrot | **Potrero Hill**	25
Gamine | **Cow Hollow**	25
Le P'tit Laurent | **Glen Pk**	24
Bodega Bistro | **Tenderloin**	24
Girl/Fig | **Sonoma/N**	24
Bistro Ralph | **Healdsburg/N**	24
Zazie | **Cole Valley**	24
Le Garage | **Sausalito/N**	24
L'Ardoise | **Castro**	24
La Note | **Berkeley/E**	23
Chez Papa Resto | **SoMa**	23
Water St. Bistro | **Petaluma/N**	23
Le Charm Bistro | **SoMa**	23
Alamo Sq. | **W Addition**	23
Bistro Liaison | **Berkeley/E**	23
Butler/Chef | **SoMa**	22
Andre's Bouchée | **Carmel/S**	22
South Park | **SoMa**	22
Plouf | **Downtown**	22
Hyde St. Bistro | **Russian Hill**	22
Baker St. Bistro | **Marina**	22
Café Claude | **Downtown**	22
Florio | **Pacific Hts**	22
French Gdn. | **Sebastopol/N**	22
Café Brioche | **Palo Alto/S**	22
Le Central | **Downtown**	21
Grand Cafe | **Downtown**	21
Charcuterie | **Healdsburg/N**	20
Cafe Bastille | **Downtown**	20
Le Zinc | **Noe Valley**	20
Café/Presse | **Downtown**	20
Chouchou | **Forest Hills**	19

FRENCH (BRASSERIE)

Absinthe | **Hayes Valley**	24
Left Bank | **multi.**	20
Luka's Taproom | **Oakland/E**	20
Café des Amis | **Cow Hollow**	19

GASTROPUB

Alembic | **Eclectic | Haight-Ashbury**	23
Bar Agricole | **Cal. | SoMa**	23
15 Romolo | **Amer. | N Beach**	22

Magnolia | Amer. | **Haight-Ashbury** 22

Salt Hse. | Amer. | **SoMa** 22

Sycamore | Amer. | **Mission** 22

Sidebar | Cal. | **Oakland/E** 22

Norman Rose | Amer. | **Napa/N** 20

Hopmonk Tav. | Eclectic | **multi.** 20

La Trappe | Belgian | **N Beach** 20

🆕 Two Sisters | Amer. | 19
Hayes Valley

🆕 Corners Tav. | Amer. | –
Walnut Creek/E

🆕 Goose/Gander | Amer. | –
St. Helena/N

GERMAN

Suppenküche | **Hayes Valley** 23

Schmidt's | **Mission** 23

Biergarten | **Hayes Valley** 23

Rosamunde | **multi.** 22

Speisekammer | **Alameda/E** 22

Guamenkitzel | **Berkeley/E** 22

Walzwerk | **Mission** 21

GREEK

Kokkari | **Downtown** 28

Evvia | **Palo Alto/S** 28

Dio Deka | **Los Gatos/S** 25

Ayola | **multi.** 22

Dipsea Cafe | **Mill Valley/N** 19

HAWAIIAN

Roy's | **Pebble Bch/S** 26

Roy's | **SoMa** 24

Ono Hawaiian | **Lakeshore** 19

HEALTH FOOD

(See also Vegetarian)

Mixt Greens | **Downtown** 23

Plant Cafe | **multi.** 22

HOT DOGS

4505 Meats | **Embarcadero** 26

Underdog | **Inner Sunset** 25

Top Dog | **multi.** 23

Caspers Hot Dogs | **multi.** 23

Showdogs | **Downtown** 21

Let's Be Frank | **multi.** 19

ICE CREAM PARLORS

Bi-Rite Creamery | **Mission** 28

Fentons | **Oakland/E** 22

INDIAN

Ajanta | **Berkeley/E** 27

Chutney | **Tenderloin** 26

Saravana Bhavan | **Sunnyvale/S** 26

All Spice | **San Mateo/S** 25

Vik's Chaat | **Berkeley/E** 25

Anokha/Lotus | **multi.** 25

Amber India | **multi.** 24

Avatar's | **multi.** 24

Shalimar | **multi.** 24

Curry Up Now | **multi.** 23

Dosa | **multi.** 23

Indian Oven | **Lower Haight** 23

Udupi Palace | **multi.** 23

Pakwan | **multi.** 23

Dasaprakash | **Santa Clara/S** 23

Roti Indian | **multi.** 23

Sakoon | **Mtn View/S** 23

Kasa Indian | **Castro** 22

Gaylord India | **Embarcadero** 22

Breads/India | **multi.** 21

Naan/Curry | **multi.** 18

INDONESIAN

Borobudur | **Nob Hill** 23

ITALIAN

(N=Northern; S=Southern)

Seven Hills | **Nob Hill** 28

Acquerello | **Polk Gulch** 28

Cucina Paradiso | S | **Petaluma/N** 27

La Ciccia | **Noe Valley** 27

Café Fiore | N | **S Lake Tahoe/E** 27

Delfina | N | **Mission** 27

Picco | **Larkspur/N** 26

La Posta | **Santa Cruz/S** 26

Diavola | **Geyserville/N** 26

Stella Alpina Osteria | 26
Burlingame/S

Quince | **Downtown** 26

Tony's Pizza | S | **N Beach** 26

Prima | N | **Walnut Creek/E** 26

Pizzaiolo | S | **Oakland/E** 26

Cook St. Helena | N | 26
St. Helena/N

Rocco's Cafe | **China Basin** 26

Sotto Mare | **N Beach** 26

Chiaroscuro | S | **Downtown** 26

Cotogna | **Downtown** 26

Dopo | **Oakland/E** 26

Riva Cucina | N | **Berkeley/E** 26

Lococo's Cucina | **Santa Rosa/N** 26

Oliveto Rest. | **Oakland/E** 26

Flour + Water | **Mission**	26	Venticello | N | **Nob Hill**	24
Rosso Pizzeria | **multi.**	26	Bacco | **Noe Valley**	24
Scopa | **Healdsburg/N**	26	Della Santina | N | **Sonoma/N**	24
Pizzeria Picco | S | **Larkspur/N**	26	Lo Coco's | S | **multi.**	24
Perbacco | **Downtown**	26	Piccino | **Dogpatch**	24
Capannina | **Cow Hollow**	26	Cafe Citti | N | **Kenwood/N**	24
Zazu | N | **Santa Rosa/N**	25	Bellanico | **Oakland/E**	24
Chantilly | N | **Redwood City/S**	25	Tony's Coal-Fired | **N Beach**	24
Gialina | **Glen Pk**	25	Poesia | S | **Castro**	24
Pasta Moon | **Half Moon Bay/S**	25	Bar Bambino | **Mission**	24
Ideale Rest. | S | **N Beach**	25	Osteria | **Palo Alto/S**	24
Bottega | **Yountville/N**	25	Bella Trattoria | S | **Inner Rich**	24
NEW Alex Rest. | **Rutherford/N**	25	Mezza Luna | S | **multi.**	24
Trattoria Corso | N | **Berkeley/E**	25	Scala's Bistro | **Downtown**	23
Pesce | N | **Russian Hill**	25	Mozzarella/Bufala | **W Portal**	23
Marcello's Pizza | **Castro**	25	Il Postale | **Sunnyvale/S**	23
Sugo | **Petaluma/N**	25	Allegro Romano | S | **Russian Hill**	23
L'Osteria | N | **N Beach**	25	Original Joe's | **San Jose/S**	23
Albona Rist. | N | **N Beach**	25	Kuleto's | N | **Downtown**	23
Incanto | N | **Noe Valley**	25	Leopold's | **Russian Hill**	23
Risibisi | N | **Petaluma/N**	25	Oliveto Cafe | **Oakland/E**	23
Bistro Don Giovanni | **Napa/N**	25	Azzurro | **Napa/N**	23
A16 | S | **Marina**	25	La Bicyclette | **Carmel/S**	23
SPQR | **Pacific Hts**	25	Osteria Coppa | N | **San Mateo/S**	23
A Bellagio | **Campbell/S**	25	Il Cane Rosso | **Embarcadero**	23
Locanda | **Mission**	25	Pane e Vino | N | **Cow Hollow**	23
Mescolanza | N | **Outer Rich**	25	Donato | N | **Redwood City/S**	23
North Bch. Rest. | N | **N Beach**	25	Mistral | **Redwood Shores/S**	23
Poggio | N | **Sausalito/N**	25	Pizzeria Tra Vigne | **St. Helena/N**	23
Tra Vigne | N | **St. Helena/N**	24	Farina | **Mission**	23
Beretta | **Mission**	24	Gabriella Café | **Santa Cruz/S**	23
Enoteca Molinari | **Oakland/E**	24	Adesso | **Oakland/E**	23
Oenotri | S | **Napa/N**	24	Uva Enoteca | **Lower Haight**	23
Barbacco | **Downtown**	24	**NEW** Forchetta/Bastoni |	23
Casanova | N | **Carmel/S**	24	**Sebastopol/N**	
Tratt. Contadina | **N Beach**	24	Emporio Rulli | **multi.**	22
Boot/Shoe | **Oakland/E**	24	Quattro | **E Palo Alto/S**	22
Rist. Milano | N | **Russian Hill**	24	La Ginestra | S | **Mill Valley/N**	22
Tratt. La Sicil. | S | **Berkeley/E**	24	Rose's Cafe | N | **Cow Hollow**	22
Zero Zero | **SoMa**	24	Cantinetta Luca | **Carmel/S**	22
Volpi's Rist. | **Petaluma/N**	24	54 Mint | S | **SoMa**	22
Lupa Trattoria | S | **Noe Valley**	24	Nob Hill Café | N | **Nob Hill**	22
Barolo | **Calistoga/N**	24	Rist. Capellini | N | **San Mateo/S**	22
Osteria Stellina | **Pt Reyes/N**	24	Pizza Antica | **multi.**	22
Postino | **Lafayette/E**	24	Aperto | **Potrero Hill**	22
Sociale | N | **Presidio Hts**	24	Acqua Pazza | S | **San Mateo/S**	22
Tommaso's | S | **N Beach**	24	Café Tiramisu | N | **Downtown**	22
Marzano | S | **Oakland/E**	24	Original Joe's (SF) | **N Beach**	22
Il Davide | N | **San Rafael/N**	24	Palio d'Asti | **Downtown**	22

CUISINES

Florio | **Pacific Hts**	22
Il Fornaio | **multi.**	22
Jackson Fillmore/Cucina | **San Anselmo/N**	22
Frantoio | N | **Mill Valley/N**	22
Bucci's | **Emeryville/E**	22
Jackson Fillmore/Cucina | **Upper Fillmore**	22
Vin Antico | **San Rafael/N**	22
Delarosa | **Marina**	22
Alioto's | S | **Fish. Wharf**	21
Firewood Cafe | **Castro**	21
Swiss Hotel | **Sonoma/N**	21
Credo | **Downtown**	21
Venezia | **Berkeley/E**	21
Luce | **SoMa**	21
Cupola Pizzeria | S | **Downtown**	21
Rustic | **Geyserville/N**	21
Americano | **Embarcadero**	21
Caffè Macaroni | S | **N Beach**	21
Stinking Rose | N | **N Beach**	21
Casa Orinda | **Orinda/E**	21
Italian Colors | **Oakland/E**	21
Peter Lowell | **Sebastopol/N**	21
Piatti | **multi.**	21
Rose Pistola | N | **N Beach**	21
Pianeta | N | **Truckee/E**	21
Ristobar | **Marina**	21
Mario's Bohemian | N | **N Beach**	21
E'Angelo | **Marina**	20
Cafe Zoetrope | S | **N Beach**	20
Emmy's Spaghetti | **Bernal Hts**	20
Ottimista | **Cow Hollow**	20
Piazza D'Angelo | **Mill Valley/N**	20
Rist. Umbria | N | **SoMa**	20
Meritage Martini | N | **Sonoma/N**	20
Uva Trattoria | **Napa/N**	19
Zuppa | S | **SoMa**	19
Pasta Pomodoro | **multi.**	19
Globe | **Downtown**	18
Buca di Beppo | **multi.**	18
NEW Campo Fina | **Healdsburg/N**	–
NEW Farina Pizza | S | **Mission**	–
NEW Mozzeria | **Mission**	–

JAPANESE
(* sushi specialist)

NEW Keiko | **Nob Hill**	29
Kiss Seafood* | **Japantown**	28
Kappou Gomi | **Outer Rich**	28
Wakuriya | **San Mateo/S**	28
Sushi Zone* | **Castro**	27
Ichi Sushi | **Bernal Hts**	27
Zushi Puzzle* | **Marina**	27
Hachi Ju Hachi* | **Saratoga/S**	27
Sushi Ran* | **Sausalito/N**	27
Nama Sushi | **Walnut Creek/E**	27
Osake* | **Santa Rosa/N**	27
Hana* | **Rohnert Pk/N**	26
Alexander's Steak | **multi.**	26
Kabuto* | **Outer Rich**	26
Sebo* | **Hayes Valley**	26
Umami* | **Cow Hollow**	26
Sakae Sushi* | **Burlingame/S**	26
Koo* | **Inner Sunset**	26
Ariake* | **Outer Rich**	26
Eiji* | **Castro**	26
Sasa | **Walnut Creek/E**	26
Jin Sho* | **Palo Alto/S**	26
Domo Sushi* | **Hayes Valley**	25
Morimoto* | **Napa/N**	25
Amasia Hide's | **Castro**	25
Chotto | **Marina**	25
Kiji Sushi Bar* | **Mission**	25
Nojo | **Hayes Valley**	25
Kirala* | **Berkeley/E**	25
Gochi | **Cupertino/S**	25
Moki's Sushi* | **Bernal Hts**	25
Sumika | **Los Altos/S**	25
Ramen Dojo | **San Mateo/S**	25
Sushi Bistro | **multi.**	25
Ryoko's* | **Downtown**	25
Ozumo* | **multi.**	25
Naomi Sushi* | **Menlo Pk/S**	25
O Chamé | **Berkeley/E**	25
Tataki* | **multi.**	25
Amakara Japanese | **Dublin/E**	24
Delica* | **Embarcadero**	24
Moshi Moshi | **Dogpatch**	24
Ebisu* | **multi.**	24
Kanpai* | **Palo Alto/S**	24
Orenchi Ramen | **Santa Clara/S**	24
Zabu Zabu | **Berkeley/E**	24
Uzen* | **Oakland/E**	24
Ippuku | **Berkeley/E**	24
Oyaji* | **Outer Rich**	24
Sushi Sam's | **San Mateo/S**	24
Tsunami Sush/Sake* | **multi.**	24
Izakaya Sozai | **Inner Sunset**	23

Sanraku* | **multi.** 23
Chaya | **Embarcadero** 23
Anzu* | **Downtown** 23
Fuki Sushi* | **Palo Alto/S** 23
NEW 903 | **Bernal Hts** 23
Yoshi's* | **Oakland/E** 23
Blowfish Sushi* | **multi.** 23
Yoshi's | **W Addition** 23
NEW Izakaya Yuzuki | 23
  Mission
Cha-Ya Veg.* | **multi.** 23
Sawa Sushi | **Sunnyvale/S** 23
Yum Yum Fish | **Outer Sunset** 23
Katana-Ya | **Downtown** 22
Hamano Sushi* | **Noe Valley** 22
2G Japanese | **Civic Ctr** 22
Godzila Sushi* | **Pacific Hts** 22
Nombe | **Mission** 22
Takara* | **Japantown** 21
NEW Ken Ken | **Mission** 21
Sushirrito* | **SoMa** 21
Benihana | **multi.** 21
Hotaru* | **San Mateo/S** 21
Nihon | **Mission** 21
Hapa Ramen | **Loc varies** 21
NEW Joshu-ya Brass.* | 21
  Berkeley/E
Ace Wasabi's* | **Marina** 20
Naked Fish* | **S Lake Tahoe/E** 20
Tex Wasabi's | **Santa Rosa/N** 20
Muracci's | **multi.** 20
Juban | **multi.** 20
Hotei* | **Inner Sunset** 20
Tokyo Go Go* | **Mission** 19
Ajisen Ramen | **Downtown** 19
Ramen Underground | 19
  Downtown
Mifune | **Japantown** 19
Hecho* | **Downtown** 18
NEW Hopscotch | **Oakland/E** -
NEW Rest. Mitsunobu | -
  Menlo Pk/S
NEW Saru Sushi | **Noe Valley** -
NEW U-Sushi* | **Downtown** -

JEWISH

Wise Sons | **multi.** 23
Miller's East | **multi.** 21
Saul's Rest./Deli | **Berkeley/E** 20
Moishe's Pippic | **Hayes Valley** 18

KOREAN

(* barbecue specialist)
To Hyang | **Inner Rich** 27
Korean Vill. BBQ | **Inner Rich** 26
Han IL Kwan | **Outer Rich** 25
HRD Coffee | **SoMa** 25
San Tung | **Inner Sunset** 24
Brother's Korean* | **Inner Rich** 24
SJ Omogari | **San Jose/S** 24
My Tofu* | **Inner Rich** 23
Ohgane Korean | **multi.** 23
Jang Su Jang* | **Santa Clara/S** 23
Sahn Maru* | **Oakland/E** 23
NEW FuseBox | **Oakland/E** -
Namu | **multi.** -

MEDITERRANEAN

Chez Panisse Café | **Berkeley/E** 28
Rivoli | **Berkeley/E** 28
Chez Panisse | **Berkeley/E** 28
Cafe Gibralter | **El Granada/S** 28
Ledford Hse. | **Albion/N** 27
Wente Vineyards | **Livermore/E** 26
Asena | **Alameda/E** 26
Esin | **Danville/E** 26
Lalime's | **Berkeley/E** 26
Frascati | **Russian Hill** 26
Campton Pl. | **Downtown** 26
Zuni Café | **Hayes Valley** 26
Central Mkt. | **Petaluma/N** 26
BayWolf | **Oakland/E** 26
Harvest Moon | **Sonoma/N** 25
Terzo | **Cow Hollow** 25
Heirloom | **Mission** 25
Insalata's | **San Anselmo/N** 25
Truly Med. | **Mission** 25
À Côté | **Oakland/E** 25
Pappo | **Alameda/E** 25
Camino | **Oakland/E** 25
Foreign Cinema | **Mission** 25
Zatar | **Berkeley/E** 25
Garibaldis | **Presidio Hts** 24
Luella | **Russian Hill** 24
Willow Wood | **Graton/N** 24
Cetrella | **Half Moon Bay/S** 24
Absinthe | **Hayes Valley** 24
Peasant/Pear | **Danville/E** 24
Mezze | **Oakland/E** 23
Hurley's | **Yountville/N** 23
Coco500 | **SoMa** 23

CUISINES

La Méditerranée	**multi.**	23
PlumpJack	**Olympic Valley/E**	23
El Dorado	**Sonoma/N**	23
71 St. Peter	**San Jose/S**	22
Monti's	**Santa Rosa/N**	22
Café Rouge	**Berkeley/E**	22
NEW Brassica	**St. Helena/N**	22
Zaré/Fly Trap	**SoMa**	22
Sidebar	**Oakland/E**	22
Rest. LuLu	**SoMa**	22
Underwood Bar	**Graton/N**	22
Ayola	**multi.**	22
Sens	**Embarcadero**	22
Arlequin Cafe	**Hayes Valley**	21
Fandango	**Pacific Grove/S**	21
Christy Hill	**Tahoe City/E**	21
Oxbow Wine	**Napa/N**	21
Pacific Crest	**Truckee/E**	21
Lavanda	**Palo Alto/S**	21
Pianeta	**Truckee/E**	21
Zibibbo	**Palo Alto/S**	20
Ottimista	**Cow Hollow**	20
MarketBar	**Embarcadero**	18

MEXICAN

La Taquiza	**Napa/N**	27
Papito	**Potrero Hill**	26
La Victoria	**San Jose/S**	25
El Castillito	**multi.**	25
La Taqueria	**Mission**	25
Loló	**Mission**	25
C Casa	**Napa/N**	25
Tamarindo	**Oakland/E**	25
Don Pisto's	**N Beach**	25
Taco Shop	**Outer Sunset**	25
Taqueria San Jose	**multi.**	24
Tacolicious	**multi.**	24
Taqueria La Bamba	**multi.**	24
Mamacita	**Marina**	24
Gracias	**Mission**	24
Nopalito	**multi.**	24
NEW La Condesa	**St. Helena/N**	24
El Huarache Loco	**multi.**	23
Taqueria Can Cun	**multi.**	23
Regalito Rosticeria	**Mission**	23
Taqueria Tlaquepaque	**San Jose/S**	23
Pancho Villa	**multi.**	23
El Farolito	**multi.**	23

3rd St. Grill	**SoMa**	23
Colibrí	**Downtown**	23
El Tonayense	**Loc varies**	23
Chilango	**Castro**	23
Xolo Taqueria	**Oakland/E**	23
Tacubaya	**Berkeley/E**	23
Aqui Cal-Mex	**multi.**	23
Picante Cocina	**Berkeley/E**	22
Doña Tomás	**Oakland/E**	22
Papalote Mex.	**multi.**	22
Tacko	**Cow Hollow**	22
El Metate	**Mission**	22
La Cumbre	**multi.**	22
La Corneta	**multi.**	22
Cactus Taqueria	**multi.**	22
Cancun	**Berkeley/E**	22
Marinitas	**San Anselmo/N**	22
Nick's Crispy	**Russian Hill**	22
NEW Mateo's Cocina	**Healdsburg/N**	21
Little Chihuahua	**multi.**	21
Juan's	**Berkeley/E**	21
Joe's Taco	**Mill Valley/N**	21
Tropisueño	**SoMa**	20
Mijita	**multi.**	20
Taqueria 3 Amigos	**multi.**	20
Tommy's Mex.	**Outer Rich**	20
Prickly Pear	**Danville/E**	19
Tres	**S Beach**	18
Guaymas	**Tiburon/N**	17
NEW Comal	**Berkeley/E**	-
NEW Copita	**Sausalito/N**	-

MIDDLE EASTERN

Saha	**Nob Hill**	26
Truly Med.	**Mission**	25
Dishdash	**Sunnyvale/S**	25
Sunrise Deli	**multi.**	24
La Méditerranée	**multi.**	23
Goood Frikin'	**Mission**	20

MONGOLIAN

Little Sheep	**multi.**	22

MOROCCAN

Aziza	**Outer Rich**	26

NEPALESE

Little Nepal	**Bernal Hts**	23

NEW ENGLAND

Old Port Lobster | **Redwood City/S** — 23

Yankee Pier | **multi.** — 19

NOODLE SHOPS

Ramen Dojo | **San Mateo/S** — 25

O Chamé | **Berkeley/E** — 25

San Tung | **Inner Sunset** — 24

Katana-Ya | **Downtown** — 22

King of Thai | **multi.** — 22

Osha Thai | **multi.** — 22

NEW Ken Ken | **Mission** — 21

Hotaru | **San Mateo/S** — 21

Hapa Ramen | **Loc varies** — 21

Citrus Club | **Haight-Ashbury** — 20

Hotei | **Inner Sunset** — 20

Ramen Underground | **Downtown** — 19

Mifune | **Japantown** — 19

NUEVO LATINO

Pasión | **Inner Sunset** — 25

Limón | **multi.** — 24

Joya | **Palo Alto/S** — 23

Destino | **Castro** — 22

PACIFIC RIM

Pacific Catch | **multi.** — 22

PAKISTANI

Chutney | **Tenderloin** — 26

Shalimar | **multi.** — 24

Pakwan | **multi.** — 23

Naan/Curry | **multi.** — 18

PAN-LATIN

Cascal | **Mtn View/S** — 23

Bocanova | **Oakland/E** — 23

Marinitas | **San Anselmo/N** — 22

Fonda Solana | **Albany/E** — 21

NEW Rumbo | **Oakland/E** — 21

César | **Oakland/E** — 20

PERSIAN

Maykadeh | **N Beach** — 23

PERUVIAN

Sazon Peruvian | **Santa Rosa/N** — 27

Pasión | **Inner Sunset** — 25

La Costanera | **Montara/S** — 25

Piqueo's | **Bernal Hts** — 24

La Mar | **Embarcadero** — 24

Mochica | **SoMa** — 24

Limón | **multi.** — 24

Fresca | **multi.** — 22

PIZZA

Cheese Board | **Berkeley/E** — 27

Diavola | **Geyserville/N** — 26

Tony's Pizza | **N Beach** — 26

Pizzaiolo | **Oakland/E** — 26

Gioia Pizzeria | **Berkeley/E** — 26

Locanda Positano | **San Carlos/S** — 26

Pizzetta 211 | **Outer Rich** — 26

Una Pizza | **SoMa** — 26

Flour + Water | **Mission** — 26

Rosso Pizzeria | **multi.** — 26

Emilia's | **Berkeley/E** — 26

Pizzeria Picco | **Larkspur/N** — 26

Pizzeria Delfina | **multi.** — 26

Zachary's Pizza | **multi.** — 26

Ragazza | **W Addition** — 25

Gialina | **Glen Pk** — 25

Arizmendi | **multi.** — 25

Marcello's Pizza | **Castro** — 25

Little Star | **multi.** — 25

NEW Redd Wood | **Yountville/N** — 25

Golden Boy | **multi.** — 25

Beretta | **Mission** — 24

Boot/Shoe | **Oakland/E** — 24

Zero Zero | **SoMa** — 24

Applewood Pizza | **Menlo Pk/S** — 24

Pazzia | **SoMa** — 24

Tommaso's | **N Beach** — 24

Marzano | **Oakland/E** — 24

Lo Coco's | **multi.** — 24

Tony's Coal-Fired | **N Beach** — 24

Red Grape | **Sonoma/N** — 24

Postrio | **Downtown** — 23

Azzurro | **Napa/N** — 23

Arinell Pizza | **multi.** — 23

Pauline's | **Mission** — 23

Pizzeria Tra Vigne | **St. Helena/N** — 23

Mombo's Pizza | **multi.** — 23

La Ginestra | **Mill Valley/N** — 22

Patxi's Pizza | **multi.** — 22

Pizza Antica | **multi.** — 22

Source | **Potrero Hill** — 22

Giorgio's | **Inner Rich** — 22

Starbelly | **Castro** — 22

Palio d'Asti	**Downtown**	22	Downtown Bakery	**Healdsburg/N**	26
Goat Hill	**multi.**	22	Saigon Sandwich	**Tenderloin**	26
Bar Bocce	**Sausalito/N**	22	4505 Meats	**Embarcadero**	26
Delarosa	**Marina**	22	Bakesale Betty	**Oakland/E**	26
Cupola Pizzeria	**Downtown**	21	Ike's Pl./Lair	**multi.**	25
Rustic	**Geyserville/N**	21	Refuge	**San Carlos/S**	25
North Bch. Pizza	**multi.**	21	Boccalone	**Embarcadero**	25
Amici's	**multi.**	21	Café Bunn	**Inner Rich**	24
Pi Bar	**Mission**	21	Gayle's Bakery	**Capitola/S**	24
Cafe Zoetrope	**N Beach**	20	Kitchenette SF	**Dogpatch**	24
Rigolo	**Presidio Hts**	18	Sentinel	**SoMa**	24
NEW Campo Fina	**Healdsburg/N**	-	Yellow Sub	**Inner Sunset**	24
NEW Del Popolo	**Downtown**	-	Southie	**Oakland/E**	24
NEW Farina Pizza	**Mission**	-	Bocadillos	**N Beach**	23
NEW Gioia Pizzeria	**Russian Hill**	-	NEW 903	**Bernal Hts**	23
NEW Mozzeria	**Mission**	-	Fort Bragg	**Ft Bragg/N**	23

POLYNESIAN

Trader Vic's	**Emeryville/E**	19

PORTUGUESE

LaSalette	**Sonoma/N**	24

PUB FOOD

Biergarten	**Hayes Valley**	23
4th St. B&G	**Downtown**	22
Wurst Rest.	**Healdsburg/N**	20
NEW Dear Mom	**Mission**	19
Gordon Biersch	**multi.**	18
Bridgetender	**Tahoe City/E**	18
NEW Southern Pacific	**Mission**	18
Half Moon Brew	**Half Moon Bay/S**	18
Public Hse.	**S Beach**	17

PUERTO RICAN

Sol Food	**San Rafael/N**	25
Parada 22	**Haight-Ashbury**	23

RUSSIAN

Katia's Tea	**Inner Rich**	20

SALVADORAN

El Zocalo	**Bernal Hts**	23
Balompie Café	**Mission**	23

SANDWICHES

(See also Delis)

Fatted Calf	**multi.**	27
Lucca Deli	**Marina**	27
Naked Lunch	**N Beach**	26

Il Cane Rosso	**Embarcadero**	23
Cheese Steak	**multi.**	23
Mixt Greens	**Downtown**	23
Amer. Grilled	**SoMa**	23
AK Subs	**SoMa**	22
Model Bakery	**multi.**	22
Boudin	**multi.**	22
4th St. B&G	**Downtown**	22
Nordstrom Cafe	**Downtown**	22
Giordano	**multi.**	22
901 Columbus	**Telegraph Hill**	22
Dinosaurs	**Castro**	21
Golden West	**Downtown**	21
Cafe Divine	**N Beach**	21
Mario's Bohemian	**N Beach**	21
Jimtown Store	**Healdsburg/N**	20
Straw	**Hayes Valley**	20
Max's	**multi.**	20
Java Beach	**Outer Sunset**	20
Spice Kit	**SoMa**	18
'Wichcraft	**Downtown**	18
NEW Melt	**multi.**	17
NEW Craftsman/Wolves	**Mission**	-
NEW Machine Coffee	**Downtown**	-
NEW Market & Rye	**multi.**	-
NEW Salumeria	**Mission**	-
NEW Split Bread	**SoMa**	-
NEW Sweet Woodruff	**Nob Hill**	-

SCANDINAVIAN

NEW Pläj	**Hayes Valley**	-

SEAFOOD

Passionfish | **Pacific Grove/S**	27
Seasons | **Downtown**	27
Swan Oyster | **Polk Gulch**	26
Marica | **Oakland/E**	26
NEW Moonraker | **Pacifica/S**	26
Sotto Mare | **N Beach**	26
Hog Island Oyster | **multi.**	26
Mendo Bistro | **Ft Bragg/N**	26
Bobo's | **Fish. Wharf**	25
Bar Crudo | **W Addition**	25
Anchor Oyster | **Castro**	25
Pesce | **Russian Hill**	25
Crab Hse. | **Fish. Wharf**	25
Willi's Seafood | **Healdsburg/N**	25
Farallon | **Downtown**	25
Cajun Pacific | **Outer Sunset**	25
Fish | **Sausalito/N**	25
Scoma's | **multi.**	25
PPQ Dungeness | **Outer Rich**	24
La Mar | **Embarcadero**	24
Sardine Factory | **Monterey/S**	24
Tadich Grill | **Downtown**	24
Walnut Creek Yacht | **Walnut Creek/E**	24
Pacific Café | **Outer Rich**	24
Flying Fish (Carmel) | **Carmel/S**	24
Hayes St. Grill | **Hayes Valley**	24
Chapter & Moon | **Ft Bragg/N**	24
Aquarius | **Santa Cruz/S**	24
Koi | **multi.**	24
Betty's Fish | **Santa Rosa/N**	24
Old Port Lobster | **Redwood City/S**	23
Waterbar | **Embarcadero**	23
Scott's Seafood | **multi.**	23
Great Eastern | **Chinatown**	23
Skool | **Potrero Hill**	23
Ferry Plaza Seafoods | **Embarcadero**	23
Alamo Sq. | **W Addition**	23
McCormick/Schmick | **San Jose/S**	23
Woodhouse Fish | **multi.**	22
Sam's Chowder | **multi.**	22
Little River Inn | **Little River/N**	22
Fish Market | **multi.**	22
Plouf | **Downtown**	22
Dante's Weird Fish | **Mission**	22
Pacific Catch | **multi.**	22
Sam's Grill | **Downtown**	22
Hog & Rocks | **Mission**	22
Catch | **Castro**	22
Dead Fish | **Crockett/E**	22
McCormick/Kuleto | **Fish. Wharf**	22
John's Grill | **Downtown**	22
Fishwife | **Pacific Grove/S**	22
Anchor & Hope | **SoMa**	22
Mayflower | **multi.**	22
C Rest. | **Monterey/S**	22
Barbara's | **Princeton Sea/S**	22
Alioto's | **Fish. Wharf**	21
Flying Fish (HMB) | **Half Moon Bay/S**	21
Waterfront | **Embarcadero**	21
Sea Salt | **Berkeley/E**	21
Nettie's Crab | **Cow Hollow**	21
Fish & Farm | **Downtown**	20
Spinnaker | **Sausalito/N**	20
Fish Story | **Napa/N**	20
Sunnyside Lodge | **Tahoe City/E**	20
Meritage Martini | **Sonoma/N**	20
Yankee Pier | **multi.**	19
Half Moon Brew | **Half Moon Bay/S**	18
Guaymas | **Tiburon/N**	17
Lake Chalet | **Oakland/E**	17
NEW Local's Corner | **Mission**	–
NEW Mission Rock | **Dogpatch**	–

SINGAPOREAN

Straits | **multi.**	21

SMALL PLATES

(See also Spanish tapas specialist)

Jole | Amer. | **Calistoga/N**	27
Picco | Italian | **Larkspur/N**	26
Tamarine | Viet. | **Palo Alto/S**	26
Willi's Wine | Eclectic | **Santa Rosa/N**	25
Va de Vi | Eclectic | **Walnut Creek/E**	25
Terzo | Med. | **Cow Hollow**	25
Willi's Seafood | Seafood | **Healdsburg/N**	25
À Côté | French/Med. | **Oakland/E**	25
Piqueo's | Peruvian | **Bernal Hts**	24
Barbacco | Italian | **Downtown**	24
Isa | French | **Marina**	24
Absinthe | French/Med. | **Hayes Valley**	24

Izakaya Sozai | Japanese | **Inner Sunset** — 23

Cascal | Pan-Latin | **Mtn View/S** — 23

Adesso | Italian | **Oakland/E** — 23

Joya | Nuevo Latino | **Palo Alto/S** — 23

Monti's | Med. | **Santa Rosa/N** — 22

Barlata | Spanish | **Oakland/E** — 22

Sycamore | Amer. | **Mission** — 22

Andalu | Eclectic | **Mission** — 22

Starbelly | Cal. | **Castro** — 22

Underwood Bar | Med. | **Graton/N** — 22

Cha Cha Cha | Carib. | **multi.** — 22

E&O Asian Kit. | Asian | **Downtown** — 21

Oxbow Wine | Cal. | **Napa/N** — 21

Straits | Singapor. | **multi.** — 21

Lavanda | Med. | **Palo Alto/S** — 21

Ristobar | Italian | **Marina** — 21

Nihon | Japanese | **Mission** — 21

Zibibbo | Med. | **Palo Alto/S** — 20

NEW Maven | Amer. | **Lower Haight** — 20

Chez Shea | Eclectic | **Half Moon Bay/S** — 19

Campanula | Amer. | **N Beach** — 19

Park Chalet | Amer. | **Outer Sunset** — 17

SOUL FOOD

Brown Sugar | **Oakland/E** — 26

Auntie April's | **Bayview** — 25

Broken Record | **Excelsior** — 24

Picán | **Oakland/E** — 24

1300/Fillmore | **W Addition** — 23

Hard Knox | **multi.** — 22

Farmerbrown | **multi.** — 22

Elite Cafe | **Pacific Hts** — 21

Home of Chicken | **multi.** — 20

SOUTH AMERICAN

Balompie Café | **Mission** — 23

SOUTHERN

Jim's Country | **Pleasanton/E** — 27

Brenda's | **Civic Ctr** — 25

Picán | **Oakland/E** — 24

Rocker Oysterfellers | **Valley Ford/N** — 24

1300/Fillmore | **W Addition** — 23

Magnolia | **Haight-Ashbury** — 22

Kate's Kit. | **Lower Haight** — 22

Front Porch | **Bernal Hts** — 22

Hard Knox | **multi.** — 22

Miss Pearl's | **Oakland/E** — 22

Blackberry Bistro | **Oakland/E** — 21

Everett/Jones BBQ | **multi.** — 21

Home of Chicken | **multi.** — 20

NEW Cedar Hill | **Marina** — 17

NEW Dixie | **Presidio** — -

SOUTHWESTERN

Rio Grill | **Carmel/S** — 23

Green Chile | **W Addition** — 23

Boogaloos | **Mission** — 20

NEW West of Pecos | **Mission** — -

SPANISH

(* tapas specialist)

Piperade | **Downtown** — 27

Contigo* | **Noe Valley** — 25

Zarzuela* | **Russian Hill** — 24

Gitane | **Downtown** — 24

Txoko | **N Beach** — 24

ZuZu* | **Napa/N** — 24

NEW Canela* | **Castro** — 24

Bocadillos* | **N Beach** — 23

Alegrias* | **Marina** — 23

Mundaka* | **Carmel/S** — 23

Esperpento* | **Mission** — 22

Barlata* | **Oakland/E** — 22

Iberia* | **Menlo Pk/S** — 22

B44* | **Downtown** — 22

César* | **Berkeley/E** — 20

STEAKHOUSES

Cole's Chop | **Napa/N** — 27

Seasons | **Downtown** — 27

Ruth's Chris | **multi.** — 27

Harris' | **Polk Gulch** — 27

Press | **St. Helena/N** — 26

House/Prime | **Polk Gulch** — 26

Alexander's Steak | **multi.** — 26

Stark's | **Santa Rosa/N** — 26

Bobo's | **Fish. Wharf** — 25

Morton's | **multi.** — 25

Sundance Steak | **Palo Alto/S** — 25

Haps Original | **Pleasanton/E** — 25

Boca | **Novato/N** — 25

Lark Creek Steak | **Downtown** — 25

Vic Stewart | **Walnut Creek/E** — 24

Arcadia | **San Jose/S** — 24

Grill/Alley | **San Jose/S** — 24

Bourbon	**Downtown**	24
Alfred's Steak	**Downtown**	23
Espetus	**multi.**	23
5A5 Steak	**Downtown**	23
El Paseo	**Mill Valley/N**	23
Forbes Mill	**multi.**	23
Izzy's Steak	**multi.**	23
Epic Roasthse.	**Embarcadero**	23
LB Steak	**multi.**	22
Cattlemens	**Petaluma/N**	22
Bob's Steak	**Downtown**	22
John's Grill	**Downtown**	22
Casa Orinda	**Orinda/E**	21
Sunnyside Lodge	**Tahoe City/E**	20
Bluestem Brass.	**SoMa**	19
NEW Lolinda	**Mission**	-

SWISS

La Fondue	**Saratoga/S**	23
Matterhorn Swiss	**Russian Hill**	21

TEAHOUSE

Lovejoy's Tea	**Noe Valley**	21
Samovar Tea	**multi.**	21
Imperial Tea	**multi.**	19

THAI

Sea Thai/Modern	**multi.**	27
Royal Thai	**San Rafael/N**	27
Thai Buddhist	**Berkeley/E**	26
Sai Jai Thai	**Tenderloin**	25
Marnee Thai	**multi.**	25
Arun	**Novato/N**	25
Basil	**SoMa**	25
Lers Ros Thai	**multi.**	25
Bangkok Thai	**multi.**	25
Thep Phanom	**Lower Haight**	24
New Krung Thai	**San Jose/S**	24
Soi4	**Oakland/E**	23
Anchalee Thai	**Berkeley/E**	23
Manora's Thai	**SoMa**	23
Pagan	**Outer Rich**	22
Khan Toke	**Outer Rich**	22
Krung Thai	**multi.**	22
King of Thai	**multi.**	22
Amarin Thai	**Mtn View/S**	22
Osha Thai	**multi.**	22
Thai Hse.	**multi.**	22
Another Monkey/Koh	**multi.**	21
Cha Am Thai	**multi.**	21

TURKISH

A La Turca	**Tenderloin**	23
Sens	**Embarcadero**	22
Troya	**Inner Rich**	22
New Kapadokia	**Redwood City/S**	21

VEGETARIAN

(* vegan)

Millennium*	**Downtown**	27
Encuentro	**Oakland/E**	26
Greens	**Marina**	25
Ravens'*	**Mendocino/N**	25
Gracias*	**Mission**	24
Udupi Palace	**multi.**	23
Dasaprakash	**Santa Clara/S**	23
Cha-Ya Veg.*	**multi.**	23
Source	**Potrero Hill**	22
Café Gratitude*	**multi.**	19

VENEZUELAN

Pica Pica	**multi.**	20

VIETNAMESE

Slanted Door	**Embarcadero**	26
Thanh Long	**Outer Sunset**	26
Saigon Sandwich	**Tenderloin**	26
Tamarine	**Palo Alto/S**	26
Vung Tau	**San Jose/S**	25
Crustacean	**Polk Gulch**	25
Café Bunn	**Inner Rich**	24
Bodega Bistro	**Tenderloin**	24
PPQ Dungeness	**Outer Rich**	24
Pho 84	**Oakland/E**	24
NEW Dragon Rouge	**Alameda/E**	24
Ana Mandara	**Fish. Wharf**	23
Out the Door	**multi.**	23
Vanessa's Bistro	**multi.**	23
Sunflower	**multi.**	23
Le Colonial	**Downtown**	23
Xanh	**Mtn View/S**	22
Zadin	**Castro**	22
Le Cheval	**multi.**	22
Pagolac	**Tenderloin**	22
Dinosaurs	**Castro**	21
Xyclo	**Oakland/E**	21
Turtle Tower	**multi.**	21
Bun Mee	**Upper Fillmore**	19
Le Soleil	**Inner Rich**	19
NEW Moss Room	**Outer Rich**	-

CUISINES

Locations

Includes names, cuisines and Food ratings.

City of San Francisco

AT&T PARK/ SOUTH BEACH

(See map on page 102)

Tsunami Sush/Sake | *Japanese*	24
Amici's | *Pizza*	21
Mijita | *Mex.*	20
MoMo's | *Amer.*	20
Burger Joint | *Burgers*	19
Tres | *Mex.*	18
Public Hse. | *Pub*	17

BAYVIEW/ HUNTER'S POINT

Auntie April's | *Soul*	25
Limón | *Peruvian*	24

BERNAL HEIGHTS

Ichi Sushi | *Japanese*	27
Moki's Sushi | *Japanese*	25
Sandbox | *Bakery*	25
Piqueo's | *Peruvian*	24
El Huarache Loco | *Mex.*	23
El Zocalo | *Salvadoran*	23
Angkor Borei | *Cambodian*	23
Little Nepal | *Nepalese*	23
NEW 903 | *Japanese/Sandwiches*	23
Liberty Cafe | *Amer.*	22
Front Porch | *Carib./Southern*	22
Locavore | *Cal.*	22
Emmy's Spaghetti | *Italian*	20

CASTRO

(See map on page 100)

Sushi Zone | *Japanese*	27
Frances | *Cal.*	27
Eiji | *Japanese*	26
Amasia Hide's | *Japanese*	25
El Castillito | *Mex.*	25
Anchor Oyster | *Seafood*	25
Ike's Pl./Lair | *Sandwiches*	25
Marcello's Pizza | *Pizza*	25
L'Ardoise | *French*	24
NEW Canela | *Spanish*	24
Poesia | *Italian*	24
Super Duper | *Burgers*	23
Chilango | *Mex.*	23

La Méditerranée | *Med./Mideast.*	23
Woodhouse Fish | *Seafood*	22
Kasa Indian | *Indian*	22
Zadin | *Viet.*	22
Chile Pies | *Dessert*	22
Eureka | *Amer.*	22
Destino | *Nuevo Latino*	22
Starbelly | *Cal.*	22
Catch | *Seafood*	22
Thai Hse. | *Thai*	22
Firewood Cafe | *Italian*	21
Dinosaurs | *Viet.*	21
Chow/Park Chow | *Amer.*	21
Brandy Ho's | *Chinese*	21
Crepevine | *Amer./French*	21
Samovar Tea | *Tea*	21
BurgerMeister | *Burgers*	20

CHINA BASIN/ DOGPATCH

Rocco's Cafe | *Italian*	26
Moshi Moshi | *Japanese*	24
Kitchenette SF | *Sandwiches*	24
Piccino | *Italian*	24
Serpentine | *Amer.*	23
Hard Knox | *Southern*	22
NEW Mission Rock | *Seafood*	-

CHINATOWN

(See map on page 98)

R & G Lounge | *Chinese*	25
Z & Y | *Chinese*	24
Bund Shanghai | *Chinese*	24
Oriental Pearl | *Chinese*	24
Jai Yun | *Chinese*	24
Great Eastern | *Chinese*	23
House/Nanking | *Chinese*	23
Hunan Home's/Gdn. | *Chinese*	22
Henry's Hunan | *Chinese*	22
ABC Cafe | *Chinese*	21
Brandy Ho's | *Chinese*	21
Yuet Lee | *Chinese*	20

COW HOLLOW

(See map on page 97)

Umami | *Japanese*	26
Capannina | *Italian*	26

Terzo	*Med.*	25
Gamine	*French*	25
Betelnut Pejiu	*Asian*	24
Roam	*Burgers*	23
Pane e Vino	*Italian*	23
NEW Umami Burger	*Burgers*	23
Rose's Cafe	*Italian*	22
Patxi's Pizza	*Pizza*	22
Tacko	*Mex.*	22
Osha Thai	*Thai*	22
La Boulange	*Bakery*	22
Nettie's Crab	*Seafood*	21
Brazen Head	*Amer.*	21
Balboa Cafe	*Amer.*	20
Ottimista	*Italian/Med.*	20
Café des Amis	*French*	19

DOWNTOWN

(See map on page 98)

Kokkari	*Greek*	28
Masa's	*French*	27
Fleur de Lys	*Cal./French*	27
Michael Mina	*Amer.*	27
Seasons	*Seafood/Steak*	27
Millennium	*Vegan*	27
Piperade	*Spanish*	27
Quince	*Italian*	26
Chiaroscuro	*Italian*	26
Cotogna	*Italian*	26
Campton Pl.	*Cal./Med.*	26
Perbacco	*Italian*	26
Morton's	*Steak*	25
Farallon	*Seafood*	25
Ryoko's	*Japanese*	25
Lark Creek Steak	*Steak*	25
Tommy Toy	*Chinese*	25
Barbacco	*Italian*	24
Wexler's	*BBQ*	24
Sunrise Deli	*Mideast.*	24
Ebisu	*Japanese*	24
Bix	*Amer./French*	24
Gitane	*French/Spanish*	24
Tadich Grill	*Seafood*	24
Wayfare Tav.	*Amer.*	24
Bourbon	*Steak*	23
Scala's Bistro	*Italian*	23
Alfred's Steak	*Steak*	23
Taqueria Can Cun	*Mex.*	23
Sanraku	*Japanese*	23

Kuleto's	*Italian*	23
Super Duper	*Burgers*	23
5A5 Steak	*Steak*	23
Postrio	*Amer.*	23
Anzu	*Japanese*	23
Unicorn	*Asian*	23
Colibrí	*Mex.*	23
Mixt Greens	*Health/Sandwiches*	23
Le Colonial	*French/Viet.*	23
Emporio Rulli	*Dessert/Italian*	22
Katana-Ya	*Japanese*	22
Sauce	*Amer.*	22
Plouf	*French*	22
Henry's Hunan	*Chinese*	22
Sam's Grill	*Seafood*	22
Café Tiramisu	*Italian*	22
King of Thai	*Thai*	22
Bob's Steak	*Steak*	22
Café Claude	*French*	22
Boudin	*Amer./Sandwiches*	22
4th St. B&G	*Pub/Sandwiches*	22
Nordstrom Cafe	*Sandwiches*	22
Palio d'Asti	*Italian*	22
NEW Per Diem	*Amer.*	22
360° Gourmet	*Eclectic*	22
Plant Cafe	*Health*	22
Il Fornaio	*Italian*	22
Jasper's Corner	*Amer.*	22
Osha Thai	*Thai*	22
Buckhorn Grill	*Amer.*	22
John's Grill	*Seafood/Steak*	22
Ayola	*Greek/Med.*	22
Claudine	*Cal.*	22
Garden Ct.	*Cal.*	22
B44	*Spanish*	22
La Boulange	*Bakery*	22
E&O Asian Kit.	*Asian*	21
Credo	*Italian*	21
Le Central	*French*	21
Cupola Pizzeria	*Italian/Pizza*	21
Cheesecake Fac.	*Amer.*	21
Rotunda	*Amer.*	21
Straits	*Singapor.*	21
Sears	*Diner*	21
Golden West	*Bakery/Sandwiches*	21
Showdogs	*Hot Dogs*	21
Grand Cafe	*French*	21
Fish & Farm	*Amer./Seafood*	20
Burger Bar	*Burgers*	20

LOCATIONS

Cafe Bastille	*French*	20
Max's	*Deli*	20
Muracci's	*Japanese*	20
Café/Presse	*French*	20
Ajisen Ramen	*Japanese*	19
Ramen Underground	*Japanese/Noodle Shop*	19
Globe	*Cal./Italian*	18
'Wichcraft	*Sandwiches*	18
Naan/Curry	*Indian/Pakistani*	18
Hecho	*Japanese*	18
NEW Melt	*Sandwiches*	17
NEW Brasserie S&P	*Cal.*	-
NEW Burritt Tavern	*Amer.*	-
NEW Del Popolo	*Pizza*	-
NEW Machine Coffee	*Coffee/Sandwiches*	-
NEW U-Sushi	*Japanese*	-

EMBARCADERO

Boulevard	*Amer.*	27
Slanted Door	*Viet.*	26
Hog Island Oyster	*Seafood*	26
4505 Meats	*Hot Dogs*	26
Boulettes Larder	*Amer.*	26
Boccalone	*Sandwiches*	25
Ozumo	*Japanese*	25
RoliRoti	*Amer.*	24
Tacolicious	*Mex.*	24
Delica	*Japanese*	24
One Market	*Amer.*	24
La Mar	*Peruvian/Seafood*	24
Blue Bottle	*Cal./Coffee*	24
Hillstone	*Amer.*	24
Chaya	*French/Japanese*	23
Waterbar	*Seafood*	23
Wise Sons	*Deli/Jewish*	23
Out the Door	*Viet.*	23
Il Cane Rosso	*Italian*	23
Mixt Greens		23
Butterfly	*Asian/Cal.*	23
Ferry Plaza Seafoods	*Seafood*	23
Epic Roasthse.	*Steak*	23
Boudin	*Amer./Sandwiches*	22
Gott's Roadside	*Diner*	22
Plant Cafe	*Health*	22
Osha Thai	*Thai*	22
Gaylord India	*Indian*	22
Sens	*Med./Turkish*	22

Town's End	*Amer./Bakery*	22
Waterfront	*Cal./Seafood*	21
Americano	*Italian*	21
Mijita	*Mex.*	20
Fog City Diner	*Amer.*	20
Imperial Tea	*Tea*	19
MarketBar	*Med.*	18
Namu	*Cal./Korean*	-

EXCELSIOR

Broken Record	*Soul*	24
Joe's Cable Car	*Burgers*	22
North Bch. Pizza	*Pizza*	21

FISHERMAN'S WHARF

(See map on page 98)

Gary Danko	*Amer.*	29
Bobo's	*Seafood/Steak*	25
Crab Hse.	*Seafood*	25
Scoma's	*Seafood*	25
In-N-Out	*Burgers*	23
Ana Mandara	*Viet.*	23
King of Thai	*Thai*	22
Boudin	*Amer./Sandwiches*	22
McCormick/Kuleto	*Seafood*	22
Boudin	*Cal.*	22
Alioto's	*Italian*	21

FOREST HILLS/ WEST PORTAL/ LAKESHORE/ PARKSIDE

Mozzarella/Bufala	*Brazilian/Italian*	23
Roti Indian	*Indian*	23
Fresca	*Peruvian*	22
Kingdom/Dumpling	*Chinese*	22
Boudin	*Amer./Sandwiches*	22
Chouchou	*French*	19
Ono Hawaiian	*Hawaiian*	19
NEW Market & Rye	*Deli/Sandwiches*	-

GLEN PARK

Gialina	*Pizza*	25
Le P'tit Laurent	*French*	24
Chenery Park	*Amer.*	23
La Corneta	*Mex.*	22
Osha Thai	*Thai*	22

HAIGHT-ASHBURY/COLE VALLEY

Zazie	*French*	24
Bacon Bacon	*Coffee*	23
Alembic	*Eclectic*	23
Parada 22	*Puerto Rican*	23
Magnolia	*Southern*	22
La Boulange	*Bakery*	22
Cha Cha Cha	*Carib.*	22
North Bch. Pizza	*Pizza*	21
Citrus Club	*Asian*	20
BurgerMeister	*Burgers*	20
Pork Store	*Amer.*	19

HAYES VALLEY/CIVIC CENTER

Fatted Calf	*Sandwiches*	27
Jardinière	*Cal./French*	27
Sebo	*Japanese*	26
Zuni Café	*Med.*	26
Domo Sushi	*Japanese*	25
Brenda's	*Creole/Southern*	25
El Castillito	*Mex.*	25
Nojo	*Amer./Japanese*	25
Bar Jules	*Amer.*	25
Chez Maman	*French*	25
Lers Ros Thai	*Thai*	25
NEW O3 Bistro	*Asian*	24
Blue Bottle	*Cal./Coffee*	24
Hayes St. Grill	*Seafood*	24
Absinthe	*French/Med.*	24
Espetus	*Brazilian*	23
Suppenküche	*German*	23
Biergarten	*German*	23
Sauce	*Amer.*	22
Patxi's Pizza	*Pizza*	22
2G Japanese	*Japanese*	22
Indigo	*Amer.*	22
La Boulange	*Bakery*	22
Farm:Table	*Amer.*	21
Arlequin Cafe	*Med.*	21
Boxing Rm.	*Cajun/Creole*	21
Stacks	*Amer.*	21
DeLessio Mkt.	*Bakery*	21
Samovar Tea	*Tea*	21
Straw	*Cal./Sandwiches*	20
Max's	*Deli*	20
NEW Two Sisters	*Amer.*	19
Moishe's Pippic	*Deli/Jewish*	18
Mel's Drive-In	*Diner*	17
Dobb's Ferry	*Amer.*	16
NEW Hayes Valley Bakeworks	*Amer./Bakery*	–
NEW Pläj	*Scandinavian*	–
NEW Rich Table	*Cal.*	–

INNER RICHMOND

To Hyang	*Korean*	27
Chapeau!	*French*	27
Richmond	*Cal.*	26
Korean Vill. BBQ	*Korean*	26
Mandalay	*Burmese*	26
Burma Superstar	*Burmese*	25
Sushi Bistro	*Japanese*	25
B Star	*Asian*	25
Café Bunn	*Sandwiches/Viet.*	24
Brother's Korean	*Korean*	24
Bella Trattoria	*Italian*	24
My Tofu	*Korean*	23
Spices	*Chinese*	23
King of Thai	*Thai*	22
Giorgio's	*Pizza*	22
Good Luck	*Chinese*	22
Troya	*Turkish*	22
Academy Cafe	*Eclectic*	21
Q Rest.	*Amer.*	20
Katia's Tea	*Russian*	20
Le Soleil	*Viet.*	19
Mel's Drive-In	*Diner*	17

INNER SUNSET

Koo	*Asian*	26
Pasión	*Nuevo Latino/Peruvian*	25
Arizmendi	*Bakery/Pizza*	25
Marnee Thai	*Thai*	25
Underdog	*Hot Dogs*	25
San Tung	*Chinese/Korean*	24
Ebisu	*Japanese*	24
Nopalito	*Mex.*	24
Craw Station	*Cajun/Creole*	24
Yellow Sub	*Sandwiches*	24
Pomelo	*Eclectic*	24
Izakaya Sozai	*Japanese*	23
Patxi's Pizza	*Pizza*	22
Pacific Catch	*Seafood*	22
Chow/Park Chow	*Amer.*	21
Crepevine	*Amer./French*	21
Hotei	*Japanese*	20
Naan/Curry	*Indian/Pakistani*	18

JAPANTOWN

Kiss Seafood	*Japanese*	28
Takara	*Japanese*	21
Benihana	*Japanese*	21
Juban	*Japanese*	20
Mifune	*Japanese*	19

LAUREL HEIGHTS/ PRESIDIO HEIGHTS

Spruce	*Amer.*	26
Garibaldis	*Cal./Med.*	24
Sociale	*Italian*	24
Hong Kong Lounge	*Chinese*	24
Ella's	*Amer.*	21
Pasta Pomodoro	*Italian*	19
Rigolo	*French*	18

LOWER HAIGHT

Thep Phanom	*Thai*	24
Indian Oven	*Indian*	23
Uva Enoteca	*Italian*	23
Kate's Kit.	*Southern*	22
Rosamunde	*German*	22
Axum Cafe	*Ethiopian*	21
Memphis Minnie	*BBQ*	20
NEW Maven	*Amer.*	20

MARINA

(See map on page 97)

Zushi Puzzle	*Japanese*	27
Atelier Crenn	*French*	27
Lucca Deli	*Deli/Sandwiches*	27
NEW Castagna	*French*	26
Chotto	*Japanese*	25
Greens	*Veg.*	25
Blue Barn	*Cal.*	25
A16	*Italian*	25
Tacolicious	*Mex.*	24
Mamacita	*Mex.*	24
Bistro Aix	*Cal./French*	24
Isa	*French*	24
Jake's Steaks	*Cheesestks.*	23
Alegrias	*Spanish*	23
Izzy's Steak	*Steak*	23
Pacific Catch	*Seafood*	22
Baker St. Bistro	*French*	22
Plant Cafe	*Health*	22
Barney's	*Burgers*	22
Delarosa	*Italian*	22
Amici's	*Pizza*	21

Ristobar	*Italian*	21
E'Angelo	*Italian*	20
Ace Wasabi's	*Japanese*	20
Let's Be Frank	*Hot Dogs*	19
NEW Cedar Hill	*Southern*	17
Mel's Drive-In	*Diner*	17

MISSION

(See map on page 100)

Bi-Rite Creamery	*Bakery/Ice Cream*	28
Tartine	*Bakery*	27
Saison	*Amer.*	27
Local Mission	*Cal.*	27
Range	*Amer.*	27
Delfina	*Italian*	27
Commonwealth	*Amer.*	26
Flour + Water	*Italian*	26
Pizzeria Delfina	*Pizza*	26
Chez Spencer	*French*	25
El Castillito	*Mex.*	25
La Taqueria	*Mex.*	25
Kiji Sushi Bar	*Japanese*	25
Universal Cafe	*Amer.*	25
Arizmendi	*Bakery/Pizza*	25
Loló	*Mex.*	25
Heirloom	*Cal./Med.*	25
Woodward's Gdn.	*Cal.*	25
Sushi Bistro	*Japanese*	25
Dynamo Donut	*Coffee*	25
Bar Tartine	*Euro.*	25
Little Star	*Pizza*	25
Mr. Pollo	*Colombian*	25
Truly Med.	*Med.*	25
Locanda	*Italian*	25
Foreign Cinema	*Cal./Med.*	25
Taqueria San Jose	*Mex.*	24
Maverick	*Amer.*	24
Beretta	*Italian*	24
Tacolicious	*Mex.*	24
Gracias	*Mex./Vegan*	24
Amber India	*Indian*	24
Limón	*Peruvian*	24
Beast/Hare	*Amer./Cal.*	24
Blue Plate	*Amer.*	24
Bar Bambino	*Italian*	24
Taqueria Can Cun	*Mex.*	23
Regalito Rosticeria	*Mex.*	23
Dosa	*Indian*	23
Pancho Villa	*Mex.*	23

Slow Club	*Amer.*	23
El Farolito	*Mex.*	23
Udupi Palace	*Indian/Veg.*	23
Wise Sons	*Deli/Jewish*	23
Arinell Pizza	*Pizza*	23
Pauline's	*Pizza*	23
Blowfish Sushi	*Japanese*	23
Schmidt's	*German*	23
Pakwan	*Pakistani*	23
Mission Cheese	*Amer.*	23
Balompie Café	*Salvadoran*	23
NEW Izakaya Yuzuki	*Japanese*	23
Mission Bch. Café	*Cal.*	23
Farina	*Italian*	23
Yamo	*Burmese*	23
Cha-Ya Veg.	*Japanese/Vegan*	23
Sunflower	*Viet.*	23
Esperpento	*Spanish*	22
Papalote Mex.	*Mex.*	22
Mission Chinese	*Chinese*	22
Dante's Weird Fish	*Seafood*	22
Sycamore	*Amer.*	22
Rosamunde	*German*	22
Hog & Rocks	*Amer.*	22
Phat Philly	*Cheesestks.*	22
Andalu	*Eclectic*	22
El Metate	*Mex.*	22
Giordano	*Sandwiches*	22
La Cumbre	*Mex.*	22
La Corneta	*Mex.*	22
Osha Thai	*Thai*	22
Garçon	*French*	22
NEW Wo Hing	*Chinese*	22
Thai Hse.	*Thai*	22
Cha Cha Cha	*Carib.*	22
Nombe	*Japanese*	22
Another Monkey/Koh	*Thai*	21
NEW Ken Ken	*Japanese/Noodle Shop*	21
Pi Bar	*Pizza*	21
Baby Blues BBQ	*BBQ*	21
Walzwerk	*German*	21
Nihon	*Japanese*	21
Pica Pica	*Venez.*	20
Goood Frikin'	*Mideast.*	20
Boogaloos	*SW*	20
Luna Park	*Amer./French*	20
Radish	*Amer.*	20
Pork Store	*Amer.*	19

Southpaw BBQ	*BBQ*	19
Tokyo Go Go	*Japanese*	19
Burger Joint	*Burgers*	19
NEW Dear Mom	*Eclectic*	19
Jay's	*Cheesestks.*	19
St. Francis	*Diner*	18
NEW Southern Pacific	*Pub*	18
Frjtz Fries	*Belgian*	18
NEW Abbot's Cellar	*Amer.*	-
NEW Central Kitchen	*Cal.*	-
NEW Craftsman/Wolves	*Bakery/Sandwiches*	-
NEW Farina Pizza	*Italian/Pizza*	-
NEW Local's Corner	*Seafood*	-
NEW Lolinda	*Argent./Steak*	-
NEW Lot 7	*Seafood*	-
NEW Mozzeria	*Pizza*	-
Namu	*Asian/Korean*	-
NEW Salumeria	*Deli/Sandwiches*	-
NEW St. Vincent Tav.	*Cal.*	-
NEW West/Pecos	*Mex.*	-

NOB HILL

(See map on page 98)

NEW Keiko	*French/Japanese*	29
Seven Hills	*Italian*	28
Saha	*Mideast.*	26
Sons/Daughters	*Amer.*	26
NEW Parallel 37	*Amer.*	24
NEW Bouche	*Cal./French*	24
Big 4	*Amer.*	24
Venticello	*Italian*	24
Borobudur	*Indonesian*	23
Nob Hill Café	*Italian*	22
NEW Sweet Woodruff	*Sandwiches*	-

NOE VALLEY

(See map on page 100)

La Ciccia	*Italian*	27
Contigo	*Spanish*	25
Firefly	*Eclectic*	25
Incanto	*Italian*	25
Tataki	*Japanese*	25
Lupa Trattoria	*Italian*	24
Bacco	*Italian*	24
Pomelo	*Eclectic*	24
Chloe's Cafe	*Amer.*	23
Fresca	*Peruvian*	22

LOCATIONS

Hamano Sushi	*Japanese*	22
Patxi's Pizza	*Pizza*	22
Henry's Hunan	*Chinese*	22
Eric's	*Chinese*	22
Barney's	*Burgers*	22
La Boulange	*Bakery*	22
Lovejoy's Tea	*Tea*	21
Little Chihuahua	*Mex.*	21
Le Zinc	*French*	20
Alice's	*Chinese*	20
Pasta Pomodoro	*Italian*	19
Toast (SF)	*Amer.*	17
NEW Saru Sushi	*Japanese*	-

NORTH BEACH

(See map on page 98)

House	*Asian*	27
Coi	*Cal./French*	27
Cafe Jacqueline	*French*	27
Naked Lunch	*Sandwiches*	26
Tony's Pizza	*Italian/Pizza*	26
Sotto Mare	*Italian/Seafood*	26
Ideale Rest.	*Italian*	25
L'Osteria	*Italian*	25
Albona Rist.	*Italian*	25
Don Pisto's	*Mex.*	25
Golden Boy	*Pizza*	25
NEW Park Tav.	*Amer.*	25
North Bch. Rest.	*Italian*	25
Taqueria San Jose	*Mex.*	24
Tratt. Contadina	*Italian*	24
Mama's on Wash.	*Amer.*	24
Tommaso's	*Italian*	24
Txoko	*Spanish*	24
Tony's Coal-Fired	*Pizza*	24
Chubby Noodle	*Asian*	24
Bocadillos	*Spanish*	23
Maykadeh	*Persian*	23
Mo's	*Amer.*	23
15 Romolo	*Amer.*	22
Original Joe's (SF)	*Amer./Italian*	22
King of Thai	*Thai*	22
Buster's Cheesesteak	*Cheesestks./Burgers*	22
Giordano	*Sandwiches*	22
La Boulange	*Bakery*	22
Caffè Macaroni	*Italian*	21
North Bch. Pizza	*Pizza*	21
Stinking Rose	*Italian*	21
Rose Pistola	*Italian*	21

Cafe Divine	*Amer./Sandwiches*	21
Mario's Bohemian	*Italian/Sandwiches*	21
Cafe Zoetrope	*Italian*	20
BurgerMeister	*Burgers*	20
La Trappe	*Belgian*	20
Campanula	*Amer.*	19
Naan/Curry	*Indian/Pakistani*	18
Bottle Cap	*Amer.*	18

OUTER RICHMOND

Kappou Gomi	*Japanese*	28
Kabuto	*Japanese*	26
Aziza	*Moroccan*	26
Pizzetta 211	*Pizza*	26
Ariake	*Japanese*	26
Han IL Kwan	*Korean*	25
Ton Kiang	*Chinese*	25
Mescolanza	*Italian*	25
PPQ Dungeness	*Seafood/Viet.*	24
Shanghai Hse.	*Chinese*	24
Pacific Café	*Seafood*	24
Oyaji	*Japanese*	24
Hong Kong Lounge	*Chinese*	24
Shanghai Dumpling	*Chinese*	24
Hakka Rest.	*Chinese*	23
Sutro's	*Cal.*	23
Pagan	*Burmese/Thai*	22
Khan Toke	*Thai*	22
Hard Knox	*Southern*	22
Mayflower	*Chinese*	22
Turtle Tower	*Viet.*	21
Cliff Hse.	*Cal.*	21
Tommy's Mex.	*Mex.*	20
NEW Moss Room	*Cal./Viet.*	-

OUTER SUNSET

Thanh Long	*Viet.*	26
Marnee Thai	*Thai*	25
Taco Shop	*Mex.*	25
Outerlands	*Amer.*	25
Cajun Pacific	*Cajun*	25
Sunrise Deli	*Mideast.*	24
Yum Yum Fish	*Japanese*	23
King of Thai	*Thai*	22
North Bch. Pizza	*Pizza*	21
Just Wonton	*Chinese*	20
Java Beach	*Sandwiches*	20
Park Chalet	*Cal.*	17
Beach Chalet	*Amer.*	17

PACIFIC HEIGHTS

Pizzeria Delfina	Pizza	26
SPQR	Italian	25
Tataki	Japanese	25
Eliza's	Chinese	23
Woodhouse Fish	Seafood	22
Florio	French/Italian	22
Godzila Sushi	Japanese	22
La Boulange	Bakery	22
Troya	Turkish	22
Elite Cafe	Amer.	21

POLK GULCH

(See map on page 98)

Acquerello	Italian	28
Ruth's Chris	Steak	27
Harris'	Steak	27
House/Prime	Amer.	26
Swan Oyster	Seafood	26
Crustacean	Asian/Viet.	25
Shalimar	Indian/Pakistani	24
Miller's East	Deli/Jewish	21

POTRERO HILL

Plow	Cal.	26
Papito	Mex.	26
Chez Papa Bistrot	French	25
Skool	Seafood	23
Sunflower	Viet.	23
Aperto	Italian	22
Source	Pizza/Veg.	22
Goat Hill	Pizza	22
NEW Market & Rye	Deli/Sandwiches	-

PRESIDIO

Presidio Social	Amer.	19
Let's Be Frank	Hot Dogs	19
NEW Dixie	Southern	-

RUSSIAN HILL

(See map on page 98)

La Folie	French	27
Frascati	Cal./Med.	26
Pesce	Italian/Seafood	25
Zarzuela	Spanish	24
Rist. Milano	Italian	24
Luella	Cal./Med.	24
Helmand Palace	Afghan	24
Allegro Romano	Italian	23
Leopold's	Austrian	23

Hyde St. Bistro	French	22
La Boulange	Bakery	22
Nick's Crispy	Mex.	22
Matterhorn Swiss	Swiss	21
NEW Gioia Pizzeria	Cal./Pizza	-

SOMA

(See map on page 102)

Benu	Amer.	27
Alexander's Steak	Japanese/Steak	26
Yank Sing	Chinese	26
Una Pizza	Pizza	26
Ame	Amer.	26
NEW AQ	Cal.	25
Fringale	French/Spanish	25
Fifth Floor	Amer./French	25
Basil	Thai	25
NEW Deli Board	Deli	25
HRD Coffee	Diner/Korean	25
Prospect	Amer.	24
Marlowe	Amer./Cal.	24
Sunrise Deli	Mideast.	24
Zero Zero	Italian/Pizza	24
Pazzia	Pizza	24
Blue Bottle	Cal./Coffee	24
Amber India	Indian	24
Sentinel	Sandwiches	24
Mochica	Peruvian	24
Roy's	Hawaiian	24
Pearl's Deluxe/Phat	Burgers	24
Sanraku	Japanese	23
Chez Papa Resto	French	23
Coco500	Cal./Med.	23
Manora's Thai	Thai	23
3rd St. Grill	Amer./Mex.	23
Town Hall	Amer.	23
Le Charm Bistro	French	23
Amer. Grilled	Amer./Sandwiches	23
Spices	Chinese	23
RN74	French	23
Mo's	Amer.	23
Bar Agricole	Cal.	23
Butler/Chef	French	22
AK Subs	Sandwiches	22
Fang	Chinese	22
54 Mint	Italian	22
Oola	Cal.	22

LOCATIONS

South Park	*French*	22
Salt Hse.	*Amer.*	22
Henry's Hunan	*Chinese*	22
Zaré/Fly Trap	*Cal./Med.*	22
Fondue Cowboy	*Fondue*	22
Citizen's Band	*Amer.*	22
360° Gourmet	*Eclectic*	22
Goat Hill	*Pizza*	22
Rest. LuLu	*French/Med.*	22
Radius	*Cal.*	22
Osha Thai	*Thai*	22
Farmerbrown	*Soul*	22
Anchor & Hope	*Seafood*	22
Ayola	*Greek/Med.*	22
La Boulange	*Bakery*	22
Another Monkey/Koh	*Thai*	21
Cha Am Thai	*Thai*	21
Luce	*Cal./Italian*	21
Sushirrito	*Japanese*	21
NEW Trace	*Amer.*	21
Turtle Tower	*Viet.*	21
25 Lusk	*Amer.*	21
Samovar Tea	*Tea*	21
Tropisueño	*Mex.*	20
Heaven's Dog	*Chinese*	20
Rist. Umbria	*Italian*	20
Bluestem Brass.	*Steak*	19
Zuppa	*Italian*	19
Spice Kit	*Asian*	18
Buca di Beppo	*Italian*	18
NEW Melt	*Sandwiches*	17
Mel's Drive-In	*Diner*	17
NEW Catheads BBQ	*BBQ*	-
NEW SoMa StrEAT	*Eclectic*	-
NEW Split Bread	*Sandwiches*	-

TELEGRAPH HILL

901 Columbus	*Sandwiches*	22

TENDERLOIN

(See map on page 98)

Canteen	*Cal.*	27
Chutney	*Indian/Pakistani*	26
Saigon Sandwich	*Sandwiches/Viet.*	26
Sai Jai Thai	*Thai*	25
Lers Ros Thai	*Thai*	25
Bodega Bistro	*Viet.*	24
Shalimar	*Indian/Pakistani*	24
Pearl's Deluxe/Phat	*Burgers*	24

A La Turca	*Turkish*	23
Pakwan	*Pakistani*	23
Burmese Kit.	*Burmese*	23
Osha Thai	*Thai*	22
Farmerbrown	*Soul*	22
Thai Hse.	*Thai*	22
Pagolac	*Viet.*	22
Turtle Tower	*Viet.*	21

UPPER FILLMORE

Baker/Banker	*Amer.*	26
Dosa	*Indian*	23
Out the Door	*Viet.*	23
La Méditerranée	*Med./Mideast.*	23
Fresca	*Peruvian*	22
Jackson Fillmore/Cucina	*Italian*	22
Bun Mee	*Viet.*	19
NEW Roostertail	*Amer.*	19

WESTERN ADDITION

State Bird	*Amer.*	27
Nopa	*Cal.*	27
Ragazza	*Pizza*	25
Bar Crudo	*Seafood*	25
Bistro Central	*French*	25
Little Star	*Pizza*	25
Nopalito	*Mex.*	24
Tsunami Sush/Sake	*Japanese*	24
Cheese Steak	*Cheesestks.*	23
Yoshi's	*Japanese*	23
Green Chile	*SW*	23
Alamo Sq.	*French/Seafood*	23
1300/Fillmore	*Soul/Southern*	23
Papalote Mex.	*Mex.*	22
Acme Burger	*Burgers*	22
Chile Pies	*Dessert*	22
Little Chihuahua	*Mex.*	21
DeLessio Mkt.	*Bakery*	21
Jay's	*Cheesestks.*	19

East of San Francisco

ALAMEDA

Asena	*Cal./Med.*	26
Burma Superstar	*Burmese*	25
Pappo	*Cal./Med.*	25
Pearl's Deluxe/Phat	*Burgers*	24
East Ocean	*Chinese*	24
NEW Dragon Rouge	*Viet.*	24
Cheese Steak	*Cheesestks.*	23

King of Thai	*Thai*	22
360° Gourmet	*Eclectic*	22
Speisekammer	*German*	22
BurgerMeister	*Burgers*	20

ALBANY

Little Star	*Pizza*	25
Caspers Hot Dogs	*Hot Dogs*	23
Fonda Solana	*Pan-Latin*	21

ANTIOCH/CONCORD

| Cheese Steak | *Cheesestks.* | 23 |
| 360° Gourmet | *Eclectic* | 22 |

BERKELEY

Chez Panisse Café	*Cal./Med.*	28
Rivoli	*Cal./Med.*	28
Chez Panisse	*Cal./Med.*	28
Ajanta	*Indian*	27
Cheese Board	*Pizza*	27
Gioia Pizzeria	*Pizza*	26
Lalime's	*Cal./Med.*	26
Riva Cucina	*Italian*	26
Thai Buddhist	*Thai*	26
Emilia's	*Pizza*	26
Zachary's Pizza	*Pizza*	26
Kirala	*Japanese*	25
Trattoria Corso	*Italian*	25
Grégoire	*French*	25
900 Grayson	*Burgers*	25
Bette's Oceanview	*Diner*	25
O Chamé	*Japanese*	25
Vik's Chaat	*Indian*	25
Bangkok Thai	*Thai*	25
Zatar	*Med.*	25
Angeline's LA Kit.	*Cajun/Creole*	24
Gather	*Cal.*	24
Sunrise Deli	*Mideast.*	24
Tratt. La Sicil.	*Italian*	24
Venus	*Cal.*	24
Zabu Zabu	*Japanese*	24
Ippuku	*Japanese*	24
Lo Coco's	*Italian*	24
La Note	*French*	23
Top Dog	*Hot Dogs*	23
Rick & Ann	*Amer.*	23
Shen Hua	*Chinese*	23
Anchalee Thai	*Thai*	23
Udupi Palace	*Indian/Veg.*	23
La Rose Bistro	*Cal./French*	23

Arinell Pizza	*Pizza*	23
Cheese Steak	*Cheesestks.*	23
La Méditerranée	*Med./Mideast.*	23
Tacubaya	*Mex.*	23
Vanessa's Bistro	*French/Viet.*	23
Cha-Ya Veg.	*Japanese/Vegan*	23
Bistro Liaison	*French*	23
Picante Cocina	*Mex.*	22
Meritage/Claremont	*Cal.*	22
Café Rouge	*Cal./Med.*	22
Revival Bar	*Cal.*	22
Cactus Taqueria	*Mex.*	22
Barney's	*Burgers*	22
Guamenkitzel	*German*	22
Le Cheval	*Viet.*	22
Cancun	*Mex.*	22
Cha Am Thai	*Thai*	21
Five	*Amer./Cal.*	21
Venezia	*Italian*	21
Sea Salt	*Seafood*	21
Breads/India	*Indian*	21
North Bch. Pizza	*Pizza*	21
Juan's	*Mex.*	21
Everett/Jones BBQ	*BBQ*	21
NEW Joshu-ya Brass.	*Japanese*	21
Crepevine	*Amer./French*	21
FatApple's	*Diner*	20
Jimmy Beans	*Diner*	20
César	*Spanish*	20
Skates on Bay	*Amer.*	20
BurgerMeister	*Burgers*	20
Saul's Rest./Deli	*Deli*	20
Café Gratitude	*Vegan*	19
Imperial Tea	*Tea*	19
T Rex BBQ	*BBQ*	18
Naan/Curry	*Indian/Pakistani*	18
NEW Comal	*Mex.*	-

CROCKETT

| Dead Fish | *Seafood* | 22 |

DANVILLE

Esin	*Amer./Med.*	26
Peasant/Pear	*Cal./Med.*	24
Bridges	*Asian/Cal.*	23
Amber Bistro	*Cal.*	23
Forbes Mill	*Steak*	23
La Boulange	*Bakery*	22
Amici's	*Pizza*	21

Chow/Park Chow	*Amer.*	21
Piatti	*Italian*	21
Prickly Pear	*Mex.*	19

DUBLIN

Amakara Japanese	*Japanese*	24
Koi	*Chinese*	24
Ohgane Korean	*Korean*	23
Caspers Hot Dogs	*Hot Dogs*	23
Amici's	*Pizza*	21
Johnny Garlic's	*Cal.*	20

EL CERRITO

FatApple's	*Diner*	20
Pasta Pomodoro	*Italian*	19

EMERYVILLE

Arizmendi	*Bakery/Pizza*	25
Bangkok Thai	*Thai*	25
Hong Kong East	*Chinese*	22
Buckhorn Grill	*Amer.*	22
Bucci's	*Cal./Italian*	22
Townhouse B&G	*Cal.*	21
Trader Vic's	*Polynesian*	19
Rudy's Can't Fail	*Diner*	19
Pasta Pomodoro	*Italian*	19

FREMONT/NEWARK

Salang Pass	*Afghan*	25
Shalimar	*Indian/Pakistani*	24
Pakwan	*Pakistani*	23

HAYWARD

Pakwan	*Pakistani*	23
Caspers Hot Dogs	*Hot Dogs*	23
Everett/Jones BBQ	*BBQ*	21

LAFAYETTE

Chevalier	*French*	26
Artisan Bistro	*Cal./French*	25
Postino	*Italian*	24
Cheese Steak	*Cheesestks.*	23
Duck Club	*Amer.*	22
Patxi's Pizza	*Pizza*	22
Bo's BBQ	*BBQ*	22
Pizza Antica	*Pizza*	22
Chow/Park Chow	*Amer.*	21
Metro	*Cal./French*	21
Yankee Pier	*New Eng./Seafood*	19

LAKE TAHOE

Evan's	*Amer.*	27
Café Fiore	*Italian*	27
Wolfdale's	*Cal.*	27
Soule Domain	*Amer.*	24
Dragonfly	*Asian/Cal.*	24
Red Hut	*Diner*	23
Moody's Bistro	*Amer.*	23
Manzanita	*Cal./French*	23
PlumpJack	*Cal./Med.*	23
Christy Hill	*Cal./Med.*	21
Pacific Crest	*Med.*	21
Pianeta	*Italian/Med.*	21
Cottonwood	*Eclectic*	20
Gar Woods	*Cal.*	20
Naked Fish	*Japanese*	20
Jake's/Lake	*Cal.*	20
Sunnyside Lodge	*Seafood/Steak*	20
Bridgetender	*Pub*	18

LIVERMORE

Wente Vineyards	*Cal./Med.*	26

OAKLAND

Commis	*Amer.*	28
Asmara	*Ethiopian*	26
Marica	*Seafood*	26
Pizzaiolo	*Italian/Pizza*	26
NEW B-Side BBQ	*BBQ*	26
Dopo	*Italian*	26
Oliveto Rest.	*Italian*	26
Café Colucci	*Ethiopian*	26
Wood Tav.	*Cal.*	26
BayWolf	*Cal./Med.*	26
Brown Sugar	*Soul*	26
Bakesale Betty	*Bakery*	26
Zachary's Pizza	*Pizza*	26
Encuentro	*Veg.*	26
Burma Superstar	*Burmese*	25
Addis Ethiopian	*Ethiopian*	25
Arizmendi	*Bakery/Pizza*	25
Grégoire	*French*	25
Tamarindo	*Mex.*	25
Ozumo	*Japanese*	25
Battambang	*Cambodian*	25
À Côté	*French/Med.*	25
Camino	*Cal./Med.*	25
NEW Haven	*Cal.*	25
Enoteca Molinari	*Italian*	24

Boot/Shoe | *Italian/Pizza*	24
Chu | *Chinese*	24
Blue Bottle | *Cal./Coffee*	24
Marzano | *Italian/Pizza*	24
Uzen | *Japanese*	24
Picán | *Southern*	24
Chop Bar | *Cal.*	24
Lo Coco's | *Italian*	24
Bellanico | *Italian*	24
Mama's Royal | *Amer.*	24
Pho 84 | *Viet.*	24
Southie | *Amer.*	24
Actual Cafe | *Cal.*	23
Plum | *Cal.*	23
Soi4 | *Thai*	23
Mezze | *Cal./Med.*	23
Top Dog | *Hot Dogs*	23
Oliveto Cafe | *Italian*	23
Flora | *Amer.*	23
Champa Gdn. | *SE Asian*	23
In-N-Out | *Burgers*	23
Nan Yang | *Burmese*	23
El Farolito | *Mex.*	23
Hawker Fare | *SE Asian*	23
Scott's Seafood | *Seafood*	23
Yoshi's | *Japanese*	23
Bocanova | *Pan-Latin*	23
Cheese Steak | *Cheesestks.*	23
Xolo Taqueria | *Mex.*	23
Ohgane Korean | *Korean*	23
Caspers Hot Dogs | *Hot Dogs*	23
Sahn Maru | *Korean*	23
Mua Lounge | *Amer.*	23
Adesso | *Italian*	23
Kincaid's | *Amer.*	23
Legendary Palace | *Chinese*	22
Doña Tomás | *Mex.*	22
Barlata | *Spanish*	22
Hudson | *Amer.*	22
Homeroom | *Amer.*	22
Fentons | *Ice Cream*	22
Sidebar | *Cal./Med.*	22
360° Gourmet | *Eclectic*	22
Cactus Taqueria | *Mex.*	22
Barney's | *Burgers*	22
Le Cheval | *Viet.*	22
Miss Pearl's | *Southern*	22
Trueburger | *Burgers*	21
Blackberry Bistro | *Southern*	21

Breads/India | *Indian*	21
Italian Colors | *Italian*	21
Metro | *Cal./French*	21
Xyclo | *Viet.*	21
NEW Rumbo | *Pan-Latin*	21
Everett/Jones BBQ | *BBQ*	21
Crepevine | *Amer./French*	21
Home of Chicken | *Southern*	20
César | *Pan-Latin*	20
Montclair Egg | *Diner*	20
Luka's Taproom | *Cal./French*	20
Rest. Peony | *Chinese*	20
Max's | *Deli*	20
Rudy's Can't Fail | *Diner*	19
Pasta Pomodoro | *Italian*	19
Lake Chalet | *Cal.*	17
NEW FuseBox | *Korean*	-
NEW Hopscotch | *Amer./Japanese*	-

ORINDA

Casa Orinda | *Italian/Steak*	21

PLEASANT HILL

Caspers Hot Dogs | *Hot Dogs*	23
Pasta Pomodoro | *Italian*	19

PLEASANTON

Jim's Country | *Southern*	27
Haps Original | *Steak*	25
Cheese Steak | *Cheesestks.*	23
Cheesecake Fac. | *Amer.*	21

RICHMOND

Caspers Hot Dogs | *Hot Dogs*	23
Hotel Mac Rest. | *Amer.*	21

SAN RAMON

Zachary's Pizza | *Pizza*	26
Cheese Steak | *Cheesestks.*	23
Izzy's Steak | *Steak*	23
Max's | *Deli*	20
Pasta Pomodoro | *Italian*	19

WALNUT CREEK

Nama Sushi | *Japanese*	27
Ruth's Chris | *Steak*	27
Prima | *Italian*	26
Sasa | *Japanese*	26
Va de Vi | *Eclectic*	25

LOCATIONS

Vic Stewart | *Steak*	24
Walnut Creek Yacht | *Seafood*	24
Lark Creek | *Amer.*	24
Scott's Seafood | *Seafood*	23
Cheese Steak | *Cheesestks.*	23
Caspers Hot Dogs | *Hot Dogs*	23
Vanessa's Bistro | *French/Viet.*	23
360° Gourmet | *Eclectic*	22
Il Fornaio | *Italian*	22
Le Cheval | *Viet.*	22
Breads/India | *Indian*	21
Home of Chicken | *Southern*	20
NEW Corners Tav. | *Amer.*	-

YOSEMITE/OAKHURST

Erna's | *Cal./French*	28
Ahwahnee | *Cal.*	22

North of San Francisco

BODEGA BAY

Terrapin Creek | *Cal.*	28
Duck Club | *Amer.*	22

CALISTOGA

Jole | *Amer.*	27
Solbar | *Cal.*	26
Barolo | *Italian*	24
All Seasons | *Cal.*	24
Brannan's Grill | *Amer.*	20

CORTE MADERA

Sea Thai/Modern | *Thai*	27
Pacific Catch | *Seafood*	22
Il Fornaio | *Italian*	22
Cheesecake Fac. | *Amer.*	21
Max's | *Deli*	20
Brick/Bottle | *Cal.*	19

FAIRFAX

Anokha/Lotus | *Indian*	25

FORESTVILLE

Farmhse. Inn | *Cal.*	27

GEYSERVILLE

Diavola | *Italian*	26
Rustic | *Italian*	21

GLEN ELLEN/
KENWOOD

Fig Cafe/Wine | *French*	26
Kenwood | *Amer./French*	25
Cafe Citti | *Italian*	24
Glen Ellen Inn | *Cal.*	24
NEW Glen Ellen Star | *Amer.*	-

GUERNEVILLE

Boon Eat/Drink | *Cal.*	24
Applewood Rest. | *Cal.*	24

HEALDSBURG/
WINDSOR

Madrona Manor | *Amer./French*	27
Downtown Bakery | *Bakery*	26
Scopa | *Italian*	26
Zazu | *Amer./Italian*	25
Chinois | *Asian*	25
Willi's Seafood | *Seafood*	25
Barndiva | *Amer.*	25
Dry Creek | *Cal.*	24
Bistro Ralph | *Cal./French*	24
Zin | *Amer.*	24
Ravenous | *Cal./Eclectic*	22
NEW Mateo's Cocina | *Mex.*	21
Charcuterie | *French*	20
Jimtown Store | *Deli*	20
Healdsburg B&G | *Amer.*	20
Spoonbar | *Cal.*	20
Johnny Garlic's | *Cal.*	20
Wurst Rest. | *Amer./Pub*	20
NEW Campo Fina | *Italian/Pizza*	-

LARKSPUR

Picco | *Italian*	26
Table Café | *Cal.*	26
Pizzeria Picco | *Pizza*	26
Avatar's | *Indian*	24
El Huarache Loco | *Mex.*	23
Emporio Rulli | *Dessert/Italian*	22
Tav./Lark Creek | *Amer.*	22
Left Bank | *French*	20
Yankee Pier | *New Eng./Seafood*	19

MENDOCINO COUNTY

Ledford Hse. | *Cal./Med.*	27
Cafe Beaujolais | *Cal./French*	26
Mendo Bistro | *Amer.*	26
Rest./Stevenswood | *Amer.*	25
Ravens' | *Vegan*	25
955 Rest. | *Amer./French*	25
Albion River Inn | *Cal.*	25

MacCallum	*Cal.*	24
Chapter & Moon	*Amer.*	24
Fort Bragg	*Bakery/Eclectic*	23
St. Orres	*Cal.*	23
Little River Inn	*Cal./Seafood*	22
Moosse Café	*Cal.*	22
Restaurant	*Amer./Eclectic*	22
Mendo Café	*Eclectic*	21
Mendocino Hotel	*Cal.*	21
North Coast Brew	*Amer.*	19

MILL VALLEY

Buckeye	*Amer./BBQ*	25
Avatar's	*Indian*	24
Pearl's Deluxe/Phat	*Burgers*	24
El Paseo	*Steak*	23
In-N-Out	*Burgers*	23
Harmony	*Chinese*	23
La Ginestra	*Italian*	22
Bungalow 44	*Amer.*	22
Pizza Antica	*Pizza*	22
Frantoio	*Italian*	22
La Boulange	*Bakery*	22
Piatti	*Italian*	21
Toast	*Amer.*	21
Joe's Taco	*Mex.*	21
NEW Hawk's Tav.	*Amer.*	21
Balboa Cafe	*Amer.*	20
Piazza D'Angelo	*Italian*	20
Pasta Pomodoro	*Italian*	19
Dipsea Cafe	*Diner/Greek*	19

NAPA

Cole's Chop	*Steak*	27
La Taquiza	*Mex.*	27
La Toque	*French*	27
Fatted Calf	*Sandwiches*	27
Hog Island Oyster	*Seafood*	26
Morimoto	*Japanese*	25
Pearl	*Cal.*	25
Farm	*Amer.*	25
C Casa	*Mex.*	25
Celadon	*Amer./Eclectic*	25
Bistro Don Giovanni	*Italian*	25
Angèle	*French*	24
Oenotri	*Italian*	24
Bank Café	*French*	24
ZuZu	*Spanish*	24
Azzurro	*Pizza*	23

In-N-Out	*Burgers*	23
Boon Fly	*Cal.*	23
Brix	*Cal./French*	23
Fumé Bistro	*Amer.*	22
Model Bakery	*Bakery*	22
Kitchen Door	*Eclectic*	22
BarBersQ	*BBQ*	22
Alexis Baking	*Bakery*	22
Gott's Roadside	*Diner*	22
Napa Wine Train	*Cal.*	22
Oxbow Wine	*Cal./Med.*	21
Norman Rose	*Amer.*	20
Pica Pica	*Venez.*	20
Fish Story	*Seafood*	20
Uva Trattoria	*Italian*	19
NEW Thomas/Fagiani's	*Amer.*	–

NOVATO

Boca	*Argent./Steak*	25
Arun	*Thai*	25
Anokha/Lotus	*Indian*	25
La Boulange	*Bakery*	22
Hilltop 1892	*Amer./Cal.*	21
Toast	*Amer.*	21
Pasta Pomodoro	*Italian*	19

OCCIDENTAL

Bistro/Copains	*French*	27

PETALUMA

Cucina Paradiso	*Italian*	27
Sea Thai/Modern	*Thai*	27
Della Fattoria	*Bakery/Eclectic*	27
Central Mkt.	*Cal./Med.*	26
Rosso Pizzeria	*Italian/Pizza*	26
Graffiti	*Eclectic*	25
Sugo	*Italian*	25
Risibisi	*Italian*	25
Volpi's Rist.	*Italian*	24
Avatar's	*Indian*	24
Water St. Bistro	*French*	23
Cattlemens	*Steak*	22
Jennie Low's	*Chinese*	21

ROSS

Marché/Fleurs	*French*	27

RUTHERFORD

Auberge du Soleil	*Cal./French*	27
NEW Alex Rest.	*Italian*	25
Rutherford Grill	*Amer.*	24

LOCATIONS

SAN ANSELMO

Insalata's	Med.	25
Jackson Fillmore/Cucina	Italian	22
Marinitas	Mex./Pan-Latin	22

SAN RAFAEL

Royal Thai	Thai	27
Arizmendi	Bakery/Pizza	25
Sol Food	Puerto Rican	25
Anokha/Lotus	Indian	25
Il Davide	Italian	24
Barney's	Burgers	22
Vin Antico	Italian	22
Amici's	Pizza	21
Miller's East	Deli/Jewish	21
Crepevine	Amer./French	21
Café Gratitude	Vegan	19

SANTA ROSA/
ROHNERT PARK

Sea Thai/Modern	Thai	27
Sazon Peruvian	Peruvian	27
La Gare	French	27
Osake	Cal./Japanese	27
Hana	Japanese	26
Lococo's Cucina	Italian	26
Rosso Pizzeria	Italian/Pizza	26
Stark's	Steak	26
Zazu	Amer./Italian	25
John Ash	Cal.	25
Willi's Wine	Eclectic	25
Bistro 29	French	25
Gary Chu's	Chinese	24
Betty's Fish	British/Seafood	24
El Farolito	Mex.	23
Flavor	Cal./Eclectic	23
Cheese Steak	Cheesestks.	23
Mombo's Pizza	Pizza	23
Monti's	Amer./Med.	22
Cattlemens	Steak	22
Fresh/Lisa	Cal./French	22
Jackson's	Cal.	21
Crepevine	Amer./French	21
Tex Wasabi's	BBQ/Japanese	20
Johnny Garlic's	Cal.	20

SAUSALITO

Sushi Ran	Japanese	27
Murray Circle	Cal.	25
Fish	Seafood	25

Scoma's	Seafood	25
Poggio	Italian	24
Le Garage	French	24
Avatar's	Indian	24
Plate Shop	Cal.	22
Bar Bocce	Pizza	22
Spinnaker	Cal./Seafood	20
NEW Copita	Mex.	–

SEBASTOPOL/
GRATON

K&L Bistro	French	25
Willow Wood	Eclectic/Med.	24
NEW Forchetta/Bastoni		23
Italian/SE Asian		
Mombo's Pizza	Pizza	23
Underwood Bar	Med.	22
French Gdn.	French	22
Peter Lowell	Italian	21
Hopmonk Tav.	Eclectic	20

SONOMA

Cafe La Haye	Amer./Cal.	27
Harvest Moon	Cal./Med.	25
Hot Box Grill	Cal.	25
Santé	Cal./French	25
LaSalette	Portug.	24
Carneros Bistro	Cal.	24
Girl/Fig	French	24
Della Santina	Italian	24
Fremont Diner	Diner	24
Red Grape	Amer./Pizza	24
El Dorado	Cal./Med.	23
Swiss Hotel	Amer./Italian	21
Hopmonk Tav.	Eclectic	20
Meritage Martini	Italian	20

ST. HELENA

Terra	Amer.	27
Meadowood Rest.	Cal.	27
Press	Amer./Steak	26
Cook St. Helena	Italian	26
Bar Terra	Amer.	25
Tra Vigne	Italian	24
Cindy's	Cal.	24
NEW La Condesa	Mex.	24
Wine Spectator	Cal.	23
Pizzeria Tra Vigne	Pizza	23
Farmstead	Amer./Cal.	22
Model Bakery	Bakery	22

Market	*Amer.*	22
NEW Brassica	*Med.*	22
Gott's Roadside	*Diner*	22
Meadowood Grill	*Cal.*	21
NEW French Blue	*Amer.*	–
NEW Goose/Gander	*Amer.*	–

TIBURON

Caprice	*Amer.*	23
Guaymas	*Mex.*	17

VALLEY FORD

Rocker Oysterfellers	*Amer./Southern*	24

WEST MARIN/OLEMA

Osteria Stellina	*Italian*	24
Nick's Cove	*Cal.*	21
Pine Cone Diner	*Diner*	21
Station Hse.	*Amer.*	17

YOUNTVILLE

French Laundry	*Amer./French*	29
Redd	*Cal.*	28
Étoile	*Cal.*	27
Bistro Jeanty	*French*	27
Ad Hoc	*Amer.*	27
Bouchon	*French*	26
Bottega	*Italian*	25
Mustards	*Amer./Cal.*	25
NEW Redd Wood	*Pizza*	25
Addendum	*Amer.*	24
Hurley's	*Cal./Med.*	23
NEW Lucy	*Cal.*	–

South of San Francisco

BIG SUR

Sierra Mar	*Cal./Eclectic*	28
Deetjen's Big Sur	*Cal.*	24
Big Sur	*Amer./Bakery*	24
Rest./Ventana	*Cal.*	23
Nepenthe	*Amer.*	18

BURLINGAME

Mingalaba	*Burmese/Chinese*	27
Stella Alpina Osteria	*Italian*	26
Sakae Sushi	*Japanese*	26
Ecco	*Cal./Continental*	25
Kabul Afghan	*Afghan*	23
Kincaid's	*Amer.*	23

Roti Indian	*Indian*	23
Copenhagen Bakery	*Bakery*	22
La Corneta	*Mex.*	22
Il Fornaio	*Italian*	22
Benihana	*Japanese*	21
Straits	*Singapor.*	21
Stacks	*Amer.*	21
Crepevine	*Amer./French*	21
Max's	*Deli*	20
Juban	*Japanese*	20
Burger Joint	*Burgers*	19

CAMPBELL

A Bellagio	*Italian*	25
Aqui Cal-Mex	*Cal./Mex.*	23
Pacific Catch	*Seafood*	22
Buca di Beppo	*Italian*	18

CARMEL/MONTEREY PENINSULA

Passionfish	*Cal./Seafood*	27
Bistro Moulin	*French*	27
Aubergine	*Cal.*	26
Roy's	*Hawaiian*	26
Casanova	*French/Italian*	24
Anton/Michel	*Continental*	24
Sardine Factory	*Amer./Seafood*	24
Pacific's Edge	*Amer./French*	24
Flying Fish (Carmel)	*Cal./Seafood*	24
Tarpy's	*Amer.*	24
Montrio Bistro	*Cal.*	24
Rio Grill	*Cal.*	23
La Bicyclette	*French/Italian*	23
Mundaka	*Spanish*	23
Andre's Bouchée	*French*	22
Cantinetta Luca	*Italian*	22
Grasing's Coastal	*Cal.*	22
Il Fornaio	*Italian*	22
Fishwife	*Cal./Seafood*	22
Carmel Bakery	*Bakery*	22
C Rest.	*Seafood*	22
Fandango	*Med.*	21
Benihana	*Japanese*	21
Mission Ranch	*Amer.*	20
Cannery/Brew	*Amer.*	19
NEW 400 Degrees	*Burgers*	–

CARMEL VALLEY

Marinus	*Cal./French*	28
Café Rustica	*Cal.*	24

CUPERTINO

Alexander's Steak | *Japanese/Steak*	26
Gochi | *Japanese*	25
Little Sheep | *Mongolian*	22
Joy Luck Palace | *Chinese*	22
Amici's | *Pizza*	21
Benihana | *Japanese*	21

FOSTER CITY

Spices | *Chinese*	23

HALF MOON BAY/ COAST

Cafe Gibraltar | *Med.*	28
Pasta Moon | *Italian*	25
La Costanera | *Peruvian*	25
Navio | *Amer.*	25
Cetrella | *Med.*	24
Mezza Luna | *Italian*	24
Duarte's | *Amer.*	23
Sam's Chowder | *Seafood*	22
Davenport | *Cal.*	22
Barbara's | *Seafood*	22
Flying Fish (HMB) | *Seafood*	21
Taqueria 3 Amigos | *Mex.*	20
Chez Shea | *Eclectic*	19
Half Moon Brew | *Pub/Seafood*	18

LOS ALTOS

Sumika | *Japanese*	25
Los Altos Grill | *Amer.*	24
Chef Chu's | *Chinese*	23
Hunan Home's/Gdn. | *Chinese*	22
Muracci's | *Japanese*	20

LOS GATOS

Manresa | *Amer.*	27
Nick's on Main | *Amer.*	26
Dio Deka | *Greek*	25
Rest. James | *Cal.*	25
Cin-Cin Wine | *Eclectic*	23
Forbes Mill | *Steak*	23

MENLO PARK

Flea St. Café | *Cal.*	26
Naomi Sushi | *Japanese*	25
Madera | *Amer.*	24
Applewood Pizza | *Pizza*	24
LB Steak | *Steak*	22

Iberia | *Spanish*	22
Cool Café | *Cal.*	21
Amici's | *Pizza*	21
Stacks | *Amer.*	21
Left Bank | *French*	20
Juban | *Japanese*	20
NEW Rest. Mitsunobu | *Japanese*	–

MILLBRAE

Kitchen | *Chinese*	24
Curry Up Now | *Indian*	23
In-N-Out | *Burgers*	23
Asian Pearl | *Chinese*	22
Mayflower | *Chinese*	22
Shanghai Dumpling | *Chinese*	21

MILPITAS

Liou's Hse. | *Chinese*	25
Mayflower | *Chinese*	22
Pasta Pomodoro | *Italian*	19

MOUNTAIN VIEW

Taqueria La Bamba | *Mex.*	24
Amber India | *Indian*	24
Chez TJ | *French*	24
In-N-Out | *Burgers*	23
Cascal | *Pan-Latin*	23
Sakoon | *Indian*	23
Xanh | *Viet.*	22
Krung Thai | *Thai*	22
Amarin Thai | *Thai*	22
Amici's | *Pizza*	21

PACIFICA/ SAN BRUNO

NEW Moonraker | *Seafood*	26
NEW Surf Spot | *Eclectic*	–

PALO ALTO/ EAST PALO ALTO

Evvia | *Greek*	28
Baumé | *French*	26
Tamarine | *Viet.*	26
Jin Sho | *Japanese*	26
Sundance Steak | *Steak*	25
Kanpai | *Japanese*	24
Amber India | *Indian*	24
Osteria | *Italian*	24
Tai Pan | *Chinese*	24
Fuki Sushi | *Japanese*	23

Scott's Seafood | *Seafood*	23
La Bodeguita/Medio | *Cuban*	23
Pampas | *Brazilian*	23
Joya | *Nuevo Latino*	23
Hunan Home's/Gdn. | *Chinese*	22
Quattro | *Italian*	22
Fish Market | *Seafood*	22
Patxi's Pizza | *Pizza*	22
Counter Palo Alto | *Burgers*	22
St. Michael's | *Cal.*	22
Il Fornaio | *Italian*	22
Café Brioche | *Cal./French*	22
Mayfield | *Bakery/Cal.*	21
Cheesecake Fac. | *Amer.*	21
Straits | *Singapor.*	21
Lavanda | *Med.*	21
Crepevine | *Amer./French*	21
Calafia | *Cal.*	20
Zibibbo | *Med.*	20
Max's | *Deli*	20
Spice Kit | *Asian*	18
Gordon Biersch | *Pub*	18
Buca di Beppo | *Italian*	18
NEW Asian Box | *Asian*	17
NEW Rangoon Ruby | *Burmese*	-

REDWOOD CITY

Chantilly | *French/Italian*	25
La Victoria | *Mex.*	25
John Bentley | *Cal.*	25
Ike's Pl./Lair | *Sandwiches*	25
Old Port Lobster | *Seafood*	23
Donato | *Italian*	23
Crouching Tiger | *Chinese*	22
New Kapadokia | *Turkish*	21
Max's | *Deli*	20
Pasta Pomodoro | *Italian*	19

REDWOOD SHORES

Mistral | *French/Italian*	23
Amici's | *Pizza*	21

SAN BRUNO

Pasta Pomodoro | *Italian*	19

SAN CARLOS/
BELMONT

Locanda Positano | *Pizza*	26
Refuge | *Belgian/Sandwiches*	25
Kabul Afghan | *Afghan*	23

Izzy's Steak | *Steak*	23
La Corneta | *Mex.*	22

SAN JOSE

La Forêt | *Continental/French*	27
Zeni | *Ethiopian*	27
Le Papillon | *French*	27
La Victoria | *Mex.*	25
Morton's | *Steak*	25
Vung Tau | *Viet.*	25
Taqueria San Jose | *Mex.*	24
New Krung Thai | *Thai*	24
Amber India | *Indian*	24
Arcadia | *Amer.*	24
Grill/Alley | *Steak*	24
SJ Omogari | *Korean*	24
Original Joe's | *Amer./Italian*	23
In-N-Out | *Burgers*	23
Taqueria Tlaquepaque | *Mex.*	23
Scott's Seafood | *Seafood*	23
Blowfish Sushi | *Japanese*	23
Cheese Steak | *Cheesestks.*	23
Aqui Cal-Mex | *Cal./Mex.*	23
McCormick/Schmick | *Seafood*	23
71 St. Peter | *Cal./Med.*	22
Fish Market | *Seafood*	22
LB Steak | *Steak*	22
Pizza Antica | *Pizza*	22
Krung Thai | *Thai*	22
360° Gourmet | *Eclectic*	22
Il Fornaio | *Italian*	22
Amici's | *Pizza*	21
Cheesecake Fac. | *Amer.*	21
Eulipia | *Amer.*	21
Straits | *Singapor.*	21
Left Bank | *French*	20
Sino | *Chinese*	20
Yankee Pier | *New Eng./Seafood*	19
Pasta Pomodoro | *Italian*	19
Gordon Biersch | *Pub*	18
Buca di Beppo | *Italian*	18

SAN MATEO

Wakuriya | *Japanese*	28
All Spice | *Indian*	25
Ramen Dojo | *Japanese/Noodle Shop*	25
Viognier | *Cal./French*	25
Golden Boy | *Pizza*	25
Sushi Sam's | *Japanese*	24

LOCATIONS

Espetus | *Brazilian* 23
Pancho Villa | *Mex.* 23
Osteria Coppa | *Italian/Pizza* 23
231 Ellsworth | *Amer.* 23
Fish Market | *Seafood* 22
Happy Cafe | *Chinese* 22
Rist. Capellini | *Italian* 22
Acqua Pazza | *Italian* 22
Little Sheep | *Mongolian* 22
La Cumbre | *Mex.* 22
Cha Cha Cha | *Carib./Cuban* 22
North Bch. Pizza | *Pizza* 21
Amici's | *Pizza* 21
Hotaru | *Japanese* 21
Attic | *Asian* 20
Taqueria 3 Amigos | *Mex.* 20
Pasta Pomodoro | *Italian* 19

SANTA CLARA

Orenchi Ramen | *Japanese* 24
Parcel 104 | *Cal.* 23
Dasaprakash | *Indian/Veg.* 23
Jang Su Jang | *Korean* 23
Fish Market | *Seafood* 22
Cheesecake Fac. | *Amer.* 21
Piatti | *Italian* 21

SANTA CRUZ/ APTOS/CAPITOLA/ SOQUEL

La Posta | *Italian* 26
Soif Wine Bar | *Cal.* 25
Oswald | *Amer.* 25
O'mei | *Chinese* 25
Gayle's Bakery | *Bakery* 24
Aquarius | *Amer.* 24
Gabriella Café | *Cal./Italian* 23
Ma Maison | *French* 23
Shadowbrook | *Cal.* 22
Café Gratitude | *Vegan* 19

SARATOGA

Hachi Ju Hachi | *Japanese* 27
Sent Sovi | *Cal.* 27
Plumed Horse | *Cal.* 25
Basin | *Amer.* 23
La Fondue | *Fondue* 23

SOUTH SF/ DALY CITY

Ebisu | *Japanese* 24
Koi | *Chinese* 24
In-N-Out | *Burgers* 23
El Farolito | *Mex.* 23
Emporio Rulli | *Dessert/Italian* 22
Nation's Giant | *Burgers* 22
Basque Cultural | *French* 21
BurgerMeister | *Burgers* 20
Yankee Pier | *New Eng./Seafood* 19
Burger Joint | *Burgers* 19

STANFORD

Ike's Pl./Lair | *Sandwiches* 25
Cool Café | *Cal.* 21

SUNNYVALE

Saravana Bhavan | *Indian* 26
Dishdash | *Mideast.* 25
Shalimar | *Indian/Pakistani* 24
Il Postale | *Italian* 23
Cheese Steak | *Cheesestks.* 23
Sawa Sushi | *Japanese* 23
Lion/Compass | *Amer.* 21
Pasta Pomodoro | *Italian* 19

WOODSIDE

Village Pub | *Amer.* 25
Station 1 | *Cal.* 25
Bella Vista | *Continental* 25
Buck's | *Amer.* 19

COW HOLLOW - MARINA

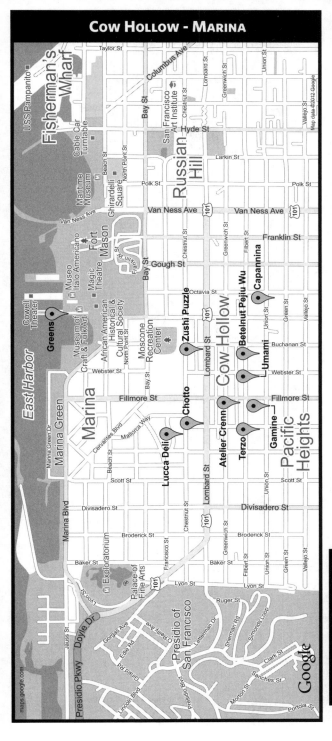

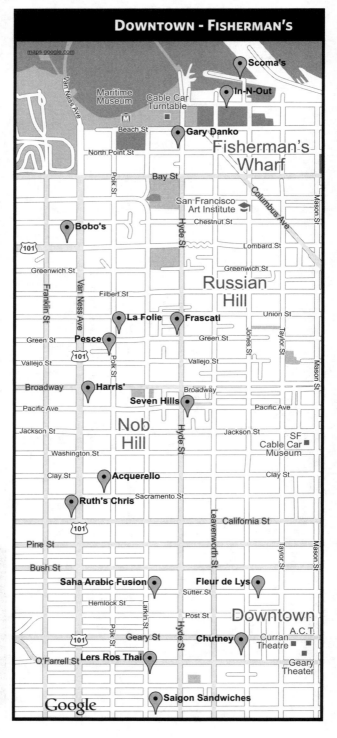

maps.google.com

Scoma's

In-N-Out

Maritime
Museum

Cable Car
Turntable

Beach St

Gary Danko

North Point St

Fisherman's
Wharf

Van Ness Ave

Polk St

Bay St

San Francisco
Art Institute

Columbus Ave

Chestnut St

101

Bobo's

Lombard St

Mason St

Greenwich St

Greenwich St

Hyde St

Franklin St

Van Ness Ave

Filbert St

Russian
Hill

Union St

La Folie

Frascati

Pesce

Green St

Green St

Jones St

Taylor St

101

Vallejo St

Vallejo St

Broadway

Harris'

Broadway

Pacific Ave

Seven Hills

Pacific Ave

Polk St

Hyde St

Jackson St

Jackson St

SF
Cable Car
Museum

Nob
Hill

Washington St

Acquerello

Clay St

Clay St

Ruth's Chris

Sacramento St

101

California St

Pine St

Leavenworth St

Taylor St

Mason St

Bush St

Saha Arabic Fusion

Fleur de Lys

Larkin St

Sutter St

Hemlock St

Post St

Downtown

A.C.T.

101

Geary St

Hyde St

Chutney

Curran
Theatre

Polk St

O'Farrell St

Lers Ros Thai

Geary
Theater

Google

Saigon Sandwiches

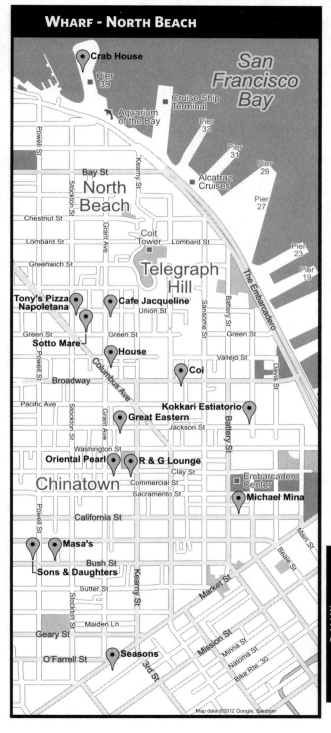

Crab House

Pier 39

San Francisco Bay

Cruise Ship Terminal

Aquarium of the Bay

Pier 33

Pier 31

Bay St

Alcatraz Cruises

Pier 29

North Beach

Pier 27

Chestnut St

Stockton St

Coit Tower

Lombard St

Lombard St

Pier 23

Greenwich St

Grant Ave

Telegraph Hill

Kearny St

Pier 19

The Embarcadero

Tony's Pizza Napoletana

Cafe Jacqueline

Union St

Sansome St

Battery St

Green St

Green St

Green St

Sotto Mare

House

Vallejo St

Powell St

Columbus Ave

Coi

Davis St

Broadway

Pacific Ave

Kokkari Estiatorio

Stockton St

Grant Ave

Great Eastern

Battery St

Jackson St

Washington St

Oriental Pearl

R & G Lounge

Clay St

Chinatown

Commercial St

Sacramento St

Embarcadero Center

Michael Mina

California St

Powell St

Masa's

Main St

Beale St

Bush St

Sons & Daughters

Sutter St

Kearny St

Stockton St

Market St

Maiden Ln

Mission St

Geary St

Minna St

Natoma St

Seasons

O'Farrell St

3rd St

Bike Rte. 30

Map data ©2012 Google, Sanborn

M A P S

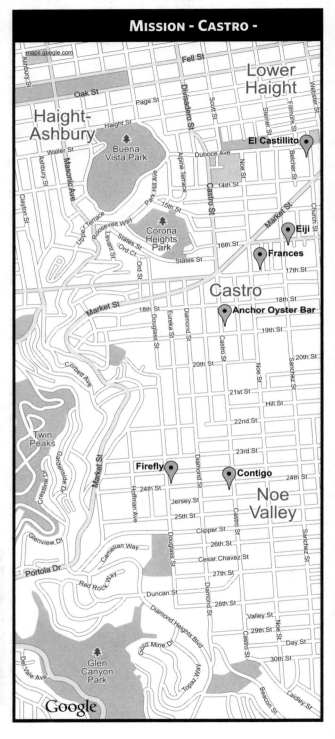

maps.google.com

Fell St

Lower
Haight

Oak St

Page St

Webster St

Ashbury St

Scott St

Divisadero St

Steiner St

Fillmore St

Haight-
Ashbury

Haight St

Buena
Vista Park

El Castillito

Belcher St

Waller St

Duboce Ave

Noe St

Ashbury St

Masonic Ave

Alpine Terrace

14th St

Clayton St

Park Hill Ave

Castro St

Upper Terrace

15th St

Market St

Church St

Roosevelt Way

Corona
Heights
Park

16th St

Eiji

Levant St

States Ave

Ord Ct

Ord St

States St

Frances

17th St

Castro

18th St

Market St

18th St

Anchor Oyster Bar

19th St

Corbett Ave

Eureka St

Douglass St

Diamond St

Castro St

20th St

20th St

Noe St

Sanchez St

21st St

Twin
Peaks

Hill St

22nd St

Gardenside Dr

Market St

23rd St

Crestline Dr

Firefly

Diamond St

Contigo

24th St

Glenview Dr

24th St

Hoffman Ave

Jersey St

Castro St

Noe
Valley

Sanchez St

Camelian Way

25th St

Clipper St

Portola Dr

Douglass St

26th St

Cesar Chavez St

Red Rock Way

27th St

Diamond St

Duncan St

28th St

Diamond Heights Blvd

Valley St

29th St

Noe St

Day St

Gold Mine Dr

Castro St

30th St

Del Vale Ave

Glen
Canyon
Park

Topaz Way

Beacon St

Laidley St

Google

Oak St
Page St
Haight St
Buchanan St
Octavia Blvd
Pearl St
Sushi Zone
12th St
S Van Ness Ave
11th St
Howard St
Dore St
Kissling St
Folsom St
Norfolk St
9th St
8th St
Dore St
101
Central Fwy
Chez Spencer
101
Central F.wy
Erie St
101
US Mint
Clinton Park
Dolores St
Landers St
Ramona Ave
Guerrero St
Valencia St
Mission St
S Van Ness Ave
14th St
Shotwell St
Folsom St
Harrison St
Alabama St
Florida St
Bryant St
16th St
15th St
16th St
Saison
17th St
Mariposa St
Capp St
Treat Ave
Mission
17th St
Tartine Bakery
Pizzeria Delfina
Commonwealth
18th St
Delfina
Range
19th St
Flour + Water
Bi-Rite Creamery
Shotwell St
20th St
Florida St
Bryant St
York St
Mission Dolores Park
Dolores St
Church St
Guerrero St
Fair Oaks St
Valencia St
Mission St
Capp St
S Van Ness Ave
Shotwell St
Treat Ave
Harrison St
Alabama St
21st St
22nd St
20th St
21st St
22nd St
23rd St
Local Mission Eatery
24th St
24th St
25th St
San Jose Ave
Bartlett St
Mission St
Folsom St
Treat Ave
Alabama St
25th St
Clipper St
Dolores St
Guerrero St
26th St
Cesar Chavez St
27th St
Incanto
Precita Ave
Mirabel Ave
Tiffany Ave
Mission St
Coleridge St
Winfield St
Elsie St
Folsom St
Alabama St
28th St
Valley St
Tataki South
La Ciccia
30th St
Bernal Heights Park
Bernal Heights Blvd
Powhattan Ave
Church St
Coleridge St
Winfield St
Eugenia Ave
Randall St
Wool St
Andover St
Anderson St
Map data ©2012 Google, Sanborn

MAPS

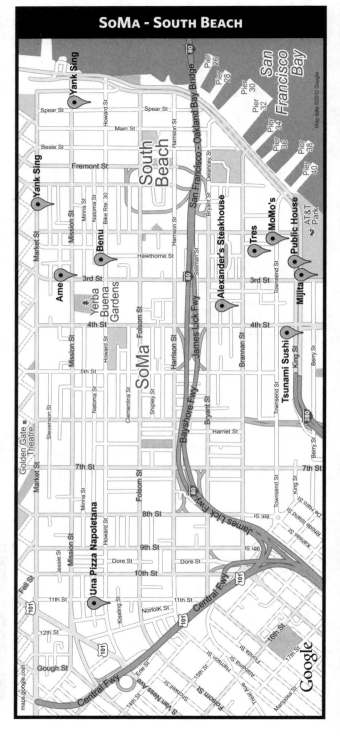

Latest openings, menus, photos and more on plus.google.com/local

CITY OF SAN FRANCISCO

Top Food

<u>29</u> Gary Danko | *American*	Local Mission | *Cal.*
<u>28</u> Kiss Seafood | *Japanese*	Fleur de Lys | *Californian/French*
Seven Hills | *Italian*	Michael Mina | *American*
Acquerello | *Italian*	Benu | *American*
Kokkari Estiatorio | *Greek*	Atelier Crenn | *French*
<u>27</u> Sushi Zone | *Japanese*	Seasons* | *Seafood/Steak*
Ichi Sushi | *Japanese*	House | *Asian*
Boulevard | *American*	Coi | *Californian/French*
Masa's | *French*	Millennium | *Vegan*
La Folie | *French*	Range | *American*
State Bird Provisions | *Amer.*	Canteen | *Californian*
La Ciccia | *Italian*	Piperade | *Spanish*
Tartine Bakery | *Bakery*	Ruth's Chris | *Steak*
Zushi Puzzle | *Japanese*	Frances | *Californian*
Saison | *American*	Delfina | *Italian*

BY CUISINE

AMERICAN (NEW)	CHINESE
<u>29</u> Gary Danko	<u>26</u> Yank Sing
<u>27</u> Boulevard	<u>25</u> Ton Kiang
State Bird Provisions	R&G Lounge
Saison	Tommy Toy's
Michael Mina	<u>24</u> San Tung

AMERICAN (TRAD.)	FRENCH
<u>26</u> House of Prime Rib	<u>27</u> Masa's
<u>24</u> Mama's on Wash.	La Folie
Bix	Fleur de Lys
Wayfare Tavern	Atelier Crenn
Hillstone	Cafe Jacqueline

BAKERIES	FRENCH (BISTRO)
<u>28</u> Bi-Rite	<u>27</u> Chapeau!
<u>27</u> Tartine Bakery	<u>25</u> Chez Spencer
<u>25</u> Arizmendi	Fringale
Dynamo Donut	Bistro Central Parc
<u>24</u> Mama's on Wash.	Chez Maman

BURGERS	INDIAN/PAKISTANI
<u>24</u> Pearl's Deluxe Burgers	<u>26</u> Chutney
<u>23</u> Super Duper	<u>24</u> Amber India
Roam Artisan Burgers	Shalimar
In-N-Out	<u>23</u> Curry Up Now
Mo's	Dosa

CALIFORNIAN	ITALIAN
<u>27</u> Local Mission	<u>28</u> Seven Hills
Coi	Acquerello
Canteen	<u>27</u> La Ciccia
Frances	Delfina
Jardinière	<u>26</u> Quince

Excludes places with low votes; *indicates a tie with restaurant above; Top Food excludes dessert-only spots

JAPANESE

28 Kiss Seafood
27 Sushi Zone
   Ichi Sushi
   Zushi Puzzle
26 Kabuto

MED./GREEK

28 Kokkari Estiatorio
26 Frascati
   Campton Place
   Zuni Café
25 Terzo

MEXICAN

25 El Castillito
   La Taqueria
   Loló
   Don Pisto's
24 Taqueria San Jose

MIDDLE EASTERN

26 Saha
24 Helmand Palace
23 A La Turca
   Maykadeh
   La Méditerranée

NOODLES

24 San Tung
22 Katana-Ya
   King of Thai
   Osha Thai
21 Hapa Ramen

PERUVIAN

25 Pasión
24 Piqueo's

La Mar Cebicheria
Mochica
Limón

PIZZA

26 Tony's Pizza
   Pizzetta 211
   Una Pizza Napoletana
   Flour + Water
   Pizzeria Delfina

SEAFOOD

26 Swan Oyster Depot
   Sotto Mare
   Hog Island Oyster Co.
25 Bar Crudo
   Anchor Oyster Bar

SPANISH/BASQUE

27 Piperade
25 Contigo
   Fringale
24 Zarzuela
   Gitane

STEAK

27 Seasons
   Ruth's Chris
   Harris'
26 House of Prime Rib
   Alexander's

VIETNAMESE

26 Slanted Door
   Thanh Long
   Saigon Sandwiches
25 Crustacean
24 Bodega Bistro

BY SPECIAL FEATURE

BREAKFAST

27 Tartine Bakery
26 Campton Pl.
   Boulettes Larder
24 Mama's on Wash.
   Zazie

BRUNCH

27 Nopa
26 Yank Sing
   Zuni Café
   Baker & Banker
   Boulettes Larder

CHILD-FRIENDLY

26 Tony's Pizza
   Yank Sing
   Pizzeria Delfina
24 Tommaso's
23 Super Duper

GOOD FOR GROUPS

28 Kokkari Estiatorio
26 Perbacco
25 AQ
   Park Tav.
   Foreign Cinema

NEWCOMERS (RATED)

- 27 State Bird Provisions
- 25 AQ
- Park Tav.
- 24 O3 Bistro
- Canela

OPEN LATE

- 27 Nopa
- 26 Chutney
- 25 Ryoko's
- Locanda
- Lers Ros Thai

OUTDOOR SEATING

- 25 Chez Spencer
- Universal Café
- Foreign Cinema
- 24 Sociale
- Isa

PEOPLE-WATCHING

- 27 Boulevard
- Michael Mina
- Jardinère
- Nopa
- 25 Park Tav.

POWER SCENES

- 29 Gary Danko
- 28 Kokkari Estiatorio
- 27 Boulevard
- Masa's
- Michael Mina

ROMANCE

- 29 Gary Danko
- 28 Acquerello
- 27 La Folie
- Jardinière
- Cafe Jacqueline

SMALL PLATES

- 25 Terzo
- 24 Piqueo's
- Barbacco
- Isa
- 23 Izakaya Sozai

TRENDY

- 27 Delfina
- Jardinère
- Nopa
- 25 AQ
- Locanda

VIEWS

- 26 Slanted Door
- 25 Greens
- 24 La Mar Cebicheria
- 23 Waterbar
- Epic Roasthouse

WINNING WINE LISTS

- 29 Gary Danko
- 28 Acquerello
- 27 Boulevard
- Masa's
- 23 RN74

BY LOCATION

CASTRO/NOE VALLEY

- 27 Sushi Zone
- La Ciccia
- Frances
- 26 Eiji
- 25 El Castillito

CHINATOWN

- 25 R & G Lounge
- 24 Oriental Pearl
- 23 Great Eastern
- House of Nanking
- 22 Hunan Home's Restaurant

COW HOLLOW/MARINA

- 27 Zushi Puzzle
- Atelier Crenn
- Lucca Deli
- 26 Umami
- Capannina

DOWNTOWN

- 28 Kokkari Estiatorio
- 27 Masa's
- Fleur de Lys
- Michael Mina
- Seasons

EMBARCADERO

- 27 Boulevard
- 26 Slanted Door
- Hog Island Oyster Co.
- 4505 Meats
- Boulettes Larder

FISHERMAN'S WHARF

- 29 Gary Danko
- 25 Bobo's
- Crab House
- Scoma's
- 23 In-N-Out

HAIGHT-ASHBURY/ COLE VALLEY

- 24 Zazie
- 23 The Alembic
- 22 Magnolia Gastropub
- La Boulange
- Cha Cha Cha

HAYES VALLEY/ CIVIC CENTER

- 27 Jardinière
- 26 Sebo
- Zuni Café
- 25 Domo Sushi
- Brenda's French Soul Food

LOWER HAIGHT

- 24 Thep Phanom Thai
- 23 Indian Oven
- Uva Enoteca
- 22 Rosamunde Sausage
- 20 Memphis Minnie's BBQ

MISSION

- 27 Tartine Bakery
- Saison
- Local Mission
- Range
- Delfina

NOB HILL/ RUSSIAN HILL

- 28 Seven Hills
- 27 La Folie
- 26 Saha Arabic Fusion
- Frascati
- Sons & Daughters

NORTH BEACH

- 27 House
- Coi
- Cafe Jacqueline
- 26 Tony's Pizza
- Sotto Mare

PACIFIC HEIGHTS/ JAPANTOWN

- 28 Kiss Seafood
- 26 Pizzeria Delfina
- 25 SPQR
- Tataki Sushi & Sake Bar
- 23 Eliza's

RICHMOND

- 27 Chapeau!
- 26 Kabuto
- Aziza
- Richmond
- Pizzetta 211

SOMA

- 27 Benu
- 26 Alexander's
- Yank Sing
- Una Pizza Napoletana
- Ame

SUNSET

- 26 Thanh Long
- Koo
- 25 Pasión
- Arizmendi
- Marnee Thai

Top Decor

28	Garden Court	26	Seasons
27	Gary Danko		Quince
	Farallon		Sutro's at the Cliff House
	Big 4		Bix
	Kokkari Estiatorio		Boulevard
	Jardinière		AQ
	Twenty Five Lusk		Grand Cafe
	Spruce		Coi
	Fleur de Lys		Masa's
	Waterbar		Acquerello

Top Service

29	Gary Danko		Michael Mina
28	Acquerello	26	Saison
	Benu		Allegro Romano
	Seasons		Atelier Crenn
27	Coi		Quince
	La Folie		Harris'
	Fleur de Lys		Big 4
	Masa's		Spruce
	Kokkari Estiatorio		Richmond
	Boulevard		La Ciccia

BEST BUYS: BANG FOR THE BUCK

1. Bi-Rite
2. Dynamo Donut
3. Blue Bottle Café
4. In-N-Out Burger
5. Saigon Sandwiches
6. Let's Be Frank
7. Arinell Pizza
8. Golden Boy
9. El Castillito
10. Ayola
11. Arizmendi
12. Yellow Submarine
13. AK Subs
14. HRD Coffee Shop
15. Java Beach Cafe
16. Buster's Cheesesteak
17. Taqueria Can Cun
18. Cheese Steak Shop
19. Marcello's Pizza
20. Taqueria San Jose

BEST BUYS: OTHER GOOD VALUES

A La Turca
American Grilled Cheese
Boccalone Salumeria
Deli Board
4505 Meats
Gioia Pizzeria
Green Chile Kitchen
Hapa Ramen
Kasa Indian Eatery
Kitchenette SF

Little Chihuahua
Naked Lunch
903
Pearl's Deluxe Burgers
Rosamunde Sausage
Showdogs
Super Duper
Truly Mediterranean
Umami Burger
Wise Sons Deli

City of San Francisco

NEW Abbot's Cellar Ⓜ *American*   `-` `-` `-` `M`

Mission | 742 Valencia St. (18th St.) | 415-626-8700 | www.abbotscellar.com
The Monk's Kettle crew takes beer-and-food pairing to the next level at this seasonal, suds-centric fine-dining spot in the Mission, where the sophisticated, midpriced New American menu is designed to complement the 120-plus beer offerings; the long dining room pays homage to a real abbot's cellar, with a surplus of exposed brick, river stones and reclaimed woods; P.S. don't miss the beer-bottle-shaped bathroom sink.

ABC Cafe Restaurant 🕭 *Chinese*   `21` `13` `15` `$23`

Chinatown | 650 Jackson St. (Wentworth St.) | 415-981-0685
Despite "not much of an atmosphere", the "fresh, hot" "dim sum every day" attracts connoisseurs to this "joint" in the heart of Chinatown; skeptics claim "there are many better Chinese places" and note that "flagging down a waitress takes some serious skills", but the "bargain-basement prices" keep its followers coming.

🔢 Absinthe ❶Ⓜ *French/Mediterranean*   `24` `23` `22` `$49`

Hayes Valley | 398 Hayes St. (Gough St.) | 415-551-1590 | www.absinthe.com
You'll feel like you're "in Paris" at this "ravishing, romantic" brasserie that's "deservedly popular" with "young hipsters" and "opera-goers" alike; this "longtime Hayes Valley gem" has "kept its wow factor" thanks to "lovely cocktails" crafted by "expert mixologists" and "fabulous" French-Med fare served by a "professional staff", even if it's "a bit pricey" and "noisy" for some.

Academy Cafe *Eclectic*   `21` `18` `17` `$21`

Inner Richmond | California Academy of Sciences | 55 Music Concourse Dr. (bet. Fulton St. & Lincoln Way) | 415-876-6121 | www.academycafesf.com
"A cut above your average museum cafe", this "surprising" self-serve Eclectic eatery inside the California Academy of Sciences offers a "culturally diverse" menu, including "tasty" "Asian dishes from Charles Phan" of Slanted Door fame; though it's "pricey" ("as expected") and "it can get really crowded", "there's something for everyone" and the "cafeteria-style" setting with an "amazing" adjoining terrace is "fabulous for families"; P.S. open to ticket-holders only.

Ace Wasabi's Rock-N-Roll Sushi *Japanese*   `20` `17` `20` `$32`

Marina | 3339 Steiner St. (bet. Chestnut & Lombard Sts.) | 415-567-4903 | www.acewasabisf.com
"Always buzzing with groups" who are undoubtedly "enjoying themselves", this "scene" is "still a trendy hangout" for the "young Marina" crowd; it's "not the most authentic Japanese restaurant" in town, and the noise-sensitive shout "bring earplugs", but "patient" servers and "above-average" "midpriced sushi" seal its status as a "party spot."

Acme Burgerhaus ❶ *Burgers*   `22` `14` `18` `$15`

Western Addition | 559 Divisadero St. (Hayes St.) | 415-346-3212
It's "all about" the "delicious" burgers – "turkey, chicken, buffalo", "ostrich, lamb", the "tasty veggie option" or straightforward Niman

Ranch beef – at this "no-frills" Western Addition patty purveyor; the variety keeps "mixed groups happy", as does an "unassuming ambiance", and already "fair" prices drop during the "amazing" happy hour, when you "can't beat" the "cheap" "draft beers."

ⓩ Acquerello ⓈⓂ *Italian*   28 | 26 | 28 | $98

Polk Gulch | 1722 Sacramento St. (bet. Polk St. & Van Ness Ave.) | 415-567-5432 | www.acquerello.com

When you're "in the most romantic of moods", this Polk Gulch "old-world" "shrine" "to haute cuisine à la Italia" is "superlative in every sense", from the "superior" wine list to the "very current" Italian prix fixe menus that are "perfection on a plate"; "well-dressed" patrons populate the "elegant", "hushed" setting in a former chapel, where "gracious" servers "anticipate" your "every need" ("the ballet should be this well choreographed"); and if it's undoubtedly "expensive", "who could put a price" on such an "exquisite" experience?

Ajisen Ramen *Japanese*   19 | 13 | 17 | $15

Downtown | Westfield San Francisco Ctr. | 865 Market St. (bet. 4th & 5th Sts.) | 415-357-0288 | www.ajisen-la.com

Shoppers jonesing for Japanese comfort food get a "ramen fix" at this "convenient" chain link in Downtown's Westfield Centre, where a "no-frills, food-court atmosphere" is the setting for "perfectly al dente" noodles swimming in a "flavorful broth"; service is speedy and tabs are "relatively cheap", but pickier types deem it just "passable" for a "craving" "on a cold day."

AK Subs Ⓢ *Sandwiches*   22 | 12 | 21 | $11

SoMa | 397 Eighth St. (bet. Folsom & Harrison Sts.) | 415-241-9600 | www.aksubs.net

Subs piled high with "bundles of meat" and "fresh veggies" are suitable "for sharing" at this SoMa "super-friendly", affordable "simple" "sandwich shop" fans deem "perfect for what it is"; you'll "get in and get out" "quickly", even "during the big lunch rush from the nearby tech startups", and breakfast is also served; P.S. open weekdays only till 4 PM.

Alamo Square Seafood Grill *French/Seafood*   23 | 20 | 22 | $32

Western Addition | 803 Fillmore St. (Grove St.) | 415-440-2828 | www.alamosquareseafoodgrill.com

"Sumptuous" French fare, including "fresh" fish cooked just "the way you like" and served "with the sauce of your choice" by a "welcoming staff", keeps this Western Addition bistro "crowded"; the daily "early-bird prix fixe" delivers lots of "bang for the buck", compensating for "cozy" confines and somewhat "plain decor."

A La Turca *Turkish*   23 | 14 | 20 | $22

Tenderloin | 869 Geary St. (Larkin St.) | 415-345-1011 | www.alaturcasf.com

"Real-deal" Istanbul eats are on the "fantastic" menu at this "unassuming" spot that's "a little Turkey in the Tenderloin"; true, it's "not glamorous", but the "top-notch" fare, from "freshly made falafel" to "juicy kebabs" and "amazing" baklava, comes in "generous" portions at "affordable" prices, and the "friendly" servers keep up a "brisk" pace.

	FOOD	DECOR	SERVICE	COST

Albona Ristorante Istriano *Italian*   `25` `18` `25` `$46`

North Beach | 545 Francisco St. (bet. Mason & Taylor Sts.) |
415-441-1040 | www.albonarestaurant.com
"Distinctive", "delicious Istrian dishes" (i.e. a "palate-pleasing"
blend of Italian, Croatian and Slovenian cuisines) make this "unpretentious gem" "very different from most North Beach spots"
say supporters, who call the "off-the-beaten-track" location "easy
to miss but hard to forget"; "get ready to bump elbows" in the "small
space", but "gracious" servers who "make you feel like family" ensure
a "totally lovely experience."

Alegrias, Food From Spain *Spanish*   `23` `19` `23` `$35`

Marina | 2018 Lombard St. (bet. Fillmore & Webster Sts.) |
415-929-8888 | www.alegriassf.com
Recalling "a Madrid neighborhood hot spot", this "energetic" Spanish
"tapas tavern" in the Marina offers "authentic" decor and "reasonably priced" small plates that "pack a lot of variety in a single
meal"; it's "like visiting a private home in Spain", with its "kind"
and "genuine" service adding to an experience that "will make you
smile for sure."

The Alembic ● *Eclectic*   `23` `20` `19` `$35`

Haight-Ashbury | 1725 Haight St. (bet. Cole & Shrader Sts.) |
415-666-0822 | www.alembicbar.com
"Forgotten classic cocktails" pair with "inventive and new" "killer bar
bites" and "unusual" mains at this Eclectic "boutique" gastropub that
brings "a little Uptown" to the "Upper Haight"; while the "small" drinks
may not be "priced accordingly", and the "witty" bartenders may cop
a "too-cool attitude", the "sexy, dimly lit" haute-saloon setting is "perfect for a first or 100th date."

∄ Alexander's Steakhouse *Japanese/Steak*   `26` `25` `26` `$90`

SoMa | 448 Brannan St. (bet. 3rd & 4th Sts.) | 415-495-1111 |
www.alexanderssteakhouse.com
See review in South of San Francisco Directory.

Alfred's Steakhouse ⓈⓂ *Steak*   `23` `22` `23` `$60`

Downtown | 659 Merchant St. (bet. Kearny & Montgomery Sts.) |
415-781-7058 | www.alfredssteakhouse.com
"Deep leather booths", "bordello-red" decor and a "well-trained"
staff that's "been there forever" take you "back to the '50s" at this
"retro fabulous" Downtown steakhouse where the beef is "prepared
precisely as requested" and "huge" martinis inspire "gin-induced
good-old-boys camaraderie"; the "mandatory" "service surcharge"
irks some meat mavens, but most maintain it's still a "much better
deal than most."

Alice's *Chinese*   `20` `18` `19` `$23`

Noe Valley | 1599 Sanchez St. (29th St.) | 415-282-8999 |
www.alicesrestaurantsf.com
For a "refreshingly fresh take on Chinese" chow – "healthy-tasting"
fare full of "crisp" veggies – Noe Valley residents rely on this "really
popular" neighborhood spot; the "pleasant" staff provides "quick service" in the "smallish dining room", and since the "fab" food is "priced
right", it's a "longtime favorite" for takeout too.

	FOOD	DECOR	SERVICE	COST

Alioto's *Italian*
21 | 20 | 21 | $45

Fisherman's Wharf | 8 Fisherman's Wharf (Taylor St.) | 415-673-0183 | www.aliotos.com

It may be "smack-dab in the middle of touristville" (aka Fisherman's Wharf), but this "nostalgic" "landmark" still seduces locals, who "get crackin'" with crab and other "dependable" Sicilian-inflected seafood; though some call it "a bit overpriced", most maintain it's "kept its mojo" thanks to "polite", "old-fashioned" servers and "fantastic views" of the "fishing boats and the Golden Gate Bridge."

Allegro Romano 🅂 *Italian*
23 | 22 | 26 | $46

Russian Hill | 1701 Jones St. (B'way) | 415-928-4002 | www.allegroromano.com

Regulars recommend you "let Lorenzo", the "fun" and "funky" chef-owner, "be your guide to an authentic meal from Roma" at this "romantic" trattoria "hidden away" in Russian Hill; it's so "teeny-tiny" that it's "hard to get in", but the tenacious are rewarded with "amazing" Italian fare and perhaps some "little extras" like "a glass of port on the house."

Amasia Hide's Sushi Bar 🅂Ⅿ *Japanese*
▽ 25 | 21 | 23 | $24

Castro | 149 Noe St. (Henry St.) | 415-861-7000

"Excellent" sushi from a "talented" chef" earns kudos for this "cute little" Japanese joint in the Castro where an "attentive" staff brings "spot-on" specials (like "half-price hot sake") and fun games while you wait ("I'm a sucker for cat's cradle and origami" says one fan); gentle prices add to reasons patrons "love this place."

Ⓩ🅽🅴🆆 Amber Dhara *Indian*
24 | 22 | 21 | $36

Mission | 680 Valencia St. (18th St.) | 415-400-5699

Ⓩ Amber India *Indian*

SoMa | 25 Yerba Buena Ln. (bet. Market & Mission Sts.) | 415-777-0500
www.amber-india.com

See review in South of San Francisco Directory.

Ame *American*
26 | 24 | 25 | $77

SoMa | St. Regis | 689 Mission St. (3rd St.) | 415-284-4040 | www.amerestaurant.com

"Culinary enthusiasts" contend it's "worth dressing up" for a "special-occasion" meal at this "high-end" SoMa "destination" in the St. Regis where Terra owners Hiro Sone and Lissa Doumani proffer "gorgeously styled", "seriously delicious" (and "very expensive") New American cuisine infused with "Asian flavors" that's "graciously" served with an "over-the-top sake menu" and "exemplary wine list"; a "quiet", "minimalist" "Zen" setting that "feels like stepping into a meditation room" adds to the "appeal of a "memorable evening."

American Grilled Cheese Kitchen *American/Sandwiches*
23 | 16 | 19 | $14

SoMa | 1 S. Park Ave. (2nd St.) | 415-243-0107 | www.theamericansf.com

Fromage fans "say cheese" at the thought of "refreshingly grown-up" "ooey-gooey grilled sandwiches" paired with "perfect" "smoky" to-

	FOOD	DECOR	SERVICE	COST

mato soup; there's "limited seating" indoors and out and often "long lines", but fans are fond of the "friendly" service and fare that doesn't "break the bank"; P.S. breakfast and lunch only, plus it stays open till the first pitch of SF Giants home night games.

Americano *Italian*

21 | 23 | 20 | $43

Embarcadero | Hotel Vitale | 8 Mission St. (The Embarcadero) | 415-278-3777 | www.americanorestaurant.com

"Right on" the Embarcadero, with a "spectacular view" of the Bay Bridge, this "upscale" Italian inside the Hotel Vitale earns kudos for "creative" and "consistent" if "somewhat pricey" plates and servers who display "exactly the right amount of charm"; still, most surveyors stick to the "vibrant happy-hour scene", when "well-dressed" "law, financial and consulting types" mingle on the "lovely" "heated patio."

☑ Amici's East Coast Pizzeria *Pizza*

21 | 17 | 20 | $22

AT&T Park | 216 King St. (bet. 3rd & 4th Sts.) | 415-546-6666
Marina | 2200 Lombard St. (Steiner St.) | 415-885-4500
www.amicis.com

For "East Coast pizza", this "no-frills" Bay Area chain is "as good as it gets" say fans of the "big" NY-style pies and their "crispy", "charred thin crusts" (available in reduced-carb and gluten-free versions too); there's also a "variety of delicious options for those not in the pizza mood", so while some find it a "bit expensive" given "what you get", most dig the "friendly" staffers and "comfortable", "family-friendly" atmosphere.

Ana Mandara *Vietnamese*

23 | 25 | 22 | $50

Fisherman's Wharf | Ghirardelli Sq. | 891 Beach St. (Polk St.) | 415-771-6800 | www.anamandara.com

A "gorgeous" "Hollywood set–like space" and "tropical patio" make diners feel like they've "temporarily left SF" at this "high-end" Vietnamese in "touristy" Fisherman's Wharf, where the "delicious", "delicately spiced" fare completes the "transporting" experience; sure, it's "not as popular as it used to be", but service is "welcoming" and the "cozy" upstairs lounge always works when "you want to impress a date."

Anchor & Hope *Seafood*

22 | 21 | 21 | $42

SoMa | 83 Minna St. (bet. 1st & 2nd Sts.) | 415-501-9100 | www.anchorandhopesf.com

"Urban sophistication meets crab shack" at this "cavernous" "nautically themed" seafooder "tucked away" in a "converted garage space" in SoMa; "life-changing" lobster rolls and "really fresh" fish are matched by the "fantastic beer list" and "fun" "young" servers, but the "lively" ambiance is a bit much for some, who shout "the noise level is off the charts."

Anchor Oyster Bar *Seafood*

25 | 18 | 22 | $36

Castro | 579 Castro St. (bet. 18th & 19th Sts.) | 415-431-3990 | www.anchoroysterbar.com

"Why go to Fisherman's Wharf" ask fans of this "cute" vintage "oyster bar" with a "nautical motif" in the Castro that's a "pearl-in-the-ocean" for "chowda" and "simple" seafood "so fresh you'll swear it was made by the Little Mermaid"; it's "fairly pricey" and "seating is tight", but the "super-friendly" staff and "limited" list of "local white wines" ensure the "hungry hordes" leave "happy as clams."

Andalu *Eclectic*

| 22 | 20 | 20 | $35 |

Mission | 3198 16th St. (Guerrero St.) | 415-621-2211 | www.andalusf.com

Even "Brussels sprouts taste unbelievable" at this "Mission hipster" where "tasty" Eclectic small plates come "at a fair price"; the "bright" "corner location" is "great for groups", and though it's "noisy" "like a train station" with "slow" service when "packed", it remains a "lively" "favorite" for "sharing tapas" while sipping "seriously delicious" sangria (and $5 margaritas on Taco Tuesdays).

Angkor Borei *Cambodian*

| 23 | 17 | 21 | $24 |

Bernal Heights | 3471 Mission St. (Cortland Ave.) | 415-550-8417 | www.cambodiankitchen.com

"Authentic Khmer cuisine" – from "exquisite vegetarian" dishes to "shrimply divine" seafood – is "beautifully prepared" at this "affordable" Cambodian that's "a real find" in Bernal Heights; it's "not much to look at" say some, but "endearing" servers and a "quiet atmosphere" add up to a "relaxed" experience.

Anzu *Japanese*

| 23 | 22 | 23 | $55 |

Downtown | Hotel Nikko | 222 Mason St. (O'Farrell St.) | 415-394-1100 | www.restaurantanzu.com

"Picture-worthy plates" including sushi and "nicely seared" steaks share the menu at this "elegant" Californian-inspired Japanese joint "hidden" "on the second floor" of Downtown's Hotel Nikko; it's "lovely" for a "well-prepared" if "pricey" dinner and "meticulously crafted cocktails" "prior to a show at the Rrazz Room" downstairs, and though some find the "hotel setting" "a bit impersonal", the "polite" service is "lovely"; P.S. Sunday's jazz brunch is a big draw.

Aperto *Italian*

| 22 | 17 | 22 | $37 |

Potrero Hill | 1434 18th St. (Connecticut St.) | 415-252-1625 | www.apertosf.com

"Housemade pastas" and "specials that change with the seasons" attract Italian enthusiasts to this "lovely" trattoria that flies "under the radar" in Potrero Hill; a "homey" space that can get "a little cramped" is compensated by "always-pleasant servers", and since you can enjoy a "well-prepared meal without taking out a loan", locals just "wish every neighborhood could have a place like this."

NEW AQ Restaurant & Bar Ⓜ *Californian*

| 25 | 26 | 21 | $52 |

SoMa | 1085 Mission St. (7th St.) | 415-341-9000 | www.aq-sf.com

"You're in for a wonderful gastronomic treat" at this "fancy" new SoMa Californian where the "clever" "menu and decor change with the seasons"; surveyors say their "senses" are "uplifted" by the "refreshingly different", "masterfully prepared" fare, "beautiful", "arty" decor and "amazing cocktail pairings", so while a few suggest "service can get overwhelmed", most simply "can't wait to see what's in store" in the months ahead.

Ariake Japanese ☒ *Japanese*

26 | 19 | 22 | $36

Outer Richmond | 5041 Geary Blvd. (bet. 14th & 15th Aves.) | 415-221-6210 | www.sfariake.com

"Generous cuts" of "brilliantly fresh" sushi plus a "variety" of "gorgeous" "specialty rolls" and cooked dishes seduce surveyors at this "cozy" (and often "packed") Outer Richmond Japanese where regulars "forget the menu" and allow the "charming" chef-owner Jin Kim to choose for them; however, you really "can't go wrong with whatever you order", and best of all, prices "won't break the bank."

Arinell Pizza ⇗ *Pizza*

23 | 8 | 15 | $8

Mission | 509 Valencia St. (16th St.) | 415-255-1303

Some of the "best NYC pizza in SF" beckons "East Coast transplants" to these "gritty hole-in-the-wall" Mission and Berkeley chain links turning out "thin, greasy" "perfection" in an "authentic" "slice you can fold"; "loud punk music and a surly staff" complete the kit, which is a "great value" when a "craving" strikes.

☒ Arizmendi *Bakery/Pizza*

25 | 13 | 21 | $11

Inner Sunset | 1331 Ninth Ave. (bet. Irving & Judah Sts.) | 415-566-3117 | www.arizmendibakery.org ☒⇗
Mission | 1268 Valencia St. (24th St.) | 415-826-9218 | www.valencia.arizmendi.coop

This "outstanding" "worker-owned co-op" with five Bay Area locations turns out "crazy good" "thin-crust" pizzas (a different vegetarian version every day) alongside "fabulous" "artisanal breads and sweets"; "service can be a little slow", seating is "sparse" and the decor "needs improvement", but "who cares when the food is this yummy and the people are so kind"; P.S. you can always "take home a partially baked pizza."

Arlequin Cafe *Mediterranean*

21 | 18 | 18 | $19

Hayes Valley | 384 Hayes St. (bet. Franklin & Gough Sts.) | 415-626-1211 | www.arlequincafe.com

"Hidden away" in "bustling" Hayes Valley, the "delightful" patio is a "tranquil sanctuary" at this "casual" Med cafe next to "sister restaurant" Absinthe; "reasonably priced" "sandwiches, salads" and pastas are "prepared with love" by a "quick and courteous" staff, and the attached wine shop is an "added perk" when you want "excellent" vino.

☒ A16 *Italian*

25 | 21 | 22 | $46

Marina | 2355 Chestnut St. (bet. Divisadero & Scott Sts.) | 415-771-2216 | www.a16sf.com

"So good" they could rename it "A-1" say fans of this ever-"trendy" Marina trattoria popular for the likes of "blistered", "wood-fired" Neapolitan pizza, "astounding salumi" and "rustic" housemade pastas; the "narrow room" is "about as fast-paced, noisy and crowded as its namesake" Italian highway, but "knowledgeable" staffers help decipher the "lesser-known labels from Southern Italy", while an "open kitchen" provides "theatrical flair"; P.S. lunch is served Wednesday–Friday.

☒ Atelier Crenn ☒☒ *French*

27 | 24 | 26 | $134

Marina | 3127 Fillmore St. (bet. Filbert & Greenwich Sts.) | 415-440-0460 | www.ateliercrenn.com

"For that special night out", "soulful host" Dominique Crenn's "groundbreaking" Marina atelier truly "shines" presenting "mind-blowing", "visually beautiful" French tasting menus that employ all "the latest bells and whistles" of "molecular gastronomy" and "push culinary boundaries" while still "tasting divine"; service is "impeccable", and although the "minimalist" decor and "small portions with high price" are "not for the meat-and-potatoes crowd", smitten surveyors insist the chef's "scope and ambition" "leaves everyone" else in town behind.

Auntie April's   *Soul Food*
25 | **15** | **21** | **$15**

Bayview | 4618 Third St. (Oakdale Ave.) | 415-643-4983 | www.auntieaprils.com

Expect to see "super-friendly" "local girl" "Auntie April herself" cooking the "authentic down-home soul food" at this "charming" "treasure" in Bayview; it's "decidedly downscale" and the commercial district neighborhood's somewhat "sketchy", but "huge portions" of "crisp" fried chicken and waffles that are "cooked just right" cause regulars to "rave" about this "solid budget choice."

Axum Cafe   *Ethiopian*
▽ **21** | **15** | **19** | **$17**

Lower Haight | 698 Haight St. (Pierce St.) | 415-252-7912 | www.axumcafe.com

Ethiopian dishes of "quality (and quantity)" are spiced "just right" at this "go-to" locale for Lower Haight East African aficionados; although the ambiance "may be lacking" and a few call it "so-so", most maintain the "fantastically cheap eats" and "real" "family feel" make it "worth a visit."

Ayola   *Greek/Mediterranean*
22 | **12** | **20** | **$10**

Downtown | 327 Kearny St. (bet. Bush & Pine Sts.) | 415-391-1154
SoMa | 118 New Montgomery St. (Mission St.) | 415-348-0808 | www.ayolasf.com

Gyros are the heroes of these "solid", "inexpensive", "quick"-service Downtown and SoMa "lunch spots" doling out "fresh", "delicious" Greek-Mediterranean staples; there's "not much eat-in space" and "the lines get long", but "the wait is worth it" for what's arguably "the best falafel around"; P.S. no dinner.

☑ Aziza   *Moroccan*
26 | **22** | **25** | **$58**

Outer Richmond | 5800 Geary Blvd. (22nd Ave.) | 415-752-2222 | www.aziza-sf.com

"Genius" chef Mourad Lahlou takes Moroccan cooking "to the next level" at this somewhat "pricey" Outer Richmond "favorite", where the "exquisitely flavored" plates showcase "innovative" "Californian touches" and the "delicately concocted" cocktails "rock the casbah"; add to that "attentive but not smothering" service and "dark", "romantic" environs and devotees dub it a "nonstop wow"; P.S. closed Tuesday.

Baby Blues BBQ   *BBQ*
21 | **15** | **19** | **$25**

Mission | 3149 Mission St. (Precita Ave.) | 415-896-4250 | www.babybluessf.com

"Transport yourself to the Midwest" at this Mission BBQ "gem" doling out "large portions" of "out-of-this-world", "Memphis-style" brisket, "juicy" ribs and "wonderful" sides ("don't miss the cornbread") accompanied by "sweet, tangy, spicy" sauces; a "funky, fun atmosphere" and "shared tables" make one forget that "parking is a real pain"; though critics claim the relatively "expensive", "mediocre" 'cue "doesn't compare to Kansas City", the majority sigh "my God, it is delicious."

	FOOD	DECOR	SERVICE	COST

Bacco Ristorante *Italian*

24	21	24	$41

Noe Valley | 737 Diamond St. (bet. Elizabeth & 24th Sts.) | 415-282-4969 | www.baccosf.com

"It's always delightful" at this "charming", "quiet" neighborhood trattoria set "in a lovely old building" – "a taste and feel of Italy right here" in "out-of-the-way" Noe Valley; "you can't go wrong" with anything on the "pretty darn authentic" menu, but they're "known for" "exceptional" housemade pasta, "daily risotto" and "regional Italian wines", graciously proffered by a "superb staff" that treats guests "like extended family."

Bacon Bacon *Coffeehouse*

23	18	22	$14

Cole Valley | 205 Frederick St. (Ashbury St.) | 415-305-1968
Location varies; see website | 415-305-1968 ⓢ
www.baconbaconsf.com

"The name says it all" at this "fave food truck" and breakfast-only take-out coffeehouse in Cole Valley, where a staff that's "nothing but wonderful" serves "all bacon, all the time"; the "yummy porky goodness" is available any way "you can think of" – including "by the 'bouquet'", on "incredible" fries or "dipped in chocolate" – so even those who "feel guilty afterwards" aver it's a "genius idea."

Baker & Banker Ⓜ *American*

26	22	25	$59

Upper Fillmore | 1701 Octavia St. (Bush St.) | 415-351-2500 | www.bakerandbanker.com

"Excellent breads" and "diet-busting" desserts "made on-site" (and sold at the adjacent "bakery/sandwich shop") begin and end "an amazing meal" at this "laid-back" neighborhood Upper Fillmore bistro where the eponymous "husband-and-wife" owners turn out "exceptional" New American dinners and "to-die-for" Sunday brunch "worth" the "upscale" tabs; while the "homey" storefront with a "little wine bar in back" can get "loud" and "crowded", the "caring" service always "shines through."

Baker Street Bistro Ⓜ *French*

22	17	21	$38

Marina | 2953 Baker St. (bet. Greenwich & Lombard Sts.) | 415-931-1475 | www.bakerstreetbistro.com

"Unpretentious" and "delicious" Gallic fare is "a real treat" at this "very romantic" Marina bistro where an "interior of the most Parisian proportions" (i.e. "tiny") means the "tables are close together", but "lovely" sidewalk seating and staffers with "a legit French accent" create a "hospitable" vibe; adding to the attraction, the *"magnifique"* "prix fixe dinner", offered to "early birds" on weekends and until closing weeknights, is undoubtedly "a bargain."

Balboa Cafe *American*

20	19	21	$36

Cow Hollow | 3199 Fillmore St. (Greenwich St.) | 415-921-3944 | www.balboacafe.com

From "socialites and politicos" to "frat boys and sorority gals", this "convivial" "institution" in Cow Hollow (with a "more family-oriented" Mill Valley sibling) is "all about the bar and the people"; the city "scene" is "loud, loud, loud", while both offer a bistro setting and "solid" mid-priced American fare including "beyond addictive" burgers plus "amazing" "classic cocktails" and a "welcoming staff", luring "regulars" to "return time and time again."

	FOOD	DECOR	SERVICE	COST

Balompie Café *Salvadoran*

| 23 | 11 | 17 | $15 |

Mission | 3349 18th St. (Capp St.) | 415 648-9199 | www.balompiecafe.com
Order the "ripest platanos", "casamiento to die for" and "best pupu-sas in town" at this "down-to-earth" Mission Salvadoran where it's "too easy to overindulge"; service is "slow" and the "decor is nothing special" ("half dive bar/half cafeteria"), but it's "super cheap" and a "great place" for "hearty food and futbol"; P.S. "excellent greasy Central American breakfast" is served until 10 AM.

Bar Agricole *Californian*

| 23 | 25 | 21 | $50 |

SoMa | 355 11th St. (bet. Folsom & Harrison Sts.) | 415-355-9400 |
www.baragricole.com
"Inventive", "locavore" Californian dinners (and "not-to-be-missed brunch") "struggle for" "supremacy" with the "even better" "killer cock-tails" "hand-mixed" by "stylish bartenders" at this "stunning", "modern" SoMa sophomore "near the clubs" that's "so cool" "you kind of want to hate it"; "portions are a bit small for the price", but service is "great" and "you can't help but love" the "Zen" interior and "beautiful patio."

Barbacco ☒ *Italian*

| 24 | 22 | 22 | $42 |

Downtown | 220 California St. (Front St.) | 415-955-1919 |
www.barbaccosf.com
They sure "know how to please the palate" at this "super-cute" "Italian osteria", "little sister" to Perbacco next door, where "hearty pastas" and a "divine" salumi selection are some of the "clever creations" that Downtowners devour at the counter and "community tables"; add in an "eclectic wine list" displayed "on an iPad" (a "fun" touch) and the "contagious" "enthusiasm" of the "helpful" staff for additional reasons why it's "so busy all the time."

Bar Bambino ☒ *Italian*

| 24 | 21 | 21 | $48 |

Mission | 2931 16th St. (bet. Capp St. & S. Van Ness Ave.) |
415-701-8466 | www.barbambino.com
Offering an "interesting take on Italian food", this "trendy" cafe/ bar in the Mission "hits all the high notes" with "superb" "cured meats", "soul-warming" entrees and "top-notch" vino; the digs are rather "small" and tabs can "add up fast", but an "outstanding" staff and a "lovely back patio" create a "good vibe" that helps transcend a "gritty" locale; P.S. sister Pronto's kiosk at 3153 17th Street serves pastries and panini Wednesday–Friday from 10:30 AM–2:30 PM.

Bar Crudo Ⓜ *Seafood*

| 25 | 19 | 19 | $43 |

Western Addition | 655 Divisadero St. (Grove St.) | 415-409-0679 |
www.barcrudo.com
"Sublime" fin fare features "innovative" "raw preparations", hooking "trendy" "hipsters" at this Western Addition seafooder in a "minimalist" setting; the "fantastic beer list" offers "exciting" options to accompany your "fabulous fish chowder" or "brilliant crudo", and though service var-ies and "it's not cheap", the "happy hour is a tremendous value."

Bar Jules Ⓜ *American*

| 25 | 20 | 23 | $43 |

Hayes Valley | 609 Hayes St. (Laguna St.) | 415-621-5482 |
www.barjules.com
A "limited" "chalkboard menu and tumblers for wine glasses" set the tone for Jessica Boncutter's deceptively "simple", "neighborhood bis-

SoMa | 1489 Folsom St. (11th St.) | 415-552-3963
www.basilthai.com

Curry connoisseurs "Thai one on" at these midpriced SoMa siblings, where "top-notch" Asian-inspired cocktails "whet your appetite" for "beautifully presented" plates fans insist are better only "in Bangkok itself"; the "cool" spaces "pleasingly blend Eastern elements" with an "industrial aesthetic" and servers ensure you "feel more than welcome", but boy, it can be "loud."

Beach Chalet Brewery & Restaurant *American*

17	22	17	$32

Outer Sunset | 1000 Great Hwy. (bet. Fulton St. & Lincoln Way) | 415-386-8439 | www.beachchalet.com

"It's all about the view" say those, who "make the trek" to Outer Sunset to "ogle the ocean" from a "lovely old building" with "fantastic WPA murals in the lobby"; the consensus on the American fare is "decent but not memorable" and "service is shaky", but the "breathtaking" setting ("high-quality" "house-brewed" beer) "keeps people coming back."

Beast & The Hare Ⓜ *American/Californian*

24	20	21	$35

Mission | 1001 Guerrero St. (22nd St.) | 415-821-1001 | www.beastandthehare.com

It's not your typical "meat and potatoes joint", so "don't expect prime rib" at this "adventurous" Mission Cal-American where a "friendly"

dinner", less so on brunch-only
and wine selection; the "dark
rie" and the "beast of th
crew proffers "kille

CITY OF S

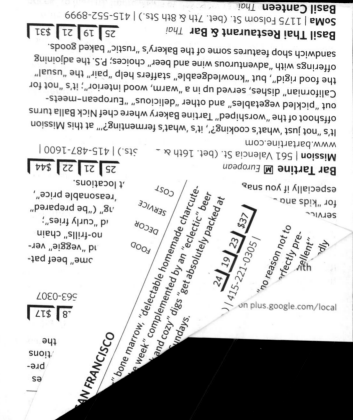

Basil Canteen *Thai*
SoMa | 1175 Folsom St. (bet. 7th & 8th Sts.) | 415-552-8999

Basil Thai Restaurant & Bar *Thai* | 25 | 19 | 21 | $31 |

...sandwich shop features some of the Bakery's "rustic" baked goods. offerings with "adventurous" wine and beer" choices; P.S, the adjoining the food rigid", but "knowledgeable" staffers help "pair" the "usual" Californian" dishes, served up in a "warm, wood interior"; it's "not for out "pickled vegetables" and other "delicious" "European–meets- offshoot of the "worshiped" Tartine Bakery where chef Nick Balla turns It's "not just what's cooking?", it's "what's fermenting?"" at this Mission www.bartartine.com

Bar Tartine *European* Ⓜ | 25 | 21 | 22 | $44 |
Mission | 561 Valencia St. (bet. 16th & ... Sts.) | 415-487-1600 |

... t locations. reasonable price", g" ("be prepared" d "curly fries"; no-frills" chain d "veggie" ver- ome" beef pat-

FOOD	DECOR	SERVICE	COST
24	19	23	$37

| 415-221-0305 |

... bone marrow, "delectable homemade charcute- ... week" complemented by an "eclectic" beer ... and cozy" digs "get absolutely packed at ... Sundays.

563-0307
| .8 | $17 |

on plus.google.com/local

SAN FRANCISCO

	FOOD	DECOR	SERVICE	COST

B44 *Spanish* — 22 | 18 | 20 | $40

Downtown | 44 Belden Pl. (bet. Bush & Pine Sts.) | 415-986-6287 | www.b44sf.com

Sitting "outside" on "quaint little" "pedestrian-only" Belden Place drinking "awesome" Iberian wines makes you "feel like you are in Barcelona" at this Downtown "paella paradise" serving "sensational" tapas and other "authentic Spanish cuisine"; "the tables are crammed quite closely together" in the "noisy" interior, but that and the owner's "infectious" enthusiasm only add to the "festive" "buzz."

Biergarten Ⓜ *German* — 23 | 21 | 19 | $19

Hayes Valley | 424 Octavia St. (bet. Fell & Linden Sts.) | 415-252-9289 | www.biergartensf.com

Suppenküche's "fabulous new" alfresco beer garden is like a "bit of Bavaria" in Hayes Valley, designed for "chowing down" on "delicious" pretzels and "authentic" German pub grub while "sipping a huge jug of beer" on "communal benches"; despite "long lines" and "embarrassingly slow" service, this "experiment" (tucked away nightly into shipping containers) is the "place to be" on a "sunny" "or even slightly chilly day (blankets are available)"; open Wednesday–Sunday, 3–9 PM.

⊉ Big 4 ☋ *American* — 24 | 27 | 26 | $62

Nob Hill | Huntington Hotel | 1075 California St. (Taylor St.) | 415-771-1140 | www.big4restaurant.com

Join the "men in suits drinking martinis" and "feel like a 19th-century railroad tycoon" at this "very civilized" (and "blessedly quiet") Nob Hill "special-occasion" "favorite" in a "classy", "old SF" setting of "dark wood" with green banquettes and "white tablecloths"; "amazing" service and "superbly prepared" American fare further justify "very expensive" tabs, but for a more moderate meal, "have a burger" and a "magic" cocktail in the "beautiful bar" with "nightly" "live" piano.

⊉ Bi-Rite Creamery *Bakery/Ice Cream* — 28 | 15 | 21 | $7

Mission | 3692 18th St. (Dolores St.) | 415-626-5600 | www.biritecreamery.com

It's "worth the fistful of Lactaid" and "miles long" wait at this Mission ice cream shop – SF's top Bang for the Buck – hawking "phenomenal" "organic" "creamy" "goodness" from "the usual to the exotic" ("two words": "salted caramel") "served by the nicest scoopers on the planet"; there's "not much room to sit", so savvy "junkies" "grab a pint" (and other "delicious desserts" from the small-batch bakery) or "go straight to the soft-serve window" to "get their fix."

Bistro Aix *Californian/French* — 24 | 21 | 23 | $42

Marina | 3340 Steiner St. (bet. Chestnut & Lombard Sts.) | 415-202-0100 | www.bistroaix.com

Regulars "love" this "highly affordable" Marina "mainstay", a "hidden gem" whose "superb", "simple", seasonal Cal-Provençal fare (plus a "mean burger") and "well-selected" wines are proffered by "friendly, helpful" servers in a "refreshing" "rustic interior"; it's a "fave" for a "romantic date or small group of friends" – just be sure to "reserve in the back 'garden' if you want to talk, not shout", with your companions.

Bistro Boudin *Californian*

| 22 | 20 | 20 | $31 |

Fisherman's Wharf | 160 Jefferson St. (Pier 43½) | 415-928-1849 |
www.bistroboudin.com

Though it's in "hyper-touristy Fisherman's Wharf", even locals are "seduced" "by the smell of sourdough" at this "second-floor" Californian situated "above the madding crowds" in its ground-level bakery; its "sublime view" of Alcatraz and "attentive" service are "definitely a welcome surprise", and the "fresh" seafood and "excellent version" of the iconic "clam chowder in a bread bowl" are "moderately priced" to boot.

Bistro Central Parc Ⓜ *French*

| 25 | 22 | 24 | $42 |

Western Addition | 560 Central Ave. (Grove St.) | 415-931-7272 |
www.bistrocentralparc.com

Regulars exchange "French-style cheek kisses" with the "fabulous" owner at this "friendly" bistro that's "a bit off the beaten path" in the Western Addition, serving "simple" yet "amazing" Gallic fare and "excellent" wines that won't "break the bank"; just "make sure" to reserve ahead for a "quiet", "romantic" dinner or "lovely" weekend brunch with "outdoor seating for sunny days."

Bix *American/French*

| 24 | 26 | 23 | $59 |

Downtown | 56 Gold St. (bet. Montgomery & Sansome Sts.) |
415-433-6300 | www.bixrestaurant.com

For a "swanky" "night on the town" or TGIF "martini" "business lunch", grab your doll and "swing" by this "Barbary Coast"–inspired supper club "tucked away in a back alley" Downtown where swells "sit at the bar" and absorb the "1930s ambiance" and "tuxed-out pianist" or head "upstairs" for "up-to-the-minute" American-French fare; it's a "class act all around" down to waiters in white jackets delivering "over-the-top service"; P.S. there's "live jazz", of course.

Blowfish Sushi To Die For *Japanese*

| 23 | 20 | 19 | $42 |

Mission | 2170 Bryant St. (20th St.) | 415-285-3848 |
www.blowfishsushi.com

"Enjoy dinner with a side of anime" at these "fun, hip" Mission and San Jose sushi outposts serving "creative sushi" and "exotic drinks" to a "younger crowd" that doesn't seem to mind the "noise"; fans who find it "overpriced" for "tiny" dinner portions go for the "daily lunch specials" "that won't kill your budget."

Blue Barn Gourmet *Californian*

| 25 | 19 | 19 | $16 |

Marina | 2105 Chestnut St. (Steiner St.) | 415-441-3232 |
www.bluebarngourmet.com

"Spectacular salads" full of "fresh organic" produce and "creatively concocted sandwiches" make a "hearty but healthy meal" at this "casual" Marina Californian where eating your veggies is "a treat"; it's a "little bit pricey" and there's "limited seating" in the "crowded" space with "cute" barnlike decor, so some suggest "call ahead and order takeout", which also shortens the "long wait."

Blue Bottle Café *Californian/Coffeehouse*

| 24 | 17 | 19 | $9 |

Embarcadero | Ferry Bldg. Mktpl. | 1 Ferry Bldg. (The Embarcadero) |
510-653-3394
SoMa | Mint Plaza | 66 Mint St. (Mission St.) | 510-653-3394

(continued)

Blue Bottle Kiosk ⌐ *Californian/Coffeehouse*
Hayes Valley | 315 Linden St. (Gough St.) | 510-653-3394
Rooftop Garden Blue Bottle
Coffee Bar *Californian/Coffeehouse*
SoMa | SFMOMA | 151 Third St. (bet. Howard & Mission Sts.) |
415-243-0455
www.bluebottlecoffee.net

Java junkies brave "crazy-long" queues to order "pricey" cups of "exquisite" "caffeine gold" from baristas who "make magic with coffee beans" at this cult chain; though a few "don't understand" the "extreme hype" and huff about the "hipper-than-thou" attitude, most maintain the "soul-satisfying" sips and "wonderful" pastries are "worth every minute" of the wait; P.S. some locations also serve a small menu of "fantastic" Californian breakfast and lunch fare.

Blue Plate *American*　　　　24 | 20 | 21 | $39
Mission | 3218 Mission St. (bet. 29th & Valencia Sts.) | 415-282-6777 |
www.blueplatesf.com

It "still rules the Outer Mission" declare devotees who "hate giving away the secret" of this "neighborhood favorite" cooking "consistently delicious", "homey" American "comfort food with a modern twist" (and made with "seasonal local ingredients"); a "top-notch" staff and "lovely garden" setting are added bonuses at this "diamond in the rough."

Bluestem Brasserie *Steak*　　　19 | 22 | 18 | $52
SoMa | 1 Yerba Buena Ln. (bet. 3rd & 4th Sts.) | 415-547-1111 |
www.bluestembrasserie.com

Between the "handsome bar area", "floor-to-ceiling windows" and "second-floor patio", this "swanky" steakhouse with an "urban" ambiance is a "wonderful" "find" for "generous" cocktails and "solid" New American fare, including "great grass-fed" beef; though it's "a bit pricey", it suits SoMa suits ready to "shake on a deal" over a "long lunch", even if the "personable" service is sometimes "a little slow."

Bobo's *Seafood/Steak*　　　　25 | 20 | 23 | $63
Fisherman's Wharf | 1450 Lombard St. (Van Ness Ave.) | 415-441-8880 |
www.boboquivaris.com

"Not your average steakhouse", thanks to the "wacky" (a few say "tacky"), "circus"-themed decor, this "surprising" Fisherman's Wharf meat and seafooder serves "sizable" portions of the likes of "perfectly cooked", "properly aged beef" and "out-of-this-world" "surf 'n' turf"; "prepare to spend a pretty penny", but count on "downing tasty cocktails" in an "intoxicating" setting graced with "exceptional service."

Bob's Steak & Chophouse *Steak*　22 | 22 | 23 | $65
Downtown | Omni Hotel | 500 California St. (Montgomery St.) |
415-273-3085 | www.bobs-steakandchop.com

Popular for business breakfasts, a "midday Manhattan" and "expense-account" lunch or an "after-work dinner" with Downtown "suits", this "pricey" "chain steakhouse" in the Omni Hotel is a "classy" setting proffering "tender" cuts of meat "cooked to perfection"; if some suggest it's "solid but not spectacular" and a smidge "stuffy", others find it a "pleasant" experience.

FOOD DECOR SERVICE COST

Bocadillos ⓧ *Spanish*
| 23 | 20 | 21 | $35 |

North Beach | 710 Montgomery St. (Washington St.) | 415-982-2622 | www.bocasf.com

Proffering "far more" than the "delicious", "well-priced" sandwiches for which it's named, Gerald Hirigoyen's all-day "modern" tapas bar in North Beach is a "favorite" for "inspired" Basque "shared plates" and "Spanish wines"; despite "no reservations" and "tight" space, "friendly" servers "always seem to find room for you" at the "convivial bar" or "communal tables" and the "party atmosphere" guarantees "a good night out."

Boccalone Salumeria *Sandwiches*
| 25 | 17 | 21 | $14 |

Embarcadero | Ferry Bldg. Mktpl. | 1 Ferry Bldg. (The Embarcadero) | 415-433-6500 | www.boccalone.com

"Choice" "craft charcuterie" from Chris Cosentino (Incanto) "rocks" at this Ferry Building pork "paradise" where "delicious" hot and cold panini and "OMG"-inducing cured meats are among the deli takeaway (unless you snag one of the four seats); "just take your Lipitor" (and wallet, as it's "pricey") and trust the "friendly" staffers to "know all things salumi" – "besides, who can argue with a cone of meat?"; P.S. closes 6 PM Monday–Saturday, 5 PM Sunday.

Bodega Bistro *Vietnamese*
| 24 | 14 | 22 | $32 |

Tenderloin | 607 Larkin St. (Eddy St.) | 415-921-1218

From "phantastic pho" to "French-inspired" Vietnamese fare to "Hanoi street food" "not found elsewhere", the eats are "amazing" at this "simple" Southeast Asian in the Tenderloin's "Little Saigon"; backers say it offers "better bang for the buck" than some competitors, and the "friendly" waiters "try very hard to please."

Boogaloos *Southwestern*
| 20 | 16 | 18 | $17 |

Mission | 3296 22nd St. (Valencia St.) | 415-824-4088 | www.boogaloossf.com

As "friendly to vegetarians, vegans and hipsters" as it is to everyday omnivores, this "trendy" Mission brunch spot "housed in an old pharmacy" has "a line around the block on weekends" for its Southwestern-influenced grub; fans swear the "unbeatable biscuits and gravy" and other "delicous" options are "worth" the "ridiculous wait", while foes cite "servers with attitudes", "loud music" and "so-so" grub as reasons to "go elsewhere."

Borobudur *Indonesian*
| 23 | 17 | 20 | $25 |

Nob Hill | 700 Post St. (Jones St.) | 415-775-1512 | www.borobudursf.com

Named for a Javanese Buddhist temple, this Indonesian is "a captivating alternative" to other Nob Hill haunts, where devotees declare each "vibrant-tasting" dish "is better than the next", from "authentic" "apps and soups" to the "amazingly generous" *rijsttafel* (rice-table dinners); it's "a good way to sample lots of traditional dishes", and if the setting is merely "modest", "moderate prices" and "friendly" servers convince most to "recommend it."

Bottle Cap Ⓜ *American*
| 18 | 15 | 19 | $38 |

North Beach | 1707 Powell St. (Columbus Ave.) | 415-529-2237 | www.bottlecapsf.com

Surveyors are split on this midpriced American that "replaced the long-standing Washington Square Bar & Grill"; fans call it a "welcome addition to North Beach", offering "inventive" cocktails and "tasty" "comfort food" with "great" live music in the "airy" dining room, while the less-impressed dub the digs "sterile" and say "pleasant" servers don't make up for "mediocre" fare; undebatable is the "outstanding location" on Washington Square Park.

NEW Bouche ●🏷🈂 *Californian/French* ▽ 24 | 22 | 21 | $44

Nob Hill | 603 Bush St. (Stockton St.) | 415-956-0396 | www.bouchesf.com

At this Nob Hill newcomer, "crazy-good" Cal-French "small plates to share or hoard" are accompanied by limited-production beers and wines and served by a "charming" staff until 1 AM; it's an "intimate" space with a "crowded bar area" overlooking the kitchen and "tight seating upstairs", but tables fashioned from old champagne riddling racks and kitschy animal bric-a-brac give it the vibe of a "hip, romantic" lair.

☒ Boudin Sourdough 22 | 19 | 19 | $18

Bakery *American/Sandwiches*

Downtown | 170 O'Farrell St. (Stockton St.) | 415-296-4740
Downtown | 619 Market St. (2nd St.) | 415-281-8200 🈂
Embarcadero | Embarcadero Ctr. | 4 Embarcadero Ctr., street level (Drumm St.) | 415-362-3330
Fisherman's Wharf | Pier 39 (Clay St.) | 415-421-0185
Parkside | 3251 20th Ave. (Buckingham Way) | 415-564-1849
www.boudinbakery.com

The "intoxicating" aroma of "freshly baked" loaves "entices" "carb lovers" into this bakery/cafe chain for "delicious" sandwiches and other "affordable" American eats, like "out-of-this-world" "creamy clam chowder in a hollowed-out sourdough round"; the "casual" "cafeteria-style" spots get "crowded", but "friendly" servers keep things moving "quickly"; P.S. at the "touristy" Fisherman's Wharf location, "kids will be amazed" watching the "skilled" bakers make "awesome" loaves in "different shapes."

Boulettes Larder *American* 26 | 18 | 21 | $35

Embarcadero | Ferry Bldg. Mktpl. | 1 Ferry Bldg. (The Embarcadero) | 415-399-1155 | www.bouletteslarder.com

"Superb" New American fare that "changes daily" according to what's "in season" is "never less than wow" (and Sunday brunch is "amazing") at this Ferry Building weekday breakfast-and-lunch spot and shop selling "lovely" prepared foods and ingredients "neatly displayed in apothecary-style jars"; sitting "at the communal table" is like "dining at the home of a truly great chef", so most forgive the "pricey" tab and sometimes "slow" service; P.S. plans are afoot to open Bouli Bar next door.

☒ Boulevard *American* 27 | 26 | 27 | $69

Embarcadero | Audiffred Bldg. | 1 Mission St. (Steuart St.) | 415-543-6084 | www.boulevardrestaurant.com

Chef-owner Nancy Oakes remains the "boss of fine dining" at her "dress-to-impress" "belle epoque" Embarcadero flagship (with a "Bay view to boot") which "works like a fine Swiss watch", proffering "magnificent, refined" American fare and "superb" wines via a "top-notch" staff; everyone from lunching "conventioneers" to "celebrities" assures it's "always crowded" and "noisy", while "year in and year out" it serves as a "go-to" for "power dinners or a romantic night out" – yes, it's "expensive, but oh so worth it."

Bourbon Steak *Steak*
24 | 23 | 24 | $85

Downtown | Westin St. Francis | 355 Powell St. (bet. Geary & Post Sts.) | 415-397-3003 | www.michaelmina.net

You may have to "save up" to visit Michael Mina's "classy", "dimly lit" Downtown steakhouse in the Westin St. Francis, but the "excellent cuts of meat" "prepared to perfection", "epic wine list" (plus "mean" cocktails) and "first-rate staff" add up to a "classy" "dining experience" for "special occasions" or "business"; and "when a restaurant serves you a trio of fries and dipping sauces instead of bread service, it's already a win."

Boxing Room *Cajun/Creole*
21 | 21 | 22 | $43

Hayes Valley | 399 Grove St. (Gough St.) | 415-430-6590 | www.boxingroomsf.com

"Every day is Mardi Gras" at this "lively" Hayes Valley "ragin' Cajun"-Creole cranking out "killer", "NOLA-worthy" "Southern-fried goodness" (read: "heavy" and "spicy") with a "Californian sensibility"; the "modern" digs "do little to recall the Old South", but the staff's "hospitality" and a "sweeping bar" pouring "well-priced" wine and beer ensure "good times", plus "where else can you get alligator?"

Brandy Ho's *Chinese*
21 | 16 | 18 | $25

Castro | 4068 18th St. (bet. Castro & Hartford Sts.) | 415-252-8000
Chinatown | 217 Columbus Ave. (bet. B'way & Pacific Ave.) | 415-788-7527
www.brandyhos.com

Some prefer this Chinese duo's "original" Chinatown location, where "the decor needs serious updating" but you can "sit at the counter" and watch your meal "prepared in giant woks over huge flames", while others favor the more "modern" "Castro outlet"; regardless, the "consistent" "no-MSG" chow ranging "from mild to off-the-charts" hot will "satisfy" your Hunan "cravings" at an "affordable" price.

NEW Brasserie S&P *Californian*
- | - | - | M
(fka Silks)

Downtown | Mandarin Oriental Hotel | 222 Sansome St. (bet. California & Pine Sts.) | 415-986-2020 | www.mandarinoriental.com

This Californian-inspired brasserie in FiDi's tony Mandarin Oriental serves a midpriced menu of eclectic small plates and entrees, while offering a bar with a section entirely devoted to gin and tonics (but there's plenty of beer, wine and bourbon too); the room – decidedly more casual than its predecessor, Silks – is decorated in neutral hues, with floor-to-ceiling windows overlooking the plaza outside.

Brazen Head ◑⌦ *American*
21 | 20 | 21 | $37

Cow Hollow | 3166 Buchanan St. (Greenwich St.) | 415-921-7600 | www.brazenheadsf.com

Whether you're on "a first date" or having a "classic" cocktail with your spouse, you'll "feel like you're having an affair" at this "dark" and "clubby" Cow Hollow American with a "secretive" air (and "no sign outside"); a "solid" menu of "reasonably priced" American fare, like "sumptuous" steak and burgers, is "served late into the night" (until 1 AM), but "don't forget your cash", because they don't take credit cards.

Brenda's French Soul Food *Creole/Southern*   25 | 18 | 20 | $24

Civic Center | 652 Polk St. (bet. Eddy & Turk Sts.) | 415-345-8100 |
www.frenchsoulfood.com

"If you miss NOLA, run", don't "walk", to this "tiny" Civic Center "joint",
where fans "line up" for "comfort Creole", from "super-creative" beignets to the "favorite" shrimp and grits, all served by a "hospitable" staff;
known for "superb" Southern breakfasts and brunches at a "low" price,
it's "now open for dinner" Wednesday–Saturday too, and a recent expansion has made the "longish wait" "much shorter"; P.S. breakfast
served Sunday until 8 PM.

Broken Record ●🕏 *Soul Food*   24 | 14 | 17 | $18

Excelsior | 1166 Geneva Ave. (Naples St.) | 415-963-1713 |
www.brokenrecordsanfrancisco.com

"The secret is out" about this "laid-back" "dive bar" in Excelsior, where
the "extraordinary" soul food cranked out by the "small kitchen" is a
"wonderful surprise"; they don't "take plastic" for the "cheap" chow, and
it's "crazy-crowded" on the "spacious" "outdoor patio", but the "good-
natured staff" and an "impressive" "whiskey selection" soften the blow.

Brother's Korean Restaurant ● *Korean*   24 | 11 | 16 | $31

Inner Richmond | 4128 Geary Blvd. (bet. 5th & 6th Aves.) | 415-387-7991
This "family-style" DIY Seoul fooder in the Inner Richmond was "pop-
ping" long "before Korean BBQ became popular" and still racks up "long
waits" for its "habit-forming" "mounds" of "finely marinated meats"
cooked over "real charcoal"; it's a "hole-in-the-wall" and service can be
lacking, plus you'll leave "smelling like smoke", but "prices are reasonable" considering it comes with "amazing" "complementary panchan."

B Star Bar *Asian*   25 | 18 | 21 | $28

Inner Richmond | 127 Clement St. (bet. 2nd & 3rd Aves.) |
415-933-9900 | www.bstarbar.com

"Fabulous" "fusion-y" Pan-Asian fare "bursts" with "huge flavor" at this
"prettier younger sister" of Burma Superstar in the Inner Richmond, serving some of its sibling's "best" Burmese dishes without the "crowds" and
"mile-long lines"; it also wins praise for "courteous" service, "reasonable
prices" and "fancy" "soju cocktails", and though some sigh "the magic"
of the original "is missing", it's "nice to be able to make reservations."

Ⓩ Buca di Beppo *Italian*   18 | 19 | 19 | $27

SoMa | 855 Howard St. (bet. 4th & 5th Sts.) | 415-543-7673 |
www.bucadibeppo.com

Bring a "big appetite and lots of friends", because the "family-style"
servings of "garlicky" Italian eats come in "epic" portions at this "crazy,
upbeat" (and "reasonably priced") "party place"; fans find the "kid-
friendly" chain a "guilty pleasure" and "never go home without" "a wide
smile", but dissenters ding the "noisy" digs and "pedestrian" pastas.

Buckhorn Grill *American*   22 | 15 | 18 | $17

Downtown | 101 Fourth St. (Howard St.) | 415-369-6150
Downtown | Westfield San Francisco Ctr. | 845 Market St.,
concourse level (bet. 4th & 5th Sts.) | 415-978-9770
www.buckhorngrill.com

"Perfectly prepared tri-tip" – "super-tender" and "nicely seasoned" –
and other meat-centric menu items come in sandwiches, on platters

FOOD | DECOR | SERVICE | COST

and in "huge", "hearty" salads that are "more than a meal" at this "cheap and cheerful" American trio Downtown and in Emeryville; they're "nothing fancy", but service is "fast" and "friendly", and you get a lot of bang "for your buck."

Bund Shanghai Restaurant *Chinese*   ▽ 24 | 13 | 21 | $23

Chinatown | 640 Jackson St. (bet. Kearny St. & Wentworth Plaza) | 415-982-0618

"Brave" (or just adventurous) eaters who "explore the entire menu" at this off-the-radar Chinatown locale will be rewarded with both dim sum delicacies and "authentic Shanghai cuisine", from some of the "best soup dumplings in town" to more unusual specialties; "service can be slow" but it exudes "genuine" "hospitality", and prices are "reasonable."

Bun Mee *Vietnamese*   19 | 16 | 17 | $15

Upper Fillmore | 2015 Fillmore St. (Pine St.) | 415-800-7696 | www.bunmee.com

With "a perfect balance" of "tasty" meat and veggies "folded into warm, crisp baguettes", the "high-quality" banh mi served at this Upper Fillmore eatery are a "fancy-pants version" of those available at "your average Vietnamese" go-to; they might be a bit "more expensive", but "you're paying" for the setting, a "delightfully retro" "little" "sliver of a cafe", as well as an "expansive" menu of salads and "amazing" sides, all served by a "friendly" staff.

Burger Bar *Burgers*   20 | 19 | 18 | $28

Downtown | Macy's | 251 Geary St., 6th fl. (bet. Powell & Stockton Sts.) | 415-296-4272 | www.burger-bar.com

"Build the burger of your dreams" with a "wide variety" of toppings at celebrity chef Hubert Keller's hamburger "heaven" inside the Downtown Macy's; "amazing" "milkshakes (alcoholic or otherwise)" and an "awesome view of Union Square" for those who "snag a window seat" add an "upscale" vibe, but critics complain the "touristy" chain is "a bit overpriced", especially in light of sometimes "slow service."

Burger Joint *Burgers*   19 | 16 | 18 | $15

AT&T Park | 242 King St. (bet. 3rd & 4th Sts.) | 415-371-1600
Mission | 807 Valencia St. (19th St.) | 415-824-3494
www.burgerjointsf.com

Fans frequent this Bay Area mini-chain for a "quick-service", "solid burger" made from "high-quality" Niman Ranch beef and "cooked how you want it"; "good milkshakes and fries round out an inexpensive meal" that "beats the fast-food options."

BurgerMeister *Burgers*   20 | 15 | 18 | $16

Castro | 138 Church St. (Duboce Ave.) | 415-437-2874
Cole Valley | 86 Carl St. (Cole St.) | 415-566-1274
North Beach | 759 Columbus Ave. (Greenwich St.) | 415-296-9907
www.burgermeistersf.com

"Big sloppy" burgers, "crisp fries" and "top-notch" milkshakes "hit the spot" at this "consistent" and "kid-friendly" Bay Area chain; the Niman Ranch patties are "better than fast-food" versions and "reasonably priced" to boot, though some note "hit-or-miss" service and suggest you won't want to "linger" since there's "not much atmosphere."

☑ Burma Superstar *Burmese*

FOOD	DECOR	SERVICE	COST
25	17	21	$26

Inner Richmond | 309 Clement St. (4th Ave.) | 415-387-2147 | www.burmasuperstar.com

"Bold" Burmese, like the "endlessly complex and addictive" tea-leaf salad, "will knock your socks off" at this "loud" trio where "courteous" servers are "helpful" to newcomers "uninitiated" into the "exotic" menu; while it beats the "trip to Rangoon", expect "ridiculous" lines at the Inner Richmond original ("you don't have to wait as long" at the East Bay offshoots) and a "cramped", "simple" setting.

Burmese Kitchen ☒ *Burmese*

FOOD	DECOR	SERVICE	COST
23	15	22	$19

Tenderloin | 452 Larkin St. (bet. Golden Gate Ave. & Turk St.) | 415-474-5569 | www.burmesekitchen.com

"Why wait in line" at more popular Myanmar hot spots when this "cozy", "casual" Tenderloin "alternative" serves "outstanding" Burmese bites "at awesomely inexpensive prices"; it doesn't have much atmosphere, but the "hardworking" staff is "so nice", and it's "great for takeout" and "delivery" too.

NEW Burritt Tavern *American*

FOOD	DECOR	SERVICE	COST
-	-	-	M

Downtown | Mystic Hotel | 417 Stockton St. (Sutter St.) | 415-400-0561 | www.burritttavern.com

Charlie Palmer's stylish new Downtown project, perched on the second floor of the Mystic Hotel and adjacent to its popular cocktail den Burritt Room, turns out moderately priced American steaks and seafood showcasing Bay Area larder; the speakeasy-style room is outfitted with clandestine curtained booths, dark wood wainscoting and vintage monochrome photos of the city.

Buster's Cheesesteak ● *Cheesesteaks/Burgers*

FOOD	DECOR	SERVICE	COST
22	13	20	$11

North Beach | 366 Columbus Ave. (Vallejo St.) | 415-392-2800 | www.busters-sf.com

"Only vegetarians" "could resist" the "tender", "juicy" cheesesteaks with "lots" of "options" (including "classic" Cheez Whiz) and "on-point" burgers at this "bargain" for Philly-style eats; though principally a "take-out joint", a few counter and sidewalk seats make it a "phenomenal" choice after hitting the North Beach bars "late at night" (open until at least 2:30 AM nightly).

Butler & The Chef Bistro Ⓜ *French*

FOOD	DECOR	SERVICE	COST
22	18	17	$22

SoMa | 155 South Park Ave. (bet. 2nd & 3rd Sts.) | 415-896-2075 | www.butlerandthechef.com

Francophiles "squeeze" into "tiny" tables at this "cozy" SoMa bistro for "classic French" breakfasts and lunch; expect a "long wait" for your "delicious" coffee and "incredible" croque monsieur (especially "on the weekends"), and the "Gallic staff can be snooty at times", but with a location facing "darling South Park", it's "absolutely lovely nonetheless."

Butterfly Ⓜ *Asian/Californian*

FOOD	DECOR	SERVICE	COST
23	23	22	$43

Embarcadero | Pier 33 (Bay St.) | 415-864-8999 | www.butterflysf.com

"Snag a window seat", because this Embarcadero eatery with a "delightful bay view" "never disappoints" with its "well-made" cocktails and "inventive" Cal-Asian cuisine served by an "attentive" staff; though a few find the tab "pricey" and note some "misses on the menu", at least the "excellent happy hour" is an "awesome" deal.

Café Bastille *French*

20	18	19	$37

Downtown | 22 Belden Pl. (bet. Bush & Pine Sts.) | 415-986-5673 |
www.cafebastillesf.com

Paris partisans longing for "the Left Bank" are willingly taken "captive prisoner" at this "charming" Downtowner that's "cozy" inside and "festive" outside, where tables line a "lively" pedestrian alleyway; "friendly" waiters with a "French accent" serve "basic" but "delicious" Gallic bistro fare that's a "treat" when you want a lot of "bang for the buck."

Café Bunn Mi ⊅ *Sandwiches/Vietnamese*

▽ 24	17	20	$13

Inner Richmond | 417 Clement St. (6th Ave.) | 415-668-8908

Not just a "hip new place" for "very affordable" bahn mi sandwiches, this "friendly" Inner Richmonder is also "popular" for its "modern" takes on Vietnamese vittles, from "healthy pho" to "delicious" soups filled "with flavor"; seating is "tight" and you might have to "hover" "for a table", so anxious eaters cope by "calling in" their order and "taking it to go"; P.S. cash only.

Café Claude *French*

22	20	21	$42

Downtown | 7 Claude Ln. (bet. Bush & Sutter Sts.) | 415-392-3515 |
www.cafeclaude.com

For an "authentic" experience "without having to exchange" dollars into Euros, Francophiles head for this "intimate" bistro "tucked away" in a Downtown alley; purists are "delighted" by the "simple" menu of "expertly prepared" "classic French" fare "expeditiously served" by waiters with "adorable" accents; "compatible" prices and "live jazz" Thursday–Saturday seal its status as a "romantic" "date spot."

Café de la Presse *French*

20	20	19	$35

Downtown | 352 Grant Ave. (bet. Bush & Sutter Sts.) | 415-249-0900 |
www.cafedelapresse.com

"Homesick French expats" and "tourists alike" assemble at this "bustling" Downtown bistro that's "exactly like a Parisian sidewalk cafe" (except the "staff is friendlier" here); "breakfast, lunch and dinner" offer a "great selection" of Gallic "favorites" at moderate prices, but some prefer simply to "sit outside" and "linger over espresso" and one of the "foreign newspapers" for sale.

Café des Amis *French*

19	24	20	$50

Cow Hollow | 2000 Union St. (Buchanan St.) | 415-563-7700 |
www.cafedesamissf.com

You "could not ask for better ambiance" at this "beautiful", "bustling" Union Street brasserie that's crammed with a "good-looking" crowd and reminds some of "a Toulouse Lautrec painting"; the service and "straight-up, well-executed" French classics offered from lunch till "late-night" are "mostly desirable", though a few say that "given the price", the experience is "missing" that certain je ne sais quoi.

Cafe Divine *American/Sandwiches*

▽ 21	22	20	$30

North Beach | 1600 Stockton St. (Union St.) | 415-986-3414 |
www.cafedivinesf.com

With its "high ceilings" and "big windows" showcasing the "view of Washington Square", this "laid-back" North Beach cafe "lives up to its name", especially if you "sit outside" or arrive during the live music offered "some nights"; the "eclectic" American menu, from sandwiches to "pizzas and salads" and more, is "well executed", and "prices are more than fair", so fans don't mind if "friendly" service is sometimes "slow."

Cafe Jacqueline M *French* 27 | 20 | 22 | $50

North Beach | 1454 Grant Ave. (bet. Green & Union Sts.) | 415-981-5565

Devotees declare "you will never find a better soufflé, savory or sweet" than the "made-to-order" "dairy puffs of love" at this "romantic" North Beach French "haunt" that "hasn't changed in 30 years"; it's "not a quick meal", and even with "puffed-up" prices and "attitude", "the experience" of seeing "adorable" Jacqueline Margulis "still beating them in the kitchen" "cannot be beat."

Café Tiramisu *Italian* 22 | 19 | 21 | $43

Downtown | 28 Belden Pl. (bet. Bush & Pine Sts.) | 415-421-7044 | www.cafetiramisu.com

"One of the stars" of Downtown's "charming" Belden Place, this "reasonably priced" ristorante offers "classic" Northern Italian fare including "a wonderful array of desserts"; "go on a sunny day", "sit outside" and "try the house Chianti" for a "convivial" experience suggest supporters who appreciate "personalized" service by the "attentive" staff.

Cafe Zoetrope *Italian* 20 | 21 | 20 | $35

North Beach | 916 Kearny St. (Columbus Ave.) | 415-291-1700 | www.cafecoppola.com

"Don't be surprised" if you see owner Francis Ford Coppola himself "relaxing at one of the outdoor tables" of this "cute" North Beach Italian "icon" where you can order "pretty much any" of the filmmaker's wines to accompany midpriced fare such as "wonderful thin-crust pizza", "delicious" pastas and "dreamy" desserts; a "friendly" staff completes the "delightful" vibe.

Caffè Macaroni S *Italian* ▽ 21 | 17 | 22 | $28

North Beach | 124 Columbus Ave. (Jackson St.) | 415-956-9737 | www.caffemacaroni.com

Chef/co-owner "Mario and his delightful wife, Stephanie", "have a knack" for "making you feel as if they are cooking and serving" "just for you" at this "super-reasonable" North Beach nook offering "robust" Southern Italian fare "reminiscent of his native Naples"; whether you've snagged an "outdoor" table or are in the "small", "casual" interior, it delivers a "pasta fix."

Cajun Pacific S M *Cajun* ▽ 25 | 18 | 21 | $32

Outer Sunset | 4542 Irving St. (47th Ave.) | 415-504-6652 | www.cajunpacific.com

"There's not much to look at in the way of decor", but the "cult following" of this tiny spot says the "great Cajun eats in the outerlands" of the Outer Sunset "more than make up for" that; it's "only open three days a week" (Thursday–Saturday), so be prepared to "make reservations" and "be patient" until the "lone server can take your order."

Campanula *American* ▽ 19 | 18 | 21 | $40

North Beach | 701 Union St. (Powell St.) | 415-829-7766 | www.campanulasf.com

"Hidden" on a North Beach corner, this New American bistro from the owners of Frascati is "a cut above" its "old-line" neighbors and makes

| | FOOD | DECOR | SERVICE | COST |

a "nice place to meet friends, share a few small plates" and enjoy "people-watching" through the "large windows"; the "gentle care" taken with the midpriced fare and "friendly", "helpful" staff help explain why it's a "neighborhood go-to" for those "in the know."

Campton Place *Californian/Mediterranean* 26 | 25 | 25 | $80
Downtown | Taj Campton Pl. Hotel | 340 Stockton St. (Sutter St.) | 415-781-5555 | www.camptonplacesf.com
More "white-glove" than "cutting-edge", this "high-end" "oasis" off Union Square "transports diners to nirvana" via "topflight" Cal-Med à la carte and tasting menus and "impressive" wines delivered with "highly professional" service in an "elegant", "formal" room where patrons "can actually carry on a conversation"; "if you're going to splurge", it's a "winning place" to host "that special evening", "amazing lunch" or "power breakfast" – while the clubby bar offers more casual bistro fare.

NEW Canela *Spanish* 24 | 20 | 22 | $35
Castro | 2272 Market St. (bet. Noe & Sanchez Sts.) | 415-552-3000 | www.canelasf.com
The Castro dining scene "is looking up" thanks to the "surprisingly delicious" Spanish fare at this newcomer on Market offering "tip-top tapas" and entrees such as paella plus "interesting" domestic and Iberian wines including "lots of half bottles" – all at "reasonable prices"; the digs are "lovely", the service "friendly" and the owners are "wonderful hosts", while the spot gets props as a "nice break from traditional" options.

Canteen Ⓜ *Californian* 27 | 15 | 21 | $49
Tenderloin | Commodore Hotel | 817 Sutter St. (bet. Leavenworth & Jones Sts.) | 415-928-8870 | www.sfcanteen.com
"It's a diner with a kitchen about the size of a closet" and "laid-back service", but Dennis Leary's Tenderloin "treasure" prepares "creative" Californian dinners (including Tuesday and Saturday prix fixes) "as good as many fine-dining establishments", at prices that are "even better"; fans prefer sitting at the counter to "watch the chef in action" and if malcontents "can't get past" the "minuscule" quarters, that's ok, as it's already "too difficult to get a reservation."

Capannina *Italian* 26 | 21 | 24 | $47
Cow Hollow | 1809 Union St. (Octavia St.) | 415-409-8001 | www.capanninasf.com
"Generous portions" of "innovative" Italian eats are "made with love" at this "cozy" Cow Hollow trattoria, where "hospitable" waiters are "happy to explain every fantastic dish"; the tables might be "too close together", but it's still "homey enough to be your neighborhood hangout", and the "prix fixe three-course dinner before 6 PM" is a "great" deal on their already "reasonable" menu.

NEW Castagna *French* ▽ 26 | 19 | 23 | $65
Marina | 2015 Chestnut St. (Fillmore St.) | 415-440-4290 | www.castagnasf.com
Run by the brothers behind shuttered Restaurant Cassis, this "great" new casual bistro gives "chic" Marina District diners "something to write home about" – French classics along with a "good" selection of wines; the petite, nautically themed storefront, navigated by an "excellent" crew, is also open during the day for quick-service lunch and brunch.

Catch *Seafood*
22 | 22 | 22 | $40

Castro | 2362 Market St. (bet. Castro & 16th Sts.) | 415-431-5000 | www.catchsf.com

"Fresh" fin fare (some swimming in "delectable" sauces) has surveyors declaring this "trendy" Castro seafooder is indeed "a catch"; the menu is "nothing fancy" and "not the cheapest", but a "great" cocktail list, "helpful" waiters who are "hotter than the food" and a "cozy" heated courtyard with an outdoor fireplace make it a "people-watching" paradise.

NEW Catheads BBQ *BBQ*
- | - | - | I

SoMa | 1665 Folsom St. (13th St.) | 415-599-6298 | www.catheadsbbq.com

"Top-notch" barbecue is on hand at this affordable new SoMa brick-and-mortar outpost of a popular pop-up, where the likes of "ribs and brisket and fixin's" riff on Midwest and Southern specialties; locally sourced meats piled onto sandwiches and combo plates (or sold by the pound) come with homemade sauces and have early adopters assuring the location's former tenant, 'cue fixture Big Nate, "would be proud."

NEW Cedar Hill *Southern*
▽ 17 | 16 | 19 | $24

Marina | 3242 Scott St. (bet. Chestnut & Lombard Sts.) | 415-834-5403 | www.cedarhillsf.com

"Great smells from the wood smoke" fill the air at this new Marina "haven for meat eaters" serving "tasty" Southern vittles such as Memphis-style ribs and a brisket sandwich; the narrow digs are decked out with mason jar chandeliers, and though service varies at this early stage, the grub's "definitely decent for these here parts."

NEW Central Kitchen *Californian*
- | - | - | M

Mission | 3000 20th St. (Florida St.) | 415-826-7004 | www.centralkitchensf.com

There's no pizza or pasta at this Mission spin-off from the Flour + Water team, just a compact menu of midpriced, locally sourced Californian cuisine gussied up with modern techniques (foams, sous vide, dehydrators); while the fare veers toward fine dining, the vibe decidedly does not: rock music blares overhead in a small black-and-white room overlooking an exhibition kitchen, while a semi-covered heated patio with communal wood tables plays host to drop-ins in the back; P.S. the adjacent daytime-only Salumeria offers a selection of lunchtime sandwiches plus grocery items such as oils and honeys.

Cha Am Thai *Thai*
21 | 16 | 20 | $23

SoMa | Museum Parc | 701 Folsom St. (3rd St.) | 415-546-9711 | www.chaamthaisf.com

You "can't go wrong with anything you order" at this "reliable" Thai twosome, whether eating at the "quaint" original "in a funky converted house" in "Berkeley's Gourmet Ghetto" or its "spacious" (separately owned) SoMa sib near Moscone Center that "caters to the convention crowd"; true, service can be "spotty", but they're "affordable" options.

Cha Cha Cha *Caribbean*
22 | 20 | 18 | $27

Haight-Ashbury | 1801 Haight St. (Shrader St.) | 415-386-7670
Mission | 2327 Mission St. (bet. 19th & 20th Sts.) | 415-824-1502
www.cha3.com

"More or less an institution", this midpriced trio with two longtime SF locations and one "much-needed" newer San Mateo branch serves "some seriously deelish grub" by way of tapas seemingly "straight from the Caribbean" and made for washing down with rather "deadly" sangria; popular with "young" groups, the vibe's "loud and lively", service varies and there's "always a wait", but add in "kitschy" "Day of the Dead" decor, and it's a "trip south with no passport needed."

The Chairman Truck 🗷Ⓜ *Chinese*　24 | 13 | 18 | $11
Location varies | 415-813-8800
The "Chairman can rule my world any day" declare devotees who "follow" this Chinese truck for "nicely turned out" dim sum, like the "transcendent" pork belly bun with "just the right amount of spices, crunchy veggies and a mouthwatering sauce"; the "little morsels" are relatively "pricey", and "sometimes long lines" leave you to "freeze your buns off in the SF fog", but it's "well worth" the wait.

☒ Chapeau! *French*　27 | 21 | 25 | $55
Inner Richmond | 126 Clement St. (bet. 2nd & 3rd Aves.) | 415-750-9787 | www.chapeausf.com
Each "exquisite" dish is "perfectly executed" and the wine list is "terrific" at this "lovely" Gallic bistro where "charming" chef Philippe does "away with snooty French stereotypes" by sending the ladies "off with a kiss on each cheek"; though a few fret about "elbow-to-elbow" seating, it's worth the "drive across town" to the Inner Richmond when you "want to feel special" "without breaking the piggy bank" (the "early-bird" specials are an especially "tremendous value").

Chaya Brasserie *French/Japanese*　23 | 22 | 21 | $51
Embarcadero | 132 The Embarcadero (Mission St.) | 415-777-8688 | www.thechaya.com
"French and Japanese" cuisines "come together" at this "stylish" hybrid on the Embarcadero with a "spectacular" Bay Bridge view; the "inventive" menu, from "fresh" sushi to more "eclectic" fare fashioned from the "highest-quality ingredients", may be "pricey" for "small portions", but "impressive" cocktails served by the "knowledgeable" staff placate the "post-work crowd" drawn to the "awesome" all-evening happy hour in the "lively" bar.

Cha-Ya Vegetarian Japanese Restaurant ⌘ *Japanese/Vegan*　23 | 14 | 18 | $22
Mission | 762 Valencia St. (bet. 18th & 19th Sts.) | 415-252-7825
An "absence of pretension and meat" defines this Mission and Berkeley duo offering "expertly prepared" and "unusual" Japanese vegan and "vegetarian treats" that are "delicious and surprisingly filling"; though the "decor leaves a lot to be desired", and flavor-seekers find the fare "a bit bland", it's "popular with a young crowd" that goes for the "reasonably priced" "Zen experience."

☒ Cheesecake Factory *American*　21 | 21 | 20 | $28
Downtown | Macy's | 251 Geary St., 8th fl. (bet. Powell & Stockton Sts.) | 415-391-4444 | www.thecheesecakefactory.com
With a menu that "competes in length with *War and Peace*", this "always packed" go-to – SF's No. 1 chain – dishes out "flavorful" midpriced American fare in portions so "gargantuan", many take their "scrumptious" signature cheesecake "home in a bag"; "long" waits and "over-

the-top" decor deter detractors, who call the "calorific" eats "uninspired", but they're outnumbered by "crowds" of admirers dubbing it a "satisfying" and "fun" "family fave" with "friendly" service.

☑ Cheese Steak Shop *Cheesesteaks*   23 | 12 | 19 | $11

Western Addition | 1716 Divisadero St. (bet. Bush & Sutter Sts.) | 415-346-3712 | www.cheesesteakshop.com

"Native Philadelphians" take a "trip down memory lane" at this "cheap" local chain, where the "hefty" cheesesteaks are as "authentic" as you'll find "this side of the Liberty Bell"; the "decor is lacking", but at least the "cheerful" servers are "fast" – a plus when getting your "gooey" "guilty pleasure" and Tastykakes "to go."

Chenery Park Ⓜ *American*   23 | 20 | 23 | $42

Glen Park | 683 Chenery St. (Diamond St.) | 415-337-8537 | www.chenerypark.com

American "comfort food" "with a Cajun twist" is "made better" with "local ingredients" at this "upscale" "neighborhood find" in "unhip Glen Park"; the Tuesday Kids Club menu makes for a meal that "both kids and parents will enjoy", and the "homey atmosphere" and "sincere" staff make it ideal for "date night" the rest of the week.

Chez Maman *French*   25 | 16 | 23 | $27

NEW **Civic Center** | 401 Gough St. (Hayes St.) | 415-355-9067
Potrero Hill | 1453 18th St. (bet. Connecticut & Missouri Sts.) | 415-824-7166
www.chezmamansf.com

"Like a Parisian corner cafe", this "tiny" Potrero Hill bistro (the "poor man's" alternative to "pricier spouse" Chez Papa Bistrot) turns out "delicious" "classics" (including "memorable" burgers) "cooked in front of you" "at the counter"; there's a "line out the door" from breakfast till late-night and only "about 14 seats", but "nobody dawdles" and the "wry" "French waiters" amuse as guests sip "wine while you wait"; P.S. there's now a Civic Center branch.

Chez Papa Bistrot *French*   25 | 19 | 22 | $43

Potrero Hill | 1401 18th St. (Missouri St.) | 415-824-8205 | www.chezpapasf.com

"Reminiscent of the fabulous bistros of Paris", from the "utterly charming" if "informal" setting to the "approachable" French fare (they perform "wizardry with mussels"), this "intimate" Potrero Hill spot is a relatively "affordable" option for "delicious" classics; it matters little that the "crowded" room can be "noisy", since the "authentic" Gallic staffers always ensure patrons feel "nurtured" "from start to finish."

Chez Papa Resto Ⓩ *French*   23 | 22 | 22 | $54

SoMa | 4 Mint Plaza (Stevenson St.) | 415-546-4134 | www.chezpaparesto.com

From the "exciting" menu to the "gracious" servers and "inviting" interior ("modern" yet still suitable for a "romantic evening"), this "happening" "find" in SoMa "fires on all cylinders"; a "hip crowd" sips "interesting cocktails" before delving into the "highly creative" (if "expensive") contemporary French fare, all adding up to an "uplifting experience", especially "if you can snag a table outside" on Mint Plaza.

Chez Spencer ⓜ *French* 25 | 22 | 23 | $65
Mission | 82 14th St. (bet. Folsom & Harrison Sts.) | 415-864-2191 | www.chezspencer.net
Laurent Katgely's "romantic" "urban retreat" "hidden" on an "industrial-looking stretch" of the Mission plies "poseurs" and "first dates" with "the genuine article" – "rich (even for French) fare" that "goes way beyond" what you'd expect; service is "exacting", and the "exposed beams", "dim lighting" and "charming" "heated terrace" "never fail to impress", but "be prepared to pay."

Chiaroscuro Ⓩ *Italian* 26 | 22 | 23 | $55
Downtown | 550 Washington St. (bet. Montgomery & Sansome Sts.) | 415-362-6012 | www.chiaroscurosf.com
"Mind-blowing" pastas made "the way a real Roman would" (chef-owner Alessandro Campitelli is a native) are highlights of the "creative" Italian menu at this "oasis" "in the shadow" of Downtown's Transamerica Pyramid; there are "no straw-wrapped Chianti bottles here", but instead "delightfully serene" (some say "stark") "modernist" decor that creates a "chic" setting for "fantastic food" and "great service."

Chilango *Mexican* 23 | 14 | 21 | $21
Castro | 235 Church St. (bet. 15th & Market Sts.) | 415-552-5700 | www.chilangorestaurantsf.com
"Too bad the secret is out" lament Castrolites "super-impressed" by the "jazzed-up" "Mexico City cuisine" prepared by a former Mexico DF chef at this new "go-to" casual cantina; "don't let the looks fool you", despite "downscale decor" (and prices), "it's not your average taqueria" – the "handmade", largely "organic" dishes are "cooked to perfection" and the staff is "lovely."

Chile Pies & Ice Cream *Dessert* 22 | 17 | 20 | $16
Western Addition | 601 Baker St. (Fulton St.) | 415-614-9411
ⓃⒺⓌ Chile Pies (Sweet & Savory) *Dessert*
Castro | 314 Church St. (15th St.) | 415-431-9411
www.chilepies.com
"Yummy pies" of both the "sweet and savory" varieties are the raison d'être of this "down-to-earth" Western Addition cafe and its Castro cousin, where after a "snack" and "a couple of craft beers", aficionados indulge in "awesome" desserts featuring a "flaky" crust or turn their attention to the "extra-sinful" "pie shake"; it may be on the "expensive" side considering the "casual" setting, but the "really nice" staff is a sweet perk.

Chloe's Cafe ⌀ *American* 23 | 16 | 20 | $20
Noe Valley | 1399 Church St. (26th St.) | 415-648-4116
"Every neighborhood should have" a "perfect little" "brunch" spot like this Noe Valley nook cranking out "flavor-packed" "scrambles", "perfect" pancakes and other "unpretentious" American eats to a "cozy" handful of tables, including some "curbside" "in the sun"; "it's not cheap" for its ilk and there's "always a morning rush no matter the day, weather or time", but "once in", the staffers "do their best to keep a smile"; P.S. no dinner.

Chotto *Japanese*

25 | 24 | 23 | $42

Marina | 3317 Steiner St. (bet. Chestnut & Lombard Sts.) | 415-441-2223 | www.chottosf.com

"Like being teleported to Tokyo minus the Harajuku girls", this "trendy" "late-night" izakaya attracts a Marina crowd with its "innovative" yet relatively "affordable" Japanese "small bites" (e.g. "bacon-wrapped mochi") and setting with handmade lanterns and barn-wood panels; the staff is "helpful", navigating offerings that are not for the "picky or bashful" plus an "excellent assortment of sake", which along with wine and snacks, is featured during happy hour; P.S. the chef left post-Survey.

Chouchou Ⓜ *French*

19 | 17 | 20 | $43

Forest Hills | 400 Dewey Blvd. (Laguna Honda Blvd.) | 415-242-0960 | www.chouchoubistro.com

A "welcoming" owner and his "caring" staff contribute to the "cozy" vibe at this "friendly" French bistro "in an unlikely spot" (Forest Hills); though it's "nothing fancy" and a few confess they "wouldn't cross town" considering the "uninspiring" interior and "crowded" confines, it's still a "nice neighborhood" spot for a relatively "reasonably priced" meal capped by a "phenomenal" tart.

❷ Chow *American*

21 | 17 | 19 | $25

Castro | 215 Church St. (bet. 15th & Market Sts.) | 415-552-2469

❷ Park Chow *American*

Inner Sunset | 1240 Ninth Ave. (bet. Irving St. & Lincoln Way) | 415-665-9912 | www.chowfoodbar.com

Those "craving" "simple" "homestyle" American fare "chow down" at this "cozy" mini-chain of "comfort food favorites" where the "varied" menu caters to "a wide range of tastes"; "quirky" decor and "efficient" and "friendly hipsters" for servers make it a "kick-back", "kid-friendly" option, even if the "bustling" spots "can be noisy at times."

Chubby Noodle ⓈⓂ *Asian*

▽ 24 | 14 | 16 | $21

North Beach | Amante's | 570 Green St. (Columbus Ave.) | 415-361-8850 | www.thechubbynoodle.com

"The novelty" of an "Asian-inspired" "pop-up" serving out of "the back" of a North Beach "neighborhood" bar is the hook at this shop from the team behind Don Pisto's, where cognoscenti hone in on "delicious" "fried chicken, garlic noodles" and other cheap eats; the unconventional setup comes complete with "old-school bartenders" offering a "plentiful selection of your favorite alcoholic beverages."

Chutney ❶ *Indian/Pakistani*

26 | 16 | 17 | $17

Tenderloin | 511 Jones St. (O'Farrell St.) | 415-931-5541

Behind an "unassuming storefront" in the Tenderloin, "order at the counter, take a number" from the "efficient" staff and wait for "brilliant" Indian-Pakistani plates, like "spot-on" chicken tikka masala and "genius" curries with "lots of complex spices"; "don't go for the decor" (though the "casual" "loftlike" space is a step up from the competition), but it's "a real find" considering the "reasonable" price.

Citizen's Band Ⓜ *American*

22 | 17 | 20 | $35

SoMa | 1198 Folsom St. (8th St.) | 415-556-4901 | www.citizensbandsf.com

"Offering no shortage of hipster appeal", this SoMa "neighborhood place" decorated with "old CB radios sitting on shelves" may look "like a diner", but the chef "seriously knows what he's doing", preparing "of-the-moment" American "down-home comfort food" (like "the crystal meth of mac 'n' cheese") for moderate tabs; "tight tables" make for a squeeze, but most are sweet on the staff and the "desserts from Pinkie's."

Citrus Club *Asian* | 20 | 15 | 18 | $17 |

Haight-Ashbury | 1790 Haight St. (Shrader St.) | 415-387-6366 | www.citrusclubsf.com

"Flavorful" Pan-Asian noodles and "gigantic bowls of soup" that "take a bite out of any sickness" "lift your spirits" on "cold" and "foggy" evenings at this Haight-Ashbury haunt; "packed" at "peak times", "the interior is nothing spectacular" and service varies, but it's a "solid standby" to "spice up your dining routine" at a "reasonable" price.

Claudine ⚄ *Californian* | ▽ 22 | 20 | 21 | $33 |

Downtown | 8 Claude Ln. (Bush St.) | 415-362-1988 | www.myclaudine.com
Tucked away "in a cute alley with no traffic", this "terrific" cafe from restaurateur Franck LeClerc (Café Claude) and chef Bridget Batson (Gitane) dishes up "affordable" Californian bistro fare for the "young" FiDi set; along with a "chic" dining room, there's a circular bar proffering local beer and wine, and a take-out gourmet market.

Cliff House Bistro *Californian* | 21 | 25 | 21 | $42 |

Outer Richmond | 1090 Point Lobos Ave. (Balboa St.) | 415-386-3330 | www.cliffhouse.com
Locals like to "dazzle out-of-towners" with "knockout views" of the "crashing" surf at this Outer Richmond cliff dweller sporting "turn-of-the-century" memorabilia; supporters suggest you "sit windowside" and "admire the sunset" while "sipping on cocktails" and digging into the "dependable" Californian cuisine, served "with a smile", while the less-impressed lament fare that's "a little lackluster" and "overpriced" to boot.

Coco500 ⚄ *Californian/Mediterranean* | 23 | 20 | 23 | $48 |

SoMa | 500 Brannan St. (4th St.) | 415-543-2222 | www.coco500.com
"Foodies" "count on" "inventive", "well-prepared" Cal-Med fare, like fried green beans and truffled flatbread (both "absolute musts), all "delivered with panache" by "friendly, efficient" servers at this SoMa bistro from Loretta Keller; the "young, hip crowd" "can be loud during prime time" (lunchtime too), and tables are "a little too close together", but its "relaxing atmosphere" and "civilized", "modern" space help it maintain "favorite" status.

Coi ⚄Ⓜ *Californian/French* | 27 | 26 | 27 | $215 |

North Beach | 373 Broadway (Montgomery St.) | 415-393-9000 | www.coirestaurant.com
Daniel Patterson's "cutting-edge" Californian-French tasting menus proffered with "splendid service" in a "minimalist" North Beach lair "put the food front and center" for a "wild" romp of "molecular gastronomy", where "fine local ingredients" are "transformed and deconstructed" into "avant-garde creations" that "almost seem like a crime to eat"; "thought-provoking" wine pairings add to an experience doubters deem "pretentious" but most call "magical" and a "worthwhile splurge" for "serious" eaters that "approaches once-in-a-lifetime" status.

Colibrí Mexican Bistro *Mexican*　　23 | 19 | 20 | $37

Downtown | 438 Geary St. (bet. Mason & Taylor Sts.) | 415-440-2737 |
www.colibrimexicanbistro.com

"Not your typical Mexican restaurant", this "lively" Downtowner "manages to modernize" south-of-the-border bites with a "creative" menu of "upscale" "regional" dishes; "fantastic" guacamole is made "to your specifications", and "complex" cocktails are concocted from an "impressive" tequila selection (the "Macho Margarita" is "an epiphany"), and while service varies from "quick" to "slow", it's "always friendly."

Commonwealth *American*　　26 | 20 | 24 | $62

Mission | 2224 Mission St. (18th St.) | 415-355-1500 |
www.commonwealthsf.com

"Some of the most thrilling food in the city" can be found at this "progressive" Mission New American, where the "wildly inventive", "beautifully composed" fare is available à la carte or in "highly recommended" tasting menus that foodies consider a "bargain" for the "quality" (plus $10 of each goes to charity); its "austere, industrial" digs may not inspire the same praise, but with "thoughtful wine pairings and "friendly, enthusiastic" service, most barely notice – and "get this, they have their own parking lot."

Contigo Ⓜ *Spanish*　　25 | 21 | 22 | $49

Noe Valley | 1320 Castro St. (24th St.) | 415-285-0250 |
www.contigosf.com

"Go with a group of adventuresome eaters" or a hot "date" to this "convivial" Noe Valley "gem" turning out "tasty" "Catalonian-by-way-of-Californian tapas" (think "fatty slices" of imported jamón and "locally sourced" produce) and "great Spanish wines" shuttled by a "warm" staff; it's not cheap, and the "tiny" "modern" digs get "hectic", but regulars love to "sit at the bar" or retreat to the "sweet" garden patio.

☑ Cotogna *Italian*　　26 | 22 | 24 | $52

Downtown | 490 Pacific St. (Montgomery St.) | 415-775-8508 |
www.cotognasf.com

Lindsay and Michael Tusk have "done it again" at this "weekday lunch spot" and "late-night" Downtown dinner destination that "shares a kitchen" with big sis Quince, offering equally "unreal pastas" and other Italian fare such as "marvelous" roasted meats and "wood-fired" pizzas (plus family-style Sunday suppers) in more "rustic" digs at a "fraction of the price"; it's also about "twice as loud" and a tough rez, but with wine for "$40" a bottle and a "cheerful" staff, "what's not to love?"

Crab House *Seafood*　　25 | 20 | 22 | $43

Fisherman's Wharf | 203 Pier 39 (The Embarcadero) | 415-434-2722 |
www.crabhouse39.com

"It's all about the crab" ("obviously") at this "no-fuss" Fisherman's Wharf seafooder, where "delicious" Dungeness are prepared every which way, including whole with a "well-seasoned" "garlic sauce" ("a big mess" but "fun" to eat); though some long for bigger portions for the price, "beautiful" waterfront views plus "fast", "friendly" service contribute to the "cool experience."

FOOD | DECOR | SERVICE | COST

NEW Craftsman & Wolves   *Bakery/Sandwiches*   - | - | - | I

Mission | 746 Valencia St. (bet. 18th & 19th Sts.) | 415-913-7713 | www.craftsman-wolves.com

Pastry whiz William Werner's über-modern contemporary patisserie in the Mission serves his signature off-the-wall confections, pastries both sweet and savory and ever-changing grab-and-go offerings along with Sightglass Coffee and tea; the cafe, filled with illuminated display cases and clean steel paneling, is so sleek it could be mistaken for a Bulgari store, albeit with significantly more affordable offerings.

Craw Station   *Cajun/Creole*   ▽ 24 | 15 | 19 | $24

Inner Sunset | 1336 Ninth Ave. (Irving St.) | 415-682-9980 | www.crawstation.com

"Fresh" seafood, like a bucket of "big" crawfish or "juicy shrimp", is seasoned from mild to "dynamite" at this wallet-friendly Inner Sunset spot, where Cajun-Creole connoisseurs "pig out" on "spicy" fare and "some nice cold beer"; service is hit-and-miss, and since most menu items you "eat with your hands", it's "not a first-date" destination, so "bring friends" who don't mind getting "messy."

Credo 🗷 *Italian*   21 | 20 | 22 | $39

Downtown | 360 Pine St. (bet. Montgomery & Sansome Sts.) | 415-693-0360 | www.credosf.com

"Fun quotes all over the walls" and "trendy" "modern decor" create an "inviting environment" at this "welcome addition" to the Downtown dining scene; the "very personable staff" serves "consistently excel-lent Italian dishes" and "solid cocktails", and since "prices are reason-able for the Financial District", devotees who "have never been disappointed" declare they are "definitely coming back."

Crepevine   *American/French*   21 | 16 | 19 | $16

Castro | 216 Church Plaza (Market St.) | 415-431-4646 ◗
Inner Sunset | 624 Irving St. (bet. 7th & 8th Aves.) | 415-681-5858 | www.crepevine.com

"Divine" crêpes, "both sweet and savory", plus "rib-sticking break-fasts", sandwiches, "super-fresh" salads – "you name it" – are on the "chalkboard menu" at this "laid-back" chain of "fast and friendly" French-American cafes; they're "not a place to impress anyone", but the "price is right" and "gigantic portions" leave "ample leftovers" for "the next day"; P.S. "cute" patio or sidewalk seating allows you to "avoid the cacophony inside."

Crustacean   *Asian/Vietnamese*   25 | 20 | 21 | $58

Polk Gulch | 1475 Polk St. (California St.) | 415-776-2722 | www.anfamily.com

"Home of the exalted roasted Dungeness crab and out-of-this-world garlic noodles" that are "worth having bad breath for a week", this Vietnamese-Asian fusioner on Polk Street "never fails" with its "finger-lickin'" fare "exploding with flavor"; it's a somewhat "fancy place" with cloth tablecloths", but that doesn't stop "friendly" servers from "strap-ping a bib" on "crabaholics", who easily overlook "expensive" tabs.

Cupkates 🅼 *Dessert*   25 | 15 | 22 | $6

Location varies; see website | 510-384-6544 | www.cupkatesbakery.com

Surveyors are sweet on this "pretty" truck that roams SF and the East Bay with a "friendly" staff doling out "unfailingly moist" cupcakes that are "pure genius"; but "get there early", since they sometimes "run out of the best flavors", like the salted caramel that "will blow your mind" – "for $3, you get a little taste of heaven."

Cupola Pizzeria *Italian/Pizza* | 21 | 19 | 19 | $34 |

Downtown | Westfield San Francisco Ctr. | 845 Market St., 4th fl. (bet. 4th & 5th Sts.) | 415-896-5600 | www.cupolasf.com

Its "high-tech decor" "makes you feel like you're in Milan", but the "top-notch" "thin-crust pizzas" blistered in an "imported" oven are "authentic" "Naples-style" at this somewhat "pricey" "sleeper" under the Westfield Centre's dome; the "innovative" Italian eats and "personable service" are a "cut above", though aesthetes admit there's "no escaping" that you're "eating in a mall."

Curry Up Now *Indian* | 23 | 14 | 18 | $12 |

Location varies; see website | 650-477-3000 | www.curryupnow.com
See review in South of San Francisco Directory.

Dante's Weird Fish ⊜ *Seafood*   ▽ | 22 | 17 | 19 | $29 |

Mission | 2193 Mission St. (18th St.) | 415-863-4744 | www.weirdfishsf.com

After a change in ownership, this retooled Mission seafooder is back in business with a revamped menu (which may not be reflected in the Food score) featuring reworked offerings like fish 'n' chips and tacos, plus reinstated vegan favorites that fans had missed; the "tiny", "hole-in-the-wall" digs have a new look too, with green walls and plant installations.

🆕 Dear Mom ● *Eclectic*   ▽ | 19 | 18 | 16 | $17 |

Mission | 2700 16th St. (Harrison St.) | 415-625-3362

An "'it' bar of the moment", this Mission pub catches many "unaware" with its "great" Eclectic grub with American, Asian and Latino influences, plus a "good revolving" menu from various vendors; the "cool, dive-y" space is like "hipster Disneyland" with a jukebox, pool table and video games, and since tabs are generally "cheap", the "crowds" have descended.

Delarosa ● *Italian* | 22 | 19 | 19 | $32 |

Marina | 2175 Chestnut St. (bet. Pierce & Steiner Sts.) | 415-673-7100 | www.delarosasf.com

"Always buzzing" with a "good-looking" "throng", this "happening" Marina Italian earns "brownie points" for its "affordable" menu of "scrumptious" "small plates" plus "super-thin" Roman pizzas (when in "doubt, just add burrata"); the antisocial aren't "big fans" of the mostly "communal tables" (either "fun or awkward, depending on the company"), but supporters are sold on the "young, fun staff", "creative" cocktails and "late-night" hours (until 1 AM).

DeLessio Market & Bakery *Bakery* | 21 | 13 | 17 | $20 |

Hayes Valley | 1695 Market St. (Gough St.) | 415-552-5559
Western Addition | Falletti's Plaza | 302 Broderick St. (Oak St.) | 415-552-8077
www.delessiomarket.com

"Mouthwatering" "buffet-style" dishes, including "absolutely decadent" mac 'n' cheese, are sold "by the pound" at this "self-serve" duo in Hayes Valley and the Western Addition, "but it's the bakery items that win me over" aver aficionados of the "amazing" cakes and tarts; the tab "can really add up", and the "cramped" quarters make it "more of a take-out than an eat-in" option, but it's worth hitting up for the "homey" fare.

☑ Delfina *Italian* | 27 | 20 | 23 | $49 |

Mission | 3621 18th St. (bet. Dolores & Guerrero Sts.) | 415-552-4055 | www.delfinasf.com

Visiting the Mission without trying Craig and Anne Stoll's "first restaurant" that started it all is "like being in Egypt and not seeing the pyramids" say the "hipsters and well-heeled boomers" who frequent this "unpretentious" trattoria for its "simple, soulful" Northern Italian cuisine "paired with great wines" by "knowledgeable" staffers; just reserve "well in advance" as it's often "crowded" (and "noisy" to boot), or you might wind up at their "pizzeria next door."

NEW Deli Board *Deli* | ▽ 25 | 13 | 20 | $13 |

SoMa | 1058 Folsom St. (bet. Russ & Moss Sts.) | 415-552-7687 | www.deliboardsf.com

"Fantastic handmade sandwiches" are the name of the game at this SoMa deli known for "amazing fixin's" and "some unique options along with your traditional roast beef or turkey; service is "great" too, just be warned seating is limited and it closes at 4 PM; P.S. its bike delivery pop-up 1058 Hoagie is set to open a brick-and-mortar outpost.

Delica *Japanese* | 24 | 15 | 18 | $21 |

Embarcadero | Ferry Bldg. Mktpl. | 1 Ferry Bldg. (The Embarcadero) | 415-834-0344 | www.delicasf.com

At lunch a "Japanese deli" with "lovely" bento boxes and "interesting salads" to "grab and go", come evening this "unassuming" Embarcadero spot offers diners "an unusual selection" of sushi that goes "beyond the California roll"; the staff is "helpful" and it makes for a "nice change of pace", though some say it's a little pricey for "small" portions.

NEW Del Popolo 🕿Ⓜ *Pizza* | - | - | - | I |

Downtown | Location varies; see website | no phone | www.delpopolosf.com

Pizzaiolo Jon Darsky, who wowed pie fanatics during his stint at Flour + Water, is now roaming the streets with this state-of-the-art mobile wood-fired pizza rig (built in a 20-ft. shipping container reoutfitted as a hearth on wheels), serving three affordable pies at a time – a classic margherita, a white pie and a daily special; the limited menu does little to dissuade the lunchtime crowds from lining up when the truck makes regular stops in the Downtown area Tuesdays–Saturdays.

Destino *Nuevo Latino* | 22 | 20 | 20 | $44 |

Castro | 1815 Market St. (bet. Guerrero St. & Octavia Blvd.) | 415-552-4451 | www.destinosf.com

A "favorite spot for a celebration", this "warm" and "welcoming" Nuevo Latino bistro coddles the Castro crowd with "superb" ceviche and "delicious" South American tapas plus "wonderful wines" and cocktails that "perfectly" "complement" the meal; "super-patient" servers happily explain the "creative" menu, but if you want to hear them, opt for an "early meal", before the "happy" "young" crowd creates an "ear-splitting" din (if they're not at sibling Pisco Lounge next door).

	FOOD	DECOR	SERVICE	COST

Dinosaurs *Vietnamese* ▽ 21 | 13 | 20 | $9

Castro | 2275 Market St. (16th St.) | 415-503-1421

Vietnamese sandwich "cravings" are satisfied at this "cheerful" Castro "hole-in-the-wall", where "friendly and efficient behind-the-counter staffers" hand out some of the "best banh mi outside of Little Saigon"; offerings are "cheap but filling", making for a "terrific value."

NEW Dixie *Southern* – | – | – | M

Presidio | 1 Letterman Dr. (Lyon St.) | 415-829-3363 | www.sfdixie.com

Fine-dining vet Joseph Humphrey (ex Meadowood) elevates classic down-home dishes with contemporary American technique at this Southern eatery, where dinner comes à la carte or as a moderately priced tasting menu and lunch is a $19 two-course prix fixe affair; set in a former Presidio army barrack, the space offers commanding views of the Palace of Fine Arts.

Dobb's Ferry ● *American* 16 | 16 | 18 | $42

Hayes Valley | 409 Gough St. (Hayes St.) | 415-551-7700 | www.dobbsferrysf.com

"Classic" New American "comfort food" is offered in "comfortable" and "unpretentious" surrounds at this Hayes Valley stop; if some find it just "so-so" (including the service) and note prices seem a "bit high for what you get", supporters argue it's "trying hard", adding it's a "good place" "when going to the symphony, opera or ballet."

Domo Sushi *Japanese* 25 | 20 | 22 | $32

Hayes Valley | 511 Laguna St. (Linden St.) | 415-861-8887 | www.domosf.com

This "intimate" Hayes Valley Japanese joint is so "teeny-tiny", "you can watch the chefs at work" as they prepare "exquisitely crafted sushi" and "put their own spin on things" with "surprising" "specialty rolls"; the "fabulous" cuts set "a new standard" say fervent locals, who also appreciate the "super-friendly staff" and "reasonable prices."

Don Pisto's ●M *Mexican* 25 | 20 | 20 | $28

North Beach | 510 Union St. (Grant Ave.) | 415-395-0939 | www.donpistos.com

It may be "surprising" that "some of the best Mexican food in the city" is "in North Beach", but those who have "stumbled upon" this "hidden gem" are "thoroughly impressed" by the "explosive flavors"; "get there early" and "expect a wait" in the "exposed-brick" interior, but once you're seated with the "loud" "hipster crowd" quaffing "addictive" margaritas, "service doesn't skip a beat."

Dosa *Indian* 23 | 23 | 21 | $38

Mission | 995 Valencia St. (21st St.) | 415-642-3672
Upper Fillmore | 1700 Fillmore St. (Post St.) | 415-441-3672
www.dosasf.com

Indian "as you've never experienced it" distinguishes this "moderately priced" duo delivering "innovative" fare, like "out-of-this-world" dosas "the size of your head" and other plates that "explode with flavor" (and so much spice you may want "lots of water" handy), all backed by "darn good cocktails"; Fillmore is "swankier", with "beautiful soaring ceilings" and "sultry" decor, while the Mission space is "more cramped", but both attract a "cult following" – luckily service remains "cordial despite being slammed", leaving most "everybody happy."

Dynamo Donut & Coffee 🅼 *Coffeehouse* 25 | 15 | 20 | $8
Mission | 2760 24th St. (bet. Hampshire & York Sts.) | 415-920-1978 | www.dynamodonut.com

"Insanely tasty" donuts, including the "favorite" maple bacon (a "no-brainer") are "too good to be true" at this petite Mission bakery, a "hipster destination" for "unsurpassed" sweets offered in "innovative", "daring combos", plus "strong, delicious" coffee poured by the "friendliest crew"; sure, it's "rather pricey", but fans swear "all hesitation melts away" after one bite.

E&O Asian Kitchen *Asian* 21 | 22 | 20 | $39
(fka E&O Trading Co.)
Downtown | 314 Sutter St. (bet. Grant Ave. & Stockton St.) | 415-693-0303 | www.eosanfrancisco.com

"One of the original 'fusion' restaurants – and still original", this recently refreshed, "cavernous" Pan-Asian "paradise" off Union Square continues to pack them in, especially for "tasty" "business lunches" or "large-group" dinners over shared "small plates"; it's a bit "pricey" for some, though "happy-hour" deals are popular in the "scene-y" downstairs lounge that serves "fantastic" "exotic cocktails"; P.S. a new menu and bar program were introduced post-Survey (though the "must"-have "corn fritters" are still being offered), along with a remodeled space.

E'Angelo 🅼 *Italian* ▽ 20 | 13 | 20 | $30
Marina | 2234 Chestnut St. (bet. Pierce & Scott Sts.) | 415-567-6164
For "a big platter" of "yummy" pasta and other "reliable" *cucina* concocted by a Friulian chef, Marina residents depend upon this "authentic" Italian that "won't break the bank"; it's just "what a neighborhood restaurant should be" maintain most, as long as "you don't mind squeezing" into the "crowded" quarters.

Ebisu *Japanese* 24 | 19 | 21 | $36
Downtown | 336 Kearny St. (bet. Bush & Pine Sts.) | 415-398-2388
Inner Sunset | 1283 Ninth Ave. (Irving St.) | 415-566-1770 🅼
www.ebisusushi.com

A "neighborhood place with citywide appeal", this "popular" 30-year-old Inner Sunset Japanese "still has them lining up for more" with a "diverse" array of "consistently high-quality" fare, from "expertly crafted rolls" and "delicate, artful sushi" to other "interesting" apps and grilled items, all at "reasonable" prices; "cheerful" servers work the "small", "family-friendly" digs, but since the wait can sometimes be "unforgiving", many get their fix at the Downtown lunch counter and quick-service SFO offshoot, which offer similarly "creative" options.

Eiji 🅼 *Japanese* 26 | 17 | 22 | $37
Castro | 317 Sanchez St. (bet. 16th & 17th Sts.) | 415-558-8149
Aside from the "unbelievable quality of the fish", "what sets apart" this "Tokyo"-style "sushi bar" in the Castro is its "delicious" "homemade *oboru*" ("silky tofu") and "out-of-this-world" "strawberry mochi"; the "cozy" digs are "so small you could miss it", but service is "friendly", so "if you can find a table and the courage to order boldly, you're in for a treat" that won't break the bank.

	FOOD	DECOR	SERVICE	COST

El Castillito *Mexican*

| | 25 | 9 | 18 | $9 |

Castro | 136 Church St. (bet. Duboce Ave. & 14th St.) | 415-621-3428 ◐
Civic Center | 370 Golden Gate Plaza (Larkin St.) | 415-292-7233
Mission | 2092 Mission St. (17th St.) | 415-621-6971 ◐⊞

"Lots of flavor" gets packed into the "to-die-for" burritos and carnitas at this Mexican trio; yes, the digs are a bit "grungy", but service is "fast", the bill is "small" and they "aren't shy with the portions" – plus you can always "get your order to go."

El Farolito ◐ *Mexican*

| | 23 | 9 | 17 | $10 |

Mission | 2779 Mission St. (bet. 23rd & 24th Sts.) | 415-824-7877 ⊞
Mission | 2950 24th St. (Mission St.) | 415-641-0758
Mission | 4817 Mission St. (Onodaga Ave.) | 415-337-5500
www.elfarolitoinc.com

"You'll never leave hungry" from these "authentic" taquerias that "don't skimp on anything", turning out "inexpensive" Mexican "comfort" food in "large portions", including "big, fat, juicy burritos"; the decor is "divey" and service can be a bit "rough around the edges", but "lines out the door at dinnertime" are "good indicators" that the grub "outweighs" all else; P.S. the Mission locales are "open late for post-drinking sustenance in the wee hours."

El Huarache Loco Ⓜ⊞ *Mexican*

| | ▽ 23 | 12 | 16 | $10 |

Bernal Heights | Alemany Farmers Mkt. | 100 Alemany Blvd. (Peralta Ave.) | 415-572-6832 | www.huaracheloco.com
See review in North of San Francisco Directory.

Elite Cafe *American*

| | 21 | 20 | 20 | $41 |

Pacific Heights | 2049 Fillmore St. (bet. California & Pine Sts.) | 415-673-5483 | www.theelitecafe.com

"New Orleans–inspired dishes", from "obscenely delicious" biscuits to "great raw bar" bites, are "the real deal" at this "wonderfully old-fashioned" American where "high-backed" booths are a "romantic" option; perhaps it's "a little pricey" ("this is Pac Heights" after all) and often "crowded", but fans affirm the "hospitality is worthy of the Big Easy."

Eliza's *Chinese*

| | 23 | 17 | 17 | $23 |

Pacific Heights | 2877 California St. (bet. Broderick & Divisadero Sts.) | 415-621-4819

"Generous portions" of "fresh-tasting" Chinese chow are "elegantly presented" at this Pacific Heights Hunan haunt, where "quality ingredients" add up to an "excellent" meal; the "lovely" modern setting and "reasonable" prices make it "a favorite for those in the know" (lunch is an especially "amazing deal"), but idlers opt for "takeout" to avoid "the bum's rush" from the "fast" waiters.

Ella's *American*

| | 21 | 15 | 18 | $25 |

Presidio Heights | 500 Presidio Ave. (California St.) | 415-441-5669 | www.ellassanfrancisco.com

Perfect for an "inventive" weekday breakfast or "fantastic" weekend brunch, "if not for a diet", this "homey" Presidio Heights cafe proffers "huge portions" of "crazy-good baked goods and other "tasty" American "comfort food"; it's "totally worth the wait" gush groupies, but the less-impressed aren't "sure what all the fuss – and the gargantuan lines – are about"; P.S. no dinner.

	FOOD	DECOR	SERVICE	COST

El Metate *Mexican*
22 | 17 | 18 | $12

Mission | 2406 Bryant St. (22nd St.) | 415-641-7209
"Bargain bites" come in the form of "authentic, flavorful" *comida,* including "well-put-together" burritos that "rock", at this Mission Mexican; service is "quick" in the "sunny, mellow" digs, and there are "outdoor tables too."

El Tonayense ∌ *Mexican*
23 | 12 | 19 | $8

Location varies; see website | 415-550-9192 | www.tonayense.com
An "SF tradition", this "mother of all" food trucks (found at locations along Harrison Street) has "been around a long time", serving up "cheap", "stand-and-eat" Mexican – "mouthwatering" burritos and "fresh", "delicious" tacos – that "will never do you wrong"; expect "quick" service and "no gimmicks", just the "basics done right."

El Zocalo ● *Salvadoran*
∇ 23 | 14 | 20 | $16

Bernal Heights | 3230 Mission St. (Valencia St.) | 415-282-2572
"If heaven has pupusas, they surely come from" this "authentic" Bernal Heights Salvadoran declare fans of its "simple" grub sold "for a song" "until 3 AM"; it might "take forever" to arrive, but that's because it's "made on the spot" "with as much love as your *tia* would bring to the table", so just "relax and enjoy the warm smiles" while you wait.

Emmy's Spaghetti Shack *Italian*
20 | 18 | 18 | $24

Bernal Heights | 18 Virginia Ave. (Mission St.) | 415-206-2086 |
www.emmysspaghettishack.com
"Heaping helpings" of "steaming" spaghetti topped by "awesome" "giant" meatballs headline the "down-home" Italian eats "for cheap" at this "loud" Bernal Heights "hipster" haven with "creative", "funky" decor; the plates aren't "particularly special" say some, who declare they could "do better at home", but "super-friendly" servers and "stellar" cocktails contribute to the "fun" vibe.

Emporio Rulli *Dessert/Italian*
22 | 20 | 18 | $20

(aka Emporio Rulli Italian Caffe at Union Square)
Downtown | Union Sq. Pavilion | 225 Stockton St. (bet. Geary & Post Sts.) |
415-433-1122 | www.rulli.com
See review in North of San Francisco Directory.

Epic Roasthouse *Steak*
23 | 25 | 21 | $70

Embarcadero | 369 The Embarcadero (bet. Folsom & Harrison Sts.) |
415-369-9955 | www.epicroasthousesf.com
A "haven for carnivores", this Embarcadero steakhouse offers "dinosaur-size cuts" and a "deep wine list" (plus a "standout" brunch) in "beautiful" waterfront environs with "breathtaking" "panoramic views" of the Bay Bridge; service gets mixed marks ("attentive" vs. "spotty") and tabs are "expensive", but "sitting outside on a pretty day is magical", and the "lively" (and comparatively "cheap") happy hour and "beer-burger-brownie deal at the upstairs bar can't be beat."

Eric's *Chinese*
22 | 16 | 19 | $22

Noe Valley | 1500 Church St. (27th St.) | 415-282-0919 |
www.ericrestaurant.com
For "flavorful", if "somewhat Americanized Chinese" "without the hassle of Chinatown", Noe Valley-ites head to this "ever-popular" neighbor-

hood "go-to"; it's "not fancy", but "welcoming" staffers, "reasonable" prices and a "homey" feel make it "just perfect" for a "low-key" meal.

Esperpento *Spanish*   22 | 16 | 18 | $25

Mission | 3295 22nd St. (Valencia St.) | 415-282-8867 | www.esperpentorestaurant.com

"Authentic tapas", "killer paella" and "delicious sangria" "remind" traveler types "of Spain" at this "cozy" Mission "hole-in-the-wall"; the "colorful" space is a "little shabby", but "mostly friendly" service, "affordable prices" and a "lively atmosphere" ensure many "come back."

Espetus Churrascaria *Brazilian*   23 | 20 | 23 | $71
(aka Espetus Churrascaria Brazilian Steakhouse)

Hayes Valley | 1686 Market St. (Gough St.) | 415-552-8792 | www.espetus.com

"Unapologetic" carnivores "with an endless appetite" "fast during the day" then "wear big clothes" to these "pretty pricey" Brazilian churrascarias in Hayes Valley and San Mateo; there's a "bountiful" buffet of "salads and side dishes", but beef buffs know not to "load up" before the "endless parade" of "delicious" "meat, meat and more meat" "served right off the skewer" by the "handsome" "wandering" staff.

Eureka Restaurant & Lounge *American*   22 | 19 | 22 | $41

Castro | 4063 18th St. (bet. Castro & Hartford Sts.) | 415-431-6000 | www.eurekarestaurant.com

Southern style and "influences from New Orleans" "jazz up" the "upscale" New American "home cooking" at this "lively" Castro bistro with a "fabulous upstairs lounge" ("ask for a table" "by the window"); "cheerful", "attentive" servers seal its status a "solid" spot "for a romantic date or cozy dinner with friends", and it even has an "upscale bar to boot."

Fang *Chinese*   22 | 19 | 19 | $36

SoMa | 660 Howard St. (bet. New Montgomery & 3rd Sts.) | 415-777-8568 | www.fangrestaurant.com

"Forgo the menu" and "put yourself" in owner "Peter Fang's hands" at this more "upscale" SoMa sibling of the "long-standing" House of Nanking; "you won't be disappointed" by the "large portions" of mid-priced "modern" Chinese chow, even if service can be "a bit stoic" – and at least you "don't have to wait on line" like at the Chinatown original.

⊠ Farallon *Seafood*   25 | 27 | 25 | $67

Downtown | 450 Post St. (bet. Mason & Powell Sts.) | 415-956-6969 | www.farallonrestaurant.com

"Dazzling", "dreamlike" "underwater" decor that "combines Dale Chihuly with Captain Nemo" "still wows" at this "special occasion" Downtowner, where the "breathtakingly fresh" fish and other "phenomenal" seafood is "hard to beat"; the tab is "a little overboard" and "you'll pay through the gills" for the "impressive" wines, but "flawless" service makes it "a treat on all counts."

Farina *Italian*   23 | 21 | 21 | $59

Mission | 3560 18th St. (Dearborn St.) | 415-565-0360 | www.farina-foods.com

For "authentic Italian like your grandmother made (if she were from Liguria)", patrons point to this "hip" Mission hang turning out "deliciously done" pastas and "world-champion pesto" in a modern, "thoughtfully" decorated space with an "upbeat atmosphere"; some might niggle over "uneven" service and "noisy" conditions, and say it's "overpriced for what you get", but it's "usually very busy" nonetheless; P.S. its pizza offshoot plies pies and more.

NEW Farina Pizza & Cucina Italiana *Italian/Pizza*

- | - | - | M

Mission | 700 Valencia St. (18th St.) | 415-565-1900 | www.farina-foods.com
Pizza cooked by a pizzaiolo from Napoli in a massive black-tiled oven built over layers of Mount Vesuvius sand gets top billing at this pizzeria offshoot of nearby Farina, but the kitchen also promises Missionites handmade pastas, grilled meats and other midpriced Neapolitan cucina; the sleek storefront outfitted with white-leather stools, a marble bar and a drop ceiling lined with graphics from a popular Italian comic strip plans to be open continuously from breakfast (for pastries and cappuccino) until late-night.

Farm:Table ₱ *American*

▽ 21 | 18 | 18 | $24

Civic Center | 754 Post St. (bet. Jones & Leavenworth Sts.) | 415-292-7089 | www.farmtablesf.com
"Just show up and order one of everything" advise admirers of this "micro-sized" eatery in the Civic Center, where a tiny, daily changing American menu featuring "simple" yet "delicious" options is offered from morning until afternoon (it closes at 3 PM); service is "friendly", and the lone communal table inside promotes a "social" experience, though with such petite digs, many take it to go.

Farmerbrown Ⓜ *Soul Food*

22 | 17 | 17 | $28

Tenderloin | 25 Mason St. (bet. Eddy & Turk Sts.) | 415-409-3276 | www.farmerbrownsf.com

Farmerbrown's Little Skillet ₱ *Soul Food*

SoMa | 360 Ritch St. (bet. 3rd & 4th Sts.) | 415-777-2777 | www.littleskilletsf.com
"Inspired soul food" "brings people back" to this "fun" Tenderloiner, where the "dark and moody ambiance", "strong" "specialty cocktails" and "all-you-can-eat live jazz brunch" contribute to the "hip" vibe; it "won't break the bank", but "ridiculous noise levels" and "so-so service" lead some to order their "super-crispy" fried chicken from the SoMa "walk-up counter" with a "limited menu" instead.

Fatted Calf *Sandwiches*

27 | 17 | 23 | $24

Hayes Valley | 320 Fell St. (Gough St.) | 415-400-5614 | www.fattedcalf.com
"More of a specialty deli" and "high-end butcher shop" "than a restaurant" (get takeaway or settle for a seat on a bench), this Napa and Hayes Valley "Valhalla of cured meats" sells "artisan sandwiches" stuffed with "sublime" charcuterie, "to-die-for" meatloaf and more; it's "not for vegetarians", but carnivores are keen on "friendly" staffers who are "extremely knowledgeable" about the "sustainably raised" fare.

Ferry Plaza Seafoods Ⓜ *Seafood*

23 | 18 | 20 | $33

Embarcadero | Ferry Bldg. Mktpl. | 1 Ferry Bldg. (The Embarcadero) | 415-274-2561 | www.ferryplazaseafood.com
Extroverts who enjoy "interaction" with the "wonderful staff" "love sitting at the bar" at this "lively" Ferry Building seafooder and market,

washing down their "impeccably fresh" fish, "spirit-warming chowder" and raw-bar bites with "delicious" wines at lunch and "early" dinners; the tab easily "adds up", but you can't put a price on the "unparalleled vista of the Bay Bridge."

15 Romolo ● *American* | 22 | 21 | 21 | $27 |

North Beach | Basque Hotel | 15 Romolo Pl. (B'way) | 415-398-1359 | www.15romolo.com

Dispensing "killer cocktails" and "quirky" American bar bites, this "hidden", back-alley "escape" from "touristy" North Beach attracts a "late-night" crowd, while luring daytime diners with an "excellent" weekend "punch-drunk brunch"; though service "takes a while" and there can be "quite the scene", the "Barbary Coast" "saloon vibe", "great jukebox" and reasonable prices appeal when "with friends" or on "a first date."

Fifth Floor 🗷Ⓜ *American/French* | 25 | 23 | 24 | $81 |

SoMa | Hotel Palomar | 12 Fourth St., 5th fl. (Market St.) | 415-348-1555 | www.fifthfloorrestaurant.com

A "special-occasion place" "hidden" away in SoMa's Hotel Palomar, this New French–New American is "firing on all cylinders" under chef David Bazirgan (ex Chez Papa Resto), who presents "creative", "complicated food prepared perfectly" and complemented by an "unparalleled" wine list; "friendly, well-informed" service and an "elegant setting" with "comfortable seating" further justify "expensive" prices, though shallower pockets hit the "busy bar" for the "burgers, bourbon and brew deal."

54 Mint 🗷 *Italian* | 22 | 21 | 21 | $43 |

SoMa | 16 Mint Plaza (Jessie St.) | 415-543-5100 | www.54mint.com

"Old-school Italian charm meets new-school decor" at this "real deal" trattoria where "authentic", "elegant" Sicilian specialties and an "intriguing" wine list result in many a "happy camper"; hidden on a "tiny alley" in SoMa, the "jumping" joint may be a "bit on the loud side", but the "welcoming" owners and "warm" servers "take care of you like family", and there's also terrace and wine-cellar seating.

Firefly *Eclectic* | 25 | 21 | 24 | $45 |

Noe Valley | 4288 24th St. (Douglass St.) | 415-821-7652 | www.fireflyrestaurant.com

A "longtime neighborhood favorite", Brad Levy's Noe Valley Eclectic still "enchants" with an "ever-changing menu" of "masterfully prepared" "upscale comfort food" that's "inventive but not overwrought"; "friendly, unpretentious service" and a "charming", "homey" setting further explain how it "gets all the details right", and though not cheap, fans deem it an "excellent value" (especially its "bargain" Sunday–Thursday prix fixe) that works for "everyday dinners as well as plan-ahead special occasions."

Firewood Cafe *Italian* | 21 | 16 | 18 | $19 |

Castro | 4248 18th St. (Diamond St.) | 415-252-0999 | www.firewoodcafe.com

"Rotisserie chicken", "awesome" pizza and "decent" pastas are among the "reliable" options at this mini-chain of "casual" Italian cafes; they're "not the place for a first date", since you "order at the counter" from the "lovely" staff and "seat yourself", but they're so "quick" and "affordable" you may "never need to cook at home again."

Fish & Farm ⧄ *American/Seafood*   20 | 18 | 20 | $47
Downtown | 339 Taylor St. (bet. Ellis & O'Farrell Sts.) | 415-474-3474 |
www.fishandfarmsf.com
"Locally sourced" ingredients from "fresh" fish to "flavorful beef" are transformed into "uncomplicated" "comfort food" at this "cozy" New American seafooder offering "value" Downtown; "efficient" servers "know their clientele", and it makes a "perfect pre-theater choice."

5A5 Steak Lounge *Steak*   23 | 24 | 22 | $66
Downtown | 244 Jackson St. (bet. Battery & Front Sts.) | 415-989-2539 |
www.5a5stk.com
Packing "a very trendy punch", this "modern" Downtown steakhouse "lounge" attracts a "cool" crowd with its "chic" "retro" design as a backdrop for "imaginative" starters and "real-deal" cuts of beef; "prompt", "accommodating" service and "killer cocktails" soften the sting of potentially "spending a small fortune."

❷ Fleur de Lys ⧄Ⓜ *Californian/French*   27 | 27 | 27 | $100
Downtown | 777 Sutter St. (bet. Jones & Taylor Sts.) | 415-673-7779 |
www.fleurdelyssf.com
Hubert Keller "never fails to wow" at his "sublime" Downtown "destination" where he shows off his *Top Chef Masters* chops by way of "exquisite" French-Californian prix fixes and "perfect" wine pairings in a "lavish", "tented" room; devotees say it's "one of a handful of restaurants left" in the area where you feel "cosseted" with "impeccable service" from start to finish, so while it's "not priced for the everyday Joe", it's definitely *the* spot to "dress up" and "celebrate good times."

Florio *French/Italian*   22 | 22 | 22 | $44
Pacific Heights | 1915 Fillmore St. (bet. Bush & Pine Sts.) | 415-775-4300 |
www.floriosf.com
"Comforting" French-Italian "brasserie cuisine" and "welcoming" service result in "clean plates and happy campers all around" at this moderate Pacific Heights bistro; a "Manhattanish atmosphere" and "great bar scene" also help make it a "neighborhood favorite."

❷ Flour + Water *Italian*   26 | 20 | 22 | $49
Mission | 2401 Harrison St. (20th St.) | 415-826-7000 |
www.flourandwater.com
Chef Thomas McNaughton's "mind-blowing" "handmade pastas" and "artisanal" "thin, wood-fired" pizzas bring "folks by the boatload" to this "all-too-hip Mission" "farm-to-table" joint pumping out "blaring techno music" while pouring "reasonably priced" wines; scoring "reservations can feel like the holy grail" (if you "just show up", expect a "two-hour wait" even for the "community table"), and the staff could "lose the 'tude", but "in the end", contented "carb"-lovers concede it's worth the dough and the "hype."

Fog City Diner *American*   20 | 20 | 20 | $35
Embarcadero | 1300 Battery St. (The Embarcadero) | 415-982-2000 |
www.fogcitydiner.com
Somehow "down-home and upscale at the same time", this "iconic" Embarcadero eatery combines "retro" diner decor with "cleverly con-

"cocted" New American "comfort food" that's "taken up a notch"; though it's "on the tourist circuit" and a few fogies call it "overpriced", "even locals" "love it" for the "top-notch" cocktails, "professional" service and resemblance to a "vintage" "railway car."

Fondue Cowboy Ⓜ️ *Fondue* ▽ 22 | 19 | 19 | $33

SoMa | 1052 Folsom St. (Russ St.) | 415-431-5100 | www.fonduecowboy.com

Buckaroos "forget the cholesterol" and "reward" themselves at this "quirky" "hipster hangout" in SoMa where the "amazing" cheese fondue comes with a "wide variety of dippers", "friendly" service and a side of "watching old Westerns" playing; there are dessert varieties too, and moderate prices, leading some to proclaim it even "better than Switzerland."

Foreign Cinema *Californian/Mediterranean* 25 | 25 | 23 | $48

Mission | 2534 Mission St. (bet. 21st & 22nd Sts.) | 415-648-7600 | www.foreigncinema.com

"Still packing them in", this "ultrahip" "Mission mecca" offers "inventive" Cal-Med fare in a "beautiful" courtyard where you can "enjoy the stars, both above and foreign" in films projected on the wall; despite the "gimmick", it "doesn't disappoint", whether for "strong cocktails" alfresco or dining "by the fire" inside, and the "cool" setting and "super" service make the experience "even more memorable"; P.S. "don't miss" brunch with "gourmet Pop Tarts."

4505 Meats 🅱️Ⓜ️🍴 *Hot Dogs* 26 | 16 | 21 | $16

Embarcadero | Ferry Bldg. Mktpl. | 1 Ferry Bldg. (The Embarcadero) | 415-255-3094 | www.4505meats.com

"They put the urge in cheeseburger" at butcher-in-chief Ryan Farr's Ferry Building "meat lover's mecca", where the likes of "bacon-studded hot dogs" and "addictive" chicharrones satisfy "anything a carnivore is craving"; there's "no seating", and tabs are relatively high, but if you "come early to avoid the crowds", "service is great" – plus "you can't beat the view" of the bay; P.S. open Thursdays and Saturdays only, until 2 PM.

4th Street Bar & Grill *Pub Food/Sandwiches* 22 | 19 | 21 | $32

Downtown | San Francisco Marquis Hotel | 55 Fourth St. (bet. Market & Misson Sts.) | 415-442-6734 | www.the4thstreetbar.com

"TVs everywhere" and an "upbeat staff" make this "extremely friendly" hang in Downtown's San Francisco Marquis Hotel a "funtastic" spot to "check out the game"; fans cheer "fresh" pub grub that's "not very expensive", and "lots of taps" (offering 18 draft beers) behind the "large bar", all making it a "great place for a group" of sports lovers.

🅾️ Frances Ⓜ️ *Californian* 27 | 20 | 25 | $58

Castro | 3870 17th St. (Pond St.) | 415-621-3870 | www.frances-sf.com

Chef-owner "Melissa Perello knows how to make her beautiful fresh ingredients speak for themselves" at this "amazing" Castro Californian showcasing her "culinary virtuosity" for "totally reasonable" prices; "getting a reservation" is as elusive as snagging a "Wonka golden ticket" (though if you're lucky, you'll find "room at the bar"), and the "cramped" space gets "way too loud", but a "friendly", "dedicated" staff along with a "brilliant" "wines-by-the-ounce" offer keeps the place "full of smiling faces."

Frascati *Californian/Mediterranean*   26 21 24 $54

Russian Hill | 1901 Hyde St. (Green St.) | 415-928-1406 | www.frascatisf.com
Atop "lovely Russian Hill" where you can "watch the cable cars pass by",
this "intimate" "date-night" destination "couldn't be more charming"
say admirers of the "well-conceived" Cal-Med menu and "thoughtfully
curated" wine list; an "attentive" staff contributes to the "cozy" environment, so most give a pass to seating that's "a bit tight" and parking
that's "a drag."

Fresca *Peruvian*   22 18 19 $35

West Portal | 24 W. Portal Ave. (Ulloa St.) | 415-759-8087
Noe Valley | 3945 24th St. (bet. Noe & Sanchez Sts.) | 415-695-0549
Upper Fillmore | 2114 Fillmore St. (Clay St.) | 415-447-2668
www.frescasf.com
"Save the plane fare to Lima" and get the "real Peruvian deal" at
this "casual", "often crowded" trio, where "spectacular" ceviche
shares the menu with "perfectly cooked seafood", "comforting lomo
saltado" and "sweet" and "fruity" sangria; dishes are "reasonably
priced" (especially during the "fabulous" weekend brunch) even if
service is sometimes "slow."

Fringale *French/Spanish*   25 20 24 $51

SoMa | 570 Fourth St. (bet. Brannan & Freelon Sts.) | 415-543-0573 |
www.fringalesf.com
Each "lovingly prepared" "dish is better than the one before" at this
"classic" Gallic-Basque bistro "that will delight even the pickiest"
Parisian with its "bang for the price" and "fantastic" wine list; "the only
downside" is "snugly placed" tables squeezed into a SoMa space that's
"a wee bit too small", but the "endlessly gracious" "French-speaking
staff" establishes a "warm and welcoming" vibe.

Frjtz Fries *Belgian*   18 15 15 $17

Mission | 590 Valencia St. (17th St.) | 415-863-8272 | www.frjtzfries.com
It's the "closest you'll come to authentic frites without flying to Brussels"
say fans of this Mission counter-serve also hailed for its "plethora" of
"divine" dipping sauces, "vast" selection of crêpes and "good brews";
the "kitschy" decor may be a little "bizarre" for some and tabs "a bit
too pricey", but that doesn't stop a "hip crowd" from keeping it "busy."

Front Porch *Caribbean/Southern*   22 19 19 $33

Bernal Heights | 65 29th St. (bet. Mission St. & San Jose Ave.) |
415-695-7800 | www.thefrontporchsf.com
"When you crave real comfort food", this midpriced Southern-Caribbean
in Bernal Heights fits the bill, turning out "hipster soul food", like "legit"
fried chicken and "spicy shrimp and grits", all served by "the friendliest" staff; sure, it can be a "little cramped", and "low tin ceilings and
lots of talkative people don't go well together", but the "cheerful" vibe
helps distract, and many leave with "no complaints"; P.S. nearby spin-
off Rock Bar is at 80 29th Street.

Gamine *French*   25 18 24 $40

Cow Hollow | 2223 Union St. (bet. Fillmore & Steiner Sts.) | 415-771-7771 |
www.gaminesf.com
Since the "small" menu of "fantastic", "authentically French" fare
served at this "homey" "little" Cow Hollow bistro comes at "com-

pletely reasonable prices", patrons profess they "could eat here every other day and very often do"; expect "close quarters", and there are "no reservations" for fewer than six, but the owner "takes personal care of his patrons", ensuring an "upbeat" vibe.

Garçon Ⓜ *French*   22 | 18 | 21 | $43

Mission | 1101 Valencia St. (22nd St.) | 415-401-8959 | www.garconsf.com
It "feels like you're in a restaurant in Paris" sigh fans of this "quaint", not-too-expensive Mission bistro "with a West Coast twist"; a few find the menu "relatively standard", but "neighborhood" regulars return often for the "authentic" dishes, "divine" cocktails and "lively" atmosphere where "friendly French service" is "not an oxymoron."

🄯 Garden Court *Californian*   22 | 28 | 23 | $54

Downtown | Palace Hotel | 2 New Montgomery St. (Market St.) | 415-546-5089 | www.sfpalace.com
"Take someone special" to this "opulent, unforgettably gorgeous" dining room in Downtown's "iconic" Palace Hotel, where the "genuinely palatial setting makes one feel like a Rockefeller (or maybe even royalty)"; the Californian breakfast and lunch fare is "average" in comparison, but the Sunday brunch offers more choices "than you can fathom", and while prices are "high", service is "attentive" and visitors rationalize "you are paying for the privilege to dine in a beautiful room."

Garibaldis *Californian/Mediterranean*   24 | 22 | 23 | $50

Presidio Heights | 347 Presidio Ave. (bet. Clay & Sacramento Sts.) | 415-563-8841 | www.garibaldisrestaurant.com
"Always packed" with "well-heeled" Presidio Heights patrons, who "start the night" with a "fabulous" cocktail or "excellent" wine, this "clubby" "neighborhood institution" serves a "broad" "seasonal" menu of "creative" Cal-Med creations; it's "pretty pricey" say some, and "too noisy at times", but "expert" servers ("attentive without being overbearing") and "chic" "modern" decor add to the "understated elegance."

🄯 Gary Danko *American*   29 | 27 | 29 | $110

Fisherman's Wharf | 800 N. Point St. (Hyde St.) | 415-749-2060 | www.garydanko.com
It's "tough enough to get to No. 1 and even harder to stay there", but Gary Danko (the man and his "truly American classic" on the Wharf) "remains the reigning and undefeated champ" for Food, Service and Popularity in the Bay Area Survey, offering "the epitome of white-tablecloth fine dining" without the "stuck-up feeling" via "exceptional", "flexible prix fixe" options and "marvelous" "custom pairings" of wine (plus an "astounding" cheese cart); it's all delivered in a "gorgeous" "jewel-box" setting by a "most gracious" staff that "treats everyone like a millionaire", and naturally, it comes "at a price", but it's widely considered a "relative bargain" compared to other "temples of gastronomy."

Gaylord India *Indian*   22 | 21 | 20 | $42

Embarcadero | 1 Embarcadero Ctr. (Sacramento St.) | 415-397-7775 | www.gaylords1.com
Around since 1980, this Embarcadero Indian is an "old favorite" for "consistent", "tasty" meals, including a "nice lunch buffet"; some lament the provisions are "a wee less impressive than they were 30 years ago", adding the white-tablecloth space "hasn't been spruced up in

years", but many still "go for the nostalgia" and rationalize the "relatively high cost" pays for the "central location" and "attentive" staff.

Gialina *Pizza*   25 | 16 | 21 | $30

Glen Park | 2842 Diamond St. (Kern St.) | 415-239-8500 | www.gialina.com

Devotees pilgrimage from "all over the city" to this "family-friendly" Glen Park pizzeria, a "small place that packs a big punch" with its "high-class" pies featuring "crispy", "almost crackerlike crusts" and lots of "inventive topping combinations", plus "memorable" salads and "lovely" wines; "service is friendly" and the space "cozy", just "go early" because it's "always crowded" with folks "begging for a table" (no reservations).

NEW **Gioia Pizzeria** Ⓜ *Californian/Pizza*   - | - | - | I

Russian Hill | 2240 Polk St. (Green St.) | 415-359-0971 | www.gioiapizzeria.com

Crossing the bridge to Russian Hill, the husband-and-wife team behind Berkeley's tiny, touted pizzeria is cranking out its signature thin-crust New York–style pies and updated old-school sandwiches in this much larger sit-down storefront decorated with vintage lighting and flea market bric-a-brac; by day, it's quick service (and you can get slices), but in the evening, table service kicks in and the expanded menu showcases NorCal-inspired pastas and entrees, accompanied by wine and beer.

Giordano Bros. *Sandwiches*   22 | 14 | 19 | $14

NEW **Mission** | 3108 16th St. (Valencia St.) | 415-437-2767 ❶
North Beach | 303 Columbus Ave. (B'way) | 415-397-2767
www.giordanobros.com

"Sandwiches hit the spot every time" at this Mission and North Beach duo where the "Primanti's-style sammies" with "french fries and cole slaw in the middle" make transplants feel like they "never left Pittsburgh"; "lots of TVs for watching games" draw sports fans who appreciate service that's still generally "fast" even when there's a "packed house" during Steelers games.

Giorgio's Pizzeria *Pizza*   22 | 15 | 21 | $20

Inner Richmond | 151 Clement St. (3rd Ave.) | 415-668-1266 | www.giorgiospizza.com

If you're "getting a little tired of all those designer pies", join Inner Richmond locals at this "solid" "family-friendly" spot that's just "like the pizza parlor you grew up going to", with its "classic, thin-crust" 'zas and "old-school" decor ("cheesy rubber grapes and red-checkered tablecloths"); "friendly" staffers and a "homey" atmosphere further cement its status as a "neighborhood favorite."

Gitane 🅱Ⓜ *French/Spanish*   24 | 25 | 22 | $53

Downtown | 6 Claude Ln. (bet. Bush & Sutter Sts.) | 415-788-6686 | www.gitanerestaurant.com

"Low lights" and a "sexy ambiance" "invite a romantic evening" at this "youth-oriented" "hideaway" Downtown, where many "first dates" begin with "creative" cocktails at the "energetic" ground-floor bar before progressing to the "richly colored" dining area upstairs for "interesting" and "delicious" French-Spanish plates; it's not cheap, but service is "warm", and many agree it "adds much-needed spice" to the city.

Globe ⬤ *Californian/Italian* | 18 | 15 | 18 | $44 |

Downtown | 290 Pacific Ave. (bet. Battery & Front Sts.) | 415-391-4132 | www.globerestaurant.com

"Wear black" to blend in at this "dark", "spare" "Manhattan-style" space Downtown "famous for its late-night fare" (as well as "ample" weekday lunches); some "service industry" folks arrive "after their own shifts" to dine on the "dependable" Cal-Italian eats, creating a "friendly feeling all around", and though old-timers opine it's "not what it used to be", service is decent and prices won't break the bank.

Goat Hill Pizza *Pizza* | 22 | 15 | 19 | $19 |

Potrero Hill | 300 Connecticut St. (18th St.) | 415-641-1440
SoMa | 171 Stillman St. (bet. 3rd & 4th Sts.) | 415-974-1303
www.goathill.com

"Amazing for kids" and anyone else craving a "quality" pie on a "perfectly cooked" "sourdough crust", this "inexpensive" Potrero Hill pizzeria is staffed by the "friendliest folks" around; it isn't "upscale", but the "budget"-minded attest you "can't beat" the "very popular" "Monday night all-you-can-eat" option, and "fast delivery" and pickup are available from their SoMa spin-off.

Godzila Sushi *Japanese* | ▽ 22 | 15 | 20 | $34 |

Pacific Heights | 1800 Divisadero St. (Bush St.) | 415-931-1773

"More Tuesday night sushi" spot than "hot-date" destination, this Pac Heights Japanese with the "cute" movie monster decor keeps 'em "coming back" with "friendly" chefs who prepare "fresh" yet "no-frills" fish and "creative rolls" rocking "zany combinations"; though picky patrons deem it "decent, but not fantastic", diehards dub it a "steal for what it is" and "worth the wait."

Golden Boy ⬤🗗 *Pizza* | 25 | 13 | 19 | $10 |

North Beach | 542 Green St. (Jasper) | 415-982-9738 | www.goldenboypizza.com

"After a night out in North Beach", this "hole-in-the-wall" is a "lifesaver", serving "thick" slices of "square" focaccia pizza; it's just the thing to "soak up the booze" proclaim "partygoers" who "grab a slice" and "go" until 2:30 AM on weekends, but "it's pretty tasty sober too" attest regulars who snag a "barstool" and soak up the "funky", "friendly" vibe; P.S. the San Mateo branch closes earlier.

Golden West 🗗 *Bakery/Sandwiches* | ▽ 21 | 6 | 19 | $14 |

Downtown | 8 Trinity Alley (bet. Montgomery & Sutter Sts.) | 415-216-6443 | www.theauwest.com

"Nothing beats the warm pastries" at this Downtown bakery/take-out shop from Dennis Leary (Canteen) that also serves up "perfect lunch" offerings, like a "variety of salads" and solid sandwiches; prices are "slightly more expensive than a typical deli" but fans find it "worth the extra dollar (or two)" for the "inventiveness and quality of ingredients"; P.S. open Monday–Friday only.

Good Luck Dim Sum 🗗 *Chinese* | 22 | 5 | 10 | $11 |

Inner Richmond | 736 Clement St. (bet. 8th & 9th Aves.) | 415-386-3388

"Ten dollars buys a feast" at this "no-frills" Inner Richmond Chinese known for dim sum that "sells so quick it's all fresh"; there are no rolling carts, seating is limited and "don't expect friendly service", but "no place has lines out the door like it", proving the "consistently good" grub for "amazingly inexpensive" prices trumps all; P.S. closes at 6:30 PM.

Goood Frikin' Chicken *Mideastern* | 20 | 11 | 17 | $18 |

Mission | 10 29th St. (Mission St.) | 415-970-2428 | www.gfcsf.com
"Just like its name says", this "simple" Mission Middle Eastern "does chicken right", sending out "tender", "juicy" birds along with "tasty" bread and "delicious" sides, like hummus and mac 'n' cheese; service is "efficient" and prices low, and though there's "lots of space", many still recommend "getting takeout and enjoying it all at home."

Gott's Roadside *Diner* | 22 | 14 | 17 | $19 |

Embarcadero | Ferry Bldg. Mktpl. | 1 Ferry Bldg. (The Embarcadero) | 866-328-3663 | www.gottsroadside.com
See review in North of San Francisco Directory.

Gracias Madre *Mexican/Vegan* | 24 | 21 | 21 | $24 |

Mission | 2211 Mission St. (18th St.) | 415-683-1346 | www.gracias-madre.com
"*Gracias!*" cry devotees of this "organic" Mexican cantina in the Mission serving up affordable, "super-creative" vegan fare "without alienating omnivores" by being too "hippie-dippie"; it's "slow" and "loud" at peak times and the "communal tables weird some people out", but regulars appreciate the "festive atmosphere", as well as the "to-die-for" nut-based desserts.

Grand Cafe *French* | 21 | 26 | 21 | $46 |

Downtown | Hotel Monaco | 501 Geary St. (Taylor St.) | 415-292-0101 | www.grandcafe-sf.com
"Majestic ceilings" and "gorgeous" "art nouveau decor" "whisk you across the pond" and to another era at this "elegant" bistro where the "varied" menu of "French favorites" has "flair"; "reliable" servers make it "perfect" for "pre- or post-theater" Downtown dining, and the "attractive" "bustling bar" is popular for more "casual" meals, though perfectionists sigh "if only the food matched decor."

Great Eastern ● *Chinese* | 23 | 13 | 16 | $30 |

Chinatown | 649 Jackson St. (bet. Grant Ave. & Kearny St.) | 415-986-2500
"Skip the chow mein and get the real goodies" at this Chinese choice "in the heart of Chinatown" – like "wonderful seafood" selected from "big tanks" full of "live sea creatures" and during the day, "superb" dim sum (order it from the "brisk" waiters, since there are "no carts"); yes, it's "crowded" (especially since "Obama stopped in" in 2012) and decor is "minimal", but prices are "very fair" considering the "high quality."

Green Chile Kitchen & Market *Southwestern* | 23 | 19 | 19 | $19 |

Western Addition | 1801 McAllister St. (Baker St.) | 415-440-9411 | www.greenchilekitchen.com
Fans tout "the best posole outside of Santa Fe" and "fantastic" green chile stew at this "family-friendly" Western Addition Southwesterner that's "as close to New Mexican cooking" as you'll find hereabouts; a "casual" setup where you "order at the counter and seat yourself", it makes for a "well-priced" and "relatively fast" meal (preferably followed by some "damn tasty" pie).

	FOOD	DECOR	SERVICE	COST

Greens ⓜ *Vegetarian* — 25 | 24 | 23 | $43

Marina | Fort Mason Ctr., Bldg. A | Marina Blvd. (Buchanan St.) | 415-771-6222 | www.greensrestaurant.com

After more then 30 years, this Marina "granddaddy of vegetarian cuisine" "still has it", continuing to set a "gold standard" with "carefully prepared" dishes that "can convince even the most meat-inclined" to go to the "greens side"; service is "warm" in the "casually elegant" space, where "huge windows" offer "dramatic" bay views (especially at sunset), so while a few quibble it's a "little overpriced", more hail its "incredible staying power."

Hakka Restaurant *Chinese* — ▽ 23 | 9 | 17 | $25

Outer Richmond | 4401 Cabrillo (45th Ave.) | 415-876-6898 | www.hakkarestaurantsanfrancisco.com

Both Cantonese "staples" and "lesser-known Hakka delights", like the "not-to-be-missed" "deep-fried pumpkin" and "scrumptious" pork belly, get "two big thumbs up" at this plain-Jane "cheap-eats" choice; way out in the Outer Richmond, it still attracts a "crowd" of connoisseurs who "appreciate real Chinese food" and "good service."

Hamano Sushi ⓜ *Japanese* — 22 | 15 | 20 | $40

Noe Valley | 1332 Castro St. (bet. Jersey & 24th Sts.) | 415-826-0825 | www.hamanosushi.com

"What you go for is the sushi" say fans of this "low-key" Noe Valley Japanese that doles out "fresh fish" (including some "unusual cuts") and "interesting rolls", all for "affordable" prices; service is "friendly" too, now if only the "modest" space would undergo a "quick makeover."

Han IL Kwan *Korean* — 25 | 15 | 19 | $26

Outer Richmond | 1802 Balboa St. (19th Ave.) | 415-752-4447

Among the "multitude of Korean restaurants" in the Outer Richmond, this one "takes the title" for "plentiful" portions of "amazing" eats, from "high-quality" barbecue to "varied" *banchan*; "you know" it's "authentic" since "tour groups come here by the busload", but they also "wipe out the seating", so "call ahead" to reserve and brace for variable service "depending on the crowd."

Hapa Ramen ⓩⓜ⇗ *Japanese/Noodle Shop* — 21 | 13 | 18 | $14

Location varies; see website | 925-212-3289 | www.haparamensf.com

Chef-owner "Richie Nakano is always trying to improve" "and it shows" in his "killer ramen stock" and handmade noodles boosted by "fresh", "innovative" flavors that make for a cheap and "tasty treat"; while some find the food-stall fare and experience a bit uneven (open Tuesdays and Thursdays at the Ferry Building and Fridays at Off the Grid in Fort Mason), others say the "steaming hot" bowls are perfect for "soothing the savage beast within"; P.S. brick-and-mortar outpost Hapa is slated for 1527 Fillmore Street.

Hard Knox Cafe *Southern* — 22 | 16 | 21 | $20

Dogpatch | 2526 Third St. (bet. 22nd & 23rd Sts.) | 415-648-3770
Outer Richmond | 2448 Clement St. (bet. 25th & 26th Aves.) | 415-752-3770
www.hardknoxcafe.com

"Rib-sticking" soul food – think "crisp" fried chicken and "guilt-inducingly good side dishes" "like grandma used to make" – "hits the spot" at this "friendly", "funky" "down-home" duo in Dogpatch and the Outer Richmond; though nitpickers scowl it's "Southern food for people who have never been to the South", most are "super-satisfied" with the "experience", down to the "unbeatable" price.

Harris' *Steak* | 27 | 25 | 26 | $71 |

Polk Gulch | 2100 Van Ness Ave. (Pacific Ave.) | 415-673-1888 | www.harrisrestaurant.com

"When you must have meat", this "timeless" Polk Gulch steakhouse "never fails" to deliver "phenomenal" "dry-aged steaks" accompanied by "tantalizing sides" and wines from a "superior" list; "oh yes, you will pay for the privilege", but it's "worth it" when enjoying an "ice-cold martini" listening to "live jazz" in the bar or being "pampered" by "professional" servers in the "elegant" "Rat Pack–style dining room."

Hayes Street Grill *Seafood* | 24 | 19 | 24 | $50 |

Hayes Valley | 320 Hayes St. (bet. Franklin & Gough Sts.) | 415-863-5545 | www.hayesstreetgrill.com

"Always a very satisfying" experience, this "elegant" yet "understated" Hayes Valley venue allows the "super-fresh" fish to "shine" in "simple" dishes that are nonetheless "exquisitely prepared"; "popular" with "concert-goers" who "overlook the dated decor" since the "professional" "staff knows how to make the curtain", it's been a seafood "stronghold" for more than 30 years.

NEW Hayes Valley | - | - | - | I |

Bakeworks ⌷ *American/Bakery*

Hayes Valley | 550 Gough St. (bet. Fulton & Grove Sts.) | 415-864-2688 | www.bakeworkssf.com

Bringing carbs and a good cause together in Hayes Valley, this non-profit bakery and cafe pumps out affordable housemade pastries, pizzas, sandwiches and 'celebrity soups' employing recipes from local chefs, plus Four Barrel coffee and Kombucha on tap; the sunny corner storefront, outfitted with reclaimed wood cabinetry and a wall of vintage rolling pins, doubles as a culinary training program for disabled, homeless or at-risk staffers.

Heaven's Dog ● *Chinese* | 20 | 19 | 18 | $39 |

SoMa | 1148 Mission St. (bet. 7th & 8th Sts.) | 415-863-6008 | www.heavensdog.com

Charles Phan hounds "chill out" at this "hip" Slanted Door sibling in a "somewhat barren" stretch of SoMa, where a "vibed-out" loungelike setting is the backdrop for "updated" Chinese "street food" and "amazing cocktails served with hand-carved ice"; diners can easily "run up a large check one bun at a time", but the "pre-theater" locale and late-night hours (until 1 AM nightly) compensate, plus there's thriftier slurping at the "noodle bar."

Hecho ⌷ *Japanese* | ▽ 18 | 19 | 18 | $61 |

Downtown | 185 Sutter St. (Kearny St.) | 415-835-6400 | www.hechosf.com

"Try it, you will not be disappointed" assure fans of this "cool concept" Downtown, where chef Joseph Manzare (Globe, Tres Agaves) serves pricey, "good-quality" sushi and an "outstanding tequila selection" (sake too) amid Japanese-cinema-inspired decor; dissenters call it an "odd fusion", but it appeals to those seeking something "a little different"; P.S. ratings do not reflect the recent arrival of master sushi chef Sachio Kojima.

Heirloom Café 🗷 *Californian/Mediterranean* 　25 | 20 | 22 | $50

Mission | 2500 Folsom St. (21st St.) | 415-821-2500 | www.heirloom-sf.com

"Up-to-date locavore food" offering "delightful combinations of flavors" is complemented by "incredible" wines "lovingly chosen" by the oenophile owner at this "cute" Mission Cal-Med; it's "a bit pricey, but worth it" say those who find it "fun to sit at a counter and see the chef at work" or "score a spot at the communal table" – and aren't bothered by "very noisy" atmospherics.

Helmand Palace *Afghan* 　24 | 16 | 20 | $34

Russian Hill | 2424 Van Ness Ave. (bet. Green & Union Sts.) | 415-362-0641 | www.helmandpalace.com

"Outstanding", "authentic" Afghan eats from "fabulous" pumpkin dishes to "lamb beyond measure" appeal to the globe-trotting gourmands drawn to the "wide choice" of "unusual" flavors offered at this "quiet" Russian Hill haunt; as for the setting, though "pleasant", "a palace it's not", but an "accommodating" staff and "very fair" prices make it a "neighborhood gem."

Henry's Hunan *Chinese* 　22 | 11 | 19 | $21

Chinatown | 924 Sansome St. (bet. B'way & Vallejo St.) | 415-956-7727
Downtown | 674 Sacramento St. (Spring St.) | 415-788-2234 🗷
Noe Valley | 1708 Church St. (bet. Day & 29th Sts.) | 415-826-9189
SoMa | 1016 Bryant St. (bet. 8th & 9th Sts.) | 415-861-5808 🗷
SoMa | 110 Natoma St. (bet. New Montgomery & 2nd Sts.) | 415-546-4999 🗷
www.henryshunanrestaurant.com

"When they ask you" "how hot", get "prepared to perspire" at this "hole-in-the-wall" Chinese chainlet, where the "distinctive" Hunan dishes "bursting" with "fresh ingredients" are "a cut above" the competition; there's "no atmosphere to speak of", but "what it lacks in charm it makes up" in the "efficiency" of the "friendly servers" and the "insanely reasonable" price.

Hillstone *American* 　24 | 22 | 24 | $41

Embarcadero | 1800 Montgomery St. (bet. Bay & Chestnut Sts.) | 415-392-9280 | www.hillstone.com

"Yes", "it's a chain", but "the formula works" affirm fans of this "airy" "modern" Embarcadero branch where "there's something for everyone" on the "fantastic" American menu, from burgers "you can't beat" to "fall-off-the-bone" babyback ribs; it's "nothing spectacular or innovative", but "well-trained" servers and nightly "soft jazz" mean most will "be back."

Hog & Rocks ● *American* 　22 | 20 | 21 | $37

Mission | 3431 19th St. (San Carlos St.) | 415-550-8627 | www.hogandrocks.com

"Oysters, oysters and more oysters" keep seafood lovers happy at this "popular" "high-end pub" in the Mission while "excellent ham" and "creative" cocktails are some of the other specialties on the menu of American small and large plates; communal tables and "friendly" staffers add to the "hoppin' vibe", especially during happy hour when the "half-shell goodies" are even more "reasonably priced."

Hog Island Oyster Co. & Bar *Seafood*   26 | 18 | 20 | $36

Embarcadero | Ferry Bldg. Mktpl. | 1 Ferry Bldg. (The Embarcadero) | 415-391-7117 | www.hogislandoysters.com

"What could be better" than to "slurp" "succulent" oysters with a "glass of champagne" or "quality craft beer" exclaim bivalve boosters, who sometimes "sit outside" "right at the water's edge" at this Embarcadero seafooder; servers who "know" and "respect" their product are always "on it" but can't eliminate the "long wait", especially during the "jammed" "half-price" "happy hour"; P.S. Napa's branch "in the Oxbow Market" lacks the "magnificent view" but has a more "mellow vibe."

Hong Kong Lounge *Chinese*   24 | 16 | 16 | $25

NEW **Laurel Heights** | 3300 Geary Blvd. (bet. Beaumont & Parker Aves.) | 415-668-8802

Outer Richmond | 5322 Geary Blvd. (bet. 17th & 18th Aves.) | 415-668-8836

Lines rivaling "the Great Wall" suggest this Outer Richmond dim sum spot is "one of the best", serving a "stunning variety" of "superb" dumplings delivered "directly from the kitchen to your table"; "quality" Chinese dinners, including "bargain" "prix fixe" options, add to the possibilities – as long as you can overlook sometimes "not so nice" staffers; P.S. for a "shorter wait" try the Laurel Heights offshoot.

Hotei *Japanese*   20 | 14 | 19 | $23

Inner Sunset | 1290 Ninth Ave. (bet. Irving St. & Lincoln Way) | 415-753-6045 | www.hoteisf.com

"Gorgeously fresh" "sushi from Ebisu", its sister spot across the street, joins forces with "Japanese noodles" that chase away the "cold" "foggy days" at this Inner Sunset eatery; though the "cozy" room can get "crowded" and a few find the fare "hit-or-miss", most "highly recommend" the "robust" ramen and "fabulous" soba at "bargain prices."

The House *Asian*   27 | 17 | 22 | $45

North Beach | 1230 Grant Ave. (bet. Columbus Ave. & Vallejo St.) | 415-986-8612 | www.thehse.com

Offering a "break from the endless Italian" options in North Beach, this "no-frills" "charmer" presents "creative Asian fusion cuisine" that's "artfully done" and might go for "a much higher price in a more upscale setting"; while the "small space" can be "cramped", fans praise the "efficient service" and a wine list that's "excellent and not too expensive."

House of Nanking *Chinese*   23 | 9 | 15 | $23

Chinatown | 919 Kearny St. (Columbus Ave.) | 415-421-1429

"They have a menu, but I'm not sure what for" say regulars of this "seedy-looking" Chinatown "hole-in-the-wall", who advise allowing the "Soup Nazi-ish" servers to "decide what you should eat" from the cheap array of "killer" Chinese chow; prepare to "line up along the sidewalk" before being seated at a "cramped" table and "bumping elbows with strangers", but – "love it or hate it" – "it's all part of the experience."

	FOOD	DECOR	SERVICE	COST

⦿ House of Prime Rib *American*   26 | 22 | 25 | $56

Polk Gulch | 1906 Van Ness Ave. (Washington St.) | 415-885-4605 |
www.houseofprimerib.net

"If you have anything other than prime rib" at this "reasonably priced"
Polk Gulch "blast from the past" "you're missing the point", as they've
got its "preparation and presentation" "down to a science", with
"courteous" servers carving "generous" slabs from big "shiny" "metal
zeppelins"; paired with "unparalleled" sides and an "irresistible" martini "delivered in its own shaker", it's an "old-school indulgence" in a
"handsome English steakhouse" setting.

HRD Coffee Shop ⦿⦿ *Diner/Korean*   25 | 8 | 22 | $11

SoMa | 521 Third St. (bet. Bayshore Frwy. & Brannan St.) | 415-543-2355 |
www.hrdcoffeeshop.com

"Bazillions of local workers" flock to this "cramped", "no-frills" Korean
diner in SoMa for "awesome fusion" breakfast eats such as kimchi
burritos and more "everyday plates"; further enticements include
prices that are "rock-bottom ridiculous" and staffers who are "friendly
even in the craziest of lunch rushes"; P.S. closes at 3 PM.

Hunan Home's Restaurant *Chinese*   22 | 13 | 19 | $25

Chinatown | 622 Jackson St. (bet. Grant Ave. & Kearny St.) | 415-982-2844 |
www.hunanhomes.com

Connoisseurs of "homestyle" Hunanese "develop a habit" at this
"reliable" Chinatown Chinese (and its Los Altos and Palo Alto offshoots), thanks to "generous" servings of "freshly made" fare and
"fabulous" sauces from "not spicy" to "really hot" (if you're "feeling strong", say "make me sweat"); though the "dated decor" has
detractors, service is "a cut above" what you'd expect "in this price
range" (i.e. "cheap").

Hyde Street Bistro *French*   22 | 19 | 20 | $44

Russian Hill | 1521 Hyde St. (bet. Jackson St. & Pacific Ave.) |
415-292-4415 | www.hydestreetbistrosf.com

"Charming enough" "for a romantic dinner", this "comfortable" bistro
atop Russian Hill is a "cozy" perch for canoodling over "simple French"
dishes like "you had in Paris"; though a few find service "lackluster",
most "feel welcomed back each time" with a "leisurely" meal that's "a
bargain to boot"; P.S. regulars suggest arriving via "cable car" to avoid
the "challenging" parking.

⦿ Ichi Sushi ⦿ *Japanese*   27 | 18 | 23 | $46

Bernal Heights | 3369 Mission St. (Godeus St.) | 415-525-4750 |
www.ichisushi.com

"Magnificent" sashimi and "traditional, superbly prepared nigiri" featuring fish that you might've "never had before", particularly if you "go
with the omakase", are sold for relatively "reasonable prices" at this
"friendly" Japanese "hole-in-the-wall" in Bernal Heights; it's "really
tiny", so "get there early", especially if you "want a seat at the bar."

Ideale Restaurant *Italian*   25 | 18 | 23 | $43

North Beach | 1315 Grant Ave. (Vallejo St.) | 415-391-4129 |
www.idealerestaurant.com

"Superb" Roman *cucina*, from "excellent" antipasti to "flawless" risotto
and "homemade pasta", is "as authentic as it gets" at this "unpreten-

tious" eatery with an "extensive" wine list; the price is "reasonable" say fans who are "transported" from "touristic North Beach "to a little trattoria in Italy" by the "homey" setting and "welcoming" "staff.

Ike's Place *Sandwiches*   25 | 12 | 18 | $13

Castro | 3489 16th St. (Sanchez St.) | 415-553-6888 | www.ilikeikesplace.com

"Ginormous" sandwiches that are "hot" and "toasty "heaven on a bun" take subs "to a new level" at this "well-hyped" Castro-ite with branches around the Bay; it's "not really a sit-down place" (the "hipster clientele" usually heads to "Dolores Park") and "insanely long lines" can stretch "round the block", so "call ahead" or "order online" to "breeze past the starving masses" and "collect" your "pricey" "prize" from the "upbeat" staff.

Il Cane Rosso *Italian*   23 | 13 | 15 | $21

Embarcadero | Ferry Bldg. Mktpl. | 1 Ferry Bldg. (The Embarcadero) | 415-391-7599 | www.canerossosf.com

"Exceptional sandwiches, salads" and rotisserie chicken comprise the "satisfying" bill of fare at this "small", "casual" Italian cafe in the Ferry Building, where the counter service can be "slow", but the prices always equal a "bargain"; "snagging a table" can be "stressful", so "if the weather's nice, take it outside" and "swoon" over the bay view.

☒ Il Fornaio *Italian*   22 | 22 | 21 | $39

Downtown | Levi's Plaza | 1265 Battery St. (bet. Filbert & Greenwich Sts.) | 415-986-0100 | www.ilfornaio.com

It's "hard to go wrong" at this "lively" Italian chain, where "wonderful" "freshly baked" breads precede "well-crafted" plates of pasta and "often exceptional" "monthly" "regional specials"; if novelty-seekers sigh it's "reliable but never exciting", it's "popular" with the "power lunch" crowd that appreciates the "professional service" and "elegant surroundings" that belie the "reasonable price."

Imperial Tea Court *Tearoom*   19 | 20 | 19 | $23

Embarcadero | Ferry Bldg. Mktpl. | 1 Ferry Bldg. (The Embarcadero) | 415-544-9830 | www.imperialtea.com

A "calm oasis" amid the "bustle of the Ferry Building" with an even "more picturesque" Berkeley branch, this "Zen" tearoom twosome is the "perfect place" to "slow down" with a pot of "exotic" tea from an "impressive selection"; the "small" menu of "excellent handmade noodles" and "incredible" dim sum may be "expensive", but oolong enthusiasts who aren't "in a hurry" are rewarded with a "lovely" experience.

Incanto *Italian*   25 | 22 | 23 | $56

Noe Valley | 1550 Church St. (bet. Duncan & 28th Sts.) | 415-641-4500 | www.incanto.biz

Plying "cuts of meat" "most people don't think of eating", Chris Cosentino's "Dante's Inferno"-themed" Noe Valley "nose-to-tail" ristorante is a "treat" for "adventurous carnivores" and "swineophiles", while those preferring something "more traditional" can stick to "rustic Italian" fare such as "spectacular salumi" and "top"-notch "handmade pastas"; "charming" servers "know what to suggest", including "flights" from the "exclusively Italian wine list", and all things considered, it doesn't cost an "offal" lot.

	FOOD	DECOR	SERVICE	COST

Indian Oven *Indian* — 23 | 18 | 22 | $29

Lower Haight | 233 Fillmore St. (bet. Haight & Waller Sts.) | 415-626-1628 | www.indianovensf.com

"Indescribably delicious" Indian eats, from "divine" curries to "beautifully prepared" meats, "never fail to please" Lower Haight habitués at this "surprisingly lovely" location with a "bright and airy" dining room; it's perpetually "packed", especially "on weekends", but a "friendly" staff that "showers you with attentive service" means most "can't wait to go back."

Indigo Ⓜ *American* — 22 | 20 | 23 | $48

Civic Center | 687 McAllister St. (Gough St.) | 415-673-9353 | www.indigorestaurant.com

"Satisfying" fare inspired by the "farmer's market" (especially the "early-bird prix fixe menu") is relatively "affordable" at this "reliable" blue-hued Civic Center New American "within walking distance of the symphony"; if a few sniff it's "nothing special", the pre-performance crowd applauds its "attentive" servers who "get you wined, dined and on your way."

Ⓩ In-N-Out Burger ● *Burgers* — 23 | 14 | 21 | $9

Fisherman's Wharf | 333 Jefferson St. (bet. Jones & Leavenworth Sts.) | 800-786-1000 | www.in-n-out.com

"California's contribution to the fast-food universe" "puts the other burger joints to shame" boast boosters of its "juicy" patties, "freshly cut" fries and "super-thick" shakes "that taste the way they did way back when"; though most of the "old-time" "cheap" chain links are "jam-packed" with cultists savvy to the "secret menu" (and who suggest ordering "animal-style everything"), "smiling" "young" servers "hustle to get your order out" "fast."

Isa *French* — 24 | 20 | 21 | $47

Marina | 3324 Steiner St. (bet. Chestnut & Lombard Sts.) | 415-567-9588 | www.isarestaurant.com

There's "lots to love" at this "lively" "small-plates palace" in the Marina, including "terrific" French nibbles, "great" wines, an "enthusiastic staff" and "dark", intimate digs that are ripe for "date night"; though some feel that the "volume-to-price ratio" isn't high, others say that costs are "reasonable", and even better with happy-hour (nightly) and prix fixe (Sunday–Thursday) deals; P.S. sitting "on the covered back terrace" is "nothing short of magical."

Izakaya Sozai Ⓜ *Japanese* — 23 | 16 | 15 | $35

Inner Sunset | 1500 Irving St. (16th Ave.) | 415-742-5122 | www.izakayasozai.com

Purists are "blown away" by the "traditional" "small plates" – like "staggeringly good" yakitori and "exceptional" ramen in a "delicious porky broth" – at this "cozy" Inner Sunset Japanese that also pours "amazing" sakes; prices are moderate, and though you'll likely have to "wait outside" for a seat in the "tiny" space, connoisseurs claim the "friendly owner" has captured "the true spirit of izakaya."

ⁿᵉʷ Izakaya Yuzuki Ⓢ *Japanese* — ▽ 23 | 18 | 21 | $39

Mission | 598 Guerrero St. (18th St.) | 415-556-9898 | www.yuzukisf.com

This new izakaya in the Mission from owner/Osaka native Yuko Hayashi specializes in "authentic Japanese dishes"; "don't expect a quick, cheap meal", but do leave time to "sample lots of amazing little bites", sho-chu, beer and sake at the walnut bar surrounded by calligraphy-style paintings and other simple adornments.

Izzy's Steaks & Chops Steak   **23 | 20 | 22 | $45**

Marina | 3345 Steiner St. (bet. Chestnut & Lombard Sts.) | 415-563-0487 | www.izzyssteaks.com

A "dimly lit" "throwback" to a previous era, this "inviting" Marina steakhouse (with "not to be overlooked" suburban siblings) caters to meat mavens with "huge portions" of "fantastic" chops, "ter-rific" "old-style" sides and a "well-priced wine list"; though "a bit pricey for everyday", budget-watchers call it a "way-better value" than the "bigger names", and "professional waiters" help create a "relaxing" vibe.

Jackson Fillmore Trattoria Ⓜ Italian   **22 | 13 | 20 | $43**

Upper Fillmore | 2506 Fillmore St. (bet. Jackson St. & Pacific Ave.) | 415-346-5288 | www.jacksonfillmoresf.com

"Home away from home" for Upper Fillmore habitués, this "itty-bitty" "neighborhood hot spot" "rolls on year after year" serving Italian fare such as "excellent" "fresh pastas" at "reasonable" tabs; "the atmosphere" alone "is worth the price of admission" say reg-ulars, who "sit at the bar" for "very personal service", but "would it kill them to spruce up the joint" inquire critics, who also wish it weren't so "loud" and "crowded."

Jai Yun Chinese   ▽ **24 | 12 | 15 | $81**

Chinatown | 680 Clay St. (Kearny St.) | 415-981-7438 | www.jaiyunrestaurant.com

"A smorgasbord of meticulously prepared dishes" comes from "inno-vative" chef-owner Nei Chia Ji at his Chinatown joint where guests "come with an open mind", choose one of three or so "prix fixe small-plate dinners" and sample "delicacies not found on most Chinese menus"; just "be prepared for a very long dinner", service that's "good, not great" and an "expensive bill" (it's "worth every penny").

Jake's Steaks Cheesesteaks   ▽ **23 | 16 | 20 | $13**

Marina | 3301 Buchanan St. (bet. Lombard & Magnolia Sts.) | 415-922-2211 | www.jakessteaks.net

"Experience Philadelphia without leaving the Bay Area" at this Marina haven of "true" cheesesteaks, Tastykakes and cheers of "go Eagles!"; service is mostly "warm", but the paraphernalia-strewn digs are small and often "noisy", so if you're looking to relax, get it to go.

ⓩ Jardinière Californian/French   **27 | 27 | 26 | $80**

Civic Center | 300 Grove St. (Franklin St.) | 415-861-5555 | www.jardiniere.com

Traci Des Jardins' "beautifully appointed" two-tier Civic Center "hot spot" "still impresses in every way", from the "always spectacular" "seasonal" Cal-French fare and "outstanding" service (especially "given the pre-theater rush") to the "Ginger Rogers movie" ambiance and central bar that "oozes glamour"; sure it's a "coin hit", but the "Monday night prix fixe" and downstairs lounge menu allow for regu-lar indulgences, and the location and "late hours" "after the opera" make it a "go-to" for the "oysters and champagne" set.

	FOOD	DECOR	SERVICE	COST

Jasper's Corner Tap & Kitchen *American*   ▽ 22 | 19 | 21 | $37

Downtown | Serrano Hotel | 401 Taylor St. (O'Farrell St.) | 415-775-7979 | www.jasperscornertap.com

"Knowledgeable" staffers serve "delicious", "good-value" American "comfort food" from breakfast through late night at this Downtown gastropub; what's more, the "contemporary" digs boast "plenty of room", with a large bi-level dining room and TV-bedecked front bar offering "great beer choices" and "stellar cocktails", including "Negroni on tap."

Java Beach Cafe *Sandwiches*   20 | 19 | 19 | $12

Outer Sunset | 1396 La Playa St. (Judah St.) | 415-665-5282
Outer Sunset | 2650 Sloat Blvd. (45th Ave.) | 415-731-2965
www.javabeachcafe.com

Popular options include a "delicious" "morning cup of joe by the beach" and "a beer and a sandwich at sunset" at this pair of "quirky" Outer Sunset "surfer hangouts" serving a "simple" menu of "quality" subs, salads and pastries; lines can be "long", but servers who are "patient" with those who "dillydally" make it a "nice hangout" nonetheless.

Jay's Cheesesteak *Cheesesteaks*   ▽ 19 | 10 | 16 | $13

Mission | 3285 21st St. (bet. Lexington & Valencia Sts.) | 415-285-5200 ✉
Western Addition | 553 Divisadero St. (bet. Fell & Hayes Sts.) | 415-771-5104
www.jayscheesesteak.com

Though foodies feel the "fat, juicy cheesesteaks" sold at these Mission and Western Addition sandwich shops are "not really like an original Philly", they "still give them props" for trying out a "San Francisco take on an East Coast classic", including a seitan-mushroom version that vegans call "to-die-for"; at the very least, it "fills a hole", and in "speedy" and cheap fashion.

Joe's Cable Car *Burgers*   22 | 17 | 19 | $20

Excelsior | 4320 Mission St. (Tingley St.) | 415-334-6699 | www.joescablecar.com

"Awesome burgers" are "what it comes down to" at this "kitschy" Excelsior diner where "Joe himself" "grinds his own fresh chuck daily" for some of the "highest-quality" patties in town; he's a "great host" who "makes sure every customer is happy", but he can't cheer up walletwatchers unprepared to "pay more than $10" for beef on a "paper plate."

John's Grill *Seafood/Steak*   22 | 23 | 21 | $46

Downtown | 63 Ellis St. (bet. Powell & Stockton Sts.) | 415-986-0069 | www.johnsgrill.com

"Any place recommended by Dashiell Hammett is good by me" aver aficionados of this "old-fashioned" Downtowner that was a setting in *The Maltese Falcon*; "the atmosphere really takes you back", as does the menu of "classic" seafood dishes, "damn good" steaks and "cocktails that would make Sam Spade proud", and "attentive" service and "live jazz" add to the experience, at prices that are "reasonable for SF."

Juban *Japanese*   20 | 17 | 19 | $32

Japantown | Kinokuniya Bldg. | 1581 Webster St. (Post St.) | 415-776-5822 | www.jubanrestaurant.com

"Bring someone who knows how to cook" quip connoisseurs of these "casual" yakinuki joints in J-town, Burlingame and Menlo Park, because "you grill your own" "fantastic" "fresh" meats on a hibachi "at your table"; it "pleases" Japanese expats and is "fun" for "kids" too, "I just wish it were a bit cheaper" sigh frugal types put off by "small" portions.

Just Wonton ☒ Chinese   ▽ 20 | 7 | 17 | $15

Outer Sunset | 1241 Vicente St. (bet. 23rd & 24th Aves.) | 415-681-2999
"Customize" your own "inexpensive and filling meal" via a "wide variety" of "delicious wontons" at this Outer Sunset Chinese "hole-in-the-wall"; rice and noodle dishes "do not disappoint" either, and the staff is "friendly" too.

Kabuto ☒ Japanese   26 | 15 | 20 | $46

Outer Richmond | 5121 Geary Blvd. (bet. 15th & 16th Aves.) | 415-752-5652 | www.kabutosushi.com
"Amazing", "extremely fresh" sushi, both "traditional" and "totally original", reels seafood fanatics into this "tiny" Outer Richmond Japanese "that knows their fish"; "adventurers" who sample the "imaginative" creations of the "talented chefs" or order the "oh-my-gawd" omakase are "rewarded" with a "unique experience", so few fret about the "long wait" to be seated in the "casual", "minimalist" dining room.

Kappou Gomi ☒ Japanese   ▽ 28 | 21 | 23 | $43

Outer Richmond | 5524 Geary Blvd. (bet. 19th & 20th Aves.) | 415-221-5353
"Adventurous" eaters "cannot go wrong" at this "low-key" Outer Richmond "jewel" proffering an "enormous menu" of 'impeccably presented", "home-cooked" "delights you won't find outside of Japan" ("there's no such thing as sushi here", but "sublime sashimi" is served); solid service and "reasonable prices" are two more reasons fans "wholeheartedly recommend" it for an "out-of-the-ordinary" experience.

Kasa Indian Eatery Indian   22 | 14 | 19 | $15

Castro | 4001 18th St. (Noe St.) | 415-621-6940 | www.kasaindian.com
"Atypical" Indian eats, such as "amazing" "kati rolls" ("like Indian burritos") and "tasty" Thali dinners attract a following to this "cheap and cheerful" Castro-ite; "portions could be bigger", but the "trendy" "young" patrons are partial to the "hipster" staff's use of "organic" "local" ingredients; P.S. "you might catch" their "cool purple truck" at locations around the Bay.

Katana-Ya ◗ Japanese   22 | 11 | 16 | $17

Downtown | 430 Geary St. (bet. Mason & Taylor Sts.) | 415-771-1280
"Get your ramen on" at this "hole-in-the-wall near Union Square", where "gigantic bowls" of "amazing", "chewy" Japanese noodles in "rich" broths (plus sushi that some deem "delicious" and others find "forgettable") are sold for "cheap prices"; "packed" quarters with a "line out the door" means "the staff expects you to get in and out" – "which is fine" by most folks.

Kate's Kitchen ⊠ Southern   ▽ 22 | 16 | 19 | $15

Lower Haight | 471 Haight St. (bet. Fillmore & Webster Sts.) | 415-626-3984 | www.kates-kitchensf.com
If you "get the large stack" of "hearty" pancakes, "for the love of God, split it", because the "amazing" Southern breakfasts and lunches

come in "very generous portions" at this Lower Haight "friendly" "hipster hangover" haunt with "cute" "checkered tablecloths"; "be prepared to wait" "on weekends" and don't forget to "bring cash", because it "doesn't disappoint" when you want "cheap" chow.

Katia's Russian Tea Room 🅼 *Russian*   ▽ 20 | 16 | 22 | $30

Inner Richmond | 600 Fifth Ave. (Balboa St.) | 415-668-9292 |
www.katias.com

Katia herself "oversees the kitchen", concocting "authentic" (and otherwise "hard to find") Russian "comfort food" (think "excellent borscht" and "great blini") at this casual "little" midpriced Inner Richmond "jewel"; their formal tea service requires advance reservations, but expect the owner "and her husband" to "provide very attentive care" when you arrive.

NEW Keiko à Nob Hill 🅼 *French/Japanese*   ▽ 29 | 27 | 28 | $123

Nob Hill | 1250 Jones St. (Clay St.) | 415-829-7141 | www.keikoanobhill.com
"Come before the news is out" advise supporters of this "great addition to Nob Hill", where chef Keiko Takahashi (ex El Paseo) turns out "elaborate preparations" of "to-die-for" Japanese-influenced French cuisine with "flavors that pop"; service that's "attentive yet nonintrusive" sets a "quiet" tone in the elegant environment, and though costs are "high", value-seekers say the "amazing tasting menu" paired with "outstanding" wines (with "lots of older French vintages") is "underpriced for what you get."

NEW Ken Ken   ▽ 21 | 16 | 18 | $24

Ramen 🅱🅼 *Japanese/Noodle Shop*
Mission | 3378 18th St. (Capp St.) | 415-967-2636 |
www.eatkenkenramen.com

A "divine wonder" is how converts describe this "cozy (albeit loud)" new Mission brick-and-mortar iteration of a popular pop-up, and though its Japanese ramen "selection is limited", it is "one of the few" to offer a vegan option; limited hours (Thursdays–Saturdays, 6–10 PM) exacerbate the "really long wait", but reasonable prices help to make it worth it.

Khan Toke Thai House *Thai*   22 | 22 | 22 | $31

Outer Richmond | 5937 Geary Blvd. (bet. 23rd & 24th Aves.) |
415-668-6654

"One of the first Thai restaurants in the city", this "lovely" 1976 spot in the Outer Richmond continues to be "popular" for fare that's "tasty" and "affordable"; but "the total experience" – "taking off your shoes", sitting on floor cushions overlooking a "beautiful garden outside" and being served by staffers "dressed in authentic attire" – is "what makes this place stand out."

Kiji Sushi Bar & Cuisine 🅱 *Japanese*   ▽ 25 | 20 | 21 | $42

Mission | 1009 Guerrero St. (bet. Alvarado & 22nd Sts.) | 415-282-0400 |
www.kijirestaurant.com

Look for the red lantern outside to find "one of the best-kept secrets" in the Mission, this "sexy-looking" Japanese whose "creative", "delectable" (and mostly sustainable) sushi comes at "a reasonable price"; "friendly, knowledgeable servers" and a "wide range of sake" only add to its allure.

Kingdom of Dumpling *Chinese*
22 | 6 | 14 | $16

Parkside | 1713 Taraval St. (27th Ave.) | 415-566-6143
This "tiny" Parkside "hole-in-the-wall" "charms the tongue" with "darn-good dumplings" and other "cheap and delicious" Chinese eats; just "don't expect service or decor" or fast in-and-out, as there are often "huge waits" – though "takeout is quick and easy."

King of Thai *Thai*
22 | 12 | 17 | $14

Downtown | 184 O'Farrell St. (bet. Powell & Stockton Sts.) | 415-677-9991 ◑
Fisherman's Wharf | 2800 Leavenworth St. (Beach St.) | 415-346-9555
Inner Richmond | 346 Clement St. (bet. 4th & 5th Aves.) | 415-831-9953 ◑
Inner Richmond | 639 Clement St. (bet. 7th & 8th Aves.) | 415-752-5198 ◑⇄
North Beach | 1268 Grant Ave. (bet. Fresno & Vallejo Sts.) | 415-391-8219 | www.kingofthainoodlehouse.com ◑
Outer Sunset | 1507 Sloat Blvd. (bet. Everglade & Springfield Drs.) | 415-566-9921 ⇄
Outer Sunset | 1541 Taraval St. (bet. 25th & 26th Aves.) | 415-682-9958 ◑
"Hungry students with a light wallet" and other penny-pinchers "shocked" at the "unbeatable" prices flock to this "casual" SF septet (and Alameda offshoot) where "large" portions of "very tasty Thai noodles" and "spicy" curries come "amazingly fast"; there's "no ambiance whatsoever", so some favor "takeout", but they're undoubtedly "convenient" when you have a "late-night" "craving" (most are open nightly until at least 1 AM).

❚ Kiss Seafood 🅈🅼 *Japanese*
28 | 18 | 25 | $83

Japantown | 1700 Laguna St. (Sutter St.) | 415-474-2866
"For the real thing" without the airfare, foodies trek to this "secret sushi spot" in Japantown where "divinely executed sushi" ("any fresher and you'd be eating underwater") and "amazingly authentic" omakase dinners are served in "living room"–sized digs; with only "12 seats" overseen by "the chef and his wife", it feels like an "honor to eat here" for guests who gush it's "well worth the money and the effort" and "virtually impossible not to leave happy."

Kitchenette SF 🅈⇄ *Sandwiches*
24 | 11 | 18 | $13

Dogpatch | American Industrial Ctr. | 958 Illinois St. (bet. 20th & 22nd Sts.) | 415-522-6628 | www.kitchenettesf.com
"If you can find it" in the "hour or two" that it's open on weekdays, you'll be rewarded with an "amazing", "decently priced" lunch at this sandwich maker operating out of a "loading dock" in Dogpatch; just "get there early", because "the waits can be a little long" and the wares "often sell out"; P.S. it's "definitely a grab and go kind of place", though there is a "wooden bench" nearby.

Koh Samui & The Monkey *Thai*
21 | 22 | 20 | $30

SoMa | 415 Brannan St. (bet. Ritch & 3rd Sts.) | 415-369-0007 | www.kohsamuiandthemonkey.com

Another Monkey *Thai*
Mission | 280 Valencia St. (14th St.) | 415-241-0288 | www.anothermonkeythai.com
"There are no monkeys" at this "hip", midpriced SoMa and Mission duo, just "wonderfully fresh", "artful Thai food" ("try the pumpkin curry") including "excellent vegetarian options" plus "cocktails in-

fused with flavors like lemongrass, basil and ginger"; despite sometimes "slow service", they're "cool"-looking choices for "groups" and "happy-hour deals."

🔲 Kokkari Estiatorio *Greek* | 28 | 27 | 27 | $59

Downtown | 200 Jackson St. (bet. Battery & Front Sts.) | 415-981-0983 | www.kokkari.com

"Politicos", "power execs" and "special-occasion" celebrants frequent this "happening" Downtown Greek for "incredible" cuisine featuring "impressive" meats spit-roasted on an open fire and "to-die-for" desserts, all brought by a "talented staff"; a "beautiful" dining room and "always-busy bar" that "retain the warmth and coziness of a taverna" add to what fans deem a "grand" "fine-dining experience" – with "a price tag that matches" (it's "worth the splurge").

Koo Ⓜ *Asian* | 26 | 19 | 22 | $42

Inner Sunset | 408 Irving St. (bet. 5th & 6th Aves.) | 415-731-7077 | www.sushikoo.com

An "excellent selection of sushi and grilled dishes", many with "inventive" Asian fusion twists, is what's on offer at this Inner Sunset site with "fast, friendly service" and "pleasant decor"; if you don't grab the "early-bird special", "expect to drop some cash", but most find it "totally worth it", especially those who "sit at the bar and watch the chefs at work."

Korean Village Wooden Charcoal BBQ House ⬤ *Korean* | ▽ 26 | 13 | 19 | $40

Inner Richmond | 4611 Geary Blvd. (10th Ave.) | 415-751-6336 | www.kvwcr.com

"If you like Korean BBQ, you can't beat" this "authentic" Inner Richmonder where you can grill "great" meats "at your table" over the eponymous wooden charcoal until 3 AM nightly; shoju and sides like "tasty" tofu soup also "keep you warm" "on cold days", so Seoul sisters shrug off the "smoky environment" and sometimes "brusque" service.

Kuleto's *Italian* | 23 | 21 | 22 | $48

Downtown | Villa Florence Hotel | 221 Powell St. (bet. Geary & O'Farrell Sts.) | 415-397-7720 | www.kuletos.com

Popular with both "out-of-towners" and locals "relaxing" "after a long day of Union Square shopping", this "fairly priced" Downtowner delivers "terrific" pastas and other Northern Italian fare in a "lively", "beautiful" setting featuring a historic carved-wood bar; if some deem the eats just "ok", "professional" servers please theatergoers with "time constraints", while those snagging "counter" seats facing the cooks claim it's "like watching the Food Channel" "in 3D."

La Boulange *Bakery* | 22 | 17 | 18 | $15

Cow Hollow | 1909 Union St. (Laguna St.) | 415-440-4450
NEW **Downtown** | 222 Sutter St. (Kearny St.) | 415-989-5010
Cole Valley | 1000 Cole St. (Parnassus St.) | 415-242-2442
Hayes Valley | 500 Hayes St. (Octavia St.) | 415-863-3376
Noe Valley | 3898 24th St. (bet. Sanchez & Vicksburg Sts.) | 415-821-1050
North Beach | 543 Columbus Ave. (bet. Green & Union Sts.) | 415-399-0714
Pacific Heights | 2043 Fillmore St. (bet. California & Pine Sts.) | 415-928-1300

(continued)

(continued)

La Boulange
Pacific Heights | 2325 Pine St. (bet. Fillmore & Steiner Sts.) | 415-440-0356
Russian Hill | 2300 Polk St. (Green St.) | 415-345-1107
SoMa | 685 Market St. (bet. Geary & Kearny Sts.) | 415-512-7610 🅱
www.laboulangebakery.com
Additional locations throughout the San Francisco area

A "sweet little spot" for "big bowls of café au lait", "incredible" "open-face sandwiches" and "delicate" pastries, these "self-serve" "Parisian patisseries" with "friendly" "staffers" are "charmers" affirm Francophiles, who arrive "early" "on weekends" when they're "always crowded"; the chain's "expanding like crazy" (and was acquired by Starbucks post-Survey), and though a few feel it was "better before the corporate makeover", most maintain it's still *"magnifique!"*

🚹 La Ciccia 🅼 *Italian*   27 | 18 | 26 | $49
Noe Valley | 291 30th St. (Church St.) | 415-550-8114 | www.laciccia.com

"Reservations are a must" as this Noe Valley venue where "exquisitely prepared" Sardinian cuisine and "exceptional", "unusual wines" are delivered in "rustic", "tiny", "cramped" digs that are "always full" and "somewhat noisy"; "wonderful" "mom-and-pop" owners and their "warm" staff "treat you like you're a member of the family", and best of all, the prices are "reasonable for the quality."

La Corneta *Mexican*   22 | 13 | 18 | $12
Glen Park | 2834 Diamond St. (bet. Bosworth & Chenery Sts.) | 415-469-8757 🍴
Mission | 2731 Mission St. (bet. 23rd & 24th Sts.) | 415-643-7001
www.lacorneta.com

"Don't let the line scare you away", it usually "moves fast" at this "no-frills", "pleasant" "cafeteria-style" Mexican quartet serving up "solid burritos" and such; what's more, everything comes in "large portions" and for "affordable prices", making it "a great value."

La Cumbre Taqueria *Mexican*   22 | 10 | 16 | $11
Mission | 515 Valencia St. (bet. 16th & 17th Sts.) | 415-863-8205
"Still a keeper", this long-standing Mission taqueria with a San Mateo twin pleases patrons with "consistently good and affordable" Mexican eats and "fresh ingredients that keep people coming back"; service is spotty and "decor is too big a word for this place", but even though it's "nothing fancy, it works" thanks to "huge burritos" that "fill you up" and "late" hours on Valencia Street (until 3 AM Friday–Saturday).

🚹 La Folie 🅶 *French*   27 | 25 | 27 | $107
Russian Hill | 2316 Polk St. (bet. Green & Union Sts.) | 415-776-5577 | www.lafolie.com

For that "special night" "splurge", Francophiles never "pass up an opportunity to dine" at "master chef" Roland Passot's Russian Hill "jewel box", where he "continues to keep his hand" "in the kitchen" and in the "ornate" dining room proffering "beautifully presented" "haute cuisine" prix fixe French dinners; it's a "lyrical experience" from the "amuse-bouche" to *"le digestif"*, enhanced by "superb", "unpretentious" service and brother George's "gorgeous wine list"; P.S. the adjacent lounge serves "unique" drinks and appetizers.

	FOOD	DECOR	SERVICE	COST

La Mar Cebicheria Peruana *Peruvian/Seafood*   24 | 23 | 21 | $52

Embarcadero | Pier 1.5 (Washington St.) | 415-397-8880 |
www.lamarcebicheria.com

"Sublime ceviche" headlines the menu of "world-class Peruvian" plates
at "celeb chef" Gastón Acurio's "very popular" South American seafooder where "knowledgeable" servers" navigate an "enchanting"
Embarcadero setting; whether you drink "sophisticated" cocktails in
the "gorgeous bar" or snag "outdoor seating" (the best for "killer" Bay
views), it's "so much fun", as long as "money is no object" and you're
prepared to "embrace" the "loud", "high-energy" "scene."

La Méditerranée *Mediterranean/Mideastern*   23 | 18 | 21 | $23

Castro | 288 Noe St. (bet. Beaver & Market Sts.) | 415-431-7210
Upper Fillmore | 2210 Fillmore St. (bet. Clay & Sacramento Sts.) |
415-921-2956
www.cafelamed.com

Devotees "dream about" the "simple" Middle Eastern–Med menu from
"savory" "phyllo treats" to "great" "meze platters" at these "reasonably priced" "standbys" in the Castro, Upper Fillmore and Berkeley;
they're "not the fanciest of restaurants", but they're "as popular as
ever" thanks to "warm", "relaxed" service and "lovely" sidewalk seating perfect for "people-watching."

L'Ardoise 🏵Ⓜ *French*   24 | 20 | 24 | $47

Castro | 151 Noe St. (Henry St.) | 415-437-2600 | www.ardoisesf.com

"Imagine that you are in a French bistro in Paris" to conjure this "charming" place in the Castro with a "closet"-sized space and "amiable", "attentive service" that make it "ideal for dates"; as for the fare, it's
"excellently prepared, beautifully plated", relatively "reasonably priced"
and complemented by a "thoughtfully chosen, varied wine selection."

Lark Creek Steak *Steak*   25 | 22 | 24 | $60

Downtown | Westfield San Francisco Ctr. | 845 Market St., 4th fl.
(bet. 4th & 5th Sts.) | 415-593-4100 | www.larkcreeksteak.com

"Sides and starters shine as brightly as the perfectly charred beef" at this
"modern steakhouse" in Downtown's Westfield Centre, where a "comfortable atmosphere" and "impeccable service" make you "forget you're
in a mall"; though it "can get expensive", "great deals" are offered at the
"cool bar" during happy hour, for a "nice respite" "after shopping."

La Taqueria 🖃 *Mexican*   25 | 10 | 17 | $12

Mission | 2889 Mission St. (bet. 24th & 25th Sts.) | 415-285-7117

For 30 years, this "true original" in the Mission has been churning out
affordable, "consistently delicious" Mexican meals comprising "awesome tacos" and "amazing" burritos that disciples call "massive mis-
siles of yummy goodness" (they're "traditional", so "they don't have
rice"); "seating is scarce" in the "no-frills", "divey" environs, so prepare
for "constant lines" – though "speedy service" keeps them moving.

La Trappe 🏵Ⓜ *Belgian*   ▽ 20 | 21 | 19 | $30

North Beach | 800 Greenwich St. (Mason St.) | 415-440-8727 |
www.latrappecafe.com

This "cozy" "brick-basement" setting could just as "easily be somewhere in Belgium" say suds lovers, who "hole up" in North Beach to mull
over the "inch-thick" list of brews (including a "mind-blowing array" of

Belgians "on tap") with "helpful" barkeeps; the "minimal" gastropub menu – "great moules frites" and other regional eats – is "a bit pricey", but who cares when the "convivial" spot has "so much character."

Le Central ☒ *French* | 21 | 19 | 21 | $43 |
Downtown | 453 Bush St. (bet. Grant Ave. & Kearny St.) | 415-391-2233 | www.lecentralbistro.com

The signature "cassoulet is first-rate" and the "people-watching" even better at this "friendly, busy" "Downtown mainstay" where all of the French bistro fare is "delicious"; a known place for a "power lunch", its location "a quick jaunt from Union Square" means it's "a nice respite from hectic shopping" too, while "fair pricing" makes it "worth a try" whatever the occasion.

Le Charm French Bistro Ⓜ *French* | 23 | 19 | 21 | $43 |
SoMa | 315 Fifth St. (bet. Folsom & Shipley Sts.) | 415-546-6128 | www.lecharm.com

Surveyors agree that the "name fits" at this "charming" SoMa bistro where the "friendly", "attentive" staff "can recommend interesting wines" to complement the "rich", "terrific" staples, all available for "reasonable prices" (especially on the "inexpensive prix fixe"); adding to the attraction, an "evening of escargot and Chablis on the patio" is especially "delightful" on Thursdays, when live jazz is offered.

Le Colonial *French/Vietnamese* | 23 | 24 | 21 | $52 |
Downtown | 20 Cosmo Pl. (bet. Jones & Taylor Sts.) | 415-931-3600 | www.lecolonialsf.com

Take "a romantic walk into an alley" for "beautiful French-Vietnamese" fare at this Theater District Downtowner with a "sensual atmosphere" recalling "pre-war Saigon"; those who deem it "pricey" suggest "make a meal of" starters or head for the lounge (with live music or DJs most nights), but wherever you perch, service is "helpful" and it's "delightful" "for groups" or "date night."

Leopold's *Austrian* | 23 | 24 | 23 | $33 |
Russian Hill | 2400 Polk St. (Union St.) | 415-474-2000 | www.leopoldssf.com

"Pretty girls" in dirndls deliver "fantastic", "hearty", "reasonably priced" Austrian fare with Italian twists at this "jovial" Russian Hill "gasthaus" where locals "chug down" "ice-cold" European brews from "boot-shaped glasses" amid Alpine "lodge decor"; the atmosphere is "really loud", but that's to be expected since it's like "Oktoberfest year-round" here.

Le P'tit Laurent *French* | 24 | 20 | 24 | $39 |
Glen Park | 699 Chenery St. (Diamond St.) | 415-334-3235 | www.leptitlaurent.net

"Big things" do indeed come in "little packages", as evidenced by this Glen Park bistro "find", where "skilled and charming" host-owner Laurent (he "runs a tight ship") and his "capable staff" deliver "consistently excellent" "classic" French fare and a "nice selection of wine" in a "tiny-triangle" of a setting; the "reasonable" price point, particularly on the Sunday–Thursday prix fixe, is a boon.

Lers Ros Thai *Thai* | 25 | 14 | 19 | $26 |
NEW **Hayes Valley** | 307 Hayes St. (Franklin St.) | 415-874-9661

(continued)

Lers Ros Thai

Tenderloin | 730 Larkin St. (O'Sarrell St.) | 415-931-6917 ◗
www.lersros.com

Some of the "best Thai in the city" draws fans to these Tenderloin and Hayes Valley spots where "flavors that are robust" and "authentic" can also be "melt-your-face-off hot"; a minority complains about "noise levels", but regulars call it an "inexpensive" place to try "funky and assertive" specials like "rabbit, boar" and "alligator", along with the more "traditional" dishes on their "crazy-long menu"; P.S. the original Larkin Street locale is "open late."

Le Soleil   *Vietnamese*   ▽ 19 | 15 | 18 | $32

Inner Richmond | 133 Clement St. (bet. 2nd & 3rd Aves.) | 415-668-4848 |
www.lesoleilusa.com

Fans gravitate to this Inner Richmond Vietnamese for its "bright, well-flavored" "classic preparations", all offered at prices that equal a "wonderful value"; though the Decor score does not reflect a recent remodel, it's just as small as it ever was.

Let's Be Frank   *Hot Dogs*   19 | 12 | 19 | $8

Marina | 3318 Steiner St. (bet. Chestnut & Lombard Sts.) | 415-674-6755
Presidio | Warming Hut Café & Bookstore | Crissy Field (Marine Dr.) |
888-233-7265 Ⓜ⇄
www.letsbefrankdogs.com

Both the original cart of this frank vendor in Crissy Field and its tiny Marina brick-and-mortar offshoot dole out "perfectly adequate" links built with "ethically raised meats" and made more "appealing" with "plentiful" fixin's; a few growl that they're "more expensive" than other hot dogs, but no one complains about the staffers – they're "friendly."

Le Zinc   *French*   20 | 18 | 18 | $40

Noe Valley | 4063 24th St. (bet. Castro & Noe Sts.) | 415-647-9400 |
www.lezinc.com

Advocates appreciate that the staffers "don't mind if you linger" at this "charming" Noe Valley French bistro, whether in the "cozy" interior at the antique zinc bar or on the "sweet hidden patio" out back; of the "reasonably priced", "unfussy" fare, the "fabulous" cheese-and-wine pairing and the prix fixe brunch ("bring a big appetite") get special kudos.

Liberty Cafe   *American*   22 | 18 | 22 | $33

Bernal Heights | 410 Cortland Ave. (bet. Andover & Bennington Sts.) |
415-695-8777 | www.thelibertycafe.com

Regulars say the recent "change in ownership didn't hurt" this longtime "neighborhood anchor in Bernal Heights", whose "consistent", "reasonably priced" American menu features the likes of "flaky, delicious" chicken pot pie; "friendly" service, a "homey" atmosphere, "delightful" outdoor seating and "cottage in the back" that "serves as a bakery in the morning and a wine bar at night" are additional reasons it's deemed a "gem."

Limón   *Peruvian*   24 | 19 | 19 | $33

Mission | 524 Valencia St. (bet. 16th & 17th Sts.) | 415-252-0918 |
www.limon-sf.com

(continued)

(continued)

Limón Rotisserie *Peruvian*
NEW **Bayview** | 5800 Third St. (Carroll Ave.) | 415-926-5665
Mission | 1001 S. Van Ness Ave. (21st St.) | 415-821-2134
www.limonrotisserie.com
Following a post-Survey switch to a more downscaled menu, the "main attraction" at this Valencia Street "modern Peruvian" is now the "fall-off-the-bone, zing-in-your-mouth rotisserie chicken" made "famous" at its "casual" spin-offs; all three locales – including the Van Ness "basement" branch and a new Bayview outpost – boast "friendly" service and "super-cheap" prices, along with "killer ceviche" and "legendary sweet potato fries" that, when "washed down with a pitcher of sangria", help make up for the "crowds" and "noise."

Little Chihuahua *Mexican* 21 | 15 | 18 | $14
Noe Valley | 4123 24th St. (Castro St.) | 415-648-4157
Western Addition | 292 Divisadero St. (bet. Haight & Page Sts.) | 415-255-8225
www.thelittlechihuahua.com
"High-quality ingredients" and unusual fillings are the hallmarks of these sustainably minded Mexican burrito-slingers in the Noe Valley and Western Addition; the "quirky decor" and "big smiles" from the counter servers help make it a "go-to" for "casual, quick takeout", albeit one with "slightly upscale" prices to match.

Little Nepal Ⓜ *Nepalese* ▽ 23 | 20 | 24 | $30
Bernal Heights | 925 Cortland Ave. (bet. Folsom & Gates Sts.) | 415-643-3881 | www.littlenepalsf.com
Everything "tastes homemade" at this "cute, little place" on the edge of the Bernal Heights shopping strip, offering "delicious" Nepalese dishes; add in "reasonable prices", a "family-friendly" atmosphere and "hospitable service", and no wonder fans say it's worth seeking out.

Little Star Pizza *Pizza* 25 | 16 | 19 | $23
Mission | 400 Valencia St. (15th St.) | 415-551-7827
Western Addition | 846 Divisadero St. (bet. Fulton & McAllister Sts.) | 415-441-1118 Ⓜ
www.littlestarpizza.com
"Heavenly deep-dish" Chicago-style pizzas with "flavorful" cornmeal crusts and "tangy, chunky tomato sauce" are offered alongside "super-crispy thin-crust" varieties at these "fair-priced" parlors; devotees say they "feel cool" in the "fun space", but because it's often "noisy" – and "no reservations" lead to "long waits" – some just "grab" and "go."

🅉 Local Mission Eatery Ⓜ *Californian* 27 | 24 | 25 | $35
Mission | 3111 24th St. (bet. Folsom & Shotwell Sts.) | 415-655-3422 | www.localmissioneatery.com
The "kitchen crew works magic" at this Mission Californian that "takes sustainability seriously" as it sends out "tasty locavore lunches" and "sophisticated" dinners, all at prices that are "reasonable for what you get"; a setting that's a "perfect mix of informal and beautiful" and "knowledgeable, friendly service" complete the picture; P.S. the "bakery in the back" whips up "amazing pastries."

	FOOD	DECOR	SERVICE	COST

NEW Local's Corner *Seafood*

| - | - | - | M |

Mission | 2500 Bryant St. (23rd St.) | 415-800-7945 | localscornersf.com
A spin-off of the nearby Local Mission Eatery, this Mission seafood-centric corner restaurant and raw bar has a locavore bent, with Bay and Pacific Northwest oysters, midpriced sustainable seafood dinners (cooked on induction burners) and natural wines and beers; the airy dining room decorated with vintage wallpaper, tin ceilings and cane chairs is open for breakfast, lunch and dinner, with plans for a special tasting menu at the chef's counter soon.

Locanda ● *Italian*

| 25 | 23 | 23 | $51 |

Mission | 557 Valencia St. (bet. 16th & 17th Sts.) | 415-863-6800 | www.locandasf.com
Proof that "everything the Stolls touch turns to gold", this "standout" Mission osteria with a "distinctly Roma attitude" delivers "fantastic" pastas, "offal" and other Southern Italian "goodness" along with "friendly" service just like "you'd expect from the Delfina crew", in an "action"-packed, "trendy" room that stays open till 1 AM nightly; add in a "buzzing" "bar scene" with "magnificent cocktails", and "valet parking" ($12 charge), and little wonder "reservations are hard to land".

Locavore Ⓜ *Californian*

| 22 | 21 | 21 | $38 |

Bernal Heights | 3215 Mission St. (Valencia St.) | 415-821-1918 | www.locavoreca.com
As the name suggests, "everything" on the ever-changing, "creative" Californian menu is "locally sourced" within 100 miles at this "fairly priced" "neighborhood" spot near Bernal Heights (now overseen by a new chef); modern rustic decor and a "friendly" staff add to the appeal.

NEW Lolinda ● *Argentinean/Steak*

| - | - | - | M |

Mission | 2522 Mission St. (21st St.) | 415-550-6970 | www.lolindasf.com
Unlike your typical churrascaria, this hip *nuevo* wood-fired grill-centric Argentinean steakhouse and small-plates hangout in the Mission from the Beretta and Starbelly team features midpriced eats inspired by Latin America, Spain and Argentina while reflecting Californian sensibilities with whole-animal utilization, sustainable meats and smaller shareable portions; the massive bi-level hang (which also includes a rooftop terrace) is outfitted with two cocktail bars for artisanal cocktails, piscos, tequilas and Latin wines.

Loló Ⓩ *Mexican*

| 25 | 23 | 23 | $33 |

Mission | 3230 22nd St. (bet. Mission & Valencia Sts.) | 415-643-5656 | www.lolosf.com
Tiny and "very eclectic", this "neighborhood jewel" turns out "somewhat random but delicious" Med-Mex fusion "small plates" that are "just as spectacular" as the "funky decor" with its "colorful" walls and collection of "cute knickknacks"; "as with everything in the Mission, it's gotten a bit too popular" but the "friendly" staff and "great value" offerings are "so worth it"; P.S. open until midnight Friday and Saturday.

L'Osteria del Forno ⌀ *Italian*

| 25 | 15 | 21 | $29 |

North Beach | 519 Columbus Ave. (bet. Green & Union Sts.) | 415-982-1124 | www.losteriadelforno.com
"Loyal neighbors" and savvy visitors alike happily "squeeze in" to this cash-only, "family-owned", "shoebox-sized" osteria "hidden" among

"the shinier" North Beach "tourist traps" to enjoy "phenomenal", "paper-thin" pizzas, "roasts" and other "real-deal" Italian fare "like grandma used to make"; waits can be "obnoxious" and the "rushed" staff and "cramped setting" don't encourage lingering, but diners "begin to ooh and aah" when it "all comes to the table."

NEW Lot 7 Ⓜ Seafood

| - | - | - | M |

Mission | 974 Valencia St. (bet. 20th & 21st Sts.) | 415-817-1212 | www.lot7sf.com

Greg Lute (Waterfront, Skates on the Bay) wields his piscine prowess on a menu of sustainable seafood at this moderately priced Mission newcomer, where the Eclectic offerings include crudo, shellfish and a fresh local catch of the day; locals drop anchor in the nautically themed, red-elm-accented space for dollar oysters and discounted drinks during happy hour (Tuesday–Friday 4–6 PM).

Lovejoy's Tea Room Ⓜ Tearoom

| 21 | 23 | 24 | $26 |

Noe Valley | 1351 Church St. (Clipper St.) | 415-648-5895 | www.lovejoystearoom.com

"Treat yourself" to an *Alice in Wonderland* tea party" – "complete with fussy, flowery decor" and "mismatched antiques" – at this midpriced Noe Valley "hangout" built for "bonding over a good cuppa", some "real scones" and "finger sandwiches"; service is fit "for queens" but "make a reservation" as it's often "filled to the brim" with kiddy birthdays, "bridal showers and other events."

Lucca Delicatessen Deli/Sandwiches

| 27 | 17 | 22 | $16 |

Marina | 2120 Chestnut St. (bet. Mallorca Way & Pierce St.) | 415-921-7873 | www.luccadeli.com

"Family-owned and -run since forever" (1929), this "institution" sells "superb sandwiches", soups, salads and pastas (the ravioli are "amazing") alongside a "wide variety" of "imported Italian ingredients", all for "fair prices"; there's "zero" decor, but it's take-out-only anyway, and perfect for an "impromptu picnic" on the nearby Marina green.

Luce Californian/Italian

| 21 | 24 | 22 | $67 |

SoMa | InterContinental Hotel | 888 Howard St. (bet. 4th & 5th Sts.) | 415-616-6566 | www.lucewinerestaurant.com

"High ceilings and marble floors" distinguish this "smart", "elegant" Cal-Ital in SoMa's InterContinental Hotel where "service is attentive but not rushed" and new chef Daniel Corey dishes up "fantastic flavor combinations" that pair well with "interesting" wines from a list focusing on Super Tuscans; if a few diners wish it were even "better for the cost", most assure it will "definitely" "not fail to please."

Luella Californian/Mediterranean

| 24 | 22 | 23 | $43 |

Russian Hill | 1896 Hyde St. (Green St.) | 415-674-4343 | www.luellasf.com

Fans "love the quintessential San Francisco feel" and "friendly" service at this "casual" "jewel on Russian Hill", where the chef "treats ingredients with TLC" while executing his Cal-Med dishes; options including a weekday prix fixe with "great choices" that's "a steal" and Sunday kids' menus bring in regulars, and it's also "a fun place to take visitors", especially "with the cable car running outside."

Luna Park   *American/French*

20 | 17 | 18 | $34

Mission | 694 Valencia St. (bet. 17th & 18th Sts.) | 415-553-8584 | www.lunaparksf.com

"Down-home" French–New American cuisine "with an edge" is served in an "energetic atmosphere" brimming with a "plethora of hipsters" ("dining and working") at this Mission "neighborhood joint"; some wish the midpriced menu had a little "more pizzazz" and the service a bit more speed, but the "cozy", "funky setting" ("booths hidden behind a curtain") makes it "worth the wait."

Lupa Trattoria   *Italian*

24 | 18 | 24 | $37

Noe Valley | 4109 24th St. (bet. Castro & Diamond Sts.) | 415-282-5872 | www.lupatrattoria.com

Now "that's Italian!" declare "loyal followers" of this "casual neighborhood trattoria" doling out "delicious" "homemade pastas" and other "classic Roman dishes" in Noe Valley; overall, the place is "small" but "cozy", the servers are "warm" and "charming", and the fare is "reasonably priced", making this a spot locals "return to again and again."

NEW Machine Coffee & Deli ☒ *Coffeehouse/Sandwiches*

- | - | - | I

Downtown | 1024 Market St. (6th St.) | 415-913-7370

Showdogs' new sibling is this affordable Downtown shop next door, featuring Four Barrel Coffee offered in presses, espressos and as hand-cast cups of single origin beans alongside a simple lineup of breakfast fare and baked goods; in-house smoked and roasted meats (overseen by Showdogs' resident charcutier Peter Temkin) are destined for build-your-own sandwiches gilded with housemade sauces, fixings and breads.

Magnolia Gastropub & Brewery ● *Southern*

22 | 20 | 18 | $29

Haight-Ashbury | 1398 Haight St. (Masonic Ave.) | 415-864-7468 | www.magnoliapub.com

"Hopsheads rejoice" at this midpriced Upper Haight microbrewery whose "insane" list of "fantastic beers" is complemented by "inventive", "delectable" Southern-inflected American bar snacks; "service is sometimes slow" (though mostly "friendly"), and it gets "over-the-top loud" inside, as it's "always packed."

Mamacita   *Mexican*

24 | 20 | 20 | $36

Marina | 2317 Chestnut St. (Scott St.) | 415-346-8494 | www.mamacitasf.com

"You'll be hard-pressed to leave anything on your plate" at this "trendy" Marina Mexican where the "wonderfully delicious tacos" and such are ferried by "chic" staffers; "ambient lighting, star-shaped chandeliers" and "tequila bottles back lit" behind the bar make for an atmosphere that could be dubbed "sex-Mex", but bear in mind that the "boisterous" vibe can turn "overwhelmingly loud" thanks to the "world-class margaritas."

Mama's on Washington Square ☒⇄ *American*

24 | 16 | 19 | $21

North Beach | 1701 Stockton St. (Filbert St.) | 415-362-6421 | www.mamas-sf.com

"Your first bite justifies the long wait in line outside" this "charming" North Beach breakfast-and-lunch "institution" where the "homestyle" American fare includes "awesome French toast" and a Monte Christo sandwich that's a "sinful delight"; "low costs" and decent service are additional reasons fans say it's "worth" the effort to squeeze into the "small", "tight space."

Mandalay *Burmese* | 26 | 19 | 23 | $27 |

Inner Richmond | 4348 California St. (bet. 5th & 6th Aves.) | 415-386-3895 | www.mandalaysf.com

Those who "don't want to wait two hours" for the popular Asian spots on Clement Street contend "the food is even better" at this "well-appointed", "reasonably priced" Inner Richmond "stalwart" where "tasty" Burmese dishes are brought by staffers who "treat everyone like royalty"; expect a bit of a line on weekends – while you used to be able to go "without a reservation", "those days are over."

Manora's Thai Cuisine *Thai* | 23 | 18 | 22 | $25 |

SoMa | 1600 Folsom St. (12th St.) | 415-861-6224 | www.manorathai.com

"Traditional Thai" fare is as "scrumptious" as it is "well priced", particularly the "great lunch deals", at this "friendly" SoMa spot that'll "make it as spicy as you want"; "fast", "gracious" service and "charming" digs also help explain how it's "succeeded this long" (since 1987).

Marcello's Pizza ●◐☞ *Pizza* | 25 | 14 | 19 | $12 |

Castro | 420 Castro St. (Market St.) | 415-863-3900 | www.marcellospizzasf.com

"Thin, crunchy, delicious" pizza with a "huge assortment of toppings" is the stock-in-trade of this "reliable" parlor where most patrons get it to go; in sum, it's an "outstanding" option for a "quick, cheap meal" "before you get your drinks on" in the Castro.

Mario's Bohemian Cigar Store Cafe *Italian/Sandwiches* | 21 | 16 | 21 | $19 |

North Beach | 566 Columbus Ave. (bet. Green & Union Sts.) | 415-362-0536

Surveyors "stop off" at this affordable North Beach Italian for "some comfort" in the form of a "pressed-meatball sandwich", "carafe of house red" and "people-watching on Washington Square"; there are "no cigars" but entering this neighborhood "joint" (around since 1972) is "like stepping into another world" and where locals are happy to "linger" over a "cappuccino."

🆕 Market & Rye *Deli/Sandwiches* | - | - | - | I |

West Portal | 68 W. Portal Ave. (Vicente St.) | 415-564-5950 | www.marketandrye.com

Potrero Hill | 300 De Haro St. (bet. 16 & 17th Sts.) | 415-252-7455 | www.marketandrye.com 🛅

This set of casual quick-service daytime delis with DIY salad bars and grab-and-go gourmet sandwiches on house-baked bread from *Top Chef* alum Ryan Scott touches down in two locations; the West Portal shop is more kid-friendly, while the Potrero Hill branch caters to the grab-and-go Design District worker bee.

MarketBar *Mediterranean* | 18 | 19 | 19 | $39 |

Embarcadero | Ferry Bldg. Mktpl. | 1 Ferry Bldg. (The Embarcadero) | 415-434-1100 | www.marketbar.com

Enjoy "a bite" in view of "the sparkling bay" on the sprawling patio of this "busy" midpriced Embarcadero brasserie in the Ferry Building;

though service varies and some say the "seasonal" Med menu "isn't quite on par" with the location, "happy hour" and "weekday lunch" are winning options "on a sunny San Francisco day."

Marlowe ⊠ *American/Californian*   24 | 19 | 22 | $42

SoMa | 330 Townsend St. (4th St.) | 415-974-5599 | www.marlowesf.com
Renowned for its market-driven, Cal-American "comfort food", including the "fabled burger", this "tiny", "bustling" SoMa bistro "not far from the ballpark" is a "favorite" of the "young, hip crowd" from lunch to late-night; it gets "insanely loud and cramped" at the communal tables, but "upbeat" staffers, "good vibes" and a "swanky" decor "make you feel like you're in Manhattan" (in a good way).

Marnee Thai *Thai*   25 | 15 | 20 | $23

Inner Sunset | 1243 Ninth Ave. (bet. Irving St. & Lincoln Way) | 415-731-9999
Outer Sunset | 2225 Irving St. (bet. 23rd & 24th Aves.) | 415-665-9500
www.marneethaisf.com
Though small, the "kitchens produce big flavors" at these Sunset Thais turning out budget-friendly "classic" dishes, including some "you can't typically get" such as "to-die-for" spicy "angel wings"; the digs may look like "a hole-in-the-wall" on a "side street" in Bangkok, complete with servers "yelling across the restaurant", but overall these "authentic" spots "set the gold standard" for local Siamese cuisine.

❷ Masa's ⊠Ⓜ *French*   27 | 26 | 27 | $127

Downtown | Hotel Vintage Ct. | 648 Bush St. (bet. Powell & Stockton Sts.) | 415-989-7154 | www.masasrestaurant.com
"Exquisite in every way", this Downtown fine-dining "landmark" continues to "dazzle" with chef Gregory Short's "sublime" New French tasting menus enlivened by "local ingredients" and "playful wine pairings", all capped off with "the best cheese and candy carts in the city"; it's all delivered with "superb service" in a "quiet", "elegant" setting for a "special-occasion experience" that's so "fabulous" there's "no other word for it – except perhaps expensive"; P.S. jackets suggested.

Matterhorn Swiss Restaurant Ⓜ *Swiss*   ▽ 21 | 21 | 21 | $43

Russian Hill | 2323 Van Ness Ave. (bet. Green & Vallejo Sts.) | 415-885-6116 | www.thematterhornrestaurant.com
"When you gotta have fondue" this "family-friendly" Alpine getaway in Russian Hill is "a little piece of Switzerland" complete with a "great wood-paneled interior" (meaning "kitschy, in a good way"); the staff is "friendly" and the "well-priced", "well-selected" wines are sure to complement the "cheesy comestibles."

𝗡𝗘𝗪 Maven ⬤ *American*   ▽ 20 | 24 | 24 | $39

Lower Haight | 598 Haight St. (Steiner St.) | 415-829-7982 | www.maven-sf.com
The "addictive" American "small plates" at this "great neighborhood hangout" in the Lower Haight are a "welcome addition" to the area's "otherwise limited dining options"; still, "the real standouts are the amazing drinks" and "good wines by the glass" served by a "knowledgeable staff" and the "beautiful bar" area replete with living wall and "long wooden tables" that "encourage a communal feeling."

FOOD · DECOR · SERVICE · COST

Maverick *American*   24 | 19 | 24 | $44

Mission | 3316 17th St. (bet. Mission & Valencia Sts.) | 415-863-3061 |
www.sfmaverick.com

"Prepared with an adult's palate in mind", the "inventive" American
menu draws fans to this "sophisticated" but "not pretentious "Mission
eatery that's "famous" for its "amazing fried chicken"; the "intimate"
setting is overseen by "cool" staffers who know their way around the
"well-planned wine list", so feel free to "leave the pairings" to them –
they'll "never steer you wrong."

Max's at the Opera *Deli*   20 | 17 | 19 | $26

Civic Center | Opera Plaza | 601 Van Ness Ave. (Golden Gate Ave.) |
415-771-7301

Max's Market Ⓢ *Deli*

Downtown | 555 California St., concourse level (Montgomery St.) |
415-788-6297
www.maxsworld.com

"Mile-high sandwiches" and "singing waiters" at the Opera locations
are the draw at this New York–style deli chain with an "upbeat atmosphere" and "old restaurant feel" that transports some patrons "back
to childhood"; "service can be spotty", but "huge" portions, including
"gargantuan" desserts, leave mavens satisfied.

Mayflower *Chinese*   22 | 16 | 16 | $28

Outer Richmond | 6255 Geary Blvd. (bet. 26th & 27th Aves.) |
415-387-8338 | www.mayflower-seafood.com

"Delicious dim sum" for "reasonable prices" makes weekends "quite
crowded" at this Outer Richmond Cantonese (with Millbrae and Milpitas
sibs), despite waits that can be "long", decor that could use an "update"
and a staff that could be "more welcoming"; in the evening, "excellent
Hong Kong–style seafood" and banquet-type dinners are offered, which
can get "expensive" but are served in a usually "quiet" atmosphere.

Maykadeh *Persian*   23 | 21 | 22 | $46

North Beach | 470 Green St. (Grant Ave.) | 415-362-8286 |
www.maykadehrestaurant.com

Kebabs "grilled to perfection" and served with "warm, soft pita bread"
are mainstays at this North Beach oasis that boasts a menu full of "fragrant", "rarified" Persian dishes served in "an attractive room" with a
"traditional atmosphere"; the staff "takes great care of their customers", and it all comes at "reasonable prices to boot."

McCormick & Kuleto's *Seafood*   22 | 25 | 22 | $48

Fisherman's Wharf | Ghirardelli Sq. | 900 N. Point St. (Larkin St.) |
415-929-1730 | www.mccormickandkuletos.com

It's the "unparalleled view" from "huge windows overlooking the bay"
that's "the star" at this Fisherman's Wharf seafooder sporting a "lengthy
menu" of "surprisingly good" (but perhaps "a little high in price") fish
dishes; it gets "crowded", which makes for sometimes "iffy" service,
and is "touristy as all get-out", but that doesn't deter all the "locals",
besides, "what do you expect in Ghiradelli Square?"

Mel's Drive-In ● *Diner*   17 | 18 | 18 | $17

Civic Center | 1050 Van Ness Ave. (bet. Geary & Myrtle Sts.) |
415-292-6358

	FOOD	DECOR	SERVICE	COST

(continued)

Mel's Drive-In

Inner Richmond | 3355 Geary Blvd. (bet. Beaumont & Parker Aves.) | 415-387-2255

Marina | 2165 Lombard St. (bet. Fillmore & Steiner Sts.) | 415-921-2867

SoMa | 801 Mission St. (4th St.) | 415-227-0793

www.melsdrive-in.com

"Take the kids" to this '50s-era chain for "good, old-fashioned" American diner food (including "breakfast anytime") served in a "retro drive-in atmosphere" complete with "jukeboxes at the tables", burgers, "frothy floats" and "fast" service; while the "basic" fare is "nothing special", these links are "open late and early in the morning" making them "dependable" spots "for a casual meal."

NEW The Melt 🖂 *Sandwiches*   17 | 14 | 17 | $13

Downtown | 1 Embarcadero Ctr. (bet. Battery & Front Sts.) | 415-813-6062

SoMa | 115 New Montgomery St. (Mission St.) | 415-691-6536

SoMa | 345 Spear St. (Folsom St.) | no phone

www.themelt.com

Flip founder Jonathan Kaplan is "taking melts" "to a whole new level" at this "quick-growing", high-tech chainlet where "miracle cookers" efficiently crank out soup-and-sandwich meals elevated by "interesting" "combos" (including dessert iterations); diners "on the run" "love" the goods, but despite an "upscale atmosphere" and "friendly service", some find prices a bit too "steep" for "bread and cheese."

Memphis Minnie's BBQ Joint *BBQ*   20 | 14 | 16 | $20

Lower Haight | 576 Haight St. (bet. Fillmore & Steiner Sts.) | 415-864-7675 | www.memphisminnies.com

Backers of the "hearty barbecue" at this Lower Haight dive call it "cheaper than flying to Memphis and every bit as tasty"; "portions are generous" but true pit fanatics say the kitchen "relies heavily" on "homemade sauces" "to compensate for" sometimes "so-so meat", while the "fast-food setting" makes some suggest getting your order "to go."

Mescolanza *Italian*   25 | 19 | 25 | $34

Outer Richmond | 2221 Clement St. (bet. 23rd & 24th Aves.) | 415-668-2221 | www.mescolanza.net

"One of the best-kept secrets" in Outer Richmond, this trattoria offers up "knockout" Northern Italian eats including "homemade pasta" and thin-crust pizzas, all at "reasonable" prices; the "charming old-world service" and "decent wine list" bring in repeat customers who relish an "intimate" atmosphere that's conducive to "quiet conversation."

⧉ Michael Mina *American*   27 | 25 | 27 | $105

Downtown | 252 California St. (Battery St.) | 415-397-9222 | www.michaelmina.net

Michael Mina "got it right" again at his more "casual" Downtown namesake offering "distinctive" Japanese-accented New American cuisine (plus "old favorites" "prepared in new ways") and "fantastic" service in a "gorgeous setting" "retained from its predecessor, Aqua"; the "no-tablecloth" vibe is more "party bistro than fine dining" – especially at the "noisy" bar filled with "suits" at lunch and a "younger crowd" later on – and the tasting menu with "spectacular" wine pairings is "pricey", but "outrageously good."

	FOOD	DECOR	SERVICE	COST

Mifune *Japanese*

19 | 13 | 15 | $21

Japantown | Japan Ctr. | 1737 Post St. (Webster St.) | 415-922-0337 | www.mifune.com

"Unpretentious" and "family-friendly", this "noodle joint" in Japantown's Japan Center fills its booths daily with regulars who slurp up its "house-made" udon and soba dishes and other "serviceable" staples; the staff can be "indifferent" and the "authentic" decor "hasn't changed" "in years", but "you can't go wrong" when you want to grab a "cheap", "fast" meal before heading to the nearby Kabuki Theater.

Mijita *Mexican*

20 | 14 | 16 | $19

South Beach | AT&T Park | 24 Willie Mays Plaza (3rd St.) | 415-644-0240 Ⓜ
Embarcadero | Ferry Bldg. Mktpl. | 1 Ferry Bldg. (The Embarcadero) | 415-399-0814
www.mijitasf.com

Fans lap up the "upscale" taqueria fare and refreshing "agua frescas" (and the tequila too) at this walk-in "lunch spot" from Traci Des Jardins (Jardinière) in the Ferry Building with outdoor seating where you can "watch the boats arrive", and its sit-down offshoot outside AT&T Park that offers a hidden entrance into the stadium; *sí*, "you can get cheaper" tacos elsewhere, but these are "miles above" most Mexican spots, thanks in part to the use of "super-fresh", mostly local ingredients.

Millennium *Vegan*

27 | 23 | 25 | $53

Downtown | Hotel California | 580 Geary St. (Jones St.) | 415-345-3900 | www.millenniumrestaurant.com

"Vegetarians' dreams come true" at this "classy" vegan eatery in Downtown's Hotel California where the "refreshingly creative" and "artfully presented" dishes even "impress and satisfy" "carnivores", down to the "amazing" dairy-free desserts; "expect to pay" for the "upscale dining" experience delivered with "attentive service" at this "magical place of culinary illusion", though a more affordable "prix fixe" menu is available Sundays–Wednesdays.

Miller's East Coast Delicatessen *Deli/Jewish*

21 | 12 | 18 | $19

(fka Miller's East Coast West Delicatessen)

Polk Gulch | 1725 Polk St. (Clay St.) | 415-563-3542 | www.millersdelisf.com

Polk Gulch mavens get their Jewish deli "fix" at this noshery (with a new San Rafael twin) dishing out "to-die-for matzo balls", "chopped liver like mom used to make" and "big, tasty" sandwiches, all for "reasonable prices"; "service is inconsistent" and the decor is "mediocre", but for an "authentic New York" experience – or at least the "glimmer" of one – it's "worth it."

Mission Beach Café *Californian*

23 | 17 | 19 | $34

Mission | 198 Guerrero St. (14th St.) | 415-861-0198 | www.missionbeachcafe.com

Weekend noshers know to get to this Mission Californian "hangout" "early" to avoid "long waits" for its "fantastic brunch" starring "divine sweet maple bacon" and "huge mimosas"; at other times, "premium" lunches and dinners come for "midrange prices" (and end with "amazing" pies), while "kind, knowledgeable servers" make even a newcomer "feel like a welcome regular" whatever the meal.

	FOOD	DECOR	SERVICE	COST

Mission Cheese ⓂAmerican   `23` `18` `20` `$24`

Mission | 736 Valencia St. (18th St.) | 415-553-8667 |
www.missioncheese.net

"Heaven on earth" for "cheeseheads", this "friendly little" Mission fro-
magerie highlights Sarah Dvorak's "carefully curated selection" of
America's "finest" artisan offerings alongside charcuterie plates and "really inventive" pressed sandwiches, plus an assortment of California
wines and beers; the space is quite "spare" and the offerings may "suffer
from small-portionitis" but still, it's "always packed" and "for good reason"; P.S. cheeses are available for purchase by the quarter-pound.

Mission Chinese Food *Chinese*   `22` `8` `15` `$24`

Mission | Lung Shan Restaurant | 2234 Mission St. (bet. 18th & 19th Sts.) |
415-863-2800 | www.missionchinesefood.com

"Insanely creative" "Chinese-inspired" dishes "like you've never had
before" are prepared with "amazing technique" and served at a "fast
pace" (but also "with love") from inside Lung Shun Restaurant at
Danny Bowien's kitchen that garners "lots of attention" and "massive"
"hipster" crowds; the "decor has improved as their fortunes have
risen" (it's "expanded to NYC"), though the place remains a "dive" –
albeit a "charitable" one that donates 75 cents per entree to the SF
Food Bank; P.S. closed Wednesdays.

🆕 Mission Rock Resort *Seafood*   `-` `-` `-` `M`

Dogpatch | 817 Terry Francois Blvd. (Mariposa St.) | 415-701-7625 |
www.missionrockresort.com

After a splashy two-million dollar renovation, this old-time waterfront
bar and grill near Mission Bay (just south of AT&T Park) lures the crowds
with an ambitious midpriced seafood-centric menu and bar program; the
sprawling two-floor wooden building features an upstairs dining room
and an oyster bar and a downstairs quick-service cafe for breakfast and
lunch, but the most coveted seats are on the decks where you can
knock back a Sailor's Shipwrecked Punch or frozen daiquiri.

Mixt Greens ⓈHealth Food/Sandwiches `23` `14` `18` `$15`

Downtown | Adam Grant Bldg. | 120 Sansome St. (bet. Bush & Pine Sts.) |
415-433-6498
Downtown | 475 Sansome St. (Commercial St.) | 415-296-9292
Downtown | JP Morgan Chase | 560 Mission St. (bet. 1st & 2nd Sts.) |
415-543-2505
Embarcadero | One Market Plaza | 70 Mission St. (bet. Spear & Steuart Sts.) |
415-296-8009 Ⓜ
www.mixtgreens.com

FiDi worker bees "love the big, caloric", "pricey" salads and "freshly
made" sandwiches offered by these lunchtime cafes, which are praised
for "inventive combinations of ingredients" and "sustainable/local/
organic" "ideals"; though the "friendly staff" can be "pretty slow" at
times, the "great outdoor seating" at the Sansome and Commercial location helps make up for "lines" that are "out the door."

Mochica *Peruvian*   `24` `18` `21` `$40`

SoMa | 937 Harrison St. (bet. 5th & 6th Sts.) | 415-278-0480 |
www.mochicasf.com

"Incredible ceviche" and other "interesting" Peruvian fare is sold for
"reasonable" rates at this "small, lively" tapas spot with "simple but

FOOD | DECOR | SERVICE | COST

tasteful decor" "in a slowly gentrifying part of SoMa"; the "approach-able wine list" is also "well priced", and "accommodating" service is another enticement.

Moishe's Pippic ⌷🗗 *Deli/Jewish*   ▽ 18 | 11 | 17 | $16

Hayes Valley | 425 Hayes St. (Gough St.) | 415-431-2440
"Chicago-style" Jewish deli fare like "piled-high" sandwiches, matzo ball soup and hot dogs is what's on the menu at this breakfast-and-lunch joint with "spare surroundings" in Hayes Valley; a few naysayers complain that it's "not even in the same league" as those in the East, but at least the prices are right.

Moki's Sushi & Pacific Grill *Japanese*   ▽ 25 | 19 | 21 | $32

Bernal Heights | 615 Cortland Ave. (bet. Anderson & Moultrie Sts.) | 415-970-9336 | www.mokisushi.com
Bernal Heights locals call this a "sushi restaurant for everyone" thanks to the "kid-friendly" items (chicken satay, fish 'n' chips, etc.) offered among the "fresh, delicious" rolls and other "high-quality" Japanese grill fare; decor that's described as "classy" "tiki", "great ser-vice" and "good prices" ensure that it remains a go-to for a "night out" in the neighborhood.

MoMo's *American*   20 | 21 | 21 | $41

South Beach | 760 Second St. (King St.) | 415-227-8660 | www.sfmomos.com
Buzzing like "a beehive during baseball season", this South Beach "fix-ture" "across the street from AT&T Park" serves New American fare that's "nothing extraordinary" but "well prepared" nonetheless; sur-veyors split on value ("reasonable" vs. "a bit expensive for what it is"), while the majority pegs the service as "friendly and knowledgeable"; P.S. the energy is especially "electric" on the patio where fans "gather for a drink" and toast the Giants.

⊠ Morton's The Steakhouse *Steak*   25 | 23 | 24 | $86

Downtown | 400 Post St. (bet. Mason & Powell Sts.) | 415-986-5830 | www.mortons.com
"Excellent prime cuts of beef cooked to perfection" are complemented by "stiff drinks", an "extensive wine list" and "huge sides" ("share them if you don't want to explode") at these Downtown and San Jose links in the "clubby" steakhouse chain; the "consistent" fare and "out-standing service" command "extremely expensive" tabs, so if you're looking for "fantastic value", "make it a point to try the happy hour", offering bargain bar bites.

Mo's *American*   23 | 16 | 20 | $21

North Beach | 1322 Grant Ave. (Vallejo St.) | 415-788-3779
SoMa | Yerba Buena Gdns. | 772 Folsom St. (4th St.) | 415-957-3779
www.mosgrill.com
"You can pay more and find fancier", but why do that ponder pa-trons of these "basic" North Beach–SoMa "institutions" serving up American fare like "super-fresh, tasty" burgers, "real strawberry" shakes and "killer" fries (plus "great" breakfast fare at Grant Avenue); add in "bargain" prices for "huge" portions, and the result is a little piece of "heaven."

Moshi Moshi *Japanese* ▽ 24 | 18 | 22 | $29

Dogpatch | 2092 Third St. (18th St.) | 415-861-8285 |
www.moshimoshisf.com

"Don't be fooled by the exterior" – this Dogpatch Japanese is a "mid-priced" "gem" proffering "solidly good" sushi, "scrumptious soba" and "great drinks" in a "casual atmosphere" that includes an "inviting outdoor patio"; even if a few assert service can be "spotty", a "loyal following" proves it's "worth it."

NEW The Moss Room *Californian/Vietnamese* – | – | – | M

Outer Richmond | California Academy of Sciences | 55 Music Concourse Dr. (Martin Luther King Jr. Blvd.) | 415-876-6121 | www.themossroom.com

Although the name remains the same, this former fine-dining subterranean at the Academy of Sciences has morphed (for the time being) into a lunch-only sit-down restaurant run by Charles Phan (who also operates the site's Academy Cafe) with a revamped menu that's similar to his signature Slanted Door–style Californian cuisine with a Vietnamese flair, plus wines and specialty cocktails; P.S. reservations are not required but non-museum-goers and members must be escorted by guest services from the front entrance.

Mozzarella di Bufala *Brazilian/Italian* ▽ 23 | 18 | 22 | $21

West Portal | 69 W. Portal Ave. (Vicente St.) | 415-661-8900 |
www.dibufala.com

West Portal residents swear this Italian-Brazilian hybrid serves some of the neighborhood's "best delivery pizza" ("try the cornmeal crust"), while those who stop by for "pleasant" in-house dining can sink their teeth into "inventive, tasty" dishes like steak with collard greens, beans and rice; P.S. the "lunch specials" are a big draw.

NEW Mozzeria *Pizza* – | – | – | I

Mission | 3228 16th St. (bet. Dolores & Guerrero Sts.) | 415-489-0963 |
www.mozzeria.com

Yes, this affordable new Italian in the Mission with sleek, "black-and-white" decor is yet another joint specializing in "authentic", wood-fired "Neapolitan pizzas", but it's also owned and operated by a "friendly", mostly deaf staff; diners can "sign with other signers", communicate with servers via iPad or simply use a pen and pad.

Mr. Pollo ●⌐ *Colombian* ▽ 25 | 10 | 20 | $27

Mission | 2823 Mission St. (bet. 24th & 25th Sts.) | 415-374-5546

"How is it possible" for this cash-only Colombian to offer up such "unbelievable, four-course" market-driven tasting menus (including the signature arepas) that will "push you out of your comfort zone" for a mere $20?, marvel fans of this "awesome hole-in-the-wall" in the Mission; the "tiny digs" may be a bit "primitive" and pacing "rather slow", but it's all still "pretty remarkable"; P.S. it's now open for lunch.

Muracci's Japanese Curry & Grill ⌐ *Japanese* 20 | 11 | 16 | $18

Downtown | 307 Kearny St. (Bush St.) | 415-773-1101 | www.muraccis.com

"Authentic, delicious" Japanese curry "warms you up from the inside out" at this "tiny" Downtown counter-service spot (open weekdays only) serving up "unique" chow and "friendly" service for a "good price"; the "line usually stretches out the door", so vets advise to "call ahead and pick up" or visit its "more serene" Los Altos sibling – which offers "table service", a "full menu" and longer hours (open weekends and evenings).

My Tofu House *Korean* 23 | 13 | 18 | $21
Inner Richmond | 4627 Geary Blvd. (bet. 10th & 11th Aves.) | 415-750-1818
Soy boys (and girls) say the house specialty – a bowl of spicy tofu soup – at this "authentic" Inner Richmond Korean is perfect "comfort food" to "warm up your soul on a foggy night"; though the decor does it no favors and service gets mixed marks, "you'll understand why this small joint fills so quickly" when the "bibimbop, barbecued meats and pancakes" arrive; P.S. "no liquor" served.

Naan 'n Curry *Indian/Pakistani* 18 | 11 | 14 | $15
Downtown | 336 O'Farrell St. (bet. Mason & Taylor Sts.) | 415-346-1443 ●
Inner Sunset | 642 Irving St. (bet. 7th & 8th Aves.) | 415-664-7225
North Beach | 533 Jackson St. (Columbus Ave.) | 415-693-0499 ●
www.naancurry.com
"Don't expect any miracles" at this "popular" quartet in San Fran and Berkeley, just "quick, filling, convenient" Pakistani-Indian grub washed down with "all-you-can-drink chai"; service is "almost nonexistent" ("order at the counter" then "get plates and utensils yourself") and decor is "dated", but at least it's "relatively cheap."

Naked Lunch ⊠Ⓜ⊄ *Sandwiches* ▽ 26 | 8 | 19 | $14
North Beach | 504 Broadway (Kearny St.) | 415-577-4951 | www.nakedlunchsf.com
"Treat yourself to lunch" at this North Beach "hole-in-the-wall" where the chef of next-door sib Txoko turns out a limited, ever-changing selection of "phenomenal" sandwiches, salads and beverages in "combinations that titillate"; Tuesday's "fried-chicken" sammie gets "a lot of hype" but "trust these guys" – whatever they're making is "worth the money" (and you can enjoy it on the patio); P.S. closed Sunday and Monday.

NEW Namu Gaji *Asian/Korean* - | - | - | M
Mission | 499 Dolores St. (18th St.) | 415-431-6268
Namu ⊠Ⓜ⊄ *Californian/Korean*
Embarcadero | Ferry Bldg. Mktpl. | 1 Ferry Bldg. (The Embarcadero) | no phone
www.namusf.com
At this new relocated Mission outpost of Namu, chef Dennis Lee presents an envelope-pushing slate of midpriced Pan-Asian–inspired, Cal-sourced izakaya fare; the casual corner spot has seating comprised of counters lining the room, a large communal table and a small chef's counter fronting the open kitchen; in addition to late-night dinner and happy-hour menus, the kitchen offers to-go fusion-Korean lunch items similar to its popular Ferry Plaza Farmer's Market stall, which still operates on Thursdays and Saturdays.

Nettie's Crab Shack *Seafood* 21 | 19 | 20 | $37
Cow Hollow | 2032 Union St. (bet. Buchanan & Webster Sts.) | 415-409-0300 | www.nettiescrabshack.com
Fans say this "cute" Cow Hollow seafood "shack" offers an "excellent" selection of "oysters, crab and fish" served at some of the "sweetest

real estate in the Marina" – "breezy" and "comfortable" inside with a lovely outdoor patio for "sipping and dipping"; while it's "not for the cheap", the "fun atmosphere" and a staff that's mostly "friendly and efficient" are added values.

Nick's Crispy Tacos ⊄ *Mexican*   22 | 13 | 15 | $14

Russian Hill | Rouge Night Club | 1500 Broadway (Polk St.) | 415-409-8226
"Restaurant by day and club by night", this somewhat "surreal taqueria" in Russian Hill (think "red velvet booths" and crystal chandeliers) serves "uh-mazing" "Baja fish" and other tacos that regulars order "Nick's way" – with both a crispy and soft tortilla; critics decry the "fratty college bar" feel, especially on $2 Taco Tuesdays, but the "cheap" eats, "super-fun" vibe and "flowing pitchers of alcohol" "always draw a crowd."

Nihon Ⓢ Ⓜ *Japanese*   21 | 20 | 15 | $46

Mission | 1779 Folsom St. (14th St.) | 415-552-4400 | www.nihon-sf.com
At this "quirky" bi-level Mission izakaya, "delicious" Japanese small plates are coupled with an "insane selection of whiskeys" (500 plus) that can be enjoyed by the pour or mixed into "inventive cocktails"; service can be "disjointed" and prices run on the "higher end", but the "laid-back" vibe in the modern digs ("quiet" dining on top and a down-stairs bar with a "great atmosphere") is so sweet most don't notice.

901 Columbus Cafe ⊄ *Sandwiches*   22 | 20 | 22 | $26

Telegraph Hill | 901 Columbus (Lombard St.) | 415-409-9001
For "chilling out" "with a latte and fabulous pastry" or a sandwich at a "reasonable" price, this "relaxing" Telegraph Hill cafe fits the bill; an "eclectic crowd", free WiFi and tables where you can "spread out" make it a "friendly little" place to "socialize", especially during the "long" happy hour (5–9:45 PM daily) when cheap beer and wine fuel the "noisy but fun" vibe.

ⓃⒺⓌ 903 Ⓜ *Japanese/Sandwiches*   ▽ 23 | 22 | 22 | $22

Bernal Heights | 903 Cortland Ave. (Gates St.) | 415-678-5759
At this new all-day sit-down offshoot of Bernal Heights cult favorite Sandbox Bakery, chef-owner Mutsumi Takehara is turning out unique, Asian-inflected savory fare – think Japanese-style sandwiches such as a fried chicken rice burger, and nightly changing entrees – washed down with Ritual coffee or a glass of wine; meals can be toted to-go or shared at communal tables in the snug back room; P.S. closes at 3 PM Sundays.

Nob Hill Café *Italian*   22 | 17 | 20 | $36

Nob Hill | 1152 Taylor St. (bet. Clay & Pleasant Sts.) | 415-776-6500 | www.nobhillcafe.com
The "old San Francisco feel" – "cute", "quaint" and "great for a date" – is only part of the story at this "low-key" Northern Italian "favorite" with a "basic" menu including "awesome gnocchi", "terrific pastas" and "thin-crust pizza"; the no-reservations policy and "reasonable prices" mean there's "always a wait", but the "wonderful atmosphere", complemented by a "friendly" staff, makes it "worth the hike to the top of Nob Hill."

Nojo *American/Japanese*   25 | 20 | 20 | $41

Hayes Valley | 231 Franklin St. (Hayes St.) | 415-896-4587 | www.nojosf.com
"Prepare yourself" for some "creative and unusual" dishes at this "fantastic" Hayes Valley American-Japanese where the likes of "duck

tongue" and "pig jowl" are brought by servers who "know what's worth trying"; while a few find the yakitori skewers and small plates "on the pricey side", a "groovy Zen decor" and a locale that's "convenient to the Symphony" tend to compensate; P.S. reservations for six or more only.

Nombe *Japanese*　　　　　　| 22 | 15 | 19 | $39 |

Mission | 2491 Mission St. (21st St.) | 415-681-7150 | www.nombesf.com
Serving "unique" Japanese street food and "steamy" bowls of ramen along with "carefully selected sakes", this "funky" Mission izakaya "hits the spot" at mealtime (including "excellent" late-night nibbles and weekend brunch); though an "odd" layout and somewhat "generic" decor don't win many fans, the generally "friendly" staff and moderate prices do.

☑ Nopa ● *Californian*　　　　| 27 | 23 | 24 | $48 |

Western Addition | 560 Divisadero St. (Hayes St.) | 415-864-8643 | www.nopasf.com
"Hipsters, urbanites" and even "local chefs" have a "restaurant crush" on this Western Addition "late-night staple" pumping out "killer", "ingredient-focused" Cal dinners and "out-of-this-world" brunch in a perennially packed, "bi-level industrial" setting; the "creative" cocktails "alone are worth" a visit and amid "the chaos", the staff "takes care of everything" with "no pretension", so it's really "one massive highlight reel", "if you can get in and handle the noise, that is."

Nopalito *Mexican*　　　　　| 24 | 17 | 20 | $29 |

NEW **Inner Sunset** | 1224 Ninth Ave. (Lincoln Way) | 415-233-9966
Western Addition | Falletti's Plaza | 306 Broderick St. (Oak St.) | 415-437-0303
www.nopalitosf.com
When it comes to "upscale" Mexican, this family-friendly Nopa sib in the Western Addition (with a new Inner Sunset location) has it "nailed", proffering "super-fresh" midpriced dishes with "local sourcing" in a "hip, bright space" and on an "enclosed patio"; the "friendly" crew and "killer margaritas" make it worth enduring "long waits" (and "table sharing"), and you can always "call head and add your name" to the list.

Nordstrom Cafe *Sandwiches*　| 22 | 19 | 21 | $23 |

Downtown | Westfield San Francisco Ctr. | 865 Market St. (5th St.) | 415-243-8500
Shopaholics head for this "comfortable" (and "convenient") department store bistro atop Westfield San Francisco Centre when they need to "unwind" with a "classy" "light lunch" of "scrumptious salads" and sandwiches and other "reliable" New American fare; despite its "mall environment", an "awesome" view, "attentive" service and "fair" prices make it a "pleasant surprise."

North Beach Pizza *Pizza*　　| 21 | 13 | 18 | $19 |

Excelsior | 4787 Mission St. (bet. Persia & Russia Aves.) | 415-586-1400
Haight-Ashbury | 800 Stanyan St. (Haight St.) | 415-751-2300 ●
North Beach | 1462 Grant Ave. (Union St.) | 415-433-2444
Outer Sunset | 3054 Taraval St. (41st Ave.) | 415-242-9100
www.northbeachpizza.net
"Gooey mozzarella", "crunchy crusts" and "exotic toppings" are hallmarks of the pies at this "family-friendly" North Beach "pizza joint" and its offspring; "decent prices" and "accommodating" service keep

the "old-fashioned" parlors "busy", but fans suggest "if it's crowded, take it home" – or opt for the "reliable" delivery.

North Beach Restaurant ● *Italian*   25 | 21 | 24 | $52

North Beach | 1512 Stockton St. (bet. Green & Union Sts.) | 415-392-1700 | www.northbeachrestaurant.com

"Fantastic, authentic" Tuscan fare (including "homemade prosciutto") and "real service from real old-style waiters" are the draws at this "classy, consistent" North Beach "old-timer" that insiders insist "hasn't diminished over the years"; "high prices" peeve the budget-minded, but for most it's "pure bliss" – especially if meals include the "excellent" house wine from the "owner's vineyard."

One Market ⌧ *American*   24 | 23 | 24 | $59

Embarcadero | 1 Market St. (bet. Spear & Steuart Sts.) | 415-777-5577 | www.onemarket.com

At this Embarcadero "splurge spot", "incredible" New American fare is "graciously" presented by a "discerning" staff and complemented by the wares of "knowledgeable sommeliers" armed with a "top-flight wine list"; "comfy banquette seating" in an "attractive" room packs in the "business-lunch" and "special-occasion" crowds, and even though a few say it "tends to be noisy", the "perfect" "views over the Embarcadero" help justify its rep as a "go-to place to impress all."

Ono Hawaiian BBQ   *Hawaiian*   19 | 12 | 16 | $11

Lakeshore | 1501 Sloat Ave. (bet. Everglade & Havenside Drs.) | 415-681-6388 | www.onohawaiianbbq.com

For a "fun change of taste", surveyors say aloha to to this "plate-lunch" specialist serving "spicy" fish cakes and other Hawaiian favorites; the "plastic, fast-food atmosphere" may lack appeal, but low costs help – plus "every meal comes with macaroni salad" – "yum!"

Oola Restaurant & Bar ● *Californian*   22 | 20 | 19 | $37

SoMa | 860 Folsom St. (bet. 4th & 5th Sts.) | 415-995-2061 | www.oola-sf.com

Chef-owner Ola Fendert's midpriced menu offers classics like "mac 'n' cheese, oysters, burgers" and "killer" ribs at this SoMa Californian where the "high ceilings", brick walls and "sexy, shimmery" decor "create a sophisticated setting"; a few grumble that service can be "spotty", but night owls savor the "interesting cocktails" and a kitchen that "stays open late" (until 1 AM on weekends).

Oriental Pearl   *Chinese*   24 | 15 | 21 | $37

Chinatown | 760 Clay St. (Grant Ave.) | 415-433-1817 | www.orientalpearlsf.com

"Excellent" dim sum ("from a menu instead of carts") and "consistently good" Chinese staples, including an "aces" Peking duck you just "have to try", earn kudos for this "Chinatown classic"; a few grumble it's "under-whelming" for "too high" a price, but more maintain you'll need to "go to Hong Kong" to find better chow – and service is "pleasant" to boot.

Original Joe's   *American/Italian*   22 | 22 | 23 | $37

North Beach | 601 Union St. (Stockton St.) | 415-775-4877 | www.originaljoessf.com

The "long-awaited rebirth" of this "classic" Italian-American joint – resurrected in North Beach after a Tenderloin fire – has fans declaring it "was worth the wait" for "hearty", "honest" fare like "heaping plates of pasta" and "reasonably priced wine"; "tuxedoed waiters" and "red booths" abound for an "early SF" vibe, and even though some say it "lacks the original's electricity", "young and old" crowds alike are "pleased" to have this "gem back in action."

Osha Thai *Thai* | 22 | 21 | 19 | $29 |

Cow Hollow | 2033 Union St. (bet. Buchanan & Webster Sts.) | 415-567-6742
NEW Downtown | 432 Sutter St. (Stockton St.) | 415-397-6742 🖂
Embarcadero | Embarcadero Ctr. | 4 Embarcadero Ctr., street level (Drumm St.) | 415-788-6742
Glen Park | 2922 Diamond St. (Bosworth St.) | 415-586-6742
Mission | 819 Valencia St. (bet. 19th & 20th Sts.) | 415-826-7738 ●
SoMa | 149 Second St. (bet. Howard & Mission Sts.) | 415-278-9991
SoMa | 311 Third St. (Folsom St.) | 415-896-6742

Osha Thai Noodle Cafe ● *Thai*

Tenderloin | 696 Geary St. (Leavenworth St.) | 415-673-2368
www.oshathai.com
"No matter the location", this "consistently good" chainlet is a "true delight" for "scrumptious" Thai dishes made with "fresh ingredients" (tip: "try the pumpkin curry"); "fast" service in "minimalist", almost "Zen"-like spaces can be expected, as well as "interesting" cocktails that are "hard to say 'no' to" and relatively "affordable" tabs – all of which draw "diverse", often "loud" crowds.

NEW O3 Bistro & Lounge 🖂 *Asian* | 24 | 22 | 22 | $31 |

Civic Center | 524 Van Ness Ave. (bet. Golden Gate Ave. & McAllister St.) | 415-934-9800 | www.o3restaurant.com
A "handy" "pre-symphony option", this Civic Center newcomer offers an "amazing" Cal-Asian menu and "delicious cocktails", all served by a generally "helpful" staff in a "dark, cozy and sexy" space; add in moderate prices and a sweet "happy hour", and it's no surprise surveyors vow to "keep going back."

Ottimista | ▽ 20 | 17 | 20 | $42 |
Enoteca-Café Ⓜ *Italian/Mediterranean*

Cow Hollow | 1838 Union St. (Octavia St.) | 415-674-8400 | www.ottimistasf.com
Cow Hollow locals "love the vibe" at this "neighborhood spot" turning out rustic Italian-Med "small plates" plus pasta and pizzas backed by a "great wine selection" that's available by the glass, bottle or *quartino*; though the bites and service are a little uneven, the "casual" atmosphere works to "meet and greet" with a drink at the bar or on the "intimate outdoor porch."

Outerlands Ⓜ *American* | 25 | 20 | 19 | $30 |

Outer Sunset | 4001 Judah St. (45th Ave.) | 415-661-6140 | www.outerlandssf.com
Helping to revitalize the Outer Sunset "one plate at a time", this "tiny" spot "out by the beach" racks up "long lines" for "rising star" Brett Cooper's "awesome", ingredient-driven New American meals and farm-to-glass cocktails, now served with table service also at lunch; the "warm" "fabulous" "homemade breads" and "quaint" "driftwood decor" provide solace from the "cold outside" (where you can

"wait a lifetime", particularly for weekend brunch), but a scheduled expansion should help.

Out the Door *Vietnamese* | 23 | 16 | 19 | $29 |

Embarcadero | Ferry Bldg. Mktpl. | 1 Ferry Bldg. (The Embarcadero) | 415-321-3740
Upper Fillmore | 2232 Bush St. (Fillmore St.) | 415-923-9575
www.outthedoors.com

Offering the "same" "modern Vietnamese" "goodness" without "the hassle of its parent", the Slanted Door, this "less-expensive" offshoot in the Upper Fillmore allows fans to "spontaneously enjoy shaking beef" and other favorites (Asian and "American breakfasts" too); the "modern" decor isn't everyone's "cup of oolong", but "friendly" service and "wine on tap" "warm things up"; the "downscale takeout" in the Ferry Building hawks lunches and "take-home" cooking "kits."

Oyaji Ⓜ *Japanese*   ▽ 24 | 18 | 18 | $41 |

Outer Richmond | 3123 Clement St. (bet. 32nd & 33rd Aves.) | 415-379-3604 | www.oyajirestaurant.com

It's one "big sushi party" at this "intimate" Outer Richmond Japanese, where the chef-owner (a "real character") produces "delicately prepared" fish and "wonderful" izakaya specialties for midpriced tabs in a "traditional" setting; regulars advise to amp up the fun, pour the *oyaji* ("old man") "a few drinks" and "let the good times roll."

Ozumo *Japanese* | 25 | 24 | 22 | $63 |

Embarcadero | 161 Steuart St. (bet. Howard & Mission Sts.) | 415-882-1333 | www.ozumo.com

"Prepare to be wowed" at this "modern, cool" Embarcadero and Oakland duo, where "remarkable" Japanese fare – including "incredible" delights from the robata grill and "fresh, creative" sushi – is supplemented by an "extensive sake menu" (80-plus choices) and "attentive" service; "expect to pay a premium" ("if you're on an expense account, go crazy"), but fans promise it's "worth every single penny."

Pacific Café *Seafood* | 24 | 18 | 23 | $34 |

Outer Richmond | 7000 Geary Blvd. (34th Ave.) | 415-387-7091 | www.pacificcafesf.com

"Get there early" warn regulars of this "no-reservations" seafooder, a "casual" Outer Richmond "classic", where "deliciously fresh, reliable" fare ensures "long lines" to get in (not to worry, there's "free wine while you wait"); the menu and decor "haven't changed since the '70s", but a "welcoming" staff that's "worked there for years" and "fair prices" keep locals "returning."

Pacific Catch *Seafood* | 22 | 17 | 20 | $26 |

Inner Sunset | 1200 Ninth Ave. (Lincoln Way) | 415-504-6905
Marina | 2027 Chestnut St. (bet. Fillmore & Steiner Sts.) | 415-440-1950
www.pacificcatch.com

"Healthy" fin fare with a pan-Pacific influence is the hook at this small chain of "casual", "affordable" seafooders whose "simple preparations" "allow the fish to stand out"; "there isn't much to the decor", but the staff "makes you feel at home" with its "attentive service" and is "welcoming to children."

Pagan Ⓜ *Burmese/Thai*   ▽ 22 | 13 | 16 | $21

Outer Richmond | 3199 Clement St. (33rd Ave.) | 415-751-2598 |
www.pagansf.com

At this "convenient" "little place" in the Outer Richmond, "two chefs" in a "tiny kitchen" produce Thai and Burmese fare (including a "tasty tea leaf salad") – and "they're both excellent"; it's "not upscale" and the "sweet staff is not always on top of things", but usually there's "no wait" and prices offer "value."

Pagolac Ⓜ⇥ *Vietnamese*   ▽ 22 | 13 | 21 | $23

Tenderloin | 655 Larkin St. (bet. Ellis & Willow Sts.) | 415-776-3234

For a "transcendant, authentic experience", order the "seven courses of beef" at this Tenderloin nook, which also whips up other "well-prepared" Vietnamese dishes replete with "fresh ingredients"; you "don't go for the atmosphere", but "friendly service" and "affordable" prices help make it "too good to miss."

Pakwan *Pakistani*   23 | 9 | 14 | $16

Mission | 3180-3182 16th St. (Guerrero St.) | 415-255-2440 ⇥
Tenderloin | 501 O'Farrell St. (Jones St.) | 415-776-0160
www.pakwanrestaurant.com

"Fragrant, scrumptious curries" and "soft, chewy naan" are "outstanding" and "cheap" at this "hole-in-the-wall" Pakistani Bay Area mini-chain; you "order at the counter" (the "staff can be gruff") and "ambiance is negligible", so "just close your eyes", or better yet, get "your order to go"; P.S. they're "BYO – always a plus."

Palio d'Asti ☒ *Italian*   22 | 21 | 22 | $46

Downtown | 640 Sacramento St. (bet. Kearny & Montgomery Sts.) | 415-395-9800 | www.paliodasti.com

With its "heartwarming" Italian standards made from "quality ingredients", "professional service" and "upscale" Tuscan-inspired trappings, this FiDi trattoria is a "great choice" for a "business lunch" or a "special meal" in the city; moderate prices, "truffle dinners in the fall" and an "awesome happy-hour special" ($1 pizza) seal the deal; P.S. scores don't reflect a post-Survey change of owner and chef.

Pancho Villa Taqueria ❶ *Mexican*   23 | 11 | 17 | $12

Mission | 3071 16th St. (bet. Mission & Valencia Sts.) | 415-864-8840 | www.smpanchovilla.com

"Frequent lines" at this "cheap, fast" taqueria duo in the Mission and San Mateo attest to the "freshness and popularity" of its "better-than-usual" "Mexican standards" ("stomach-busting" burritos, "refreshing" agua fresca "with chunks of real fruit") that make up for an interior that's "nothing special" "featuring uncomfortable stools"; a staff providing "speedy counter service" "tries very hard to accommodate."

Pane e Vino *Italian*   23 | 19 | 23 | $41

Cow Hollow | 1715 Union St. (Gough St.) | 415-346-2111 | www.paneevinotrattoria.com

"In a city filled with" "neighborhood Italian joints", this Cow Hollow trattoria is "one of the better", with "unpretentious but delicious" Northern Italian fare, a "great wine selection" and an "affable staff"; though the "homey", "kid-friendly" space can get "crowded" and parking can be a "problem", fans say "bravo" to its overall "value."

Papalote Mexican Grill *Mexican*

22 | 12 | 16 | $14

Mission | 3409 24th St. (Valencia St.) | 415-970-8815
Western Addition | 1777 Fulton St. (Masonic Ave.) | 415-776-0106
www.papalote-sf.com

"Hipsters stream out the door" at this Mission and Western Addition taqueria duo serving "unusually interesting" and "non-greasy" Mexican fare including "fantastic" "burritos" and salsa that "alone is worth a trip" ("buy a jar to take home"); purists say they're "not really authentic", and since the no-frills spaces get "pretty cramped", regulars "phone in" and get their affordable grub to-go.

Papito *Mexican*

▽ 26 | 19 | 22 | $20

Potrero Hill | 317 Connecticut St. (bet. 18th & 19th Sts.) | 415-695-0147 | www.papitosf.com

Potrero Hill locals plead "don't visit" their "favorite tiny neighborhood spot", a Chez Papa sibling bringing "French flair" and "organic" ingredients to "Mexican soul" food – they'd rather keep it for themselves; it's "not expensive" and most enjoy being fussed over by charming garçons while sipping a "refreshing" sangria at the "nice copper bar" or sitting "outside" at one of the sidewalk tables, so "what's not to like?"

Parada 22 *Puerto Rican*

▽ 23 | 18 | 22 | $17

Haight-Ashbury | 1805 Haight St. (Shrader St.) | 415-750-1111 | www.parada22.com

At this "adorable little" Haight-Ashbury storefront, a "super-friendly" staff serves "rib-sticking Puerto Rican comfort food done right" (including "red beans so good" fans "could swim in a tub of them"); "cheap prices" for "good-sized portions" washed down with a "half-pitcher of sangria" are the makings of a "good night."

NEW Parallel 37 *American*

▽ 24 | 22 | 22 | $66

Nob Hill | Ritz-Carlton San Francisco | 600 Stockton St. (California St.) | 415-773-6168 | www.parallel37sf.com

This "more casual", "hip" new incarnation for "fine dining" inside the Nob Hill Ritz-Carlton "still impresses" with "well-executed" New American fare that's less-expensive than the previous "haute" menu here; a few stalwarts "mourn the loss" of the "elegant special-occasion" spot of yore and service reviews are mixed, but the "stylish" cocktail lounge has quickly become a "chic spot for drinks."

Park Chalet
Garden Restaurant *Californian*

17 | 22 | 18 | $30

Outer Sunset | 1000 Great Hwy. (bet. Fulton St. & Lincoln Way) | 415-386-8439 | www.parkchalet.com

Facing Golden Gate Park, this Outer Sunset hangout "welcomes all" with an "outdoor vibe" and "house-brewed beer" to accompany "tasty" midpriced Cal–New American grub served by a "happy staff"; unlike the adjacent Beach Chalet, there's no water "view", still, sitting on the patio with the "ocean air in your face" is "heaven."

NEW Park Tavern Ⓜ *American*

25 | 25 | 23 | $53

North Beach | 1652 Stockton St. (bet. Filbert & Union Sts.) | 415-989-7300 | www.parktavernsf.com

There's "a certain magic" to this "happening" new "see-and-be-seen" North Beach tavern with "great views of the park" that's often "jammed"

FOOD | DECOR | SERVICE | COST

with "politicos", the "social" set and clientele "of all ages" "eating and drinking well" in the "cool"-looking space; the "imaginative", market-driven New American fare (including the famed "Marlowe burger") is delivered with service that's "always pro", and a late-night bar adds to the "lively" vibe.

Pasión *Nuevo Latino/Peruvian*
25 | 24 | 22 | $39

Inner Sunset | 737 Irving St. (bet. 8th & 9th Aves.) | 415-742-5727 | www.pasionsf.com

Chef Jose Calvo-Perez serves Nuevo Latino–Peruvian fare (including "delicious" ceviche and "fantastic" entrees) cat this "imaginative" Inner Sunset offshoot of his father's Fresca chain; service is sometimes "slow", and the "energetic environment" with a bright, "beautiful" Inca-inspired mural can "get noisy", but admirers swear the "happy hour is a steal."

Pasta Pomodoro *Italian*
19 | 17 | 20 | $22

Laurel Heights | 3611 California St. (Spruce St.) | 415-831-0900
Noe Valley | 4000 24th St. (Noe St.) | 415-920-9904
www.pastapomodoro.com

"Friendly" staffers, "comfortable, inviting" decor and "uncomplicated", "inexpensive" Italian fare (including a "wide selection" to fix a "pasta craving") are the hallmarks of this "semi-fast chain"; it's popular with "families and friends", and though it sometimes looks "like a day care center early evenings", it "can always be depended upon to please."

Patxi's Pizza *Pizza*
22 | 16 | 18 | $22
(fka Patxi's Chicago Pizza)

NEW **Inner Sunset** | 822 Irving St. (9th Ave.) | 415-759-9000
Cow Hollow | 3318 Fillmore St. (Lombard St.) | 415-345-3995
Hayes Valley | 511 Hayes St. (bet. Laguna & Octavia Sts.) | 415-558-9991
Noe Valley | 4042 24th St. (bet. Castro & Noe Sts.) | 415-285-2000
www.patxispizza.com

Even displaced Chicagoans swear the "deep-dish", "decadent stuffed pizzas" at this Bay Area chain are "the real deal" (though some "prefer the thin-crust" pies); since they're "always packed" with "families", the ambiance "tends to be noisy" and "waits are long" (locals know to "call ahead" for "half-baked pizzas" to finish up at home), and while service can be "slow" and the "decor could use work", it's a "great deal" that's "totally worth the calories."

Pauline's Pizza 🚫Ⓜ *Pizza*
23 | 14 | 20 | $28

Mission | 260 Valencia St. (bet. Duboce Ave. & 14th St.) | 415-552-2050

Pauline's Wines 🚫Ⓜ *Pizza*

Mission | 260 Valencia St. (bet. Duboce Ave. & 14th St.) | 415-552-2050
www.paulinespizza.com

They've been "getting it right" for decades at this "family-friendly" lo-cavore pizzeria in the Mission offering "unusual toppings" ("the pizza-of-the-day is the way to go") and "fresh salads" harvested "from their own farm"; although it can "be kind of pricey" and "parking may be an issue", "carafes" of house wine quaffed in the no-frills main room or in the nearby vino bar help lessen the sting.

	FOOD	DECOR	SERVICE	COST

Pazzia ⊠ *Pizza* ▽ | 24 | 15 | 23 | $35 |

SoMa | 337 Third St. (bet. Folsom & Harrison Sts.) | 415-512-1693
SoMa habitués "squeeze" into this "solid neighborhood Italian" for "standout" "thin-crust pizza", "wonderful housemade pastas" and other "authentic" fare accompanied by a "surprisingly affordable wine list"; while the "friendly" atmosphere generated by the staff and "charming owner" is part of the "attraction", regulars suggest asking for an "outdoor table" if it's "too noisy inside."

Pearl's Deluxe Burgers *Burgers* | 24 | 13 | 19 | $13 |

SoMa | 1001 Market St. (6th St.) | no phone
Tenderloin | 708 Post St. (Jones St.) | 415-409-6120
www.pearlsdeluxe.com
Diners who "take burgers seriously" suggest trying the "juicy" patties at this quartet of Bay Area eateries where the lineup includes "healthy options" (e.g. grass-fed beef, "buffalo, veggie and turkey") along with "to-die-for shakes" and "O-rings"; there are "prices to match" the sometimes "exotic ingredients", and if you're looking for ambiance, "go somewhere else."

⊠ Perbacco ⊠ *Italian* | 26 | 23 | 24 | $56 |

Downtown | 230 California St. (bet. Battery & Front Sts.) | 415-955-0663 | www.perbaccosf.com
"Ambrosial" Piedmont-inflected Italian cuisine (both "traditional and innovative") and "exceptional" wines delivered with "knowledgeable" service lure a "sophisticated, classy crowd" to this FiDi Barbacco sib; a "special-occasion" and "business-lunch standby", the large, brick-lined room retains an "intimate atmosphere", though conversationalists get tables "upstairs" ("away from the noise").

NEW Per Diem *American* ▽ | 22 | 23 | 21 | $30 |

Downtown | 43 Sutter St. (bet. Montgomery & Sansome Sts.) | 415-989-0300 | www.perdiemsf.com
This "super-hip" "new hot spot" enlivens a "sleepy stretch of the FiDi" for Downtowners looking to spend their per diem on "artisanal" cocktails plus "excellent" pizzas and other "hearty" midpriced Cal-Italian-type American fare; service pleases in the two-story space with a "beautiful design" that's a modern take on Gold Rush–era decor; P.S. lunch served weekdays only.

Pesce *Italian/Seafood* | 25 | 18 | 24 | $40 |

Russian Hill | 2227 Polk St. (bet. Green & Vallejo Sts.) | 415-928-8025 | www.pescebarsf.com
"Meet a friend" at this "tiny" and "casual" midpriced Russian Hill ristorante where "Venetian-inspired" seafood and "terrific" pastas are served "tapas"-style and are enhanced by cocktails and "wonderful wines"; an "attentive staff" and "friendly" vibe compensate for somewhat "austere" quarters, and regulars say "if you want to talk, go early."

Phat Philly *Cheesesteaks* ▽ | 22 | 12 | 19 | $13 |

Mission | 3388 24th St. (Valencia St.) | 415-550-7428 | www.phatphilly.com
Showing "extreme dedication" to "authentic" Philly cheesesteaks (including Amaroso rolls) plus improvement "on the real thing" with the likes of American Kobe beef, a tofu option and cheddar-beer sauce fans "could eat a bowl of" earns kudos for this Mission sandwich

shop run by "friendly guys"; while the main attraction's "not über-cheap" and can take "a while to be prepped", "inexpensive beer" and Tastykakes are pluses.

Pi Bar ● *Pizza* ▽ 21 | 18 | 20 | $20

Mission | 1432 Valencia St. (25th St.) | 415-970-9670 | www.pibarsf.com

"Authentic NY–style, thin-crust pizza" and a "small but stellar rotating beer selection" delivered with "friendly" service make this pie purveyor a "popular Mission haunt"; the "simple, casual" digs are "perfect for a post-work" stop, especially during "hap-Pi hour" when suds go for $3.14 (the clever regular price of a slice); P.S. it also "opens at 3:14" PM.

Pica Pica Maize Kitchen *Venezuelan* 20 | 14 | 17 | $16

Mission | 401 Valencia St. (15th St.) | 415-400-5453 | www.picapickitchen.com

See review in North of San Francisco Directory.

Piccino Ⓜ *Italian* 24 | 22 | 21 | $37

Dogpatch | 1001 Minnesota St. (22nd St.) | 415-824-4224 | www.piccinocafe.com

Situated in "modern" "digs" in The Yellow Building, this Cal-Italian "gem" continues to draw Dogpatch "regulars" with its "superb" "thin-crust pizza", "imaginative salads" and "inventive small plates", all "made from the freshest ingredients"; servers who are "über-friendly" add to the "solid value", as does "sitting at the bar watching the magic happen" in the "bright, airy room."

Piperade Ⓧ *Spanish* 27 | 22 | 24 | $56

Downtown | 1015 Battery St. (bet. Green & Union Sts.) | 415-391-2555 | www.piperade.com

Chef-owner Gerald Hirigoyen "brings the Basque dining experience to life" at this "delightful", "out-of-the-way" Downtowner featuring "rustic", "authentic" regional classics and "affordable" wines from the area, all delivered with a "level of hospitality" that "just keeps getting better"; the "exposed-brick" digs are "filled at lunch with business" folk, but the "cozy" ambiance works for a "date", dinner with "friends" or any occasion calling for "flavor" and a bit of "flair."

Piqueo's *Peruvian* 24 | 18 | 22 | $36

Bernal Heights | 830 Cortland Ave. (Gates St.) | 415-282-8812 | www.piqueos.com

At this "neighborhood jewel" in Bernal Heights, chef-owner Carlos Altamirano creates "beautifully presented" midpriced Peruvian fare "with a modern flair" featuring "easy-to-share small plates" (called "piqueos" in Peru) including "amazing ceviche" plus entrees; it's "loud and crowded" and "can be hard to get into" but has a "sexy atmosphere" and the "staff is very knowledgeable", especially "about the wines."

Pizzeria Delfina *Pizza* 26 | 17 | 20 | $30

Mission | 3611 18th St. (Guerrero St.) | 415-437-6800
Pacific Heights | 2406 California St. (bet. Fillmore & Steiner Sts.) | 415-440-1189
www.pizzeriadelfina.com

"Insanely good", "beautifully charred" Neapolitan-style pies with "innovative toppings" à la "Delfina proper" (its big sis) have fans of this

	FOOD	DECOR	SERVICE	COST

Mission–Pac Heights duo vowing they "won't eat pizza anyplace else"; it's no "one-trick pony" though, also offering "delicious" salads, antipasti and wines as staffers efficiently "swim their way through the sea of hipsters" – while those adverse to "long lines" and "loud music" order "ahead for takeout."

Pizzetta 211 ⊄ *Pizza*

26	15	19	$25

Outer Richmond | 211 23rd Ave. (California St.) | 415-379-9880 | www.pizzetta211.com

"Thin-crust artisanal pizzas" with toppings such as farm-fresh "eggs, pancetta, butternut squash" and other locavore ingredients that change weekly make this bare-bones pizzeria "one of the great hidden secrets" of the Outer Richmond; service is "spotty", but diehards arrive "early" to "snag" one of the few seats, and "dress warmly" lest they be relegated to "eating outside"; P.S. "cash only."

NEW Pläj *Scandinavian*

–	–	–	M

Hayes Valley | Inn At The Opera | 333 Fulton St. (bet. Franklin & Gough Sts.) | 415-863-8400 | www.plajrestaurant.com

San Francisco finally has its first Scandinavian restaurant with this Hayes Valley newcomer (pronounced 'play') offering midpriced small plates of traditional Swedish dishes made with locally sourced ingredients; the former Ovations space is now filled with hardwoods and orange accents, and there's a small bar that stocks Scandinavian beers, European spirits like Bols Genever and plenty of vodka.

Plant Cafe Organic *Health Food*

22	19	17	$26

Downtown | 101 California St. (bet. California & Front Sts.) | 415-693-9730 Ⓩ

Embarcadero | Pier 3 (bet. B'way & Washington St.) | 415-984-1973

Marina | 3352 Steiner St. (bet. Chestnut & Lombard Sts.) | 415-931-2777 www.theplantcafe.com

"Tasty", "organic" Californian cuisine served "in a cool atmosphere" is the concept that keeps this trio of crunchy cafes turning out "awesome" "housemade veggie burgers", "fresh vegetable juices" and other "affordable" clean-living staples; the staff can get "slammed during the lunch rush", but fans appreciate being able "to eat out with friends and not blow your diet"; P.S. the Embarcadero location's patio has "beautiful views of the bay."

Plouf *French*

22	16	18	$40

Downtown | 40 Belden Pl. (bet. Bush & Pine Sts.) | 415-986-6491 | www.ploufsf.com

"Feel like you're in Europe" at this "industrial"-chic Downtown seafooder, where Francophiles declare the "mussels and fries" ("prepared many different ways") "are the best this side of Belgium"; "the French waiters" can be "nonchalant" and the outdoor seating on Belden Place can get "jammed", but it's still a "go-to place" for a "romantic" tête-à-tête at a moderate tab.

Plow *Californian*

26	19	21	$24

Potrero Hill | 1299 18th St. (Texas St.) | 415-821-7569 | www.eatatplow.com

"Delicious breakfast and lunch dishes" (including "amazing home fries" and lemon ricotta pancakes "to die for") made of "locally sourced ingredients" have daytime diners coming "early" to avoid a "torturous" wait at this Potrero Hill Californian cafe; while the nothing-fancy interior of reclaimed wood floors and oak-barrel tables belies the sometimes pricey tabs, "friendly service" and a no-pressure vibe help make this a "favorite" of the "young crowd."

Poesia *Italian*
24 | 20 | 23 | $48

Castro | 4072 18th St. (bet. Castro & Hartford Sts.) | 415-252-9325 | www.poesiasf.com

"Handmade pasta" and other "homey Italian food" from the Calabria region pairs with "Italian cinema classics" "projected on the wall" at this "vibrant", "intimate" Castro osteria; while some feel the "portions are small" for the price tag and "tables are close together", the "friendly" staffers "really do treat you like part of the family."

Pomelo *Eclectic*
24 | 16 | 22 | $25

Inner Sunset | 92 Judah St. (bet. 5th & 6th Aves.) | 415-731-6175
Noe Valley | 1793 Church St. (30th St.) | 415-285-2257
www.pomelosf.com

With menus featuring "a variety of dishes" influenced by cuisines from "around the world", this Eclectic duo serves "fresh" "global" grub cosmopolitans consider an "awesome value"; service can be uneven at both the "microscopic" Inner Sunset outpost and the "noisier" Noe Valley locale, but diners like that they "can watch the chef cook" in the vibrant and sunny rooms' open kitchens.

Pork Store Café *American*
19 | 11 | 16 | $16

Haight-Ashbury | 1451 Haight St. (bet. Ashbury St. & Masonic Ave.) | 415-864-6981
Mission | 3122 16th St. (Valencia St.) | 415-626-5523
www.porkstorecafe.com

At this "greasy-spoon" "breakfast-and-lunch" duo in the Haight and the Mission, "hangover" sufferers forget "Saturday night sins" with "huge" portions of "excellent-value", "diner-style" classics (and a "make-your-own" "Bloody Mary bar"); despite "lightning-fast" service, there can be "long waits", so regulars "crawl out of bed early" to get their pick of tables in the "tiny" space; P.S. the 16th Street location is open until 3 AM Thursday–Saturday.

Postrio *American*
23 | 22 | 21 | $64

Downtown | Prescott Hotel | 545 Post St. (bet. Mason & Taylor Sts.) | 415-776-7825 | www.postrio.com

Though no longer the Downtown "landmark" of its Wolfgang Puck days, this "simple cafe" still turns out "wonderful" "personal pizzas" and American "bar food" with "friendly", "timely" service; though the tab can be "pricey", it's a longtime "favorite" that works "for a quick bite" "after shopping" or "pre-theater", but one can only "descend the stairs like a star" to the "beautiful" "main dining room" for breakfast or private parties.

PPQ Dungeness Island *Seafood/Vietnamese*
24 | 14 | 19 | $30

Outer Richmond | 2332 Clement St. (25th Ave.) | 415-386-8266

"If you like crab", this Vietnamese in the Outer Richmond "is the place to go" for "delicious", "transcendent" takes on the crustacean; while the faux-tropical space can get "quite crowded" and parking in the area is about the "roughest in the city", fans applaud the relatively "cheap" prices and service that can accommodate "large groups" in the upstairs dining room.

Presidio Social Club *American*   19 | 22 | 19 | $41

Presidio | 563 Ruger St. (Lombard St.) | 415-885-1888 | www.presidiosocialclub.com

"Tucked away in the trees in the Presidio", this "vintage" military barracks turned "casual" American serves up a "time warp back to the '20s" to go with the "quirky", updated renditions of "down-home" eats presented on "mess hall plates" and "lovely old-fashioned cocktails" poured into "circa 1954" glassware; service can be "slow" but "prices are reasonable", and "you can't beat lunch on the outside deck on warm, sunny days."

Prospect *American*   24 | 24 | 24 | $62

SoMa | Infiniti Towers | 300 Spear St. (Folsom St.) | 415-247-7770 | www.prospectsf.com

If "creative food" like "crispy trotters" and "well-made" cocktails are "what you crave", this New American "casual sister" to Nancy Oakes' "more upscale Boulevard" is "a likely prospect"; its "spiffy" "New York–ish" decor, "impeccable service" and "yuppie crowd" are reflective of its locale in a "tony" SoMa "high-rise", but if you've got an "expense" account, "first-rate" dinners and "Sunday brunch" will "surprise and delight", while the "robust bar scene" is HQ for "happy hour" deals and drinks.

Public House *Pub Food*   17 | 21 | 17 | $29

South Beach | AT&T Park | 24 Willie Mays Plaza (3rd St.) | 415-644-0240 | www.publichousesf.com

Boasting its "own entrance to AT&T Park", this mega gastropub offers a "vast" beer selection to accompany "elegant" "bar food" at moderate prices from chef Traci Des Jardins (Jardinière); it hits a home run for "pre-game festivities" (just "get there early" because "the line is longer than Timmy Lincecum's locks"), but "even on non-game days", diehards "stop by for a pint" and to "watch sports on the telly."

Q Restaurant & Wine Bar *American*   20 | 18 | 20 | $29

Inner Richmond | 225 Clement St. (bet. 3rd & 4th Aves.) | 415-752-2298 | www.qrestaurant.com

"Quirky, quick and quintessentially yummy", this Inner Richmond American with a "youthful vibe" and "playgroundlike dining room" complete with "magnetic letters on the walls" is "comfort-food central", turning out the likes of "mac 'n' cheese, Tater Tots" and "BBQ ribs" for a "truly reasonable price"; service can be spotty and the grub's a little "hit-and-miss", but devotees say this "funky" spot will "make you smile."

⚡ Quince 🗷 *Italian*   26 | 26 | 26 | $124

Downtown | 470 Pacific Ave. (bet. Montgomery St. & Pacific Ave.) | 415-775-8500 | www.quincerestaurant.com

"Pasta magician" Michael Tusk and his wife, Lindsay, "wow" at their "fancy" Downtown Cal-Italian that's filled with "movers and shakers" "wining and dining" on "compelling", "high-end" tasting menus and "fabulous" (albeit "expensive") vintages delivered with "thoughtful service"; it's "fantastic in every way" with a "palace"–like interior and "a bill to match", so while some "tsk" it's all "a bit precious", to others it's the stuff of "dreams."

Radish   *American*   ▽ | 20 | 18 | 20 | $22

Mission | 3465 19th St. (Lexington St.) | 415-834-5441 | www.radishsf.com
Located in a little "off the beaten path" in the Mission, this "chill" neighborhood haunt serves brunch through "late-night" offering "huge portions" of "affordable" "real" American food ("lots of fresh veggies, whole grains and wheat-free options"); while the "lovely" red-walled space's "hipster quotient is off-the-charts" (the "cool kids" make up much of the clientele and staff), guests get "seated quickly" and with "no sass."

Radius 🅜🅜 *Californian*   ▽ | 22 | 18 | 22 | $49

SoMa | 1123 Folsom St. (Langton St.) | 415-525-3676 | www.radiussf.com
SoMa "locavores" embrace this sit-down dinner Californian (and its adjacent "quick-lunch cafe") on Folsom Street's emerging "Restaurant Row", where a "welcoming" staff ferries out "creative" and "delicious" cuisine and wine – all "sourced within a 100-mile 'radius' of the restaurant (hence the name)"; "prices are reasonable for the quality", and the rustic-industrial setting includes a patio.

Ragazza   *Pizza* | 25 | 19 | 21 | $33

Western Addition | 311 Divisadero St. (bet. Oak & Page Sts.) | 415-255-1133 | www.ragazzasf.com
A "nice respite" from the crowds at older sister Gialina, this "fantastic neighborhood spot" in the Western Addition turns out "the same" seasonally driven "wood-fired" pizza, pasta and sides at moderate prices; a "nice wine list" and "very friendly" crew are the "icing on the cake", just "don't go with too many people" as the "small" space lined with "old family photographs" "doesn't take reservations."

Ramen Underground ⊬🍴 *Japanese/Noodle Shop*   ▽ | 19 | 12 | 18 | $15

Downtown | 355 Kearny St. (Pine St.) | 415-765-9909
Big "satisfying bowls" of "perfect" ramen floating in "rich and flavorful" broth that hits the spot "on a cold day" are the draw at this tiny Downtown Japanese "hole-in-the-wall" newly opened by a Katana-Ya vet; the bill can get "a bit pricey" since you pay "an extra dollar" per additional topping, and since the "tiny" room can get "crowded", regulars who want a fix "just call ahead for takeout."

R & G Lounge   *Chinese* | 25 | 14 | 16 | $36

Chinatown | 631 Kearny St. (bet. Clay & Sacramento Sts.) | 415-982-7877 | www.rnglounge.com
Plates of "salt-and-pepper crabs keep luring you back" to this Cantonese favorite, considered some of the "best Chinese" in Chinatown, if not "the Bay"; "make reservations and bring your patience", as service is "brusque" and "rushed", though "tourists" and "locals" alike say this "taste of Hong Kong–style dining" (especially in the basic "downstairs" room) is "worth every yuan."

Range   *American* | 27 | 21 | 25 | $55

Mission | 842 Valencia St. (bet. 19th & 20th Sts.) | 415-282-8283 | www.rangesf.com
Offering "imaginative", "seasonal" American fare made "without gimmicks" from a husband-and-wife-team, this "hipster haunt" has

Missionites thinking it may just be the "perfect" eatery; the "awesome" service (including the "entertaining" "mixologists" at the "hopping" bar) helps make it "wonderful enough for a special occasion", and though the "cozy" digs can get a "bit crowded and noisy", the vibe is relaxed enough to "sneak in on a Tuesday just because."

Regalito Rosticeria *Mexican*

23 | 20 | 23 | $29

Mission | 3481 18th St. (bet. Lexington & Valencia Sts.) | 415-503-0650 | www.regalitosf.com

At this "authentic, high-quality" "gem" "in the heart of the Mission", "organic ingredients" make for "delicious, fresh Mexican" "rotisserie" fare that's more "sophisticated and subtle" than you might expect; the "cute place" can get crowded, but the "friendly" servers are most "accommodating", while prices are moderate; P.S. connoisseurs "check out" Pigalito Night on Tuesdays, when the menu features "a whole pig."

Restaurant LuLu *French/Mediterranean*

22 | 21 | 20 | $46

SoMa | 816 Folsom St. (bet. 4th & 5th Sts.) | 415-495-5775 | www.restaurantlulu.com

There's a "lively" "buzz" about this SoMa French-Mediterranean stalwart serving "homey", "hearty" "family-style" eats in a "noisy but fun" "cavernous room" with an "open kitchen", rotisserie and "wood-burning stove"; critics call out "pricey" tabs and uneven service, but most "enjoy being together" here, plus there's a "nice wine list" to boost the mood.

The Richmond 🗷 *Californian*

26 | 18 | 26 | $45

Inner Richmond | 615 Balboa St. (bet. 7th & 8th Aves.) | 415-379-8988 | www.therichmondsf.com

"Fine dining for a terrific price" is on offer at this Inner Richmond Californian with "gracious service" and a "friendly chef" who turns out "quality" dishes from an ever-changing menu; "affordable" wines and a prix fixe option make dinner in this "unassuming yet sexy little dining room" seem like an "outstanding bargain", and regulars predict "you will leave feeling glad that you came."

NEW Rich Table *Californian*

- | - | - | M

Hayes Valley | 199 Gough St. (Oak St.) | 415-355-9085 | www.richtablesf.com

Husband-and-wife chef team Evan and Sarah Rich have opened their own Hayes Valley haunt, serving daily changing, midpriced Northern Californian fare with cocktails and wine on tap; the 50-seat corner space is cozy and casual, with tables and walls made from salvaged barn wood and an exhibition kitchen anchoring the room.

Rigolo *French*

∇ 18 | 13 | 13 | $19

Presidio Heights | Laurel Village Shopping Ctr. | 3465 California St. (bet. Laurel & Locust Sts.) | 415-876-7777 | www.rigolocafe.com

Pascal Rigo's Presidio Heights cafe serves sandwiches, pizzas and casual French plates that are perfect options for a "quick" bite any time of day; with its "play area" and "children's menu", it "gets noisy midday", and some contend it's actually "a little overpriced" for a counter-service spot, but it's still a fine "place to hang with coffee and a pastry", especially after shopping in Laurel Village.

Ristobar ⓜ *Italian*

| 21 | 23 | 20 | $43 |

Marina | 2300 Chestnut St. (Scott St.) | 415-923-6464 | www.ristobarsf.com

Boasting decor that's "beyond beyond" – think "frescoed ceilings" and a Venetian-glass "chandelier" – this "date"-worthy Marina Italian turns out pasta, pizza and other "solid" "small plates" that encourage "sharing"; it's easy to indulge "way too much" thanks to "excellent" wines and "the best desserts" overseen by owner/pastry chef Gary Rulli (Emporio Rulli), all delivered with "accommodating" service.

Ristorante Milano *Italian*

| 24 | 17 | 23 | $46 |

Russian Hill | 1448 Pacific Ave. (bet. Hyde & Larkin Sts.) | 415-673-2961 | www.milanosf.com

Gnocchi cognoscenti hope this "first-rate Northern Italian" in Russian Hill "stays unknown" to a wider audience so they can continue to get a table in the "tiny" dining room that fills up fast; "gracious" service, "fabulous" "handmade pastas" and other classic dishes are the main draws, and regulars contend that even "higher-priced" competitors don't always "match" this "neighborhood standby."

Ristorante Umbria ⓢ *Italian*

▽ | 20 | 18 | 20 | $34 |

SoMa | 198 Second St. (Howard St.) | 415-546-6985 | www.ristoranteumbria.com

"Details" are important at this "sweet, old-school Italian" where the "Umbrian cuisine" is "solidly executed" and "the owner glad-hands all patrons"; some say service "can be abrupt", but most find this "loud, popular" SoMa spot "completely charming" and "perfect for lunch" or for dinner "before a show" at the nearby Yerba Buena Center or Metreon.

RN74 *French*

| 23 | 24 | 22 | $63 |

SoMa | Millennium Tower | 301 Mission St. (bet. Beale & Freemont Sts.) | 415-543-7474 | www.rn74.com

Oenophiles happily "jump aboard" Michael Mina's "swank" SoMa bistro done up like a "European train station" where the drama of the "revolving" "timetable board" advertising bottle "bargains" "nearly eclipses" the "solid", "high-ticket" New French fare; it's aces for a "client lunch" and "happy hour" is a "scream" (as in "loud") when the "beautiful people" and "tech" titans crowd in, but the vino, chosen with prowess by Rajat Parr and crew, is what really "makes it special."

Roam Artisan Burgers *Burgers*

| 23 | 16 | 18 | $18 |

Cow Hollow | 1785 Union St. (bet. Gough & Octavia Sts.) | 415-440-7626 | www.roamburgers.com

Patty partisans "go to sleep thinking about the burgers" at this Cow Hollow den dedicated to "sustainable" ingredients in their "juicy, grass-fed" beef, all-natural bison, "harvest turkey" and "amazing" veggie options gilded with "unique toppings" and washed down with "thick, delicious" shakes; you may have to "jockey for a table" at this counter-service spot, but connoisseurs "love" to customize their orders to taste, and for a "fair price" too.

Rocco's Cafe ⓟ *Italian*

| 26 | 20 | 22 | $25 |

China Basin | 1131 Folsom St. (7th St.) | 415-554-0522 | www.roccoscafe.com

"Nothing but good, basic, well-made" Italian fare is what you'll find at this old-school China Basin cafe that's open all day and specializes in "good-size portions" of "homestyle cooking"; a "warm" atmosphere and "efficient service" add incentive, all for a "price that can't be beat", which is why regulars call it "da best."

RoliRoti 🏝 Ⓜ⊘ *American*   24 | 14 | 18 | $12

Embarcadero | Ferry Bldg. Mktpl. | 1 Ferry Bldg. (The Embarcadero) | 510-780-0300 | www.roliroti.com

Addicts wait forever for the "to-die-for" porchetta sandwich from this food truck and mobile rotisserie at Ferry Plaza and farmer's markets about town, an item hailed as "a glorious creation of spit-roasted pork", "crispy crackling" and "crusty bread"; the "fat, juicy chickens dripping onto a bed of potatoes and garlic" are also "worth" the "long line" and "splurge" at this "meat nirvana."

🆕 Roostertail 🏝 *American*   ▽ 19 | 16 | 16 | $18

Upper Fillmore | 1963 Sutter St. (Fillmore St.) | 415-776-6783 | www.roostertailsf.com

A set of Postrio alums are behind this new fast-casual rotisserie off Upper Fillmore that cooks up a daily slate of "filling" spit-roasted meats (the chicken is "perfection"), Southern-inspired "sandwiches and salads" and Americana desserts like ice cream floats; the "counter" service and "no-frills" room work best for a "cheap night out with kids" but it's all available to go and you can call ahead for curbside service.

Rosamunde Sausage Grill ⊘ *German*   22 | 11 | 14 | $13

Lower Haight | 545 Haight St. (bet. Fillmore & Steiner Sts.) | 415-437-6851
Mission | 2832 Mission St. (bet. 24th & 25th Sts.) | 415-970-9015 ◑
www.rosamundesausagegrill.com

These link purveyors dispensing "delicious housemade sausages" "blow your standard hot dog out of the water" insist fans who call them "a SF must" and a "great value" too; at the original Lower Haight "hole-in-the-wall", customers go "next door to Toronado" for a "cold one to wash it down", while patrons of the roomier Mission outpost sample "favorite German beers on tap."

Rose Pistola *Italian*   21 | 19 | 20 | $48

North Beach | 532 Columbus Ave. (bet. Green & Union Sts.) | 415-399-0499 | www.rosepistola.com

"Solid" rustic Ligurian cuisine – "delicious" pastas, "good-quality" fish and "thin-crust" pizzas from the wood-fired oven – plus "an active bar" scene in an "open, comfortable space" still draws them in at this North Beach Italian stalwart; though some say the tab is "kind of pricey", service is "attentive" and many like to "linger" and "people-watch", especially at one of the "outdoor tables" or window seats facing Columbus Avenue.

Rose's Cafe *Italian*   22 | 20 | 21 | $33

Cow Hollow | 2298 Union St. (Steiner St.) | 415-775-2200 | www.rosescafesf.com

"Union Street swells" often stop by this all-day cafe offering the kind of "delicious" Italian eats and "welcoming feel" that make it a "neighborhood favorite"; a "popular" spot to "grab brunch with the girls" (their signature "breakfast pizza" is not to be missed), it gets "crowded on weekends" and the "outdoor seating" fills up quickly "when it's sunny"; even so, reservations are accepted for dinner only.

Roti Indian Bistro *Indian*
23 | 18 | 21 | $29

West Portal | 53 W. Portal Ave. (bet. Ulloa & Vicente Sts.) | 415-665-7684 | www.rotibistro.com

"Upscale yet friendly and casual", this Indian pair in Burlingame and West Portal turns out "delicious" "traditional" fare as well as more "innovative dishes", including abundant vegetarian options; service is generally "accommodating" in the modern, warm-hued settings, and while some find the fare a bit "costly", fans say portions are "huge."

The Rotunda *American*
21 | 25 | 21 | $43

Downtown | Neiman Marcus | 150 Stockton St. (bet. Geary & O'Farrell Sts.) | 415-362-4777 | www.neimanmarcus.com

"After dropping a fortune" in the Downtown Neiman Marcus, shoppers head to this "elegant" in-store cafe with a signature "stained-glass ceiling" for "pricey" American standards including lobster club sandwiches and "huge popovers with strawberry butter"; service could "be more attentive" and it's "a mad rush during the holidays", but all considered, it's a "place to feel very special"; P.S. no dinner served.

Roy's *Hawaiian*
24 | 23 | 24 | $54

SoMa | 575 Mission St. (bet. 1st & 2nd Sts.) | 415-777-0277 | www.roysrestaurant.com

It's "like walking out of San Francisco and onto Maui" at this SoMa outpost of the island chain with its "wide selection of fish" presented with Roy Yamaguchi's "Hawaiian-fusion twist" and "spectacular service"; while a few critics wish the decor were more beach "than office building" and say they "only come when someone else is paying", it's a "favorite for special occasions" and the prix fixe menus are "unbeatable."

⊠ Ruth's Chris Steak House *Steak*
27 | 23 | 25 | $65

Polk Gulch | 1601 Van Ness Ave. (California St.) | 415-673-0557 | www.ruthschris.com

Meat mavens "can hear the sizzle" just thinking about this "high-end" chain with outposts in Polk Gulch and Walnut Creek, where the "perfectly prepared" "luxury steaks" are paired with "huge" "delicious" sides, "wonderful" cocktails and followed by "scrumptious" desserts; service is "always excellent" and most agree it's a "reliable" choice for a satisfying meal "in every way."

Ryoko's ◑ *Japanese*
25 | 20 | 22 | $42

Downtown | 619 Taylor St. (bet. Post & Sutter Sts.) | 415-775-1028 | www.ryokos.com

For a "notorious, late-night" "basement sushi bar", this Downtown den puts out "fresh", "well-executed" fin fare, offering "great quality at the right price"; while it's probably "not the best sushi you ever had", it's an "energetic, fun, divey" spot for "after-clubbing munchies" (serving until 1:30 AM), plus there's a "DJ in the corner" some nights.

Saha Arabic Fusion ⊠Ⓜ *Mideastern*
26 | 23 | 25 | $42

Nob Hill | Carlton Hotel | 1075 Sutter St. (bet. Hyde & Larkin Sts.) | 415-345-9547 | www.sahasf.com

"Creative, zesty dishes" showcasing "complex" "Arab-fusion" flavors (with plenty of vegetarian, "vegan and gluten-free options") can be found at this Middle Eastern "gem" "hidden inside" the Carlton Hotel on the Nob Hill–Tenderloin border; the "helpful" staff and "affordable

---

FOOD | DECOR | SERVICE | COST

wine list" add to the "romantic" ambiance that "belies" the somewhat "rough neighborhood outside."

Saigon Sandwiches ⌀ *Sandwiches/Vietnamese*   26 | 4 | 14 | $7
Tenderloin | 560 Larkin St. (bet. Eddy & Turk Sts.) | 415-474-5698
"Lines run out the door" at this famed Tenderloin "hole-in-the-wall" dispensing "ridiculously inexpensive" ($3.50) Vietnamese sandwiches featuring "crusty rolls" stuffed with "exactly the right ratio of ingredients", including "tofu or meat", "chopped greens" and "tangy carrot-slaw"; it's "takeout only" and closes at 5 PM, yet devotees insist you'll get the "best bang for your banh mi" at this "quick-service" spot.

Sai Jai Thai *Thai*   ∇ 25 | 12 | 19 | $15
Tenderloin | 771 O'Farrell St. (Hyde St.) | 415-673-5774
"Authentic Thai" is dished out at this dive on a "sketchy block" in the Tenderloin, where fans find some of the most "flavorful" cheap eats "in the city"; newcomers note: "these folks will make it super-spicy if you ask" and deliver it with "friendly service" to boot.

🛛 Saison 🅱🅼 *American*   27 | 23 | 26 | $257
Mission | 2124 Folsom St. (17th St.) | 415-828-7990 | www.saisonsf.com
Experience "epic" dining at this 18-seat "temple of gastronomy" in the Mission where chef Joshua Skenes "wows" in his "open kitchen" preparing "off-the-charts" New American tasting menus matched with "sublime wine pairings"; don't be fooled by the "unpretentious" service and blaring "rock music" – despite "tiny portions", "you and your date can drop a grand here" (at the chef's counter); P.S. prepaid online reservations required.

Salt House *American*   22 | 21 | 20 | $48
SoMa | 545 Mission St. (bet. 1st & 2nd Sts.) | 415-543-8900 | www.salthousesf.com
Like this "sister" shops, Town Hall and Anchor & Hope, this "hip" SoMa boîte with its "delicious" New American eats is a go-to favorite for "after-work drinks, a bite with friends" or date night; a "bustling" "bar scene" can make it "incredibly loud" in the "cool" "old" brick-lined room, but that's "all part of the appeal" to the "buzzy young crowd" too buzzed to notice the occasionally "slow" service.

ⁿᵉʷ Salumeria *Deli/Sandwiches*   – | – | – | I
Mission | 3000 20th St. (Florida St.) | 415-471-2998 | www.salumeriasf.com
This petite, old-world–style Mission deli from the Flour + Water team sells spit-roasted meat, antipasti and fresh pastas, plus morning pastries, fresh cheeses and fancy meat-centric sandwiches built on house-baked bread; it's primarily an affordable take-out spot (open from 9 AM–7 PM), but seating is available until about 4 PM at communal tables on the patio that sits between it and sibling Central Kitchen.

Samovar Tea Lounge *Tearoom*   21 | 21 | 20 | $25
Castro | 498 Sanchez St. (18th St.) | 415-626-4700
Hayes Valley | 297 Page St. (Laguna St.) | 415-861-0303
SoMa | 730 Howard St. (bet. 3rd & 4th Sts.) | 415-227-9400
www.samovarlife.com
"Fine teas from around the world" and an "inventive" yet "limited" Asian-inspired menu "can be sampled" at this trio of "peaceful tea rooms" per-

FOOD DECOR SERVICE COST

fect for "a meditative experience" or "afternoon date" (particularly in SoMa with its "urban spectacular" views of the Yerba Buena gardens); still, service is a bit "uneven", and while the tea is "properly brewed", even aficionados agree it's "pretty pricey for what you get."

Sam's ChowderMobile 🅱🅼 *Seafood*   22 | 20 | 19 | $35
Location varies; see website | 650-712-0245 | www.samschowdermobile.com
See review in South of San Francisco Directory.

Sam's Grill & Seafood Restaurant 🅱 *Seafood*   22 | 18 | 22 | $42
Downtown | 374 Bush St. (bet. Kearny & Montgomery Sts.) | 415-421-0594
"Consistently terrific seafood" is what you find at this circa-1867 "San Francisco treasure" with "the look and feel of a Spencer Tracy movie" – think "martinis, curtained booths" and "crusty" waiters in tuxes who are all "grizzled pros"; while tabs can be "pricey", some believe this "historic" spot still offers "the best value Downtown", plus "the bar pours good drinks" and best of all, it "feels like home."

Sandbox Bakery *Bakery*   ▽ 25 | 16 | 20 | $13
Bernal Heights | 833 Cortland Ave. (bet. Cortland Ave. & Gates St.) | 415-642-8580 | www.sandboxbakerysf.com
Fans "flock" to this "French bakery with a Japanese twist" in Bernal Heights for "sweet and savory snacks and pastries" plus "great coffee" and "unique" "bento-style lunch items"; though it "ain't cheap" for what you get and there's no indoor seating, sidewalk "benches" and a "nice staff" will "do just fine" for most; P.S. closes at 3 PM.

Sanraku *Japanese*   23 | 16 | 19 | $33
Downtown | 704 Sutter St. (Taylor St.) | 415-771-0803
Sanraku Metreon *Japanese*
SoMa | Metreon | 101 Fourth St. (Howard St.) | 415-369-6166
www.sanraku.com
"You're not going to get a lot of wacky rolls" but "if you're jonesing" for "fresh", well-"crafted" sushi, "excellent bento boxes" and other "authentic Japanese" staples, washed down by some good sake, this "small", "crowded" Downtown spot and its larger, recently remodeled SoMa Metreon sib are "hard to beat"; both offer "reasonable prices" and "fast, courteous service."

San Tung *Chinese/Korean*   24 | 11 | 13 | $21
Inner Sunset | 1031 Irving St. (bet. 11th & 12th Aves.) | 415-242-0828 | www.santungrestaurant.com
"Crunchy, sticky, lick-your-fingers" good, the "dry fried chicken wings" cause a commotion at this Inner Sunset "Chinese-Korean" "dive" that also offers "hand-pulled noodles" and other specialties; patrons endure "long lines", "slow service" and "dull" decor, but most say the "reasonable" prices for "heaven on a plate" make this place "worth the hassle."

🆕 Saru Sushi Bar 🅼 *Japanese*   - | - | - | I
Noe Valley | 3856 24th St. (Vicksburg St.) | 415-400-4510 | www.akaisarusf.com
Noe Valleyites dine "cheek by jowl" at this "tiny" Japanese newcomer offering "fresh, delicious" classic and nouveau sushi and a "carefully thought-out" sake list; the renovated room run by an "extremely

friendly" staff juxtaposes traditional wood paneling with exposed concrete walls decorated with monkeys (from whence the name comes).

Sauce ● _American_

| 22 | 17 | 23 | $44 |

NEW **Downtown** | 56 Belden Pl. (bet. Bush & Pine Sts.) | 415-397-8800
Hayes Valley | 131 Gough St. (Oak St.) | 415-252-1369
www.saucesf.com

"Ballet" and "Symphony" patrons "get saucy" at this "little Hayes Valley charmer" nearby (with a new Downtown sib) that offers a "quirky take on classic comfort food"; the "tables are a bit close" and the "bland decor" leaves some "underwhelmed", but the "friendly, professional" service and changing menu of "tasty American tapas" do the trick for most, plus you can linger until 2 AM nightly.

Scala's Bistro _Italian_

| 23 | 23 | 23 | $50 |

Downtown | Sir Francis Drake Hotel | 432 Powell St. (bet. Post & Sutter Sts.) | 415-395-8555 | www.scalasbistro.com

"Memorable" Italian fare gives "high satisfaction" to diners at this "bustling" bistro in Downtown's Sir Francis Drake Hotel, where patrons praise the "helpful" staff and warm "Tuscan atmosphere" inside the "classic, old SF" room; chatty types quibble that "talking won't be possible" over the "extra-loud" din; still, the majority feels it's an "outstanding value" and "a breath of fresh air in the overpriced Union Square" area.

Schmidt's _German_

| 23 | 19 | 21 | $27 |

Mission | 2400 Folsom St. (20th St.) | 415-401-0200 | www.schmidts-sf.com

"Casual" and "non-kitschy", this German beer hall in the Mission from the owners of nearby Walzwerk dishes up a "limited menu" of "amazing sausages", "spaetzle", "apple strudel" and other usual suspects, along with a "killer" selection of Deutsch beers on tap; prices are "reasonable" for the "filling" fare served at "communal" tables in basic surroundings, but "be forewarned – when they say 'large beer', they mean it."

☑ Scoma's _Seafood_

| 25 | 21 | 22 | $49 |

Fisherman's Wharf | Pier 47 | 1 Al Scoma Way (Jefferson St.) | 415-771-4383 | www.scomas.com

"Seafood right off the boat" is the attraction at these "classic" waterfront locales in Fisherman's Wharf and Sausalito; they do get "crowded" and some insist they're "resting on their laurels", but loyalists say the service is "friendly", the wines "top-notch" and while tabs can be "expensive", it's still a "great value" for fish this "fresh" and "tasty."

Sears Fine Food _Diner_

| 21 | 15 | 19 | $22 |

Downtown | 439 Powell St. (bet. Post & Sutter Sts.) | 415-986-0700 | www.searsfinefood.com

"Little" "Swedish pancakes" served with warm maple syrup "melt in your mouth" at this Downtown "legend", where there's typically a "long line in the morning"; the interior is "nostalgic", though "a bit noisy", but service is "decent" and there's also a menu of "American diner food" that goes beyond breakfast, while tabs are "relatively light on the wallet."

☑ Seasons _Seafood/Steak_

| 27 | 26 | 28 | $70 |

Downtown | Four Seasons Hotel San Francisco | 757 Market St., 5th fl. (bet. 3rd & 4th Sts.) | 415-633-3838 | www.fourseasons.com

Situated on the fifth floor of the Downtown Four Seasons, this "elegant" steak and seafooder offers "perfectly prepared" dishes delivered with "exceptional service" in a "stylish" but "understated atmosphere" with a "great view" of the city to boot; it's "pricey" but "worth it", especially as a place "to impress a client" or celebrate a very "special occasion"; P.S. opens for breakfast at 6:30 AM daily.

Sebo ☒ Japanese
26 | 18 | 22 | $81

Hayes Valley | 517 Hayes St. (bet. Laguna & Octavia Sts.) | 415-864-2122 | www.sebosf.com

Self-proclaimed "sushi experts" say "if you love fresh fish" and pre-mium sake, this "traditional Tokyo-style" bar in Hayes Valley is quite a catch with its "inventive", "seasonal" seafood "you've never heard of before" that's "flown in daily from Japan" then fussed over "to bring out its maximum umami"; regulars sit at the counter to "watch them make art" that comes at "exorbitant prices"; P.S. closed Monday.

Sens Restaurant ☒ Mediterranean/Turkish
22 | 22 | 21 | $41

Embarcadero | Embarcadero Ctr. | 4 Embarcadero Ctr., promenade level (Drumm St.) | 415-362-0645 | www.sens-sf.com

"Reliable" Mediterranean "comfort food" and a "spacious setting" in the Embarcadero Center make this destination a "mainstay" for "busi-ness lunches", "group" dining and "alfresco happy hour"; but it's the "lovely" "views of the bay and Ferry Building" that make it a "cool place to hang out" and enjoy mezes and cocktails while being waited on by "accommodating" servers; P.S. closed weekends.

The Sentinel ☒ Sandwiches
▽ 24 | 9 | 18 | $13

SoMa | 37 New Montgomery St. (bet. Market & Mission Sts.) | 415-284-9960 | www.thesentinelsf.com

Lines run "long" at this SoMa "takeout-only" shop from Dennis Leary (Canteen, Golden West) cranking out "superb" morning pastries and "incredible" "artisanal sandwiches" on "fantastic breads"; "they fre-quently sell out", but regulars "don't mind spending a little extra" for the "tastiest lunch you can get"; P.S. open weekdays only till 2:30 PM.

Serpentine American
23 | 21 | 21 | $42

Dogpatch | 2495 Third St. (22nd St.) | 415-252-2000 | www.serpentinesf.com

"Impressive creations" make this "trendy" New American "Dogpatch gem" a "perennial brunch favorite", while also serving up "excellent" cocktails and "delicious" lunch and dinner fare with a focus on "local" and "sustainable" ingredients; fans "love the industrial feel" – "high ceilings and concrete" (which means it gets "noisy") – as well as the "friendly" staff and "fair" prices, and despite the occasional menu "miss", most leave "full and happy."

☒ Seven Hills ☒ Italian
28 | 22 | 26 | $47

Nob Hill | 1550 Hyde St. (Pacific Ave.) | 415-775-1550 | www.sevenhillssf.com

"Creative" farm-to-table cuisine inspired by Rome (a seven-hilled city like SF) includes "amazing" "housemade giant raviolis" at this "darling", "intimate" Nob Hill trattoria that also offers an "inter-esting" selection of "well-priced" wines chosen by "two master sommeliers"; "the caliber of cooking is comparable to more expensive places", plus a "lively" noise level and "welcoming" servers help create a "friendly" atmosphere.

	FOOD	DECOR	SERVICE	COST

Shalimar ⊅ *Indian/Pakistani* — 24 | 7 | 14 | $16

Polk Gulch | 1409 Polk St. (Pine St.) | 415-776-4642
Tenderloin | 532 Jones St. (Geary St.) | 415-928-0333 ◐
www.shalimarsf.com

"Ignore the decor" (i.e. lack thereof) and "fast-food service" and relish the "insanely good" and "spicy" "cheap eats" at this Indian-Pakistani chainlet that loyalists say puts its "imitators" to shame; a few balk at the "greasy fare" and "shabby digs" but others remind "you go here to eat, not hang out."

Shanghai Dumpling King *Chinese* — 24 | 5 | 14 | $18

Outer Richmond | 3319 Balboa St. (34th Ave.) | 415-387-2088

"What a dump" but "what perfect dumplings" are on offer at this Outer Richmond Chinese, where adventurous eaters "turn a blind eye" to the "no-frills" decor and the "distance" from other parts of town to slurp down Shanghainese delicacies; you may have to "share your table", but it's so "super-cheap" and service so "helpful" that after "one taste", you'll be this king's "advocate for life."

Shanghai House ⊅ *Chinese* — ▽ 24 | 11 | 13 | $23

Outer Richmond | 3641 Balboa St. (bet. 37th & 38th Aves.) | 415-831-9288

Diners are wowed by the "excellent homemade" Chinese fare, including scrumptious "soup dumplings", at this "small", "simple place" in Outer Richmond, which some say serves "the best Shanghainese in San Francisco"; service can be "slow" and decor is nonexistent "but the food makes up for it"; P.S. cash only.

Showdogs *Hot Dogs* — ▽ 21 | 12 | 15 | $14

Downtown | 1020 Market St. (6th St.) | 415-558-9560 |
www.showdogssf.com

"You wouldn't think hot dogs could be so tasty", but this upscale Downtown shop slinging luxury "links" and "homemade" condiments is worth applauding "loudly"; sandwiches (e.g. "an excellent fried-chicken" one) and a "surprising range of hearty breakfasts" are also offered, and if tabs are "a little pricey", the "variety and creativity" plus a "great beer" selection make it "best" in show for grabbing a bite near the theater district.

Skool *Seafood* — 23 | 22 | 21 | $41

Potrero Hill | 1725 Alameda St. (De Haro St.) | 415-255-8800 |
www.skoolsf.com

Located in Potrero Hill, this "secluded", "Japanese-influenced" seafooder gets "straight A's" for its "fresh", "innovative" eats and "great cocktails" ably served by an "informed" crew in a "way-cool" "modern" setting; "the only demerit is for an ocean-sized roar", especially during a "happy hour" attracting "a zillion young sweet things", but "reasonable prices" and a "beautiful patio" earn "extra credit."

Z Slanted Door *Vietnamese* — 26 | 23 | 23 | $53

Embarcadero | Ferry Bldg. Mktpl. | 1 Ferry Bldg. (The Embarcadero) |
415-861-8032 | www.slanteddoor.com

At this "picture-perfect" location on the Embarcadero waterfront, Charles Phan's "legendary", "modern" Vietnamese "masterpiece" presents "off-the-charts delicious" small plates and "unique" wines "beautifully" paired by the "hip" (albeit "slammed") staff in a "stunning" "glass setting"; yes, it's "loud" and "pricey", but the "fab Bay views" alone are worth "every penny" and the "fight through the crowds at the Ferry Building", if only for a "late lunch" or to "sit at the bar" "with the locals."

Slow Club American
23 | 18 | 21 | $37

Mission | 2501 Mariposa St. (Hampshire St.) | 415-241-9390 | www.slowclub.com

"Mission cool" paired with "fresh" "local" ingredients from a "seasonal" New American menu characterize this "popular" "neighborhood" "go-to" in a "noisy" "industrial" space; "hipsters" come for the "not-too-pricey" fare, "solid" brunch and "impressive" cocktails, while service is generally "knowing."

Sociale Ⓢ Italian
24 | 22 | 23 | $51

Presidio Heights | 3665 Sacramento St. (bet. Locust & Spruce Sts.) | 415-921-3200 | www.caffesociale.com

Down a "side alley" in Presidio Heights, this "charming" "hideaway" serving "first-rate" "seasonal" "Northern Italian" fare is a neighborhood "favorite" for a "romantic dinner" or "catch-up time with good friends", particularly on the "secret patio"; the "tiny" dining room's "tight seating" means "you'll get to know your neighbors" and the tabs are "a bit pricey", but the "friendly" staff is "gracious and knowledgeable."

NEW SoMa StrEAT Food Park Eclectic
- | - | - | I

SoMa | 428 11th St. (Bryant St.) | 925-256-0816 | www.somastreatfoodpark.com

This new SoMa outdoor venue, the city's first permanent food-truck pod, hosts a rotating slate of the area's best trucks for low-priced lunch and dinner (all day on weekends) and has a covered heated seating area that includes bathrooms, free WiFi and a projection system for movie screenings (and eventually, a liquor license); P.S. you can check @SoMaStrEatFood on Twitter to see the daily lineup.

Sons & Daughters ⓈⓂ American
26 | 20 | 23 | $101

Nob Hill | 708 Bush St. (bet. Mason & Powell Sts.) | 415-391-8311 | www.sonsanddaughterssf.com

The "brilliant" young chefs behind this "tiny" Nob Hill "gem" have "foodies" "purring with delight" over their New American "tasting menus" enlivened with "a dash of molecular gastronomy" and game-changing "wine pairings"; it's all "a bit precious" and prices have crept up while "portions" remain "microscopic", but the savvy staff is disarmingly "playful" and the open kitchen adds to the experience.

Sotto Mare Ⓢ Italian/Seafood
26 | 17 | 22 | $34

North Beach | 552 Green St. (Columbus Ave.) | 415-398-3181 | www.sottomaresf.com

You'll find fish, pasta and "that's about it" at this "eccentric" yet "excellent" Italian seafooder in North Beach, which "looks like a dive bar" "full of neighbors" who sit "at the counter" (or "outside when it's sunny") feasting on what may be the "best cioppino in the city"; overall, expect "good value" on "huge portions" of "simple", "fresh" fare along with "decent" service in an atmosphere that's "boisterous" "fun."

Source   *Pizza/Vegetarian*   ▽ 22 | 17 | 21 | $20

Potrero Hill | 11 Division St. (De Haro St.) | 415-864-9000 | www.source-sf.com

"Innovative", "world-conscious" vegetarian fare, including "incredibly convincing faux meats" and "pizzas baked in a dragon-shaped oven", is accompanied by "ultrafiltered water and air" and "vibrational music" that aims to "make you feel good" at this Potrero Hill cafe; while the spare decor may be a bit "blah" for some, the staff gets kudos and it's all "sure to please on gastronomic, sensory and conscientious levels."

NEW Southern Pacific Brewery ◑ *Pub Food* ▽ 18 | 22 | 16 | $21

Mission | 620 Treat St. (19th St.) | 415-341-0152 | www.southernpacificbrewing.com

"You have to know where it is to find it", but when you do, this massive new Mission gastropub in a converted machine warehouse on a dead-end street has "great atmosphere"; while service may still need a little work, it's already "crowded" with folks enjoying the house craft brews, artisan cocktails and elevated pub grub served for lunch and dinner; P.S. open till 2 AM Thursday–Sunday.

South Park Cafe ⌧ *French*   22 | 19 | 21 | $42

SoMa | 108 South Park St. (bet. 2nd & 3rd Sts.) | 415-495-7275 | www.southparkcafesf.com

"Tucked away" in SoMa, this bistro "calls Paris to mind" with its "simple, affordable and authentic" "French cuisine" served in a "low-key" atmosphere that's "intimate enough to have a conversation"; service pleases, but the lovely parkside location is a plus at this "old classic" that's still considered a "neighborhood gem."

Southpaw BBQ   *BBQ*   ▽ 19 | 18 | 22 | $30

Mission | 2170 Mission St. (bet. 17th & 18th Sts.) | 415-934-9300 | www.southpawbbqsf.com

Bringing good ol' "Southern food" to the Mission, this "delightful" upscale "great barbecue" joint and microbrewery decked out with vintage photos cranks out the likes of brisket, brined chicken and "ribs done right"; the vast "selection of sauces" (Memphis, Alabama and eastern North Carolina styles) boost the flavor, and the all-American whiskeys, wines and suds add to the appeal.

Spice Kit ⌧ *Asian*   ▽ 18 | 13 | 18 | $15

SoMa | 405 Howard St. (bet. 1st & Fremont Sts.) | 415-882-4581 | www.spicekit.com

"Customizable" organic Californian takes on "traditional Asian street food" like banh mi draws FiDi habitués to this affordable breakfast, lunch and dinner spot; the fare "isn't exactly authentic" and "takeout" is popular since there's scant seating, but the "concept" brings much-needed "culinary diversity" to the neighborhood; P.S. a new Palo Alto location is scheduled to open in August 2012.

Spices ⊅ *Chinese*   ▽ 23 | 12 | 17 | $20

SoMa | 294 Eighth Ave. (Clement Ave.) | 415-752-8884

(continued)

(continued)

Spices II ● *Chinese*

Inner Richmond | 291 Sixth Ave. (Clement St.) | 415-752-8885
www.spicesrestaurantonline.com

Better "get ready to drink a lot of water" if you go to this "authentic" "Sichuan-style" trio, where the "hot, hot, hot" specialties are "abundant and interesting" and feature "every texture in the catalog"; while the decor and service don't inspire much goodwill, the lunch and dinner fare "might induce you to head to the embassy for your Chinese visa."

NEW Split Bread *Sandwiches*

\- | \- | \- | I

SoMa | The Metreon | 145 Fourth St. (Mission St.) | 415-603-2000 | www.splitbread.com

This high-tech new SoMa sandwich shop, the first in a new chain from the Mixt Greens folks, features spit-roasted meats, local veggies, housemade condiments and artisan bread, but what sets it apart is that ordering is done via QR codes scanned from smart phones in advance or at one of the Carrera marble-topped digital kiosks and paid for via credit or debit cards; everything is available to-go or in the sleek room filled with retro globe chandeliers and high barstool seating.

SPQR *Italian*

25 | 19 | 21 | $53

Pacific Heights | 1911 Fillmore St. (bet. Bush & Pine Sts.) | 415-771-7779 | www.spqrsf.com

Fans insist "you should try" the "fantastico" Italian fare at this "urbane" Pac Heights "osteria" (a sibling of A16) turning out "heavenly pastas" and other "soulful" yet "extremely creative" dishes (as well as a weekend lunch) and pouring "amazing" "lesser-known" wines; the "tiny" room gets "crowded and noisy", but service is "fine" and "sitting at the chef's counter" watching "the action unfold" is a "reward" in itself.

Z Spruce *American*

26 | 27 | 26 | $69

Presidio Heights | 3640 Sacramento St. (bet. Locust & Spruce Sts.) | 415-931-5100 | www.sprucesf.com

"Elegant barely covers it" say diners dazzled by this "swanky" "gem" "buried" in Presidio Heights where "young turks and grande dames" spruced-up in "high heels and jewels" hobnob and "treat" themselves to seasonal New American fare and "pricey" wines; high tabs may give some "indigestion", but even if just "dropping into the bar" for a "manly burger", the "staff goes out of its way to make you feel special."

Stacks *American*

21 | 16 | 19 | $20

Hayes Valley | 501 Hayes St. (Octavia St.) | 415-241-9011 | www.stacksrestaurant.com

"You can consume your body weight" in "delicious scrambles and pancakes" at this threesome of "upbeat" diners in Hayes Valley, Burlingame and Menlo Park, where lunch is also a "cut above"; service that always comes "with a smile" and "decent prices" help make waiting in the "obscene lines on weekend mornings" seem totally "worth it."

Starbelly *Californian*

22 | **20** | **19** | **$34**

Castro | 3583 16th St. (Market St.) | 415-252-7500 | www.starbellysf.com

"Creative drinks and rustic comfort food" are on order at this Castro Californian, where the menu includes "delicious pizzas" and "unique beers on tap", and the "back patio" is perfect for lunch "on a warm day"; though dissenters say service isn't always "on the ball", at least it's "well priced for the area."

🄽 NEW State Bird Provisions ⌧ *American*

27 | **18** | **23** | **$50**

Western Addition | 1529 Fillmore St. (bet. Geary Blvd. & O'Farrell St.) | 415-795-1272 | www.statebirdsf.com

Rubicon alums Stuart Brioza and Nicole Krasinski are behind this American newcomer in an urban-cozy Western Addition storefront that's "spinning heads" with "clever" "small plates" and larger dishes served "dim-sum style"; because enthusiasts "order so many plates" from the "knowledgeable" staff, the tab can creep up, still, there's a reason it's "packed" with chefs "on their day off"; P.S. dinner only Monday–Thursday, closed Sundays.

St. Francis Fountain *Diner*

18 | **19** | **18** | **$16**

Mission | 2801 24th St. (York St.) | 415-826-4200 | www.stfrancisfountainsf.com

"Hipsters" populate this all-day Mission "soda fountain" where "old-time charm" and "super-reasonable" prices come with "good ol' greasy" "addictive diner fare"; service is "usually courteous" and a "vintage candy counter" and "satisfying" veggie dishes are unexpected perks.

Stinking Rose *Italian*

21 | **21** | **21** | **$37**

North Beach | 325 Columbus Ave. (bet. B'way & Vallejo Sts.) | 415-781-7673 | www.thestinkingrose.com

"Get your stink on" at this "kitschy" Cal-Italian in North Beach, where "they season their garlic with food" in dishes such as "40-clove chicken" and "even ice cream"; "friendly" service and "decent" prices add to the "unique experience" that bulb-lovers say both "locals and tourists" "must try at least once."

Straits Restaurant *Singaporean*

21 | **20** | **19** | **$36**

Downtown | Westfield San Francisco Ctr. | 845 Market St., 4th fl. (bet. 4th & 5th Sts.) | 415-668-1783 | www.straitsrestaurants.com

"Creative cuisine and a fun atmosphere" make this "beautiful" Pan-Asian restaurant-cum-nightclub in the Downtown Westfield Centre (with three sibs to the south) the place where "the hip hang out" to sample the midpriced "small plates" and other fare on the "interesting" "Singapore-style" menu; the music can be "very loud" and the service "incredibly slow", but most appreciate the "strong drinks."

Straw *Californian/Sandwiches*

▽ **20** | **18** | **23** | **$22**

Hayes Valley | 203 Octavia St. (Page St.) | 415-431-3663 | www.strawsf.com

"Let your inner child out" at this affordable Hayes Valley cafe, where a "whimsical" carnival theme features a "Tilt-a-Whirl booth" and a "quirky", "upscale" Californian take on "circus food" including a Bearded Lady sandwich, a "burger on a donut" and a "cotton-candy cocktail"; the "helpful", "efficient" staff adds to an experience fans declare "worth the line."

	FOOD	DECOR	SERVICE	COST

NEW St. Vincent Tavern & Wine Merchant 🗷 *Californian*

-	-	-	M

(fka Heart Wine Bar)

Mission | 1270 Valencia St. (bet. 23rd & 24th Sts.) | 415-285-1200 | www.stvincentsf.com

At this winecentric Mission tavern from David Lynch (former wine director for Quince and Manhattan's Babbo), the midpriced Californian gastropub fare is designed to complement the artisanal vino and local craft beers, not the other way around; there's a list of 100 kinds under $100, all available by the bottle or half-bottle, which can be enjoyed in the narrow, rustic space dominated by a zinc-topped bar and a large storage container (holding some special reserve vintages) or eventually, taken to go.

Sunflower Restaurant *Vietnamese*

23	13	20	$19

Mission | 3111 16th St. (bet. Albion & Valencia Sts.) | 415-626-5022
Potrero Hill | 288 Connecticut St. (18th St.) | 415-861-2336
www.sunflowersf.com

"Locals already know and love" these Vietnamese "gems" with "to-die-for" pho and other "stellar" dishes, including "excellent vegetarian choices"; at the small, centrally located Mission original, there can be a "wait", while the newer Potrero Hill locale is deemed "more attractive", but "quick service" and "inexpensive" tabs appeal at both venues.

Sunrise Deli *Mideastern*

▽ 24	11	19	$13

Downtown | 89 Belden Pl. (Pine St.) | 415-362-2800
Outer Sunset | 2115 Irving St. (22nd Ave.) | 415-664-8210
SoMa | 54 Second St. (Pine St.) | 415-495-9999
www.sunrisedeli.net

"They aren't kidding about the falafels" and "hummus (made the correct way)" at this Middle Eastern shop in the Outer Sunset, with outposts for its "cheap eats" Downtown and in SoMa and Berkeley; there's not much to recommend the decor, but fans praise its "platters for entertaining" while saying "the rest of the menu is average at best."

Super Duper *Burgers*

23	16	19	$14

Castro | 2304 Market St. (bet. Noe & 16th Sts.) | 415-558-8123
Downtown | 721 Market St. (bet. 3rd & 4th Sts.) | 415-538-3437
www.superdupersf.com

Patty partisans agree the "name not only describes the food, but the prices" and "super-fast" service at these "sustainable" Bay Area burger joints notable for their "organic" ingredients, "amazing" vegetarian variations and "homemade pickles"; though "industrial" in feel, they let you "subdue" "beefy" "guilty-pleasure" "cravings" without the guilt, plus you can "add alcohol to your milkshake", while "mini"-sized options and "choco-dipped" "soft serve" placate the "pint-sized" set.

Suppenküche *German*

23	19	19	$31

Hayes Valley | 525 Laguna St. (Hayes St.) | 415-252-9289 | www.suppenkuche.com

"From the pretzel to the schnitzel", this Hayes Valley hofbräuhaus serves "large portions" of some of the "the best German food around" backed by an "incredible beer selection", all "excellently priced"; "shoulder-to-shoulder crowds" make it "noisy as a rock concert" and sometimes "hard to get good service", but "das Boot" (a glass boot full of brew) makes fans say *sehr gut!*"

Sushi Bistro *Japanese*

| 25 | 22 | 24 | $33 |

Inner Richmond | 431 Balboa St. (bet. 5th & 6th Aves.) | 415-933-7100 🅂 🅼
Mission | 2809 24th St. (Potero Ave.) | 415-282-2001
www.sushibistro.com

"Funky versions of old favorites" are offered at these Japanese siblings in Inner Richmond and the Mission serving "super-fresh" sushi and "well-prepared rolls" that twist tradition with ingredients like jalapeño; most agree you "get what you pay for", and when you factor in "exceptionally friendly" service, it's no wonder these are "welcome neighborhood finds."

Sushirrito 🅂 *Japanese*

| 21 | 10 | 17 | $13 |

SoMa | 59 New Montgomery St. (Market St.) | 415-495-7655 |
www.sushirrito.com

"Gimmicky? yes", but the "burrito-sized" rolls (hence the name) "made to order" with quality ingredients like "fresh fish" and "local organic veggies" are "deliiiiicious" swear devotees of this quick-service, Japanese-inspired SoMa take-out shop with "lines out the door" for their "cheap eats"; choices are limited and frankly it's "way too much" food to finish, but "courageous" lunch-goers "try anyway"; P.S. not open on "weekends or for dinner."

🅉 Sushi Zone 🅂✂ *Japanese*

| 27 | 15 | 18 | $32 |

Castro | 1815 Market St. (bet. Guerrero St. & Octavia Blvd.) | 415-621-1114
Like those "tiny Tokyo restaurants", this "crazy-packed" Castro Japanese with just a "few seats" delivers "fantastically fresh" sushi, a "ridiculously long sake list" and "a whole lot of character" for a reasonable price; the sushi "isn't exactly authentic" ("mango and macadamia nuts") but they "don't skimp on portions", just "prepare yourself" for a "long wait."

Sutro's at the Cliff House *Californian*

| 23 | 26 | 23 | $51 |

Outer Richmond | 1090 Point Lobos Ave. (Balboa St.) | 415-386-3330 |
www.cliffhouse.com

"Watch the sunset out of massive windows" with "unsurpassed views of the Pacific Coast" at the Outer Richmond's historic Cliff House, where the seafood-focused Californian cuisine and "top-notch" "professional" service leave newcomers "pleasantly surprised"; since prices are a bit steep ("you are definitely paying for" the location), this is one "must-do spot for out-of-town guests" that locals save for a "treat" or "special occasion."

Swan Oyster Depot 🅂✂ *Seafood*

| 26 | 13 | 22 | $35 |

Polk Gulch | 1517 Polk St. (bet. California & Sacramento Sts.) |
415-673-1101

"Just a food counter inside a fish market", this century-old Polk Gulch "institution" serves "the freshest seafood imaginable" until 5:30 PM; the "uncomfortable stool seating" is "as informal as the docks" but "the crew behind the counter" treats you "as one of their own", so while detractors say it's "not worth the price and wait", some supporters consider it "a strong contender for last meal on earth."

FOOD | DECOR | SERVICE | COST

ᴺᴱᵂ Sweet Woodruff *Sandwiches*

-｜-｜-｜I

Nob Hill | 798 Sutter St. (Jones St.) | 415-292-9090 |
www.sweetwoodruffsf.com

The latest offspring from the Sons & Daughters crew, this gourmet
American in Lower Nob Hill proffers a rotating slate of artisan sandwiches, small plates and desserts – all priced under $10; the tiny cor-
ner storefront is set up primarily for takeout, though 11 stools line the
reclaimed-wood counter for those inclined to perch; P.S. open 7 AM–
9:30 PM daily.

The Sycamore *American*

▽ 22 | 19 | 21 | $20

Mission | 2140 Mission St. (bet. 17th & 18th Sts.) | 415-252-7704 |
www.thesycamoresf.com

Place your order with the barkeep at this "warm" and "quirky" American
that's "a breath of fresh air on a grungy" Mission "stretch" serving fare
like "sliders", sandwiches and "pork belly donuts"; "novelty treats"
like "board games" contribute to the "great vibe", as do the "bottomless mimosas" at brunch and fine "beer list", all of which can be enjoyed in the "sunny courtyard" day or night.

Tacko *Mexican*

22 | 18 | 18 | $17

Cow Hollow | 3115 Fillmore St. (Filbert St.) | 415-796-3534 | www.tacko.co

"Tack on over" to this Cow Hollow taqueria for an "oddball combination" of "Mexico and New England" that nonetheless "works beautifully", from its "lobster rolls" "as good as any you'd get in Bar Harbor"
to chef-owner Nick Fasanella's "signature tacos" prepared his "way"
with a "crispy shell"; the service and nautical decor earn mixed reviews, but moderate tabs and "buckets of margaritas" encourage patrons to keep "coming back."

Tacolicious *Mexican*

24 | 19 | 20 | $23

Embarcadero | Ferry Bldg. Mktpl. | 1 Ferry Bldg. (The Embarcadero) |
no phone 🅱🅼⇅
Marina | 2031 Chestnut St. (Fillmore St.) | 415-346-1966 | 🅼
ᴺᴱᵂ **Mission** | 741 Valencia St. (18th St.) | 415-626-1344
www.tacoliciioussf.com

Sceney yet "friendly", these "upscale" Marina and Mission Mexicans
(siblings of the original Thursday Ferry Building lunch stall) turn out
"creative" "twists on tacos" "from duck confit to skirt steak" boosted
by "fine ingredients" and "amazing salsas"; margaritas pack a "punch"
plus there's a "mind-blowing tequila collection" at the Mission location's adjacent bar, Mosto; P.S. a Palo Alto branch is in the works for
632 Emerson Street.

Taco Shop At Underdog's ◑ *Mexican*

▽ 25 | 15 | 21 | $15

Outer Sunset | 1824 Irving St. (19th Ave.) | 415-566-8700 |
www.underdogssf.com

"College students", Outer Sunset locals and dudes "on the way back
from the beach" frequent this "very neighborhood" taqueria-cum–sports
bar with all the essentials – "lots of TVs", "cold beer on draft", "crispy
tacos" and "good prices" – from chef/co-owner Nick Fasanella (ex Nick's
Crispy Tacos); the "cozy", football paraphernalia–filled room gets
"crowded on game days", but "even when they're slammed", the crew
still "has time to refill your chips."

𝗭 Tadich Grill ⓈΖ *Seafood*   24 | 22 | 23 | $45

Downtown | 240 California St. (bet. Battery & Front Sts.) | 415-391-1849 |
www.tadichgrill.com

In business since 1849, this "classic, film-noir"-worthy "seafood temple"
Downtown has "old-time SF atmosphere" in every detail from the "19th-
century booths" to the "jokingly grumpy servers" that are "straight from
central casting"; sure, the "menu never changes", but since "fresh fish at
its best" and "classic cocktails" "never go out of fashion", schools of
"business folk", "tourists" and "nostalgic" types still "wait their turn in
line" and keep things "noisy and crowded, especially at lunchtime."

Takara *Japanese*   ▽ 21 | 12 | 20 | $28

Japantown | 22 Peace Plaza (bet. Laguna & Webster Sts.) | 415-921-2000 |
www.takararestaurant.com

Putting "a modern flair on traditional sushi" while also turning out
"more authentic dishes", this "well-lit" Japanese "hidden away" in the
Japantown mall is a "favorite among locals" (including "families") who
appreciate the "genteel" service and "lunch specials" that are "a bargain" for the "excellent quality."

Taqueria Can Cun ●Ζ *Mexican*   23 | 9 | 16 | $10

Downtown | 1003 Market St. (6th St.) | 415-864-6773
Mission | 2288 Mission St. (19th St.) | 415-252-9560
Mission | 3211 Mission St. (Valencia St.) | 415-550-1414

"Plump", "satisfying" burritos and "super" tacos are the main draw at
this "superb" taqueria trio offering "one of the best value meals in all
of SF"; the atmosphere is "no-frills" but late hours at the two Mission
locales still attract plenty of "hipsters", and the "cheap", "mouthwatering" Mexican fare wins over most everyone else.

Taqueria San Jose *Mexican*   24 | 14 | 18 | $12

Mission | 2830 Mission St. (24th St.) | 415-282-0203 |
www.taqueriasanjose1since1980.com

Taqueria San Jose No. 3 ⓈⓂ *Mexican*

North Beach | 2257 Mason St. (Francisco St.) | 415-749-0826

High demand for the "great-value burritos" and "carnitas tacos" can
create "nightmare lines" at this bare-bones Mission Mexican stalwart
(with newer offshoots in North Beach and San Jose); decor and service
are not its strong points, so repeat customers advise figuring out your
order "before you reach the counter."

𝗭 Tartine Bakery *Bakery*   27 | 15 | 16 | $17

Mission | 600 Guerrero St. (18th St.) | 415-487-2600 |
www.tartinebakery.com

There's "no sign outside" this "ne plus ultra" of "French-inflected"
bakeries in the Mission, "just mesmerizing aromas" and "omnipresent
queues that snake out the door", whether at "breakfast or 4:45 PM"
when the "pricey" "rustic loaves" leave the oven; it's a "carb-lover's
Eden" of "buttery" pastries, "ginormous" "hot pressed sandwiches"
and a "barista" pulling espresso, and while seating is "limited" and
service can be "slow", all's forgiven with that first "precious bite."

Tataki South *Japanese*   25 | 17 | 19 | $32

Noe Valley | 1740 Church St. (Day St.) | 415-282-1889

(continued)

(continued)

Tataki Sushi & Sake Bar *Japanese*
Pacific Heights | 2815 California St. (Divisadero St.) |
415-931-1182
www.tatakisushibar.com

"Snob-worthy", "responsibly acquired fish" and "creative rolls" (including "several vegan options") can be had if you brave "the waits to get in" at these "small", "modern" Japanese joints in Pac Heights and Noe Valley; service reviews are mixed and tabs are "a little pricey" but the "sustainable" fare means you can eat "guilt-free"; P.S. those who "go early" can "catch the happy-hour deals" and "sit down right away."

Terzo *Mediterranean*
25 | 24 | 23 | $54
Cow Hollow | 3011 Steiner St. (Union St.) | 415-441-3200 |
www.terzosf.com

Regulars "order a lot of small plates to share" at this Cow Hollow Mediterranean where chef Mark Gordon "keeps whipping up delectable new dishes" that are "organic and seasonal"; prices can be "fairly high", but a "romantic interior" and "incredible servers" are in the package, plus there's a half-off "wine deal" Sunday–Wednesday.

NEW Thai House 530 *Thai*
22 | 16 | 18 | $19
Mission | 530 Valencia St. (16th St.) | 415-503-1500 |
www.thaihouse530.com

Thai House Express *Thai*
Castro | 599 Castro St. (19th St.) | 415-864-5000
Tenderloin | 901 Larkin St. (Geary St.) | 415-441-2248 ●
www.thaiexpresssf.com

"Solid", "super-cheap" Thai standards make this "efficient", family-run chainlet a "favorite before-the-bars haunt" in the Castro and Tenderloin, the latter open till midnight nightly; meanwhile, the swanky new annex in the Mission offers more Pan-Asian options for the same "inexpensive" price point.

Thanh Long Ⓜ *Vietnamese*
26 | 16 | 20 | $51
Outer Sunset | 4101 Judah St. (46th Ave.) | 415-665-1146 |
www.anfamily.com

You don't have to wait for "the arrival of Dungeness crab season" to "get down and dirty" with a "nutcracker and plastic bib" and "dig in" to "roasted" crustaceans and "amazing" Vietnamese-style noodles (smothered with enough garlic "to sink a boatful of vampires") at this "remote" Outer Sunset stalwart; for "frozen" seafood, it's pretty "pricy" but "nice" drinks and "valet parking" help offset the variable service and sometimes "noisy" ambiance.

Thep Phanom Thai Cuisine *Thai*
24 | 16 | 21 | $31
Lower Haight | 400 Waller St. (Fillmore St.) | 415-431-2526 |
www.thepphanom.com

Presenting "phenomenally fresh and tasty" fare in a "small" "dimly lit" Lower Haight Victorian, this long-running Thai "never fails" to deliver a "more formal" Siamese dining experience ("not Westernized at all") "complete with authentically costumed" staff, "classically prepared dishes" and "traditional" decor; it "gets crowded" and as result "service can be spotty" but prices are reasonable.

	FOOD	DECOR	SERVICE	COST

3rd Street Grill ⌧ *American/Mexican* | 23 | 21 | 22 | $26 |

SoMa | 695 Third St. (Townsend St.) | 415-538-0804

For a "quick lunch" in SoMa or a "delicious" burger or burrito "before or after the big game" at AT&T Park, this American-Mexican hybrid gets "two thumbs" up; it's "usually not too busy" and "great" service and reasonable tabs assure most "definitely would go back."

1300 on Fillmore *Soul Food/Southern* | 23 | 24 | 23 | $45 |

Western Addition | 1300 Fillmore St. (Eddy St.) | 415-771-7100 | www.1300fillmore.com

"Putting the soul back in soul food", this "dimly lit" "boîte" offers "refined" Southern-inspired eats amid "historical photos" that "embrace" the Western Addition's "jazz" tradition; sure, it's "somewhat pricey", but the "luxe" setting, "expertly crafted cocktails" and "charming" service make for a "glamorous" night out, especially when live music adds a "festive" touch.

360° Gourmet *Eclectic* | 22 | 19 | 21 | $26 |

Downtown | 50 Post St. (bet. Kearny & Montgomery Sts.) | 415-398-4800
SoMa | 1 Market St. (bet. Spear & Steuart Sts.) | 415-357-1190
www.360gb.com

You get "a lot of burrito for the price" at this "basic" chainlet dishing out an Eclectic menu of wraps, bowls, quesadillas and such – customized with mix-and-match sauce options like curry and teriyaki; the Downtown and SoMa branches draw a "lunch-hour crowd" craving a "filling, inexpensive meal" of "flavorful" fare plus "quick service with a smile", while some of the other locations also stay open for dinner.

3-Sum Eats ⊄ *American* | 25 | 17 | 22 | $15 |

Location varies; see website | 415-375-2790 | www.3-sumeats.com

"Rave-able, crave-able" New American eats, like a "moist" and "crispy" fried chicken sandwich that achieves "maximum crunchiness" through a layer of cornflakes, are "the bomb" at SF's No. 1 food truck, where "*Top Chef* alum Ryan Scott" is behind the wheel; "the wait can be long" for the "sinful" snacks, but "the guys working there are beyond nice", and the "generous portions" come at "reasonable prices."

Toast *American* | 17 | 15 | 19 | $21 |

Noe Valley | 1748 Church St. (Day St.) | 415-282-4328
Noe Valley | 3991 24th St. (Noe St.) | 415-642-6328
www.toasteatery.com

They're "just like the diners of old, without the greasiness and attitude", proclaim boosters of this Noe Valley duo; some lament the "lack of space", and say "it'll cost you more than you expect", but locals go for the "casual" vibe and family-friendly, "simple fare" with "fast service" – "nothing more, nothing less."

To Hyang Ⓜ *Korean* | ▽ 27 | 12 | 20 | $29 |

Inner Richmond | 3815 Geary Blvd. (bet. 2nd & 3rd Aves.) | 415-668-8186

It may fly under the radar, but this "no-frills" "real deal" in the Inner Richmond dishes out "amazing" affordable Korean and is "filled with locals" and avid eaters (including a visit by TV's Tony Bourdain); the menu's "not for the squeamish" and "when they say spicy, they mean it", but everything from the soy sauce and kimchi to the infused soju drinks is "housemade."

FOOD | DECOR | SERVICE | COST

Tokyo Go Go *Japanese*   ▽ 19 | 17 | 17 | $32

Mission | 3174 16th St. (bet. Guerrero & Valencia Sts.) | 415-864-2288 |
www.tokyogogo.com

"Stark" decor may set the tone at this Mission Japanese, but patrons are "thankful" that's "not reflected in" its "artfully" plated sushi and other "pretty pricey" specialties; service that's "hit-or-miss" and fare that's at times just "ok" are compensated by a "central location" on 16th Street and a "good happy hour."

Tommaso's 🅼 *Italian*   24 | 17 | 21 | $33

North Beach | 1042 Kearny St. (bet. B'way & Pacific Ave.) | 415-398-9696 |
www.tommasosnorthbeach.com

"Long before" there was a pizzeria "on every corner", this "old-school" North Beach Italian "institution" was firing up pies out of its "original wood-burning oven"; it's "not showy", just a "charmingly downscale" spot doling out Neapolitan "comfort food" at a "dockworker's price" by folks who "make you feel like family" – but "expect to wait" because there are "no reservations."

Tommy's Mexican Restaurant *Mexican*   20 | 17 | 21 | $28

Outer Richmond | 5929 Geary Blvd. (bet. 23rd & 24th Aves.) |
415-387-4747 | www.tommystequila.com

"Delicious" margaritas "by the pitcher" and a "mind-blowing" "selection of sipping tequila" curated by "the original tequila ambassador" Julio Bermejo make this "family-run" Outer Richmond Mexican featuring "authentic Yucatán favorites" ultra-"popular" with locals and fans from afar; something of a "neighborhood dive", it can get "very crowded", but servers that "are tops" and moderate prices help fuel the "fiesta."

Tommy Toy's Cuisine Chinoise *Chinese*   25 | 25 | 25 | $64

Downtown | 655 Montgomery St. (bet. Clay & Washington Sts.) |
415-397-4888 | www.tommytoys.com

More "upscale" than the "Chinatown favorites" nearby, this "most dignified and beautiful" Downtown stalwart puts a "gourmet" twist on what's called "the best Cantonese food this side of a five-star Hong Kong restaurant"; a "professional staff", "dim candlelight" and centuries-old tapestries lend a "classic ambiance", and since tabs can get "expensive", wallet-watchers contend that "lunch specials are the way to go."

Ton Kiang *Chinese*   25 | 14 | 18 | $28

Outer Richmond | 5821 Geary Blvd. (bet. 22nd & 23rd Aves.) |
415-387-8273 | www.tonkiang.net

"Order your heart out" at this "two-floor" Outer Richmond "institution" where a "dazzling" variety of dim sum is "served all day", joined by "Hakka cuisine" at dinner; "it's not the cheapest" and could use "sprucing up", plus there are "long" waits "weekend mornings", but for "delectable" Chinese food without the "drive to Chinatown", it's "the place to go."

Tony's Coal-Fired Pizza & Slice House 🅼 *Pizza*   24 | 15 | 18 | $20

North Beach | 1556 Stockon St. (Union St.) | 415-835-9888 |
www.tonyspizzanapoletana.com

"Now that's a slice of pizza" announce fans of renowned pizzaiolo Tony Gemignani's "take-out haven" offering single servings of his signature pies ("so many choices") to folks who "don't want to brave the crowds next door" at this famed North Beach 'za HQ; other "fast, great eats" include a mean "Chicago beef sandwich", but since there's no seating, most take their orders across the street to Washington Square Park.

Tony's Pizza Napoletana ☒ *Italian/Pizza*   26 | 18 | 20 | $29
North Beach | 1570 Stockton St. (Union St.) | 415-835-9888 | www.tonyspizzanapoletana.com
"It's hard to find a better pie" than those among the "great variety" of "award-winning" pizzas ("Sicilian, Californian, Roman" even "gluten-free") that famed chef-owner Tony Gemignani tosses and cooks to a crisp in seven types of ovens at his "lively" "North Beach gem"; tabs are "somewhat pricey", but the "excellent wine list" and "friendly" servers help soothe after a "brutal" wait for a table.

Town Hall *American*   23 | 21 | 22 | $50
SoMa | 342 Howard St. (Fremont St.) | 415-908-3900 | www.townhallsf.com
"Not your grandmother's biscuits 'n' ham", the "upscale Southern-inspired" American eats (including "dessert to die for") at this "cozy" SoMa "tavern" keep it "always jam-packed" with "lotsa SF celebs and po-liticos" and "corporate" types knocking back "after-work drinks"; tabs are "kinda pricey" and things can get "noisy" both at the bar and the out-door tables, but the "friendly and warm" staff stays "on top of things."

Town's End Restaurant & Bakery ☒ *American/Bakery*   22 | 16 | 21 | $31
Embarcadero | South Beach Marina Apts. | 2 Townsend St. (The Embarcadero) | 415-512-0749 | www.townsendrb.com
"Since way before" AT&T Park arrived nearby, this "terrific breakfast/brunch" Embarcadero "waterfront" spot has been turning out "reli-able" American grub and "baked goods" (including "mini-muffins" that arrive "as you sit down") that are "worth the calories" – and won't "break the bank"; the "relaxed" setting includes some outdoor seats, and the "attentive, happy" staff will "do anything to make you happy"; P.S. no longer serving dinner.

NEW Trace *American* (fka XYZ)   ▽ 21 | 15 | 22 | $53
SoMa | W San Francisco | 181 Third St. (Howard St.) | 415-817-7836 | www.trace-sf.com
"Imaginative", "well-prepared" (and "pricey") farm-to-table small and large plates take center stage at this "trendy" American at SoMa's W Hotel; the "geometric", "modern decor" is a little too "cool" for some (like "dining in a stylish refrigerator") and it's "noisy beyond belief", but an accommodating staff helps compensate.

Trattoria Contadina *Italian*   24 | 18 | 22 | $39
North Beach | 1800 Mason St. (Union St.) | 415-982-5728 | www.trattoriacontadina.com
"Out of the way" from "tourist-heavy Columbus" Avenue, this "cheer-ful" North Beach "classic" "is where the locals go" to enjoy "unpreten-tious", "old-school" Italian standards (including "housemade gnocchi" and "delicious pasta sauces") for "little money"; staffers provide "pleasant service", but since the "cozy" quarters can get "crowded", regulars say make a "reservation" or "eat at the bar to skip the wait."

Tres *Mexican*
(fka Tres Agaves)

18	18	18	$32

South Beach | 130 Townsend St. (bet. 2nd & 3rd Sts.) | 415-227-0500 | www.tressf.com

"Flights of tequila" and "killer margaritas" paired with "creative Mexican" fare leave fans "feeling all warm inside" at this South Beach cantina and lounge; "proximity to AT&T Park" and a "back patio" help make it a top "post-game hangout", but more sober surveyors find it a little too "crowded" and "pricey" for merely "decent" grub.

Tropisueño *Mexican*

20	18	18	$26

SoMa | 75 Yerba Buena Ln. (bet. Market & Mission Sts.) | 415-243-0299 | www.tropisueno.com

"Taco shop by day, sit-down restaurant by night", this SoMa Mexican gets praise for its "homemade salsas", "fresh chips" and "chile-salt rimmed margaritas"; service is generally "convivial", so the wood-and-tile hacienda-style space is often "crowded", and if prices are "on the high end" for its ilk, it's "in an area that doesn't have much" else like it.

Troya *Turkish*

22	17	23	$29

Inner Richmond | 349 Clement St. (5th Ave.) | 415-379-6000
NEW **Pacific Heights** | 2125 Fillmore St. (bet. California & Sacramento Sts.) | 415-563-1000
www.troyasf.com

It's "like a trip to Istanbul" at this "unassuming" "neighborhood" Inner Richmond Turk, thanks to "authentic" cuisine served in a room lined with black-and-white photos of the old country, where a "friendly" staff also plies "wine and meze" during the "terrific happy hour"; P.S. a new unrated Pac Heights offshoot ups the ante with weekend brunch and a more modern design.

Truly Mediterranean *Mediterranean*

▽ 25	8	16	$13

Mission | 3109 16th St. (bet. Guerrero & Valencia Sts.) | 415-252-7482 | www.trulymedsf.com

Truly a gyro hero, this Mission hole-in-the-wall cranks out "fantastic", "cheap" Med–Middle Eastern eats (e.g. "super tasty shawarma", "died-and-gone-to-heaven" halvah); the helpful crew is "willing to mix it up if you have diet needs", and "late" hours (till midnight on week-ends) and a location "within walking distance of many cool bars" make it easy to "grab dinner", but seating is scant, so many just "pop in" and "get it to go."

Tsunami Sushi & Sake Bar ●🗷 *Japanese*

24	22	20	$41

South Beach | 301 King St. (4th St.) | 415-284-0111 | www.nihon-sf.com
Western Addition | 1306 Fulton St. (Divisadero St.) | 415-567-7664 | www.dajanigroup.net

"Delicious sake flights" pair with "fresh and tasty sushi" and "izakaya-style tapas" at this Japanese duo in Western Addition and South Beach, where "hipsters" fill the "chic" rooms, particularly during the "great happy hour"; though "service can be snobby" and the upscale experi-ence "comes at a price", it's still "a cozy spot" that fits the bill for "a lively date" or "catching up" with friend.

	FOOD	DECOR	SERVICE	COST

Turtle Tower Restaurant *Vietnamese* · 21 | 7 | 14 | $13

Outer Richmond | 5716 Geary Blvd. (21st St.) | 415-221-9890 ⊄
SoMa | 501 Sixth St. (Bryant St.) | 415-904-9888
Tenderloin | 631 Larkin St. (bet. Eddy & Ellis Sts.) | 415-409-3333 ⊄
www.turtletowersf.com

"No-nonsense pho" – Vietnamese noodle soup that's "simple and soothing" with a "light, clean broth" – "fills you up without emptying your wallet" at this "hole-in-the-wall" noodle shop in the Tenderloin (with offshoots in SoMa and the Outer Richmond); service is "quick", but these "go-to spots" still "get packed" with "experienced" slurpers who "come here in droves", meaning "you might end up sharing a table."

⚡ Twenty Five Lusk *American* · 21 | 27 | 21 | $60

SoMa | 25 Lusk St. (bet. 3rd & 4th Sts.) | 415-495-5875 | www.25lusk.com
One of the city's "coolest dining spaces", this "trendy" "loft"-like SoMa locale features exposed wooden beams, "dim lighting" and hanging "fireplaces" in the downstairs lounge that's regularly populated with "beautiful people"; add in "obliging servers" and it's a "perfect" place to impress "for a client dinner or romantic date"; the "creative" New American fare is pretty "sleek" too, and "you'll definitely pay for the experience."

2G Japanese Brasserie *Japanese* · 22 | 21 | 21 | $42

Civic Center | Opera Plaza | 601 Van Ness Ave. (Golden Gate Ave.) | 415-292-9997 | www.2gjapanese.com
"Hidden inside the Opera Plaza complex", this "reasonably priced" Civic Center Japanese offers a "varied" menu ranging from "artistic" and "unusual dishes" to "beautifully prepared" "traditional" fare; "super-helpful servers" make it a "haven" for "symphony attendees" who need to catch the curtain, but less-rushed fin fanatics "make sure" to order the omakase and soak up the "ambiance."

🆕 Two Sisters Bar & Books Ⓜ⊄ *American* · ▽ 19 | 21 | 21 | $23

Hayes Valley | 579 Hayes St. (Laguna St.) | 415-863-3655 | www.2sistersbarandbooks.com
Reminiscent of midcentury Vienna or a Jane Austin novel, this "quaint" gastropub in Hayes Valley offers gussied-up, retro-inspired American snacks, dinners and weekend brunch in a narrow, old-timey Victorian storefront where hipsters can "sit at the bar" and "peruse" used books as they drink; it "has a lot of promise", though literary types sigh that the tomes are mostly "for decor"; P.S. cash only.

Txoko ✗Ⓜ *Spanish* · 24 | 21 | 23 | $41

North Beach | 504 Broadway (Kearny St.) | 415-500-2744 | www.txokosf.com
"From the talented pair behind Naked Lunch" this late-night "Basque-inspired" boîte in North Beach turns out "awesome, creative", locally sourced bites and a few large plates that all "pair perfectly" with the cocktails and Iberian wines; "service can be slow" but prices are moderate, and the dark, rustic space (former home of the Beat-era Enrico's) and the "European"-style sidewalk tables are prime settings "for a romantic evening."

	FOOD	DECOR	SERVICE	COST

Udupi Palace ⊘ Indian/Vegetarian — 23 | 13 | 18 | $16

Mission | 1007 Valencia St. (21st St.) | 415-970-8000 |
www.udupipalaceca.com

"Even carnivores love" the vegetarian fare at this "authentic" South
Indian Mission and Berkeley duo, including "huge, spicy uttapams",
"dosas packed with flavor" and other "truly delicious dishes"; "don't
be fooled" by shabby exteriors, as these venues offer "fast" and
"cheerful" service, a "family-friendly" environment and "unbeatable
quality for the price."

Umami Japanese — 26 | 24 | 22 | $43

Cow Hollow | 2909 Webster St. (Union St.) | 415-346-3431 |
www.umamisf.com

Taking "sushi to a different level", this Cow Hollow Japanese "hot
spot" turns out "amazingly fresh" and "inventive combinations" of raw
fish as well as "Asian fusion" specialties like "Kobe beef sliders" and
"ahi tacos"; "daring cocktails" and the "cool interior" of "dark wood"
and "dim" lighting stoke the "lively" vibe, while fans call the "wallet-
happy" "sumo hour" (nightly 5:30–7 PM) offering discounted bites
and "half-off" bottles among "the best in town."

NEW Umami Burger Burgers — 23 | 16 | 18 | $23

Cow Hollow | 2184 Union St. (Fillmore St.) | 415-440-8626 |
www.umamiburger.com

Converts attest this Cow Hollow link in a "popular" LA chain "lives up
to its hype" serving "innovative, juicy burgers" in "amazing" "flavor
combinations" with "housemade condiments" adding "another di-
mension"; the "simple" space is "small", and if service can be "a little
lax" and "portions could be a little larger" for the price, local offerings
like Anchor Steam beer and Humphry Slocombe ice cream compensate, so "come early to avoid a wait."

Una Pizza Napoletana ⑤Ⓜ Pizza — 26 | 16 | 16 | $29

SoMa | 210 11th St. (Howard St.) | 415-861-3444 | www.unapizza.com
"True Neopolitan" pies emerge from the central blue-tiled "imported"
"oven-cum-altar" at this SoMa "church of pizza" presided over by
Anthony Mangieri; "when he runs out of dough, no more for you", but
if you're good with the "long waits", "crazy" prices and limitations –
"no substitutions", "no meat", "no desserts" – "purists" praise the
"sublime" pies as "the best" in town; P.S. open Wednesday–Saturday.

Underdog ⊘ Hot Dogs — 25 | 15 | 20 | $18

Inner Sunset | 1634 Irving St. (bet. 17th & 18th Aves.) | 415-665-8881 |
www.underdogorganic.com

"Cheap and tasty" franks are "handcrafted" from "organic" ingredients at this Inner Sunset "find" also offering "veggie-friendly" options
(including "vegan sausages" and desserts); the staff is "friendly" and
the atmosphere's "chill", but since it's "the size of a shoebox", regulars
suggest "taking your dogs to the park."

Unicorn Pan Asian Cuisine ⑤ Asian — 23 | 22 | 20 | $31

Downtown | 191 Pine St. (Battery St.) | 415-982-9828 |
www.unicorndining.com

Situated "in the heart of the Financial District", this Pan-Asian favorite
of the "business-lunch crowd" offers "creative interpretations of clas-

sic" dishes that are "beautifully presented" and served by a "friendly staff" in an "interesting" setting with glass sculptures, dark wood and "dim" lighting; "vegetarian options" are an added plus, as are "ample portions" and "reasonable prices."

Universal Cafe Ⓜ *American*

FOOD	DECOR	SERVICE	COST
25	20	21	$37

Mission | 2814 19th St. (bet. Bryant & Florida Sts.) | 415-821-4608 | www.universalcafe.net

"Fresh" ingredients "handpicked" "from local markets" assure the "outstanding" New American cuisine at this "down-to-earth" Mission "gem" is "on par" with nearby hot spots "but with less fuss" and at a "better price"; the "small, sunny front deck" and one of the "best brunches in the city" attract a "stylish" "crowd" of local "hipsters", and while the "vibe" is "friendly and enjoyable", there's sometimes a "long wait."

NEW U-Sushi Ⓢ *Japanese*

FOOD	DECOR	SERVICE	COST
-	-	-	I

Downtown | 525 Market St. (1st St.) | 415-543-7655 | www.u-sushi.com

This clever, have-it-your-way, quick-service sushi spot Downtown (from the owner of Ozumo) brings the power of robotics to the plate; customers customize their maki with a choice of fish, rice, wrapper, sauce, etc., and let it roll, courtesy of a 'robot automation' machine that cuts it into even pieces – and voilà, lunch (or an early dinner) is served; P.S. the tiny storefront is takeout only; open Monday–Friday.

Uva Enoteca *Italian*

FOOD	DECOR	SERVICE	COST
23	21	22	$37

Lower Haight | 568 Haight St. (bet. Fillmore & Steiner Sts.) | 415-829-2024 | www.uvaenoteca.com

"Surrounded by bars and BBQ joints", this Lower Haight "diamond in the rough" offers a "small", midpriced Italian menu of "delicious" pizzas, salumi and "cheese plates", along with a "well-crafted wine list" that the "approachable", "knowledgeable" staff will help translate; "tables are a little close", but the "cozy" atmosphere is "great for a date" and the "justifiably well-known happy hour" and "bottomless Bellinis" at brunch are nice perks.

Venticello *Italian*

FOOD	DECOR	SERVICE	COST
24	23	23	$51

Nob Hill | 1257 Taylor St. (Washington St.) | 415-922-2545 | www.venticello.com

"Like dining in an exquisite home in a previous century", this "warm and cozy" Nob Hill "neighborhood gem" turns out Northern Italian cooking "just like mama's", including "homemade pastas" and "wood-fired pizzas" ferried by "charming" servers; all in all, it's a "very SF experience" with views out "the large window" of the "crooked street" and "cable cars going by", so "locals" "keep coming back again and again."

Walzwerk Ⓜ *German*

FOOD	DECOR	SERVICE	COST
21	15	17	$28

Mission | 381 S. Van Ness Ave. (bet. 14th & 15th Sts.) | 415-551-7181 | www.walzwerk.com

Images of "Marx, Engels and Lenin stare down" from the walls of this "unusual" East German place in the Mission offering up "the best of everything from behind the Iron Curtain"; the atmosphere may feel a bit "cold" and service can range from "dutiful" to "snooty" but "authentic" "tasty" fare like "sausages, schnitzel and sauerbraten" paired with "excellent imported beers" ensures many "leave happy."

	FOOD	DECOR	SERVICE	COST

Waterbar *Seafood* | 23 | 27 | 23 | $57 |

Embarcadero | 399 The Embarcadero (Folsom St.) | 415-284-9922 |
www.waterbarsf.com
"Tourists" join local fish-fanciers at this "gorgeous" (if "crowded")
Embarcadero seafooder whose "incredibly warm and friendly" staff
ferries "creative", sustainable "fin fare" in a setting with "stunning"
water "views" (both the Bay and the "cool large aquarium" columns inside); sure, it's "pricey", but the "jumping bar" offers "deals on the half
shell" (i.e. $1 oysters) daily till 6 PM.

Waterfront Restaurant ● *Californian/Seafood* | 21 | 24 | 20 | $49 |

Embarcadero | Pier 7 (B'way) | 415-391-2696 |
www.waterfrontsf.com
"Breathtaking" Bay Bridge "views from every table", both indoors and
from the "tented patio", make this Embarcadero seafooder a "wonderful place to relax" and absorb the "beautiful setting"; the Californian
fare is deemed "well executed" while service is "pleasant" if at times
"uneven", and the "cost"-conscious "go for lunch" when the "same
food" comes at "lower prices"; P.S. the Food score may not reflect
a chef change.

Wayfare Tavern *American* | 24 | 24 | 22 | $52 |

Downtown | 558 Sacramento St. (bet. Montgomery & Sansome Sts.) |
415-772-9060 | www.wayfaretavern.com
Food Network groupies mix with FiDi "suits" at celeb chef Tyler
Florence's "see-and-be-seen" "power lunch" (and dinner) spot, where
"attentive" servers bring "gut-busting", "upscale" (read: "pricey")
American fare and "mean drinks" in an "old-school British pub" setting
filled with "taxidermy"; it's "less tavern-ish" (and "frenetic") upstairs,
but fans say "the best seats in the house" are at the bar, "looking into
the open kitchen."

🆕 West of Pecos *Southwestern* | - | - | - | M |

Mission | 550 Valencia St. (bet. 16th & 17th Sts.) | 415-252-7000 |
www.westofpecos.com
The Wild West comes to the Mission at this Southwestern venture
from the Woodhouse Fish Company boys, where Santa Fe native son
Leo Varos slings midpriced, chile-spiced fare made with local, sustainable ingredients; the dining room, entered through saloonlike swing-
ing doors and flanked by adobe-style fireplaces, seems straight out of
a Georgia O'Keeffe tableau with its steer-skull decor, while a side bar
beckons imbibers with beer, cocktails and the hard stuff (tequila,
mezcal or whiskey).

Wexler's 🖾 *BBQ* | 24 | 21 | 22 | $41 |

Downtown | 568 Sacramento St. (Montgomery St.) | 415-983-0102 |
www.wexlerssf.com
"Not your typical BBQ joint with peanut shells on the floor", this
"very modern" Downtown American furnishing "inventive seasonal cocktails" and comfort food that's both "sophisticated" and
"offbeat" draws the "hip FiDi" crowd; "calling it 'barbecue' is a
stretch" and "service is hit-or-miss", but the "awesome atmosphere" is smoking good "for drinks" or a "date"; P.S. their lunch truck
is out back weekdays.

	FOOD	DECOR	SERVICE	COST

'Wichcraft *Sandwiches*
18 | 14 | 15 | $16

Downtown | Westfield San Francisco Ctr. | 868 Mission St., ground fl. (bet. 4th & 5th Sts.) | 415-593-3895 | www.wichcraftnyc.com

"Tom Colicchio knows how to make a sammich!" say fans of the celeb chef's Westfield Centre outpost with its "well-made", "creative sandwiches" and dreamy "sweet" "creamwiches" served in a "cafeteria"-style setting; cost-conscious types say the "NYC" transplant's relatively "high-end prices" for "small" portions just "don't cut it in SF", still, it's "not bad for a quick lunch while shopping."

Wise Sons Jewish Delicatessen Ⓜ *Deli/Jewish*
23 | 14 | 19 | $19

Embarcadero | Ferry Bldg. Mktpl. | 1 Ferry Bldg. (The Embarcadero) | 415-787-3354 Ⓢ

NEW **Mission** | 3150 24th St. (Shotwell St.) | 415-787-3354 www.wisesonsdeli.com

"Why did we have to wait so long?" wonder fans of this new Mission brick-and-mortar offshoot of the "popular" Jewish deli pop-up (still operating Tuesdays at the Ferry Building) turning out "housemade" versions of "traditional" classics, such as "sublime pastrami" and "to-die-for" chocolate babka, "updated with locally sourced ingredients"; though a bit pricey, it's an "instant hit", and only offers lunch, brunch and Friday night dinner, so expect "crazy" lines.

NEW Wo Hing General Store *Chinese*
22 | 22 | 22 | $39

Mission | 584 Valencia St. (bet. 16th & 17th Sts.) | 415-552-2510 | www.wohinggeneralstore.com

Charles Phan is back in the Mission where he started at this "great re-do of the old Slanted Door space" where he's wokking up "excellent Chinese street food" and homestyle eats upgraded with local, seasonal ingredients for dinner; the "upscale" bi-level room is aces for late-night "drinks" and "people-watching" but a few find it a bit "too pricey" and "ordinary" for the pedigree.

Woodhouse Fish Company *Seafood*
22 | 17 | 20 | $32

Castro | 2073 Market St. (14th St.) | 415-437-2722
Pacific Heights | 1914 Fillmore St. (bet. Bush & Pine Sts.) | 415-437-2722 www.woodhousefish.com

"Meaty" "crab" and "lobster rolls" "never fail" to please at this New England–style seafood duo in Pac Heights and the Castro where "flavorful, affordable" seafood ("who can beat $1 oysters on Tuesdays?") is served by a "cheery", "helpful" staff; the "low-key", "nautical"-themed joints are "popular with locals" and "there are no reservations", so "be prepared to wait."

Woodward's Garden Ⓢ Ⓜ *Californian*
25 | 16 | 22 | $53

Mission | 1700 Mission St. (Duboce Ave.) | 415-621-7122 | www.woodwardsgarden.com

Despite being "almost under the freeway", this "little" "oldie but goodie" in the Mission is "still" a surprisingly "charming" and "quiet" place to enjoy a "casual" dinner "with close friends or a date"; the "creative" Cal cuisine (prepared right "in front of you" in the "open kitchen") is "matched by" an "excellent wine selection" and a "warm reception" that compensate for its "iffy" locale.

	FOOD	DECOR	SERVICE	COST

Yamo ☒⊕ *Burmese*

| | 23 | 7 | 14 | $11 |

Mission | 3406 18th St. (Mission St.) | 415-553-8911

It "feels like you're in Rangoon" "sitting shoulder-to-shoulder, slurping housemade noodles" at this "quintessential hole-in-wall" in the Mission dishing out "cheap", "delicious" Burmese grub; service can be brusque but it's "quick", even so, there are "often long lines" and veterans sometimes "call ahead for takeout" to avoid them.

☑ Yank Sing *Chinese*

| | 26 | 18 | 20 | $38 |

SoMa | Rincon Ctr. | 101 Spear St. (bet. Howard & Mission Sts.) | 415-957-9300
SoMa | 49 Stevenson St. (bet. 1st & 2nd Sts.) | 415-541-4949
www.yanksing.com

Fans insist "the pinnacle of SF dim sum" can be found in SoMa, "not Chinatown", at this "cavernous" "white-tablecloth" Chinese brunch/lunch spot in Rincon Center and its "smaller" nearby branch where an "endless" "flurry" of the "prettiest" and "best-variety" dumplings get "wheeled" from "kitchen to table in record time" by "efficient" servers; expect "Disneyland waits" and it can get "pricey" for "rookies" who don't "pace" themselves, but most agree "it's worth it."

Yellow Submarine ⊕ *Sandwiches*

| | 24 | 13 | 18 | $10 |

Inner Sunset | 503 Irving St. (6th Ave.) | 415-681-5652

"Huge, delicious" "hot subs" ("a medium" easily equals "two meals") dressed with "awesome" "secret sauce" are the draw at this "venerable" Inner Sunset sandwich shop with low prices, "quick" service and a notable lack of decor; true, "there's not really anything healthy on the menu", but this place is a "solid" choice all the same.

Yoshi's San Francisco *Japanese*

| | 23 | 25 | 20 | $48 |

Western Addition | Fillmore Heritage Ctr. | 1330 Fillmore St. (Eddy St.) | 415-655-5600 | www.yoshis.com

All the makings of a "great date night" are offered at this "sophisticated" Western Addition club/restaurant (sibling of the popular Oakland venue) including "world-class live jazz", "a great lounge for cocktails" and "classic" Japanese fare with a touch of "Californian inventiveness" that's "worth a trip even if you're not going to a concert"; "service can be slow" and tabs a bit "expensive" for "small portions", but this "pretty cool" place is "worth it."

Yuet Lee ❶ *Chinese*

| | 20 | 6 | 11 | $26 |

Chinatown | 1300 Stockton St. (B'way) | 415-982-6020

Regulars say it "hasn't changed" since the '70s (when it opened) at this Chinatown "classic" still serving "authentic" Cantonese seafood for "reasonable prices"; the "decor is garish" and it can be "hard to find a seat", but service is "fast" plus it's open till 3 AM Friday–Saturday for a "late-night Chinese" fix.

Yum Yum Fish *Japanese*

| | ▽ 23 | 8 | 16 | $20 |

Outer Sunset | 2181 Irving St. (23rd Ave.) | 415-566-6433 | www.yumyumfishsushi.com

With only a handful of seats, this sardine-sized Outer Sunset storefront is really more of a walk-up seafood counter with "fresh fish for sale" and "fantastic" "take-out sushi" for "cheap" prices; but backers say look past the "no-frills, hole-in-the-wall ambiance" and basic ser-

vice and you'll be "impressed with the quality of the rolls" and other
Japanese fin fare; P.S. last order is at 7:15 PM.

Zadin *Vietnamese*   ▽ 22 | 21 | 23 | $29

Castro | 4039 18th St. (Hartford St.) | 415-626-2260 | www.zadinsf.com
"Significantly better than you'd expect" to find on this stretch in the
Castro, this "quiet", "relaxing" spot turns out "great noodle soups"
and an array of Vietnamese vittles (some "quite spicy") at "reasonable prices"; the fact that "nearly everything is gluten-free or can be
made" so is a big perk for some, and the "delightful" atmosphere and
"excellent" service have all-around appeal.

Z & Y *Chinese*   ▽ 24 | 14 | 16 | $21

Chinatown | 655 Jackson St. (bet. Grant Ave. & Kearny St.) |
415-981-8988 | www.zandyrestaurant.com
"For those who like their food with lots of heat", this Chinatown dive
doles out "incredibly authentic Sichuanese" cuisine that's "generous
with the peppers", resulting in "tasty, spicy" dishes; it's "not much to
look at" and service is nothing special, but the "good, honest food"
makes up for it and the two-hour validated parking at the nearby
Portsmouth Square Garage is an added bonus.

Zaré at Fly Trap ⊠ *Californian/Mediterranean* 22 | 21 | 22 | $46

SoMa | 606 Folsom St. (2nd St.) | 415-243-0580 | www.zareflytrap.com
Chef-owner "Hoss Zaré brings his Persian culture to life" at this SoMa
"gem" where some of the "most pleasant folks you're ever going to
meet" proffer "memorable drinks" and "flavorful" Cal-Med meals elevated by the "interesting use of spices"; it's "noisy", but the "inviting"
atmosphere and "hopping bar" attract regulars like flypaper, be it for
"a first date, happy hour" or some "real food before a Giants game."

Zarzuela ⊠Ⓜ *Spanish*   24 | 19 | 22 | $42

Russian Hill | 2000 Hyde St. (Union St.) | 415-346-0800
"I hope they stay here forever" sigh supporters of this "terrific neighborhood tapas place in Russian Hill" that's "right on the cable car line"
and serves "authentic Spanish food" along with "first-rate" "sangria";
an "accommodating staff" and "good value" help compensate for the
"no-reservations" policy in a room that's "small" and often "crowded",
but still has "charm."

Zazie *French*   24 | 20 | 21 | $28

Cole Valley | 941 Cole St. (bet. Carl St. & Parnassus Ave.) | 415-564-5332 |
www.zaziesf.com
"*C'est magnifique!*" exclaim locals about this "small" but "dependable"
"slice of Paris in Cole Valley" open all day that draws a "roaringly busy"
weekend brunch crowd with "unbearably long" lines for a table
(thankfully, there's a "warm and friendly" staff); another option is a
"great-value", "delicious" French meal on the "magical" "outdoor patio", where Bring Your Dog to Dinner commences every Monday.

Zero Zero *Italian/Pizza*   24 | 21 | 21 | $36

SoMa | 826 Folsom St. (4th St.) | 415-348-8800 | www.zerozerosf.com
Neapolitan pizzas are "so in vogue" and this "swanky" SoMa Italian
stands out with its "phenomenal" "thin-crust, flame-kissed" pies (including a "seasonal" option) plus antipasti and pastas courtesy of

chef-owner Bruce Hill; crowded from brunch through dinner, "noise levels are high", but tabs are "decent" and service gets a nod, as do "terrific" cocktails; P.S. "build-your-own" sundaes are a hit with all ages.

Zuni Café M _Mediterranean_   26 | 22 | 23 | $52

Hayes Valley | 1658 Market St. (bet. Franklin & Gough Sts.) | 415-552-2522 | www.zunicafe.com

Everyone from theatergoers to the "digerati" "buzz" about "the roast chicken" (and the burgers "if you can get there for lunch or after 10 PM") at Judy Rodgers' "quintessential San Francisco bistro" in Hayes Valley that has turned out "satisfying" "wood-fired" Med meals "since the '70s"; the "bustling" zinc bar is still the "best place for oysters", a "well-mixed cocktail" and "people-watching", so despite murmurs of occasional "attitude" from the servers, "wild horses couldn't keep" fans away.

Zuppa _Italian_   19 | 18 | 19 | $39

SoMa | 564 Fourth St. (bet. Brannan & Bryant Sts.) | 415-777-5900 | www.zuppa-sf.com

You'll have to veer "off the beaten path" in SoMa to find this "relaxing", "rustic Italian" offering the likes of pizzas, pastas and "phenomenal roasted whole chicken"; it's a "little noisy" (credit the concrete-walled "industrial design") and service has its ups and downs, but regulars deem it a "gem" nonetheless.

Zushi Puzzle ⊠ _Japanese_   27 | 11 | 19 | $52

Marina | 1910 Lombard St. (Buchanan St.) | 415-931-9319 | www.zushipuzzle.com

"Some of the very best" and "freshest sushi" including "inventive special rolls" draws fin fans to this unassuming Marina locale; it "lacks atmosphere" and table service can be "awkward", but "sit at the bar" and let "master" chef Roger Chong "make selections" to "give your taste buds the ride of their life" – albeit also a "shock" to your wallet.

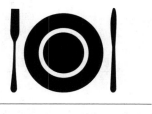

EAST OF SAN FRANCISCO

Top Food

BY CUISINE

Excludes places with low votes

BY SPECIAL FEATURE

BREAKFAST/BRUNCH

- **28** Erna's Elderberry
- **25** Bette's Oceanview
- Camino
- **24** Venus
- **23** La Note

CHILD-FRIENDLY

- **26** Zachary's Pizza
- **24** Lo Coco's
- Bellanico
- **22** Picante Cocina
- **21** Chow

MEET FOR A DRINK

- **23** Flora
- Adesso
- **22** Barlata
- Revival Bar
- **20** Luka's Taproom

NEWCOMERS (RATED)

- **25** Haven
- **24** Dragon Rouge
- **21** Rumbo Al Sur

OPEN LATE

- **23** In-N-Out
- Caspers Hot Dogs
- Adesso
- **21** Fonda Solana
- **20** Home of Chicken/Waffles

OUTDOOR SEATING

- **26** Wente Vineyards
- Prima
- **25** À Côté
- **24** Gather
- **23** La Note

PEOPLE-WATCHING

- **28** Chez Panisse Café
- **26** Wood Tav.
- **25** Va de Vi
- Ozumo
- À Côté

ROMANCE

- **28** Erna's Elderberry
- Chez Panisse
- **27** Wolfdale's
- **26** Wente Vineyards
- Lalime's

SMALL PLATES

- **25** Va de Vi
- À Côté
- **23** Adesso
- **22** Barlata

TRENDY

- **23** Plum
- Flora
- Hawker Fare
- Adesso
- **22** Revival Bar

VIEWS

- **27** Wolfdale's
- **26** Wente Vineyards
- **23** Bocanova
- **22** Ahwahnee Dining
- **20** Skates on Bay

WINNING WINE LISTS

- **28** Erna's Elderberry
- Chez Panisse Café
- Chez Panisse
- **23** Adesso
- **20** César

BY LOCATION

BERKELEY

- **28** Chez Panisse Café
- Rivoli
- Chez Panisse
- **27** Ajanta
- Cheese Board Pizzeria

LAKE TAHOE AREA

- **27** Wolfdale's
- **24** Dragonfly
- **23** PlumpJack Cafe
- **20** Gar Woods Grill & Pier
- Jake's on the Lake

OAKLAND

- **28** Commis
- **26** Asmara Restaurant
- Marica
- Pizzaiolo
- Dopo

Top Decor

28	Erna's Elderberry		Skates on the Bay
	Ahwahnee Dining	24	Wolfdale's
27	Wente Vineyards		Esin
	Meritage at The Claremont		Lake Chalet
25	Sasa		Haven
	Postino		Picán
	Bocanova		Duck Club
	Vic Stewart's		Ozumo
	Gar Woods Grill & Pier		Chez Panisse Café
	Chez Panisse		Rivoli

Top Service

28	Erna's Elderberry		Wente Vineyards
27	Chez Panisse		Jim's Country
26	Wolfdale's		Riva Cucina
	Commis		BayWolf
	Chez Panisse Café	24	Lalime's
	Esin		Vic Stewart's
	Asena Restaurant		Prima
25	Ruth's Chris		Postino
	Rivoli		Ajanta
	Marica		Sasa

BEST BUYS: BANG FOR THE BUCK

1. Blue Bottle
2. Top Dog
3. Caspers Hot Dogs
4. In-N-Out Burger
5. Arinell Pizza
6. Arizmendi
7. Jim's Country
8. Cheese Steak Shop
9. El Farolito
10. Cheese Board Pizzeria
11. Bakesale Betty
12. Cancun
13. Pearl's Deluxe Burgers
14. Actual Cafe
15. Cactus Taqueria
16. Gioia Pizzeria
17. La Boulange
18. Trueburger
19. Picante Cocina Mexicana
20. Montclair Egg Shop

BEST BUYS: OTHER GOOD VALUES

Bo's BBQ
Brown Sugar Kitchen
B-Side BBQ
Burma Superstar
Chow
Emilia's Pizzeria
Fentons Creamery
Grégoire
Hawker Fare
Homeroom
Le Cheval
Mama's Royal
Pizza Antica
Shen Hua
Tacubaya
Udupi Palace
Venus
Vik's Chaat
Xolo Taqueria
Zachary's Chicago Pizza

East of San Francisco

Z À Côté *French/Mediterranean* | 25 | 21 | 23 | $42 |
Oakland | 5478 College Ave. (Taft Ave.) | 510-655-6469 |
www.acoterestaurant.com
"California meets Provence" in the "excellent small plates" at this
"hopping" Mediterranean in Oakland's Rockridge serving "French
food for real people"; thanks to a menu that "changes often", "eclectic" wine list and "amazing" cocktails, patrons "party in the front" or
"enjoy a quiet meal" in the "secluded" garden – either way, staffers are
"always on their game."

Actual Cafe *Californian* | 23 | 22 | 21 | $16 |
Oakland | 6334 San Pablo Pl. (Alcatraz Ave.) | 510-653-8386 |
www.actualcafe.com
"Everything is fresh, including the attitude" at this "hip, scruffy, bike-
friendly" Oakland "neighborhood hang" where "lots of different types"
"mix and mingle" over Californian eats like "gigantically awesome"
salads, sandwiches, coffee, "fresh juices" and "homemade sodas" – all
"inexpensive" and served by an "unfailingly polite" staff; P.S. weekends
are "laptop- and cell phone–free", while there's "free live music" most
Saturday and Sunday nights.

Addis Ethiopian *Ethiopian* | 25 | 18 | 22 | $21 |
Oakland | 6100 Telegraph Ave. (61st St.) | 510-653-3456 |
www.addisethiopian.com
"Come hungry" to "eat phenomenal food with your fingers" at this "authentic" Ethiopian that's like "Africa on Telegraph"; while the "decor is
a bit funky", "service is very friendly" and dishes like *kitfo* (minced,
seasoned beef) and tofu tibs are "top-notch" at "modest prices", plus
"they even serve African beer."

Adesso ●☑ *Italian* | 23 | 19 | 21 | $33 |
Oakland | 4395 Piedmont Ave. (Pleasant Valley Ave.) | 510-601-0305 |
www.dopoadesso.com
Prepare for "a salumi celebration" at this "bustling" Italian "charcuterie lover's dream" (and Dopo sibling), where "Piedmont Avenue
hipsters" wash down "superb cured meat" with "atypical Italian
wines" and "imaginative mixologist-style cocktails"; heartier eaters bemoan "small plates" that are "a bit" on the "pricey" side, but
most happily "meet a friend for happy hour" and nibble away on the
"fantastic artisanal food."

Z Ahwahnee Dining Room *Californian* | 22 | 28 | 23 | $59 |
Yosemite | Ahwahnee Hotel | 1 Ahwahnee Way (Tecoya Rd.) |
Yosemite National Park | 209-372-1489 | www.yosemitepark.com
National park visitors enjoy "glamping" under the "vaulted ceiling"
of this "grand", "historic" hotel dining room with "extraordinarily
beautiful" decor; most are "too busy" admiring the "majestic
mountains" and "breathtaking views of Yosemite Valley and Falls"
to "remember" the "surprisingly good" albeit "pricey" Cal-American
fare and "old-school service", but generally agree the "fantastic"
Sunday brunch and special "Bracebridge" dinners "should be on
everyone's bucket list."

FOOD | DECOR | SERVICE | COST

☑ Ajanta *Indian*

| 27 | 22 | 24 | $31 |

Berkeley | 1888 Solano Ave. (bet. Fresno Ave. & The Alameda) | 510-526-4373 | www.ajantarestaurant.com

"Charming" chef-owner Lachu Moorjani "takes Indian cuisine to a whole new level" at this "one-of-a-kind" "white-tablecloth" spot catering to "Berkeley sensitivities" with an "imaginative changing menu" of "mostly organic" "regional and seasonal" dishes paired with a "very good local wine list"; though "pricey by student standards", the "sumptuous" room and "ever-so-friendly" staff ensure that a meal here is "head and shoulders above" the rest.

Amakara Japanese *Japanese*

| 24 | 21 | 20 | $35 |

Dublin | 7222 Regional St. (Amador Valley Blvd.) | 925-803-8485 | www.amakaraco.com

"Who would have expected such quality in a strip mall?" ask devotees of this "innovative" Dubliner with a menu of cold and hot fare that's "more interesting than your typical neighborhood Japanese" spot and offers spacious quarters to boot; "informed" staffers plus the likes of "California rolls with real crab meat" and "deliciously fresh sashimi" make it "well worth the money."

Amber Bistro ☒ *Californian*

| 23 | 21 | 22 | $38 |

Danville | 500 Hartz Ave. (Church St.) | 925-552-5238 | www.amberbistro.com

This "small bistro" and "watering hole" in Danville remains a "reliable" "local spot" for grabbing a "casual" Californian lunch or dinner washed down with "delicious cocktails"; "small plates", a "prix fixe dinner" and "great happy-hour deals" "keep the cost down", and while the room gets "very noisy" and "service is hit-or-miss", you can't beat the outdoor seating in summer.

☑ Amici's East Coast Pizzeria *Pizza*

| 21 | 17 | 20 | $22 |

Danville | Rose Garden Ctr. | 720 Camino Ramon (Sycamore Valley Rd.) | 925-837-9800
Dublin | 4640 Tassajara Rd. (bet. Central Pkwy. & Dublin Blvd.) | 925-875-1600
www.amicis.com

See review in City of San Francisco Directory.

Anchalee Thai Cuisine *Thai*

| 23 | 21 | 23 | $26 |

Berkeley | 1094 Dwight Way (bet. San Pablo Ave. & 10th St.) | 510-848-4015 | www.anchaleethai.com

"Creative" eats come with "mouthwatering" presentations at this "unique, unassuming Thai" in Berkeley; modest tabs and "great service" make it versatile for a "date or family dinner", just "keep the party size small" because the "pleasant" dining room with exposed brick is "tiny."

Angeline's Louisiana Kitchen *Cajun/Creole*

| 24 | 20 | 21 | $28 |

Berkeley | 2261 Shattuck Ave. (bet. Bancroft Way & Kittredge St.) | 510-548-6900 | www.angelineskitchen.com

When "your inner Cajun" or Creole calls, answer with the likes of "crawfish étouffée", "amazing" fried chicken, "must-try" hush puppies and "scrumptious beignets" at this Berkeley answer to NOLA that "could fry ice if they had to"; though the decor is "plain", prices are "reasonable", while "jazzy music" and "friendly service warm it up."

	FOOD	DECOR	SERVICE	COST

Arinell Pizza ⌿ *Pizza* · 23 | 8 | 15 | $8

Berkeley | 2119 Shattuck Ave. (Addison St.) | 510-841-4035
See review in City of San Francisco Directory.

⭐ Arizmendi *Bakery/Pizza* · 25 | 13 | 21 | $11

Emeryville | 4301 San Pablo Ave. (43rd St.) | 510-547-0550 |
www.arizmendibakery.org
Oakland | 3265 Lakeshore Ave. (MacArthur Frwy.) | 510-268-8849 |
www.lakeshore.arizmendi.coop
See review in City of San Francisco Directory.

Artisan Bistro Ⓜ *Californian/French* · 25 | 20 | 23 | $49

Lafayette | 1005 Brown Ave. (Mt. Diablo Blvd.) | 925-962-0882 |
www.artisanlafayette.com
Offering "just the right blend of amazing local, fresh cuisine and fabulous
service", this Cal-French "treasure" "in a converted house" appeals to
Layfayette locals seeking a "gourmet" meal at a "more affordable price";
an "inventive and oft-changing menu" keeps things interesting, but
sensitive surveyors advise "sit on the lovely patio, or bring earplugs."

⭐ Asena · 26 | 20 | 26 | $29
Restaurant Ⓢ *Californian/Mediterranean*

Alameda | 2508 Santa Clara Ave. (Everett St.) | 510-521-4100 |
www.asenarestaurant.com
"Fresh ingredients, sublime flavors" and "mouthwatering" "homemade
bread" make this midpriced Alameda Cal-Med a "beloved" "local staple" that "always knocks it out of the park" ("the lamb dishes are outstanding"); thanks to "old-school elegance", "warm and inviting owners"
and staffers that "take you into their family", islanders claim they've
"never had a bad meal here."

Asmara Restaurant Ⓜ *Ethiopian* · 26 | 17 | 21 | $20

Oakland | 5020 Telegraph Ave. (51st St.) | 510-547-5100 |
www.asmararestaurant.com
Become a "connoisseur of Ethiopian cuisine" while scooping up "delicious and inexpensive" specialties with injera bread that's "perfectly
tangy and wonderfully textured" at this "friendly" Oakland "favorite";
some caution one room is "romantic" but the other is "cafeterialike",
so for "intimate" dining "with your hands", choose accordingly (and
don't miss the "addictive" "honey wine").

Bakesale Betty Ⓢ Ⓜ *Bakery* · 26 | 12 | 21 | $13

Oakland | 5098 Telegraph Ave. (51st St.) | 510-985-1213 |
www.bakesalebetty.com
Braving "crazy-long lines" is "worth it" at this "quirky", affordable
Oakland bakery takeout assure fans of its "incredible fried chicken
sandwich", a "hefty, mouthwatering" "taste feast" topped with "jalapeño slaw"; "extremely friendly and efficient" staffers "crank out" the
limited menu, including "unparalleled" chicken pot pies, "marvelous"
strawberry shortcake and "cookies the size of your head"; P.S. the
Broadway location has closed.

Bangkok Thai *Thai* · 25 | 20 | 21 | $21

Berkeley | 1459 University Ave. (Acton St.) | 510-848-6483

(continued)

(continued)

Bangkok Thai

Emeryville | Public Mkt. | 5959 Shellmound St. (bet. Powell & 65th Sts.) | 510-601-1038

www.bangkokthaicuisine.com

"Quick and fresh" fare with "just the right amount of spice" is the draw at this "very pleasant" yet "inexpensive" Berkeley Thai with an Emeryville sibling in the Public Market; both have a "casual atmosphere" and the "huge benefit" of parking nearby.

Barlata *Spanish* `22` `19` `19` `$36`

Oakland | 4901 Telegraph Ave. (49th St.) | 510-450-0678 | www.barlata.com

Those "into Spanish food" head to this "lively" tapas bar in Oakland's "up-and-coming Temescal district", from the "owner of B44", that's akin to "being in Barcelona" with its "authentic" specialties – some "served in a can (*lata*)" – plus "superb drinks" and Iberian wines that "merit a tip of the hat"; it's "too loud" and a bit "overpriced" for a few, but the "happy-hour deals" are a "best bet."

Barney's Gourmet Hamburgers *Burgers* `22` `16` `18` `$17`

Berkeley | 1591 Solano Ave. (Ordway St.) | 510-526-8185
Berkeley | 1600 Shattuck Ave. (Cedar St.) | 510-849-2827
Oakland | 4162 Piedmont Ave. (Linda Ave.) | 510-655-7180
Oakland | 5819 College Ave. (Chabot Rd.) | 510-601-0444
www.barneyshamburgers.com

See review in City of San Francisco Directory.

Battambang *Cambodian* ▽ `25` `16` `22` `$21`

Oakland | 850 Broadway (bet. 8th & 9th Sts.) | 510-839-8815

"You won't be disappointed" or "leave hungry" after dining at this "affordable", "family-run" Southeast Asian that has been feeding "amazing", "authentic" Cambodian fare to Oakland fans for "over 15 years"; it's a "dependable standby" where the "delicious" dishes and "very attentive service" make up for the "nice-but-nothing-fancy" decor.

BayWolf *Californian/Mediterranean* `26` `22` `25` `$52`

Oakland | 3853 Piedmont Ave. (Rio Vista Ave.) | 510-655-6004 | www.baywolf.com

Michael Wild's "spectacular" "30-plus-year-old Oakland dining institution" can still "be counted on every time" for "superb" seasonal Cal-Med "slow meals" ("the duck is a must") paired with "interesting wines" that "won't break the bank"; "it may not be new or sexy", but the "aim-to-please staff" and "lovely" "converted home" setting with "enclosed front porch" "keep it in the game" "for business or special occasions."

Bellanico Restaurant & Wine Bar *Italian* `24` `19` `23` `$38`

Oakland | 4238 Park Blvd. (Wellington St.) | 510-336-1180 | www.bellanico.net

"Robust", "developed flavors and attention to detail" mark the "inventive" Italian fare "prepared with respect and love" at this "jam-packed" Glenview "neighborhood trattoria" (sibling of SF's Aperto); service is "warm and welcoming", plus there's "always an affordable prix fixe option" – and "don't miss the wine flights."

Bette's Oceanview Diner *Diner*
25 | 18 | 21 | $20

Berkeley | 1807 Fourth St. (bet. Hearst Ave. & Virginia St.) | 510-644-3230 | www.bettesdiner.com

For 30 years, this "retro-chic" "Berkeley landmark" has been dishing out its "exciting twist on nostalgic diner food" – like "gourmet scrapple" and "soufflé pancakes" – with "fast, pleasant service" at "fair prices"; there's a "long, long wait" for the "amazing", "hearty" breakfasts, but "your taste buds will thank you", so "bring the *Chron,* grab a cuppa joe and chill"; P.S. no dinner.

Bistro Liaison *French*
23 | 21 | 22 | $40

Berkeley | 1849 Shattuck Ave. (Hearst Ave.) | 510-849-2155 | www.liaisonbistro.com

There's "no jet lag" involved to savor "classic dishes prepared flawlessly" at this "little slice of France" in Berkeley "sans the French attitude"; fans look past "hellishly tight quarters" for "heavenly" midpriced bistro fare served by "expert", "friendly" servers – and "the wine-club dinners are huge fun."

Blackberry Bistro *Southern*
21 | 16 | 18 | $19

Oakland | 4240 Park Blvd. (Wellington St.) | 510-336-1088 | www.theblackberrybistro.com

"Great breakfast eats" like "homemade biscuits", "crêpes", "tofu scramble" and vanilla-orange French toast are "standouts" at this "cozy yet hip" daytime-only Southern "neighborhood gem"; it can get "very busy" on weekends, and "limited space can lead to substantial waits", but "winning" service helps compensate; P.S. it's a "find for early Sunday brunch."

Blue Bottle Roastery & Coffee Bar *Californian/Coffeehouse*
24 | 17 | 19 | $9

Oakland | 300 Webster St. (3rd St.) | 510-653-3394 | www.bluebottlecoffee.net

See review in City of San Francisco Directory.

Bocanova *Pan-Latin*
23 | 25 | 22 | $41

Oakland | Jack London Sq. | 55 Webster St. (Embarcadero W.) | 510-444-1233 | www.bocanova.com

A "bright spot" in Jack London Square for a "relaxed and sociable meal", this "hip" "waterfront" Oaklander pleases the "beautiful crowd" with "excellent", "innovative" Pan-Latin shared plates, "incredible desserts" and "not-to-be-missed specialty cocktails"; the "attentive" staff also gets props, but it's the "sexy" setting, particularly the "lovely patio" where you can "watch the boats", that really "steals the show."

Boot & Shoe Service Ⓜ *Italian/Pizza*
24 | 20 | 21 | $31

Oakland | 3308 Grand Ave. (Elmwood Ave.) | 510-763-2668 | www.bootandshoeservice.com

"Amazing" thin-crust pizza with "über-fresh" toppings and "unique" appetizers, washed down with "fantastic cocktails", justify the "long waits" at this "hip" "offshoot of Pizzaiolo" in Oakland, packed with "twenty- and thirtysomethings" who "don't seem to mind" the "way-too-loud" music or "communal tables"; P.S. beside having the "friendliest" staff, it now serves "awesome" weekend brunch plus breakfast and lunch.

FOOD DECOR SERVICE COST

Bo's Barbecue 🅼 *BBQ*   22 | 14 | 17 | $24
Lafayette | 3422 Mt. Diablo Blvd. (Brown Ave.) | 925-283-7133 |
www.bosbarbecue-catering.com
"Don't go looking for atmosphere" (or "table service" for that matter) as
this Lafayette 'cue joint is "all about the food" – such as the "best brisket
around" – and an "excellent selection of beer and wine" "to match";
some say it's "inconsistent" and "pricier than it should be", but for a special "treat", "try going [on Saturday night] when a jazz group is playing."

Breads of India & Gourmet Curries *Indian*   21 | 15 | 17 | $24
Berkeley | 2448 Sacramento St. (Dwight Way) | 510-848-7684
Oakland | 948 Clay St. (bet. 9th & 10th Sts.) | 510-834-7684 🆂
Walnut Creek | 1358 N. Main St. (bet. Cypress & Duncan Sts.) |
925-256-7684 🅼
www.breadsofindia.com
Patrons praise the "generous variety of breads from all over India", along
with "tempting curries" and other dishes on the "changing daily menu"
at this East Bay trio; service varies, and the traditional decor is "nice"
enough, but best of all there's a "small price tag."

Bridges Restaurant *Asian/Californian*   23 | 23 | 23 | $47
Danville | 44 Church St. (Hartz Ave.) | 925-820-7200 |
www.bridgesdanville.com
"Still a great place to go", this Danville "old standby" that won fame in
Mrs. Doubtfire appeals with its "delicious" "Asian-influenced" Californian
fare ferried by "gracious and attentive" servers in a "contemporary"
setting; added draws are a "terrific happy-hour menu" (5 PM till closing weeknights) with prices that "can't be beat", and a summertime
patio with "live music."

Bridgetender Tavern *Pub Food*   ▽ 18 | 21 | 18 | $24
Tahoe City | 65 W. Lake Blvd. (Rte. 89) | 530-583-3342 |
www.tahoebridgetender.com
For "a burger and a beer", this affordable "old favorite" in Tahoe City
overlooking the Truckee River is "perfect for what it is"; surveyors say it's
particularly fine for "sitting outside" in the summer "after rafting" or a
"bike ride", but the "pretty good" pub grub, "atmosphere and service"
make this South Lake spot a "fun" place "to hang" year-round.

Brown Sugar Kitchen *Soul Food*   26 | 18 | 22 | $22
Oakland | 2534 Mandela Pkwy. (26th St.) | 510-839-7685 |
www.brownsugarkitchen.com
"Amazing fried chicken" and a "cornmeal waffle" so "ethereal" you
almost "have to hold it down so it won't float away" are among the
"down-home" fare with "nouveau flair" at this midpriced West
Oakland soul food "paradise" from chef Tanya Holland; the "wait is insane but well worth it", though the 3 PM closing time leaves devotees
longing for "longer hours."

🆕 B-Side Barbecue 🅼 *BBQ*   ▽ 26 | 23 | 24 | $20
Oakland | 3303 San Pablo Ave. (34th St.) | 510-595-0227 |
www.bsidebbq.com
Brown Sugar Kitchen's "Tanya Holland has outdone herself" at her
new West Oakland "authentic Southern BBQ" joint where "you can
smell" the "finger-licking-good (literally)" "smoky" meats "from blocks

away"; portions are large "enough to feed two", but "don't overlook the sublime mac 'n' cheese" or "delicious pickled vegetables"; despite an "iffy" locale and "limited seating", it's already jammed with "large crowds" for lunch and "early dinner."

Bucci's 🅱 *Californian/Italian*

| 22 | 21 | 22 | $35 |

Emeryville | 6121 Hollis St. (bet. 59th & 61st Sts.) | 510-547-4725 | www.buccis.com

"Mama Bucci is almost always on hand to make it feel like home" at this "relaxed" Emeryville Cal-Italian, a "reliable 'go-to' place" for a "civilized lunch" or "last-minute" "dinner on a Friday night when you don't feel like cooking"; regulars rave about the "wonderful food", "knowledgeable and friendly staff", "spacious" "art-filled interior" and "oasis patio", confirming "it only gets better with time."

Buckhorn Grill *American*

| 22 | 15 | 18 | $17 |

Emeryville | 5614 Bay Ave. (Shellmound St.) | 510-654-2996 | www.buckhorngrill.com

See review in City of San Francisco Directory.

BurgerMeister *Burgers*

| 20 | 15 | 18 | $16 |

Alameda | 2319 Central Ave. (bet. Oak & Park Sts.) | 510-865-3032
Berkeley | 2237 Shattuck Ave. (Kittredge St.) | 510-649-1700
www.burgermeistersf.com

See review in City of San Francisco Directory.

🇿 Burma Superstar *Burmese*

| 25 | 17 | 21 | $26 |

Alameda | 1345 Park St. (bet. Alameda & Central Aves.) | 510-522-6200
Oakland | 4721 Telegraph Ave. (bet. 47th & 48th Sts.) | 510-652-2900
www.burmasuperstar.com

See review in City of San Francisco Directory.

Cactus Taqueria *Mexican*

| 22 | 14 | 17 | $14 |

Berkeley | 1881 Solano Ave. (bet. Fresno Ave. & The Alameda) | 510-528-1881
Oakland | 5642 College Ave. (Keith Ave.) | 510-658-6180
www.cactustaqueria.com

"Fresh Mexican" bites are "a real bargain" at this Berkeley and Rockridge "counter service" duo offering "extras most taquerias don't" – such as an "extraordinary selection of intriguing salsas" in bright, casual digs; expect "long lines, and tons of kiddies" unless you "come after 7 PM", otherwise the "loud" scene can be like "a form of torture."

Café Colucci *Ethiopian*

| 26 | 20 | 21 | $20 |

Oakland | 6427 Telegraph Ave. (bet. Alcatraz Ave. & 65th St.) | 510-601-7999 | www.cafecolucci.com

Fans "always leave satisfied" by this budget-friendly Oakland Ethiopian's "fresh and flavorful" dishes that are enhanced with "spices that you can't get at most restaurants"; order "a big variety" to "share", then settle into the "cozy atmosphere", since service is "friendly" but "slow."

Café Fiore *Italian*

| ▽ 27 | 23 | 26 | $43 |

South Lake Tahoe | 1169 Ski Run Blvd. (Tamarack Ave.) | 530-541-2908 | www.cafefiore.com

Hidden "away from the glitz of casinos", this "intimate" Northern Italian in South Lake Tahoe watched over by a "friendly staff" proffers a "wonderful menu of daily specials and a solid wine list", all making it "worth the trip round the lake"; the cozy candlelit cabin also ranks "high on the romantic scale", but it's not cheap, and "reservations are a must" for the seven tables (plus a few more on the patio during summer).

Café Gratitude *Vegan*
19 | **16** | **17** | **$22**

Berkeley | 1730 Shattuck Ave. (bet. Francisco & Virginia Sts.) | 510-725-4418 | www.cafegratitude.com

Backers of this "hippie-dippie" vegan and "raw-food" chainlet on a "mission" call its "nutritious" fare "creative" and "surprisingly flavorful", if reactions to its "devoted" staff vary with those seeking "food, not dogma" quipping "I'd be grateful for lower prices"; likewise "communal tables can be a blessing or a curse", but believers insist the experience will make you "feel like a better person."

Café Rouge *Californian/Mediterranean*
22 | **19** | **21** | **$40**

Berkeley | Market Plaza | 1782 Fourth St. (bet. Hearst Ave. & Virginia St.) | 510-525-1440 | www.caferouge.net

"Carnivorous chomping" is the name of the game at this midpriced Fourth Street Cal-Med "known for" its "superior" organic meats including burgers "freshly ground at the on-site butcher shop" and "cooked to perfection"; clock-watchers say "service can be slow", but "dollar oysters are a great deal", and outdoor seating offers "some of the best dog-watching in the Bay Area."

Camino *Californian/Mediterranean*
25 | **22** | **22** | **$48**

Oakland | 3917 Grand Ave. (Sunny Slope Ave.) | 510-547-5035 | www.caminorestaurant.com

Chef/co-owner Russell Moore (ex Chez Panisse) is practically "out-Alice-ing" mentor Alice Waters at his "fairly simple" yet "utterly delicious" Cal-Med Oaklander where "almost everything" is cooked in a "huge fireplace", resulting in "marvelous flavors" and a "warm environment" to boot; though some call it "a bit overpriced" while others are "underwhelmed" by service that "can be on or off" and "cafeteria-style" "farm-table" seating, once dinner arrives, "the annoyances of life melt away"; P.S. closed Tuesdays.

Cancun *Mexican*
22 | **18** | **18** | **$13**

Berkeley | 2134 Allston Way (Shattuck Ave.) | 510-549-0964

"Great, fresh food, much of which the restaurant grows" at its Sonoma farm, helps set this Berkeley "self-service" Mexican apart; "quality" ingredients that are "organic, with normal pricing", plus the "amazing salsa bar" mean it's "mobbed during peak hours."

Casa Orinda *Italian/Steak*
21 | **19** | **22** | **$34**

Orinda | 20 Bryant Way (bet. Davis Rd. & Moraga Way) | 925-254-2981 | www.casaorinda.net

"Like walking into a spaghetti Western", this Orinda Italian steakhouse "time capsule" with Old West decor is the kind of "retro" "hangout" where "waiters remember repeat customers" and bartenders "make old-fashioned drinks" as families and an "older crowd" "chow down" on "hearty" prime rib and "dynamite Southern fried chicken"; some say it's "pricier than it should be", still most find it "as comfortable as an old bathrobe."

	FOOD	DECOR	SERVICE	COST

Caspers Hot Dogs *Hot Dogs*

23 | 12 | 21 | $8

Albany | 545 San Pablo Ave. (bet. Brighton Ave. & Garfield St.) | 510-527-6611
Dublin | 6998 Village Pkwy. (bet. Amador Valley & Dublin Blvds.) | 925-828-2224
Hayward | 21670 Foothill Blvd. (Grove Way) | 510-581-9064
Hayward | 951 C St. (bet. Main St. & Mission Blvd.) | 510-537-7300
Oakland | 5440 Telegraph Ave. (55th St.) | 510-652-1668
Pleasant Hill | 6 Vivian Dr. (Contra Costa Blvd.) | 925-687-6030 ◗
Richmond | 2530 MacDonald Ave. (Civic Center St.) | 510-235-6492
Walnut Creek | 1280 Newell Hill Pl. (bet. Newell Ave. & San Miguel Dr.) | 925-930-9154
www.caspershotdogs.com

You "can't go wrong" with the "old-school" franks at this East Bay "institution", where "the scene is pure '50s" and the grub comes "the way hot dogs should be served" – "with a snap to them" on "steamed buns" with "plenty of condiments" to pile on top; "old-time counter girls" who "call you 'hon'" add to a "classic" experience that's "well worth" the tiny tab.

César ◗ *Spanish*

20 | 20 | 19 | $34

(fka César España)
Berkeley | 1515 Shattuck Ave. (bet. Cedar & Vine Sts.) | 510-883-0222 | www.cesarberkeley.com
César Latino *Pan-Latin*
Oakland | 4039 Piedmont Ave. (Glen Ave.) | 510-985-1200 | www.barcesar.com

"*Viva España*" effuse fans of this moderately priced, "reliable late-night standby" in Berkeley's "Gourmet Ghetto" serving up "tasty tapas" and paella (its Oakland cousin plies a Pan-Latin menu) with a side of "people-watching" in "bistro"-style digs that "open to the street"; service can be "hit-or-miss", and it's "noisy" and "crowded" at night, but conversationalists assure "you can actually hear each other talk" at lunch; P.S. no reservations.

Cha Am Thai *Thai*

21 | 16 | 20 | $23

Berkeley | 1543 Shattuck Ave. (Cedar St.) | 510-848-9664 | www.chaamberkeley.com
See review in City of San Francisco Directory.

Champa Garden *SE Asian*

23 | 14 | 18 | $20

Oakland | 2102 Eighth Ave. (21st St.) | 510-238-8819 | www.champagarden.com

"Fresh, authentic, flavorful Southeast Asian cuisine" surfaces in Oakland's San Antonio neighborhood at this local "gem" offering a mix of Thai, Laotian, Vietnamese and Lue "dishes you can't get anywhere else"; ignore the "obscure location" and "spotty" service admirers say, and go for "budget-friendly" plates "served with generous helpings of fresh herbs."

Cha-Ya Vegetarian Japanese

23 | 14 | 18 | $22

Restaurant ⊟ *Japanese/Vegan*
Berkeley | 1686 Shattuck Ave. (bet. Lincoln & Virginia Sts.) | 510-981-1213
See review in City of San Francisco Directory.

FOOD DECOR SERVICE COST

☑ Cheese Board Pizzeria ☒ *Pizza* — 27 | 15 | 20 | $13

Berkeley | 1512 Shattuck Ave. (Vine St.) | 510-549-3055 |
www.cheeseboardcollective.coop

"Long lines tell the story" of the "life-changing" veggie-only pizzas at
this "worker-owned" "Gourmet Ghetto" pizzeria/bakery and cheese
shop, where "super-cheap" whole pies and "generous" slices, "crafted
with "cheese-monger standards", have a "cult following"; sure, there's
only one "exotic" choice per day and seats are "scarce", but even a
"carnivorous fiend" will "come hungry and leave happy."

☑ Cheesecake Factory *American* — 21 | 21 | 20 | $28

Pleasanton | Stoneridge Mall | 1350 Stoneridge Mall Rd. (Foothill Rd.) |
925-463-1311 | www.thecheesecakefactory.com
See review in City of San Francisco Directory.

☑ Cheese Steak Shop *Cheesesteaks* — 23 | 12 | 19 | $11

Alameda | Blanding Shopping Ctr. | 2671 Blanding Ave. (Tilden Way) |
510-522-5555
Concord | 3478 Clayton Rd. (Roslyn Dr.) | 925-687-6116
Berkeley | 1054 University Ave. (bet. San Pablo Ave. & 10th St.) |
510-845-8689
Lafayette | 3455 Mt. Diablo Blvd. (2nd St.) | 925-283-1234
Oakland | 3308 Lakeshore Ave. (bet. Lake Park Ave. & Mandana Blvd.) |
510-832-6717
Pleasanton | Gateway Square Shopping Ctr. | 4825 Hopyard Rd.
(Stoneridge Dr.) | 925-734-0293
San Ramon | Crow Canyon Crest Shopping Ctr. | 3110 Crow Canyon Pl.
(Crow Canyon Rd.) | 925-242-1112
Walnut Creek | 1626 Cypress St. (bet. California Blvd. & Locust St.) |
925-934-7017
www.cheesesteakshop.com
See review in City of San Francisco Directory.

Chevalier ⓜ *French* — 26 | 21 | 23 | $54

Lafayette | 960 Moraga Rd. (Moraga Blvd.) | 925-385-0793 |
www.chevalierrestaurant.com

It's "worth staying local" in Lafayette for "excellent classic French"
cuisine from a "personable" chef-owner who's "genuinely excited
to cook"; though wallet-watchers note it's "expensive", the "lovely"
outdoor patio, "old-fashioned service" and "unstuffy atmosphere"
make this a "special-celebration spot", and besides, "the prix fixe is
a good value."

☑ Chez Panisse ☒ *Californian/Mediterranean* — 28 | 25 | 27 | $87

Berkeley | 1517 Shattuck Ave. (bet. Cedar & Vine Sts.) | 510-548-5525 |
www.chezpanisse.com

"After 40 years", Alice Waters' "iconic" Berkeley "landmark" is "maybe
not cutting-edge" anymore and the "high priestess" herself is "seldom
seen", but it remains a "mecca" for "ethereal locavore" Cal-Med meals
"served simply and without ego", accompanied by "fantastic wines"
and "outstanding service"; while the "adherence to purity" strikes
some as "almost comical" at times, and the "very expensive", "limited
daily menus make it a gamble for picky eaters", devotees insist "you
owe it to yourself" to "stroll through" the kitchen of this "understated"
Craftsman bungalow "where it all began", to "find out why."

	FOOD	DECOR	SERVICE	COST

⬿ Chez Panisse

Café ⊠ *Californian/Mediterranean*

| 28 | 24 | 26 | $54 |

Berkeley | 1517 Shattuck Ave. (bet. Cedar & Vine Sts.) | 510-548-5049 | www.chezpanisse.com

"Incredible" "farm-to-table" Cal-Med meals ("including pizza") built on produce that tastes "like it was picked that morning" (and "it was!") draw "budget-conscious" food lovers to this "more-relaxed", "easier"-to-access sibling of Alice Waters' Berkeley "high temple" downstairs, where an à la carte menu is served "with the same care and commitment", but at a more "earthly price"; the "homey" "Craftsman setting" and "gracious" staff add to the experience of an "enjoyable" lunch or "casual" pre-theater dinner, and groupies can still take a spin "through the kitchen."

Chop Bar *Californian*

| 24 | 20 | 23 | $29 |

Oakland | 247 Fourth St. (Alice St.) | 510-834-2467 | www.oaklandchopbar.com

"Comfort service" matches the "comfort food" at this "comfortable yet edgy" Californian that's "one of the hottest dinner spots in Jack London" Square; locals swear "they must have the cows in the back room, the ground beef tastes so fresh", while "reasonable prices", "wine on tap" and a setting with a garage-door front add to the "laid-back" vibe; P.S. open all day.

⬿ Chow *American*

| 21 | 17 | 19 | $25 |

Danville | 445 Railroad Ave. (Hartz Ave.) | 925-838-4510
Lafayette | La Fiesta Sq. | 53 Lafayette Circle (Mt. Diablo Blvd.) | 925-962-2469
www.chowfoodbar.com
See review in City of San Francisco Directory.

Christy Hill *Californian/Mediterranean*

| ▽ 21 | 24 | 21 | $56 |

Tahoe City | 115 Grove St. (Rte. 28) | 530-583-8551 | www.christyhill.com

"Nearly every seat" of this "cozy" Tahoe City stalwart "is oriented" to maximize the "stunning views" of the lake – "if you can make it for sun-set", fans joke "you wouldn't even need to eat to be satisfied"; but luckily, the "pricey" Cal-Med dinners and bar menu have their own appeal, and there's "good wine" to boot; P.S. in summer, guests can "sit outside."

Chu *Chinese*

| ▽ 24 | 22 | 23 | $31 |

Oakland | 5362 College Ave. (bet. Bryant & Manila Aves.) | 510-601-8818 | www.restaurantchu.com

"Generous" portions of "fresh", "innovative variants on standard Chinese fare" – including housemade noodles – are delivered with "pleasant" service at this midpriced North Oaklander; "go for the art-work" and the "beautiful" modern decor advise some, while others talk up the "outstanding" happy hour (4 PM-7 PM daily, plus 9 PM-12 PM Friday and Saturday).

⬛NEW Comal *Mexican*

| - | - | - | M |

Berkeley | 2020 Shattuck Ave. (bet. Addison St. & University Ave.) | 510-926-6300 | www.comalberkeley.com

Matt Gandin (ex Delfina) oversees the large *platos fuertes* and the smaller antojitos at this huge new Downtown Berkeley late-night

Mexican, where the midpriced traditional fare is fused with NorCal sensibilities and ingredients, and drinks feature small-batch agave spirits (think tequila, mescal and bacanora); the sprawling, rustic indoor/outdoor space has concrete walls, long communal tables and weathered wood and steel accents, plus a 2,500-sq.-ft. patio with its own full bar, covered dining area and alfresco beer garden.

Ⓩ Commis Ⓜ *American* 28 | 21 | 26 | $98
Oakland | 3859 Piedmont Ave. (Rio Vista Ave.) | 510-653-3902 | www.commisrestaurant.com

Buckle in for a "gastronomical ride" at this "unmarked" Oakland New American from "genius" chef-owner James Syhabout, whose "adventurous" "molecular gastronomy–imbued" prix fixes are chockfull of "unbelievably delicious" "oddball combinations" that fans dub "worldview-altering"; "first-class" service helps elevate the "tiny", "spartan" digs, and while reservations are "hard to get", diners with an "open mind" (and deep bank account) are in for one of "the best high-end dining experiences in the area."

NEW Corners Tavern *American* – | – | – | M
Walnut Creek | Broadway Plaza Shopping Ctr. | 1342 Broadway Plaza (S. Main St.) | 925-948-8711 | www.cornerstavern.com

San Francisco's Town Hall gang turned the old Bing Crosby's into this midpriced American gastropub in Walnut Creek, reflecting their trademark blend of down-home yet sophisticated cuisine; clubby sofas, a horseshoe bar and antique snake cages filled with quirky dioramas define the lounge, while the light and airy mural-lined dining room opens onto patio seating in good weather.

Cottonwood *Eclectic* ▽ 20 | 21 | 22 | $41
Truckee | 10142 Rue Hilltop (Brockway Rd.) | 530-587-5711 | www.cottonwoodrestaurant.com

"Great upscale comfort food" (including a signature Caesar salad "made the way it should be") and a "nice view" "overlooking Truckee" make this moderate Eclectic housed in a historic ski lodge "the place to come" for "rejuvenation" "after a day on the slopes" or for a relaxing meal on the deck in summer; casual environs and solid service help assure "everybody feels comfortable", while weekly live music adds to the "fun atmosphere."

Crepevine *American/French* 21 | 16 | 19 | $16
Berkeley | 1600 Shattuck Ave. (Cedar St.) | 510-705-1836
Oakland | 5600 College Ave. (Ocean View Dr.) | 510-658-2026 ●
www.crepevine.com
See review in City of San Francisco Directory.

Dead Fish *Seafood* 22 | 22 | 21 | $41
Crockett | 20050 San Pablo Ave. (Merchant St.) | 510-787-3323 | www.thedeadfish.com

"If you want a place with a view", this Crockett seafooder overlooking the Carquinez Straits fits the bill say aficionados who also go for the "satisfying", occasionally "inspiring" eclectic roundup of dishes, including its "famous" crab; "service is prompt", and though a few surveyors find the tabs "a bit pricey for what you get", the "patio is perfect" for soaking up the scenery.

Doña Tomás M *Mexican* 22 | 18 | 20 | $36

Oakland | 5004 Telegraph Ave. (bet. 49th & 51st Sts.) | 510-450-0522 | www.donatomas.com

An "emphasis on fresh, seasonal ingredients" and a "modern twist – or two" add up to "flavorful", "well-prepared" Mexican plates (including "carnitas from heaven") at this Oakland "institution" where "friendly" (if "slow") staffers also offer up "tasty drinks" that "pack a wallop"; sure, it gets "a bit crowded and noisy", and some find it "pricey" for the genre, but most agree it's "worth the extra money" and recommend "eating outside if weather is nice."

Dopo Ⓩ *Italian* 26 | 18 | 22 | $38

Oakland | 4293 Piedmont Ave. (bet. Echo & Glen Eden Aves.) | 510-652-3676 | www.dopoadesso.com

Regulars rave about the "innovative Italian cuisine" at this midpriced Oakland "trattoria" that dishes out "delicate" "handmade pastas", "authentic pizza" and cured meats with flavors that "shine"; "uneven" service, "cramped quarters" and "no reservations" for fewer than six are a bit of "a downer", but "eating at the bar and watching the chefs work is great."

Dragonfly *Asian/Californian* 24 | 21 | 21 | $44

Truckee | Porter Simon Bldg. | 10118 Donner Pass Rd., 2nd fl. (Spring St.) | 530-587-0557 | www.dragonflycuisine.com

"Creative Asian-inspired Californian cuisine" (including sushi) draws fans to this second-floor Truckee stop, where regulars recommend "eating outside if you can" for "spectacular views of the mountains" and trains "coming and going over nearby Donner Pass"; it's not cheap, but realists remind "you get what you pay for."

NEW Dragon Rouge *Vietnamese* 24 | 18 | 22 | $22

Alameda | 2337 Blanding Ave. (29th Ave.) | 510-521-1800 | www.dragonrougerestaurant.com

"Newly relocated" to a "great new space right on the waterfront", this "delightful, family-run" Alameda Vietnamese offers "inventive items" "with a Cali twist"; though "a bit pricey compared to places in Oakland's Chinatown", "distinct flavors", an "attentive staff", "surprise entertainment" and a "lively bar scene" make it a "local gem."

Duck Club *American* 22 | 24 | 22 | $49

Lafayette | Lafayette Park Hotel & Spa | 3287 Mt. Diablo Blvd. (Pleasant Hill Rd.) | 925-283-7108 | www.lafayetteparkhotel.com

You can "treat someone to an upscale experience without going broke" at this "high-end" hotel restaurant duo offering "well-prepared" New American fare in a "quiet, elegant" setting; Bodega Bay has "nice ocean views" ("get a table by the window at sunset") while Lafayette has a "lively" happy hour, and service at both is "lovely."

East Ocean Seafood *Chinese* 24 | 17 | 19 | $25

Alameda | 1713 Webster St. (bet. Buena Vista & Pacific Aves.) | 510-865-3381 | www.eastoceanseafoodrestaurant.com

"Crowds line up" at this Alameda "family-run" "dim sum temple" serving "authentic and flavorful" "Cantonese" Chinese fare for "reasonable" prices; it's "often very busy" with "banquet-style" "parties on weekend nights", but the staff is so "helpful" that "even the dim sum pushcart servers can explain dishes in English"; P.S. dim sum served 10 AM–2:30 PM.

El Farolito *Mexican* — 23 | 9 | 17 | $10
Oakland | 3646 International Blvd. (Terminal St.) | 510-533-9194 | www.elfarolitoinc.com
See review in City of San Francisco Directory.

Emilia's Pizzeria 🖼️Ⓜ️⇗ *Pizza* — ▽ 26 | 8 | 21 | $18
Berkeley | 2995 Shattuck Ave. (Ashby Ave.) | 510-704-1794 | www.emiliaspizzeria.com
"Light crust, very fresh" "ingredients" and "the right ratio of cheese" have pals of "East Coast–style pizza" phoning the instant this "small", "hard-to-find" Berkeley "storefront" opens "to reserve" a "time slot" for "pickup"; some complain the "one-size" "pies aren't worth" the "rigmarole", but regulars advise "put the number on speed dial"; P.S. only eight seats.

Encuentro Cafe & Wine Bar 🖼️Ⓜ️ *Vegetarian* — ▽ 26 | 23 | 23 | $30
Oakland | 202 Second St. (Jackson St.) | 510-832-9463 | www.encuentrooakland.com
Even "meat eaters" won't feel they've "missed out" at this Jack London District vegetarian where the midpriced menu of small plates is filled with "satisfying" flavors and "seasonal ingredients"; though some cite "long waits", a "friendly" staff that's "knowledgeable" about the "interesting" wine selection helps compensate.

Enoteca Molinari 🖼️Ⓜ️ *Italian* — ▽ 24 | 20 | 23 | $37
Oakland | 5474 College Ave. (Taft Ave.) | 510-428-4078 | www.enoteca-molinari.com
"Italian food that sparkles with flavor" "delights" locals who squeeze into the "tight" quarters of this "homey and intimate" Oakland enoteca; "portions are a bit small", but "prices are low" enough, and "pleasant" service and an "extensive selection of Italian wines" add to the allure.

Z Erna's Elderberry House *Californian/French* — 28 | 28 | 28 | $96
Oakhurst | Château du Sureau | 48688 Victoria Ln. (Hwy. 41) | 559-683-6800 | www.elderberryhouse.com
"Anyone visiting Yosemite" "must" stop by this Oakhurst "special-occasion" spot for a "taste of Europe in the Sierras" by way of the "fantastic" New French–Californian prix fixes often proffered by the "charming" "Erna herself" in an "elegant" "fairy-tale" setting; it's "very expensive", but "nothing compares" for miles around, and if you stay overnight at the "adjacent château", Sunday brunch is "exquisite" too.

Esin Restaurant & Bar *American/Mediterranean* — 26 | 24 | 26 | $46
Danville | Rose Garden Ctr. | 750 Camino Ramon (Sycamore Valley Rd.) | 925-314-0974 | www.esinrestaurant.com
"Locals would like to keep" this Danville New American–Med to themselves, touting its "inventive", "beautifully prepared" menu that "changes seasonally", "exceptional" service and "elegant" (but "still child-friendly") atmosphere; "order dessert first and plan your dinner around it" advise insiders, as pastry chef/co-owner "Esin makes all" the "glorious" treats "in house."

	FOOD	DECOR	SERVICE	COST

Evan's American Gourmet Cafe *American*   ▽ 27 | 24 | 27 | $60

South Lake Tahoe | 536 Emerald Bay Rd. (15th St.) | 530-542-1990 |
www.evanstahoe.com

"Exquisitely prepared" New American plates that would be "wonderful for anywhere" are considered especially "priceless for Tahoe" at this "special-occasion" destination; staffers make diners feel like "invited guests" in the "intimate" converted cabin surrounds, so fans find it "worth the pricey tab."

Everett & Jones Barbeque *BBQ*   21 | 13 | 16 | $21

Berkeley | 1955 San Pablo Ave. (University Ave.) |
510-548-8261 ⌂
Hayward | 296 A St. (Filbert St.) | 510-581-3222
Oakland | Jack London Sq. | 126 Broadway (bet. Embarcadero W. & 2nd St.) | 510-663-2350
www.eandjbbq.com

"Smack your lips and lick your fingers" – "they really know how to serve up some 'cue" in "delicious heaping abundance" at this BBQ trio; just beware that there's counter service and "no frills" at Berkeley and Hayward, while Oakland is slightly "more expensive" with "sit-down" service.

FatApple's *Diner*   20 | 15 | 20 | $20

Berkeley | 1346 Martin Luther King Jr. Way (bet. Berryman & Rose Sts.) |
510-526-2260
El Cerrito | 7525 Fairmount Ave. (bet. Carmel & Ramona Aves.) |
510-528-3433

"Old-fashioned, wholesome" "dishes" including "wonderful homemade desserts and pastry" from the "attached bakeries" are the draw at this East Bay duo in Berkeley and El Cerrito; some feel the savory fare is "totally eclipsed by the pies", while others claim the "plethora of children" could "send most nonparents running", but "reasonable" prices and "friendly servers" keep many coming back.

Fentons Creamery *Ice Cream*   22 | 17 | 19 | $17

Oakland | 4226 Piedmont Ave. (bet. Entrada & Glenwood Aves.) |
510-658-7000
Oakland | Oakland Int'l Airport | Terminal 2 (Ron Cowan Pkwy.) |
no phone
www.fentonscreamery.com

"Take a step back in time" at this "classic" Oakland "ice cream parlor" with "friendly" service offering "ginormous" sundaes and cones from a "list of flavors as long as your arm"; "be prepared to make new friends in line" advise fans who mostly "stick to the ice cream" or "terrific crab sandwiches" and "share" to avoid "a bellyache"; P.S. it's also "a nice treat at the airport."

Five *American/Californian*   21 | 22 | 20 | $41

Berkeley | Hotel Shattuck Plaza | 2086 Allston Way (Oxford St.) |
510-225-6055 | www.five-berkeley.com

"Eye-popping decor", thanks to the "tasteful renovation" of an "elegant old hotel", creates a "lovely" "retro atmosphere" at this Berkeley Cal-American where "colorful, creative dishes" are served by a "polished" staff; the location makes it "one of the best places for before or after the theater", and it's "not noisy, as it used to be."

Flora 🅱️Ⓜ️ *American*　23 | 22 | 22 | $42

Oakland | 1900 Telegraph Ave. (19th St.) | 510-286-0100 |
www.floraoakland.com

"Exotic cocktails" plus "fantastic attention to detail" in its "refined and
confident" New American fare proffered amid "swanky" "art deco"
"decor" make this "uptown hipster" haven one of Oakland's "great"
spots for a "date night"; "warm service" adds to the "romantic" vibe,
and though it can get "too loud" and a bit "pricey", it's in a prime "location near the Fox and Paramount theaters."

Fonda Solana ● *Pan-Latin*　21 | 19 | 18 | $34

Albany | 1501 Solano Ave. (Curtis St.) | 510-559-9006 |
www.fondasolana.com

An Albany "late-night place", this Pan-Latin "hangout" draws a "lively
crowd" for its "high-quality south-of-the-border" small plates topped
off by "delish drinks"; bigger eaters moan "it costs a fortune to fill up",
but "recession pricing" at happy hours (5 PM–7 PM and 9 PM till close)
and "courteous", "efficient service" let everyone "leave happy."

Forbes Mill Steakhouse *Steak*　23 | 21 | 22 | $58

Danville | Livery Mercantile | 200 Sycamore Valley Rd. W.
(San Ramon Valley Blvd.) | 925-552-0505 |
www.forbesmillsteakhouse.com
See review in South of San Francisco Directory.

🆕 FuseBox 🅱️Ⓜ️⇻ *Korean*　– | – | – | I

Oakland | 2311 Magnolia St. (Grand Ave.) | 510-444-3100 |
www.fuseboxoakland.com

Capturing the spirit of those tiny out-of-the-way soju *bangs* (or
taverns) in Korea, this casual Korean-American 'kochi-gui pub'
tucked away in industrial West Oakland dishes out affordable
grilled and fried snacks, along with housemade banchan and playful Americanized inventions such as a po' boy fried chicken sandwich;
like any good izakaya, it's stocked with plenty of beer, sake and soju,
which diners can knock back from stools in the minimalist wood-lined
digs or the sunny courtyard; P.S. open for lunch Wednesday–Friday to
start, but dinner is forthcoming.

Gar Woods Grill & Pier *Californian*　20 | 25 | 21 | $40

Carnelian Bay | 5000 N. Lake Blvd. (Center St.) | 530-546-3366 |
www.garwoods.com

"It's hard to beat sitting on the deck" with a "delicious fruity rum"
cocktail at this moderate Carnelian Bay hang where the "killer drinks"
are offered alongside Californian nibbles; sure, the "awesome view" of
Lake Tahoe "bests the food", but service is "better than expected" –
and it's really all about the "fabulous atmosphere" anyway.

Gather *Californian*　24 | 22 | 22 | $37

Berkeley | David Brower Ctr. | 2200 Oxford St. (Allston Way) |
510-809-0400 | www.gatherrestaurant.com

"Innovative combinations of the freshest local ingredients" "showcase" the Bay Area's bounty at this "very Berkeley" Californian,
where you can "go whole hog" or "whole vegan" since many of the
"exciting, well-prepared" midpriced offerings (including the "exquisite" charcuterie) are meat-free; "eco-friendly" stylings are as

expected, and though visitors disagree on service ("efficient" vs. "slow"), most agree it works "when you want to be healthy and feel good about your dining experience."

Gaumenkitzel ☒ German   ▽ 22 | 18 | 23 | $24

Berkeley | 2121 San Pablo Ave. (Cowper St.) | 510-647-5016 | www.gaumenkitzel.net

"Charming owners" from Hamburg are behind this Berkeley bakery/cafe offering "authentic" flavors in "light" and "modern" German fare like spaetzle and beef roulade, plus "delicious pastries" and a "good selection" of *bier*; it's all offered at "decent prices", and although the "bare-bones" room feels "a bit sterile" to some, most appreciate the "warm" service.

Gioia Pizzeria Pizza   26 | 9 | 18 | $14

Berkeley | 1586 Hopkins St. (bet. McGee & Monterey Aves.) | 510-528-4692 | www.gioiapizzeria.com

It's just "like Brooklyn" say expats enamored with this affordable Berkeley slice shop run by a "friendly" couple firing up "unbelievably good" "real NY-style" "thin-blistered crusts", then crowning them with "innovative" seasonal "California-style toppings"; in a space the "size of a walk-in closet", "there's no real seating or service" and "always a line", so some "call ahead" for "a whole pie to go"; a new SF outpost boasts larger digs and a bigger menu.

Grégoire French   25 | 10 | 18 | $20

Berkeley | 2109 Cedar St. (bet. Shattuck Ave. & Walnut St.) | 510-883-1893
Oakland | 4001 Piedmont Ave. (40th St.) | 510-547-3444
www.gregoirerestaurant.com

Offering "off-the-wall" "tasty" fare, this oft "packed" North Berkeley and Oakland French duo "wows" with "beautifully prepared" "gourmet fast food", like "deliciously creative" sandwiches and "divine" potato puffs in "small" digs best suited to takeout (albeit "upscale takeout"); though some say it's "a little too expensive" for grub that you "eat out of a cardboard box", most agree it offers some of the "best" quick bites around.

Haps Original Steaks & Seafood Steak   25 | 23 | 23 | $62

Pleasanton | 122 W. Neal St. (Main St.) | 925-600-9200 | www.hapsoriginal.com

"Upscale dining with down-home service" makes this "good old-fashioned" Pleasanton chophouse popular for "celebrations"; there's "old-school" "decor" and "budget-buster" tabs, but "great prime ribs" and "huge" steaks keep 'em coming to this "throwback" "joint."

⬛NEW Haven Californian   25 | 24 | 21 | $54

Oakland | 44 Webster St. (Embarcadero W.) | 510-663-4440 | www.havenoakland.com

"Heaven" is what acolytes rename this "adventurous entry into Daniel Patterson's empire" (Coi, Plum), a converted Jack London Square warehouse where chef Kim Alter works "magic in the open kitchen" conjuring a "divine", "innovative" Californian menu ("standouts include the Brussels sprouts and the smoked pasta"); "snazzy" stonework-and-wood digs plus mostly "attentive" service are boons, and though "your wallet will be a lot lighter", you'll leave "happy"; P.S. "the best deal is the tasting menu" – "you'll be dazzled."

Hawker Fare ⊠ *SE Asian*

23 | 15 | 17 | $23

Oakland | 2300 Webster St. (23rd St.) | 510-832-8896 |
www.hawkerfare.com

Locals feel "blessed" by Commis chef James Syhabout's "street food, not haute cuisine" at this "playful" Southeast Asian in Oakland, where "organic produce", "pastured meats" and "impeccable technique" "elevate the humble rice bowl"; "expect to wait" in the tiny, graffiti-covered storefront where you'll be "seated cheek-to-pierced-jowl next to people much hipper than you" shouting over the "blare of the hip-hop" – but it's all "inventive, cheap fun."

Home of Chicken & Waffles ● *Southern*

20 | 15 | 17 | $18

Oakland | 444 Embarcadero W. (B'way) | 510-836-4446
Walnut Creek | 1653 Mt. Diablo Blvd. (S. California Blvd.) | 925-280-1653
www.homeofchickenandwaffles.com

For "chicken and waffles" like "mama used to make" served up with "Southern hospitality", this pair is an East Bay "go-to"; decor is "cute and cool", and they're "a post-bar-hopping staple" "for cheap eats, especially late at night when everything else is closed."

Homeroom ☒ *American*

22 | 19 | 21 | $18

Oakland | 400 40th St. (Shafter Ave.) | 510-597-0400 |
www.homeroom510.com

"Childhood comfort food comes of age" at this "retro schoolroom" look-alike in Oakland's Temescal, where "everyone from babies to hipsters" "keeps coming back" to try the many iterations of "tasty", "filling" "mac 'n' cheese like your mother never made" (goat cheese, Mexican, vegan and gluten-free among them); it's "tiny" and the line to get in "can be long", but it's "worth it" considering the "reasonable prices", not to mention "grown-up" concoctions like beer floats.

Hong Kong East Ocean
Seafood Restaurant *Chinese*

22 | 20 | 16 | $37

Emeryville | 3199 Powell St. (Anchor Dr.) | 510-655-3388 | www.hkeo.us

The "spectacular view" at this "Hong Kong"–style Emeryville Chinese "overlooks the bay", and "the food is good enough to complement it" when "big family groups" order dim sum from the menu (since there are "no carts coming around"); just be warned, it "can be pricey" because "you're basically paying for the ambiance."

NEW Hopscotch ☒ *American/Japanese*

– | – | – | M

Oakland | 1915 San Pablo Ave. (bet. 19th & 20th Sts.) | 510-788-6217 |
www.hopscotchoakland.com

Situated in Oakland's up-and-coming Uptown District, this new mid-priced diner serves whimsical Japanese-inspired regional American fare from a Yoshi's vet; the 40-seat storefront is chock-full of greaser-era diner gear like black-and-white-checkered floors and cherry-red vinyl swivel counter seats, but oversized windows and framed mirrors hung just so lend the space an airy, modern feel.

Hotel Mac Restaurant & Bar *American*

21 | 22 | 21 | $42

Richmond | Hotel Mac | 50 Washington Ave. (bet. Cottage & Tewksbury Aves.) | 510-233-0576 | www.hotelmac.net

"Take your sweetie" to this "charming" historic Point Richmond hotel built in 1911 (think pressed-tin ceilings and lots of brass and wood) for "solid American" "fine dining" that's "elegant without being preten-tious"; a "friendly staff", "adequate portions", "good specials" and a weekday "happy hour" that's "a steal" further make this a "hidden gem."

Hudson *American* 22 | 22 | 22 | $46

Oakland | 5356 College Ave. (Manila Ave.) | 510-595-4000 | www.hudsonoakland.com

"Top-notch" "wood-fired pizzas" and "seasonal dishes" that are "in-ventive without going overboard" plus "superb" bar "concoctions" have "hipsters" saying this Rockridge New American has "really hit its stride" and is "worth every penny"; the staff is "lively", but the "unex-pectedly cool" interior can be "noisy up front", so "ask for the back room" if you want to "carry on a conversation."

⚡ Il Fornaio *Italian* 22 | 22 | 21 | $39

Walnut Creek | 1430 Mt. Diablo Blvd. (bet. B'way & Main St.) | 925-296-0100 | www.ilfornaio.com
See review in City of San Francisco Directory.

Imperial Tea Court *Tearoom* 19 | 20 | 19 | $23

Berkeley | Epicurious Garden | 1511 Shattuck Ave. (bet. Cedar & Vine Sts.) | 510-540-8888 | www.imperialtea.com
See review in City of San Francisco Directory.

⚡ In-N-Out Burger ● *Burgers* 23 | 14 | 21 | $9

Oakland | 8300 Oakport St. (Edgewater Dr.) | 800-786-1000 | www.in-n-out.com
See review in City of San Francisco Directory.

Ippuku *Japanese* 24 | 23 | 21 | $41

Berkeley | 2130 Center St. (bet. Oxford St. & Shattuck Ave.) | 510-665-1969 | www.ippukuberkeley.com

"Live dangerously" at this "friendly" Japanese izakaya near the Downtown Berkeley BART station, where "two guys and a hibachi" re-ward "adventurous eaters" with "amazing" yakitori and other dishes featuring "various chicken parts" that might "challenge" your "com-fort zone"; just "bring plenty of yen", as the fare and the "interesting" shochus and sakes that "go with them" can "add up quickly."

Italian Colors *Italian* 21 | 20 | 22 | $35

Oakland | 2220 Mountain Blvd. (Scout Rd.) | 510-482-8094 | www.italiancolorsrestaurant.com

"They recognize regulars" at this Montclair "hangout" where the "Italian comfort food" "is not gourmet", but is "a big step above pizza-parlor spa-ghetti"; the "friendly staff" is "accommodating with kids", and the "ac-complished guitarist" Wednesday–Saturday nights is "a definite plus."

Izzy's Steaks & Chops *Steak* 23 | 20 | 22 | $45

San Ramon | 200 Montgomery St. (bet. Alcosta Blvd. & Market Pl.) | 925-830-8620 | www.izzyssteaks.com
See review in City of San Francisco Directory.

Jake's on the Lake *Californian* 20 | 23 | 21 | $39

Tahoe City | Boatworks Mall | 780 N. Lake Blvd. (Jackpine St.) | 530-583-0188 | www.jakestahoe.com

"Spectacular" views make this "retro" Tahoe City waterfront grill "worth a splurge", especially "if you're on their outside deck"; "friendly service" and live music in the bar on weekends are boons, and though the menu is "secondary", it's "decent" if "a bit formulaic", though "the hula pie is worth driving four hours for."

Jimmy Beans *Diner*

| 20 | 11 | 16 | $18 |

Berkeley | 1290 Sixth St. (Gilman St.) | 510-528-3435 | www.jimmybeans.com

Fans of this diner in a "weird" West Berkeley location say it serves "ordinary items made with panache and grace", including all-day breakfast ("don't miss the silver-dollar pancakes"); there's "no table service during the day" and the "funky setting" leaves something to be desired", but the $15 three-course dinners are "a great bargain."

⚡ Jim's Country Style Restaurant *Southern*

| 27 | 16 | 25 | $14 |

Pleasanton | 5400 Sunol Blvd. (Bernal Ave.) | 925-426-7019

Pleasanton "locals" have "been overeating" "forever" at this "classic homestyle family place" that dishes up "great" Southern fare "for the price"; it "isn't fancy", but "excellent breakfasts", "large portions" and "friendly" service mean it's "always packed" "on the weekends."

NEW Johnny Garlic's *Californian*

| 20 | 18 | 20 | $30 |

Dublin | 4920 Dublin Blvd. (Hacienda Dr.) | 925-248-2347 | www.johnnygarlics.com

See review in North of San Francisco Directory.

NEW Joshu-ya Brasserie *Japanese* (fka Joshu-ya Sushi Bar)

| ▽ 21 | 18 | 19 | $22 |

Berkeley | 2441 Dwight Way (Telegraph Ave.) | 510-848-5260 | www.joshu-ya.com

"Surprisingly good sushi for a university location" is cut at this affordable Berkeley Japanese eatery where the new chef-owner seems "to have some great ideas" such as inventive tapas – and even a burger at lunch; the renovated dining room has a "cool atmosphere" and service is "decent", plus there's a garden patio.

Juan's Place *Mexican*

| 21 | 14 | 20 | $18 |

Berkeley | 941 Carleton St. (9th St.) | 510-845-6904

"Always crowded with Cal students", this "reliable" "Berkeley mainstay" doles out "amazing" flour tortilla chips and "greasy, filling" Mexican mains, all presented in "huge portions" and washed down with "great wine margaritas"; "don't expect frills", but do count on "accommodating", "friendly service", "reasonable prices" and plenty of "kitsch."

NEW Kincaid's *American*

| 23 | 22 | 21 | $47 |

Oakland | 1 Franklin St. (Water St.) | 510-835-8600 | www.kincaids.com

See review in South of San Francisco Directory.

King of Thai Noodles *Thai*

| 22 | 12 | 17 | $14 |

Alameda | 1635 Park St. (Pacific Ave.) | 510-522-8200

See review in City of San Francisco Directory.

Kirala *Japanese*

| 25 | 16 | 19 | $36 |

Berkeley | 2100 Ward St. (Shattuck Ave.) | 510-549-3486

(continued)

Kirala 2 *Japanese*
Berkeley | Epicurious Gdn. | 1511 Shattuck Ave. (bet. Cedar & Vine Sts.) | 510-649-1384
www.kiralaberkeley.com
"Serious sushi and Japanese-food lovers" endure "epic" waits for "outstanding fresh fish", "amazing robata" and "even better" "udon dishes" at this "deservedly busy" "go-to place" for a "sublime dining experience" in Berkeley; "try coming when the doors open or two hours later" to avoid "standing in line"; P.S. get bento boxes and premade rolls to go at the takeout-only Epicurious Garden branch.

Koi Palace @ Dublin *Chinese*   24 | 18 | 15 | $35
(fka Koi Garden)
Dublin | Ulferts Ctr. | 4288 Dublin Blvd. (bet. Glynnis Rose Dr. & John Monego Ct.) | 925-833-9090 | www.koipalace.com
See review in South of San Francisco Directory.

La Boulange *Bakery*   22 | 17 | 18 | $15
Danville | 405 Railroad Ave. (Hartz Ave.) | 925-838-1200 |
www.laboulangebakery.com
See review in City of San Francisco Directory.

Lake Chalet *Californian*   17 | 24 | 18 | $38
Oakland | Lake Merritt Boathse. | 1520 Lakeside Dr. (bet. 14th & 17th Sts.) | 510-208-5253 | www.thelakechalet.com
With an "absolutely fabulous setting" in a "beautifully renovated boathouse" on Lake Merritt, diners just "wish the food and service" were "as good as" the "spectacular location" of this Oakland Californian; "happy-hour prices are really great" though, so "go, enjoy the view", "have snacks, appetizers, drinks" and hope "they get their act together."

Lalime's *Californian/Mediterranean*   26 | 22 | 24 | $51
Berkeley | 1329 Gilman St. (bet. Neilson St. & Peralta Ave.) | 510-527-9838 | www.lalimes.com
"First", and fans say "still the best", of the K2 restaurant group's ventures, this Berkeley Cal-Med is "a neighborhood gem if there ever was one", proffering a "changing menu" of "seasonal" "locally sourced" cuisine and "very good wines" in a "romantic" "Craftsman-style" "bungalow"; service "offered with genuine smiles" and "fun theme nights" keep them coming back, plus it's "relatively" affordable, making it a "go-to favorite" of locals who've been celebrating "special occasions" here "since it began."

La Méditerranée *Mediterranean/Mideastern*   23 | 18 | 21 | $23
Berkeley | 2936 College Ave. (bet. Ashby Ave. & Russell St.) | 510-540-7773 | www.cafelamed.com
See review in City of San Francisco Directory.

La Note *French*   23 | 21 | 20 | $26
Berkeley | 2377 Shattuck Ave. (bet. Channing Way & Durant Ave.) | 510-843-1535 | www.lanoterestaurant.com
"Sensational" "French countryside–inspired" breakfasts starring "creative" pancakes and omelets and "bowl-size café au lait" make this "affordable" cafe with a "charming" "Provence vibe" "renowned" in

Berkeley; "get there early" to avoid the "long lines during the weekend" or come for dinner (Fridays–Sundays only) when it's less "crowded" and "noisy"; P.S. a "lovely garden" is open in good weather.

Lark Creek *American*   24 | 21 | 23 | $44

Walnut Creek | 1360 Locust St. (bet. Cypress St. & Mt. Diablo Blvd.) | 925-256-1234 | www.larkcreek.com

"Delicious" Traditional American "comfort food" is made with "farm-fresh ingredients" and served with "verve" by a "caring staff" at this "classic standby" in Walnut Creek, whose "warm, welcoming" setting features an open kitchen inside and sidewalk seating out; though some feel prices are "on the expensive side", the "exceptional desserts" and "excellent" wines help keep it on the list of places "you can always depend on."

La Rose Bistro Ⓜ *Californian/French*   23 | 17 | 21 | $35

Berkeley | 2037 Shattuck Sq. (bet. Addison St. & University Ave.) | 510-644-1913 | www.larosebistro.com

"Nobody seems to know about" this "small, cozy" Berkeley bistro that offers a Californian-French menu accompanied by "lovely" service; loyalists say it offers "great value" "for the money" and makes a "nice, quiet lunch place" or "great pre-theater option."

Le Cheval *Vietnamese*   22 | 18 | 20 | $28

Oakland | 1007 Clay St. (10th St.) | 510-763-8495
Walnut Creek | 1375 N. Broadway (bet. Cypress & Duncan Sts.) | 925-938-2288 Ⓜ

Le Petit Cheval Ⓩ⇗ *Vietnamese*

Berkeley | YWCA | 2600 Bancroft Way (Bowditch St.) | 510-704-8018
www.lecheval.com

Regulars at the Walnut Creek outpost find it the most "comfortable" of this Vietnamese trio serving a "wide range of tasty dishes including clay pots", pho and banh mi at "reasonable prices"; the Berkeley outlet is best for a "quick lunch", while Oakland fans are "still impressed" with the original, now reopened at its previous Clay Street address.

Legendary Palace *Chinese*   ▽ 22 | 16 | 18 | $20

Oakland | 708 Franklin St. (7th St.) | 510-663-9188

At this Oakland "dim sum factory" that "packs them in", lots of chefs prepare a big roster of wok, dim sum and BBQ items amid "gaudy decor"; service is decent, and it's all "noisy fun", but best of all, "it's dirt-cheap."

Little Star Pizza *Pizza*   25 | 16 | 19 | $23

Albany | 1175 Solano Ave. (Cornell Ave.) | 510-526-7827 |
www.littlestarpizza.com
See review in City of San Francisco Directory.

Lo Coco's Restaurant & Pizzeria Ⓜ *Italian*   24 | 17 | 22 | $27

Berkeley | 1400 Shattuck Ave. (Rose St.) | 510-843-3745
Oakland | 4270 Piedmont Ave. (Echo Ave.) | 510-652-6222 ⇗
www.lococospizzeria.com

"Truly authentic", "reasonably priced" "Sicilian food" is the draw at this "lovely little Italian" pair with a "happy, bustling, warm atmosphere"; "homemade pasta and sauces" are "so good" you "want to cry", the pizza is like "grandmother used to make" and "the bread is out of this world", all leaving patrons "satisfied and full."

Luka's Taproom & Lounge ● *Californian/French*

| 20 | 15 | 17 | $27 |

Oakland | 2221 Broadway (W. Grand Ave.) | 510-451-4677 |
www.lukasoakland.com

Expect "comfort food" with Californian-French "flair" at this mid-priced brasserie that's an "anchor" for the Uptown Oakland "hipster" "food scene"; there's a "classy beer selection" and the "Belgian fries with three different sauces" are a "must-have", but "the burger is what you come back for" – assuming you don't mind variable service and a "loud and lively crowd."

Mama's Royal Cafe ⊅ *American*

| 24 | 15 | 20 | $18 |

Oakland | 4012 Broadway (40th St.) | 510-547-7600 |
www.mamasroyalcafeoakland.com

"You feel like you're in a '70s time warp" at this "funky" "longtime" Oakland "breakfast favorite" with "strong coffee", "generous servings" and waitresses who "call you hon"; the "often local and organically sourced" chow is "still solid after all these years" (including the "shockingly delicious" home fries), adding up to a "good value" that's "worth" the "long waits."

Manzanita

Lake Tahoe *Californian/French*

| ▽ 23 | 25 | 21 | $63 |

Truckee | Ritz-Carlton Lake Tahoe | 13031 Ritz Carlton Highlands Ct. (Hwy. 267) | 530-562-3050 | www.manzanitalaketahoe.com

"It's worth a trip on the gondola" to enjoy the "out-of-this-world" views from this Truckee restaurant/bar in the Ritz-Carlton, perched "halfway up the mountain" of the Northstar Resort; the "outstanding", if pricey, Cal-French food from celebrity chef Traci Des Jardins (Jardinière) and "attentive service" make it a "welcome addition" to the local dining scene, and a meal outside on the seasonal terrace is truly "a wonderful experience."

Marica *Seafood*

| 26 | 21 | 25 | $40 |

Oakland | 5301 College Ave. (B'way) | 510-985-8388 |
www.maricafood.wordpress.com

"Shh, don't tell anyone" plead Rockridgers who are "blown away" by this "small" neighborhood "gem" serving some of the most "inventive" seafood "for the price" in the East Bay; add in "a cool, old wooden bar", a "friendly staff" and specials like "oysters for $1" and the "early-bird prix fixe", and it's no wonder it's a "local favorite."

Marzano *Italian/Pizza*

| 24 | 21 | 23 | $35 |

Oakland | 4214 Park Blvd. (Glenfield Ave.) | 510-531-4500 |
www.marzanorestaurant.com

There are "so many great menu items" at this "neighborhood" Italian in Oakland, and it's "difficult to choose" among dishes such as antipasti, Neapolitan pies that taste like they were "shipped from Italy" and "hearty entrees" that are pulled from the "wood-burning pizza oven"; prices are "not bad at all", and the "delightful staff" adds to the appeal.

	FOOD	DECOR	SERVICE	COST

Max's Diner & Bar 🗷 *Deli*　　20 | 17 | 19 | $26

Oakland | Oakland City Ctr. | 500 12th St. (bet. B'way & Clay St.) |
510-451-6297

Max's Restaurant of San Ramon *Deli*

San Ramon | 2015 Crow Canyon Pl. (Crow Canyon Rd.) |
925-277-9300
www.maxsworld.com

See review in City of San Francisco Directory.

Meritage at　　22 | 26 | 23 | $58
The Claremont *Californian*

Berkeley | The Claremont Hotel | 41 Tunnel Rd. (Claremont Ave.) |
510-292-4562 | www.meritageclaremont.com

"Sink into luxury with a gorgeous view" that takes in "San Francisco
Bay as far as the Golden Gate" at this "knockout" Californian situated in Berkeley's "majestic Claremont Hotel"; surveyors have
praise for "beautiful, inventive dishes served with flair" by a "superior" staff and find the brunch "outstanding", while the "live piano"
adds a "retro feel."

Metro ● *Californian/French*　　21 | 18 | 20 | $39

Lafayette | 3524 Mt. Diablo Blvd. (bet. 1st St. & Moraga Rd.) |
925-284-4422 | www.metrolafayette.com

🆕 **Metro Montclair** *Californian/French*

Oakland | 2058 Mountain Blvd. (La Salle Ave.) | 510-339-3322 |
www.montclairmetro.com

When the "weather cooperates", the "lovely" "patio" is a "favorite" for
alfresco dining at this midpriced Cal-French in "sleepy Lafayette"
(with an Oakland sibling), where a "tantalizing" menu is filled with
"upscale comfort food"; service can be "spotty" and the modern setting can get "noisy" due to a "lively bar scene", so those seeking solace
should "eat outside or wear earplugs."

Mezze *Californian/Mediterranean*　　23 | 22 | 23 | $38

Oakland | 3407 Lakeshore Ave. (bet. Mandana Blvd. & Trestle Glen Rd.) |
510-663-2500 | www.mezze.com

Regulars contend that "every neighborhood should have a place"
like this Oakland "warm and welcoming" "Lakeshore District"
Californian-Mediterranean "staple" with its "adventurous spirit",
where there's "always something new, flavorful and exciting to try"
from the "eclectic menu" with a "creative spin"; the budget-minded
say the "the prix fixe" dinner option is a "good value", plus there's no
corkage Monday–Wednesday.

Miss Pearl's　　22 | 22 | 22 | $33
Restaurant & Lounge *Southern*
(fka Miss Pearl's Jam House)

Oakland | Waterfront Plaza Hotel | 1 Broadway (Embarcadero W.) |
510-444-7171 | www.jdvhotels.com

After a flood in 2011, this Jack London Square spot with a "very
pretty" "view of the harbor" and San Francisco modernized its decor
as a backdrop for its Southern menu; regulars "love the changes" including "new menu items" from chef Eddie Blyden, and service
remains "very friendly."

Montclair Egg Shop *Diner*

20 | 18 | 19 | $16

Oakland | 6126 Medau Pl. (Moraga Ave.) | 510-339-9554

"Eggs Benedict in various forms is a specialty" at this affordable Oakland daytime diner where a "friendly" staff serves up breakfast, lunch and brunch; "bring the entire family" to enjoy the "fun train collection", but remember, it's "a small place" so you may have to "wait for a table on weekends" (and parking "can be tricky").

Moody's Bistro & Lounge *American*

∇ 23 | 17 | 24 | $48

Truckee | Truckee Hotel | 10007 Bridge St. (Donner Pass Rd.) | 530-587-8688 | www.moodysbistro.com

Despite some changes in menu and decor, this "real find" in Truckee remains "just as homey as ever", serving pizzas and American eats with a "focus on quality dishes"; you can still "find a wine for any budget", and catch the live "jazz" regulars "love."

Mua Lounge ● *American*

23 | 23 | 20 | $30

Oakland | 2442 Webster St. (B'way) | 510-238-1100 | www.muaoakland.com

"Throngs of hipsters" flock to this Oakland "converted car repair shop" filled with "funky artwork" in search of "a fun night out", with "cocktails" and "fantastic", "mostly small-plate" midpriced American fare; service is decent but "after dinner" "the place turns into a club", so those who'd rather avoid "the blaring DJ" should go at lunch (Friday only); P.S. "great for big groups."

Naan 'n Curry *Indian/Pakistani*

18 | 11 | 14 | $15

Berkeley | 2366 Telegraph Ave. (bet. Channing Way & Durant Ave.) | 510-841-6226 | www.naancurry.com

See review in City of San Francisco Directory.

Naked Fish *Japanese*

∇ 20 | 18 | 18 | $35

South Lake Tahoe | 3940 Lake Tahoe Blvd. (bet. Hwy. 50 & Pioneer Trail) | 530-541-3474 | www.thenakedfish.com

"It's not just sushi" that's served at this Hawaiian-influenced Japanese spot in South Lake Tahoe – there are "a lot of other creative fish dishes" among the menu's hot entrees, plus a changing list of sake, wine and beer; the new lounge next door offers small plates and appetizers to help ease the wait for the sushi bar – and a big-screen TV too.

Nama Sushi & Teriyaki *Japanese*

∇ 27 | 16 | 22 | $25

Walnut Creek | 1502 Sunnyvale Ave. (Sunnyvale Ave.) | 925-932-9540

Fin fanciers say the chef "is a creative master when it comes to raw fish" at this "casual", "always" "busy" Japanese hidden in a Walnut Creek strip mall just off Highway 680; some belly up to the L-shaped bar for "awesome sushi", but there are also tables, and warm dishes including "great tempura" at "moderate" prices, all delivered with "great service."

Nan Yang Rockridge *Burmese*

23 | 17 | 23 | $26

Oakland | 6048 College Ave. (Claremont Ave.) | 510-655-3298 | www.nanyangrockridge.com

"Reliably delicious", "beautiful" dishes are filled with "delightful flavor combinations" at this midpriced Rockridge "neighborhood" Burmese; patrons suggest "ask Philip", the chef/co-owner, "to select your meal for you and he'll create a perfect balance" of "favorite" items like "garlic noodles" and "ginger salad", while those who find the "pleasant" setting a bit too minimal advise "get a seat by the window."

900 Grayson 🅾 *Burgers*   25 | 18 | 22 | $23

Berkeley | 900 Grayson St. (7th St.) | 510-704-9900 | www.900grayson.com

"Prepare to confess" after meeting the "Demon Lover", this "funky" Californian's "sinful" version of chicken and waffles from a menu of "classics with a twist", plus an "outstanding" burger; sure, the place is in the "hinterlands" of Berkeley, and Saturday brunch lines are "out the door", but it's "worth squeezing" in for such "comforting" fare and "warm", "efficient" service; P.S. closes 3 PM weekdays and 2:30 PM Saturday.

North Beach Pizza ❶ *Pizza*   21 | 13 | 18 | $19

Berkeley | 1598 University Ave. (California St.) | 510-849-9800 | www.northbeachpizza.net

See review in City of San Francisco Directory.

O Chamé *Japanese*   25 | 24 | 22 | $35

Berkeley | 1830 Fourth St. (bet. Hearst Ave. & Virginia St.) | 510-841-8783 | www.ochame.com

Lunch or dinner at this "Zenlike" retreat on Berkeley's Fourth Street is "always an education in restraint and refinement", thanks to the "beautifully composed" bowls of noodles and other "unique", "lovingly prepared" Japanese fare made with the "freshest local ingredients"; tabs are a bit "pricey", but service from the "accommodating staff" and a pour from the "plentiful" sake menu never fail to "warm your soul."

Ohgane Korean *Korean*   23 | 16 | 16 | $27

Dublin | 7877 Amador Valley Blvd. (Regional St.) | 925-875-1232
Oakland | 3915 Broadway (40th St.) | 510-594-8300
www.ohgane.com

"Tabletop grills" make this East Bay twosome "a fun place to take newcomers" to Korean fare suggest surveyors who praise the "high-quality ingredients" and the wood-charcoal barbecue; service varies, but moderate prices add to the good feeling; P.S. the Oakland location has a "huge dining room."

Oliveto Cafe *Italian*   23 | 18 | 20 | $38

Oakland | 5655 College Ave. (Shafter Ave.) | 510-547-5356 | www.oliveto.com

When East Bay diners "miss Europe", this "little cafe" located "steps from the Rockridge BART" fits the bill with cappuccinos and "quick bites" from the "limited" but "satisfying" "locally sourced" Italian menu that's a cheaper "alternative to what's cooking at its big brother" upstairs; "people-watching" patrons appreciate that the "friendly" crew lets you "stay a long time", and early-birds chirp cheerfully for the "breakfast pizza."

Oliveto Restaurant *Italian*   26 | 23 | 23 | $57

Oakland | 5655 College Ave. (Shafter Ave.) | 510-547-5356 | www.oliveto.com

Having experienced a "big-time comeback" with the 2010 arrival of chef Jonah Rhodehamel, this "deservedly popular" Rockbridge Northern Italian continues to reach "sublime heights" with its "innovative", "locally sourced fare", especially when paired with "extraordinary" vino suggested by an "attentive" staff; while some say it's "high-priced", even those with "bridge-a-phobia" feel it's "worth a trip" on a "special occasion" or for its well-known "themed dinners" ("whole hog, tomato or oceanic").

Ozumo *Japanese* | 25 | 24 | 22 | $63 |

Oakland | 2251 Broadway (W. Grand Ave.) | 510-286-9866 |
www.ozumo.com
See review in City of San Francisco Directory.

Pacific Crest Grill at   ∇ | 21 | 17 | 23 | $43 |
Bar of America *Mediterranean*

Truckee | 10042 Donner Pass Rd. (Bridge St.) | 530-587-2626 |
www.barofamerica.net
Sierra sojourners "make a point to stop in Truckee" at this "favorite" white-tablecloth bistro (run by the owners of Pianetta and Christy Hill) to dine on "great burgers and fries" or "fresh" Cal-Med plates; it's a "calmer experience" than that at next-door honky-tonk sibling Bar of America, which shares its stock of "notable wines" and plays live music on the weekend, adding to the appeal.

Pakwan *Pakistani* | 23 | 9 | 14 | $16 |

Fremont | 41068 Fremont Blvd. (Irvington Ave.) | 510-226-6234 Ⓜ♿
Hayward | 25168 Mission Blvd. (Central Blvd.) | 510-538-2401
www.pakwanrestaurant.com
See review in City of San Francisco Directory.

Pappo Ⓜ *Californian/Mediterranean* | 25 | 20 | 22 | $42 |

Alameda | 2320 Central Ave. (bet. Oak & Park Sts.) | 510-337-9100 |
www.papporestaurant.com
"Expertly balanced flavors" from a "talented chef" who lets "the seasonal ingredients shine through" bring "big-city food" to "tiny Alameda" at this "intimate", "relaxed" Cal-Med; true, the "menu" is "small", but it's also "exciting" and "changes frequently", while service is "quietly efficient" and prices are "reasonable."

Pasta Pomodoro *Italian* | 19 | 17 | 20 | $22 |

El Cerrito | 5040 El Cerrito Plaza (Fairmount Ave.) | 510-225-0128
Emeryville | Bay Street Mall | 5614 Shellmound St. (Powell St.) |
510-923-1173
Oakland | 5500 College Ave. (Lawton Ave.) | 510-923-0900
Pleasant Hill | 45 Crescent Dr. (Contra Costa Blvd.) | 925-363-9641
San Ramon | 146 Sunset Dr. (Bollinger Canyon Rd.) | 925-867-1407
www.pastapomodoro.com
See review in City of San Francisco Directory.

Patxi's Pizza *Pizza* | 22 | 16 | 18 | $22 |
(fka Patxi's Chicago Pizza)

Lafayette | The Clocktower | 3577 Mt. Diablo Blvd. (Lafayette Circle) |
925-299-0700 | www.patxispizza.com
See review in City of San Francisco Directory.

Pearl's Deluxe Burgers *Burgers* | 24 | 13 | 19 | $13 |

Alameda | 2254 S. Shore Blvd. (Park St.) | 510-864-1015 |
www.pearlsdeluxe.com
See review in City of San Francisco Directory.

The Peasant &
the Pear ☑ *Californian/Mediterranean*

| 24 | 21 | 23 | $42 |

Danville | The Clock Tower | 267 Hartz Ave. (bet. Linda Mesa & Prospect Aves.) | 925-820-6611 | www.thepeasantandthepear.com

Chef-owner Rodney Worth "gets it right", offering "unpretentious but excellent" "comfort food" for "reasonable prices" at this Danville Cal-Med; staffers make you "feel like they care", and the "intimate", "relaxed atmosphere" is "perfect for a first date", particularly on the "outside patio" where there's "live music" Thursday–Saturday nights from April–November.

Pho 84 ☒ *Vietnamese*

| 24 | 16 | 20 | $19 |

Oakland | 354 17th St. (bet. Franklin & Webster Sts.) | 510-832-1338 | www.pho84.com

"Wonderful spices", "fresh ingredients" and "perfectly cooked" meat that's "so very tender" make this Oakland Vietnamese "the place to go" for "authentic pho" and other specialties; although the decor is pretty basic, and there's "always a long line" at lunch waiting to "slurp up" a "great deal", staffers are largely "welcoming" (and dinner is more "leisurely and relaxing").

Pianeta *Italian/Mediterranean*

| ∇ 21 | 18 | 18 | $57 |

Truckee | 10096 Donner Pass Rd. (Brockway Rd.) | 530-587-4694 | www.pianetarestaurant.com

"Well-done" hearty specialties (such as housemade pasta) hit the spot on "a cold day" and are matched by a serious wine cellar at this year-round Truckee Italian-Med with friendly service and a "warm, welcoming" old world–setting; sure, "you pay a little more" (it's in a "tourist area", after all), but "what the heck, you're on vacation" justify Tahoe travelers.

Piatti *Italian*

| 21 | 21 | 21 | $37 |

Danville | 100 Sycamore Valley Rd. W. (San Ramon Valley Blvd.) | 925-838-2082 | www.piatti.com

"Enormous portions" of "tasty" Italian specialties "at good prices" assure "you can't go wrong" at this "vibrant" (if a bit "noisy") Bay Area chain where dolce vita details include "fresh potted herbs on the table" (and, in Mill Valley, a "spectacular" water view); most agree it fits the bill for "business lunches" or celebratory dinners for "large parties", plus service is "fast and attentive."

Picán *Southern*

| 24 | 24 | 22 | $46 |

Oakland | 2295 Broadway (23rd St.) | 510-834-1000 | www.picanrestaurant.com

"Southern sassy meets Northern Californian" "urban chic", and the result is a "classy, sexy, high-end soul food" stop where "all of Oakland feels at home" and the "fried chicken is so good", it's "just like mom never made"; though service is "inconsistent" and the chow is "not diet", fans will "happily eat veggies the rest of the week" to atone.

Picante Cocina Mexicana *Mexican*

| 22 | 16 | 20 | $16 |

Berkeley | 1328 Sixth St. (bet. Camelia & Gilman Sts.) | 510-525-3121 | www.picanteberkeley.com

"Watch them make corn tortillas right in front of you" at this "large, festive" "cafeteria-style" "Berkeley institution" with "family atmosphere" and "consistently" "tasty" Mexican fare built with "quality in-gredients"; it can be "noisy" with "lots of kids" and "long lines", but fans adore the "full bar", "quick service" and "ultrareasonable pricing", plus the "little outdoor garden" is "delightful" in nice weather.

Pizza Antica   Pizza   22 | 18 | 19 | $25

Lafayette | 3600 Mt. Diablo Blvd. (Dewing Ave.) | 925-299-0500 | www.pizzaantica.com
See review in South of San Francisco Directory.

Pizzaiolo ⌧ Italian/Pizza   26 | 20 | 21 | $38

Oakland | 5008 Telegraph Ave. (bet. 49th & 51st Sts.) | 510-652-4888 | www.pizzaiolooakland.com
Most patrons visit this Oakland Italian for its "spectacular" "wood-fired pizzas" crowned with "delicious" and sometimes "unusual" toppings, but say "don't overlook" the "incredible salads" and other "sublime dishes" where the "fresh ingredients" "sing out" amid the "boisterous surroundings"; while service "varies" and some complain about the "price-to-portion ratio", most agree it's still "worth it"; P.S. "make a reservation" or "the wait" can be "intimidating."

Plum   Californian   23 | 21 | 22 | $51

Oakland | 2214 Broadway (W. Grand Ave.) | 510-444-7586 | www.plumoakland.com
Daniel Patterson's "exciting" Oakland outpost "gets mobbed" for its "remarkably inventive" (albeit sometimes "bizarre") Californian small plates ably served by a "hipster staff" in a "snazzy" yet "casual" set-ting featuring "giant" photos of plums; fans love to "sit at the counter" and watch the chefs "create their masterpieces", which are "a bargain" compared to tabs at "sister Coi in SF", but a few ding the "micro-sized" meals and "uncomfortable" "hardwood" seats; P.S. the adjacent Plum Bar offers "nice" farm-to-glass cocktails and bar snacks.

PlumpJack Cafe   Californian/Mediterranean   23 | 21 | 21 | $54

Olympic Valley | PlumpJack Squaw Valley Inn | 1920 Squaw Valley Rd. (Hwy. 89) | 530-583-1576 | www.plumpjackcafe.com
At this resort restaurant in North Tahoe's Olympic Valley, après-skiers chill out while digging into seasonally focused Cal-Med cuisine matched with a "huge", "reasonably priced" wine list; though tabs may be "expen-sive" and service could use a tweak, the "young" crowd populating the "cozy", rustic digs and at the adjacent bar doesn't seem to mind.

Postino   Italian   24 | 25 | 24 | $50

Lafayette | 3565 Mt. Diablo Blvd. (Lafayette Circle) | 925-299-8700 | www.postinorestaurant.com
"Intimate dining rooms" featuring exposed brick and fireplaces in "a lovely old building", as well as attractive "outdoor seating", make this Lafayette "oasis" a "beautiful setting" for a "fantastic" "high-end, high-class" Italian meal; "attentive" servers and a "nice wine list" add up to an "overall good choice", particularly for a "date" or "special occasion."

Prickly Pear Cantina   Mexican   19 | 19 | 21 | $25

Danville | Blackhawk Plaza | 3421 Blackhawk Plaza Circle (Camino Tassajara) | 925-984-2363 | www.thepricklypearcantina.com
"There's nothing prickly" about this "cavernous" Mexican "cantina" from chef-owner Rodney Worth (The Peasant & the Pear) that offers

up a "great-value", "creative menu" along with "killer margaritas"; the few grumbles about "inconsistent" food are muffled by a "serene" setting inside Danville's Blackhawk Plaza enhanced by a "lovely patio" and a "friendly staff."

Prima *Italian*

26 | 24 | 24 | $48

Walnut Creek | 1522 N. Main St. (bet. Bonanza St. & Lincoln Ave.) | 925-935-7780 | www.primawine.com

A "perennial favorite", this "excellent" Walnut Creek Italian "continues to wow" with chef-owner Peter Chastain's "authentic, sophisticated" dishes and an "amazing" wine list (featuring bottles available at its next-door wine shop); dissenters call it "pricey" and "a little pretentious", but most agree the "excellent ambiance" with service to match helps make it a "lovely place" for "date night" or a "formal occasion."

Red Hut Café *Diner*

∇ 23 | 16 | 20 | $18

South Lake Tahoe | 2723 Lake Tahoe Blvd. (Al Tahoe Blvd.) | 530-541-9024
South Lake Tahoe | Ski Run Ctr. | 3660 Lake Tahoe Blvd. (bet. Hwy. 50 & Ski Run Blvd.) | 530-544-1595
www.redhutcafe.com

"You get plenty for your money" at these "casual" South Lake Tahoe diners slinging "homestyle" breakfast-and-lunch fare like "biscuits and gravy" and some of "the best" waffles going in a "homey atmosphere"; the vintage, '50s-style decor is nothing special, but competent service helps make these "local hangouts" "worth every penny"; the Ski Run location also offers dinner and has an "ice cream shop."

Restaurant Peony *Chinese*

20 | 13 | 14 | $25

Oakland | Pacific Renaissance Plaza | 388 Ninth St. (bet. Franklin & Webster Sts.) | 510-286-8866 | www.restaurantpeony.com

"Ignore the ambiance" and "forget the service" (which can be downright "indifferent") because the "huge selection" of "spectacular" dim sum (and other Chinese specialties) is the real draw at this "popular" Oakland "extravaganza"; the weekend "crowds" are often "daunting" and some find the menu "a bit pricey" for what it is, but it packs 'em in all the same.

Revival Bar & Kitchen ●Ⓜ *Californian*

22 | 22 | 21 | $42

Berkeley | 2102 Shattuck Ave. (Addison St.) | 510-549-9950 | www.revivalbarandkitchen.com

"Local, sustainable", "snout-to-tail" cuisine "that holds up" against "the competitive Berkeley standard" makes for "perfect pre-theater" or late-night dining at chef-owner Amy Murray's "quirky but imaginative" Californian, where dishes star "seasonal ingredients" "prepared at the peak of freshness"; alas, it's sometimes "so noisy you can't hold a conversation", but "knowledgeable" staffers, a "cozy atmosphere", "decent prices" and "inventive drinks" keep it a "cool scene."

Rick & Ann's *American*

23 | 17 | 20 | $25

Berkeley | 2922 Domingo Ave. (bet. Ashby & Claremont Aves.) | 510-649-8538 | www.rickandanns.com

Berkeleyites "keep coming back" for the "great American chow" made from "locally sourced", "high-quality" ingredients at this inexpensive, "family-friendly" joint that offers plenty of "healthy and unique options" for breakfast through dinner; there are often "long lines on

weekends", but service comes "with a smile" and the "feel-good food
for the soul" is "worth the wait"; P.S. no dinner Mondays.

Riva Cucina ⚏Ⓜ️ *Italian* | 26 | 22 | 25 | $39 |

Berkeley | 800 Heinz Ave. (7th St.) | 510-841-7482 | www.rivacucina.com
"*Perfetto*" agree fans of this "hidden" "slice of Italy" "tucked away
amid the warehouses of West Berkeley" that's a "casual place for serious" Emilia-Romagna–inspired cuisine with "a touch of locavore creativity"; the midpriced eats are delivered with "excellent", "personal
service" in a "lovely", "peaceful" dining room, making this place "feel
like a find"; P.S. closed Sundays and Mondays.

⚏ Rivoli *Californian/Mediterranean* | 28 | 24 | 25 | $51 |

Berkeley | 1539 Solano Ave. (bet. Neilson St. & Peralta Ave.) |
510-526-2542 | www.rivolirestaurant.com
"Still great after all these years", this "exceptional" "neighborhood
standby" "on the outskirts of Berkeley" is run by a husband-and-wife
team who know how to "keep it simple" but still wow, delivering "consistently scrumptious" Cal-Med fare paired with well-curated wines
and "fantastic" service; the "petite" but "romantic setting" overlooking a "secret garden" "never fails to impress", leading fans to say this
"gem" "equals or surpasses" some "more expensive" rivals.

Rudy's Can't Fail Café ⚫ *Diner* | 19 | 19 | 18 | $19 |

Emeryville | 4081 Hollis St. (Park Ave.) | 510-594-1221
Oakland | 1805 Telegraph Ave. (bet. 18th & 19th Sts.) | 510-251-9400
www.iamrudy.com
"Just what a diner should be", this pair of "hipster hangouts" in
Emeryville and Oakland are "open late", serve "solid", "homey"
American grub all day long and are manned by an "indifferent", "tatted-
up staff"; there's enough "kitsch decor" (including "funky Barbies")
and "loud" music in the "punk rock–meets-playroom settings" to
"keep kids of all ages entertained", and given the decent prices, many
"can't fail to stop here" when they need a "greasy fix."

🆕 Rumbo Al Sur Ⓜ️ *Pan-Latin* | 21 | 21 | 21 | $40 |

Oakland | 4239 Park Blvd. (Wellington St.) | 510-479-1208
Offering an "interesting twist on tapas", this "fabulous" midpriced
Pan-Latin bistro is a "great addition" to Oakland's Glenview area,
cranking out "unusual" and "spicy" fare complemented by South
American wines, Mexican beers and an "extensive tequila menu"
(served straight-up or mixed into "interesting" cocktails); even as "a
new kid on the block", service has "its act together" and the "lively
bar" crowd comes ready to rumba.

⚏ Ruth's Chris Steak House *Steak* | 27 | 23 | 25 | $65 |

Walnut Creek | 1553 Olympic Blvd. (bet. Locust & Main Sts.) |
925-977-3477 | www.ruthschris.com
See review in City of San Francisco Directory.

Sahn Maru Korean BBQ *Korean*   ▽ | 23 | 10 | 18 | $21 |

Oakland | 4315 Telegraph Ave. (43rd St.) | 510-653-3366 |
www.sahnmarukoreanbbq.com
"Solid", reasonably priced Korean fare – including unusual items like
black goat stew – is served up at this Oakland joint amid lackluster de-

cor that's full of bric-a-brac; just concentrate on the signature barbecue dishes like bulgogi and kalbi accompanied by a "great selection of sides" (banchan) and ferried by "really nice people."

Salang Pass Afghan   ▽ 25 | 19 | 20 | $23

Fremont | 37462 Freemont Blvd. (Peralta Blvd.) | 510-795-9200 | www.salangrestaurant.com

Fremont's "little Kabul" has "its gem" in this affordable, "low-key Afghani" offering "warm service" and an "excellent variety" of "authentic, well-prepared" "kebabs", "curries", "*aushak*" (Afghan-style ravioli) and other "delightful surprises" including "terrific" "vegetarian options"; "come with your family or a large group of friends", and try the "traditional floor seating" in a special section draped with colorful fabric to resemble a tent.

Sasa Japanese   26 | 25 | 24 | $45

Walnut Creek | 1432 N. Main St. (Cypress Dr.) | 925-210-0188 | www.sasawc.com

"Mouthwatering combinations" from an "interesting izakaya-style menu" – plus "creative cocktails", a "superb" staff and "wow-factor" decor – have turned this Walnut Creek Japanese into a "trendy hot spot"; though some complain it's "noisy" and a little "overpriced", the "exquisite presentations" and "creative" dishes, including "innovative" sushi, are sure to please; P.S. the plant-filled "outdoor" patio is a "delightful" plus.

Saul's Restaurant & Delicatessen Deli   20 | 15 | 18 | $22

Berkeley | 1475 Shattuck Ave. (bet. Rose & Vine Sts.) | 510-848-3354 | www.saulsdeli.com

"Authentic Jewish comfort food" like at a "real East Coast deli – only better" (since it's "taken up a notch with good Californian ingredients") means "you cannot go wrong" at this "old-fashioned" Berkeley standby with "pleasant" service; while a few might kvetch about "small", "overpriced" portions, there's always a "wait" on "weekends."

⌷ Scott's Seafood Seafood   23 | 22 | 23 | $44

Walnut Creek | 1333 N. California Blvd. (Bonanza St.) | 925-934-1300 | www.scottswc.com

⌷ Scott's Seafood Restaurant Seafood

Oakland | 2 Broadway (Embarcadero W.) | 510-444-3456 | www.scottseastbay.com

"After all these years", these seafooders remain "good for a chain", with an "extensive menu" of "well-prepared" fin fare plus "classic" cocktails and "excellent house wines" to wash it down; "charming" servers enhance the "high-class" (some say "old-fashioned") vibe, reflected in tabs that can run on the "pricey" side; P.S. Oakland and San Jose offer "beautiful" waterfront views.

Sea Salt Seafood   21 | 17 | 19 | $37

Berkeley | 2512 San Pablo Ave. (Dwight Way) | 510-883-1720 | www.seasaltrestaurant.com

"One of the Lalime's spin-offs", this Berkeley "sustainable" seafood spot offers "fresh" and "simple" fin fare – like the "excellent" fish 'n' chips, beloved lobster rolls and a trout BLT that's "worth the visit alone" – served by "friendly" staffers in a "casual" setting with "patio" seating; prices are "reasonable", and "happy-hour deals" with "imaginative cocktails" and "dollar oysters" add value.

Shalimar ⊘ *Indian/Pakistani* | 24 | 7 | 14 | $16 |
Fremont | 3325 Walnut Ave. (bet. Liberty St. & Paseo Padre Pkwy.) | 510-494-1919 | www.shalimarsf.com
See review in City of San Francisco Directory.

Shen Hua *Chinese* | 23 | 18 | 20 | $25 |
Berkeley | 2914 College Ave. (bet. Ashby Ave. & Russell St.) | 510-883-1777
"Fantastic Chinese with a kick" and the "fastest service on the planet" has Berkeley denizens saying "you can't go wrong" at this "big, airy" "warehouse"-like spot that's "extremely kid-friendly"; sure, it gets "loud" and the fare, for some, seems "more American than authentic", but "reasonable" prices and "gargantuan" cocktails keep fans "going back."

Sidebar ⊠ *Californian/Mediterranean* | 22 | 20 | 20 | $36 |
Oakland | 542 Grand Ave. (bet. Euclid Ave. & MacArthur Blvd.) | 510-452-9500 | www.sidebar-oakland.com
"Local, casual cuisine" attracts an "eclectic crowd" to this "hip" Oakland gastropub dishing out Cal-Med fare and run by "veteran folks" (from the defunct Zax Tavern); though perfectionists find it "predictably good but rarely outstanding", "inventive cocktails" and "cool" service in a "comfortable" space with a U-shaped copper bar add to the "value."

Skates on the Bay *American* | 20 | 25 | 21 | $40 |
Berkeley | 100 Seawall Dr. (University Ave.) | 510-549-1900 | www.skatesonthebay.com
While "the food's quite good" at this midpriced American with a "terrific location right on the water" in the Berkeley Marina, it's the "breathtaking views of San Francisco and the bridges across the bay" that steal the show; though service can be "spotty", fans maintain this locale is "more than just a tourist trap", and a recent renovation should make it even more "popular for happy hour" and "special occasions."

Soi4 *Thai* | 23 | 19 | 22 | $33 |
Oakland | 5421 College Ave. (bet. Kales & Manila Aves.) | 510-655-0889 | www.soifour.com
"If this is Thai street food, then bring on more streets like it" praise proponents of the "unconventional but tasty" "Bangkok-style" dishes that are "attractively presented" at this "stylish/casual" Oaklander with floor-to-ceiling windows and "modern" decor; add in "gracious" servers who are adept at "explaining dishes like they cooked them themselves" to see why it's a "local favorite."

Soule Domain *American* | ∇ 24 | 24 | 24 | $53 |
Kings Beach | 9983 Cove Ave. (Stateline Rd.) | 530-546-7529 | www.souledomain.com
Tahoe travelers and locals say it's "always a treat to go back" to this "gem" hidden behind a Kings Beach strip mall, thanks to the chef-owner and his "knowledgeable staff"; the American fare and "great wine selection" make it a standout for the area, while the vintage "cozy" log cabin digs seem built for "fireplace nights."

FOOD | DECOR | SERVICE | COST

Southie *American* | 24 | 15 | 23 | $20

Oakland | 6311 College Ave. (bet. Alcatraz Ave. & 63rd St.) | 510-654-0100 | www.southieoakland.com

Whether for "breakfast, lunch or dinner", they're "slinging some great dishes" at this pint-size New American "Wood Tavern spin-off" in Oakland, including "incredible, original sandwiches" by day and small bites at night, plus "great beers on tap"; it "might seem a little pricey, but it's well worth it" for "good-quality" eats with a "warm and friendly" vibe.

Speisekammer Ⓜ *German* | 22 | 18 | 21 | $29

Alameda | 2424 Lincoln Ave. (Everett St.) | 510-522-1300 | www.speisekammer.com

"Get your schnitzel fix" at this "real-deal" Alameda German that turns out "comfort classics" – the "kasespaetzle" (i.e. mac 'n' cheese) "will rock your world" – and a "great selection" of Deutsch "biers" served in "liter steins" by "personable" staffers; the decor is as "authentic" as the midpriced menu, making you feel like you're "in Munich", particularly outside on the spacious patio that's popular "for a party."

Sunnyside Lodge Restaurant *Seafood/Steak* | ▽ 20 | 24 | 21 | $39

Tahoe City | 1850 W. Lake Blvd. (bet. Pineland Dr. & Sequoia Ave.) | 530-583-7200 | www.sunnysideresort.com

"Right on the lake" in Tahoe City, this midpriced surf 'n' turfer is equally "perfect" for "lunch or brunch" on the "sunny deck" in the summer or inside by the fire where it "feels like home" to the "snow" bunnies who "return" every year; "it's all about" the "inviting" "ambiance" and "breathtaking" views, though the food and service are certainly "good enough"; P.S. it's dinner-only during the winter months.

Sunrise Deli Ⓢ Ⓜ *Mideastern* | ▽ 24 | 11 | 19 | $13

Berkeley | 2456 Bancroft Way (Telegraph Ave.) | 510-845-9400 | www.sunrisedeli.net

See review in City of San Francisco Directory.

Tacubaya *Mexican* | 23 | 15 | 17 | $17

Berkeley | 1788 Fourth St. (bet. Hearst Ave. & Virginia St.) | 510-525-5160 | www.tacubaya.net

"Sophisticated" Mexican fare draws noshers to this "cafeteria"-style "taqueria" (an "offshoot of Doña Tomás") tucked among Berkeley's Fourth Street shops, where "fantastic fresh corn tortillas" provide "authentic flavor" and the "seasonal menu" makes "you feel like there's a chef in the kitchen, not a CEO"; the decor isn't much to look at, but "outdoor seating", "efficient service" and "super-cheap" tabs compensate.

Tamarindo Antojeria Mexicana Ⓢ *Mexican* | 25 | 21 | 21 | $34

Oakland | 468 Eighth St. (bet. B'way & Washington St.) | 510-444-1944 | www.tamarindoantojeria.com

"Fine Mexican dining" in "a modern, trendy setting" brings Oaklanders Downtown for "fresh and flavorful" small plates that are "cleverly reinvented" with "depth", "complexity" and "gourmet ingredients"; the "small portions disappoint a little" "compared to the prices", but "caring" service plus "excellent margaritas" and a "great tequila selection" help to ease any shortcomings.

Thai Buddhist Temple
Mongkolratanaram Buffet Ⓜ✉ _Thai_

▽ 26 | 13 | 18 | $12

Berkeley | Wat Mongkolratanaram Buddhist Temple | 1911 Russell St.
(bet. Martin Luther King Jr. Way & Otis St.) | 510-849-3419

"Berkeley's best-kept culinary secret" might just be the "Sunday morning festivities" "in the courtyard" of this "actual Thai temple" that hosts a once-a-week, "very casual" "Thai food buffet" where "locals" and "temple-goers" congregate for "cheap and delicious" Siamese home cooking and exchanging "friendly namastes" (greetings); "don't expect a fine-dining experience" (there's only "garden seating"), but it's "definitely worth a try" "at least once."

360° Gourmet _Eclectic_

22 | 19 | 21 | $26

Alameda | 853 Marina Village Pkwy. (Constitution Way) | 510-814-9003
Concord | 1975 Diamond Blvd. (Willow Pass Rd.) | no phone
Oakland | Oakland Int'l Airport, Terminal 1 | 1 Airport Dr.
(Ron Cowan Pkwy.) | no phone
Walnut Creek | 1558 Newell Ave. (Main St.) | 925-935-1026
www.360gb.com
See review in City of San Francisco Directory.

Top Dog _Hot Dogs_

23 | 10 | 18 | $8

Berkeley | 2160 Center St. (Oxford St.) | 510-849-0176
Berkeley | 2503 Hearst Ave. (Euclid Ave.) | 510-843-1241
Berkeley | 2534 Durant Ave. | 510-843-5967 ◐
Oakland | 3272 Lakeshore Ave. (Trestle Glen Rd.) | 510-419-0333
Oakland | CVS | 5100 Broadway (51st St.) | 510-601-1187
www.topdoghotdogs.com

"Every type of sausage you can imagine" – "kielbasa", "calabrese", "veggie", "chicken apple", "bird dog" (turkey) and more – is "cooked perfectly and ready when you are" at this Berkeley trio with two sister outlets in Oakland; there's not much in the way of decor, but the offerings make for "quick" and "delicious drunk food", especially since Durant Avenue is "open late."

Townhouse Bar & Grill Ⓢ _Californian_

21 | 19 | 21 | $39

Emeryville | 5862 Doyle St. (bet. 59th & Powell Sts.) | 510-652-6151 |
www.townhousebarandgrill.com

"Hidden inside" a townhouse, this "semi-fancy" "favorite" in a former Emeryville "speakeasy" pulls off the "right balance of comfort and creativity", proffering "flavorful" Californian "comfort food" in "old-time" surroundings (think potbelly stove, wood beams and "brass chandeliers"); add in "friendly" staffers and a "nice outdoor patio", and no wonder most maintain "it's not just another place to grab a bite."

Trader Vic's Ⓜ _Polynesian_

19 | 23 | 20 | $45

Emeryville | 9 Anchor Dr. (Powell St.) | 510-653-3400 |
www.tradervicsemeryville.com

Take "a mini tropical vacation" at this "truly timeless" Polynesian in Emeryville complete with "island atmosphere" and "fancy" "tiki drinks"; "critics" contending this "institution" is "past its prime" with merely "average" fare and service are missing the point that a couple of "old-fashioned" mai tais and "great pupus" still make for a "fun night" – plus there's a "spectacular" bay view; P.S. the Palo Alto branch has closed.

Trattoria Corso *Italian*
25 | 19 | 22 | $42

Berkeley | 1788 Shattuck Ave. (Delaware St.) | 510-704-8004 |
www.trattoriacorso.com

Rivoli's "smaller, more casual" trattoria sister near the Berkeley Rep
serves up "divine pasta" and other "rustic" Florentine-style cucina
plus "top-rate" wines at "value prices"; while it gets "noisy" at times,
a "friendly and patient" staff and "black-and-white Italian movies
playing in the background" at the bar "overlooking the kitchen" add to
the "charming atmosphere."

Trattoria La Siciliana ⊅ *Italian*
24 | 17 | 18 | $33

Berkeley | 2993 College Ave. (bet. Ashby Ave. & Webster St.) |
510-704-1474 | www.trattoriasiciliana.com

"Fairly priced" and "family owned", this Berkeley Sicilian serves "unpretentious" fare that is "simple" and "beautiful", starting with the
"delicious" bread and "oil dip"; the wait is "horrific", the "cramped
quarters" are "always crowded" and "the kitchen is as slow as a Rome
traffic jam" – i.e. it's a "real", "authentic" Italian "find"; P.S. "cash only."

T Rex Barbecue *BBQ*
18 | 17 | 17 | $29

Berkeley | 1300 10th St. (Gilman St.) | 510-527-0099 | www.t-rex-bbq.com

Berkleyites seeking a "primal meat-eating experience" frequent this
"upscale BBQ" (from the "Lalime's family" of eateries) offering favorites like "beef brisket, babyback ribs" and "Southern fried chicken" in
a "cavernous open space" with "a full bar and TV screens"; the "staff
doesn't rush you" through the "comfort food at a comfortable price",
and an "excellent happy hour" tops it off.

Trueburger ⓔ *Burgers*
21 | 13 | 18 | $14

Oakland | 146 Grand Ave. (bet. Harrison & Valdez Sts.) | 510-208-5678 |
www.trueburgeroakland.com

Two Bay Wolf alums "focus on a single dish with such zeal, we all come
out ahead" at this Oakland bastion of "juicy" burgers made from "freshly
ground" meat ("vegetarian" options too) and served on buns that "beg
to be squeezed"; an "epic" mural of the city distinguishes the space, and
prices "won't break the bank"; dinner Wednesday–Saturday only.

Udupi Palace ⊅ *Indian/Vegetarian*
23 | 13 | 18 | $16

Berkeley | 1901-1903 University Ave. (Martin Luther King Jr. Way) |
510-843-6600 | www.udupipalaceca.com

See review in City of San Francisco Directory.

Uzen ⓔ *Japanese*
∇ 24 | 16 | 21 | $31

Oakland | 5415 College Ave. (bet. Kales & Manila Aves.) | 510-654-7753

"Restraint, balance and subtlety are the rules" at this "very bright, very
small" but "oh-so-delicious" Oakland Japanese serving "impeccably
fresh", "well-priced" sushi, "amazing" udon and other "traditional"
dishes in a "stark, modern" setting; "selection is limited", but the
"staff is attentive" and the "quality remains great."

Va de Vi *Eclectic*
25 | 22 | 22 | $44

Walnut Creek | 1511 Mt. Diablo Blvd. (Main St.) | 925-979-0100 |
www.va-de-vi-bistro.com

"Graze your way through" your meal on "haute cuisine small plates"
paired with "tempting wine flights" and delivered by "helpful" servers

at this "hip" Eclectic Walnut Creek eatery offering a sophisticated "combination of flavors"; some gripe that the "tiny" "tapas" "add up fa$t!" and tables are a bit too "close" for comfort, but groupies gush that "sharing oohs" with your neighbors is "the best part."

Vanessa's Bistro *French/Vietnamese*   23 | 19 | 21 | $37

Berkeley | 1715 Solano Ave. (Ensenada Ave.) | 510-525-8300 | www.vanessasbistro.com

Vanessa's Bistro 2 *French/Vietnamese*

Walnut Creek | 1329 N. Main St. (Duncan St.) | 925-891-4790 | www.vanessasbistro2.com

"Imaginative", "gorgeously presented" French-Vietnamese cuisine is "a tasty gourmet twist on home cooking" at this "family-run" East Bay duo (the Berkeley original and a newer, larger Walnut Creek locale) where a menu of mostly "small plates" "makes it easy to take advantage of the variety"; while service reviews are mixed, most applaud the "top-notch food at midrange prices."

Venezia *Italian*   21 | 23 | 22 | $34

Berkeley | 1799 University Ave. (Grant St.) | 510-849-4681 | www.caffevenezia.com

"Look up and you might catch a glimpse of someone's undies" amid the "clothes drying on the line" (don't worry, it's all part of the "witty", faux–"Italian village decor") at this midpriced Berkeley "standby" serving up "solid" pastas, pizzas and other classics; admirers applaud service that's "beyond attentive" and a menu with "something for everybody", including "out-of-town guests", "kids" and "large parties."

Venus *Californian*   24 | 20 | 22 | $32

Berkeley | 2327 Shattuck Ave. (bet. Bancroft Way & Durant Ave.) | 510-540-5950 | www.venusrestaurant.net

"Everyone leaves contented" at this "funky" Berkeley Californian, where "consistently delectable" dishes are "put together with great care and integrity" using "organic, sustainable" and "seasonal" ingredients; granted, it gets "loud and crowded" in the "cozy" dining room, but "friendly" servers help compensate, as do the "many vegetarian options" and "moderate" prices.

Vic Stewart's Ⓜ *Steak*   24 | 25 | 24 | $57

Walnut Creek | 850 S. Broadway (bet. Mt. Diablo Blvd. & Newell Ave.) | 925-943-5666 | www.vicstewarts.com

"It doesn't get much more romantic" than dining in a "private" compartment of an old "railroad parlor car" at this "standby steakhouse" located in a historic, circa-1891 "train station"; "a mainstay in Walnut Creek for many years", it's "a dazzling choice for carnivores", and while tabs are "quite expensive", service is "outstanding."

Vik's Chaat Corner *Indian*   25 | 11 | 13 | $14

Berkeley | 2390 Fourth St. (Channing Way) | 510-644-4432 | www.vikschaatcorner.com

"Authentic South Indian snacks" and "stuff you won't see anywhere else" are among the "delicious" "street food" at this "easy-on-the-wallet" Berkeley quick-service cafe; seats can be "hard to get" in the "warehouse" space with "all of the charm of the Mumbai airport crossed with your school cafeteria", but the "small Indian grocery market" up front is a boon for home cooks; P.S. 6 PM closing Monday–Thursday, 8 PM Friday–Sunday.

Walnut Creek Yacht Club ☒ *Seafood*   24 | 19 | 22 | $42

Walnut Creek | 1555 Bonanza St. (Locust St.) | 925-944-3474 | www.walnutcreekyachtclub.com

Though this "popular" Walnut Creek spot is "miles from any body of water", the seafood on its ever-changing menu is "so fresh it almost bites you"; alas, it can get "very loud" and the nautical decor is not to everyone's taste, but "a comfy neighborhood vibe" and "friendly" service help make up for "crowds" and "pricey" tabs.

☒ Wente Vineyards,   26 | 27 | 25 | $58
The Restaurant at *Californian/Mediterranean*

Livermore | 5050 Arroyo Rd. (Wetmore Rd.) | 925-456-2450 | www.wentevineyards.com

It's "heaven" dining "on the patio" in a "gorgeous setting" "among the vineyards" at this "sophisticated" Livermore "destination"; "naturally", there's a "fantastic wine list", and the chef "pulls out the stops" for his "exciting, seasonal menu" of Cal-Med cuisine "served with pride and attention", making it "worth a trip" to this "out-of-the-way" location.

☒ Wolfdale's *Californian*   27 | 24 | 26 | $56

Tahoe City | 640 N. Lake Blvd. (bet. Grove St. & Pioneer Way) | 530-583-5700 | www.wolfdales.com

"Elegant" meals are "worth going out of your way" for at this "special-occasion" North Shore "favorite" in Tahoe City that "remains great after 30 years", offering a unique East-meets-West Californian menu and a "fine wine list" in an upscale lakeside setting; it's not cheap, but "the chef knows his stuff", and "great views" from the deck, a bocce court and happy-hour specials add to the appeal.

Wood Tavern *Californian*   26 | 19 | 23 | $44

Oakland | 6317 College Ave. (bet. Alcatraz Ave. & 63rd St.) | 510-654-6607 | www.woodtavern.net

"Pick anything on the menu" and "you won't be disappointed" at this "perpetually packed" Rockridge Californian that "lives up to all the hype" with "divine" "gourmet comfort food" delivered by "respectful servers" at a price that's "right"; sure, "the noise level requires texting your dinner partner", but admirers really "don't care" if they "can't hear", as they're "too busy eating."

Xolo Taqueria ☒ *Mexican*   ▽ 23 | 19 | 21 | $12

Oakland | 1916 Telegraph Ave. (19th St.) | 510-986-0151 | www.xolotaqueria.com

"Tasty, updated Mexican" fare is on offer at this "large", quick-service taqueria (sibling to "Tacubaya and Doña Tomás") in Oakland's Uptown that redefines "what a burrito" (or a taco) "can be" with "unique" options; the low prices and "cool vibe", not to mention the proximity to the "Fox Theater", make it popular for "after-concert."

Xyclo *Vietnamese*   21 | 18 | 20 | $28

Oakland | 4218 Piedmont Ave. (bet. Entrada & Ridgeway Aves.) | 510-654-2681 | www.xyclorestaurant.com

"Everything tastes bright" at this Oakland "neighborhood favorite" that "brings a fresh approach to Vietnamese cuisine" with its "creative dishes"; the modern decor with lots of warm wood "puts out a fancy vibe", yet the fare is still "affordable" and the place is "family-friendly", with a staff that's "very attentive."

Yankee Pier *New England/Seafood* | 19 | 16 | 19 | $34 |

Lafayette | Lafayette Mercantile Bldg. | 3593 Mt. Diablo Blvd. (bet. Dewing Ave. & Lafayette Circle) | 925-283-4100 | www.yankeepier.com
See review in North of San Francisco Directory.

Yoshi's at Jack London Square *Japanese* | 23 | 23 | 23 | $44 |

Oakland | Jack London Sq. | 510 Embarcadero W. (bet. Clay & Washington Sts.) | 510-238-9200 | www.yoshis.com
"Beyond the jazz", it's worth "checking out" the dining room attached to this "world-class" Oakland music club, serving "fabulous" sushi and "imaginative Japanese-fusion cuisine" by a chef who "really knows his flavors"; yes, it's a tad "pricey", but those in the groove appreciate the "cool vibe" and "splendid service", plus you "get dibs on seating for performances" if you eat here.

Zabu Zabu *Japanese*   ∇ | 24 | 22 | 20 | $32 |

Berkeley | 1919 Addison St. (bet. Martin Luther King Jr. Way & Milvia St.) | 510-848-9228 | www.zabu-zabu.com
"Unlimited" shabu-shabu is the "outstanding signature" dish at this affordable Berkeley Japanese that also offers a host of staples like sushi rolls, dumplings and tempura; a "hard-to-find" location is a drawback, but the payoff comes in "heaping plates" perfect for sharing delivered with "friendly" service.

☒ Zachary's Chicago Pizza *Pizza* | 26 | 15 | 19 | $21 |

Berkeley | 1853 Solano Ave. (The Alameda) | 510-525-5950
Oakland | 5801 College Ave. (bet. Claremont Ave. & Grove Shafter Frwy.) | 510-655-6385
San Ramon | Crow Canyon Crest Shopping Ctr. | 3110 Crow Canyon Pl. (Crow Canyon Rd.) | 925-244-1222
www.zacharys.com
"Stuffed" or "thin-crust" pies that give "other pizzas inferiority complexes" pack the "crowds" into this East Bay trio of parlors despite their "basic" decor, variable service and somewhat "pricey" tabs; the "buttery, flaky" crusts topped with "zesty", "chunky" tomato sauce are "highly addictive", just "prepare for a wait" or "call ahead" and get it "to go."

Zatar ☒Ⓜ⇪ *Mediterranean* | 25 | 20 | 23 | $37 |

Berkeley | 1981 Shattuck Ave. (University Ave.) | 510-841-1981 | www.zatarrestaurant.com
"Fresh" ingredients including produce grown by the married chef-owners in "their own organic garden" contribute to the eclectic "Mediterranean-inspired" menu at this Berkeley charmer; at times service can be "a little slow", but the "small", "cozy place" with "enchanting decor" has moderate prices; P.S. open Wednesday–Saturday.

Latest openings, menus, photos and more on plus.google.com/local

NORTH OF SAN FRANCISCO

Top Food

29 French Laundry | *Amer./Fr.*	Étoile | *Californian*
28 Redd | *Californian*	Sea Modern Thai | *Thai*
27 Cucina Paradiso | *Italian*	Della Fattoria | *Bakery/Eclectic*
Bistro des Copains | *French*	Meadowood Rest. | *Cal.*
Farmhouse Inn | *Cal.*	Royal Thai* | *Thai*
Cole's Chop House | *Steak*	Bistro Jeanty | *French*
Madrona Manor | *Amer./Fr.*	La Toque | *French*
Terra | *American*	Marché aux Fleurs | *French*
Auberge du Soleil | *Cal./Fr.*	La Gare | *French*
Sushi Ran | *Japanese*	Osake | *Cal./Japanese*

BY CUISINE

AMERICAN
29 French Laundry
27 Madrona Manor
Terra
Cafe La Haye
26 Ad Hoc

CALIFORNIAN
28 Redd
27 Farmhouse Inn
Auberge du Soleil
Étoile
Meadowood Rest.

ECLECTIC
27 Della Fattoria
25 Graffiti
Willi's Wine Bar
Celadon
24 Willow Wood

FRENCH
27 Bistro des Copains
Bistro Jeanty
La Toque
Marché aux Fleurs
La Gare

ITALIAN
27 Cucina Paradiso
26 Picco

Diavola
Cook St. Helena
Lococo's Cucina Rustica

JAPANESE
27 Sushi Ran
Osake
26 Hana Japanese
25 Morimoto Napa
20 Tex Wasabi's

MEDITERRANEAN
26 Central Market
25 Harvest Moon Café
Insalata's
24 Willow Wood
23 Hurley's

PIZZA
26 Diavola
Rosso Pizzeria
Pizzeria Picco
25 Arizmendi
Redd Wood

SEAFOOD/STEAK
27 Cole's Chop House
26 Press
Hog Island Oyster Co.
Stark's Steakhouse
Willi's Seafood

Excludes places with low votes, unless otherwise indicated; *indicates a tie with restaurant above

BY SPECIAL FEATURE

BREAKFAST/BRUNCH

- 28 Redd
- 26 Downtown Bakery
- 25 Buckeye
- 24 Fremont Diner
- Willow Wood

CHILD-FRIENDLY

- 26 Cook St. Helena
- Rosso Pizzeria
- 25 Fish
- 23 Pizzeria Tra Vigne
- 22 Gott's Roadside

NEWCOMERS (RATED)

- 25 Alex Restaurant
- Redd Wood
- 22 Brassica
- 21 Mateo's Cocina Latine
- Hawk's Tavern

OUTDOOR SEATING

- 27 Madrona Manor
- Auberge du Soleil
- 25 Bistro Don Giovanni
- 24 Tra Vigne
- Angèle

PEOPLE-WATCHING

- 26 Bouchon
- Picco
- Solbar
- 25 Morimoto
- 20 Spoonbar

ROMANCE

- 29 French Laundry
- 27 Farmhouse Inn
- Madrona Manor
- Terra
- Auberge du Soleil

SMALL PLATES

- 26 Picco
- 25 Willi's Wine Bar
- Willi's Seafood
- 22 Monti's Rotisserie
- Underwood

VIEWS

- 27 Auberge du Soleil
- Étoile
- Meadowood Rest.
- 25 Murray Circle
- 23 Brix

WINE BARS

- 27 Sushi Ran
- Étoile
- 26 Fig Café & Wine Bar
- 25 Willi's Wine Bar
- 21 Oxbow Wine Merchant∇

WINNING WINE LISTS

- 29 French Laundry
- 28 Redd
- 27 Terra
- Étoile
- La Toque

BY LOCATION

MARIN COUNTY

- 27 Sushi Ran
- Sea Thai Bistro
- Royal Thai
- Marché aux Fleurs
- 26 Picco

MENDOCINO COUNTY

- 26 Cafe Beaujolais
- Mendo Bistro
- 955 Restaurant
- Albion River Inn
- 24 MacCallum House

NAPA COUNTY

- 29 French Laundry
- 28 Redd
- 27 Cole's Chop House
- Terra
- Auberge du Soleil

SONOMA COUNTY

- 27 Cucina Paradiso
- Bistro des Copains
- Farmhouse Inn
- Madrona Manor
- Sea Thai Bistro

Top Decor

28	Auberge du Soleil			Graffiti

28 Auberge du Soleil

27 Caprice
French Laundry
Étoile

26 Farm
Meadowood Rest.
Madrona Manor
Murray Circle
El Paseo
Napa Valley Wine Train

Graffiti
Farmhouse Inn

25 Tra Vigne
John Ash & Co.
Cole's Chop House
Dry Creek Kitchen
Press
Rustic
Mendocino Hotel Rest.
Terra

Top Service

28 French Laundry

27 Madrona Manor
Meadowood Rest.
Terra
Étoile
Farmhouse Inn*
Auberge du Soleil

26 Bistro des Copains
Cucina Paradiso
Marché aux Fleurs

La Toque
La Gare
Redd

25 Cafe La Haye
Ad Hoc
Cole's Chop House
Bistro 29
Central Market
Sea Thai Bistro
Press

BEST BUYS: BANG FOR THE BUCK

1. In-N-Out
2. Arizmendi
3. Cheese Steak Shop
4. El Farolito
5. Pearl's Phat Burgers
6. Downtown Bakery & Creamery
7. Model Bakery
8. La Boulange
9. Sol Food
10. Crepevine
11. Pica Pica Maize Kitchen
12. Betty's Fish & Chips
13. Barney's Gourmet Hamburgers
14. Mombo's Pizza
15. Emporio Rulli
16. Joe's Taco Lounge & Salsaria
17. Avatar's
18. Jimtown Store
19. C Casa
20. Royal Thai

BEST BUYS: OTHER GOOD VALUES

Alexis Baking Company
Amici's
Azzurro Pizzeria
Cafe Citti
Café Lotus
Cucina Paradiso
Della Fattoria
Diavola Pizzeria
Fremont Diner
Gott's Roadside

Graffiti
Hopmonk Tavern
Pizza Antica
Pizzeria Picco
Pizzeria Tra Vigne
Rosso Pizzeria
Sazon Peruvian
Sea Thai
Sugo
Willow Wood

North of San Francisco

☑ Addendum M *American* | 24 | 15 | 19 | $21 |

Yountville | 6476 Washington St. (bet. Mission St. & Oak Circle) |
707-944-1565 | www.adhocrestaurant.com

Thomas Keller fans say his seasonal American take-out joint dishing
out the chef's famous buttermilk fried chicken and "BBQ plates"
along with beer and wine from a small garden shack just behind Ad
Hoc is the "best food you'll ever have in a parking lot"; the bird is "everything it's cracked up to be" and the "amazing" brisket is "no slouch
either" – though it's pretty "pricey" for a boxed lunch and "picnic
bench" seating; P.S. open from early spring to late fall, for lunch
Thursday–Saturday only.

☑ Ad Hoc *American* | 27 | 22 | 25 | $68 |

Yountville | 6476 Washington St. (bet. Mission St. & Oak Circle) |
707-944-2487 | www.adhocrestaurant.com

With its "no-nonsense" decor and "seemingly pedestrian meat-and-
potatoes" menu, Thomas Keller's "casually magnificent" Yountville
American offers "family-style" set dinners and "outstanding Sunday
brunches" "executed with a precision that belies its free-wheeling
name"; true, wine comes in "water glasses" and rock music fills the air,
but service is "high-end" and that "famous fried chicken" ("served every other Monday" and daily at neighboring Addendum) is "pricey"
but "worth every penny."

Albion River Inn Restaurant *Californian* | 25 | 24 | 24 | $49 |

Albion | Albion River Inn | 3790 N. Hwy. 1 (Albion-Little River Rd.) |
707-937-1919 | www.albionriverinn.com

Whether you "stay the night or head up to Mendocino town" afterwards,
"by all means take a ride" on "the world's most scenic coastal high-
ways" to this "romantic getaway" in Albion that's a "win on all fronts";
sure, the "drop-dead gorgeous oceanfront views" are what "elevate" it
to "an extraordinary experience", but the "wonderful" Californian cuisine is "matched by warm, attentive service", an "extensive wine list"
and an "amazing collection of single malts" (125 kinds).

Alexis Baking Company *Bakery* | 22 | 14 | 17 | $19 |
(aka ABC)

Napa | 1517 Third St. (bet. Church & School Sts.) | 707-258-1827 |
www.alexisbakingcompany.com

You're more likely to "run into locals" than tourists at this "wonderful little" bakery/diner in Napa that "keeps it simple" with a
"unique take on breakfast" ("best huevos rancheros ever"), daily
lunch specials and "off-the-charts" "homemade bread and pastries"; there's "no dinner", and the service and decor is "chaotic" at
best, but many deem it the "best brunch place in town" providing you
"get there before the crowds."

NEW Alex Restaurant M *Italian* | 25 | 22 | 23 | $62 |

Rutherford | 1140 Rutherford Rd. (Rte. 29/St. Helena Hwy.) |
707-967-5500 | www.alexitalianrestaurant.com

An "excellent addition to upvalley fine dining", this sommelier-backed
Rutherford newcomer (occupying the space that formerly housed La

Toque) lures in "locals" with "pricey" but "distinctive", "authentic" cuisine from Liguria and Emilia-Romagna prepared by a former Bottega chef; early adopters give props to the "excellent Italian wine list, with affordable choices" and recommend a "table by the fireplace" or on the "patio when the weather is good", though early critics warn service can be "inconsistent", it can also be "excellent."

All Seasons Bistro Ⓜ *Californian*   24 | 21 | 23 | $37

Calistoga | 1400 Lincoln Ave. (Washington St.) | 707-942-9111 | www.allseasonsnapavalley.net

"Tastefully prepared" plates offered in "charming" bistro environs make this Calistoga Californian a "pleasant" "place to escape", especially since service is "friendly" too; the wine selection is "excellent" but you can also bring a bottle from the on-site retail shop (for a corkage fee).

🄿 Amici's East Coast Pizzeria *Pizza*   21 | 17 | 20 | $22

San Rafael | 1242 Fourth St. (bet. B & C Sts.) | 415-455-9777 | www.amicis.com

See review in City of San Francisco Directory.

Angèle *French*   24 | 23 | 23 | $49

Napa | Hatt/Napa Mill Bldg. | 540 Main St. (5th St.) | 707-252-8115 | www.angelerestaurant.com

"It's hard to beat" the "amazing" ambiance "indoors and out" at this "posh little bistro" set in an old boathouse "on the banks of the Napa River" where "consistently good", midpriced, "upscale French comfort food", a "lovely" dog-friendly patio and a slightly "snooty" staff combine to "remind one of the South of France"; a bar pouring "excellent cocktails" and wines keeps it "crowded with locals"; P.S. the arrival of a new chef is not reflected in the Food score.

Applewood Restaurant Ⓜ *Californian*   24 | 21 | 23 | $51

Guerneville | Applewood Inn, Restaurant & Spa | 13555 Hwy. 116 (River Rd.) | 707-869-9093 | www.applewoodinn.com

Like a "cosmopolitan retreat among the redwoods", this Guerneville "Euro-style inn" "hits all the right notes" serving Californian fare including tasting menus delivered with "unpretentious" service that "exceeds expectations"; though it's not cheap, a "romantic" "country" setting warmed by a "cozy fireplace" and an "approachable and exciting" wine list add to reasons most would gladly "drive back up to the middle of nowhere"; P.S. closed Monday–Tuesday.

🄿 Arizmendi Ⓩ *Bakery/Pizza*   25 | 13 | 21 | $11

San Rafael | 1002 Fourth St. (bet. A St. & Lootens Pl.) | 415-456-4093 | www.fourthstreet.arizmendi.coop

See review in City of San Francisco Directory.

Arun Ⓩ *Thai*   ▽ 25 | 22 | 22 | $19

Novato | 385 Bel Marin Keys Blvd. (Hamilton Dr.) | 415-883-8017

In a "neighborhood of business offices", this Novato "gem" stands out with "authentic, hearty" Thai cooking that will "satisfy and comfort"; the earth-toned space can be "tight", especially during its "popular lunch", but service is "quick" and tabs budget-friendly, so most agree it's a "great find."

☑ Auberge du Soleil Restaurant *Californian/French*

| 27 | 28 | 27 | $88 |

Rutherford | Auberge du Soleil | 180 Rutherford Hill Rd. (Silverado Trail) | 707-967-3111 | www.aubergedusoleil.com

"If you want to woo someone, this is the place" with its spectacular" "views of the Napa Valley", "superb" Cal-French "fusion" cuisine and "incredible wine list" bolstered by "intuitive, hover-free" service, all making for a Rutherford "jewel" and all-around "perfect" spot for a "special occasion"; acolytes assure it's "expensive but worth it", while the bar menu or "lunch on the deck" are more affordable options at a "destination" that's a slice of "heaven."

Avatar's ⊠ *Indian*

| 24 | 13 | 23 | $20 |

Sausalito | 2656 Bridgeway (Coloma St.) | 415-332-8083

Avatar's Punjabi Burrito *Indian*

NEW **Larkspur** | 574 Magnolia Ave. (Doherty Dr.) | 415-945-1808
Mill Valley | 15 Madrona St. (bet. Lovell & Throckmorton Aves.) | 415-381-8293 ⊠
Petaluma | 131 Kentucky St. (bet. Washington St. & Western Ave.) | 707-765-9775
www.enjoyavatars.com

Prepare to "wolf down" "exotic", "flavor-filled" Punjabi burritos, "incomparable" enchiladas and other"innovative Indian fusion cuisine" at this "budget-friendly" foursome tended by the "friendliest servers" who "guide you through the crazy fun menu"; sure, they're "spartan in atmosphere" (and Mill Valley has few seats), but since they're "exceptionally habit forming", most insist "you'll likely become a regular."

Azzurro Pizzeria e Enoteca *Pizza*

| 23 | 20 | 21 | $27 |

Napa | 1260 Main St. (Clinton St.) | 707-255-5552 | www.azzurropizzeria.com

The 'in' "place for pizza in Napa", this "local go-to" dishes "delicious" thin-crust pies complemented by a "nice selection of wines"; service is "fast" and prices area modest, so despite a "cool", "happening" vibe, it's still a "no-reservations, no-fuss" pick.

Balboa Cafe *American*

| 20 | 19 | 21 | $36 |

Mill Valley | 38 Miller Ave. (Sunnyside Ave.) | 415-381-7321 | www.balboacafe.com

See review in City of San Francisco Directory.

Bank Café & Bar *French*

▽ | 24 | 20 | 21 | $40 |

Napa | Westin Verasa Napa | 1314 McKinstry St. (Soscol Ave.) | 707-257-5151 | www.latoque.com

Ken Frank's casual, all-day French in the Westin Verasa Napa delivers "La Toque–quality" regional à la carte and prix fixe meals at prices that won't break the bank; the "blessedly quiet" room and "nice ambiance" make it a "great place" "to unwind at the end of the day", particularly if the more formal dining room "next door" "is not an option."

BarBersQ *BBQ*

| 22 | 18 | 21 | $33 |

Napa | Bel Aire Plaza | 3900 Bel Aire Plaza (Trancas St.) | 707-224-6600 | www.barbersq.com

A "reliable go-to" when you have a 'cue "craving", this Napa BBQ joint delivers "consistently good" "down-home" eats bolstered by "local wine pairings"; its "relaxed" "strip-mall" setting is "pleasant" enough, service gets solid marks and prices are "reasonable", so it's a "locals' spot" that also appeals as a "place to bring the kids when visiting wine country."

Bar Bocce *Pizza* | 22 | 21 | 19 | $31
Sausalito | 1250 Bridgeway (bet. Pine & Turney Sts.) | 415-331-0555 | www.barbocce.com

Take a "micro vacation" at this "right-on-the-water" Sausalito hang offering a midpriced menu of "creative" sourdough pizza, "amazing salads" and "delicious" cask wine in "tiny" digs elevated by a fire pit-enhanced back patio and bocce court; sure, service can sometimes be "slow", but with a "laid-back" vibe and "breathtaking view overlooking the harbor", many ask "what's the rush?"

Barndiva 🅼 *American* | 25 | 24 | 23 | $49
Healdsburg | 231 Center St. (Matheson St.) | 707-431-0100 | www.barndiva.com

"A true wine country experience" awaits at this "charming and rustic" Healdsburg American where "knowledgeable" servers deliver "inspiring", "beautifully presented" plates displaying an "imaginative use of" "farm-fresh" ingredients; the "art-filled" interior has a "relaxed" atmosphere and outside is "spacious and gorgeous", so the only "small minus" is tabs some "wish were more barnlike."

Barney's Gourmet Hamburgers *Burgers* | 22 | 16 | 18 | $17
San Rafael | 1020 Court St. (4th St.) | 415-454-4594 | www.barneyshamburgers.com

See review in City of San Francisco Directory.

Barolo *Italian* | ▽ 24 | 21 | 21 | $37
Calistoga | Mount View Hotel | 1457 Lincoln Ave. (bet. Fair Way & Washington St.) | 707-942-9900 | www.barolocalistoga.com

"Italian comfort food" dished out in "comfy digs" makes this "unassuming neighborhood spot" inside the Mount View Hotel something of a Calistoga "hidden gem"; "friendly service" and a "good wine" list add to the "great value", and insiders "love the happy-hour drink prices."

Bar Terra *American* | ▽ 25 | 24 | 24 | $57
St. Helena | 1345 Railroad Ave. (bet. Adams St. & Hunt Ave.) | 707-963-8931 | www.terrarestaurant.com

Hiro Sone's "creative" à la carte menu features Asian-inflected New American "small plates" that are "excellent" ("as always") along with cocktails "that raise the bar on artisanal mixology" at this "casual" lounge offshoot of St. Helena's more formal Terra restaurant next door; the "lively" atmosphere and "friendly banter" between "knowledgeable" barkeeps and regulars make for a welcome "respite" from the stuffier "wine country" options.

Betty's Fish & Chips *British/Seafood* | 24 | 14 | 22 | $18
Santa Rosa | 4046 Sonoma Hwy. (bet. Bush Creek Rd. & Mission Blvd.) | 707-539-0899

"Take the whole family" to this "folksy" Santa Rosa seafooder with a "long-standing reputation" for some of the "best fish 'n' chips" and "even better pies"; sure, the "kitschy nautical decor" is "nothing to write home about", the space is "small" and tabs are "a little pricey"

NORTH OF SAN FRANCISCO

FOOD DECOR SERVICE COST

for the genre, but "friendly" staffers and a "homey atmosphere" still help keep it "busy and crowded."

☑ Bistro des Copains Ⓜ *French*   27 | 21 | 26 | $42

Occidental | 3782 Bohemian Hwy. (bet. Coleman Valley & Graton Rds.) | 707-874-2436 | www.bistrodescopains.com

"Worth going out of your way for – and you have to", this "*très charmant*" Gallic "sleeper" in the "remote" "hamlet of Occidental" offers "fabulous", "imaginative" Provençal dinners (including a "fine prix fixe" and "free corkage" on Sonoma wines on Thursdays); the kitchen's "beehive ovens" "add to the warm", "welcoming" feel that you get from the "friendliest" staff, making it truly a "bistro of friends" that attracts both "locals and tourists"; P.S. Wednesday–Sunday only.

Bistro Don Giovanni *Italian*   25 | 23 | 23 | $45

Napa | 4110 Howard Ln. (bet. Oak Knoll & Salvador Aves.) | 707-224-3300 | www.bistrodongiovanni.com

"Despite all the new upstarts", it's still "sublime" to "sit on the terrace" "surrounded by vineyards" at this "stunningly beautiful" yet "unpretentious" "Italian bistro" in Napa that's "favored by locals" for its "excellent" *cucina*, "good wine list" and "the warmest greeting"; it all comes at a "fair price", though the noise-sensitive note that the "Tuscan-ish" room and "fun bar" can get quite "loud", especially when the "horde of tourists descends."

Bistro Jeanty *French*   27 | 23 | 24 | $54

Yountville | 6510 Washington St. (Mulberry St.) | 707-944-0103 | www.bistrojeanty.com

"Francophiles" practically "hear Edith Piaf at the bar" at Philippe Jeanty's "celebrated" Yountville bistro that's "as authentic as a Left Bank beret", with "gracious" garçons proffering "crave-worthy French comfort food" at "fair prices"; if you can "ignore the calories" and a menu that "doesn't change", it's an "enchanting" lunch or dinner spot, particularly with "a glass of Pastis in the courtyard" or around the "communal table."

Bistro Ralph *Californian/French*   24 | 19 | 23 | $46

Healdsburg | 109 Plaza St. (bet. Center St. & Healdsburg Ave.) | 707-433-1380 | www.bistroralph.com

"Count on Ralph" Tingle to "mingle with the crowd" at his "classic", "convivial" bistro on Healdsburg Square that's been delivering "consistently well-prepared", "seasonal" French-Cal cuisine, plus a "fantastic Sonoma wine list" and "killer" martinis, since "before all the others came to town"; always "on the money", it's staffed by "the most personable" crew, and "you'll see lots of locals" alongside the "tourists", especially at lunch on the patio.

Bistro 29 ☒Ⓜ *French*   25 | 21 | 25 | $41

Santa Rosa | 620 Fifth St. (bet. D St. & Mendocino Ave.) | 707-546-2929 | www.bistro29.com

"Outstanding" "French cuisine in an intimate bistro" setting sums up this Santa Rosa "go-to", where "warm", "attentive" servers and an "excellent-value midweek prix fixe" (Tuesday–Thursday) also work in its favor; add in "affordable prices" and it's "one of the best kept secrets in Sonoma County."

Share your reviews on plus.google.com/local   283

Boca *Argentinean/Steak* | 25 | 22 | 22 | $41 |

Novato | 340 Ignacio Blvd. (Rte. 101) | 415-883-0901 |
www.bocasteak.com

Situated in Novato, this "Argentinean-style steakhouse" also offers
other "well-prepared" choices, like "delicious" salads and "don't-miss"
sides, to go along with its "to-die-for" chops; the wood-accented
space is "cozy", the "bar draws a festive happy-hour crowd" and service is generally "attentive", so if some consider prices on the "high"
side, they're still "reasonable for what you get."

Boon Eat + Drink *Californian* ▽ | 24 | 18 | 22 | $37 |

Guerneville | 16248 Main St. (bet. 4th & Mill Sts.) | 707-869-0780 |
www.eatatboon.com

"By far the hippest" eatery in town, this bistro "rocks Guerneville
to a new level" with its "fresh" Californian fare (some featuring
produce from their hotel garden nearby) plus local microbrews and
a "nice selection of Russian River wines"; the "minimalist" digs
with a front patio can get "crowded" and no reservations means there
often can be a "wait", but most surveyors feel it's "an unexpected find"
"at a reasonable price."

Boon Fly Café *Californian* | 23 | 19 | 21 | $33 |

Napa | Carneros Inn | 4048 Sonoma Hwy. (Old Sonoma Rd.) |
707-299-4900 | www.thecarnerosinn.com

A "great stop" "between Napa and Sonoma", this "unpretentious"
"roadside cafe" offers "inventive", "moderately priced" Californian
"comfort food" in Napa's Carneros Inn and makes a "fun place" to
"kick back" before or after "wine tasting"; mornings are a "mob
scene" due to "amazing brunch" specials like "made-to-order donuts" and "bacon Bloody Marys", but it's open "all day" and run by
a "friendly" staff, making it a "satisfying" "alternative to the pricey"
wine country options.

Z Bottega *Italian* | 25 | 24 | 23 | $59 |

Yountville | V Mktpl. | 6525 Washington St. (Yount St.) | 707-945-1050 |
www.botteganapavalley.com

"You don't have to be a TV-chef groupie to appreciate" Michael
Chiarello's Yountville "smash hit" where the "ultimate showman" extends his "personal greetings" and "charms" your palate with "rustic"
Italian fare and "well-priced wines" delivered with "TLC" in a "beautiful" villa setting complete with seating by an outdoor fireplace; it's
"noisy" and a tad "touristy" but also considered a relative "bargain"
for the area, making it "tough to get in."

Z Bouchon *French* | 26 | 24 | 24 | $58 |

Yountville | 6534 Washington St. (Yount St.) | 707-944-8037 |
www.bouchonbistro.com

"With the hand of Thomas Keller directing", you'll be surprised how
much more "affordable" this lunch-through-dinner Yountville French
can be than the chef's nearby French Laundry, while still offering "fabulous", "nicely done" classics; the "atmosphere could be mistaken for
a Parisian bistro", down to the "zinc bar" and garçons navigating the
"crowded" "small tables" with "finesse"; P.S. the pâtisserie next door
purveys "wonderful" take-out fare.

Brannan's Grill *American*   20 | 20 | 19 | $36

Calistoga | 1374 Lincoln Ave. (Washington St.) | 707-942-2233 |
www.brannansgrill.com

"Sit by the big fireplace" or dine by the "large open windows" "on summer nights" and "watch the tourists go by" this "comfy" New American
devotees dub a "Calistoga classic", offering "nice beef, fish and other
selections to please every taste"; some say both food and service are
"hit-or-miss", but it's still considered one of the area's "better
establishments" – with "smooth jazz on weekends."

NEW Brassica Ⓜ *Mediterranean*   22 | 21 | 23 | $48
(fka Go Fish)

St. Helena | 641 Main St. (Mills Ln.) | 707-963-0700 |
www.brassicanapavalley.com

Chef-owner Cindy Pawlcyn's "makeover of Go Fish" is a "delight"
say fans of her "refreshed" St. Helena locale offering "interesting",
"delicious" Med small and large plates enhanced by a "stunning assortment of wines by the glass" (many "on tap"); the "cozy" interior,
"huge" patio and "extraordinarily attentive" staff remain, so while it's
still a "work in progress", most feel it's a off to a "good start."

Brick & Bottle *Californian*   19 | 18 | 20 | $36

Corte Madera | 55 Tamal Vista Blvd. (Sandpiper Circle) | 415-924-3366 |
www.brickandbottle.com

"Sincere" service, "reliable" "comfort food" (especially the "divine"
pimiento burger) and a "casual" vibe help make this Corte Madera
Californian a "regular go-to spot"; even those who dub it "nothing special" appreciate its "vibrant bar area" and moderate prices.

Brix *Californian/French*   23 | 24 | 23 | $53

Napa | 7377 St. Helena Hwy. (Yount Mill Rd.) | 707-944-2749 | www.brix.com

A "favorite place to stop while wine tasting", this Napa longtimer garners praise for its "beautiful vineyard setting", "wonderful" view "onto
grapevines and hills" and "gorgeous" on-site garden" that supplies ingredients for the "elegantly prepared" French-inflected Californian
cuisine; "attentive" service further results in a "relaxed atmosphere",
and while it borders on "expensive", most agree it offers a "good
value for your dollar."

🔲 Buckeye Roadhouse *American/BBQ*   25 | 24 | 24 | $47

Mill Valley | 15 Shoreline Hwy. (Hwy. 101) | 415-331-2600 |
www.buckeyeroadhouse.com

"Consistently excellent" American "comfort food with a flair" ("brisket to
die for", "addicting oysters", "fantastic pork chops") and the "best martinis north of the Golden Gate Bridge" make this "happening" Mill Valley
"landmark" "a must-stop"; the "inviting" "lodgelike interior", "professional servers and valet parking" "complete the special-occasion feel
you can afford every day" – if you're part of "the moneyed Marin set."

Bungalow 44 *American*   22 | 21 | 21 | $44

Mill Valley | 44 E. Blithedale Ave. (Sunnyside Ave.) | 415-381-2500 |
www.bungalow44.com

"Comfort food meets haute cuisine" at this Mill Valley New American,
where "modern versions of great classics" are "hearty" and flavorful"
and service is generally "accommodating"; the "always animated" bar

can be a "happening pick-up scene" ("lots of cougars" and the male equivalent), but the covered patio can be a "calm" refuge.

Cafe Beaujolais *Californian/French* 26 | 22 | 24 | $51

Mendocino | 961 Ukiah St. (bet. Evergreen & School Sts.) | 707-937-5614 | www.cafebeaujolais.com

"Still a favorite", this "quaint" Mendocino Cal-French delivers "dependably excellent" "seasonal" fare and "local" wines with "outstanding service"; the "homey" Victorian farmhouse setting suits "conversation at lunchtime" (Wednesday–Sunday only) or a "romantic" dinner ("especially" in the "atrium"), all at prices that are "not out of control"; P.S. "homemade breads" and pastries sold at the to-go bakery window are an added "treat."

Cafe Citti *Italian* 24 | 16 | 21 | $24

Kenwood | 9049 Sonoma Hwy./Hwy. 12 (Shaw Ave.) | 707-833-2690 | www.cafecitti.com

"While wine-tasting in Sonoma", "locals and tourists" make a "quick stop" at this "unpretentious" Kenwood "roadhouse" for "heartwarming" Tuscan "trattoria" fare loaded with "plenty of garlic"; yes, counter "service and decor are minimal" (with "picnic tables" "when it's warm"), but it "simply works" – and it's "priced to please."

Café Gratitude *Vegan* 19 | 16 | 17 | $22

San Rafael | 2200 Fourth St. (W. Crescent Dr.) | 415-578-4928 | www.cafegratitude.com

See review in East of San Francisco Directory.

Cafe La Haye 🅂Ⓜ *American/Californian* 27 | 20 | 25 | $54

Sonoma | 140 E. Napa St. (bet. 1st & 2nd Sts.) | 707-935-5994 | www.cafelahaye.com

"Exceptional" Cal-American fare at a relatively "reasonable cost" draws "an eclectic grouping of locals and weekend tourists" to this "absolutely terrific" "gem on the Sonoma square" that's praised as even "better than most in better-known Napa"; "despite" the "jewel-box" setting ("wish it were a bit larger"), "it all comes together nicely" with a "superb wine list" and "spectacular service" – that is, "if you can get a rez."

NEW Campo Fina *Italian/Pizza* - | - | - | M

Healdsburg | 330 Healdsburg Ave. (North St.) | 707-395-4640 | www.campo-fina.com

This casual new all-day Italian spin-off from the nearby Scopa folks in Healdsburg turns out affordable Italian cicchetti (small plates) and wood-oven-fired pizzas complemented by reasonably priced Boot and wine-country vino, locally brewed beer and wine cocktails; the family-friendly dining room features exposed-brick walls, red leather booths and reclaimed fixtures that pay homage to its past as a turn-of-the-century saloon, but the real action is outside on the 65-seat covered back patio where diners can try their hand on the bocce court.

🅩 The Caprice *American* 23 | 27 | 24 | $59

Tiburon | 2000 Paradise Dr. (Mar W. St.) | 415-435-3400 | www.thecaprice.com

Perhaps Marin's "best-kept secret", this "special-occasion" "favorite" in Tiburon offers "magnificent" views "of the Golden Gate Bridge and

San Francisco" Bay that are particularly "outstanding at sunset"; while some find the American menu "a bit pricey", others say the fare and service "deliver it well" and all agree that the "terrific setting" "can't be beat" for "pure romance."

Carneros Bistro & Wine Bar *Californian* ▽ 24 | 22 | 24 | $50

Sonoma | The Lodge at Sonoma | 1325 Broadway (bet. Clay St. & Leveroni Rd.) | 707-931-2042 | www.thelodgeatsonoma.com

"Uniformly excellent" "upscale" fare and locally procured wines are delivered by an "exceedingly attentive and pleasant" staff at this "understated" Sonoma Californian that's "unusually great for being in a hotel"; other assets include an "elegant" dining room that opens onto an organic herb garden.

Cattlemens Steakhouse *Steak* 22 | 19 | 21 | $36

Petaluma | 5012 Petaluma Blvd. N. (McDowell Blvd.) | 707-763-4114
Santa Rosa | 2400 Midway Dr. (Farmers Ln.) | 707-546-1446
www.beststeakinthewest.com

"Add sizzle to your life" at these "family-oriented" chophouse chain links where "meat lovers rejoice" over "generous" portions of "consistently good" cuts in casual, Western-themed surrounds; add in "friendly" staffers and "good prices" and most give it a "yee haw."

C Casa *Mexican* 25 | 16 | 18 | $20

Napa | Oxbow Public Mkt. | 610 First St. (bet. Silverado Trail & Soscol Ave.) | 707-226-7700 | www.myccasa.com

Fans cheer "holy taco!" for the "imaginative", "fabulously prepared" offerings at this Napa counter-serve "tucked away" in the Oxbow Public Market that also dishes other "gourmet Mexican street food" (including breakfast fare); finding a seat can sometimes be a "challenge" and diners seesaw on the cost – is it "cheap" or "a little pricey"? – but given the "fresh, interesting flavors", most can't help going "back for more."

Celadon *American/Eclectic* 25 | 22 | 24 | $49

Napa | The Historic Napa Mill | 500 Main St. (5th St.) | 707-254-9690 | www.celadonnapa.com

Greg Cole's Napa "institution" (and sibling of Cole's Chop House) is where "locals go to eat" "luscious" American-Eclectic "gourmet comfort food" in the "rejuvenated river area"; whether you sit near the fire pit on the "airy" patio or in the "cozy" dining room of the historic building, it's a "great all-around experience" replete with "wonderful" wines and the "generous host" himself, who "always takes time" with the "efficient" staff to "make sure everything is perfect."

Central Market *Californian/Mediterranean* 26 | 21 | 25 | $39

Petaluma | 42 Petaluma Blvd. (Western Ave.) | 707-778-9900 | www.centralmarketpetaluma.com

"Original" Cal-Med "slow food" is the focus of the "brilliantly prepared", "locally sourced" menu, bolstered by "wonderful" wine pairings, at this "Petaluma gem" from "gracious host-chef-owner" Tony Najiola; a few "wish the atmosphere were a bit less casual", but since it's "not too darn expensive for fine dining", most are happy to keep it a Sonoma County "secret" – the kind of place where "chefs dine on their nights off."

FOOD DECOR SERVICE COST

Chapter & Moon ⓜ *American* ▽ 24 | 17 | 21 | $32

Fort Bragg | 32150 N. Harbor Dr. (Main St.) | 707-962-1643
Proffering a "tiny menu" of "very good fish dishes" and "top-flight" traditional American "comfort foods" with "immense flavor" (including
"delicious" breakfasts and brunches) from a modest oak-walled shack
at the end of a pier, this "Fort Bragg jewel" is "worthy of a detour";
aside from cooking up some of the "best value on the North Coast",
you can't beat the "wonderful location overlooking" Noyo Harbor.

Charcuterie *French* 20 | 17 | 21 | $33

Healdsburg | Healdsburg Plaza | 335 Healdsburg Ave. (Plaza St.) |
707-431-7213 | www.charcuteriehealdsburg.com
"If pork is your thing", this "good-value" pig-themed "French country" bistro "on the Healdsburg square" offers "consistently" "creative
(and distinctly" Gallic) preparations that "change frequently", all
served up by "friendly and unpretentious" staffers; while "portions are
large", the quarters can come off as "cramped", still, the place exudes
a "comfort feel."

🄴 Cheesecake Factory *American* 21 | 21 | 20 | $28

Corte Madera | The Village at Corte Madera | 1736 Redwood Hwy.
(Hwy. 101) | 415-945-0777 | www.thecheesecakefactory.com
See review in City of San Francisco Directory.

🄴 Cheese Steak Shop *Cheesesteaks* 23 | 12 | 19 | $11

Santa Rosa | 750 Stony Point Rd. (Sebastopol Rd.) | 707-527-9877 |
www.cheesesteakshop.com
See review in City of San Francisco Directory.

Chinois *Asian* ▽ 25 | 23 | 25 | $34

Windsor | 186 Windsor River Rd. (Bell Rd.) | 707-838-4667 |
www.chinoisbistro.com
There's "something to please everyone" at this upscale Asian fusion
bistro in "unassuming" Windsor presenting a "mix of dim sum", Chinese
and Southeast Asian cuisines "all rolled into one"; the fare is "light and
bright" with "flavors" that "just shine", especially when served with
soju, sake and a serious wine list by a skilled staff in a room appointed
with authentic Eastern furnishings; P.S. lunch served weekdays only.

Cindy's Backstreet Kitchen *Californian* 24 | 22 | 24 | $46

St. Helena | 1327 Railroad Ave. (bet. Adams St. & Hunt Ave.) |
707-963-1200 | www.cindysbackstreetkitchen.com
"Napa stalwart chef" Cindy Pawlcyn (Mustards) oversees this "idio-
syncratic" St. Helena "country kitchen", turning out a "variety" of
"well-done" Californian dishes with "Latin flavors" that make for an
"utterly delightful" (and "decently priced") "wine-country lunch" or
"unpretentious" evening – "especially in the summer under the fig tree";
while wayfarers call it a "must-stop", the "homey vibe", "chatty" bar
scene and "spot-on service" keep it a "big hangout for locals" as well.

🄴 Cole's Chop House *Steak* 27 | 25 | 25 | $71

Napa | 1122 Main St. (bet. 1st & Pearl Sts.) | 707-224-6328 |
www.coleschophouse.com
"As good as any NY steakhouse" but "with a Napa Valley twist", this
"classic" "carnivore heaven" from Greg Cole (Celadon) proffers "big

portions" of "top-notch" meat "cooked to your exact specifications" and paired "wonderfully with those great big Napa cabs"; set in a "landmark building", it boasts a "fine ambiance" and "service to match", so "high prices" aren't exactly a surprise.

Cook St. Helena *Italian*

26 | 18 | 23 | $46

St. Helena | 1310 Main St. (Hunt Ave.) | 707-963-7088 | www.cooksthelena.com

"Eat well with locals" at this St. Helena Italian turning out "pasta done right" and other "well-prepared", "locally sourced" eats via "friendly" servers; the "vintage chic" storefront is "tiny", so expect "insanely crowded conditions", especially since such "quality" meals rarely come so "reasonably priced."

NEW Copita *Mexican*

- | - | - | M

Sausalito | 739 Bridgeway (Anchor St.) | 415-331-7400 | www.copitarestaurant.com

Cookbook author and TV personality Joanne Weir and restaurateur Larry Mindel (Poggio, Il Fornaio) team up at this affordable, seasonally driven tequileria and Mexican cantina in Sausalito; a custom wood-fired rotisserie serves as the colorful venue's focal point in digs with a communal table and a mahogany-topped bar, though the most coveted tables are on the sidewalk outside.

Crepevine ● *American/French*

21 | 16 | 19 | $16

San Rafael | 908 Fourth St. (Lootens Pl.) | 415-257-8822
Santa Rosa | 740 Farmers Ave. (Sonoma Ave.) | 707-577-8822
www.crepevine.com

See review in City of San Francisco Directory.

☑ Cucina Paradiso ☒ *Italian*

27 | 23 | 26 | $37

Petaluma | 114 Petaluma Blvd. N. (bet. Washington St. & Western Ave.) | 707-782-1130 | www.cucinaparadisopetaluma.com

"Lots of regulars" call this Petaluma Italian a "favorite", praising its "sophisticated flavors" and "well-executed" dishes, especially the "exceptional homemade pastas"; the trattoria-style space can get a "bit noisy", but service is "welcoming" and with such "reasonable prices", most consider it an "amazing deal."

Cucina Restaurant & Wine Bar ☒ *Italian*

∇ 22 | 17 | 21 | $37

San Anselmo | 510 San Anselmo Ave. (Tunstead Ave.) | 415-454-2942 | www.cucinarestaurantandwinebar.com

"Simple and delicious" is the bottom line on this "reasonably priced" San Anselmo Italian that "consistently delivers homey meals" known to "pack a powerful punch of flavor"; "friendly" service elevates the casual, trattoria-style environs, and "perfectly made desserts" end things on a sweet note.

Della Fattoria Downtown Café *Bakery/Eclectic*

27 | 20 | 21 | $24

Petaluma | 141 Petaluma Blvd. N. (bet. Washington St. & Western Ave.) | 707-763-0161 | www.dellafattoria.com

"Heaven in Petaluma" is how fans describe this Eclectic bakery/cafe "popular" for "fabulous in-house baked bread and pastries", "giant bowl"–sized lattes and "well-made" breakfasts and lunches (plus "hearty" dinners on Friday); the "casual" space is "charming" despite often "crowded" conditions ("getting a table on a Saturday morning is almost as hard as winning the lottery"), and the "staff is gracious", so though it's "a little on the pricey side", admirers remind "you get what you pay for."

Della Santina's *Italian*   24 | 22 | 24 | $42

Sonoma | 133 E. Napa St. (1st St.) | 707-935-0576 | www.dellasantinas.com

Enoteca Della Santina Ⓜ *Italian*

Sonoma | 127 E. Napa St. (bet. 1st & 2nd Sts.) | 707-938-4200 | www.enotecadellasantina.com

"Just off the square in historic Sonoma" lies this "family-run" trattoria (and adjoining enoteca) where they "greet you with a warm welcome" and send out "well-presented", "homestyle" meals that "only mama knows how to cook"; with "fair prices" it's a "local and visitor favorite", especially in the outdoor courtyard that's "delightful on a warm day."

Diavola Pizzeria &   26 | 20 | 22 | $34
Salumeria *Italian*

Geyserville | 21021 Geyserville Ave. (Hwy. 128) | 707-814-0111 | www.diavolapizzeria.com

"Unreal pizzas", "don't-miss" salumi and other "simple yet extraordinary" dishes make for a "sophisticated but casual meal" at this "worth-the-schlep" Geyersville Italian set in an early 1900's building; service gets few complaints, and with "reasonable" prices, it's a "wine country bargain", just "expect to wait" because it's small and "always crowded with locals."

Dipsea Cafe *Diner/Greek*   19 | 16 | 18 | $22

Mill Valley | 200 Shoreline Hwy. (Tennessee Valley Rd.) | 415-381-0298 | www.dipseacafe.com

On weekends there's "always a line out the door" for the "highly addictive" "hearty" breakfasts at this "cheery" Mill Valley American diner that adds Greek specialties at dinner (offered Wednesday–Sunday only); some are turned off by the "noisy" environs and somewhat "spotty" service, adding it's "nothing outstanding", but "sitting outside is pleasant" and "inexpensive" tabs don't hurt either.

Downtown Bakery &   26 | 13 | 19 | $15
Creamery ⌷ *Bakery*

Healdsburg | 308 Center St. (bet. Matheson & Plaza Sts.) | 707-431-2719 | www.downtownbakery.net

A "hometown institution", this "world-class" bakery/cafe is "worth a special detour" to Healdsburg for "seriously good sticky buns", "don't-miss" donut muffins and other "excellent baked goods", plus "refreshing" ice cream and "simple" breakfasts and lunches (a cafe menu is served Friday–Monday); inside is small, so many "take out to the plaza across the street"; P.S. no credit cards.

Dry Creek Kitchen *Californian*   24 | 25 | 24 | $66

Healdsburg | Hotel Healdsburg | 317 Healdsburg Ave. (Matheson St.) | 707-431-0330 | www.charliepalmer.com

"Deliciously prepared" dishes are "elevated by imaginative combinations" and "sing when paired with the Sonoma wines" at this "worth-a-voyage" Healdsburg Californian from chef-restaurateur Charlie Palmer; the "blissful" setting is "exactly what you would want", with "large open doors" and a "vine-draped arbor", and service is "high-quality" too, so while some sniff it's "overpriced and overpraised", more find it a "capital-letter keeper", especially given its "enlightened" vino policy (no corkage on local labels).

Duck Club *American*

| 22 | 24 | 22 | $49 |

Bodega Bay | Bodega Bay Lodge & Spa | 103 S. Hwy. 1 (Doran Park Rd.) | 707-875-3525 | www.bodegabaylodge.com
See review in East of San Francisco Directory.

El Dorado Kitchen *Californian/Mediterranean*

| 23 | 23 | 22 | $46 |

Sonoma | El Dorado Hotel | 405 First St. W. (Spain St.) | 707-996-3030 | www.eldoradosonoma.com
"Solid" Cal-Med cooking "hits the spot" at this dining room in Sonoma's El Dorado Hotel, where the "innovative" offerings are set down by "thoroughly professional" staffers in "sophisticated", contemporary surroundings; it may be a "bit pricey for regular dining", but it's still "worth a stop", "especially when you can be out on the patio."

El Farolito *Mexican*

| 23 | 9 | 17 | $10 |

Rohnert Park | 6466 Redwood Dr. (Laguna Dr.) | 707-588-8013
Santa Rosa | 565 Sebastopol Rd. (Avalon Ave.) | 707-526-7444 | www.elfarolitoinc.com ◗
See review in City of San Francisco Directory.

NEW El Huarache Loco *Mexican*

| ▽ 23 | 12 | 16 | $10 |

Larkspur | 1803 Larkspur Landing Circle (Lincoln Village Circle) | 415-925-1403 | www.huaracheloco.com
Marinites are going *loco* for the new brick-and-mortar home to Veronica Salazar's "authentically delicious" "Mexican street food", like the namesake huarache (sandal-shaped tortillas stuffed with beans and topped with meat and veggies) and "warm, filling" breakfasts; the "fresh, cheap eats" are served in a traditional sit-down dining room outfitted with leather-back chairs and wrought-iron chandeliers; P.S. a stall at the Alemany Farmers Market is open weekends 8 AM–3 PM.

El Paseo *Steak*

| 23 | 26 | 21 | $73 |

Mill Valley | 17 Throckmorton Ave. (E. Blithedale Ave.) | 415-388-0741 | www.elpaseomillvalley.com
With Tyler Florence and Sammy Hagar at the helm, this "beautiful" Mill Valley spot – a "charming rabbit warren of cozy rooms" hidden at the end of a "brick path" – is "younger and louder" than ever, turning out "fabulously decadent" steaks and other American "comfort food"; the bar is a "sexy place to hang out", but service is "hit-or-miss" and high prices mean visits to this "chophouse" are often limited to a "special 'big night out.'"

Emporio Rulli *Dessert/Italian*

| 22 | 20 | 18 | $20 |

Larkspur | 464 Magnolia Ave. (bet. Cane & Ward Sts.) | 415-924-7478 | www.rulli.com
It's like "taking a short vacation in Italy" at this "bustling" cafe chain that turns out an "amazing" array of "authentic" pastries, "tasty" panini

sandwiches and "strong" coffee drinks from "well-trained baristas";
the "bustling" Larkspur original is "cozy", Union Square offers "excellent people-watching on the square" and SFO branches are an "escape
from fast food."

⨀ Étoile *Californian*   27 | 27 | 27 | $93

Yountville | Domaine Chandon Winery | 1 California Dr. (Rte. 29/
St. Helena Hwy.) | 707-944-2892 | www.chandon.com

"Imaginative, well-executed" "works of culinary art" and "excellent" wines, all presented by "unfailingly helpful" servers, make
this "high-end" Californinan at the Domaine Chandon Winery
"worthy of celebration"; the "casually elegant" dining room features a "huge expanse of windows that showcases the beautiful
surroundings" and the patio is just as "magical", so it's a "splurge"-
worthy experience especially "perfect for a night out sans kids";
P.S. closed Tuesday and Wednesday.

Farm Ⓜ *American*   25 | 26 | 24 | $65

Napa | Carneros Inn | 4048 Sonoma Hwy. (Old Sonoma Rd.) |
707-299-4883 | www.thecarnerosinn.com

It "probably doesn't get much better than this" Napa New American
where "refined" fare built on "superb, locally sourced" ingredients is
served in a setting featuring a "lovely, open architectural design, cozy
banquettes, fireplaces" and "covered outdoor seating"; "lovely" service and a "special selection of regional wines" complete the experience that's "expensive" but "satisfying."

⨀ Farmhouse Inn &   27 | 26 | 27 | $90
Restaurant *Californian*

Forestville | Farmhouse Inn | 7871 River Rd. (Wohler Rd.) |
707-887-3300 | www.farmhouseinn.com

"Set in a charming old farmhouse", this Forestville Californian has "a
lot to be proud of", from the "skillful execution" of "complex" prix
fixe dinners highlighting "incredible flavor combinations" to the "top-
notch" servers and "master" sommeliers who help guests navigate the
"nearly encyclopedic wine list"; the "quaint romantic setting" is "elegant" but "with zero pretense", though "high prices" mean many
save it as a "special treat for a for a special occasion"; P.S. it's open
Thursday–Monday only.

Farmstead *American/Californian*   22 | 23 | 21 | $47

St. Helena | Long Meadow Ranch | 738 Main St. (Charter Oak Ave.) |
707-963-9181 | www.farmsteadnapa.com

"As the name would suggest", this Cal-New American in St. Helena
serves "satisfying" "farm-to-table" "comfort food" offered in a "bright"
and "airy" "barnlike" setting that works for both a "large family meal
or more intimate couples dinner"; it's not cheap and a few gripe "quiet
tables are hard to come by", but "charming" service, a "sane corkage
policy" ($2 donated to charity) and a "huge garden for summer and
fall dining" help keep it a Napa "go-to."

Fatted Calf *Sandwiches*   27 | 17 | 23 | $24

Napa | Oxbow Public Mkt. | 644 First St. (bet. Silverado Trail & Soscol Ave.) |
707-256-3684 | www.fattedcalf.com

See review in City of San Francisco Directory.

Fig Cafe & Winebar *French*

26 | 20 | 24 | $37

Glen Ellen | 13690 Arnold Dr. (O'Donnell Ln.) | 707-938-2130 | www.thefigcafe.com

Locals "hate that more out-of-towners are learning about" this "casual" onetime "hidden treasure" (sister to Girl & the Fig) in Glen Ellen, where the "fantastic" French "comfort food" is "wine country fare at its best", service is "attentive" and prices are "fair"; it stocks "interesting" vinos but many "bring their own sips" due to "free corkage", which means "the only downside is no-reservations, so come prepared to wait."

Fish ⊅ *Seafood*

25 | 15 | 15 | $32

Sausalito | 350 Harbor Dr. (Gates 5 Rd.) | 415-331-3474 | www.331fish.com

Surveyors suggest you "go fish" at this "bare-bones" midpriced Sausalito shack "overlooking the harbor", where "some of the cleanest, freshest catch anywhere" gets a further boost from a "thoughtful wine and beer list"; "you seat yourselves on picnic tables inside or out", and though it can be a "drag to stand in line to order" and many "hate that it's cash-only", at least patrons "feel great about the whole experience" given its dedication to "sustainable, locally sourced" ingredients.

Fish Story *Seafood*

20 | 21 | 20 | $47

Napa | Napa Riverfront | 790 Main St. (3rd St.) | 707-251-5600 | www.fishstorynapa.com

"Solidly executed" fin fare made with sustainable seafood (a "big plus") and an "inviting" locale on the Napa riverfront mean there's "nothing fishy" about this "wine country delight"; still, some snipe it's "underwhelming" with "hit-or-miss" grub, though most concede it's "value-priced for the area" and "comfortable when you don't want a big-deal" meal.

Flavor *Californian/Eclectic*

23 | 20 | 20 | $31

Santa Rosa | 96 Old Courthouse Sq. (bet. 3rd & 4th Sts.) | 707-573-9600 | www.flavorbistro.com

"A local favorite", this "bustling" Santa Rosa bistro situated "right on old courthouse square" dishes out a "wide-ranging" Californian-Eclectic menu filled with "consistently good comfort food"; a few surveyors grumble that the offerings are "not very imaginative", but regulars are charmed by the generally "congenial service", "decent prices" and "pleasant setting."

NEW Forchetta/Bastoni *Italian/SE Asian*

∇ 23 | 22 | 21 | $32

Sebastopol | Sonoma Plaza | 6948 Sebastopol Ave. (Bodega Ave.) | 707-829-9500 | www.forchettabastoni.com

Run by a husband-and-wife team set on stopping the revolving-door syndrome at this centrally located Sebastopol location, this "novel dual restaurant" has an upstairs featuring "affordable" Southeast Asian "street food" and a "larger" ground-floor dining room for "well-prepared Italian specialties"; whether diners prefer sticks or forks (as the name translates), the stylish setting with a "young vibe" and a "nice bar" is fast becoming a popular "late-night place to be."

Fort Bragg Bakery 🗷Ⓜ⇱ *Bakery/Eclectic* ▽ 23 | 15 | 19 | $19

Fort Bragg | 360 N. Franklin St. (Laurel St.) | 707-964-9647 |
www.fortbraggbakery.com

An out-of-the-way Fort Bragg locale doesn't deter fans from "sensational" pastries and breads, plus solid lunch fare like thin-crust pizza
and "delicious sandwiches" at this European-inspired bakery/cafe run
by Christopher Kump (ex Cafe Beaujolais); wines and local brews are
also on offer, making it an overall "nice stop", just "get there early" before they run out of favorites.

Frantoio *Italian* 22 | 22 | 22 | $45

Mill Valley | 152 Shoreline Hwy. (Hwy. 101) | 415-289-5777 |
www.frantoio.com

It's "reliable in every way" say loyalists of this moderate Mill Valley
Italian where the "classics never fail", service is mostly "attentive" and
the operational olive oil press is "a sight to see"; the Tuscan-themed
space is also "attractive" (if occasionally "noisy"), so it's an easy "go-
to" that's "nice enough" for "special events."

Fremont Diner *Diner* 24 | 16 | 19 | $21

Sonoma | 2698 Fremont Dr. (S. Central Ave.) | 707-938-7370 |
www.thefremontdiner.com

"Imaginative twists" elevate "down-home" diner favorites" to "simply
fabulous" proportions at this Sonoma "roadside find", where a "friendly"
staff keeps watch over the "small", "funky" space and outdoor patio;
it's often "crowded" (and "justifiably so") so "get there early" advise
fans who wish they'd add "more indoor seating" and "extend their operating hours" (it closes at 3 PM during the week and 4 on weekends).

𝗡𝗘𝗪 French Blue *American* - | - | - | M

St. Helena | 1429 Main St. (bet. Adams & Pine Sts.) | 707-968-9200 |
www.frenchbluenapa.com

This all-day, walk-in-only New American (owned by winemaker and
Press proprietor Leslie Rudd) in Downtown St. Helena turns out moderately priced farm-to-table fare, largely sourced from the organic ingredients grown nearby in Rudd's own garden; it's all served in a cozy,
rustic setting equipped with a wood-burning oven and fireplace, and
complemented by a Napa-focused wine list and craft cocktails.

French Garden Ⓜ *French* 22 | 21 | 22 | $38

Sebastopol | 8050 Bodega Ave. (Pleasant Hill Rd.) | 707-824-2030 |
www.frenchgardenrestaurant.com

From "foodies to grannies" there's "something for everyone" at this
"affordably priced" French bistro on the "outskirts of Sebastopol"
where the "true farm-to-table cuisine" features produce from its own
garden; other pluses include "quality" service and a "spacious patio"
perfect for 'lingering."

𝗭 French Laundry *American/French* 29 | 27 | 28 | $297

Yountville | 6640 Washington St. (Creek St.) | 707-944-2380 |
www.frenchlaundry.com

"Words can't even describe" the "experience of a lifetime" say food
lovers who've had the "thrill" of landing a reservation and making "the
trek" to Thomas Keller's "culinary Everest" in Yountville where the
"heavenly" New American–French tasting menus "feature ingredients

treated with the utmost respect and care" and the "impeccable" service is "like a coordinated dance"; it's all "too precious" for some and wines cost "a fortune", but acolytes insist "you'll go to your grave (in a pauper's field) remembering this meal" and the "exquisite" "gardens outside the stone building."

Fresh by Lisa Hemenway *Californian/French*   22 | 16 | 19 | $28

Santa Rosa | 5755 Mountain Hawk Way (Hwy. 12) | 707-595-1048 | www.freshbylisahemenway.com

"If you can get past eating in the middle of a grocery store" fans say you'll be rewarded with cooking that's "fresh indeed" at this Santa Rosa Cal-French spot; "reasonable" checks and "local wine choices" are also welcome parts of the experience, though a few fed up with "long waits" for food prefer the take-out counter.

Fumé Bistro & Bar *American*   22 | 17 | 22 | $41

Napa | 4050 Byway E. (Avalon Ct.) | 707-257-1999 | www.fumebistro.com

So far "tourists have missed" this Napa "locals' hangout", a "reliable wine-country haunt" where the "solid" American fare is "priced reasonably" and set down by "friendly" servers; not everyone's a fan of the artwork-enhanced surrounds, but it still has a "warm ambiance", and the "lively bar scene" helps.

Gary Chu's Ⓜ *Chinese*   24 | 21 | 22 | $31

Santa Rosa | 611 Fifth St. (bet. D St. & Mendocino Ave.) | 707-526-5840 | www.garychus.com

For some of the "best Chinese in Sonoma County", diners hit up this midpriced Santa Rosa "favorite", where the "flavors meld perfectly" and many of the "delicious" dishes feature "interesting twists"; modern stylings contribute to a "pleasant atmosphere" and service gets few complaints, so though a few cityites scoff "anyone who has lived in San Francisco will be disappointed", loyalists point out it's "been here for a long time so it must be doing something right."

Girl & the Fig *French*   24 | 22 | 23 | $45

Sonoma | Sonoma Hotel | 110 W. Spain St. (1st St.) | 707-938-3634 | www.thegirlandthefig.com

A wine country "icon" right "in the heart of Sonoma square", this 15-year-old bistro from restaurateur Sondra Bernstein "shows no signs of getting tired" say fans citing the "imaginative" "Provence-inspired" creations "prepared simply and well", plus "swoon"-worthy cocktails and a "great selection" of wines "filled with Rhône varietals"; the "convivial" room can get "noisy", but the outdoor patio is "charming", and with "friendly" service and "value" tabs (at least for the area), it's still a "standout."

Glen Ellen Inn *Californian*   ▽ 24 | 21 | 23 | $41

Glen Ellen | 13670 Arnold Dr. (Warm Springs Rd.) | 707-996-6409 | www.glenelleninn.com

"Well off the beaten path", this Glen Ellen Californian run by a husband-and-wife team is a "real find", offering "creative, high-quality" dishes, including many with a French accent, all at moderate prices; the "charming", homey surrounds are ripe for "romance" and service is "attentive" too.

	FOOD	DECOR	SERVICE	COST

NEW Glen Ellen Star *American*   — | — | — | M

Glen Ellen | 13648 Arnold Dr. (Warm Springs Rd.) | 707-343-1384 | www.glenellenstar.com

This Glen Ellen bistro run by a husband-and-wife team armed with plenty of culinary pedigree (he's cooked at The French Laundry and NYC's Corton, her family runs a winery) specializes in rustic-yet-refined, wood-fired New American cuisine, complemented by pre-mium wines on tap (plus some special reserve and boutique bottles); it's all presented in a tiny dining room with a farmhouse vibe and an enclosed, heated patio for semi-alfresco dining; P.S. the handmade ice cream is also offered to go.

NEW Goose & Gander ● *American*   — | — | — | M

St. Helena | 1245 Spring St. (Oak Ave.) | 707-967-8779 | www.goosegander.com

Roosting in a Prohibition-era Downtown St. Helena Arts and Crafts bungalow (once home to legendary bootlegger Walter Martini and the former Martini House), this upscale gastropub lures locals and tourists alike with midpriced, ingredient-driven rustic American lunch and dinner fare; the space has a wood-beamed, two-story dining room, a landscaped patio and a speakeasy-style basement wine bar where industry folks rub elbows over retro cocktails and late-night nibbles.

Gott's Roadside *Diner*   22 | 14 | 17 | $19
(fka Taylor's Automatic Refresher)

Napa | Oxbow Public Mkt. | 644 First St. (McKinstry St.) | 707-224-6900
St. Helena | 933 Main St. (bet. Charter Oak Ave. & Mitchell Dr.) | 707-963-3486
www.gottsroadside.com

"A 21st-century version of a 1950s burger joint", this "self-serve" trio with "epic lines" puts a "gourmet twist" on everything, adding "amazing" ahi poke tacos and "top-notch wines" to "traditional diner" standards; though it's relatively "pricey", you "gott-sa try it" insist fans, who are "childishly happy" on "sunny days" sitting at "picnic tables on the lawn" in St. Helena (the Napa and SF spin-offs have indoor seating too).

Graffiti *Eclectic*   25 | 26 | 24 | $36

Petaluma | 101 Second St. (C St.) | 707-765-4567 | www.graffitipetaluma.com

An "excellent location overlooking the Petaluma River" makes this midpriced Eclectic a "fantastic place to eat" say fans who also cheer the "creative" cooking, including "many small dishes and interesting large plates"; a "warm and efficient" crew tends to diners in the window-lined dining room or out on the patio that's especially "great in good weather", so the few who grumble it "never seems to wow" are in the minority.

Guaymas *Mexican*   17 | 22 | 17 | $35

Tiburon | 5 Main St. (Tiburon Blvd.) | 415-435-6300 | www.guaymasrestaurant.com

"Watch the ferries come in" from the patio at this "festive, crowded" Mexican seafooder in Tiburon with a "beautiful setting right on the bay"; it has a "fun atmosphere, especially with a pitcher of margaritas" and though a few grouse about "slow service" and "overpriced" fare that's "inconsistent", "the view is always spectacular."

Hana Japanese Restaurant *Japanese* 26 | 18 | 24 | $50

Rohnert Park | 101 Golf Course Dr. (Roberts Lake Rd.) | 707-586-0270 | www.hanajapanese.com

"Don't miss the sushi" at this Rohnert Park Japanese where "genius" chef-owner Ken Tominaga "makes sure every dish is of top quality", from "pristine raw fish" that's "beautifully arranged and served", to the "well-prepared" cooked items, all of which are complemented by a "wide selection of sake" and set down by "attentive" staffers; yes, it's in the "oddest" strip-mall location, the decor is somewhat "non-existent" and it's "not cheap", but most are still happy to pay for such a "memorable" experience.

Harmony Restaurant *Chinese* 23 | 23 | 21 | $38

Mill Valley | Strawberry Vill. | 800 Redwood Hwy. (Belvedere Dr.) | 415-381-5300 | www.harmonyrestaurantgroup.com

It's "worth a visit" to this Chinese spot in a Mill Valley shopping center for its "contemporary dim sum" (served for both lunch and dinner) promising "carefully selected" "local, organic ingredients", "bright flavors" and no MSG; it seems a "bit pricey" to some, but a "sophisticated" setting and "timely, gracious service" are part of the deal.

Harvest Moon Café *Californian/Mediterranean* 25 | 19 | 22 | $46

Sonoma | 487 First St. W. (Napa St.) | 707-933-8160 | www.harvestmooncafesonoma.com

"Delightful memories" are made at this "little jewel on Sonoma Square", where a husband-and-wife team provides "friendly, attentive" service while turning out "sublime", "reasonably priced" Cal-Med dinners (and Sunday brunches) based on "whatever is fresh that day"; the "casual", "homey" interior is somewhat "cramped", so insiders head for the "pleasant" back garden that's like "a bit of Provence."

NEW Hawk's Tavern *American* 21 | 21 | 21 | $35

Mill Valley | 507 Miller Ave. (Reed St.) | 415-388-3474 | www.hawkstavern.com

"Delicious" small and large plates at "reasonable prices" keep this "trendy" Mill Valley American "gastropub" from celebrity chef Tyler Florence "always busy" with locals who "drop in for a beer or glass of wine" (or just to "nosh") at the "funky" bar or on the porch; while a few gripe about "long waits", the service is "pleasant" and there's brunch too.

Healdsburg Bar & Grill *American* 20 | 18 | 19 | $29

Healdsburg | 245 Healdsburg Ave. (bet. Matheson & Mill Sts.) | 707-433-3333 | www.healdsburgbarandgrill.com

Despite its Cyrus pedigree, "don't expect haute cuisine" at this "super-casual" bar and grill in Healdsburg, where "inspired" mid-priced American pub grub (including a "great burger") is served by an "exceptionally nice" staff in a kid-friendly setting; something of the local *Cheers*, it's a natural to "watch the game" or linger at lunchtime "on the patio", and there's a "pretty good wine list" to boot.

Hilltop 1892 *American/Californian*   21 | 24 | 24 | $36

Novato | 850 Lamont Ave. (Redwood Blvd.) | 415-893-1892 |
www.hilltop1892.com

"Welcome back" say longtime regulars of this "landmark restaurant on
top of a Novato hill", where new owners have renovated the Craftsman-
style setting and "updated the menu" of "high-quality", moderately
priced Traditional American fare with Californian spins; solid service
is a bonus, but it's the "terrific views" that really steal the show.

Hog Island Oyster Co. & Bar *Seafood*   26 | 18 | 20 | $36

Napa | Oxbow Public Mkt. | 610 First St. (bet. Silverado Trail & Soscol Ave.) |
707-251-8113 | www.hogislandoysters.com
See review in City of San Francisco Directory.

Hopmonk Tavern *Eclectic*   20 | 19 | 20 | $26

Sebastopol | 230 Petaluma Ave. (bet. Abbott Ave. & Burnett St.) |
707-829-7300
Sonoma | 691 Broadway (Andrieux St.) | 707-935-9100
www.hopmonk.com

"Everybody finds something they like" among the "reasonably priced"
Eclectic pub food, but it's the "fine selection of local and imported
beers" that really draw "lively, young" types to these Sebastopol and
Sonoma "hangouts" from Dean Biersch of Gordon Biersch; the atmosphere's particularly "wonderful in summer" on the "super" fire pit–
blessed patio and downright "funky" on the weekends thanks to the
"fantastic sounds" of local bands.

Hot Box Grill Ⓜ *Californian*   25 | 16 | 23 | $46

Sonoma | 18350 Hwy. 12 (Boyes Blvd.) | 707-939-8383 |
www.hotboxgrill.com

The "dining room looks ordinary, but the food is certainly not" at this
Boyes Hot Spring sophomore from a former Cafe La Haye chef, who
whips up an "amazing", "innovative" chalkboard menu of "rich"
Californian fare; some find the prices "steep considering the neighborhood", but for others, it's "the find of the decade."

Hurley's Restaurant &   23 | 22 | 23 | $51
Bar *Californian/Mediterranean*

Yountville | 6518 Washington St. (Yount St.) | 707-944-2345 |
www.hurleysrestaurant.com

"You always feel welcome" at this Yountville site where chef Bob
Hurley prepares "consistent" Californian cuisine with a "flavorful"
Mediterranean twist (game preparations are particularly "wonder-
ful"); diners feel prices are relatively "reasonable", especially the
lunch prix fixe, making it a "great place to bring out-of-town guests";
P.S. "love the patio."

Il Davide Ⓜ *Italian*   24 | 20 | 24 | $41

San Rafael | 901 A St. (bet. 3rd & 4th Sts.) | 415-454-8080 |
www.ildavide.net

"Refined" Tuscan fare rife with "unique flavor combinations" comes
from chef-owner David Haydon, and a "warm reception" comes
from his "superb" staff at this "outstanding" San Rafael ristorante; the
"lovely", "lively" atmosphere also pleases, but the best feature may be
its "reasonable prices", particularly lunch specials "you can't beat."

⨂ Il Fornaio *Italian* — 22 | 22 | 21 | $39

Corte Madera | Town Center Corte Madera | 223 Corte Madera Town Ctr.
(Madera Blvd.) | 415-927-4400 | www.ilfornaio.com
See review in City of San Francisco Directory.

⨂ In-N-Out Burger ● *Burgers* — 23 | 14 | 21 | $9

Mill Valley | 798 Redwood Hwy. (Belvedere Dr.)
Napa | 820 Imola Ave./Hwy. 121 (Gasser Dr. & Soscol Ave.)
800-786-1000 | www.in-n-out.com
See review in City of San Francisco Directory.

Insalata's *Mediterranean* — 25 | 23 | 23 | $42

San Anselmo | 120 Sir Francis Drake Blvd. (Barber Ave.) | 415-457-7700 |
www.insalatas.com
Chef-owner Heidi Krahling serves "luscious" Med dishes "usually
with local ingredients" and at "fair prices" at this San Anselmo spot;
"friendly service", a "well-stocked wine cellar" and an airy, "welcoming"
room help make it just the thing for "special occasions", while "interesting takeout" is a boon for "Marin ladies who don't want to cook."

Jackson's *Californian* — 21 | 22 | 21 | $34

Santa Rosa | 135 Fourth St. (Davis St.) | 707-545-6900 |
www.jacksonsbarandoven.com
"Well-prepared Californian-style bar food" including "delicious" wood-
fired pizza is sold for "affordable prices" at this "charming" Santa Rosa
"casual spot"; after-work revelers and other scene-seekers go for the
"high-energy" atmosphere, especially at the long, "beautiful bar" where
"fabulous drinks" are concocted.

Jennie Low's Chinese Cuisine *Chinese* — ▽ 21 | 17 | 22 | $23

Petaluma | 140 Second St. (C St.) | 707-762-6888 | www.jennielow.com
"Pleasantly reliable" is the word on this Petaluma Chinese, from surveyors saying it "makes an effort to offer healthy preparations like
steaming, less oil" and "more vegetables"; though it sports "not the
best decor on the block", "moderate prices" and an "efficient staff"
mean it's "a great place to take a group for a family-style meal."

Jimtown Store *Deli* — 20 | 17 | 17 | $19

Healdsburg | 6706 Hwy. 128 (bet. Red Winery Rd. & Sausal Ln.) |
707-433-1212 | www.jimtown.com
"On your way to and from the wineries in Alexander Valley", you "must
stop" at this "quaint" "old country store" outside of Healdsburg, offering "substantial", "well-prepared" deli sandwiches along with "antiques,
collectibles, old-fashioned candy" and "ice-cream treats"; hit the "comfortable patio" or, better still, "put together a picnic"; P.S. closes at
5 PM, earlier off-season.

Joe's Taco Lounge & Salsaria *Mexican* — 21 | 19 | 20 | $20

Mill Valley | 382 Miller Ave. (bet. Evergreen & Montford Aves.) |
415-383-8164
This "quirky" taqueria with "an amazing hot sauce collection" is a "Mill
Valley favorite" of "just about everyone", dishing out "tasty" "fresh"
Mexican fare with a "bucket of beers" or "wine margaritas" to wash it
down; "lightning service" and "reasonable prices" keep it packed and
"loud as heck", and patrons profess "that's what makes it fun."

John Ash & Co. *Californian*

| 25 | 25 | 24 | $59 |

Santa Rosa | 4330 Barnes Rd. (River Rd.) | 707-527-7687 | www.vintnersinn.com

"Superb food in harmony with glorious decor" distinguishes this recently "revitalized" Santa Rosa Californian boasting a "romantic setting" "overlooking the vineyards"; the locavore dishes are "beautifully presented" by a "polite, prompt" staff also offering an "extensive" selection of Sonoma-centric vintages, and while it's "expensive", it's deemed "worth it", whether for a "special occasion" or "after a day at the wineries."

Johnny Garlic's *Californian*

| 20 | 18 | 20 | $30 |

Windsor | 8988 Brooks Rd. S. (Los Amigos Rd.) | 707-836-8300
NEW **Santa Rosa** | 1460 Farmers Ln. (bet. Bennet Valley Rd. & Hoen Frontage Rd.) | 707-571-1800
www.johnnygarlics.com

"TV chef" Guy Fieri owns these midpriced Bay Area chain links serving "dependable" Californian cuisine "with flair" in a "fun" "pub-type" atmosphere that can get "a little frenetic"; though some "expect more" "wow", and service varies, "portions are decent" and "all seem to be having a good time"; P.S. "they aren't kidding about the garlic."

Jole *American*

| ▽ 27 | 20 | 22 | $54 |

Calistoga | Mount View Hotel | 1457 Lincoln Ave. (bet. Fair Way & Washington St.) | 707-942-5938 | www.jolerestaurant.com

"Top-quality local ingredients" are whipped into "innovative" New American small plates offered à la carte or in "constantly changing, never-boring" tasting menus at this "wonderful" Calistoga option with a "cute" "neighborhood feel"; though it's on the "expensive" side, "helpful" service and a selection of small-production wines add value, making it "worth the drive" from afar.

K&L Bistro *French*

| 25 | 19 | 24 | $46 |

Sebastopol | 119 S. Main St. (bet. Bodega Ave. & Burnett St.) | 707-823-6614 | www.klbistro.com

"A little bit of Paris" in Sebastapol, this "sophisticated" bistro with "small-town friendliness" is a local "go-to" for "delicious" French fare paired with "excellent" wines; some say they get "a little claustrophobic" inside, but most don't mind the "small storefront" setting in light of the "reasonable prices", not to mention staffers who serve with "professionalism and good cheer."

Kenwood Ⓜ *American/French*

| 25 | 22 | 25 | $55 |

Kenwood | 9900 Sonoma Hwy./Hwy. 12 (Libby Ave.) | 707-833-6326 | www.kenwoodrestaurant.com

Nestled "in the middle of Sonoma Valley's vineyards", this "comfortable" Kenwood "country restaurant" is cited for its "reliable", "delicious" American-French fare, "exceptional wine list" and "high-quality" service; however, it's the "wonderful views" from the patio that really help to make "every visit special."

Kitchen Door *Eclectic*

| 22 | 17 | 17 | $30 |

Napa | Oxbow Public Mkt. | 610 First St. (bet. Silverado Trail & Soscal Ave.) | 707-226-1560 | www.kitchendoornapa.com

Todd Humphries (of the defunct Martini House) "has another winner" in this "casual" cafe in Napa's Oxbow Market proffering "innovative"

Eclectic eats from a "rustic" "open kitchen" for "down-to-earth prices"; those bothered by the "cafeteria-type ordering" will be happy to learn that full table service started post-Survey at brunch, lunch and dinner, both inside and on the "lovely" "deck" overlooking the river.

La Boulange *Bakery*   22 | 17 | 18 | $15

Mill Valley | Strawberry Vill. | 800 Redwood Hwy. (Belvedere Dr.) | 415-381-1260
Novato | Hamilton Mktpl. | 5800 Nave Dr. (bet. N. Hamilton Pkwy. & Roblar Dr.) | 415-382-8594
www.laboulangebakery.com
See review in City of San Francisco Directory.

NEW La Condesa *Mexican*   ∇ 24 | 18 | 18 | $43

St. Helena | 1320 Main St. (bet. Adams St. & Hunt Ave.) | 707-967-8111 | www.lacondesanapavalley.com
"Fantastic", "inventive", somewhat "pricey" Mexican *comida* comes to St. Helena by way of this "friendly", colorful new offshoot of an "up-scale" Austin hot spot; there's "no shortage of tequila" here – in fact, there's almost "too many to choose from" – the effects of which make it often as "loud" as a "bowling alley."

La Gare M *French*   27 | 22 | 26 | $44

Santa Rosa | 208 Wilson St. (3rd St.) | 707-528-4355 | www.lagarerestaurant.com
"A favorite of Santa Rosans" for over 30 years, this French "destina-tion" transports followers with its "cozy" decor "reminiscent" of a "country inn" as a backdrop for "superlative" renditions of classics from "rack of lamb" to "frogs' legs"; a "warm, hospitable" staff "makes you feel like family", and while it's all "a little dated", most savor the "step back in time."

La Ginestra M *Italian*   ∇ 22 | 16 | 20 | $30

Mill Valley | 127 Throckmorton Ave. (bet. Madrona St. & Miller Ave.) | 415-388-0224 | www.laginestramv.com
"To-die-for homemade ravioli" is the highlight at this "little", "old-style" Southern Italian that's "been around Mill Valley for years" (since 1964); the homey decor, "terrific service" and "reasonable prices" make it a "great family-dining" place, suitable for "everyday" and "special-occasion" dinners alike.

LaSalette *Portuguese*   24 | 19 | 23 | $45

Sonoma | Mercado Ctr. | 452 First St. E. (bet. Napa & Spain Sts.) | 707-938-1927 | www.lasalette-restaurant.com
"Save the airfare to Portugal" suggest fans of this "lovely", "friendly oasis" "tucked away" "off the square" in Sonoma, where chef-owner Manny Azevedo cooks "eye-opening" Portuguese dishes "in an open oven" and staffers "seem to genuinely care"; prices won't break the bank, while the space is "cramped" but "pleasant", making "outside on the patio" the seating of choice "in good weather."

La Taquiza ⊠ *Mexican*   ∇ 27 | 15 | 17 | $13

Napa | 2007 Redwood Rd. (Solano Ave.) | 707-224-2320 | www.lataquizanapa.com
A former French Laundry baker and his wife are behind this "simple" Mexican take-out taqueria in Napa, where nearly everything on the

fish-centric menu is so "wonderfully fresh" and "authentic", you "could be sitting on the pier in Ensenada"; though word is "the service and the decor are not so great", at least you can get in and out "quick."

La Toque   *French*   27 | 25 | 26 | $98

Napa | Westin Verasa Napa | 1314 McKinstry St. (Soscol Ave.) | 707-257-5157 | www.latoque.com

For all the drama of "ultrafine dining" without the "snooty" attitude, "few restaurants equal" Ken Frank's Napa "special-occasion" New French inside the Westin Verasa where "superb" prix fixes come paired with "killer international" wines courtesy of "amazing sommeliers"; "if your budget can stand it, book the chef's kitchen table", although you'll still receive "top-notch" treatment (with prices to match) in the "comfortable" "modern" dining room; P.S. the adjacent Bank Bar offers a less-expensive menu throughout the day.

Ledford House Ⓜ *Californian/Mediterranean*   ▽ 27 | 26 | 24 | $41

Albion | 3000 N. Hwy. 1 (Spring Grove Rd.) | 707-937-0282 | www.ledfordhouse.com

At this place that's "perched on a bluff" in Albion on the Mendocino coast, husband-and-wife chef-owners "make sure you are happy" with "fabulous", slightly expensive Californian-Mediterranean fare, matched with area wines and "wonderful" service; insiders know to "be there by sunset" for the most "panoramic views", though the "lovely room" and nightly live music are their own draws – no wonder it's always full of folks celebrating "birthdays, anniversaries and special occasions."

Left Bank   *French*   20 | 21 | 19 | $39

Larkspur | Blue Rock Inn | 507 Magnolia Ave. (Ward St.) | 415-927-3331 | www.leftbank.com

"Dependable" brasserie fare at moderate prices is the deal at this "bustling", "family-friendly" French trio (co-owned by La Folie chef Roland Passot) boasting "attractive decor"; service can be either "prompt" or "slow" depending on the staffer (though most are "friendly"), but each branch has outdoor seating that's indisputably "relaxing."

Le Garage   *French*   24 | 19 | 22 | $42

Sausalito | 85 Liberty Ship Way (Marinship Way) | 415-332-5625 | www.legaragebistrosausalito.com

Take your "taste buds for service" at this slightly pricey converted repair shop "on the water in Sausalito", where "accented" staffers in "auto-repair overalls" deliver "fantastic" French bistro fare; some surveyors don't like that it "gets loud when it's full (and it's usually full)", but everyone loves when "the weather's warm" and the steel-and-glass doors are rolled up, allowing an unobstructed "view of the yachts" at the Schoonmaker Point Marina.

Little River Inn Restaurant   *Californian/Seafood*   22 | 21 | 24 | $45

Little River | Little River Inn | 7901 N. Hwy. 1 (Little River Airport Rd.) | 707-937-5942 | www.littleriverinn.com

Choose between the "beautiful" dining room with an "unexpected" "garden view" or "bliss at the bar", which boasts a "perfect" vista of the "Pacific coastline" at this "welcoming" "destination" attached to a "historic inn" in Mendocino's Little River; in addition to "delicious" if a bit "expensive" Cal seafood and a "superb wine list", "buttery" "Swedish pancakes" seduce the brunch bunch who "spend the weekend" here for a "romantic" "getaway."

Lococo's Cucina Rustica ☒ *Italian* 26 | 20 | 23 | $36

Santa Rosa | 117 Fourth St. (Wilson St.) | 707-523-2227 | www.lococos.net
As "perfect for a romantic evening" as it is for "families needing a night out without breaking the bank", this "cute" Downtown Santa Rosa ristorante dishes out "fabulous", "rich" fare including "fine pastas and pizzas"; "accommodating" staffers "add to your dining pleasure", but just bear in mind that it's quite "popular", thus "frenetic" and "difficult to get into on weekends."

Lotus Cuisine of India *Indian* 25 | 21 | 23 | $24

San Rafael | 704 Fourth St. (Tamalpais Ave.) | 415-456-5808 | www.lotusrestaurant.com

Anokha Cuisine of India *Indian*

Novato | 811 Grant Ave. (bet. Reichert & Sherman Aves.) | 415-892-3440 | www.anokharestaurant.com

Café Lotus *Indian*

Fairfax | 1912 Sir Francis Drake Blvd. (bet. Claus & Taylor Drs.) | 415-457-7836 | www.cafelotusfairfax.com
"Exquisite flavors of India shine" at this Bay Area trio offering "authentic", "perfectly seasoned" dishes, including "lots of gluten-free options", all at "reasonable" prices; diners "love the retractable roof" at the San Rafael original and the "convivial" atmosphere in Novato (both also have "tasty lunch buffets"), while the cafe is pegged as a "hole-in-the-wall", but all boast generally "friendly, helpful" service.

NEW Lucy Restaurant & Bar *Californian* – | – | – | E
(fka Bardessono)

Yountville | Bardessono Hotel & Spa | 6526 Yount St. (bet. Finnel Rd. & Washington St.) | 707-204-6030 | www.bardessono.com
"Chef Scargle is giving real and new meaning to farm-to-table" at this all-day eatery in Yountville's LEED-certified Bardessono Hotel and Spa, where he offers a pricey, garden-centric Californian menu with many of the ingredients grown on-site; the casual dining room boasts a dramatic, 21-ft.-long communal table, but guests can also dine on the patio or at the bar pouring artisan cocktails.

MacCallum House *Californian* 24 | 24 | 21 | $57

Mendocino | MacCallum House Inn | 45020 Albion St. (bet. Hesser & Kasten Sts.) | 707-937-5763 | www.maccallumhouse.com
"Take a break from those gorgeous Pacific vistas" nearby to focus on the "creative", "indulgent" fare and "interesting" cocktails offered at this "intimate" Californian in a "Victorian marvel"–cum-B&B "in the heart of beautiful Mendocino"; while service might be a bit "uneven", overnight guests (and in-the-know locals) contend the breakfast is "worth rising" for; P.S. a table "near the fireplace" is particularly "romantic."

☑ Madrona Manor 27 | 26 | 27 | $104
Restaurant ☒ *American/French*

Healdsburg | Madrona Manor | 1001 Westside Rd. (W. Dry Creek Rd.) | 707-433-4231 | www.madronamanor.com
"Prepare to be spoiled" at this "fine old manor" house inn/restaurant in Healdsburg surrounded by gorgeous gardens and filled with

"museum-quality furnishings" that make for a "magical" setting in which to enjoy "outstanding", "beautifully presented" French–New American cuisine; it's "very pricey", but considering the "classy service", "interesting wine pairings" and culinary "theatrics", it's more of "an event" than a meal and "worth it for special occasions"; P.S. closed Monday and Tuesday.

Marché aux Fleurs 🏵Ⓜ *French* | 27 | 24 | 26 | $55 |

Ross | 23 Ross Common (Lagunitas Rd.) | 415-925-9200 | www.marcheauxfleursrestaurant.com

"Loyal" Ross locals "keep coming back" to this "cozy, rustic" bistro for the "gracious" husband-wife owners' "brilliant" New French cuisine made with "farmer's-market" finds (the "menu lists the pedigree of each ingredient"), matched by a "superb wine list featuring many excellent boutique wineries"; though it's a bit of a "splurge", fans deem it as suitable for a "casual" "weeknight" meal as a "special occasion", both even more "fabulous" when the "beautiful garden patio" is open.

Marinitas *Mexican/Pan-Latin* | 22 | 20 | 19 | $32 |

San Anselmo | 218 Sir Francis Drake Blvd. (Bank St.) | 415-454-8900 | www.marinitas.net

A "contemporary" mix of "upscale" Pan-Latin eats starring "tasty" Argentinean steak and ceviche is washed down with "great margaritas" at this San Anselmo cantina with a "pleasant, dimly lit atmosphere" and "friendly staff"; it's usually "impossible to carry on a conversation in normal tones", but "most people come for the fun", "uplifting" "party scene" anyway.

Market *American* | 22 | 20 | 21 | $44 |

St. Helena | 1347 Main St. (bet. Adams St. & Hunt Ave.) | 707-963-3799 | www.marketsthelena.com

Both visitors on "a Sunday drive in wine country" and "fiercely loyal" St. Helena locals say "this place never fails to delight", with "flavorful, well-prepared" Traditional American comfort food that's "fairly priced for the quality"; bedecked with "stone walls and rich woodwork", the room is often "fully booked", but the "staff handles it well"; P.S. the "old-time-y bar" and no corkage fees are "added attractions."

🆕 Mateo's Cocina Latina *Mexican* | 21 | 20 | 19 | $38 |

Healdsburg | 214 Healdsburg Ave. (bet. Matheson & Mill Sts.) | 707-433-1520 | www.mateoscocinalatina.com

"Forget about burritos", "inspired impresario" Mateo Granados (ex Dry Creek Kitchen) is "redefining Mexican cooking" at his "hip" new midpriced cantina in Healdsburg where "inventively presented", locally sourced Yucatán cuisine and "tongue-tingling" sauces meet in "revelatory ways"; critics note it's "still working out the service kinks", but the garden "patio" and "excellent" tequila bar menu are nice perks.

Max's Cafe of Corte Madera *Deli* | 20 | 17 | 19 | $26 |

Corte Madera | 60 Madera Blvd. (Hwy. 101) | 415-924-6297 | www.maxsworld.com

See review in City of San Francisco Directory.

Meadowood, The Grill *Californian*   21 | 20 | 22 | $47
(aka The Grill at Meadowood)
St. Helena | Meadowood Napa Valley | 900 Meadowood Ln. (Silverado Trail) | 707-968-3144 | www.meadowood.com

Surveyors looking for a "relaxing" "getaway" are drawn to the "low-key elegance" and "fantastic" fairway "views" that surround this "casual" "country club"–esque Californian grill at St. Helena's Meadowood resort, where a "friendly" staff serves breakfast through dinner; "while it pales in comparison" to the experience at its high-end upstairs sibling, if you can "grab a table on the veranda", it makes for a "memorable meal."

Meadowood, The Restaurant ⊠ *Californian*   27 | 26 | 27 | $150
(aka The Restaurant at Meadowood)
St. Helena | Meadowood Napa Valley | 900 Meadowood Ln. (Silverado Trail) | 707-967-1205 | www.meadowood.com

Hidden in a "high-end" St. Helena "country club"–like resort with "serene views of forest" and "croquet fields", this gourmet "delight" is "a shrine to cuisine" under the helm of chef Christopher Kostow, who displays "pure artistry" with his "stellar" Californian tasting menus (and "whimsical presentations"); "fantastic premium" wines add to the "great experience", as does a "perfectly" coordinated "small army of servers" at your "every beck and call" in the revamped dining room (reopened post-Survey); it's definitely a "sky-is-the-limit" tab, but "worth the splurge."

Mendo Bistro *American*   26 | 21 | 25 | $38
Fort Bragg | The Company Store | 301 N. Main St. (Redwood Ave.) | 707-964-4974 | www.mendobistro.com

Chef Nicholas Petti's surprisingly "creative" New American in "remote" Fort Bragg is "worth the trip" for its "fresh" seafood selections ("prepared almost any way you like") and "the best crab cakes in Northern California" (when in season); "affordable" "Mendocino wines", a "caring staff" and a "beautiful view" of Downtown from the "high-ceilinged" former Company Store make the experience especially "memorable."

Mendocino Café *Eclectic*   21 | 17 | 21 | $27
Mendocino | 10451 Lansing St. (Albion St.) | 707-937-6141 | www.mendocinocafe.com

"Comfortable and cozy", this affordable low-key cafe in "pricey Mendocino" offers a "broad menu" of mostly "organic", "Asian-influenced" Eclectic eats (the "yummy" Thai burrito is a particular "favorite"); a few wonder whether the fare should be described as "fusion or confusion", but who cares when you can "grab a seat on the deck" and enjoy "breathtaking views" over the water.

Mendocino Hotel Restaurant *Californian*   21 | 25 | 22 | $41
Mendocino | Mendocino Hotel | 45080 Main St. (bet. Kasten & Lansing Sts.) | 707-937-0511 | www.mendocinohotel.com

When on a "getaway up in the redwoods", be sure to stop at this "gorgeous" hotel in "one of the most beautiful little towns on earth" (that would be Mendocino), proffering "hearty" bistro eats in the "oak and Victoriana–festooned" Lobby Lounge, locally sourced Californian cuisine in the "dark, quiet, romantic" dining room and "old world charm" throughout; indeed, it "will take you back in time", with "enjoyable" service and not-too-expensive prices to boot.

Meritage Martini
Oyster Bar & Grille *Italian*

▽ 20 | 17 | 20 | $44

Sonoma | 165 W. Napa St. (bet. 1st & 2nd Sts.) | 707-938-9430 | www.sonomameritage.com

"For good food and convivial company", locals head to this Northern Italian near Sonoma Plaza serving "well-prepared" fare and oysters that are half off during daily happy hours; as for the service and decor, the staff is "friendly and efficient" and the "hand-blown glass fixtures are beautiful."

🆕 Miller's
East Coast Delicatessen *Deli/Jewish*

21 | 12 | 18 | $19

San Rafael | Montecito Shopping Ctr. | 421 Third St. (Grand Ave.) | 415-453-3354 | www.millersdelisf.com

See review in City of San Francisco Directory.

Model Bakery *Bakery*

22 | 14 | 18 | $14

Napa | Oxbow Public Mkt. | 644 First St. (bet. Silverado Trail & Soscol Ave.) | 707-963-8192

St. Helena | 1357 Main St. (bet. Adams St. & Hunt Ave.) | 707-963-8192

www.themodelbakery.com

Although these "low-key" St. Helena–Napa "coffee stops" are "primarily" "neighborhood" bakeries, they also offer reasonably priced fare for a "casual breakfast or lunch", including "great tartine sandwiches", "tasty pizzas" and "delicious" pastries; "service can be slow" and the Main Street original has more "local ambiance", but both bake up their "famous" English muffins that are "out of this world."

Mombo's Pizza *Pizza*

23 | 7 | 19 | $16

Santa Rosa | 1880 Mendocino Ave. (Silva Ave.) | 707-528-3278

Sebastopol | 560 Gravenstein Hwy. N. (Covert Ln.) | 707-823-7492

www.mombospizza.com

Some transplants call the "reasonably priced" thin-crust pizzas served at this pair of Sonoma County parlors the most "excellent" they've eaten "since leaving NY" ("don't miss the pesto pizza"); since both locales are of the "hole-in-the-wall", counter-service variety, "most patrons order takeout or delivery"; P.S. the Sebastopol location carries wine along with beer from local Moonlight Brewery.

Monti's Rotisserie &
Bar *American/Mediterranean*

22 | 20 | 21 | $37

Santa Rosa | Montgomery Village Shopping Ctr. | 714 Village Ct. (Farmers Ln.) | 707-568-4404 | www.starkrestaurants.com

"Creative food *can* be had in a shopping center" attest fans of this "neighborhood restaurant" in Santa Rosa, where the midpriced New American–Med fare is "dependably delicious" and delivered by a "willing staff"; dining "near the wood-fired oven" (where "fantastic" "nightly rotisserie specials" are cooked) in the terra-cotta, wood and wrought-iron–accented interior is "cozy" on "winter nights", while a patio beckons when the weather's warm.

Moosse Café *Californian*

22 | 20 | 22 | $34

Mendocino | The Blue Heron Inn | 390 Kasten St. (Albion St.) | 707-937-4323 | www.themoosse.com

Visitors and locals alike consider this "charming" cafe at the cozy Blue Heron Inn a "favorite" for its "original", midpriced Cal cuisine proffered by a "friendly" crew; whether at a table "near the fireplace" in the "intimate" dining room or on the "garden patio" with a "view of the ocean", it's "one of the loveliest spots in Mendocino" for "lunch or dinner."

Morimoto Napa *Japanese*

25 | 24 | 22 | $74

Napa | 610 Main St. (5th St.) | 707-252-1600 | www.morimotonapa.com

Like "your typical Morimoto" kitchen, even basic dishes such as "toro tartare" and "tableside tofu" are "turned into creative" "masterpieces" at this "hip" riverfront Japanese in Downtown Napa that lures star-struck "tourists" with "beautifully presented", "haute" seafood and "one-of-a-kind drinks" in *Architectural Digest*–worthy surroundings; some prefer to "eat out on the terrace" to escape the "rowdy, loud bar scene" and say service is not up to "*Iron Chef*" standards, but most contend it "almost lives up to the incredible hype" so long as diners have the main ingredient – "moolah!"

Murray Circle *Californian*

25 | 26 | 24 | $62

Sausalito | Cavallo Point Resort in Fort Baker | 602 Murray Circle (Sausalito Lateral Rd.) | 415-339-4750 | www.murraycircle.com

"The old officer's club" is alive and well at this "creative" Californian in a former Sausalito army fort that serves some of the "most innovative" food in Marin, be it for brunch "on the porch" while you "watch the sailboats cruise" or dinner "in the bar" by "the fireplace"; overall, "the view, the history" and the "like-clockwork" service make it "well worth the schlep" "across the Golden Gate Bridge."

Mustards Grill *American/Californian*

25 | 21 | 23 | $50

Yountville | 7399 St. Helena Hwy./Hwy. 29 (bet. Oakville Grade Rd. & Washington St.) | 707-944-2424 | www.mustardsgrill.com

Cindy Pawlcyn's "classic" "roadside bistro" outside Yountville "continues to stop traffic" at "lunch and dinner" with its "hearty portions" of "inventive" Cal–New American "comfort food" (with vegetables from their own garden) served with "amazing grace" in "relaxed", "noisy", "kitschy" digs; it's "pricey" and reservations are "essential" as even the bar gets "crowed" with everyone from "first-time foodies" to local "winemakers."

Napa Valley Wine Train *Californian*

22 | 26 | 24 | $89

Napa | 1275 McKinstry St. (bet. 1st St. & Soscol Ave.) | 707-253-2111 | www.winetrain.com

It's "always a fun experience" "sampling wines" and "fine" Californian cuisine as this "old-fashioned train" chugs past Napa's "beautiful vineyards"; sure, some snobs snarl there are "better options for a valley visit", but far more deem the upscale excursion a "scenic and taste treat" that "everyone should do . . . once."

Nick's Cove *Californian*

21 | 22 | 21 | $44

Marshall | Nick's Cove & Cottages | 23240 Hwy. 1 (4 mi. north of Marshall-Petaluma Rd.) | 415-723-1071 | www.nickscove.com

Previously owned by SF restaurant impresario Pat Kuleto, this "rustic", "retro-fish house" (and cottages for overnight guests) on Tomales Bay in Marshall recently "changed hands" and has undergone a "reimagining" including a new chef and live music; just add in "a fireplace, an ocean view and beautifully prepared seafood" and "what's not to love?"; P.S. midweek specials include a $25 prix fixe and half-off bottles from the extensive wine list.

955 Restaurant Ⓜ *American/French* 25 | 22 | 22 | $44
Mendocino | 955 Ukiah St. (School St.) | 707-937-1955 | www.955restaurant.com

Despite its off-the-beaten-path address, this longtime Mendocino "locals' secret" draws them in with "creative", reasonably priced New American–French fare and a staff overseen by husband-and-wife "owner-operators"; additionally, "no one is in a hurry" here, which always makes for a "relaxing atmosphere" in the "peaceful and beautiful" setting.

Norman Rose Tavern *American* 20 | 19 | 19 | $37
Napa | 1401 First St. (Franklin St.) | 707-258-1516 | www.normanrosenapa.com

At this "clubbyish" American gastropub in Downtown Napa, the "hard-to-beat" burgers and other locally sourced "bar food" are paired with "good wine" and suds, helping to "keep this place jam-packed daily" and into the night; while some feel service could use some work, and surveyors disagree on prices (some say "fair", others cry foul), the "nice atmosphere" helps make it a "go-to" for many.

North Coast Brewing Company *American* 19 | 16 | 18 | $28
Fort Bragg | 455 N. Main St. (Pine St.) | 707-964-3400 | www.northcoastbrewing.com

"In the heart of Fort Bragg", and across the street from the "fabulous microbrewery" that crafts the suds on tap here, this "family-friendly" American grill serves up "decent" pub grub along with an "upbeat vibe"; modest prices add to the allure, but in the end, it's "all about the beer."

Oenotri *Italian* 24 | 20 | 22 | $49
Napa | Napa Sq. | 1425 First St. (bet. Franklin & School Sts.) | 707-252-1022 | www.oenotri.com

The Oliveto alums behind this "trendy" Southern Italian let their "roots show" with "creative pastas", "killer pizza" and "salumi plates", made in an "open kitchen" and paired with "interesting" Boot vinos; it's "on the expensive side" for "small portions" and often so "crowded" it can be "hard to have a conversation", but many say this bit of "Naples" in Napa is still "worth the trip"; P.S. Saturday and Sunday open for dinner only.

Osake Ⓩ *Californian/Japanese* 27 | 21 | 24 | $38
Santa Rosa | 2446 Patio Ct. (Farmers Ln.) | 707-542-8282 | www.garychus.com

"Park yourself at the sushi bar" at this "austere" Santa Rosa Japanese, where chef-owner Gary Chu "puts on quite a show" as he "turns out amazing, creative" dishes in "generous portions" before a "rowdy, feel-good crowd"; it's all a "bit pricey", but most agree the service is "wonderful", and both the "delicious" food and attendant "theatrics" are "unmatchable" in the area.

FOOD DECOR SERVICE COST

Osteria Stellina *Italian*   24 | 17 | 21 | $42
Point Reyes Station | 11285 Hwy. 1 (bet. 2nd & 3rd Sts.) |
415-663-9988 | www.osteriastellina.com
The kind of "place a traveler dreams of finding", this "unpretentious"
Italian in "bucolic" Point Reyes Station transforms ingredients from "local waters" and "surrounding farms" into "delicious", "rustic" dishes
("get the goat") paired with "outstanding" wine; true, the "ordinary"-
looking room can get "crowded" and "super loud", but "fair prices"
and "pleasant" service compensate.

Oxbow Wine   ▽ 21 | 20 | 22 | $30
Merchant *Californian/Mediterranean*
Napa | Oxbow Public Mkt. | 610 First St. (bet. Silverado Trail &
Soscol Ave.) | 707-257-5200 | www.oxbowwinemerchant.com
Located in Oxbow Public Market, this Cal-Med shop/restaurant doles
out "tastings" of an "amazing" wine, cheese and cured meats inventory,
as well as more substantial Cal-Med "small plates" throughout the
day; while it may be a "little too pricey" for an order-at-the-counter
place, the outdoor seating on the Napa River adds to the appeal.

Pacific Catch *Seafood*   22 | 17 | 20 | $26
Corte Madera | Town Ctr. Corte Madera | 133 Corte Madera Town Ctr.
(off Hwy. 101) | 415-927-3474 | www.pacificcatch.com
See review in City of San Francisco Directory.

Pasta Pomodoro *Italian*   19 | 17 | 20 | $22
Mill Valley | Strawberry Vill. | 800 Redwood Hwy. (Belvedere Dr.) |
415-388-1692
Novato | Vintage Oaks at Novato | 140 Vintage Way (Rowland Blvd.) |
415-899-1861
www.pastapomodoro.com
See review in City of San Francisco Directory.

Pearl ⊠Ⓜ *Californian*   ▽ 25 | 18 | 24 | $37
Napa | 1339 Pearl St. (bet. Franklin & Polk Sts.) | 707-224-9161 |
www.therestaurantpearl.com
Patrons say this Californian is indeed a "pearl" among the "upscale" options in Downtown Napa – a "cute" (if "rather bare") bistro that entices
"regulars and touristas" with "awesome oysters" and other "simple" but
"excellent" homestyle cooking; "reasonable" prices, "smiling" service
and "gracious owners" who are "there to greet you" add to the appeal.

Pearl's Phat Burgers *Burgers*   24 | 13 | 19 | $13
Mill Valley | 8 E. Blithedale Ave. (Camino Alto) | 415-381-6010 |
www.pearlsdeluxe.com
See review in City of San Francisco Directory.

Peter Lowell's *Italian*   ▽ 21 | 16 | 15 | $32
Sebastopol | 7385 Healdsburg Ave. (Florence Ave.) | 707-829-1077 |
www.peterlowells.com
"Interesting creations" of "healthy food" anchor this "popular"
Sebastopol hangout serving midpriced, organic "farm-to-table" Italian
and "local" biodynamic wines; regulars warn "don't eat here if you're
in a hurry" (service can be "on the slow side") and wish the "modern"
LEED-certified space would "expand" since limited seating sometimes
means "sharing a table" both in the main room and on the "great" patio.

Piatti *Italian*

21 | 21 | 21 | $37

Mill Valley | 625 Redwood Hwy. (Hwy. 101) | 415-380-2525 | www.piatti.com
See review in East of San Francisco Directory.

Piazza D'Angelo *Italian*

20 | 19 | 20 | $39

Mill Valley | 22 Miller Ave. (bet. Sunnyside & Throckmorton Aves.) |
415-388-2000 | www.piazzadangelo.com
Near town square in Mill Valley, this "happening" Italian is a "longtime
local favorite", with "satisfying" renditions of the classics (including
"wood-fired pizza") that come with tabs that "aren't over the top";
while a "packed" bar offers "great people-watching", a "super" staff
oversees the "ever-crowded", oft-"noisy" dining room, bedecked with
a "wood-burning fireplace."

Pica Pica Maize Kitchen *Venezuelan*

20 | 14 | 17 | $16

Napa | Oxbow Public Mkt. | 610 First St. (bet. Silverado Trail &
Soscol Ave.) | 707-251-3757 | www.picapicakitchen.com
"Fresh Venezuelan street fare" is the "unusual" specialty at these casual
spots in San Francisco's Mission District and the Napa Oxbow Market,
where "arepas" – "little corn pillows of goodness" with meat or vegetable fillings – and "maize'wiches" made with sweet corn bread "provide a break from tacos and burritos"; though service can be uneven,
there's "great value" to be had, and newcomers "can't wait to go back."

Picco *Italian*

26 | 21 | 23 | $47

Larkspur | 320 Magnolia Ave. (King St.) | 415-924-0300 |
www.restaurantpicco.com
Central Marin locals frequent this Larkspur Cal-Italian "go-to" "with a
tableful of friends" to "try everything" from the menu of "innovative
small plates"; despite the "thirsty and hungry" crowds, service is "excellent", and while the "bustling" "bar scene" lends a "roadhouse"
vibe, this "casual eatery" is still a tad more serious than the popular
sister "pizzeria next door."

Pine Cone Diner ✍ *Diner*

▽ 21 | 15 | 14 | $16

Point Reyes Station | 60 Fourth St. (B St.) | 415-663-1536 |
www.pineconediner.com
A Point Reyes Station sojourn "isn't complete without at least one
meal" at this "hip" breakfast-and-lunch-only spot with "un-ironic"
1950s decor inside and "picnic-bench-style tables" outside; veterans
note there can be long "waits" ("especially on nice days") and the
"prickly" service "can be incredibly slow", but fans put up with it all for
the "delicious", "dressed-up" diner chow.

Pizza Antica *Pizza*

22 | 18 | 19 | $25

Mill Valley | Strawberry Vill. | 800 Redwood Hwy. (Belvedere Dr.) |
415-383-0600 | www.pizzaantica.com
See review in South of San Francisco Directory.

Pizzeria Picco *Pizza*

26 | 13 | 17 | $27

Larkspur | 316 Magnolia Ave. (King St.) | 415-945-8900 |
www.pizzeriapicco.com
Larkspur's "secret is out" about this "tiny", "upscale pizzeria" (the fancier, next-door sib to Picco) cranking out "truly divine", "Neapolitan"-
by-way-of-Californian "wood-fired pizzas" and "amazingly fresh" salads,

capped off by equally "crave-worthy" wines and "soft-serve" (drizzled with "olive oil or chocolate dipped"); despite being "mobbed" by "hungry people" "waiting patiently" to nab a "barstool" or sidewalk table, staffers "handle the crowds well", though many regulars just grab a "frozen" pie "to take home."

Pizzeria Tra Vigne   *Pizza*
| 23 | 16 | 18 | $28 |

St. Helena | Inn at Southbridge | 1016 Main St. (bet. Charter Oak Ave. & Pope St.) | 707-967-9999 | www.pizzeriatravigne.com

"In the land of the pretentious meal", this Downtown St. Helena Italian is a "casual", "not-too-pricey" alternative that "never disappoints" with its "wonderful pizzas", pastas and salads; since the roomy space is often "full of local families", it can get "noisy", but service is "friendly" and the "outdoor dining is very pleasant", "particularly in summer", while a "good choice of draft beers" and "no-corkage" policy sweeten the deal.

Plate Shop   Ⓜ *Californian*
| ▽ 22 | 18 | 21 | $46 |

Sausalito | 39 Caledonia St. (Johnson St.) | 415-887-9047 | www.plateshop.net

Chef Peter Erickson (of shuttered 1550 Hyde) creates "delicious" Californian "smallish plates worth sharing" using the bounty of the on-site garden in this Sausalito industrial setting that (like the name) nods to the area's ship-building past; service varies, and though the bill can add up, tipplers appreciate the curated wine list and "farm-to-glass cocktails."

Poggio   *Italian*
| 24 | 24 | 23 | $47 |

Sausalito | Casa Madrona | 777 Bridgeway (Bay St.) | 415-332-7771 | www.poggiotrattoria.com

It's "one of the first places tourists see as they leave the ferry landing", but this trattoria right on Sausalito's main drag is also "popular with locals" enamored of the "garden-inspired", "wood-fired" offerings, both inside the "supremely comfortable" dining room and "on the sidewalk where you can "watch the world go by"; "knowledgeable" service and a "wonderful wine list" complete a package that has fans returning "again and again."

Press   *American/Steak*
| 26 | 25 | 25 | $73 |

St. Helena | 587 St. Helena Hwy. (White Ln.) | 707-967-0550 | www.pressthelena.com

"Carnivores" rave about this St. Helena American's "exceptional" "charred red meat" plus sides "on a par with any steakhouse" and "big", all-Napa reds (including "old vintages") from an impressive cellar; a full-court press of "attentive" servers work the "beautiful", modern farmhouse-style quarters, and while regulars advise "take your cholesterol pills and your wallet", thrifty sorts seek out "the bar menu for a lighter tab."

Ravenous Cafe   Ⓜ *Californian/Eclectic*
| 22 | 19 | 20 | $41 |

Healdsburg | 117 North St. (Center St.) | 707-431-1302

This Healdsburg "perennial favorite" has relocated post-Survey from its Center Street bungalow back to its original tiny digs next to the Raven Theater, where there are only eight tables; the old crew is still serving up a full-fledged, daily changing "handwritten menu" of "fantastic", "fresh" Cal-Eclectic eats (some old favorites and some new ones), along with "terrific wines" and "warm vibes", all at a "reasonable price"; P.S. open Wednesday–Sunday for lunch and dinner.

Ravens' Restaurant *Vegan*   ▽ 25 | 22 | 21 | $44

Mendocino | Stanford Inn & Spa | 44850 Comptche Ukiah Rd. (Hwy. 1) | 707-937-5615 | www.ravensrestaurant.com

"Anyone not completely obsessed with meat will be happy", and maybe "learn some things about food", at this "gorgeous" Mendocino farm and inn serving "innovative" vegan and vegetarian dishes that "could easily grace the tables of the Bay Area's best"; though some suggest service can "fall a little flat" and pronounce prices "expensive", more agree an experience here is "pleasing on many levels."

Ɽ Redd *Californian*   28 | 23 | 26 | $70

Yountville | 6480 Washington St. (Oak Circle) | 707-944-2222 | www.reddnapavalley.com

Richard Reddington's "upscale without being stuffy" "special-occasion restaurant" is "a standout in Yountville's sea of greats", only with far "less show" and at "a fraction of the cost", presenting "brilliant" Californian cuisine (with "playful" East-meets-West "combinations") that's as "pleasing to the eye as to the palate"; the "simple, modern" indoor/outdoor digs may be "too cool" for some, but "impeccable without hovering" service plus a "deep wine list" (along with cheaper options for lunch or at the bar) leave most "with a foodie glow."

NEW Redd Wood *Pizza*   25 | 22 | 22 | $45

Yountville | 6755 Washington St. (bet. Burgundy Way & Madison St.) | 707-299-5030 | www.redd-wood.com

It's "no surprise" that Richard Reddington's "casual" Italian "just down the street" from his more formal Redd is a "spectacular" "new addition" to Yountville's restaurant scene, especially given the "excellent" pizzas fresh "out of the wood-burning oven", handmade pastas, salumi and other expertly prepared, "soulful" dishes accompanied by affordable local wines; understandably, tables in the "cozy" room overlooking the kitchen or on the "patio" are already tough to score.

Red Grape Pizzeria ❶ *American/Pizza*   24 | 17 | 21 | $26

Sonoma | 529 First St. W. (Napa St.) | 707-996-4103 | www.theredgrape.com

"Why go elsewhere for pizza in Sonoma?" ask fans of this "go-to place" for "fantastic, thin-crust" pies and a "varied menu" of "delicious" if basic American chow served by a "young, enthusiastic and efficient" staff; nitpickers call it "a little pricey for the ambiance" (think light-wood paneling and a concrete floor), but it's "always packed" nonetheless.

The Restaurant *American/Eclectic*   ▽ 22 | 18 | 23 | $60

Fort Bragg | 418 N. Main St. (Laurel St.) | 707-964-9800 | www.therestaurantfortbragg.com

Around "since 1973", this "neighborhood" "hidden gem" has been offering "surprisingly fine dining" in the "small town" of Fort Bragg; the husband-and-wife owners "provide outstanding service" along with "reliably good" (if not cheap) Eclectic–New American dinners in a "charming" dining room filled with "beautiful original oil paintings" by noted local artist Olaf Palm; P.S. closed Tuesday–Wednesday.

Restaurant at Stevenswood *American*   ▽ 25 | 21 | 21 | $64

Little River | Stevenswood Lodge | 8211 Shoreline Hwy./N. Hwy. 1
(1 mi. south of Mendocino) | 707-937-2810 | www.stevenswood.com

Situated in a Little River forest resort on the Mendocino coast, this "beautiful" New American presents a "small" but "excellent" menu of "brilliantly prepared and presented" fare; the "intimate" woodsy dining room, overseen by a "kind" staff "gets all the details right" from a roaring fireplace to "lovely background dinner music" to "delicious" breakfasts that "go far beyond" the usual; P.S. dinner is not served Wednesdays.

Risibisi *Italian*   25 | 21 | 23 | $45

Petaluma | 154 Petaluma Blvd. N. (bet. Washington & Western Sts.) |
707-766-7600 | www.risibisirestaurant.com

Serving "satisfying and luxurious" dishes that are a "mashup of California and Italy", this "congenial" Petaluma ristorante features a "cozy", "intimate" space that makes it a "nice choice" for a "quiet, private tête-à-tête"; a "warm" staff that "works very hard to please you" seals the deal – and it's a "good value" to boot.

Rocker Oysterfellers Ⓜ *American/Southern* ▽ 24 | 18 | 21 | $41

Valley Ford | Valley Ford Hotel | 14415 Hwy. 1 (School St.) |
707-876-1983 | www.rockeroysterfellers.com

Set in a restored roadside hotel, this "funky" Valley Ford saloon dishes out oysters, po' boys and other "heavenly" Southern comforts with the hospitality to match; it's a "favorite stop" en route to Bodega Bay whether you "eat in the bar" or "outside in the summer", particularly on Thursdays when they offer $1 Tomales Bays ; P.S. dinner is served Thursday–Sunday and there's Saturday lunch and Sunday brunch.

🆕 Rosso Pizzeria &   26 | 19 | 24 | $29
Mozzarella Bar *Italian/Pizza*

Petaluma | 151 Petaluma Blvd. S. (C St.) | 707-772-5177

Rosso Pizzeria & Wine Bar *Italian/Pizza*

Santa Rosa | Creekside Ctr. | 53 Montgomery Dr. (2nd St.) |
707-544-3221
www.rossopizzeria.com

They may be "hard to find", but these pizza tsars in Santa Rosa and Petaluma are "worth the search" for "awesome", "blistered" wood-fired pies made with "top-notch ingredients" and "cracker-thin" crusts; "unusual charcuterie", an "outstanding" list of "fairly priced" biodynamic wines and a "friendly, knowledgeable" staff add to the appeal of the "pretty basic" spots, as do "excellent daily specials" that "rarely miss a beat."

Royal Thai *Thai*   27 | 21 | 23 | $24

San Rafael | 610 Third St. (Irwin St.) | 415-485-1074 |
www.royalthaisanrafael.com

"Unwavering" for some "three decades", this "pleasant, centrally located, old house" in San Rafael turns out "terrific Thai" that customers call the "best in Marin"; "you could throw a dart at the menu and not go wrong" with offerings like the "yummy pad Thai", curries and crêpes, all "at good prices" and served by a "pleasant, efficient" staff, all adding up to "a winner."

FOOD | DECOR | SERVICE | COST

Rustic, Francis's Favorites *Italian*   21 | 25 | 24 | $44

Geyserville | Francis Ford Coppola Winery | 300 Via Archimedes (Fredson Rd.) | 707-857-1400 | www.franciscoppolawinery.com

Boasting "one of the best views in the wine country", "fab movie memorabilia" for "flick buffs" and a "gorgeous swimming pool" and "bocce court" "for the entire family", Frances Ford Coppola's indoor/outdoor winery restaurant could have only been "designed by a master showman"; it's "a little corny", but "large portions" of "flavorful" Italian fare and pizzas served by a "friendly staff" make this "destination" "worth the trip to Geyserville."

Rutherford Grill *American*   24 | 22 | 23 | $41

Rutherford | 1180 Rutherford Rd. (Hwy. 29) | 707-963-1792 | www.hillstone.com

Some of the "best comfort food in wine country" (including "knife-and-fork" ribs and "to-die-for" artichokes) and "no corkage fee" make it "hard to drive past" Rutherford's "hopping" member of the Hillstone chain – "high praise when you consider the area"; alas, there's often a "wait for a table", so insiders recommend passing the time sipping a glass from the "nicely priced" reserve wine list – and playing it cool "if a famous vintner is seated beside you at the bar."

Santé *Californian/French*   ▽ 25 | 23 | 24 | $82

Sonoma | Fairmont Sonoma Mission Inn & Spa | 100 Boyes Blvd. (Sonoma Hwy.) | 707-939-2415 | www.fairmont.com

It's got "some of the best food in Sonoma County" say supporters of this upscale destination whose "outstanding" Cal-French fare – infused with "quality ingredients" and "tasting as good as it looks" – is paired with an "extensive wine list" (about 600 vinos); while dissenters question the "hype" surrounding the place, "attentive but not hovering" service and sophisticated decor win over most, even if it all "comes at a price."

Sazon Peruvian Cuisine *Peruvian*   ▽ 27 | 16 | 25 | $24

Santa Rosa | 1129 Sebastopol Rd. (bet. Burbank & Roseland Sts.) | 707-523-4346 | www.sazonsr.com

"Don't let the exterior deter you" advise admirers of this Santa Rosa "revelation" with a nondescript facade – inside the "small" space, there are "lots of colors" with "bright flavors to match", largely in the "incredible" ceviche; "foodies" ready for an "adventure in eating" dive right in, but for novices, the "knowledgeable" staff provides guidance, helping make a Peruvian meal here a "fabulous time", and for not too much dinero.

⊠ Scoma's Sausalito *Seafood*   25 | 21 | 22 | $49

Sausalito | 588 Bridgeway (Princess St.) | 415-332-9551 | www.scomassausalito.com

See review in City of San Francisco Directory.

Scopa *Italian*   26 | 18 | 23 | $47

Healdsburg | 109 Plaza St. (bet. Center St. & Healdsburg Ave.) | 707-433-5282 | www.scopahealdsburg.com

"If you want to feel like a local in Healdsburg", make tracks to this "boisterous" Italian hidden "under an old barber shop sign" for "absolutely wonderful" "pizza, pasta and starters" that will "put a smile on your face"; it's "always packed" (so "make a reservation well ahead") and the "tiny, tiny" quarters mean tables are a "bit too tight", but a "delightful staff" smooths over any bumps; P.S. area vintners pour their latest on Winemaker Wednesdays.

Sea Modern Thai ▣ *Thai* | 27 | 22 | 25 | $33 |

Petaluma | 500 Petaluma Blvd. S. (G St.) | 707-766-6633

Sea Thai Bistro *Thai*

Corte Madera | 60 Corte Madera (Redwood Ave.) | 415-927-8333 ▣
Santa Rosa | 2323 Sonoma Ave. (Farmers Ln.) | 707-528-8333
www.seathaibistro.com

"Even if you're not that into Thai", fans say "you'll love" this "upscale" North Bay trio that whips up "fabulous" fusion fare with a "modern twist" ("pad Thai and chicken satay it ain't"); things can get "loud", but "wonderful, warm" service and "sleek" decor help ensure most "come back" for more "adventurous eating"; P.S. fish-phobes take note: the name is an abbreviation for 'Southeast Asia.'

Solbar *Californian* | 26 | 24 | 24 | $57 |

Calistoga | Solage Resort | 755 Silverado Trail (bet. Brannan St. & Pickett Rd.) | 707-226-0850 | www.solbarnv.com

"Super wines" and an "inventive" Californian menu with "something for everybody" ("light for the spa crowd, and hearty for the rest") reveal the chef's French Laundry roots at this "beautiful" "poolside" spot at Calistoga's Solage Resort; inside the "trendy" interior, "young" "glitterati" are attended to by a "knowledgeable" staff, and while romantics profess there's "nothing better than dining on the patio", bottom-line sorts call the prices "most attractive."

Sol Food *Puerto Rican* | 25 | 17 | 18 | $18 |

San Rafael | 811 Fourth St. (Lincoln Ave.) | 415-451-4765
San Rafael | 901 Lincoln Ave. (3rd St.) | 415-451-4765 ◖
www.solfoodrestaurant.com

For "value"-priced island fare that "soothes the soul", locals happily "brave the line" at this "deservedly packed" San Rafaelite doling out "high-quality" Puerto Rican staples (e.g. "plantains so sweet they could be dessert"); a "friendly staff" works the "bright-colored" dining room, which is usually "noisy" and sometimes "chaotic" – prompting impatient types to hit its "next-door take-out place" and "sit on the curb to eat"; P.S. there's a pickup location on Fourth Street.

The Spinnaker *Californian/Seafood* | 20 | 23 | 21 | $40 |

Sausalito | 100 Spinnaker Dr. (Bridgeway) | 415-332-1500 |
www.thespinnaker.com

"Bay, seals, city views, sailboats" – it's all about the "exceptional" vistas at this "old-style" Sausalito stalwart nestled in a "water location" across from San Francisco; the Californian-seafood menu is "solid", and while service isn't as "swoon-worthy" as the locale, the place remains a "favorite" for "special occasions" and "out-of-town guests."

Spoonbar *Californian* | 20 | 23 | 21 | $44 |

Healdsburg | H2hotel | 219 Healdsburg Ave. (bet. Mill & W. Matheson Sts.) | 707-433-7222 | www.spoonbar.com

Injecting a little "urban hip" into "Sonoma wine country", this "ultra-modern" Californian in Downtown Healdsburg offers "imaginative",

NORTH OF SAN FRANCISCO

FOOD | DECOR | SERVICE | COST

"locally sourced" cuisine, "wonderful cocktails", "friendly service" and a "super-fun atmosphere"; it's a great place to meet up "with friends", especially "in the summer when the windows/doors are open" giving the place "an alfresco feel no matter where you sit"; P.S. the post-Survey installment of former Aziza chef Louis Maldonado is not reflected in the Food score.

Stark's Steakhouse *Steak*   26 | 24 | 23 | $54

Santa Rosa | 521 Adams St. (W. 7th St.) | 707-546-5100 |
www.starkrestaurants.com
Carnivores congregate at this "classic" American steakhouse with "vintage yet chic" decor, a "go-to spot for special celebrations" in Santa Rosa with "professional" service delivering "dry-aged" beef that "melts in your mouth" and "even better sides"; "it's pricey" alright, but thrifty types can economize at the "amazing happy hour", one of the "best values in town."

Station House Cafe *American*   17 | 15 | 16 | $30

Point Reyes Station | 11180 State Rte. 1 (2nd St.) | 415-663-1515 |
www.stationhousecafe.com
If you're hankering for "hearty portions" of locally sourced "comfort food" "after a day of hiking", surveyors suggest this "old standby" in Point Reyes Station; the chow may be "nothing extraordinary", but at least outdoorsy types dig sitting on the "lovely patio" next to the "fountain and flowering trellis"; P.S. closed Wednesdays.

St. Orres Restaurant *Californian*   ▽ 23 | 26 | 21 | $63

Gualala | St. Orres Hotel | 36601 S. Hwy. 1 (Seaside School Rd.) |
707-884-3335 | www.saintorres.com
Chef/co-owner Rosemary Campiformio continues to ensure everyone is "happy" and well-fed at her "romantic" "Russian-domed" retreat nestled in the "coastal redwoods" of Gualala by delivering "creative" all-inclusive Californian dinners ("wild game dishes are a big favorite") matched by a "thoughtful local wine list"; sure, you'll pay today's prices to dine in a "throwback" "hippie atmosphere", but it's "well worth the trip" for the "unique setting" alone.

Sugo *Italian*   ▽ 25 | 20 | 23 | $30

Petaluma | 5 Petaluma Blvd. S. (B St.) | 707-782-9298 |
www.sugopetaluma.com
There's "something for everyone" at this "intimate" Petaluman proffering a "well-thought-out menu" of "excellent" Italian fare crafted from "fresh ingredients", plus most everything is made in-house; a "gracious" staff and "reasonable" prices keep patrons smiling in the "contemporary" space (think "cement floors and high ceilings"), as do the movies projected on a wall.

⧉ Sushi Ran *Japanese*   27 | 21 | 24 | $61

Sausalito | 107 Caledonia St. (bet. Pine & Turney Sts.) | 415-332-3620 |
www.sushiran.com
Sausalitans feel "lucky" to have had this "destination" Japanese around for "almost 30 years", while non-local sushi fans say it's "worth crossing the bridge" for the "remarkable" "daily deliveries from Toykyo's Tsukiji fish market" and other "cooked delights" ably served in a "peaceful" setting; "the sake bar next door" works for lunch or biding

time, so despite "high prices", "once you've eaten" here, "there's no going back."

Swiss Hotel Restaurant ● *American/Italian* | 21 | 19 | 22 | $33 |

Sonoma | 18 W. Spain St. (1st St.) | 707-938-2884 | www.swisshotelsonoma.com

"Set in a wonderful old hotel" on Sonoma Plaza, this "reasonably priced" "institution" (it opened in 1929) fills the bill if you're hankering for a "home-cooked meal feel" after a day of "wine tasting"; "townies" and visitors alike cherish the "well-prepared" Italian and American fare in an "old-time atmosphere" – especially the "divine" "leafy back patio" and the "front veranda" for "sundown drinks."

Table Café 🅢🅜 *Californian* | ▽ 26 | 18 | 24 | $19 |

Larkspur | 1167 Magnolia Ave. (Estelle Ave.) | 415-461-6787 | www.table-cafe.com

"Delicate, delicious" Cal cuisine is "lovingly prepared" at this "little neighborhood" spot in Larkspur specializing in "superb dosas"; the sustainable "local fare" is "always fresh and organic", and whether you opt for "outdoor seating" or "healthy takeout", you're almost sure to "leave happy" – usually with "awesome brownies" or other home-made desserts in hand.

Tavern at Lark Creek *American* | 22 | 25 | 23 | $42 |

Larkspur | 234 Magnolia Ave. (Madrone Ave.) | 415-924-7766 | www.tavernatlarkcreek.com

Today's "more casual" "reincarnation of the old" Lark Creek Inn in Larkspur remains a "Marin County favorite" for "family celebrations", while the "sunny" Victorian digs have become "increasingly popular" for its "dependable" New American "tavern food" and "incredible" desserts; "it's a tad more affordable" too, and though service varies, "the atmosphere is unbeatable", particularly outside for "Sunday brunch."

🅩 Terra *American* | 27 | 25 | 27 | $91 |

St. Helena | 1345 Railroad Ave. (bet. Adams St. & Hunt Ave.) | 707-963-8931 | www.terrarestaurant.com

Ame owners Hiro Sone and Lissa Doumani's "wine-country classic" in St. Helena still dazzles diners with "innovative" New American dishes, plus "terrific desserts" and an "extensive wine list", all served with "unmatchable" "hospitality" in a "romantic" "country-elegant" stone farmhouse; "the build-your-own tasting menu" might be the "best" "fine-dining" deal in Napa, and those desiring a "more laid-back" meal can head next door for Bar Terra's equally "creative" "small plates."

Terrapin Creek 🅜 *Californian* | ▽ 28 | 21 | 25 | $46 |

Bodega Bay | 1580 Eastshore Rd. (Hwy. 1) | 707-875-2700 | www.terrapincreekcafe.com

It's "worth the drive out to Bodega Bay" to this "real jewel" that "brings in the crowds" thanks to "utterly charming" chef-owners who "work the floor" and prepare "exceptional", "adventurous", locally sourced Californian fare "with none of the pretension" or tabs you'd expect; it's a "relaxing" setting with a small patio overlooking the water, and all "so good it's almost a pleasure to pay"; P.S. open Thursday–Sunday.

Tex Wasabi's   *BBQ/Japanese*

| 20 | 18 | 20 | $34 |

Santa Rosa | 515 Fourth St. (4th St.) | 707-544-8399 | www.texwasabis.com

Popular Food Networker Guy Fieri churns out "unique" "Asian-BBQ fusion" (i.e. "pork sliders and ribs" share the menu with sushi) at this Santa Rosa branch of his modestly priced franchise; a "twentysomething crowd" fills the "slick, dark" space to imbibe "yummy drinks", but some snap it's "more hype than substance."

NEW The Thomas & Fagiani's Bar ● *American*

| - | - | - | M |

Napa | 813 Main St. (3rd St.) | 707-226-7821 | www.thethomas-napa.com

Bringing a touch of NYC to Downtown Napa, this tri-level New American canteen and raw bar from Manhattan's Farmerie brothers (Public, Saxon & Parole) set in a historical building aims to be a key new dining and nightlife player; the second floor serves as the main dining room replete with wine wall and open kitchen for midpriced rustic wood-fired dishes with international touches, while the ground-floor Fagiani's Bar offers classic cocktails and bar bites until midnight and a rooftop bar overlooks the Napa River.

Toast   *American*

| 21 | 16 | 19 | $23 |

Mill Valley | 31 Sunnyside Ave. (bet. E. Blithedale & Miller Aves.) | 415-388-2500 | www.toastmillvalley.com
Novato | Hamilton Mktpl. | 5800 Nave Dr. (bet. N. Hamilton Pkwy. & Roblar Dr.) | 415-382-1144 | www.toastnovato.com

"Just what you want in a neighborhood diner" – "ample portions" of "good ol' American" eats served all day long at "bargain" prices – is what patrons find at this Mill Valley locale and its larger Novato offshoot; service can be iffy and reviews are mixed on the toast-inspired decor (with pockmarked walls on Nave Drive resembling actual bread), but the lively, "friendly" atmosphere makes it a suitable (if sometimes "noisy") spot to take the "kids."

Tra Vigne   *Italian*

| 24 | 25 | 23 | $57 |

St. Helena | 1050 Charter Oak Ave. (Main St.) | 707-963-4444 | www.travignerestaurant.com

"There's a reason" this St. Helena Tuscan "treasure" has "been around forever" – it's the "wine country – casual" setting (complete with "delightful" courtyard), servers who "know their stuff" and an "inventive menu" starring "delicious" Northern Italian *cucina* crafted from "fresh local ingredients"; it can be a "little pricey", but the fact there's "no corkage fee" on the first bottle is a "big plus", enabling even spendthrifts to declare it's "worth the trip."

Underwood Bar & Bistro Ⓜ *Mediterranean*

| 22 | 20 | 22 | $42 |

Graton | 9113 Graton Rd. (Edison St.) | 707-823-7023 | www.underwoodgraton.com

"After a day" in Sonoma County, this "charming" bistro in "out-of-the-way" Grafton is "well worth" seeking out for "unpretentious", reasonably priced Mediterranean fare – and perhaps some fancy cocktails at the "terrific bar"; the "cozy" digs can get "noisy and busy" "even at lunch, when the local wine growers get into their product", but "exceptional service" and late-night hours are pluses.

	FOOD	DECOR	SERVICE	COST

Uva Trattoria & Bar ⓜ *Italian* — 19 | 19 | 22 | $35

Napa | 1040 Clinton St. (bet. Brown & Main Sts.) | 707-255-6646 | www.uvatrattoria.com

There's "great" free "live music" in the air and "decent" Italian chow (pasta, pizza, etc.) on the plates at this Downtown Napa eatery with an "energetic" vibe; "friendly" servers add to the appeal, as do "reasonable" tabs aided by a BYO policy that waives the corkage on the first bottle.

Vin Antico *Italian* — 22 | 21 | 20 | $41

San Rafael | 881 Fourth St. (bet. Cijos St. & Lootens Pl.) | 415-454-4492 | www.vinantico.com

"*Fantastico* farm-to-table" Cal-Italian fare is the lure at this "sleek nugget" in Downtown San Rafael that "locals love"; "attractive decor" with "lots of dark woods" and tables "close together" creates a "romantic" ambiance, and though service can be "spotty" and bills "on the pricey side", the "city" atmosphere keeps it "fun and delish."

Volpi's Ristorante & Bar ⓜ *Italian* — ▽ 24 | 21 | 23 | $34

Petaluma | 124 Washington St. (bet. Keller St. & Telephone Alley) | 707-762-2371

Peddling "hearty portions" of "family-style" classics, this "old-world Italian joint" in Petaluma is a "throwback in every way" – and "satisfies" with "every cliché" in the process, from the "checkered tablecloths" to the "speakeasy"-like "bar in back"; "you'll be stuffed when you leave", and the "friendly staff" even busts out "accordion music frequently" to round out the "down-home charm."

Water Street Bistro *French* — ▽ 23 | 20 | 21 | $32

Petaluma | 100 Petaluma Blvd. N. (Western Ave.) | 707-763-9563 | www.waterstreetbistro.net

"Don't let the low price fool you" – this "terrific local" cafe run by a "wonderful chef"-owner is *the* Petaluma stop for breakfast and lunch", offering "fresh, seasonal" French-inflected fare served by a "knowledgeable staff"; specials frequently "get sold out", and since the "super-homey" setting can get a "bit cramped", regulars vie for tables "on the riverside patio"; P.S. monthly Saturday night dinners require reservations.

Willi's Seafood & Raw Bar *Seafood* — 25 | 21 | 22 | $46

Healdsburg | 403 Healdsburg Ave. (North St.) | 707-433-9191 | www.willisseafood.net

"Seafood lovers" descend upon this Healdsburg "pearl" for small bites of "fresh, local" fish, "lobster rolls to die for" and selections from a "great raw bar" (all complemented by "a wine list to match");"friendly, efficient" servers work the "airy" dining space and "lively bar", but those "tasty" tapas, bivalves and libations can "add up to a hefty check."

Willi's Wine Bar *Eclectic* — 25 | 20 | 23 | $46

Santa Rosa | 4404 Old Redwood Hwy. (Ursuline Rd.) | 707-526-3096 | www.williswinebar.net

Despite its "roadhouse" "exterior", locals insist this Eclectic "Santa Rosa gem outshines many of its Napa Valley rivals" with "truly exceptional", "innovative" "small plates" and "memorable" wine pairings; it gets "crowded and noisy", and those "tiny" tidbits "can easily" add up "to a big bill", but it's still an "utterly charming place to pop in for a drink and a bite", especially on the "lovely" patio.

Willow Wood
Market Cafe *Eclectic/Mediterranean*
24 | 20 | 20 | $29

Graton | 9020 Graton Rd. (Edison St.) | 707-823-0233 | www.willowwoodgraton.com

Cranking out possibly "the best brunch/lunch for many miles around", this "adorable" "off-the-beaten-path" country store/cafe with a "nice patio" in Graton is a "great casual place" to "meet and greet in Western Sonoma county"; "despite slightly cramped quarters", the midpriced Eclectic-Med eats are "not your typical boring" choices, and it's a "reliable" alternative to sister Underwood.

Wine Spectator Greystone *Californian*
23 | 23 | 22 | $49

St. Helena | Culinary Institute of America | 2555 Main St. (bet. Deer Park Rd. & Pratt Ave.) | 707-967-1010 | www.ciachef.edu

Home to the CIA in St. Helena, this "beautiful" stone building is "a very special place", where "students" and "seasoned chefs" work side-by-side in an "open kitchen" to turn out "imaginative", "well-prepared" Californian fare that's paired with "playful wine flights"; it's "pricey" considering "it's a training ground" for waiters and cooks, but "lunch on the patio with views of the local vineyards makes any visit to Napa Valley a treat."

Wurst Restaurant *American/Pub Food*
▽ 20 | 14 | 18 | $17

Healdsburg | 22 Matheson St. (Healdsburg Ave.) | 707-395-0214

Fans of wurst call this "sausage heaven" and American pub "the best" thanks to the "Midwest"-made and local dogs (plus a burger that's "da bomb") that are a welcome antidote to Healdsburg's usual "overpriced eats"; it's an "extremely casual", "friendly" spot to "relax and have a beer and a brat", and "when the weather's good" the patio gets "jammed."

Yankee Pier *New England/Seafood*
19 | 16 | 19 | $34

Larkspur | 286 Magnolia Ave. (bet. King St. & William Ave.) | 415-924-7676 | www.yankeepier.com

"Fresh, sustainable" seafood served in a "casual" atmosphere is the hallmark of this "kid-friendly" local chainlet; while believers savor the "New England clam shack" fare (including "must-try" lobster rolls and chowder), skeptics call the offerings "pricey for what you get"; P.S. the SFO branch "makes a flight delay quite nice."

Zazu Ⓜ *American/Italian*
25 | 20 | 23 | $49

Santa Rosa | 3535 Guerneville Rd. (Willowside Rd.) | 707-523-4814
NEW Zazu on the
River Shack *American/Italian*
Healdsburg | Davis Family Vineyards | 52 Front St. (Hudson St.) | no phone
www.zazurestaurant.com

It may "look like a country dive", but this Santa Rosa "roadhouse" is the setting for an "adventurous", "farm-to-table" New American–Northern Italian menu that'll "knock your socks off", complemented by a "killer" "Sonoma-centric" wine list, all courtesy of chef-owners Duskie Estes and John Stewart (aka "the king and queen of pork"); the vibe's "convivial" and the tab's "hefty", though the thrice-weekly "prix

NORTH OF SAN FRANCISCO

| | FOOD | DECOR | SERVICE | COST |

fixes" are a bargain "treat"; P.S. newcomer Zazu on the River in Healdsburg offers sandwiches, salads and salumi to the winery set.

Zin *American*

| | 24 | 21 | 23 | $46 |

Healdsburg | 344 Center St. (North St.) | 707-473-0946 | www.zinrestaurant.com

"Consistently delicious", "imaginative" New American fare featuring homegrown produce and housemade condiments comes with a "great wine selection" at this Healdsburg local "favorite"; the "casual, attentive staff" keeps things "cozy" in an "industrial" setting that can get "noisy", but prices are "reasonable in an overpriced neighborhood" and patrons return "again and again."

ZuZu *Spanish*

| | 24 | 19 | 22 | $44 |

Napa | 829 Main St. (bet. 2nd & 3rd Sts.) | 707-224-8555 | www.zuzunapa.com

Situated on Napa's Riverfront, this "cozy" Spaniard "standby" with a "really nice" staff offers "well-executed tapas" and "outstanding" wines ("many Spanish" varietals "along with Napa bottles") in a "relaxed, casual atmosphere"; it's neither "fine dining" nor cheap, but devotees dub it a "find" that's "well worth" the sometimes "long wait"; P.S. no reservations.

Latest openings, menus, photos and more on plus.google.com/local

SOUTH OF SAN FRANCISCO

Top Food

28 | Marinus | *Californian/French*
Sierra Mar | *Cal./Eclectic*
Evvia | *Greek*
Cafe Gibraltar | *Med.*

27 | Passionfish | *Cal./Seafood*
La Forêt | *Continental/French*
Manresa | *American*
Le Papillon | *French*
Sent Sovi | *Californian*
Bistro Moulin | *French*

Mingalaba | *Burmese/Chinese*

26 | Alexander's | *Japanese/Steak*
Stella Alpina Osteria | *Italian*
Aubergine | *Californian*
Baumé | *French*
Flea St. Café | *Californian*
Nick's on Main | *American*
Roy's at Pebble Beach | *Haw.*
Tamarine | *Vietnamese*
Jin Sho | *Japanese*

BY CUISINE

AMERICAN

27 | Manresa
26 | Nick's on Main
25 | Village Pub
24 | Madera
Big Sur Bakery

ASIAN

27 | Mingalaba
26 | Tamarine
25 | Vung Tau
24 | New Krung Thai
Koi Palace

CALIFORNIAN

28 | Marinus
Sierra Mar
27 | Sent Sovi
26 | Aubergine
Flea St. Café

CONTINENTAL

27 | La Forêt
25 | Ecco
Bella Vista
24 | Anton & Michel

FRENCH

28 | Marinus
27 | La Forêt
Le Papillon
Bistro Moulin
26 | Baumé

INDIAN

25 | All Spice
24 | Amber India
Shalimar
23 | Curry Up Now
Roti Indian Bistro

ITALIAN

26 | Stella Alpina Osteria
25 | Pasta Moon
A Bellagio
24 | Casanova
Osteria

JAPANESE

26 | Alexander's
Jin Sho
25 | Gochi
Ramen Dojo
24 | Orenchi Ramen

MED./GREEK

28 | Evvia
Cafe Gibraltar
25 | Dio Deka
24 | Cetrella
22 | 71 Saint Peter

SEAFOOD

27 | Passionfish
24 | Sardine Factory
Flying Fish Grill (Carmel)
Koi Palace
23 | Old Port Lobster

Excludes places with low votes

BY SPECIAL FEATURE

BREAKFAST/BRUNCH

27 La Forêt
24 Madera
    Gayle's Bakery
    Big Sur Bakery
23 Gabriella Café

OUTDOOR SEATING

28 Sierra Mar
26 Roy's at Pebble Beach
24 Casanova
    Anton & Michel
22 Sam's Chowder House

PEOPLE-WATCHING

28 Evvia
26 Flea St. Café
    Tamarine
25 Dio Deka
    Village Pub

ROMANCE

28 Marinus
    Sierra Mar
27 La Forêt
    Le Papillon
24 Casanova

SINGLES SCENES

23 Cin-Cin Wine Bar
    Cascal
    Joya
22 Xanh
20 Sino

SMALL PLATES

26 Tamarine
23 Cascal
    Joya
21 Straits
    Lavanda

VIEWS

28 Sierra Mar
26 Roy's at Pebble Beach
25 La Costanera
24 Pacific's Edge
19 Nepenthe

WINNING WINE LISTS

28 Marinus
    Sierra Mar
27 Passionfish
25 Village Pub
    Plumed Horse

BY LOCATION

CARMEL/MONTEREY

28 Marinus
27 Bistro Moulin
26 Aubergine
24 Casanova
    Anton & Michel

HALF MOON BAY/ COAST

28 Cafe Gibraltar
25 Pasta Moon
    La Costanera
24 Cetrella
    Caffè Mezza Luna

LOS GATOS

27 Manresa
26 Nick's on Main
25 Dio Deka
23 Cin-Cin Wine
    Forbes Mill

PALO ALTO/ MENLO PARK

28 Evvia
26 Baumé
    Flea St. Café
    Tamarine
    Jin Sho

PENINSULA

27 Mingalaba
26 Stella Alpina Osteria
25 Village Pub
    John Bentley's
23 Old Port Lobster

SANTA CRUZ/ CAPITOLA

24 Gayle's Bakery
23 Gabriella Café
22 Shadowbrook
19 Café Gratitude

Top Decor

29	Sierra Mar		Nepenthe
			Aubergine
28	Marinus	25	Evvia
	Pacific's Edge		Dio Deka
27	Roy's at Pebble Beach		Chantilly
			Manresa
26	La Forêt		La Costanera
	Plumed Horse		Alexander's
	Restaurant at Ventana		
	Madera	24	Village Pub
	Quattro Restaurant		Joya Restaurant
	Shadowbrook		

Top Service

27	Marinus		Quattro Restaurant
	Sierra Mar		Alexander's
	Baumé		Evvia
	Manresa	25	Aubergine
	La Forêt		John Bentley's
26	Cafe Gibraltar		Plumed Horse
	Chantilly		Station 1 Restaurant*
	Bistro Moulin		Flea St. Café
	Le Papillon		All Spice
	Sent Sovi	24	Morton's

BEST BUYS: BANG FOR THE BUCK

1. In-N-Out	11. Pancho Villa Taqueria
2. La Victoria Taqueria	12. La Cumbre Taqueria
3. Taqueria La Bamba	13. Carmel Bakery
4. Nation's Giant Hamburgers	14. Taqueria 3 Amigos
5. Cheese Steak Shop	15. Ramen Dojo
6. Taqueria San Jose	16. Burger Joint
7. El Farolito	17. Aqui Cal-Mex Grill
8. Curry Up Now	18. Taqueria Tlaquepaque
9. Ike's Lair/Place	19. Crepevine
10. La Corneta	20. BurgerMeister

BEST BUYS: OTHER GOOD VALUES

Amici's	Mingalaba
Applewood Pizza	Orenchi Ramen
Asian Box	Pacific Catch
Bun Bo Hue	Patxi's Pizza
Cool Café	Pizza Antica
Counter Palo Alto	Rangoon Ruby
Dasaprakash	Shalimar
Dishdash	SJ Omogari
Gayle's Bakery	Vung Tau
Krung Thai	Zeni

* Indicates a tie with restaurant above

South of San Francisco

A Bellagio *Italian*
25 | 22 | 24 | $44

Campbell | 33 S. Central Ave. (Orchard City Dr.) | 408-370-7705 |
www.abellagio.com

"Slightly old school with modern sensibilities", this "truly Italian" Campbell trattoria has an "on-point" staff delivering "beautifully plated entrees" in a setting where locals "can actually have a conversation without shouting"; adding to the allure, prices are considered "reasonable" and you can even hit "the terrace with a glass of wine."

Acqua Pazza ⓜ *Italian*
22 | 20 | 23 | $36

San Mateo | 201 E. Third Ave. (Ellsworth Ave.) | 650-375-0903 |
www.acqua-pazza.com

"Authentic" Italian "classics" are on offer at this "reasonably priced" San Mateo trattoria owned by three brothers from Naples; "friendly" servers help create a "warm", "homey feel" in the "lively" bi-level space, so even if a few find the cooking "uninspired", most agree it's generally a "pleasant place to be."

☒ Alexander's Steakhouse *Japanese/Steak*
26 | 25 | 26 | $90

Cupertino | Cupertino Sq. | 10330 N. Wolfe Rd. (bet. Rte. 280 & Stevens Creek Blvd.) | 408-446-2222 | www.alexanderssteakhouse.com

"Huge" portions of "awesome aged meats" are "grilled to perfection" at this "posh" "temple" to beef that "raises the bar" for carnivores in Cupertino and SoMa; it fuses "Japanese cuisine" with a "classic steakhouse" and service is "exemplary", though diners who haven't "launched a successful IPO" can suffer "sticker shock" from the "über-pricey" tab; P.S. a Palo Alto seafood offshoot is in the works.

All Spice ☒ⓜ *Indian*
25 | 23 | 25 | $49

San Mateo | 1602 S. El Camino Real (Borel Ave.) | 650-627-4303 |
www.allspicerestaurant.com

"It's worth searching" for this "jewel-box Victorian" "hidden on El Camino" in San Mateo where chef/co-owner Sachin Chopra (Sakoon) "artfully presents" a "superbly inventive fusion" of "fragrant", "traditional" Indian spices and "modern" Californian sensibilities; the "polite, helpful" service overseen by his co-owner wife, Shoshana, in the "gorgeous, homey setting" creates a "very hospitable" atmosphere for enjoying one of the "nicest" "special-occasion" meals "for the money" (particularly since "they sorted out their liquor license").

Amarin Thai Cuisine *Thai*
22 | 18 | 18 | $22

Mountain View | 174 Castro St. (W. Evelyn Ave.) | 650-988-9323 |
www.amarinthaicuisine.com

"Consistently good" fare makes this "popular" Mountain View Thai a "go-to" for "simmered-to-perfection" curries and other "authentic" dishes made with "well-balanced and flavorful sauces"; service gets mixed marks ("friendly" vs. "flaky") and it can feel "congested" during "rush hour", but "reasonable prices" still ensure it's a "favorite."

☒NEW Amber Dhara *Indian*
24 | 22 | 21 | $36

Palo Alto | 150 University Ave. (High St.) | 650-329-9644

(continued)

(continued)

☑ Amber India *Indian*

Mountain View | Olive Tree Shopping Ctr. | 2290 W. El Camino Real
(bet. Ortega & Rengstorff Aves.) | 650-968-7511
San Jose | Santana Row | 377 Santana Row (Olsen Dr.) | 408-248-5400

☑ Amber Café *Indian*

Mountain View | 600 W. El Camino Real (View St.) | 650-968-1751
www.amber-india.com

Definitely diverse, from the "ravishing" SoMa and San Jose spots to the "casual" Cafe "popular with groups of techies" in Mountain View, this "vibrant" curry chainlet (with a new Mission branch) shares a "broad" menu that's "fit for a maharajah" – ranging from the "awesome" "staple" "butter chicken" to some "seriously hot stuff" – as well as "attentive" service; "bargain" buffets (except at Amber Café) are an "affordable" alternative to the sometimes "pricey" plates.

☑ Amici's East Coast Pizzeria *Pizza*   21 | 17 | 20 | $22

Cupertino | 10310 S. De Anza Blvd. (bet. Pacifica Dr. & Rodrigues Ave.) | 408-252-3333
Menlo Park | 880 Santa Cruz Ave. (Evelyn St.) | 650-329-8888
Mountain View | 790 Castro St. (Yosemite Ave.) | 650-961-6666
Redwood Shores | 226 Redwood Shores Pkwy. (Twin Dolphin Dr.) | 650-654-3333
San Jose | 225 W. Santa Clara St. (Almaden Ave.) | 408-289-9000
San Mateo | 69 E. Third Ave. (bet. El Camino Real & San Mateo Dr.) | 650-342-9392
www.amicis.com
See review in City of San Francisco Directory.

Andre's Bouchée *French*   22 | 23 | 23 | $60
(fka Bouchée)

Carmel | Mission St. (bet. Ocean & 7th Aves.) | 831-626-7880 | www.andresbouchee.com

Even under "new ownership", this "French family-owned-and-operated" bistro and wine bar remains "one of the nicest places to eat" in Carmel; the "intimate, inviting atmosphere" sets the stage for enjoying monsieur Andre Lemaire's "fabulously traditional" Gallic fare paired with a "stellar wine list and sommelier" and proffered by "friendly, attentive" garçons; P.S. dinner only.

Anton & Michel Restaurant *Continental*   24 | 24 | 24 | $55

Carmel | Mission St. (bet. Ocean & 7th Aves.) | 831-624-2406 | www.antonandmichel.com

This "elegant", "old-school" Carmel Continental has been serving "deliciously straightforward" fare for more than 30 years in a "lovely old-world setting" replete with "pretty fountains" and working fireplaces; some say "the atmosphere is dated" and "expert" staff is "stuffy", while others counter "who can resist" the "dining room theater" of "tableside cooking" including rack of lamb, Caesar salad and "flaming desserts"?

Applewood Pizza *Pizza*   24 | 14 | 18 | $18

Menlo Park | 1001 El Camino Real (Ravenswood Ave.) | 650-324-3486 | www.applewoodpizza.com

"Classic sauces", "lots of cheese" and "flavorful toppings in interesting combinations" result in "fully loaded" pies that "satisfy all taste buds" at this "reasonably priced" Menlo Park pizzeria; yes, the "decor leaves something to be desired" and service "could be better", but its "selection of beers is hard to match" and prices are quite "reasonable" too.

Aquarius *American*   ∇ 24 | 25 | 22 | $50

Santa Cruz | Santa Cruz Dream Inn | 175 W. Cliff Dr. (Bay St.) | 831-460-5012 | www.aquariussantacruz.com

The "view of the beach is amazing" while the "quality" New American fare is a "pleasant surprise" at this picturesque breakfast-through-dinner waterfront restaurant in the Dream Inn that attempts to usher the age of fine dining into crunchy Santa Cruz; the staff can be "great", if the tabs are a little pricey.

Aqui Cal-Mex Grill *Californian/Mexican*   23 | 19 | 19 | $18

Campbell | 201 E. Campbell Ave. (bet. 2nd & 3rd Sts.) | 408-374-2784
San Jose | 10630 S. De Anza Blvd. (Kirwin Ln.) | 408-996-1443
San Jose | 1145 Lincoln Ave. (bet. Minnesota Ave. & Willow St.) | 408-995-0381
San Jose | 5679 Snell Ave. (Blossom Hill Rd.) | 408-362-3456
www.aquicalmex.com

"Creative", "well-prepared" Mexican dishes with a "distinctly Californian slant" are paired with "strong margaritas" and "must-order sangria swirls" at this counter-serve Campbell chain link; "service is prompt", the atmosphere is "casual" and you "can't beat the price" – no surprise it's a "favorite neighborhood hangout."

Arcadia *American*   24 | 21 | 23 | $53

San Jose | San Jose Marriott | 100 W. San Carlos St. (Market St.) | 408-278-4555 | www.michaelmina.net

"Standard upscale" steakhouse fare gets a boost from "well-prepared" New American offerings (lobster pot pie, lamb sliders, charcuterie) at this "opulent" San Jose Marriott eatery from Michael Mina; "attentive" service and "modern" decor add "date"-night appeal, just "bring your credit card" as tabs are a "bit pricey."

NEW Asian Box *Asian*   ∇ 17 | 16 | 17 | $16

Palo Alto | Town & Country Vill. | 855 El Camino Real (Embarcadero Rd.) | no phone | www.asianboxpaloalto.com

Grace Nguyen (ex Slanted Door) and husband Chad Newton (ex Fish & Farm) peddle "really good", affordable, sustainable Asian street food at this take-out/eat-in/fast-casual newcomer in a Palo Alto shopping center; everything is gluten-free and customizable with choice of proteins, fixings and housemade sauces (including the "very hot Hot Box It"), and washed down with Vietnamese iced coffee, iced tea and eventually beer and wine; additional outlets in Mountain View and Burlingame are in the works.

Asian Pearl Seafood Restaurant ● *Chinese*   22 | 18 | 18 | $30

Millbrae | 1671 El Camino Real (Park Pl.) | 650-616-8288

The portions are "big" and the dim sum "creative" at this Millbrae Chinese turning out "tasty", "traditional" cuisine delivered by "friendly" (if "slow") servers; some find the decor "lackluster" and note it can get "noisy" (it's "not a date place"), but "affordable" tabs help.

	FOOD	DECOR	SERVICE	COST

Attic ☒Ⓜ *Asian*   `20` `18` `19` `$30`

San Mateo | 234 S. B St. (bet. 2nd & 3rd Aves.) | 650-342-4506 |
www.atticrestaurant.com

Locals contend "San Mateo needs more eateries like this" "slightly
trendy" Pan-Asian "tucked above" its own "hopping" bar (Under the
Attic) where revelers can enjoy "great happy-hour drink specials" "before going upstairs" to the main dining room where a "friendly" crew
proffers an "interesting mix" of "solid", midpriced "modern" Filipino and
Pan-Asian eats; those who've tried it have been "pleasantly surprised."

Aubergine   *Californian*   `26` `26` `25` `$116`
(aka L'Auberge Carmel)

Carmel | L'Auberge Carmel | Monte Verde St. (7th Ave.) | 831-624-8578 |
www.laubergecarmel.com

"Nothing else comes close" to this "intimate" Relais & Châteaux "treasure" that's "wonderful in every way", where the "truly gifted chef"
crafts "fabulous", "extraordinarily creative", "gorgeous" Californian
tasting menus emphasizing "fresh and local ingredients"; "portions
are still small" (as is the jewel-box setting), and "second mortgages
might be needed to pay the tab", but the "refined service" enhanced
with "spot-on wine parings" from a "stunning" list "rounds out an incredible" "special-occasion dining experience" that's "worth it."

Barbara's Fish Trap ⊘ *Seafood*   `22` `14` `18` `$24`

Princeton by the Sea | 281 Capistrano Rd. (Hwy. 1) | 650-728-7049

A "fresh seafood shack, with the emphasis on shack", Barbara's is a
"perennial favorite" in Princeton by the Sea for reasonably priced
chowder, fish 'n' chips and "everything fried"; though there's "usually
a line" ("get there by 11 AM" to "beat the senior crowd"), "the wait
isn't too long" and "you can walk by the water" or order from the take-
out window for "outdoor picnic table seating"; cash only.

The Basin   *American*   `23` `20` `23` `$44`

Saratoga | 14572 Big Basin Way (5th St.) | 408-867-1906 |
www.thebasin.com

"Kudos" go to this "popular" Saratoga American for its "commitment
to sustainable seafood" and organic ingredients plus a "great staff to
match"; the menu offers enough "intriguing twists" to keep things "interesting", and if the "cozy" setting gets "a bit loud", the outdoor patio
makes an "excellent" choice on a "warm summer night."

Basque Cultural Center Ⓜ *French*   `21` `16` `20` `$31`

South San Francisco | Basque Cultural Ctr. | 599 Railroad Ave. (bet. Orange &
Spruce Aves.) | 650-583-8091 | www.basqueculturalcenter.com

"For a wonderful cross-cultural experience", "watch jai alai", "enjoy the
company of families from the old country" and dig into "huge quantities
of very good", "hearty", "family-style" fare served with "big drinks" at
this "authentic" Basque "club" in South SF; service is "a bit slow" and it's
a bit "short on atmosphere", but "high on value" and "fun for a group."

Baumé Ⓜ *French*   `26` `24` `27` `$231`

Palo Alto | 201 S. California Ave. (Park Blvd.) | 650-328-8899 |
www.baumerestaurant.com

Bruno Chemel's "amazing", "gorgeous" New French prix fixe menus
are "like a science experiment gone wild" ("lots of liquid nitrogen" and

"gimmicks") at this "total foodie" destination in "sleepy Palo Alto" that delivers serious "wow factor"; an "impeccable" staff does an equally fine job in the "chic" space, so while "minuscule" portions do "give a literal meaning to molecular gastronomy", most concede it's "worth the splurge"; P.S. closed Monday–Tuesday.

Bella Vista ⧄Ⓜ *Continental*   25 | 24 | 24 | $60

Woodside | 13451 Skyline Blvd. (5 mi. south of Rte. 92) | 650-851-1229 | www.bvrestaurant.com

"Tucked away among redwoods", this "romantic", "elegant" Woodside Continental is a "special place" where "outstanding", "old-school" fare is ferried by "delightful servers" who help navigate the "impressive" wine list; "ask for a table by the window" and enjoy the "stunning views" at this "slice of history"; P.S. don't miss the "flawless" dessert soufflés.

Benihana *Japanese*   21 | 20 | 22 | $39

Burlingame | 1496 Old Bayshore Hwy. (Mahler Rd.) | 650-342-5202
Monterey | 136 Olivier St. (Scott St.) | 831-644-9007
Cupertino | Cupertino Sq. | 2074 Vallco Fashion Park (Vallco Pkwy.) | 408-253-1221
www.benihana.com
See review in City of San Francisco Directory.

Big Sur Bakery & Restaurant *American/Bakery*   24 | 18 | 21 | $36

Big Sur | 47540 Hwy. 1 (½ mi. south of Pfeiffer State Park) | 831-667-0520 | www.bigsurbakery.com

"A fun place to stop on your way to Big Sur", this "low-key" roadside bakery/restaurant may be known for its "really wonderful" "desserts and pastries", but its "limited" yet "creative" American "comfort-food" menu, including "wood-fired pizzas", is "surprisingly good" too; the indoor/outdoor setting is "rustic" and service is "laid-back", but it offers some of the "best value" around; P.S. no dinner on Mondays.

⧄ Bistro Moulin *French*   27 | 20 | 26 | $47

Monterey | 867 Wave St. (bet. David & Irving Aves.) | 831-333-1200 | www.bistromoulin.com

Providing a "quaint break" from the "nearby Cannery Row" tourist joints, this "charming" French spot "run by the chef and his wife" is the locals' "go-to" place for a "nice dinner out" in Monterey; the "intimate" space may be otherwise "nondescript", but the "fantastic" bistro fare and "excellent" wines, delivered by "an attentive and well-informed" staff, ensure it's "always a treat."

Blowfish Sushi To Die For *Japanese*   23 | 20 | 19 | $42

San Jose | Santana Row | 335 Santana Row (Alyssum Ln.) | 408-345-3848 | www.blowfishsushi.com
See review in City of San Francisco Directory.

⧄ Buca di Beppo *Italian*   18 | 19 | 19 | $27

Campbell | Pruneyard Shopping Ctr. | 1875 S. Bascom Ave. (Campbell Ave.) | 408-377-7722
Palo Alto | 643 Emerson St. (bet. Forest & Hamilton Aves.) | 650-329-0665
San Jose | Oakridge Mall | 925 Blossom Hill Rd. (bet. Santa Teresa & Winfield Blvds.) | 408-226-1444
www.bucadibeppo.com
See review in City of San Francisco Directory.

Buck's *American*
19 | 22 | 21 | $26

Woodside | 3062 Woodside Rd. (Cañada Rd.) | 650-851-8010 |
www.buckswoodside.com

"Deli gone wild" describes this affordable all-day eatery in Woodside
that's "still the place for your local VC sighting" over "hearty" "American
comfort food"; while service is spotty and the eats may be "average"
(though breakfasts are "fabulous"), it's the "funky memorabilia" "all over
the ceiling and walls" – including a "replica of the space shuttle" and
"Cracker Jack toys" – that draws the crowds to this "tarted-up diner."

Burger Joint *Burgers*
19 | 16 | 18 | $15

Burlingame | 1401 Burlingame Ave. (Primrose Rd.) | 650-558-9232
South San Francisco | San Francisco Int'l Airport | Int'l Terminal,
Boarding Area A (Hwy. 101) | 650-821-0582
www.burgerjointsf.com

See review in City of San Francisco Directory.

BurgerMeister *Burgers*
20 | 15 | 18 | $16

Daly City | Serramonte Ctr. | 3 Serramonte Ctr. (Junipero Serra Frwy.) |
650-994-1515
Daly City | 507 Westlake Ctr. (John Daly Blvd.) | 650-755-1941
www.burgermeistersf.com

See review in City of San Francisco Directory.

Café Brioche *Californian/French*
22 | 19 | 20 | $33

Palo Alto | 445 S. California Ave. (bet. Ash St. & El Camino Real) |
650-326-8640 | www.cafebrioche-paloalto.com

A "tasty", "something-for-everyone" menu that's part "country French"
and part Californian draws a "loyal local clientele" to this "busy" Palo
Alto cafe; with "warm" (if occasionally "slow") service, "cozy", "bistro"
surrounds and "reasonable prices", it's a "go-to" for a "nice brunch
with friends" or a "casual date night."

⚡ Cafe Gibraltar Ⓜ *Mediterranean*
28 | 23 | 26 | $43

El Granada | 425 Ave. Alhambra (Palma St.) | 650-560-9039 |
www.cafegibraltar.com

Chef/co-owner and "perfectionist" Jose Luis Ugalde's "inventive"
"seasonal organic" Mediterranean cuisine, paired with "unusual
wines to match", makes for a "treat" "altogether much better than" little El Granada "has any right to" say appreciative fans who find it "unforgettable"; add in "knowledgeable service that allows the fabulous
food to star" and a "serene" atmosphere (replete with a peekaboo
"view to die for") and you see why it's "so worth the trip."

NEW Café Gratitude *Vegan*
19 | 16 | 17 | $22

Santa Cruz | 103 Lincoln Ln. (Pacific Ave.) | 831-427-9583 |
www.cafegratitude.com

See review in East of San Francisco Directory.

Café Rustica Ⓜ *Californian*
24 | 19 | 21 | $38

Carmel Valley | 10 Del Fino Pl. (bet. Carmel Valley & Pilot Rds.) |
831-659-4444 | www.caferusticacarmel.com

"Delicious", "well-prepared" plates in "picturesque" digs with a "patio
overlooking the beautiful hills" make this "rustic yet refined" Californian
a "highlight of Carmel Valley"; service is generally "friendly" and it's
"priced right" too, so regulars shrug "what more could you ask for?"

Calafia *Californian*

20 | 18 | 18 | $32

Palo Alto | Town & Country Vill. | 855 El Camino Real (Embarcadero Rd.) | 650-322-9200 | www.calafiapaloalto.com

Ex-Google chef Charlie Ayers "knows what he's doing" say fans of this "bustling" Californian that "fits the Palo Alto scene" with an "extensive" (if slightly "schizophrenic") menu of "imaginative", "satisfying" dishes, including "healthy" choices and "numerous" vegan options, served by a "friendly, speedy" staff; sure, some find it just "so-so" and complain of "noisy" conditions, but more champion its "casual, comfortable" setting and insist it's "perfect for feeding a mixed group"; P.S. the adjacent market offers grab-and-go items.

Cannery Row
Brewing Company ● *American*

19 | 21 | 18 | $31

Monterey | 95 Prescott Ave. (Wave St.) | 831-643-2722 | www.canneryrowbrewingcompany.com

"One of the best draft beer selections" around (70-plus) lures hopsheads to this Monterey "sports bar" also vending burgers and other affordable American pub grub; its Cannery Row locale can result in a "touristy crowd" and "service can get spotty", but with outdoor fire pits and a "casual" vibe, most agree it's still a "quality place."

Cantinetta Luca *Italian*

22 | 20 | 20 | $52

Carmel | Dolores St. (bet. Ocean & 7th Aves.) | 831-625-6500 | www.cantinettaluca.com

For a "casual yet consistently good" Italian meal, this "lively" Carmel "locals'" "favorite" (with an adjacent "precious food shop" Salumeria) turns out "outstanding" "housemade salumi, crispy pizzas and enveloping pastas"; it's a bit "pricey" and the "rustic" digs with an "open oven in the back" can be "noisy", but everything's "high style – including the decor and clientele."

Carmel Bakery *Bakery*

22 | 16 | 19 | $13

Carmel | Ocean Ave. (Lincoln St.) | 831-626-8885

Dispensing "traditional European-style pastries and coffee", Bavarian soft pretzels, "homemade soups and large sandwiches", this Carmel bakery "institution" dating to 1906 is a "great place to stop on Ocean Avenue" to "fuel up" in the morning or grab "take-out lunch" "after a day of shopping"; P.S. open 7 AM-7 PM.

Casanova *French/Italian*

24 | 24 | 23 | $54

Carmel | Fifth Ave. (bet. Mission & San Carlos Sts.) | 831-625-0501 | www.casanovarestaurant.com

Perhaps the "most romantic place" around, this "quaint" Carmel "favorite" proffers "spectacular" French-Italian fare in "many small dining rooms", including one housing a table from France where Vincent Van Gogh took his meals; ask the "charming" staff for a seat on "the outdoor patio" for "date night" (and never mind the "tourists"); P.S. lunch is less "expensive."

Cascal *Pan-Latin*

23 | 22 | 20 | $35

Mountain View | 400 Castro St. (California St.) | 650-940-9500 | www.cascalrestaurant.com

"Get a large group of friends together" and hit up this "popular" Mountain View Pan-Latin for "interesting", "full-of-flavor" tapas and "bigger entrees" "washed down easily" with "must-have" sangria in a "lively", "colorful" space tended by a "helpful" staff; inside can be "insanely loud" ("bring your megaphone"), but outdoors is "quieter and less crammed", and if penny-pinchers find it a bit "pricey", the "killer happy hour" is a "cheap-ish" alternative.

Cetrella Ⓜ *Mediterranean*   24 | 24 | 23 | $48

Half Moon Bay | 845 Main St. (Monte Vista Ln.) | 650-726-4090 | www.cetrella.com

This "romantic" "special-occasion spot" centered around a double-sided stone fireplace has "been around Half Moon Bay for a while", drawing in supporters with its "artistically presented" Mediterranean cuisine; an "imaginative wine list" and "bargain" midweek prix fixe add to the appeal, plus there's "live jazz" on Fridays and Saturdays and service is generally "gracious", so surveyors say it's "well worth the drive."

Cha Cha Cha Cuba *Caribbean/Cuban*   22 | 20 | 18 | $27

San Mateo | 112 S. B St. (First Ave.) | 650-347-2900 | www.chacuba.com

See review in City of San Francisco Directory.

Chantilly ⓧ *French/Italian*   25 | 25 | 26 | $69

Redwood City | 3001 El Camino Real (Selby Ln.) | 650-321-4080 | www.chantillyrestaurant.com

"Always reliable", this "first-class" Redwood City "favorite" offers "old-world charm" with its "perfectly prepared" French–Northern Italian menu; if the "slightly formal setting" is suited to "clients of a certain age" and tabs are "costly", it remains an "elegant" choice "for a celebration" where "you can hear yourself talk" and, thanks to "flawless" service, "feel really special."

⒵ Cheesecake Factory *American*   21 | 21 | 20 | $28

Palo Alto | 375 University Ave. (bet. Florence & Waverly Sts.) | 650-473-9622

San Jose | 925 Blossom Hill Rd. (bet. Santa Teresa & Winfield Blvds.) | 408-225-6948

Santa Clara | Westfield Shoppingtown Valley Fair | 3041 Stevens Creek Blvd. (Santana Row) | 408-246-0092

www.thecheesecakefactory.com

See review in City of San Francisco Directory.

⒵ Cheese Steak Shop *Cheesesteaks*   23 | 12 | 19 | $11

San Jose | Monterey Plaza | 5524 Monterey Rd. (Blossom Hill Rd.) | 408-972-0271

Sunnyvale | 832 W. El Camino Real (Hollenbeck Ave.) | 408-530-8159

www.cheesesteakshop.com

See review in City of San Francisco Directory.

Chef Chu's *Chinese*   23 | 16 | 21 | $27

Los Altos | 1067 N. San Antonio Rd. (El Camino Real) | 650-948-2696 | www.chefchu.com

"Year after year", locals return for the "delicious" Chinese fare at this "Los Altos institution" that's "family-run" and a family "favorite"; if the "decor is a little dated", the "somewhat Americanized" menu ferried by "a devoted staff' gives "quality value" and "far outshines its surroundings."

Chez Shea *Eclectic* ∇ | 19 | 15 | 16 | $24

Half Moon Bay | 408 Main St. (Mill St.) | 650-560-9234 | www.chez-shea.com

"Foods from around the world" are on offer at this "little sister" of Cafe Gibraltar that's a "dependable stop in Half Moon Bay" for "flavorful, fresh" Eclectic fare "without breaking your wallet"; it's "crowded with tourists" on weekends and "locals during the week" thanks to "fast, friendly service", and a "small patio" expands the seating options.

Chez TJ ⌧ Ⓜ *French* 24 | 23 | 24 | $111

Mountain View | 938 Villa St. (bet. Bryant & Franklin Sts.) | 650-964-7466 | www.cheztj.com

When "someone else is paying", Mountain View locals choose this "venerable" "special-occasion" prix fixe specialist offering "extremely creative", "three-hour-plus" New French "*gastronomique* menus" built around "vegetables from the house garden" and "served with precision" in a "romantic" old Victorian "cottage"; acolytes assure "if you're into" "epic" "wine pairings" and savor "very slow" "pacing between courses", the "kitchen wizardry" is "worth the wait."

Cin-Cin Wine Bar & Restaurant ⌧ *Eclectic* 23 | 19 | 23 | $39

Los Gatos | 368 Village Ln. (Almendra Ave.) | 408-354-8006 | www.cincinwinebar.com

Stock up on "hearty little plates" to "share with friends" or "colleagues after work" at this Los Gatos sib to Cascal, a "chic" "neighborhood" Eclectic sporting "flavors from all over the world" matched by a "well-thought-out" wine list; the prices can "sneak up on you", but service is "always pleasant" and the scene "fun and festive", so be prepared for a "noisy" night out – and the temptation to "nibble off the plates of strangers."

Cool Café *Californian* 21 | 17 | 17 | $20

Menlo Park | Menlo Business Park | 1525 O'Brien Dr. (University Ave.) | 650-325-3665 ⌧
Stanford | Stanford Univ. Cantor Arts Ctr. | 328 Lomita Dr. (Museum Way) | 650-725-4758 Ⓜ
www.cooleatz.com

A "great getaway in the middle of a school day" or "in between viewing art" at Stanford's Cantor Arts Center say locals of this Californian eatery (with a weekday Menlo Park sib), where the "healthy, tasty" offerings are best enjoyed on the outdoor patio overlooking the Rodin sculpture garden; a few find it "a tad pricey" given the "cafeteria"-style setup, but more argue the "quality, service and proximity to a free museum make it worth the occasional visit."

Copenhagen Bakery & Cafe *Bakery* 22 | 16 | 19 | $19

Burlingame | 1216 Burlingame Ave. (Lorton Ave.) | 650-342-1357 | www.copenhagenbakery.com

"Your waistline won't thank you, but your mouth will" at this Burlingame bakery/cafe where the "dynamite pastries" make a "mean breakfast", the "hearty", open-faced sandwiches and "large" salads "fuel shopping sprees at neighboring stores" and "simple" dinner fare includes pasta and entrees like schnitzel; affordable tabs also keep it "crowded", even if the surrounds and service could be improved.

Counter Palo Alto *Burgers* 22 | 16 | 19 | $18

Palo Alto | 369 S. California Ave. (Ash St.) | 650-321-3900 | www.thecounterburger.com

"Big, messy, exactly-how-you-want-it burgers" star at this "busy" Palo Alto chain link known for a "staggering number of sophisticated toppings" (it's "not for the indecisive"), plus "to-die-for onion strings", "perfectly cooked" sweet potato fries and "thick" shakes; the "attitude-free" staff can be a little "scattered" and you may want to "take earplugs if you're noise-sensitive" but with "fair prices" it's still an "appealing" pick.

Crepevine *American/French* 21 | 16 | 19 | $16

Burlingame | 1310 Burlingame St. (Primrose Rd.) | 650-344-1310 | www.crapevine.com
Palo Alto | 367 University Blvd. (bet. Florance & Waverley Sts.) | 650-323-9000 | www.crepevine.com
See review in City of San Francisco Directory.

C Restaurant & Bar *Seafood* ∇ 22 | 26 | 21 | $48

Monterey | InterContinental The Clement Monterey | 750 Cannery Row (bet. David & Prescott Aves.) | 831-375-4800 | www.thecrestaurant-monterey.com

Score a "seat by the wall of windows" for a "spectacular view of Monterey Bay" at this "modern" dining room in the InterContinental The Clement Monterey; the seasonal, seafood-focused menu doesn't come cheap, but fans declare it "worth the price."

Crouching Tiger *Chinese* 22 | 18 | 18 | $20

Redwood City | 2644 Broadway St. (El Camino Real) | 650-298-8881 | www.crouchingtigerrestaurant.com

"Spicy" Sichuan specialties will make "you sweat" at this Redwood City Chinese where the "consistently tasty" fare is offered at "reasonable prices"; "quick service" and a "comfortable setting" enhanced with paintings up the "family-friendly" appeal.

Curry Up Now *Indian* 23 | 14 | 18 | $12

Millbrae | 129 S. B St. (bet. 1st & 2nd Aves.) | 650-477-3000 | www.curryupnow.com

"Putting Indian food in a tortilla" is a "brilliant idea" concur curry connoisseurs, who "break into a joyful Bollywood dance" thinking of their "super-spicy" chicken tikka masala burritos and "delicious" "deconstructed samosas" (both "a bargain"); "the line can be long" at the trucks that traverse San Francisco and the Peninsula and a "brick-and-mortar" sibling in Millbrae, but at least you can "order ahead online."

Dasaprakash *Indian/Vegetarian* ∇ 23 | 19 | 20 | $19

Santa Clara | 2636 Homestead Rd. (bet. Kiely Blvd. & Layton St.) | 408-246-8292 | www.dasaprakash.com

"An exotic adventure for your taste buds" awaits at this "reasonably priced" Santa Clara Indian where "even meat eaters will love" the "very good" "all-vegetarian" offerings; a "helpful" staff "navigates new customers through the menu" and tables that are "far enough apart" mean "you can eat peacefully" and "actually converse with your friends."

Davenport Roadhouse Restaurant & Inn Ⓜ *Californian*
▽ 22 | 20 | 21 | $25

Davenport | 1 Davenport Ave. (Cabrillo Hwy./Hwy. 1) | 831-426-8801 | www.davenportroadhouse.com

An "unexpected treat" when "you're driving up the coast from Santa Cruz", this "secluded" Davenport Californian offers "solid meals at solid prices"; set in a former school, it has a "funky atmosphere" with lots of wood and brick, and since service gets few complaints it's an overall "good stop."

Deetjen's Big Sur Restaurant *Californian*
▽ 24 | 25 | 23 | $47

Big Sur | Deetjen's Big Sur Inn | 48865 Hwy. 1 (30 mi. south of Carmel) | 831-667-2378 | www.deetjens.com

Set in "historic" Big Sur Inn, this "romantic" Californian offers a "menu that rivals the beauty" of its surroundings, delivering locally sourced fare in an "antiques-filled", candlelit room that exudes a "nostalgic atmosphere"; tabs verge on "expensive, but "gourmet-minded travelers" insist it's a "must."

Dio Deka *Greek*
25 | 25 | 24 | $62

Los Gatos | Hotel Los Gatos | 210 E. Main St. (High School Ct.) | 408-354-7700 | www.diodeka.com

There's "not a single blah dish" at this Hotel Los Gatos Greek say fans cheering the "modern take" on "traditional" Greek fare; "friendly" staffers tend to "lots of beautiful people" in the "bustling" "upscale" space, and though tabs are "expensive", many "don't mind paying higher prices" for "special-occasion bliss."

Dishdash Ⓢ *Mideastern*
25 | 18 | 20 | $25

Sunnyvale | 190 S. Murphy Ave. (Washington Ave.) | 408-774-1889 | www.dishdash.com

Dish n Dash Ⓢ *Mideastern*

Sunnyvale | 736 N. Mathilda Ave. (San Anselmo) | 408-530-9200 | www.dishndashrestaurant.com

"Incredibly flavorful" fare in "generous portions" keeps this Sunnyvale Middle Eastern "packed to the rafters", especially since prices are "reasonable" and "service is generally very friendly and accommodating despite the crowds"; though the "long wait" is a "con", fans advise you just "have another cocktail while you wait" – or head over to its North Mathilda Avenue quick-serve offshoot, a "perfect alternative", with "fresh, filling" fare (wraps, salads, smoothies) fit for an "economy budget."

Donato Enoteca *Italian*
23 | 22 | 22 | $42

Redwood City | 1041 Middlefield Rd. (bet. Jefferson Ave. & Main St.) | 650-701-1000 | www.donatoenoteca.com

You'll feel "close to Tuscany" at this moderately priced Redwood City Italian where the "passionate" chef-owner sends out "deliciously satisfying pizza" and other "consistently good" offerings, including a number of "imaginative", "out-of-the-ordinary" dishes; the staff is "attentive", and while the "relaxing" surroundings are good for "family night", they're also thought to be "romantic" enough for "date night", especially when surveyors are sitting "outdoors under the heated lamps."

Duarte's Tavern *American*   23 | 15 | 20 | $28

Pescadero | 202 Stage Rd. (Pescadero Creek Rd.) | 650-879-0464 | www.duartestavern.com

For "comfort food at its best" diners "take a step back in time" at this "historic" Pescadero tavern, a "coastal tradition" for "incredible pies", "super-rich" soups (especially the "justly famous" artichoke) and other "tasty" "old-time" American eats, all at moderate prices; service is "personable" and the "knotty-pine-paneled dining room" is joined by an "inviting bar" that's "just the kind of place" to "waste an entire afternoon."

Ebisu ●Ⓜ *Japanese*   24 | 19 | 21 | $36

South San Francisco | San Francisco Int'l Airport | International Terminal (Hwy. 101) | 650-588-2549 | www.ebisusushi.com
See review in City of San Francisco Directory.

Ecco Restaurant Ⓢ *Californian/Continental*   25 | 23 | 24 | $54

Burlingame | 322 Lorton Ave. (bet. Burlingame & Donnelly Aves.) | 650-342-7355 | www.eccorestaurant.com

"Delicately prepared, beautifully presented" Continental-Cal cuisine and "warm", "attentive" service keep this Burlingame longtimer "one of the more consistently reliable" choices around; "relaxed, pretty" surrounds are yet another reason fans find "pricey" tabs "worth it."

El Farolito *Mexican*   23 | 9 | 17 | $10

South San Francisco | 394 Grand Ave. (Maple Ave.) | 650-737-0138 | www.elfarolitoinc.com
See review in City of San Francisco Directory.

Emporio Rulli *Dessert/Italian*   22 | 20 | 18 | $20

South San Francisco | San Francisco Int'l Airport | Domestic Terminal 3 (Hwy. 101) | 888-887-8554
South San Francisco | San Francisco Int'l Airport | Lower Int'l Loop (Hwy. 101) | 888-887-8554
South San Francisco | San Francisco Int'l Airport | Upper Int'l Loop (Hwy. 101) | 888-887-8554 ●
www.rulli.com
See review in North of San Francisco Directory.

Espetus Churrascaria *Brazilian*   23 | 20 | 23 | $71
(aka Espetus Churrascaria Brazilian Steakhouse)

San Mateo | 710 S. B St. (bet. 7th & 8th Aves.) | 650-342-8700 | www.espetus.com
See review in City of San Francisco Directory.

Eulipia Restaurant & Bar Ⓜ *American*   ▽ 21 | 18 | 22 | $40

San Jose | 374 S. First St. (bet. San Carlos & San Salvador Sts.) | 408-280-6161 | www.eulipia.com

With a convenient location near the opera and California Theatre, plus service that's "aware patrons need to get to seats on time" and solid eats, this moderately priced San Jose New American is a "superior theater prelim"; still, a few critics contend it's "a bit passé" after 35 years in business, but it fits the bill.

	FOOD	DECOR	SERVICE	COST

☑ Evvia *Greek*   28 | 25 | 26 | $55

Palo Alto | 420 Emerson St. (bet. Lytton & University Aves.) |
650-326-0983 | www.evvia.net

The "upscale Greek cuisine" at this "top-tier" Palo Altan (little sis of
SF's Kokkari) is "blessed by the gods of Mount Olympus" cheer fans
touting the "otherworldly" lamb, "expertly grilled fish" and other "succulent" specialties, all delivered via "friendly", "engaging" servers; its
"lively atmosphere is pleasure-enhancing" too, and though it gets
"noisy and densely packed in" at "prime hours", most agree it's "always a favorite – especially if someone else is picking up the tab."

Fandango *Mediterranean*   21 | 21 | 21 | $48

Pacific Grove | 223 17th St. (bet. Laurel & Lighthouse Aves.) |
831-372-3456 | www.fandangorestaurant.com

After 25 years, this Pacific Grove Mediterranean "still has it" say fans
praising its "well-prepared" fare and "killer wine list", both so "extensive" "the only problem is choosing what to eat and drink"; a few find
the offerings a bit "uninspired", but "polished" service and a "charming converted house atmosphere" help win many over.

The Fish Market *Seafood*   22 | 18 | 20 | $30

Palo Alto | 3150 El Camino Real (bet. Page Mill Rd. & Hansen Way) |
650-493-9188
San Jose | 1007 Blossom Hill Rd. (Winfield Blvd.) | 408-269-3474
San Mateo | 1855 S. Norfolk (Fashion Island Blvd.) | 650-349-3474
Santa Clara | 3775 El Camino Real (Halford Ave.) | 408-246-3474
www.thefishmarket.com

"Fresh fish" for a "fair price" has fans hooked on this "consistent" San
Mateo chain link "right on the water" (and its siblings); downstairs is
a "casual", "bare-bones" setup where the "action" and "chatter" is at
the oyster bar ("watch the chefs in action"), while the "upscale" Top
of the Market offers a "quieter" vibe for a "business lunch or intimate
dinner"; P.S. get your "seafood fix" to-go from the on-site retail space.

Fishwife at Asilomar Beach *Californian/Seafood*   22 | 16 | 20 | $30

Pacific Grove | 1996½ Sunset Dr. (Asilomar Ave.) | 831-375-7107 |
www.fishwife.com

"Locals love" this "low-key" Pacific Grove Californian where you "don't
have to dress up" to enjoy the "consistently good" sustainably caught
seafood-focused offerings made more "interesting" by a "Caribbean
touch"; "prices are fair", the staff is "friendly" and the "cheerfully decorated" space is "close enough to the beach for a nice postprandial
stroll", so don't be surprised if it's "crowded."

Flea St. Café ⓜ *Californian*   26 | 22 | 25 | $57

Menlo Park | 3607 Alameda de las Pulgas (Avy Ave.) | 650-854-1226 |
www.cooleatz.com

Still "bringing fresh, local, organic" ingredients "to your table", chef-
owner Jesse Ziff Cool works the room at this "inventive" Cal-New
American "Menlo Park mainstay", where her "commitment to sustainability" extends even to the recycled-glass bar where "interesting
California wines" and farm-fresh cocktails are poured; the "elegant"
setting and "top-notch" service make it HQ on the Peninsula for "business dinners" or "bringing your honey", and it's easier to "splurge"
knowing it's all "good for the earth."

	FOOD	DECOR	SERVICE	COST

Flying Fish Grill *Californian/Seafood* | 24 | 20 | 23 | $46

Carmel | Carmel Plaza | Mission St. (bet. Ocean & 7th Aves.) |
831-625-1962

"One of Carmel's consistent stars", this "serene" Californian from
chef/co-owner Kenny Fukumoto "skillfully delivers" "innovative" fin
fare with Asian touches via "courteous, understated" servers; hidden
in the lower level of a shopping plaza, it has an "inviting cellar ambiance", and while not cheap, the "cozy", "softly lit" environs make it a
"welcome escape" from the "hectic" tourist scene.

Flying Fish Grill *Seafood* | 21 | 15 | 18 | $25

Half Moon Bay | 211 San Mateo Rd. (Main St.) | 650-712-1125 |
www.flyingfishgrill.net

After "expanding into a much larger space", the "legendary" fish tacos
are just "as good" say loyalists of this Half Moon Bay Californian that's
still a "quick stop" for your seafood "fix"; otherwise, solid service can
sometimes be "slow", and while a few complain it's merely "average",
more cite "value" tabs and label it their "too-tired-to-cook place."

Forbes Mill Steakhouse *Steak* | 23 | 21 | 22 | $58

Los Gatos | 206 N. Santa Cruz Ave. (Royce St.) | 408-395-6434 |
www.forbesmillsteakhouse.com

Expect "butter soft" filets and other "prime" "slabs of beef", plus
"enough steak alternatives" to satisfy a "diverse" group at this "upscale"
chophouse duo in Danville and Los Gatos; "stylish" wood-accented
decor adds more "special-occasion sparkle" and service is "helpful",
so even if a few find it merely "ok", more (especially those with "deep
pockets") label it a "favorite."

NEW 400 Degrees *Burgers* | - | - | - | I

Carmel | Mission St. (7th St.) | 831-244-0040 | 400degrees.com

Providing a much-needed casual, affordable dining option in Downtown
Carmel is this new all-day, late-night gourmet burger joint from the
folks behind Cantinetta Luca and Aubergine; the name comes from
the custom-made cast iron griddle on which the kitchen cooks the
house-blended patties that come with local veggies and fresh condiments, plus a selection of fries and salads, and the eco-modern digs
include a dog-friendly heated patio; P.S. also offered: natural sodas,
milkshakes, beer and wines available by the glass or half bottle.

Fuki Sushi *Japanese* | 23 | 20 | 20 | $42

Palo Alto | 4119 El Camino Real (bet. Arastradero & Page Mill Rds.) |
650-494-9383 | www.fukisushi.com

"Very fresh" fish has backers calling this "Palo Alto's best sushi place",
where the "beautifully prepared" fin fare "melts in your mouth like
butter"; cooked Japanese dishes are also offered, and the "pleasantly
personal" staff and "traditional setting" including "takami seating"
make for a "nice place to take clients" – but "bring your company
credit card" as it's "kind of expensive."

Gabriella Café *Californian/Italian* | 23 | 20 | 21 | $35

Santa Cruz | 910 Cedar St. (bet. Church & Locust Sts.) |
831-457-1677 | www.gabriellacafe.com

"Local and organic" ingredients take the "imaginative" fare up a notch
at this midpriced Santa Cruz Cal-Italian; a few complain it can be "up

and down" and the "tiny" space can get "tight", but "low lighting" and "cozy" surrounds make it "excellent for date night" – providing "you really like your neighbors."

Gayle's Bakery & Rosticceria *Bakery*   24 | 14 | 18 | $18

Capitola | Upper Capitola Shopping Ctr. | 504 Bay Ave. (Capitola Ave.) | 831-462-1200 | www.gaylesbakery.com

"People come from miles away" to visit this Capitola bakery/cafe and load up on "upscale picnic" provisions, like "tasty prepared meals", "delicious" sandwiches and "excellent baked goods"; though primarily a "stop and go" spot, you can "try to find somewhere to sit" on the enclosed patio – either way you'll be served by "friendly" staffers

Gochi Japanese Fusion Tapas 🏠 *Japanese*   25 | 20 | 20 | $39

Cupertino | 19980 Homestead Rd. (bet. Blarney & Heron Aves.) | 408-725-0542 | www.gochifusiontapas.com

The "enormous" menu of "delicious" "izakaya-style" fusion fare is "best enjoyed in groups with a healthy appetite for variety" at this "popular" midpriced Cupertino Japanese offering "traditional" dishes alongside more "interesting" choices, like "awesome pizzas", plus "smooth, sweet sake" and "ice cold beer"; the decor is "authentic" with "lots of tatami-style seating" and service is generally "friendly" (if a little "slow"), so it's "frequently crowded", making reservations "highly recommended."

NEW Golden Boy *Pizza*   25 | 13 | 19 | $10

San Mateo | 234 Main St. (2nd Ave.) | no phone | www.goldenboypizza.com
See review in City of San Francisco Directory.

Gordon Biersch *Pub Food*   18 | 17 | 18 | $27

Palo Alto | 640 Emerson St. (bet. Forest & Hamilton Aves.) | 650-323-7723
San Jose | 33 E. San Fernando St. (bet. 1st & 2nd Sts.) | 408-294-6785
www.gordonbiersch.com

"Hearty" American pub grub "complements" a "rotating selection" of "glorious" "locally" brewed suds at these "packed" Palo Alto and San Jose links in a national chain; although the affordable eats are "nothing to write home about" (excepting the "addictive garlic fries") and the "friendly" servers are "a little slow", if you "stick to simple things" like "burgers and brewskis" you'll have "fun" with the "loud" "young crowd."

Grasing's Coastal Cuisine *Californian*   22 | 21 | 21 | $45

Carmel | Jordan Ctr. | Sixth Ave. (Mission St.) | 831-624-6562 | www.grasings.com

"Locally sustained" ingredients meet "excellent preparations" at Kurt Grasing's Carmel Californian, where a "great wine list" and "enthusiastic" service add to the appeal; a "bar menu offers more affordable choices" and you can even "bring your dog" to the "beautiful" patio for a "quiet, locals'" experience.

Grill on the Alley *Steak*   24 | 21 | 22 | $53

San Jose | Fairmont San Jose | 172 S. Market St. (San Carlos St.) | 408-294-2244 | www.thegrill.com

"Meat lovers" congregate at this chophouse chain link in San Jose's Fairmont Hotel for "large" cuts in contemporary environs with a "kind of New York vibe"; service is generally "attentive", and though prices seem "set for the expense-account crowd", happy-hour specials in the "comfy, alive" bar are a less costly alternative.

Hachi Ju Hachi Ⓜ *Japanese* ▽ 27 | 16 | 24 | $52
Saratoga | 14480 Big Basin Way (3rd St.) | 408-647-2258 |
www.hachijuhachi88.com
"Authentic", "humble and honest" fare draws fans to this Saratoga Japanese; the decor is "spartan" and the check will lighten your wallet, but service gets high marks and it's always enjoyable to "sit at the bar" and watch the chef "in action."

Half Moon Bay
Brewing Company *Pub Food/Seafood* 18 | 19 | 18 | $28
Half Moon Bay | 390 Capistrano Rd. (bet. Cabrillo Hwy. & Prospect Way) |
650-728-2739 | www.hmbbrewingco.com
An "easy place to hang out", this Half Moon Bay stop vends Californian "high-end brewpub" eats and"excellent beers" to a "large après-beach crowd" and "lots of locals"; the interior is "nothing special" and service can be a bit "slapdashy", but "sitting" outside by the fire pit and "enjoying the ocean view" still can't be beat.

Happy Cafe Restaurant Ⓜ⇔ *Chinese* ▽ 22 | 5 | 14 | $17
San Mateo | 250 S. B St. (bet. 2nd & 3rd Aves.) | 650-340-7138 |
www.happycaferestaurant.blogspot.com
"A true hole-in-the-wall", this San Mateo Shanghainese attracts diners with "authentic Chinese home cooking", like noodles (a "main draw") and "amazingly good" soup dumplings; "tables can be cramped" in the "tiny" digs, but "inexpensive" tabs help, and hey, you "go for the food" anyway; P.S. closed Mondays and Tuesdays.

Hotaru *Japanese* 21 | 13 | 17 | $24
San Mateo | 33 E. Third Ave. (bet. El Camino Real & San Mateo Dr.) |
650-343-1152 | www.hotarurestaurant.com
There's always a "line out the door" at this "small storefront" Japanese in San Mateo providing a "consistent", "straightforward" selection of sushi, udon, teriyaki, et al.; "the decor is lacking some flair" and the staff makes some feel "rushed", but at the end of the day "no one cares" because it's so "cheap."

Hunan Home's Restaurant *Chinese* 22 | 13 | 19 | $25
Los Altos | 4880 El Camino Real (bet. Jordan Ave. & Los Altos Sq.) |
650-965-8888 | www.hunanhomes.com
Hunan Garden *Chinese*
Palo Alto | 3345 El Camino Real (bet. Fernando & Lambert Aves.) |
650-565-8868 | www.chineserestauranthunangarden.com
See review in City of San Francisco Directory.

Iberia *Spanish* 22 | 19 | 17 | $46
Menlo Park | 1026 Alma St. (Ravenswood Ave.) | 650-325-8981 |
www.iberiarestaurant.com
Be it "tapas by the fireplace" in "the beautiful bar" or more substantial meals in the dining room or on the patio, fans say this "romantic hideaway in Menlo Park" "consistently provides a fantastic Spanish dining experience"; a few find it "overpriced", but most "would go there again."

	FOOD	DECOR	SERVICE	COST

Ike's Lair *Sandwiches*   25 | 12 | 18 | $13

Redwood City | 2655 Broadway (El Camino Real) | 650-365-2200 |
www.ikeslair.com

Ike's Place *Sandwiches*

Stanford | Stanford Univ. Huang Engineering Ctr. | 475 Via Ortega Dr.
(Campus Dr.) | 650-322-1766 | www.ilikeikesplace.com
See review in City of San Francisco Directory.

∎ Il Fornaio *Italian*   22 | 22 | 21 | $39

Burlingame | 327 Lorton Ave. (bet. Bellevue & Donnelly Aves.) |
650-375-8000
Carmel | The Pine Inn | Ocean Ave. (Monte Verde St.) | 831-622-5100
Palo Alto | Garden Court Hotel | 520 Cowper St. (bet. Hamilton &
University Aves.) | 650-853-3888
San Jose | Sainte Claire Hotel | 302 S. Market St. (bet. San Carlos &
San Salvador Sts.) | 408-271-3366
www.ilfornaio.com
See review in City of San Francisco Directory.

Il Postale *Italian*   23 | 19 | 22 | $34

Sunnyvale | 127 W. Washington Ave. (bet. Frances St. & Murphy Ave.) |
408-733-9600 | www.ilpostale.com
At this former Sunnyvale post office, the "sweet, attentive" staff doles
out "huge portions" of "luscious Italian"-American fare; the "small" setting "fills up pretty fast" (and gets "loud"), so "be sure you call for a
reservation" (accepted only for parties of five or more).

∎ In-N-Out Burger ◐ *Burgers*   23 | 14 | 21 | $9

Millbrae | 11 Rollins Rd. (bet. Adrian Rd. & Millbrae Ave.)
Mountain View | 1159 N. Rengstorff Ave. (Leghorn St.)
Mountain View | 53 W. El Camino Real (bet. Bay St. & Grant Rd.)
San Jose | 550 Newhall Dr. (Chestnut St.)
San Jose | 5611 Santa Teresa Blvd. (bet. Blossom Hill Rd. & Summerbrook Ln.)
Daly City | 260 Washington St. (Sullivan Ave.)
800-786-1000 | www.in-n-out.com
See review in City of San Francisco Directory.

Izzy's Steaks & Chops *Steak*   23 | 20 | 22 | $45

San Carlos | 525 Skyway Rd. (bet. Airport Way & Monte Vista Dr.) |
650-654-2822 | www.izzyssteaks.com
See review in City of San Francisco Directory.

Jang Su Jang *Korean*   23 | 18 | 18 | $30

Santa Clara | Lawrence Plaza | 3561 El Camino Real (bet. Flora Vista Ave. &
Lawrence Expwy.) | 408-246-1212 | www.jangsujang.com
Santa Clarans assure that "you will always get a great and reliable
Korean meal" at this modern-looking venue offering both "kitchen-
cooked" fare and grill-it-yourself barbecue, and if it's perhaps "a little
pricier than other places" of its ilk, it's "worth it"; though service is
"quick", count on "long waits if you don't have a reservation."

Jin Sho ⊠ *Japanese*   26 | 19 | 18 | $49

Palo Alto | 454 S. California Ave. (bet. Ash St. & El Camino Real) |
650-321-3454 | www.jinshorestaurant.com
"Impeccable" "melt-in-your-mouth" sushi and cooked fare is "expertly
prepared" by former Nobu chefs – and "at a price" ("worth it") – at this

FOOD DECOR SERVICE COST

"modern" Palo Alto Japanese; service can be "a little slow", but that just leaves more time to savor the "highly recommend" omakase, which can be paired with a sake sampler.

John Bentley's ☒ *Californian*   25 | 22 | 25 | $55
Redwood City | 2915 El Camino Real (Selby Ln.) | 650-365-7777 |
www.johnbentleys.com

A "tempting array" of "heavenly", "farm-fresh" cuisine makes the "somewhat pricey" tabs "worth it" at this "warm, inviting" Redwood City Californian from the eponymous chef-owner; a "terrific" staff and "fine selection of wines" help make it ripe "for that special occasion", but it's also "great for a good meal any time."

Joya Restaurant *Nuevo Latino*   23 | 24 | 20 | $41
Palo Alto | 339 University Ave. (Florence St.) | 650-853-9800 |
www.joyarestaurant.com

"Impressively hip for Downtown Palo Alto", this "contemporary" Nuevo Latino provides its "beautiful, smart" habitués with "terrific tapas" and an "epic beverage list", all delivered by "friendly", "attentive" staffers; many find the costs somewhat "pricey", but conclude it's "worth a visit" if only to revel in the "young", "groovy vibe" typical of a "more metropolitan area."

Joy Luck Palace *Chinese*   22 | 16 | 16 | $25
Cupertino | 10911 N. Wolfe Rd. (Homestead Rd.) | 408-255-6988

"Arrive early" for lunch, because there's usually "a wait" to get into this Cupertino strip-mall spot, where "dim sum's the treat" and a "ridiculously good value for the price"; "typical Chinese" dinners are also offered in the large space, which features private rooms and "spare but speedy service."

Juban *Japanese*   20 | 17 | 19 | $32
Burlingame | 1204 Broadway (bet. Laguna & Paloma Aves.) | 650-347-2300
Menlo Park | 712 Santa Cruz Ave. (bet. Chestnut & Maloney Sts.) |
650-473-6458
www.jubanrestaurant.com
See review in City of San Francisco Directory.

Kabul Afghan Cuisine *Afghan*   23 | 18 | 21 | $30
Burlingame | 1101 Burlingame Ave. (California Dr.) | 650-343-2075
San Carlos | San Carlos Plaza | 135 El Camino Real (bet. Harbour Blvd. & Holly St.) | 650-594-2840
www.kabulcuisine.com

Loyal patrons of "many years" "deeply appreciate" the "fantastic lamb dishes", "wonderful kebabs" and other "exotic", "hearty" Afghan fare prepared at these spots in San Carlos and Downtown Burlingame; the settings are kind of "plain", but that matters not in light of the "fast, friendly service", "generous portions" and "reasonable prices."

Kanpai ☒ *Japanese*   ▽ 24 | 19 | 20 | $38
Palo Alto | 330 Lytton Ave. (bet. Bryant & Florence Sts.) |
650-325-2696 | www.kanpaipaloalto.com

"Outstanding Japanese cuisine for surprisingly little money" sums up this Palo Altan where the sushi is "fresh" and "creative"; the "small" space is "always crowded", but the "friendly staff" fosters a "cozy atmosphere", while the "superb" sake selection helps keep everyone relaxed.

Kincaid's Bayhouse *American*
23 | **22** | **21** | **$47**

Burlingame | 60 Bay View Pl. (Airport Blvd.) | 650-342-9844 | www.kincaids.com

"After all these years", this Burlingame branch of a small national chain is still a "standby" for "appetizing" Traditional American dishes complemented by "excellent" wines and "special occasions" involving "big groups"; "friendly" service and "fabulous views of the bay" ("get a window table") are two more aspects that make the somewhat "costly" checks "worth it."

The Kitchen ● *Chinese*
▽ **24** | **16** | **17** | **$32**

Millbrae | 279 El Camino Real (La Cruz Ave.) | 650-692-9688 | www.thekitchenmillbrae.com

It's a "real winner" say fans of this Millbrae Chinese that dishes up "well-prepared" dim sum (available only at lunch); while the service is "so-so" and the decor not notable, crowds of families on weekends attest to the "excellent" Cantonese cuisine and moderate prices.

Koi Palace *Chinese*
24 | **18** | **15** | **$35**

Daly City | Serramonte Plaza | 365 Gellert Blvd. (bet. Hickey & Serramonte Blvds.) | 650-992-9000 | www.koipalace.com

"Packing the house every weekend", this "upscale" Daly City and Dublin duo delivers an "astounding selection" of "to-die-for" dim sum in addition to "stellar seafood" and "elaborate" Cantonese-style banquet dinners in a setting complete with a tranquil koi pond and rows of fish tanks that's nonetheless "a zoo"; waits can be "ridiculous", the "service is spotty" and "it costs more" than some others in its genre, but the "crowds can't be wrong."

Krung Thai *Thai*
22 | **17** | **18** | **$23**

Mountain View | San Antonio Shopping Ctr. | 590 Showers Dr. (bet. California & Latham Sts.) | 650-559-0366 | www.originalkrungthai.com
San Jose | 642 S. Winchester Blvd. (bet. Moorpark Ave. & Riddle Rd.) | 408-260-8224 | www.newkrungthai.com

Fans attest these San Jose and Mountain View twins are among "the best places to go for authentic" Siamese "curries and pad Thai"; since they're "always busy" and can get "very crowded", "friendly" service varies, nonetheless they're "great" for lunch with "business colleagues" or dinner "with friends or family"; P.S. the similarly named New Krung Thai is separately owned.

La Bicyclette *French/Italian*
23 | **19** | **20** | **$38**

Carmel | Seventh Ave. (Dolores St.) | 831-622-9899

Turning out "unpretentious", "delicious" fare for three decades, this "cozy" Carmel French-Italian "gathering spot" is still "hopping", thanks to the "darling" bistro decor, "tasty" pizzas and "authentic and fresh" bread from the word-burning oven, along with a prix fixe menu that may be the "best value in town" (some of the organic vegetables hail from the local middle school); P.S. the wines are "excellent."

La Bodeguita del Medio ⊠ *Cuban*
23 | **20** | **20** | **$36**

Palo Alto | 463 S. California Ave. (El Camino Real) | 650-326-7762 | www.labodeguita.com

"Popular and trendy", this Palo Alto Cuban transports with "well-prepared" midpriced dishes, "strong" drinks and a cigar lounge that's "as close to Havana heaven as you'll get"; the servers "really care" and Cuban artwork adds ambiance, as do "roomy tables" spaced "far enough" apart for "quiet conversation."

La Corneta *Mexican*   22 | 13 | 18 | $12

Burlingame | 1123 Burlingame Ave. (bet. Hatch Ln. & Lorton Ave.) | 650-340-1300
San Carlos | 1147 San Carlos Ave. (bet. El Camino Real & Laurel St.) | 650-551-1400
www.lacorneta.com
See review in City of San Francisco Directory.

La Costanera Ⓜ *Peruvian*   25 | 25 | 23 | $49

Montara | 8150 Cabrillo Hwy. (bet. 1st & 2nd Sts.) | 650-728-1600 | www.lacostanerarestaurant.com
"Start with a pisco sour" at the beach bar of this Montara waterfront Peruvian, then move upstairs for "views of the Pacific" to go with the "authentic" dishes; it's "a little out of the way" and "a bit pricey", but service is generally "accommodating" and most agree the "delicious" fare from chef-owner Carlos Altamirano (SF's Piqueo and Mochica) is "not to be missed."

La Cumbre Taqueria *Mexican*   22 | 10 | 16 | $11

San Mateo | 28 N. B St. (bet. Baldwin & Tilton Aves.) | 650-344-8989
See review in City of San Francisco Directory.

La Fondue *Fondue*   23 | 23 | 22 | $65

Saratoga | 14550 Big Basin Way (4th St.) | 408-867-3332 | www.lafondue.com
Cheese lovers, carnivores and chocoholics alike are "very fondue this place" in Saratoga, where diners dip bread, meat, fruit and cake into tabletop pots; the "two-hour dinner experience" in rooms with "creative", "eclectic decor" is "fun for groups", "older kids" and "date night" too, and service is "good", but some gripe it's "overpriced" "considering you do all the cooking yourself."

🔁 La Forêt Ⓜ *Continental/French*   27 | 26 | 27 | $63

San Jose | 21747 Bertram Rd. (Almaden Rd.) | 408-997-3458 | www.laforetrestaurant.com
"Tucked away in a rural alcove of San Jose" yet only "20 minutes to Downtown", this "hidden gem" for an "upscale" "special dinner" has a creekside location "on the edge of Silicon Valley" that "adds to the mystique"; service is as "classy" as the setting, while "traditional" dishes on the Continental-French menu are a "treat for the eyes and palate" (with "over-the-top prices" to match).

La Posta Ⓜ *Italian*   ▽ 26 | 19 | 21 | $37

Santa Cruz | 538 Seabright Ave. (Watson St.) | 831-457-2782 | www.lapostarestaurant.com
Behind a modest storefront in Santa Cruz's happening Seabright neighborhood, this "fantastic" spot doles out "inventive", "superlative" Italian fare and "outstanding Italian wines" for "reasonable prices"; "wonderful" staffers and a "vibrant bar scene" are draws on any evening, but locals make a point to stop by on Tuesdays for 'neighborhood nights', featuring a "steal" of a meal deal and live "traditional music."

Lavanda *Mediterranean*
21 | 20 | 21 | $46

Palo Alto | 185 University Ave. (Emerson St.) | 650-321-3514 | www.lavandarestaurant.com

"Unique" Italian-centric Mediterranean and Croatian cuisines are on the menu at this "great location in the heart of Palo Alto" offering small and large plates plus "excellent wines"; what's more, the "friendly and efficient" staff adds to meals that the "hip", "international clientele" deems "a pleasure"; P.S. it's "somewhat pricey", but for a more "reasonable" check, come for Sunday's prix fixe dinner.

La Victoria Taqueria ● *Mexican*
25 | 12 | 17 | $10

Redwood City | 847 Main St. (B'way) | 650-366-1070
San Jose | 131 W. Santa Clara St. (bet. Market & San Pedro Sts.) | 408-993-8230
San Jose | 140 E. San Carlos St. (bet. 3rd & 4th Sts.) | 408-298-5335
San Jose | 5015 Almaden Expwy. (Cherry Ave.) | 408-978-7666
www.lavicsj.com

"Two words: orange sauce" say "La Vic" regulars of the "addictive" house condiment for "killer burritos", "tasty carne asada" and other Mexican classics at this taqueria chainlet; "hungry college kids" inhale "day and night" at the San Carlos "Victorian-era house across from SJ State" – a South Bay "institution", it can get "overcrowded", thanks to "fast" service and cheap tabs.

LB Steak *Steak*
22 | 23 | 21 | $57

NEW Menlo Park | 898 Santa Cruz Ave. (University Dr.) | 650-321-8980
San Jose | Santana Row | 334 Santana Row (Alyssum Ln.) | 408-244-1180
www.lbsteak.com

"The cowhide chairs tell you they are serious about their steak" at this "classy, modern" French-flavored meatery co-owned by Roland Passot (La Folie) in San Jose's "bustling Santana Row" and Menlo Park, a "go-to" for dates, business meals and "groups"; though the prices are "high", service is "informative" and the "Cal-strong" wine list is "great."

Left Bank *French*
20 | 21 | 19 | $39

Menlo Park | 635 Santa Cruz Ave. (Doyle St.) | 650-473-6543
San Jose | Santana Row | 377 Santana Row (Olsen Dr.) | 408-984-3500
www.leftbank.com

See review in North of San Francisco Directory.

⊠ Le Papillon *French*
27 | 24 | 26 | $91

San Jose | 410 Saratoga Ave. (Kiely Blvd.) | 408-296-3730 | www.lepapillon.com

Despite its "odd location next to a strip mall" in San Jose, this "elegant" circa-1977 "gem" "never fails to exceed all expectations" thanks to its "amazing", "unforgettable" New French creations (which can be "matched well with wines") and "impeccable service" from "friendly, knowledgeable" staffers; the "upscale" experience may be "expensive", but fans say it's "worth it" for a "romantic date" or "special occasion."

Lion & Compass ⊠ *American*
21 | 19 | 22 | $50

Sunnyvale | 1023 N. Fair Oaks Ave. (Weddell Dr.) | 408-745-1260 | www.lionandcompass.com

"The place to see and be seen in Silicon Valley", this Sunnyvale stalwart "still delivers" "fine" New American fare with "old-school service"; a few ding the "dated" decor, declaring it "detracts from the experience", but it's still a popular place for "business lunches", especially if you're wielding a "corporate credit card."

Liou's House Ⓜ *Chinese* ▽ 25 | 11 | 18 | $19

Milpitas | 1245 Jacklin Rd. (Park Victoria Dr.) | 408-263-9888
Hidden in a "humble" strip mall next to a miniature golf course, this affordable off-the-radar spot showcases "authentic" Hunan and Taiwanese specialties by chef James Liou (formerly of Chef Chu's); it's "a level above most of the Chinese places in Milpitas" despite the spare decor.

Little Sheep Mongolian Hot Pot *Mongolian* 22 | 17 | 16 | $29

Cupertino | 19062 Stevens Creek Blvd. (bet. Judy & Tantau Aves.) | 408-996-9919
San Mateo | 215 S. Ellsworth Ave. (bet. 2nd & 3rd Aves.) | 650-343-2566
www.littlesheephotpot.com
"Legions of hungry patrons" line up "to be first" at this Mongolian hot-pot chain where each table gets a "boiling cauldron" of "rich", "flavorful broth" in which to cook "many different vegetable and meat options" ("satisfying", but maybe "pricey for the amount you get"); though servers are "brisk", they "don't rush you out with the check", meaning it gets and stays "crowded", especially on weekends.

Locanda Positano Ⓜ *Pizza* ▽ 26 | 21 | 22 | $36

San Carlos | 617 Laurel St. (San Carlos Ave.) | 650-591-5700 | www.locanda-positano.com
Injecting a little "hip NYC ambiance" into the mid-Peninsula, this "hotspot" trattoria in San Carlos is a worthy "Acqua Pazza sister" doling out "awesome", "genuine Napoli-style pizza" and other "reasonably priced" staples (including a "to-die-for" Nutella calzone); it gets "busy" and "a bit noisy", but the "warm" staff makes you "feel welcome" whether you "grab a table outside" or stay inside to watch the pizzaiolo in action.

Los Altos Grill *American* 24 | 21 | 21 | $39

Los Altos | 233 Third St. (W. Hawthorne Ave.) | 650-948-3524 | www.hillstone.com
Like its parent, Hillstone, this "classy" Los Altos option specializes in American "comfort food" – e.g. "fabulous" grilled artichokes, "to-die-for" ribs – for which you "get your money's worth"; the "warm-wood" and fireplace–blessed dining room is a "great place" to take "kids" and "parents" alike, while the "lively bar" is a "pickup scene" where "well-heeled patrons" "partake of martinis" crafted by "top-notch" 'tenders; P.S. "there's no corkage fee if you bring your own wine."

Madera *American* 24 | 26 | 24 | $68

Menlo Park | Rosewood Sand Hill | 2825 Sand Hill Rd. (Hwy. 280) | 650-561-1540 | www.maderasandhill.com
"VCs eat and meet" at the "Silicon Valley power scene" that is this Peninsula New American located at the Rosewood Sand Hill Hotel, where tech types "pitch business ideas" in the "gorgeous" room featuring a wall of windows; service is "top-notch", the seasonally focused cuisine is "impeccably prepared" (though very "expensive") and if it gets too "noisy and crowded", a table on the patio can be quieter with "great views of the Santa Cruz Mountains" to boot.

	FOOD	DECOR	SERVICE	COST

Ma Maison ⓜ French   ▽ 23 | 24 | 24 | $44

Aptos | 9051 Soquel Dr. (Rio Del Mar Blvd.) | 831-688-5566 |
www.mamaisonrestaurant.com

"Tucked away" in a "little", "old house along the main drag" in Aptos,
this bistro run by a Parisian chef-owner may fly under the radar, but the
"outstanding service" and "consistently excellent" "country French" fare
make it "one of the better alternatives in town"; it's not too expensive
and is great for lunch on the patio or "special nights" by the fireplace.

☒ Manresa ⓜ American   27 | 25 | 27 | $163

Los Gatos | 320 Village Ln. (bet. N. Santa Cruz & University Aves.) |
408-354-4330 | www.manresarestaurant.com

It "doesn't get more farm-to-table" than at this "crown jewel on the
Peninsula" where "thought-provoking" New American fare emerges
from chef-owner David Kinch's Los Gatos "atelier/kitchen" in the form
of "innovative" tasting menus built around "pristine ingredients" from
a biodynamic farm; the newly "remodeled" dining room and cocktail
lounge have a "modern" look that "befits" the "three-hour" "ultra-
high-end" "extravaganza", and when you add in the "superbly choreographed service", it's "no wonder it costs so much."

☒ Marinus ⓜ Californian/French   28 | 28 | 27 | $93

Carmel Valley | Bernardus Lodge | 415 W. Carmel Valley Rd.
(Laureles Grade Rd.) | 831-658-3595 | www.bernardus.com

Way beyond the typical "hotel restaurant", this Carmel Valley "gem"
at Bernardus Lodge boasts a "beautiful" setting and "inviting" revamped decor as a backdrop for Cal Stamenov's "impeccable" Cal–New
French menus that "push the envelope" while pleasing vegetarians, locavores and omnivores alike; service is "top-of-the-line" and the wine
list is "staggering" (with "prices to match"), so overall it's "well worth
the trip for a special occasion" and even better to "stay the night so
you can savor every glass."

Max's Cafe of Redwood City Deli   20 | 17 | 19 | $26

Redwood City | Sequoia Station | 1001 El Camino Real (James Ave.) |
650-365-6297

Max's Opera Cafe of Palo Alto Deli

Palo Alto | Stanford Shopping Ctr. | 711 Stanford Shopping Ctr.
(Sand Hill Rd.) | 650-323-6297

Max's Restaurant and Bar Deli

Burlingame | 1250 Old Bayshore Hwy. (B'way) | 650-342-6297
www.maxsworld.com

See review in City of San Francisco Directory.

Mayfield Bakery & Café Bakery/Californian   21 | 19 | 19 | $34

Palo Alto | Town & Country Vill. | 855 El Camino Real (Embarcadero Rd.) |
650-853-9200 | www.mayfieldbakery.com

"On the doorstep of Stanford" in Palo Alto's Town & Country shopping center, this "great little sis to Spruce and Village Pub" turns
out "imaginative" Californian dishes from a "beautiful open kitchen";
the dining room, featuring whitewashed wood, can get "noisy"
when "crowded", so some suggest "go late" – when the "friendly"
staff "offers you a loaf of bread to take home" from the adjacent bakery ("oh, that bread!").

Mayflower *Chinese* | 22 | 16 | 16 | $28 |

Milpitas | 428 Barber Ln. (Bellew Dr.) | 408-922-2700

Hong Kong Flower Lounge *Chinese*

Millbrae | 51 Millbrae Ave. (bet. B'way & El Camino Real) |
650-692-6666
www.mayflower-seafood.com
See review in City of San Francisco Directory.

McCormick & Schmick's *Seafood* | 23 | 22 | 22 | $46 |

San Jose | Fairmont San Jose | 170 S. Market St. (San Carlos St.) |
408-283-7200 | www.mccormickandschmicks.com

"Simply prepared fish" mixed with "fancier" fare works for "business lunches" and even "better for dinner" say patrons of this chain link inside the Fairmont San Jose; while a few find the "corporate" vibe "boring", the majority gives a thumbs-up to the wood-and-brass decor and "friendly, accommodating" staff and says that although tabs can be "pricey", there are "great" happy-hour specials.

Mezza Luna *Italian* | 24 | 21 | 23 | $38 |

Princeton by the Sea | 459 Prospect Way (Capistrano Rd.) |
650-728-8108 | www.mezzalunabythesea.com

Caffè Mezza Luna *Italian*

Half Moon Bay | Harbor Vill. | 240 Capistrano Rd. (Hwy. 1) | 650-560-0137

It's like "eating in Italy" at this Princeton by the Sea "standby" where the "authentic, mouthwateringly delicious" Southern Italian fare comes at "value" prices; "attentive" staffers and a "casual", fireplace-enhanced setting with harbor views help make it feel like a "retreat"; P.S. the Half Moon Bay cafe offshoot serves gelato, pastries, salads and sandwiches.

Z Mingalaba *Burmese/Chinese* | 27 | 17 | 21 | $24 |

Burlingame | 1213 Burlingame Ave. (bet. Lorton Ave. & Park Rd.) |
650-343-3228 | www.mingalabarestaurant.com

Burlingamers who've braved the nearly "prohibitive lines" outside this "bang-for-your-buck" sib of SF's Mandalay say they "understand why it's so crowded" once they've tasted its "unbelievable" Chinese cuisine with "delicious" "Burmese twists"; since the "staff is quite knowledgeable" about the "exotic" eats, it's an "outstanding" place to "bring out-of-towners for something they can't get back home."

Mission Ranch Restaurant *American* | 20 | 23 | 23 | $49 |

Carmel | 26270 Dolores St. (14th Ave.) | 831-625-9040 |
www.missionranchcarmel.com

"You're on Clint Eastwood's turf" at this eatery inside a Carmel hotel, actually a "rambling farmhouse" (restored by the film star) "overlooking the foothills" and a "sheep pasture", where "American comfort food" is served by a "friendly", "experienced" staff; it's quite "popular" and it doesn't take reservations, so it's usally best to "show up early" for drinks at the "lively" piano bar or on the patio where you can "watch the sunset."

Mistral *French/Italian* | 23 | 21 | 20 | $42 |

Redwood Shores | 370-6 Bridge Pkwy. (Marine Pkwy.) | 650-802-9222 |
www.mistraldining.com

"Tucked away" in a "pleasant location" in Redwood Shores, this "great neighborhood place" with solid service "never disappoints" for "casual", not-too-pricey French-Italian lunches, brunches and dinners, or just "grabbing a drink"; there's a "nice ambiance" inside, but the "covered, temperature-controlled patio" is the place to be with its "beautiful" views of the lagoon.

Montrio Bistro *Californian*
24 | 23 | 22 | $48

Monterey | 414 Calle Principal (Franklin St.) | 831-648-8880 | www.montrio.com

"Beautifully crafted" New American fare with Californian, French and Italian influences, "wonderful cocktails" and "a well-considered wine list" keep this "gem" in a "cute, renovated firehouse" in Downtown Monterey "always crowded" (and somewhat "noisy"); factor in "great service" and prices that are only a tad "expensive", and no wonder admirers say they "love everything about this place."

NEW Moonraker *Seafood*
∇ 26 | 23 | 22 | $36

Pacifica | Best Western Plus Lighthouse Hotel | 105 Rockaway Beach Ave. (Cabrillo Hwy./Hwy. 1) | 650-557-7025 | www.moonrakerpacifica.com

Both tourists and locals enjoy grabbing an "overstuffed booth" next to the "floor-to-ceiling windows" to "watch the sun set over the ocean" with an "inventive" "cocktail in hand" at this "newly remodeled" "seaside spot" in the Pacifica Best Western; the service and "San Francisco–style" seasonal seafood get props, plus the "early-bird" and "happy-hour" specials are ways to avoid big tabs while enjoying "the million-dollar view."

☑ Morton's The Steakhouse *Steak*
25 | 23 | 24 | $86

San Jose | 177 Park Ave. (bet. Almaden Blvd. & Market St.) | 408-947-7000 | www.mortons.com

See review in City of San Francisco Directory.

Mundaka *Spanish*
∇ 23 | 20 | 23 | $40

Carmel | San Carlos St. (bet. Ocean & 7th Aves.) | 831-624-7400 | www.mundakacarmel.com

It's right "off the main drag" in staid Carmel, but there's "nothing boring" about this "cool" "tapas bar" presenting a nightly changing slate of "inventive" "small plates" by local chef Brandon Miller; it's not your typical Spanish fare but the "helpful staff won't steer you wrong", plus "reasonable wine prices", "funky decor" and "live music" ensure it's "a party every night."

Muracci's Japanese
Curry & Grill ☒ *Japanese*
20 | 11 | 16 | $18

Los Altos | 244 State St. (bet. 2nd & 3rd Sts.) | 650-917-1101 | www.muraccis.com

See review in City of San Francisco Directory.

Naomi Sushi Ⓜ *Japanese*
∇ 25 | 15 | 24 | $28

Menlo Park | 1328 El Camino Real (bet. Glenwood & Oak Grove Aves.) | 650-321-6902 | www.naomisushi.com

This "go-to" Japanese located in Menlo Park is "full all the time" with locals who "love the sushi" (especially the omakase menu); the "prices are good", fish "fresh" and staff "friendly", though the "no-frills" decor is so "cozy" that some surveyors feel as if they are "sitting on top of strangers."

	FOOD	DECOR	SERVICE	COST

Nation's Giant Hamburgers ● *Burgers*   22 | 13 | 16 | $10

Daly City | Westlake Shopping Ctr. | 301 S. Mayfair Ave. (John Daly Blvd.) | 650-755-8880 | www.nationsrestaurants.com

"Burgers and pie – what's not to like?" ask proponents of this "casual" 24-hour Daly City chain link proffering "big, juicy" chopped beef that's "goodness on a bun", "huge" breakfasts and "ridiculous portions" of "fresh-made" desserts; it's "noisy" and you'll "wait on yourself" at the counter, but no matter – most agree "it's worth it."

Navio *American*   ▽ 25 | 28 | 27 | $78

Half Moon Bay | Ritz-Carlton Half Moon Bay | 1 Miramontes Point Rd. (Hwy. 1) | 650-712-7055 | www.ritzcarlton.com

"Overlooking the Pacific", the "beautiful", boatlike dining room at the Ritz-Carlton Half Moon Bay provides a "perfect environment" for enjoying "exquisitely prepared", "locally sourced" American cuisine served by an "impeccable" staff; it's "not cheap", but fans fawn it's "worth every penny", especially for a "special occasion" or the "amazing Sunday brunch."

Nepenthe *American*   18 | 26 | 18 | $38

Big Sur | 48510 Hwy. 1 (¼ mi. south of Ventana Inn & Spa) | 831-667-2345 | www.nepenthebigsur.com

You "can see forever" from the terrace of this "legendary spot" ("once Orson Welles and Rita Hayworth's hideout"), a "hippie" hang on a Big Sur cliffside that offers a "limited" midpriced American menu, but also possibly the "best location in California"; while it may attract "a lot of tourists", and the staff can have an "attitude", the "view" makes it "a must-stop on your trip down the coast."

New Kapadokia 🈂Ⓜ *Turkish*   21 | 16 | 20 | $28

Redwood City | 2399 Broadway St. (Winslow St.) | 650-368-5500 | www.newkapadokia.com

"Each dish brings a glimpse of Turkey (no travel needed)" at this Redwood City Ottoman, where it's "easy to order too much" – and eat too much, since the "authentic" chow is "well prepared and tasty" and comes in "interesting flavor combinations"; the "narrow" space has the "feel of a coffee shop" but isn't "as busy as it deserves to be", considering the "modest" prices, "friendly" staff and convenience to "downtown events."

New Krung Thai Restaurant *Thai*   24 | 21 | 19 | $28

San Jose | 580 N. Winchester Blvd. (Forest Ave.) | 408-248-3435 | www.newkrungthai.com

"Delectable" Thai fare assures that this "consistent" San Jose favorite does a brisk business (i.e. it can get "really crowded"); while "it doesn't take reservations" and tends to get "noisy", undeterred devotees "bring friends" to "try more things" – a luxury afforded by modest prices.

Nick's on Main 🈂Ⓜ *American*   26 | 20 | 24 | $50

Los Gatos | 35 E. Main St. (College Ave.) | 408-399-6457 | www.nicksonmainst.com

At his "tiny" Los Gatos "gem", chef-owner and "gracious host" Nick Difu turns out "creative" New American dishes in a "warm, cozy setting" manned by a "personable" staff; tables are so "close together" you'll surely "get to know your fellow diners", and it gets "extremely noisy", but fans happily "put up with it" because "neighborhood restaurants don't get better than this"; P.S. reservations are a must.

North Beach Pizza ● *Pizza*   21 | 13 | 18 | $19
San Mateo | 240 E. Third Ave. (B St.) | 650-344-5000 | www.northbeachpizza.net
See review in City of San Francisco Directory.

Old Port Lobster Shack *Seafood*   23 | 13 | 17 | $29
Redwood City | 851 Veteran's Blvd. (bet. Jefferson Ave. & Middlefield Rd.) | 650-366-2400 | www.oplobster.com
When displaced "Maine-iacs" "crave real back-East" "lobstah", this reproduction of a "shack on a wharf" in a "nondescript strip mall" in Redwood City (with a second location in Portola Valley) fits the bill with lobster rolls filled with "plump, tasty chunks", not to mention "clam chowdah" and "microbrews from New England"; even diehards admit it's "pricey", but "place your order then sit" at the "picnic tables" and "all that's missing" from the mini vacation is the "smell of sea air and swooping seagulls."

O'mei Ⓜ *Chinese*   ▽ 25 | 15 | 21 | $30
Santa Cruz | 2316 Mission St. (Fair Ave.) | 831-425-8458
It's "well worth the trip" to this Santa Cruz strip-mailer for some of the more "unusual" and (often spicy) Sichuan fare around (acolytes swear by "anything that has Chinese bacon in it"); service gets the job done, and considering the moderate prices, the menu's a "wow."

Orenchi Ramen ⓈⓂ⇄ *Japanese*   24 | 13 | 17 | $17
Santa Clara | Lawrence Station Shopping Ctr. | 3540 Homestead Rd. (Lawrence Expwy.) | 408-246-2955 | www.orenchiramen.com
"Ramen snobs" "inhale" the "delicious", "perfectly balanced" broth and "fresh noodles" at this Santa Clara Japanese; despite its "unlikely" strip-mall location, it's "extremely popular", so regulars of the spare space warn "arrive early or expect to wait" ("it doesn't take reservations").

Original Joe's ● *American/Italian*   23 | 19 | 23 | $32
(aka Joe's, OJ's)
San Jose | 301 S. First St. (San Carlos St.) | 408-292-7030 | www.originaljoes.com
"Sit at the counter and enjoy the show" at this Downtown San Jose "tradition", where "engaging", "old-world" waiters in tuxes transport "humongous portions" of "hearty", "straight-up" Italian to everyone from "out-of-town guests" to "mad men drinking martinis"; while a few critics argue it's a "bit expensive", longtimers counter that prices are "fair", especially because you'll have "more than enough to take home" – including a side of "nostalgia."

Osteria Ⓢ *Italian*   24 | 16 | 20 | $36
Palo Alto | 247 Hamilton Ave. (Ramona St.) | 650-328-5700
An "old standby" in Palo Alto, this "family-run" Italian has been "consistently good" for decades (it opened in 1981), turning out "smooth-as-silk" pastas, "well-made" sauces and other "simple, dependable" Italian fare; it can get "crowded and noisy", with seats packed "so close together" that "some of your clams might

creep into your neighbor's fettucine", but most agree the "food, service and price are right."

Osteria Coppa *Italian/Pizza*   23 | 18 | 21 | $41

San Mateo | 139 S. B St. (bet. 1st & 2nd Aves.) | 650-579-6021 | www.osteriacoppa.com

At this "sophisticated" "neighborhood Tuscan" in Downtown San Mateo, locals dig into "seriously good" "handmade pasta", "delightful" pizzas and other "unfussy but elegant" Italian fare, complemented by an "affordable", Boot-heavy wine list; the "bustling" bar can get "noisy" and the "charming" servers "need a bit of polish", but for "happy hour or a night out", the "cool, modern" spot is "fun, fast and filling."

Oswald Restaurant ⓜ *American*   ▽ 25 | 19 | 23 | $42

Santa Cruz | 121 Soquel Ave. (bet. Front St. & Pacific Ave.) | 831-423-7427 | www.oswaldrestaurant.com

"Hipsters, surfers, professors and over-30s" flock to this "happening place" in Downtown Santa Cruz where an "outstanding" crew proffers "fantastic", ingredient-driven New American plates and "innovative drinks" in a starkly modern setting; it "can be noisy", but the "Wednesday prix fixe" for $29 is "a steal to say the least"; P.S. open for lunch on Fridays only.

Pacific Catch *Seafood*   22 | 17 | 20 | $26

Campbell | The Pruneyard | 1875 S. Bascom Ave. (Campbell Ave.) | 408-879-9091 | www.pacificcatch.com
See review in City of San Francisco Directory.

❷ Pacific's Edge *American/French*   24 | 28 | 23 | $83

Carmel | Hyatt Carmel Highlands | 120 Highlands Dr. (Hwy. 1) | 831-622-5445 | www.pacificsedge.com

"You really do feel that you're at the Pacific's edge" when you walk into this "romantic" Hyatt Carmel Highlands restaurant that's "seemingly suspended over the ocean", all the better to enjoy the "superb" American-French fare, "professional" service and "expansive wine list" full of "big names"; some snarl it's "outrageously expensive", but those who "go early" enough to "see the sun sink beneath the sea" assure "you pay for what you get."

Pampas *Brazilian*   23 | 22 | 22 | $55

Palo Alto | 529 Alma St. (bet. Hamilton & University Aves.) | 650-327-1323 | www.pampaspaloalto.com

"All the perfectly seasoned meat you can eat" comes to your table via "super-friendly" skewer-wielding waiters at this "upscale" Palo Alto Brazilian churrascaria featuring "tender, well-marinated" "rodizio meats" and an "amazing buffet" (get-your-money's-worth types "don't eat for three days before" a meal here, and "skip the salad bar"); "great caipirinhas" and vintages from the "excellent" wine list help "wash down all of that meat", and on weekends, a "live band" contributes to the "cool" ambiance.

Pancho Villa Taqueria *Mexican*   23 | 11 | 17 | $12

San Mateo | 365 S. B St. (bet. 3rd & 4th Aves.) | 650-343-4123 | www.smpanchovilla.com
See review in City of San Francisco Directory.

	FOOD	DECOR	SERVICE	COST

Parcel 104 *Californian*   23 | 20 | 22 | $63

Santa Clara | Santa Clara Marriott | 2700 Mission College Blvd.
(bet. Freedom Circle & Great America Pkwy.) | 408-970-6104 |
www.parcel104.com

"Don't be fooled" by a location "hidden" in the Santa Clara Marriott: chef
Bradley Ogden's "upscale eatery" (named for the pear orchard that once
grew here) "stands out on its own", with "creative", "locally sourced"
"seasonal" Californian cuisine and "lovely" wine pairings; the staff is
"friendly and helpful", and while the Frank Lloyd Wright–inspired room
can feel "cavernous", "noisy" and "busy", it's still a "favorite place for
business meals" among Silicon Valley sorts; P.S. tabs can get "expensive", so insiders seek out the "insane happy-hour deals."

☑ Passionfish *Californian/Seafood*   27 | 20 | 24 | $46

Pacific Grove | 701 Lighthouse Ave. (Congress Ave.) | 831-655-3311 |
www.passionfish.net

"Inventively" prepared "sustainable fish" ("no guilt here") joins "slow-
cooked meat options" on the "fairly priced" menu delivered by "knowledgeable" servers at this Pacific Grove Californian; oenophiles insist
"it's all about the wine list" featuring "hard-to-find" cult faves priced
"near retail" – either way, there's ample compensation for the "modern" room's "cramped quarters."

Pasta Moon *Italian*   25 | 21 | 24 | $41

Half Moon Bay | 315 Main St. (Kelly St.) | 650-726-5125 |
www.pastamoon.com

"Pasta is the strong suit" (natch) at this "romantic" Half Moon Bay
"destination", where "farmers, foragers and fishermen" provide
the "fresh local ingredients" that go into the "delicious" Cal-Italian
fare; staffers who "strive to make you feel welcome", along with
"reasonable prices" and a "good selection" of "all-Italian wines",
help make it a "go-to place" for residents, and "worth the trip" for diners farther afield too.

Pasta Pomodoro *Italian*   19 | 17 | 20 | $22

Milpitas | 181 Ranch Dr. (McCarthy Blvd.) | 408-582-0160
Redwood City | 490 El Camino Real (Whipple Ave.) | 650-474-2400
San Bruno | Bayhill Ctr. | 811 Cherry Ave. (San Bruno Ave.) |
650-583-6622
San Jose | 1205 The Alameda (Julian St.) | 408-292-9929
San Jose | Camden Park | 2083 Camden Ave. (Union Ave.) |
408-371-2600
San Jose | 378 Santana Row (Olsen Dr.) | 408-241-2200
San Jose | Evergreen Mkt. | 4898 San Felipe Rd. (Yerba Buena Blvd.) |
408-532-0271
San Mateo | Bay Meadows | 1060 Park Pl. (Saratoga Dr.) | 650-574-2600
Sunnyvale | 300 W. El Camino Real (Mathilda Ave.) | 408-789-0037
www.pastapomodoro.com
See review in City of San Francisco Directory.

Patxi's Pizza *Pizza*   22 | 16 | 18 | $22
(fka Patxi's Chicago Pizza)

Palo Alto | 441 Emerson St. (bet. Lytton & University Aves.) |
650-473-9999 | www.patxispizza.com
See review in City of San Francisco Directory.

	FOOD	DECOR	SERVICE	COST

Piatti *Italian*
| | 21 | 21 | 21 | $37 |

Santa Clara | 3905 Rivermark Plaza (Montague Expwy.) | 408-330-9212 |
www.piatti.com
See review in East of San Francisco Directory.

Pizza Antica *Pizza*
| | 22 | 18 | 19 | $25 |

San Jose | Santana Row | 334 Santana Row (Alyssum Ln.) | 408-557-8373 |
www.pizzaantica.com
"Lots of families with kids" flock to these suburban Bay Area outposts of the Californian chain of "casual" Italians for "solid salads"
and "thin-crust, wood-fired pizzas"; "service can be spotty" while
tabs can get "pricey", and since the "noisy", "cavernous" spaces
can get "very busy", regulars advise "get there prior to 5 PM" to "avoid
a long wait."

Plumed Horse ☒ *Californian*
| | 25 | 26 | 25 | $87 |

Saratoga | 14555 Big Basin Way (4th St.) | 408-867-4711 |
www.plumedhorse.com
It's "one big wow" "from the moment you walk in" to the "stylish"
"modern" digs at this "first-class" Saratoga "special-occasion"
Californian; the "top-notch" tasting menus and "constant filling" of
your "champagne glass" can add up (you'll likely spend "gobs of
money"), but details including an "over-the-top" wine collection
stored in a "glass-bottomed" room show they're "trying very hard."

Quattro Restaurant & Bar *Italian*
| | 22 | 26 | 26 | $59 |

East Palo Alto | Four Seasons Hotel Silicon Valley at East Palo Alto |
2050 University Ave. (Woodland Ave.) | 650-470-2889 |
www.fourseasons.com
Though the "beautiful setting" in the Four Seasons East Palo Alto may
suggest otherwise, the room is "full of the dotcom crowd, so Levi's are
"ok" at this "refined" Italian; "very good food" and "excellent service"
round out the "delightful, relaxing" experience, and though budget-
minded sorts complain the menu is "overpriced", in early 2012 half the
dining room was given over to Intermezzo, a wine-and-nibbles specialist featuring smaller plates at smaller prices.

Ramen Dojo *Japanese/Noodle Shop*
| | 25 | 15 | 16 | $15 |

San Mateo | 805 S. B St. (bet. 8th & 9th Aves.) | 650-401-6568
Serious slurpers line up "before they open" at this "really small"
San Mateo noodle shop for arguably "the most" "frickin' delicious"
"bowl of ramen" available "outside Japan"; there's little to choose
from other than "three "different levels of spiciness" and miscella-
neous toppings, but service is "super fast" for these "cheap eats";
P.S. closed Tuesdays.

ᴺᴱᵂ Rangoon Ruby *Burmese*
| | - | - | - | M |

Palo Alto | 445 Emerson St. (bet. Lytton & University Aves.) |
650-323-6543 | www.rangoonruby.com
This Palo Alto Burmese offers a budget-friendly greatest-hits menu of
traditional favorites (with an abundance of vegetarian options) incor-
porating influences from Indian, Thai and Chinese cuisines; the modern dining room is filled with white tablecloths, and the jade-topped
mahogany bar serves tropically inclined libations, including the midcentury cocktail for which the restaurant is named.

	FOOD	DECOR	SERVICE	COST

Refuge ⊠ *Belgian/Sandwiches*
25 | 16 | 20 | $26

San Carlos | 963 Laurel St. (Morse Blvd.) | 650-598-9813 |
www.refugesc.com

At this "casual place" in San Carlos, a "simple, perfect" menu "focuses on what they do best" – "thick-cut, housemade" pastrami sandwiches ("take a heart specialist along"), nine-oz. burgers and one of the Peninsula's "best selections of Belgian brews"; the budget-minded call it "rather expensive", but "big portions" and a "small-town-bar" ambiance have out-of-towners sighing "I only wish it were in my neighborhood."

Restaurant at Ventana *Californian*
23 | 26 | 24 | $69

Big Sur | Ventana Inn & Spa | 48123 Hwy. 1 (Coast Ridge Rd.) |
831-667-2331 | www.ventanainn.com

"Get away from it all" at this "terrific" Californian, a "special spot" in a "breathtaking" inn where patrons dine in the "warm, comfortable" interior or on a terrace affording "incredible" vistas of Big Sur and the Pacific; the "high-quality" dishes and "accommodating" service come with "above-average" tabs, but since you're also "paying for the vew", insiders insist on going during the day or "at sunset."

Restaurant James Randall ⊠Ⓜ *Californian*
▽ 25 | 22 | 25 | $59

Los Gatos | 303 N. Santa Cruz Ave. (Bachman Ave.) | 408-395-4441 |
www.restaurantjamesrandall.com

"There's always something new to try" at this "well-kept secret" in Los Gatos, a "family-run" operation set in a "quaint" "small house" where the "outstanding" eclectic Californian menu "changes" regularly; the price is right, and the adjacent "hip wine bar" hawking "special cocktails" and bar bites makes suburbanites feel like they're "back in civilization."

⁣🆕 Restaurant Mitsunobu Ⓜ *Japanese*
– | – | – | E

Menlo Park | 325 Sharon Park Dr. (Sand Hill Rd.) | 650-234-1084 |
www.rmitsunobu.com

"Following the Kaygetsu tradition", this new high-end contemporary Japanese situated on the site of that shuttered Menlo Park favorite regales Peninsula diners with "excellent" service and seasonal keiseki dinners (albeit with a Californian twist) overseen by its predecessor's executive chef; prix fixe and à la carte menus offer sushi, sashimi and cooked small plates, along with an array of premium sakes; P.S. serves lunch Tuesday–Friday.

Rio Grill *Californian*
23 | 20 | 22 | $43

Carmel | Crossroads Shopping Ctr. | 101 Crossroads Blvd. (Rio Rd.) |
831-625-5436 | www.riogrill.com

"After so many years" (since 1983), "locals" and visitors alike are still smitten by this "spirited, breezy" Carmel grill serving "generous portions" of "grilled foods", "great veggies" and other "well-prepared" "Californian cuisine with a Southwestern touch"; patrons look beyond the "shopping-center location", as the "inventive dishes", "awesome" wine selection (listed on an iPad) and "knowledgeable servers" make it "worth returning to again and again."

Ristorante Capellini *Italian*
22 | 21 | 20 | $40

San Mateo | 310 Baldwin Ave. (B St.) | 650-348-2296 | www.capellinis.com
More than 20 years after opening in a 1925 bank building, this San Mateo Italian is "still going strong", turning out "consistent", "de-

licious" and "authentic" "old-school" fare at moderate prices; the "quaint, elegant" multilevel space designed by restaurant impresario Pat Kuleto can get "noisy" when "crowded", but the "friendly" staff is "professional", and the "nice wine list" and "full bar" help make it a "go-to" "after a bad day at work."

Roti Indian Bistro *Indian*
23 | 18 | 21 | $29

Burlingame | 209 Park Rd. (bet. Burlingame & Howard Aves.) |
650-340-7684 | www.rotibistro.com
See review in City of San Francisco Directory.

☒ Roy's at Pebble Beach *Hawaiian*
26 | 27 | 24 | $62

Pebble Beach | The Inn at Spanish Bay | 2700 17 Mile Dr. (Palmero Way.) |
831-647-7423 | www.roysrestaurant.com
Like "all Roy's restaurants", this Pebble Beach golf resort locale proffers "outstanding Hawaiian-style" "Asian fusion" delivered by a "super-attentive" staff for "upscale prices", but what really "sets it apart" are the "superlative views over Spanish Bay" visible through "floor-to-ceiling windows" that "make every table" a "choice" one; it's particularly "enchanting" for "lunch followed by a walk on the beach" or next to the "fire pit" where you can "catch the bagpiper" "at sundown."

Sakae Sushi Noboru *Japanese*
▽ 26 | 18 | 20 | $71

Burlingame | 243 California Dr. (bet. Burlingame & Howard Aves.) |
650-348-4064 | www.sakaesushi.com
"Fresh from Japan", the fin fare at this Burlingame spot is "flown in from the Tokyo fish market" several times a week, making for "superb and unusual" sushi that some call "the best on the peninsula", while "tasty" cooked dishes such as tempura are also available; gracious service and a "good selection of sakes" help compensate for uninspired decor and tabs that can add up fast.

Sakoon *Indian*
23 | 21 | 21 | $28

Mountain View | 357 Castro St. (bet. California & Dana Sts.) |
650-965-2000 | www.sakoonrestaurant.com
"Funky" lighting, "comfortable banquettes" and bright colors set the scene for "imaginative, well-seasoned" "fusion fare" (including "excellent vegetarian choices") at this "upscale", über-"hip" Indian in Mountain View; surveyors can't agree on service, but most applaud the "great lunch buffet" – and it's a "deal" at that.

Sam's Chowder House *Seafood*
22 | 20 | 19 | $35

Half Moon Bay | 4210 N. Cabrillo Hwy. (Capistrano Rd.) |
650-712-0245 | www.samschowderhouse.com
"Dreamy lobster rolls" and "exceptional clam chowder" make this seafood cliffhanger in Half Moon Bay "feel like the Eastern seaboard", only with "vast views of the Pacific"; a few think it's "a little pricey", but even that "doesn't keep the crowds away" thanks to a patio that's one of the "best places" around for "alfresco dining"; P.S. Sam's Chowdermobile makes stops about town (www.samschowdermobile.com).

Saravana Bhavan *Indian*
▽ 26 | 13 | 18 | $15

Sunnyvale | 1305 S. Mary Ave. (Fremont Ave.) | 408-616-7755 |
www.saravanaabhavan-ca.com
Don't let the basic decor and building that "looks like a converted Howard Johnson's" fool you: this "casual" Sunnyvale South Indian

offers "adventure" in the form of a "really delicious" vegetarian menu ("dominated by dosas" with a "variety of chutneys") and "amazing" desserts; sure, service is merely "average", but most "enjoy the experience" nonetheless.

Sardine Factory *American/Seafood*   24 | 23 | 23 | $61

Monterey | 701 Wave St. (Prescott Ave.) | 831-373-3775 | www.sardinefactory.com

There's still plenty of "history" at this "Cannery Row classic" (*"Play Misty for Me* was filmed here"), but this American seafooder "has had a rebirth" and the "food has become outstanding" thanks to chef Brant Good; surveyors are attractive to the "many little rooms" (especially the "beautiful atrium" complete with a glass dome) and details like the "ice swans", as well as a "professional staff" that "impresses."

Sawa Sushi Ⓢ *Japanese*   ▽ 23 | 17 | 23 | $96

Sunnyvale | 1042 E. El Camino Real (Henderson Ave.) | 408-241-7292 | www.sawasushi.net

Sushi groupies concur there's no "comparison" to the "quality" and "delight" received at this long-running, high-end Japanese in a Sunnyvale strip mall; private lunches and nightly dinners (especially the ever-changing omakase menu) are "expensive" (and come with "an attitude as well"), but the "interaction" with chef-owner Steve Sawa, and the attendant "enlightenment of the senses is worth the small hurdle of getting in" to the minimalist space; P.S. closed Sunday.

Z Scott's of Palo Alto *Seafood*   23 | 22 | 23 | $44

Palo Alto | Town & Country Vill. | 855 El Camino Real (Embarcadero Rd.) | 650-323-1555 | www.scottsseafoodpa.com

Z Scott's of San Jose *Seafood*

San Jose | 185 Park Ave. (bet. Almaden Blvd. & Market St.) | 408-212-7287 | www.scottsseafoodsj.com

See review in East of San Francisco Directory.

Z Sent Sovi Ⓜ *Californian*   27 | 22 | 26 | $124

Saratoga | 14583 Big Basin Way (5th St.) | 408-867-3110 | www.sentsovi.com

"There is no cozier, friendlier fine dining" in the South Bay than at this "little spot" in Saratoga where "enthusiastic" husband-and-wife chef-owners offer "imaginative" Californian cuisine and "excellent" wines in a "homey" yet "romantic setting"; it's "not inexpensive", but regulars return for the "prix fixe menus" and "special events year-round" that have a "fresh, seasonal focus."

71 Saint Peter Ⓢ *Californian/Mediterranean*   22 | 20 | 21 | $38

San Jose | San Pedro Sq. | 71 N. San Pedro St. (bet. Santa Clara & St. John Sts.) | 408-971-8523 | www.71saintpeter.com

For an "intimate" dinner, this "charming" Cal-Med bistro in San Jose's San Pedro Square is a midpriced "favorite" that "always delivers" a "delightful dining experience" with "well-prepared", "seasonal" "farm-to-table" fare; if a few find it "nothing too exciting", most maintain that the "beautiful" patio and "above and beyond accommodating" owners make it a "fabulous date-night choice."

Shadowbrook *Californian*

22 | 26 | 23 | $50

Capitola | 1750 Wharf Rd. (Capitola Rd.) | 831-475-1511 |
www.shadowbrook-capitola.com

Capitolans "have been going for years" to this "elegant" "special place"
to ride the "cute little" tram through "gorgeous gardens" to the "quirky"
dining rooms that "appear at every twist and turn" and have "nice
views" of Soquel Creek; the Californian menu features "delicious" fare
(doubters deem it "ordinary") and service is "attentive", but regulars
recommend having a "bite in the bar" to get the whole "great experience" at a lower price point.

Shalimar *Indian/Pakistani*

24 | 7 | 14 | $16

Sunnyvale | 1146 W. El Camino Real (bet. Bernardo & Grape Aves.) |
408-530-0300 | www.shalimarsv.com
See review in City of San Francisco Directory.

Shanghai Dumpling Shop *Chinese*

21 | 9 | 13 | $19

Millbrae | 455 Broadway (Taylor Blvd.) | 650-697-0682
At Millbrae's "low-key dumpling house" (not to be confused with the
similarly named Shanghai Dumpling King in Outer Richmond), many
"families" and "groups of friends" come for the "addicting" morsels
filled with "lots of juice"; though "decor is basic" and service can be
"efficient if a bit harried", many say the "value is tremendous", so "expect long lines if you go on the weekend."

☑ Sierra Mar *Californian/Eclectic*

28 | 29 | 27 | $93

Big Sur | Post Ranch Inn | Hwy. 1 (30 mi. south of Carmel) |
831-667-2200 | www.postranchinn.com
Diners have their heads in the clouds, almost literally, as they gaze
out over the "seemingly infinite horizon" through the "floor-to-
ceiling windows" of this "exclusive" locale perched "on the edge of
a cliff overlooking the ocean" in Big Sur's Post Ranch Inn; voted the
Bay Area's No. 1 for Decor, it's a truly "amazing setting" for "sensational" Cal-Eclectic meals paired with "world-class" wines, but
while "the view is priceless" and service is "outstanding", tabs match
the sky-high location.

Sino *Chinese*

20 | 22 | 17 | $36

San Jose | Santana Row | 377 Santana Row (Olsen Dr.) | 408-247-8880 |
www.sinorestaurant.com
A "large, pleasing array of dim sum", "interesting" Chinese-influenced
fare and "excellent" cocktails (both "boozy and nonalcoholic") await
the "youngish" set at this Santana Row "scene"; "service needs some
work" and a "nightclub atmosphere" means the "crowded" space gets
"noisy", but overall it's a "a fun place" – as long as you're prepared for
the "pricey" tabs.

SJ Omogari ☑ *Korean*

▽ 24 | 11 | 21 | $20

San Jose | 154 E. Jackson St. (4th St.) | 408-288-8134 |
www.omogari.biz
"It's all about the meat jun" – breaded and sautéed strips of marinated
beef – at this "family-run" San Jose Korean, where the "authentic",
"delicious" meals include "free green tea ice cream" and kimchee
that's made fresh twice daily; the decor won't win any awards, but
"friendly service" and modest prices compensate.

Soif Wine Bar *Californian*   ▽ 25 | 21 | 23 | $39

Santa Cruz | 105 Walnut Ave. (Pacific Ave.) | 831-423-2020 |
www.soifwine.com

For "food-and-wine combinations" that "cannot be beat", oenophiles gravitate to this Santa Cruz La Posta sibling offering an "amazing" cellar and a slate of "small and large" Californian plates "as opulent or spartan as you like"; a "knowledgeable" staff and "cozy" setting make it an "easy, friendly environment" even if for "just a glass of wine at the bar."

NEW Spice Kit *Asian*   ▽ 18 | 13 | 18 | $15

Palo Alto | 3340 S. Carolina Ave. (Birch St.) | 650-326-1698 |
www.spicekit.com

See review in City of San Francisco Directory.

Spices 🗷Ⓜ *Chinese*   ▽ 23 | 12 | 17 | $20

Foster City | 929 Edgewater Blvd. (Beach Park Blvd.) | 650-358-8886 |
www.spicesrestaurantonline.com

See review in City of San Francisco Directory.

Stacks *American*   21 | 16 | 19 | $20

Burlingame | 361 California Dr. (Lorton Ave.) | 650-579-1384
Menlo Park | 600 Santa Cruz Ave. (El Camino Real) | 650-838-0066
www.stacksrestaurant.com

See review in City of San Francisco Directory.

Station 1 Restaurant Ⓜ *Californian*   25 | 21 | 25 | $72

Woodside | 2991 Woodside Rd. (Mountain Home Rd.) |
650-851-4988 | www.station1restaurant.com

Nestled in a "small, rustic" former firehouse, this "new-ish" Woodside Californian offers a "superb" prix fixe menu focused on "seasonal items" that's "always a delightful surprise"; it can be "expensive", especially if you indulge in the "delicious" pre-Prohibition cocktails or pours from the "imaginative" wine list, but "personable" staffers who "remember you after your first visit" help extinguish most concerns.

Stella Alpina Osteria *Italian*   26 | 21 | 24 | $49

Burlingame | 401 Primrose Rd. (Chapin Ave.) | 650-347-5733 |
www.stellaalpinaosteria.com

"Romantic" sorts smart enough to "make reservations several days ahead" "squeeze into" this "lovely" "neighborhood osteria" in Burlingame for "consistently wonderful" Northern Italian fare prepared with "excellent ingredients" (tip: "don't miss" the "amazing truffle gnocchi"); tabs can be a "bit pricey", but the "warm, inviting" vibe makes it even more alluring.

St. Michael's Alley 🗷Ⓜ *Californian*   22 | 21 | 22 | $42

Palo Alto | 140 Homer Ave. (High St.) | 650-326-2530 |
www.stmikes.com

"Sitting outside is a delight" at this "off-the-beaten-path" Palo Altan proffering midpriced Californian cuisine with a "twist", though the interior – a collection of "intimate rooms" with "interesting decor" – also has its fans; even the less-impressed agree the "worth-the-wait weekend brunch" served at the eatery's original location (806 Emerson Street) is among the "best in town."

Straits Restaurant *Singaporean*

| 21 | 20 | 19 | $36 |

Burlingame | 1100 Burlingame Ave. (California Dr.) | 650-373-7883
San Jose | Santana Row | 333 Santana Row (Alyssum Ln.) | 408-246-6320
www.straitsrestaurants.com

Straits Cafe *Singaporean*

Palo Alto | 3295 El Camino Real (Lambert Ave.) | 650-494-7168 | www.straitscafepaloalto.com
See review in City of San Francisco Directory.

Sumika Ⓜ *Japanese*

▽ | 25 | 14 | 19 | $37 |

Los Altos | 236 Central Plaza (bet. 2nd & 3rd Sts.) | 650-917-1822 | www.sumikagrill.com

The "amazing" skewers "tempt you to order one more (and then one more)" at this "absolutely authentic" yakitori bar in Los Altos, which "grills anything and everything" and serves up Japanese specialties like "oyako-don done right"; there's little decor and spendy tabs ("prices match the quality"), but in-the-know eaters attest it's "worth the effort"; P.S. the secret to the "charcoalicous" taste? "distinctive oak wood" imported from Japan.

Sundance The Steakhouse *Steak*
(fka Sundance Mine Company)

| 25 | 23 | 23 | $50 |

Palo Alto | 1921 El Camino Real (Stanford Ave.) | 650-321-6798 | www.sundancethesteakhouse.com

"Parents with their Stanford offspring" and "business-lunchers" alike flock to this "splendid" Palo Alto carnivorium for "protein on the hoof", including "consistently delicious" steaks, seafood and "fresh" salads shuttled by "knowledgeable" servers in a "classy" yet "comfortable" setting; if all that "big meat" comes with "bigger prices", thrifty tipsters advise checking out the 'Sunset Dinner' for a "delicious, yet affordable, date night."

🆕 The Surf Spot *Eclectic*

| - | - | - | M |

Pacifica | 4627 Pacific Coast Hwy. (Reina Del Mar Ave.) | 877-625-2929 | www.surfspoteats.com

Sporting a name and beachy vibe that's inspired by surf destinations around the globe, this casual new all-day coastside hangout in Pacifica features an Eclectic slate of locally sourced affordable international comfort food that changes with the seasons; in addition to its 180-seat indoor dining room, guests can hang 10 on the expansive lawn where they can play volleyball, chill by the fire pit or listen to live music on weekends while knocking back some good libations.

Sushi Sam's Edomata ⓈⓂ *Japanese*

| 24 | 13 | 19 | $41 |

San Mateo | 218 E. Third St. (bet. B St. & Ellsworth Ave.) | 650-344-0888 | www.sushisams.com

"Sit at the bar" and "order the omakase (at least 10 pieces)" as Sam "works his magic" at this "reasonably priced" San Mateo sushi joint, which also features a limited menu of cooked Japanese favorites; it's set in a "spartan" space and can be "noisy", but since it offers such "awesome fish" and "delicious" desserts, there are often "lines out the door", so "call ahead to get on the list."

Tai Pan *Chinese*

24 | 22 | 22 | $38

Palo Alto | 560 Waverley St. (bet. Hamilton & University Aves.) | 650-329-9168 | www.taipanpaloalto.com

It's "worth the gas money to drive" to Palo Alto swear supporters of this "linen-napkins-and-white-tablecloths" Chinese proffering "authentic" Hong Kong–style chow, including "delicious" dim sum ordered off a menu and "served piping hot from the kitchen" ("no carts"); "professional" servers do the "elegant surroundings" justice, and if the "price is higher" here, it's only because you're paying for "quality."

Tamarine *Vietnamese*

26 | 23 | 23 | $50

Palo Alto | 546 University Ave. (bet. Cowper & Webster Sts.) | 650-325-8500 | www.tamarinerestaurant.com

"Sit back and be dazzled" at this "inventive" (if "pricey") Palo Alto Vietnamese that attracts a "congenial" crowd with its "beautifully presented" small plates from a menu that "changes regularly" and "excellent cocktails"; it's "always packed", so "reserve ahead" and don't be surprised if it's "noisy and cramped", but no matter: service that's "attentive without being cloying", "gorgeous design" and that "fabulous" food add up to a "winning combination."

Taqueria La Bamba *Mexican*

24 | 10 | 18 | $10

Mountain View | 152 Castro St. (Evelyn Ave.) | 650-965-2755
Mountain View | 2058 Old Middlefield Way (N. Rengstorff Ave.) | 650-965-2755
Mountain View | 580 N. Rengstorff Ave. (Middlefield Rd.) | 650-965-2755
www.labambamexicanrestaurants.com

"Silicon Valley yuppies" and other locals line up for "excellent burritos" at this "family-owned and -operated" Mountain View Mexican that "never fails to satisfy"; the "super-speedy" cooks provide the only "entertainment" in the "no-frills" ambiance, but "you're not eating the decor" – just "tasty" (and inexpensive) "carnitas and grilled chicken."

Taqueria San Jose *Mexican*

24 | 14 | 18 | $12

San Jose | 235 E. Santa Clara St. (6th St.) | 408-288-8616
See review in City of San Francisco Directory.

Taqueria 3 Amigos *Mexican*

20 | 12 | 17 | $12

Half Moon Bay | 270 S. Cabrillo Hwy. (Kelly Ave.) | 650-726-6080
San Mateo | 243 S. B St. (3rd Ave.) | 650-347-4513 ◗

They're only "taco joints", so don't expect "luxe" decor, but this duo of late-night "fast-food" Mexicans in Half Moon Bay and Downtown San Mateo "do brisk business" (both "dine-in or takeout"); "an all-you-can-eat chips-and-salsa bar" and "reasonable prices" are additional reasons why these counter-service taquerias are "packed all weekend" with "tourists" and locals.

Taqueria Tlaquepaque *Mexican*

23 | 13 | 18 | $16

San Jose | 2222 Lincoln Ave. (bet. Curtner & Franquette Aves.) | 408-978-3665
San Jose | 699 Curtner Ave. (Canoas Garden Ave.) | 408-448-1230 ⊠
San Jose | 721 Willow St. (Delmas Ave.) | 408-287-9777

"Faithful fanatics" of "old-school" "Mexican grub" like "chile verde burritos" and "enchiladas suizas" flock to this San Jose trio that's

	FOOD	DECOR	SERVICE	COST

"priced right"; it "may not be the prettiest" and "service is just ok", but you won't care after a round of "addicting" "Mexican beer with tequila" to help wash down the "generous portions."

Tarpy's Roadhouse *American*   24 | 24 | 23 | $37

Monterey | 2999 Monterey-Salinas Hwy. (Canyon Del Rey Blvd.) | 831-647-1444 | www.tarpys.com
"Delicious" American "comfort food with a twist" is turned out at this "casual", midpriced "sister restaurant to the Rio Grill" situated in a sprawling "old, restored" stone "roadhouse"; it's "a little out of the way" in Monterey but "worth the drive" for the "quaint" "atmosphere inside or out" plus a "well-stocked" bar and "great wines" that ensure "lots of fun" for brunch, "lunch with girls" or dinner "with family."

360° Gourmet *Eclectic*   22 | 19 | 21 | $26

San Jose | San Jose Int'l Airport, Terminal A | 2077 Airport Blvd. (Bayshore Frwy.) | no phone | www.360gb.com
See review in City of San Francisco Directory.

231 Ellsworth 🅂 *American*   23 | 21 | 23 | $53

San Mateo | 231 S. Ellsworth Ave. (bet. 2nd & 3rd Aves.) | 650-347-7231 | www.231ellsworth.com
Serving New American cuisine, this "special-occasion" Downtown San Mateo destination offers a "terrific" chef's menu in an "intimate setting" suitable for "quiet conversation" or "business meals"; admirers praise the "attentive but not smothering" service, and though some deem it "slightly overpriced", fans keep coming back for the "amazing wine selection" and "elegant yet casual" attitude.

Village Pub *American*   25 | 24 | 24 | $67

Woodside | 2967 Woodside Rd. (Whiskey Hill Rd.) | 650-851-9888 | www.thevillagepub.net
Despite the "folksy name", this "Woodside delight" is a "favorite of the venture capital set", who slip into the "clubby" confines and treat themselves to "outstanding" "seasonal" American eats and "grand cru by the glass"; a "seasoned staff" "makes you feel special", and while "the table next to you is probably closing a billion dollar deal", plebeians can "make do" with a burger and "Prohibition-era drink" at the moderately priced bar.

Viognier 🅂 *Californian/French*   25 | 22 | 23 | $65

San Mateo | Draeger's Mktpl. | 222 E. Fourth Ave. (bet. B St. & Ellswoth Ave.) | 650-685-3727 | www.viognierrestaurant.com
Flush foodies ferret out this "wonderful" Cal-French "fine-dining" spot perched in an "unlikely setting" above a San Mateo "grocery store"; "haute cuisine with a conscience" ("locally available, sustainable and in season"), a "knowledgeable" staff and "ever-changing" "tasting menus" help patrons "escape the top-of-a-market feel" – as does the "phenomenal" wine list with 1,700 plus selections.

Vung Tau *Vietnamese*   25 | 18 | 18 | $25

San Jose | 535 E. Santa Clara St. (12th St.) | 408-288-9055 | www.vungtaurestaurant.com
"More upscale than the average pho place", this reasonably priced, family-run Vietnamese in San Jose (with a "midrange" outpost in Milpitas, a "budget" locale in Newark and sibling Tamarine in Palo

Alto) distinguishes itself with "flavorful, comforting" "traditional" dishes that are "authentic" but made with "an interesting twist"; amid the "simple", "nicely furnished" digs, "friendly" servers are "knowledgeable about portion sizes" and "help steer novice diners in the right direction."

Wakuriya Ⓜ *Japanese* ▽ 28 | 22 | 29 | $117
(aka Japanese Kitchen Wakuriya)
San Mateo | Crystal Springs Village Shopping Ctr. | 115 De Anza Blvd. (bet. Parrott Dr. & Polhemus Rd.) | 650-286-0410 | www.wakuriya.com
At their "tiny", "haute Japanese" in a San Mateo strip mall, "husband-and-wife duo" Katsuhiro and Mayumi Yamasaki (of the defunct Kaygetsu) present seasonally changing "kaiseki-style" dinners ("nine delicious courses" of "wow") while making guests "feel like the only ones dining"; it's "hard to get into" (and quite "expensive"), but for such a "memorable experience", it's worth "calling one month in advance", as "reservations are a must"; P.S. open Wednesday–Sunday.

Xanh *Vietnamese* 22 | 22 | 19 | $33
Mountain View | 110 Castro St. (Evelyn Ave.) | 650-964-1888 | www.xanhrestaurant.com
Even the service is "slick" at this "high-end", "ultramodern" Mountain View Vietnamese, where a "hip" throng assembles to sample "fancy drinks" and an "interesting" menu of "consistently delicious" dishes awash in "explosive and diverse flavors"; if some suggest the "eye-catching" style (e.g. "wall of water") and "clubby vibe" is "over the top" for the "'burbs", they can hit the "bountiful" lunch buffet instead and avoid the "loud" evening scene.

Yankee Pier *New England/Seafood* 19 | 16 | 19 | $34
San Jose | Santana Row | 378 Santana Row (Olsen Dr.) | 408-244-1244
South San Francisco | San Francisco Int'l Airport | United Domestic Departure Terminal 3 (Hwy. 101) | 650-821-8938 www.yankeepier.com
See review in North of San Francisco Directory.

Zeni *Ethiopian* ▽ 27 | 20 | 20 | $22
San Jose | Plaza Shopping Ctr. | 1320 Saratoga Ave. (Payne Ave.) | 408-615-8282 | www.zenirestaurant.com
"Wash up and eat with your hands" at this "fabulous", "family-run" Ethiopian in San Jose, where "adventurous" types revel in using "wonderful injera" to "scoop up" the "tasty, spicy" chow (and wash it down with honey wine); weekends get "lively", so you may have to "wait a bit" for a table in the "traditional" space where you "sit on cusions at low tables", but disciples decree "it's worth it."

Zibibbo Ⓩ *Mediterranean* 20 | 19 | 19 | $45
Palo Alto | 430 Kipling St. (bet. Lytton & University Aves.) | 650-328-6722 | www.zibibborestaurant.com
This "pleasant" Palo Alto outpost of SF's Restaurant Lulu delivers "solid" "Mediterranean goodies" (including "small plates") to everyone from couples on a "date" to biz types entertaining "clients or potential recruits"; the unimpressed knock a "spacious layout" that can get "noisy" and "inconsistent" service and chow, but for many it remains an "old standby."

Latest openings, menus, photos and more on plus.google.com/local

ALPHABETICAL
PAGE INDEX

All places are in San Francisco unless otherwise noted (East of San Francisco=E; North of San Francisco=N; South of San Francisco=S).

Wine Vintage Chart

This chart is based on a 30-point scale. The ratings (by U. of South Carolina law professor **Howard Stravitz**) reflect vintage quality and the wine's readiness to drink. A dash means the wine is past its peak or too young to rate. Loire ratings are for dry whites.

Whites	95	96	97	98	99	00	01	02	03	04	05	06	07	08	09	10
France:																
Alsace	24	23	23	25	23	25	26	22	21	22	23	21	26	26	23	26
Burgundy	27	26	22	21	24	24	23	27	23	26	26	25	26	25	25	-
Loire Valley	-	-	-	-	-	-	-	25	20	22	27	23	24	24	24	25
Champagne	26	27	24	25	25	25	21	26	21	-	-	-	-	-	-	-
Sauternes	21	23	25	23	24	24	29	24	26	21	26	25	27	24	27	-
California:																
Chardonnay	-	-	-	-	22	21	24	25	22	26	29	24	27	23	27	-
Sauvignon Blanc	-	-	-	-	-	-	-	-	-	25	24	27	25	24	25	-
Austria:																
Grüner V./Riesl.	22	-	25	22	26	22	23	25	25	24	23	26	25	24	25	-
Germany:	22	26	22	25	24	-	29	25	26	27	28	26	26	26	26	-

Reds	95	96	97	98	99	00	01	02	03	04	05	06	07	08	09	10
France:																
Bordeaux	25	25	24	25	24	29	26	24	26	25	28	24	24	25	27	-
Burgundy	26	27	25	24	27	22	23	25	25	23	28	24	24	25	27	-
Rhône	26	22	23	27	26	27	26	-	26	25	27	25	26	23	27	-
Beaujolais	-	-	-	-	-	-	-	-	-	-	27	25	24	23	28	25
California:																
Cab./Merlot	27	24	28	23	25	-	27	26	25	24	26	24	27	26	25	-
Pinot Noir	-	-	-	-	-	26	25	24	25	26	24	27	24	26	-	-
Zinfandel	-	-	-	-	-	25	24	26	24	23	21	26	23	25	-	-
Oregon:																
Pinot Noir	-	-	-	-	-	-	26	24	25	24	25	24	27	24	-	-
Italy:																
Tuscany	25	24	29	24	27	24	27	-	24	27	25	26	25	24	-	-
Piedmont	21	27	26	25	26	28	27	-	24	27	26	26	27	26	-	-
Spain:																
Rioja	26	24	25	22	25	24	28	-	23	27	26	24	25	26	-	-
Ribera del Duero/ Priorat	25	26	24	25	25	24	27	-	24	27	26	24	25	27	-	-
Australia:																
Shiraz/Cab.	23	25	24	26	24	24	26	26	25	25	26	21	23	26	24	-
Chile:	-	-	-	-	24	22	25	23	24	24	27	25	24	26	24	-
Argentina:																
Malbec	-	-	-	-	-	-	-	-	-	25	26	27	26	26	25	-